European Studies in Social Psychology

Social identity and intergroup relations

European studies in social psychology

This series will consist mainly of specially commissioned volumes on specific themes, particularly those linking work in social psychology with other disciplines. It will also include occasional volumes of 'Current Research'.

The series is jointly published by the Cambridge University Press and the Editions de la Maison des Sciences de l'Homme, in close collaboration with the Laboratoire Européen de Psychologie Sociale of the Maison, as part of the joint publishing agreement established in 1977 between the Fondation de la Maison des Sciences de l'Homme and the Syndics of the Cambridge University Press.

Cette collection est publiée en co-édition par Cambridge University Press et les Editions de la Maison des Sciences de l'Homme en collaboration étroite avec le Laboratoire Européen de Psychologie Sociale de la Maison.

Elle comprend essentiellement des ouvrages sur des thèmes spécifiques permettant de mettre en rapport la psychologie sociale et d'autres disciplines, avec à l'occasion des volumes consacrés à des 'recherches en cours'. Il s'intègre dans le programme de co-édition etabli en 1977 par la Fondation de la Maison des Sciences de l'Homme et les Syndics de Cambridge University Press.

Already published:

Social markers in speech, edited by Klaus R. Scherer and Howard Giles
Advances in the social psychology of language, edited by Colin Fraser and Klaus R. Scherer
The analysis of action: recent theoretical and empirical advances, edited by Mario von Cranach and Rom Harré

Social identity
and intergroup relations

Edited by
Henri Tajfel

Cambridge University Press

Cambridge
London   New York   New Rochelle
Melbourne   Sydney

Editions de la Maison des Sciences de l'Homme
Paris

CAMBRIDGE UNIVERSITY PRESS
Cambridge, New York, Melbourne, Madrid, Cape Town, Singapore,
São Paulo, Delhi, Dubai, Tokyo, Mexico City

Cambridge University Press
The Edinburgh Building, Cambridge CB2 8RU, UK

Published in the United States of America by Cambridge University Press, New York

www.cambridge.org
Information on this title: www.cambridge.org/9780521153652

First published 1982
First paperback printing 2010

A catalogue record for this publication is available from the British Library

Library of Congress Catalogue Card Number: 81-21676

ISBN 978-0-521-24616-3 Hardback
ISBN 978-0-521-15365-2 Paperback

Contents

Part I
The cognitive construction of groups

Part II
The dynamics of interaction between groups:
Experimental studies

Conclusion

Contributors

EMILIANA BONALDO
Istituto di Psicologia, Università di Padova

RICHARD Y. BOURHIS
Department of Psychology, McMaster University

RUPERT J. BROWN
Social Psychology Research Unit, University of Kent at Canterbury

BRIAN CADDICK
Department of Social Work, University of Bristol

ED CAIRNS
Department of Psychology, The New University of Ulster at Coleraine

DORA CAPOZZA
Istituto di Psicologia, Università di Padova

JEAN-CLAUDE DESCHAMPS
Département de Psychologie, Université de Lausanne

ALBA DI MAGGIO
Istituto di Psicologia, Università di Padova

MILES HEWSTONE
Department of Experimental Psychology, University of Oxford

PETER HILL
(formerly) Department of Psychology, University of Bristol

MURRAY HORWITZ
Department of Psychology, Boston College, Boston, Mass.

JOS M.F. JASPARS
Department of Experimental Psychology, University of Oxford

KARMELA LIEBKIND
Department of Social Psychology, University of Helsinki

CLAUDE LOUCHE
Département Informatique, Université des Sciences et Techniques du Languedoc, Montpellier

SIK HUNG NG
Department of Psychology, University of Otago

JACOB M. RABBIE
Instituut voor sociale psychologie, Rijksuniversiteit te Utrecht

STEPHEN REICHER
Department of Psychology, University of Bristol

GORDON F. ROSS
Work Research Unit, Department of Employment, London

HENRI TAJFEL
Department of Psychology, University of Bristol

JOHN C. TURNER
Department of Psychology, University of Bristol

SUWARSIH WARNAEN
Department of Psychology, University of Indonesia

MARGARET WETHERELL
Psychological Laboratories, University of St Andrews

Preface

This is a book about relations between social groups and their conflicts, about the role played in these conflicts by the individuals' affiliations with their groups (or their 'social identity'), and about the psychological processes which are responsible for the formation of groups. While maintaining its unity of focus upon the themes just mentioned and the perspectives adopted to discuss them, the book contains at the same time a great deal of diversity. The topics discussed include the psychology of crowds, the psychological effects of differences in power between groups, the ways in which people's membership of various groups affects their differing views about the causes of social events, the effects of the perceived illegitimacy of the existing social arrangements upon people's attitudes towards their own social group and others, the conditions in which members of certain groups become 'depersonalized' by other people, and some aspects of the psychology of historical, ethnic, professional and industrial conflicts or tensions. Some chapters are mainly theoretical or speculative, others contain descriptions of experimental studies, and still others report on research done in field settings. The 'populations' or respondents participating in these field studies include Catholics and Protestants in Northern Ireland, Italian students from the North and the South of the country, German- and Italian-speaking inhabitants of South Tyrol, members of numerous ethnic groups in Indonesia, the Swedish-speaking inhabitants of a small community in Finland, polytechnic and university lecturers in Britain, and French trade unionists. Through all this diversity some *general* questions are asked about the social psychology of relations between human groups and, whenever possible, the beginnings of a few answers are provided.

It has been a pleasure to have had the opportunity and the privilege of putting this book together. In 1978 another book appeared on similar themes, concerned with 'differentiation between social groups', which I also edited. In the intervening period of less than three years, a great deal of new thinking and research about intergroup relations has been done in various countries, much of it adopting a perspective similar to that of the first book but also containing disagreement, criticisms and new, awkward questions asked within this wider common framework. This book exemplifies all these aspects of the recent work.

I am grateful to my friends and colleagues from universities in several countries, and to those who are in my own university, or who had been there and moved elsewhere, for agreeing to adopt this book as a channel for the diffusion of their work. In addition, I have particular reasons to be grateful for the hospitality shown to me in Helsinki and Padua where first contacts quickly led to a decision to cooperate in a common enterprise. The contacts with most other contributors to this book go back to a longer past of cooperative work, agreements as well as disagreements, and, most of all, the sharing of a conviction that the work on problems discussed in this book is important both for the development of social psychology and for a better understanding of various facets of our social reality.

The Social Science Research Council (UK) supported in various ways the work on which are based five chapters of the book. The Laboratoire Européen de Psychologie Sociale (LEPS) organized a conference at Rennes at which many discussions directly relevant to this book were held, and two of its chapters were presented in their preliminary versions. The Fonds National Suisse de la Recherche Scientifique, the University of Otago Research Committee, the Netherlands Organization for the Advancement of Pure Research (ZWO), the Fulbright Scholarship Scheme, the French Centre National de la Recherche Scientifique, the Italian National Council of Research (CNR) and several other institutions also supported, directly or indirectly, the work from which various chapters have resulted. I am grateful to my colleagues on the editorial committee of the Cambridge University Press – Maison des Sciences de l'Homme series of *European Studies in Social Psychology* for their help and advice. It is also a special pleasure to be able to express, yet once again, my indebtedness to Alma Foster for her help in bringing this text to the point where it became fit to be sent to the publishers.

The final version of this book was completed in surroundings of unmatched beauty in which ideal conditions for work were also provided. I wish to thank the Rockefeller Foundation for offering me its hospitality for a month in its superb Villa Serbelloni in Bellagio. My special thanks go to the Administrator of the Villa, Roberto Celli, its hostess, Jo Ardovino, and their staff. They achieved the difficult blend of lightness of touch with seriousness of purpose, of which the result was a number of very happy 'resident scholars' at the Villa.

H. TAJFEL

Bellagio, April 1981

Introduction

HENRI TAJFEL

It has been said many times in recent years that the study of intergroup relations remained for too long at the edges of the 'mainstream' of social psychology. The possible reasons for this odd neglect of one of the most fundamental issues of our times have also been abundantly discussed. This is why there will be no return to these complaints and their various justifications either in this Introduction or in the remainder of this book. We are now in the position of being able to look forward rather than backwards. In addition to a good deal of new research in the United States and elsewhere, the preoccupation with intergroup relations (including the social psychology of social conflict) has been for some years now at the centre of interest of an increasing number of social psychologists in Europe and has become one of the clearly visible and major trends of research amongst them. In addition to a large number of research reports and theoretical discussions published in the last decade in a variety of journals, several books have appeared very recently whose purpose it was to achieve new integrations, to present new research, to take stock or to review critically the whole area or some parts of it. In addition, discussions of intergroup relations are claiming a very much larger share of the text than has been the custom for a long time in some of the new textbooks for students published in Europe.

This book must be seen as a part of this general trend. It represents some of the facets of these new developments, and it is most of all a 'working' book. It is this in the sense that none of its chapters aims to present general reviews or summaries of established trends of research. The four chapters of Part I are all 'speculative', as their aim is to present new theoretical approaches to problems, some of which have been with us for a long time. They are in the nature of blueprints for new research, in most cases research which is already proceeding as this book goes into production. The remaining eleven chapters of Parts II and III combine, in each case, the description of one or more empirical studies (and of a large number of

AO

such studies in the case of chapter 9 by Horwitz and Rabbie and chapter 10 by Cairns) with extensive discussions of the background of the research which can be found either in theoretical preoccupations or in aspects of social reality (or in both). To the question of 'why we have done what we have done' the answers are found in some cases in terms of an existing (and sometimes acute) issue of intergroup relations, and in other cases in terms of a perceived need for the widening or modification of a theoretical perspective. As editor of this book, I felt it was important that an opportunity should be given to discuss these various background preoccupations more fully than is usually possible in standardized journal articles or in more general summaries. The second question implicit in all of these chapters is: 'So what?' This question is often more difficult to answer, by far. It will be for the reader to decide if and how the various contributors have managed to deal with it successfully.

A few further preliminary points must be made before a brief description is made of the structure of the book and the nature of its chapters. (A fuller discussion of some of the major empirical and theoretical issues which are raised in the book will be found in the concluding chapter.) First, the definition of terms: 'social identity' and 'intergroup relations'. The former of these has led in the past to many confusions. As was the case in some previous publications, our purpose here is *not* to unravel, conceptually or empirically, the *general* issues of identity or of the individual's self-concept. To quote:

For the purpose of this discussion, social identity will be understood as that *part* of the individuals' self-concept which derives from their knowledge of their membership of a social group (or groups) together with the value and emotional significance attached to that membership. It will be clear that this is a limited definition of 'identity' or 'social identity'. This limitation is deliberate, and it has two aims. The first is not to enter into endless and often sterile discussions as to what 'is' identity. The second is to enable us to use this limited concept in the discussions which follow. There is no doubt that the image or concept that an individual has of himself or herself is infinitely more complex, both in its contents and its derivations, than 'social identity' as defined and circumscribed here. We are not, however, concerned ... with the origins and development of individual identity or self-awareness. The aims are much more modest: the assumption is made that, however rich and complex may be the individuals' view of themselves in relation to the surrounding world, social and physical, *some* aspects of that view are contributed by the membership of certain social groups or categories. Some of these memberships are more salient than others; and some may vary in salience in time and as a function of a variety of social situations. Our explicit preoccupation is with the effects of the nature and subjective importance of these memberships on those aspects of an individual's behaviour which are pertinent to intergroup relations – without in the least denying that this does not enable us to make any statements about the 'self' in general, or about social behaviour in *other* contexts. 'Social identity' as defined here is thus best considered as a shorthand term used to describe (i) limited aspects of the concept of self which are (ii) relevant to certain limited aspects of social behaviour. (Tajfel, 1981[1], p255)

The social psychology of intergroup relations is concerned with intergroup behaviour and attitudes. Here again, we shall adopt a definition used in the past and first proposed by Sherif (1966) when he wrote: 'Whenever individuals belonging to one group interact, collectively or individually, with another group or its members *in terms of their group identifications* we have an instance of intergroup behaviour' (p12, italics in the original).

This is therefore a book about the role played by social identity, as defined above, in the ways people form groups and behave towards one another as members of groups which find themselves, or are perceived to be, in a great variety of relationships. It is *not* a book about the concept of identity, although some pertinent aspects of 'individual' as distinct from 'social' identity do enter into the arguments presented by Turner in chapter 1 and Deschamps in chapter 3. The assessment of 'self' as seen against the background of an individual's group membership also finds its way into the data and discussions presented by Jaspars and Warnaen in chapter 12 and by Liebkind in chapter 13.

The obvious gap in these preliminary definitional exercises is in the absence of a discussion of the term 'group'. This is a deliberate omission as two very different conceptions of group and group formation are presented in the book. One will be found in chapter 1 by Turner, with its applications to the social psychology of crowd behaviour extensively discussed by Reicher in chapter 2. Another conception deriving from a substantial body of research and going back in its roots to the work of Lewin (1948), will be found in the arguments presented by Horwitz and Rabbie in chapter 9. Both these views are discussed in the concluding chapter.

The four chapters of Part I are all concerned, in their different ways, with the cognitive aspects of group functioning and intergroup relations. The common purpose is to unravel the psychological processes which are responsible for the 'cognitive construction of groups' (one's own and others), for the formation or functioning within a group of shared perspectives upon certain aspects of social reality.

In chapter 1, Turner widens the earlier ideas about social categorization and social identity starting from their previous applications to the field of *inter*group behaviour and concluding that they can also be used for the explanation of *in*group formation. One way to set his views in context is to consider the manner in which he modifies the significance of what has been referred to in the past as the 'interpersonal – intergroup' continuum of social interaction. The two 'extremes' of this hypothetical continuum were defined as follows: 'What is meant by "purely" interpersonal is any social encounter between two or more people in which *all* the interaction that takes place is determined by the personal relationships between the individuals and by their respective individual characteristics. The "intergroup" extreme is that in which *all* of the behaviour of two or more individuals towards each other is determined by their membership of different social groups or categories.' (Tajfel, 1981, p240. See also Brown and Turner, 1981, for a recent extensive discussion.) In Turner's usage, this continuum becomes one moving from 'purely' interpersonal to 'purely' *group* behaviour; i.e. the concern is with the conditions which lead individuals to define themselves and act as members of a group rather than in their individual capacity. In discussing the processes which may be involved, Turner stands on their head the traditional definitions or descriptions of groups in terms of cohesion and face-to-face interaction. A *sufficient* condition for group formation is to be found, according to him, in processes of social influence which lead individuals to internalize certain social norms, to see themselves in appropriate circumstances as embodying these norms in their attitudes and social behaviour, and thus to define their social location in terms of certain selected group affiliations. This can happen, as Turner shows with the help of some empirical examples, *independently* of group cohesion or of direct interaction with other people. It could be said that the term 'social category' probably becomes here of more practical use in theory and research than 'social group', as the latter has been traditionally associated with cohesion and face-to-face interaction. These ideas may help to encompass more easily in social psychology the wider social entities which have been neglected because of the discipline's long-lasting fascination with 'small groups'. We shall return to this issue in the concluding chapter of this book.

Turner's chapter was discussed in this Introduction at some length because it provides an opening for the remainder of the book in exemplifying the preoccupation of most of the chapters with an analysis of group processes which, although they are (trivially) located *in* individuals, cannot be properly understood unless the individual level of analysis is clearly transcended. Chapter 2 by Reicher provides an excellent example of one application of these views. It is concerned with a problem which is not only as old as the day when social psychology experienced its first *prise de conscience* as a discipline in its own right, but very much older. The history of ideas about 'crowd psychology' is full of myths related more closely to the social and political biases of the various writers on the subject than to attempts at establishing the validity of the presumed 'facts'. Reicher reviews critically in his chapter these older ideas from Le Bon onwards, and continues – no less critically – with a review of contemporary work. The remainder of his chapter is an attempt to establish a theoretical alternative for the understanding of the social psychology of crowds. In this attempt, Turner's ideas about social *identification*, discussed in chapter 1, are applied to the formation and behaviour of crowds as social groups, not different in many ways from a variety of other social groups.

With chapter 3 by Deschamps we come to problems of social identity as they concern relations between groups rather than group formation. Deschamps introduces the issue of power which also looms large in two other chapters of the book (7 and 15) and is implicit in some of the others (e.g. chapters 10 and 11). His general perspective or approach is similar to that of most other contributors: the role of social categorization and social identity in intergroup relations must be analysed in ways which take *explicitly* into account the wider social contexts within which the groups function. He is, however, critical of earlier research on social categorization which ignored the distinction that must be made between social groups which 'dominate' and those which are 'dominated'. Deschamps's concern is with one particular aspect of this distinction: its effects on the conception that people have of themselves, or rather their achievement of *individuality*. Members of dominating groups are often capable of imposing a view of the world in which the norm or the point of reference in relation to which other people are defined comes from the centre where the power resides. People belonging to these groups who are at the centre of the social system need not be defined in terms of their group affiliations: they are mainly conceived of as individuals. At the same time, the social categorizations imposed upon those who are in peripheral or dominated groups account for much of the way in which they define themselves and are defined by others. The achievement or the *construction* for oneself of full individuality is the privilege of social power. The forms of social identity become a function of social differentials. Deschamps provides in his chapter some evidence, mainly linguistic, for his views. As he admits, much more evidence will have to follow to substantiate his stark socio-cognitive differentiations.

There is, however, no dearth of evidence for the type of socio-cognitive differentiations which are the subject of chapter 4 by Hewstone and Jaspars. Attribution theory has held for some years *one* of the centres of the stage in social psychology. Whichever way one may wish to define 'attribution', there is no doubt that it has to do with causality of behaviour – behaviour of other people and sometimes also one's own – as it is perceived in various conditions of social interaction. In Deschamps's discussion, people's conception of their individuality is seen as affected by the cognitive effects of relations of power between groups. In the traditional attribution theory the perception of the causes of behaviour of other people is analysed in terms of complex networks of inter-individual interactions, and of individual costs and benefits. There is an interesting convergence between Deschamps's insistence on the need to introduce intergroup power differentials if we are to understand the way in which individuals construct their own and others' identity, and the theory of social attribution proposed by Hewstone and Jaspars in which they insist that the significance of group affiliations must be taken into account if we are to understand the way in which people construe the causality of the behaviour of others.

Part II of the book is devoted to experimental studies. But, as will be seen, a clear distinction must be made for several reasons between its first four chapters and chapter 9 by Horwitz and Rabbie. Chapters 5, 6, 7 and 8 are concerned, in their different ways, with evaluations, extensions, testing and critiques of a theoretical perspective to which most chapters of this book are related in one way or another. The common denominator of all the chapters of Part II is the preoccupation with the *dynamics* of intergroup relations. This is why the introductions to the experimental studies ('Why we have done what we have done?') are as important as the studies themselves, and in each case they amount to a theoretical essay.

The social dynamics underlying the perception of social reality are considered in chapter 5 by Caddick. In a situation in which status and other divisions between groups are fairly rigidly drawn or stratified, how should one account for the *psychological* determinants of the transition from the acceptance of *status quo* to its rejection and to movements towards change? One of the answers appears to be in terms of the rejection of the existing social reality as the only *possible* objective state of affairs, and consequently the development of 'cognitive alternatives' to the present situation. In turn, it can be assumed that this rejection of the *status quo* is powerfully fuelled by the perception of the existing social arrangements as being unstable or illegitimate or both. There is still not much direct evidence that this is the case. The concept of 'illegitimacy' implies, however, that the criteria on the basis of which judgements are made about a social situation as being 'legitimate' or 'illegitimate' must enter the argument; and – by the same token – equity theory presents additional possibilities for the explanation of movements towards change. Caddick examines the competing claims of two theoretical perspectives, both of which are summarized in his chapter. He is not able to reach firm conclusions. This is undoubtedly an important problem which badly requires a good deal of new thinking and research.

In chapter 6 Brown and Ross, also, deal with the role of perceived illegitimacy in intergroup relations, discussed by Caddick in the preceding chapter; they do this against a background of the argument that many of the previous experiments on social identity in intergroup relations confined themselves to static situations in which conclusions were drawn from one frozen moment of time. In their discussion and study they introduce some of the variables of change and development in the relations between groups. The major questions are: What happens to the evaluations of the group by its own members and to intergroup discrimination when status differences between groups are associated with harsh treatment or lenient treatment of one group by another? How do these forms of treatment affect the attitudes towards themselves and others of groups which are of higher and lower status?

The dynamics of relations between groups are also the background to the discussion and studies presented by Ng in chapter 7. Just as Brown and Ross are concerned with the effects of differential treatments of one group by another, so Ng concentrates upon the differences in power. As is the case in chapter 6, he finds much of the previous research 'static' and is critical of many of the earlier social categorization experiments because all, or most, of them chose situations which were so arranged that members of various groups could take decisions about members of out-groups with equal power on both sides. When this is not so, as is the case in Ng's experiments, it is found that, as distinct from the results of many of the earlier experiments, 'outgroup discrimination is not a necessary outcome of social categorization, but is contingent upon a permissive intergroup power relation'. Ng's position is best summarized in his own words: 'There may be diverse causes of discrimination, some of which are more minimal than others. Yet there can be no minimal and sufficient cause apart from one which is embedded in, and mediated by, the social arrangement of power.'

Wetherell's attack in chapter 8 comes from a different quarter. Can the results of many of the earlier studies, showing that a transient categorization of people into groups based on trivial criteria is a *sufficient* condition for intergroup discrimination to occur, be generalized to non-Western cultural contexts? And to what extent were the methods used in these earlier experiments conducive to discrimination which would not appear, or at least would be tempered, if other methods were used? The experiments described in the chapter attempt to tackle both these questions. Different sets of results seem to point in different directions, but there is little doubt that they raise important questions concerning the cross-cultural validity of assumptions about intergroup behaviour which are made on the basis of the researchers' experience of data from one cultural milieu, however wide it may be. There is nothing new to this caveat, but Wetherell's discussion and her results open new *concrete* possibilities of research.

The chapter by Horwitz and Rabbie was placed at the end of Part II because it describes a perspective on the study of intergroup relations which is different in many ways from the perspective represented in most of the other chapters. It is also more than a description of particular experimental studies focusing upon one major issue in intergroup relations. The authors summarize a large number of studies which are relevant to a variety of problems in intergroup relations and which together amount to a separate theoretical statement. Because of this, chapter 9 can be considered as a sounding board for many of the ideas presented in other chapters of this book. The focus is essentially Lewinian, and it is upon the *interdependence* of individuals as the basic criterion for group formation and for the development of relations with other groups. It was felt that the inclusion of a point of view, highly salient in its difference from the approach adopted in much of the remainder of the book, was a necessary rounding up of a volume of studies which is, after all, not concerned (as must be obvious from the chapters previously described) with accumulating positive evidence for one particular set of assumptions, but with discussing problems in the social psychology of intergroup relations which are important and have often remained unresolved.

In Part III we move to concrete social contexts and field studies. Cairns starts off in chapter 10 with a discussion of the conflict in Northern Ireland. The social, historical, political and economic causality of the present situation must undoubtedly remain prior to the analysis of any of its psychological concomitants. And yet these psychological effects are obviously there and they loom large in everybody's daily life. This is abundantly shown in the evidence, brought together by Cairns from a variety of sources. He has also been able to show that this evidence can be synthesized more easily, that it can make more systematic *sense*, if it is refocused and rearranged in terms of people's search for a positive and distinctive identity which they wish to derive – in the context of a long-standing conflict – from their respective group memberships.

Similar points can be made about chapter 11 by Capozza, Bonaldo and Di Maggio. They also deal with two long-standing intergroup situations of tensions, at least one of which erupted at times in violence. The discussion by the Paduan workers is based on three studies, two of which – separated by fifteen years – relate to the South–North attitudes in selected populations in Padua. The change-over time in ingroup and reciprocal group perceptions is discussed in their chapter against the background of the socio-political and economic changes which took place in Italy between the early sixties and the late seventies. The third study, based on data from South Tyrol where there is a historical background of acute conflict, presents a curious convergence with the Northern Irish situation: the existence of a minority in one setting which becomes in turn a majority in a wider setting.

There is a contrast between these two chapters and the Indonesian study by Jaspars and Warnaen which is the subject of chapter 12. Conflicts of interests or of attitudes do not enter explicitly either into the data or the background of ethnic multiplicity, at least as it is described in the chapter. There are some indications that in the ethnic melting pot of the Indonesian capital, where many groups cohabit, there exists a higher salience than is the case in the provinces of people's group membership, of their social identity and of the social comparisons with others in which they engage; and some even stronger indications that *one* minority group – the Chinese – is conceived by others as being somewhat beyond the pale. The 'generalized social comparison model' which Jaspars and Warnaen construct from this background will be discussed in the concluding chapter of the book.

The Finnish study of the Swedish-speaking minority described by Liebkind in chapter 13 has three aims: to present the details of the historical and social background of the minority; to use an intensive technique (the Role Construct Repertory Grid) on a small population; and to show that some *general* conclusions can be drawn from this combination of data. One of the main conclusions seems to be that, as the vitality of a minority language decreases, so there is an increase from one generation to the next of *one* (and perhaps, in these conditions, the first) amongst the strategies of adaptation which may be open to minorities in some circumstances: a trend towards assimilation.

In the last two chapters of Part III, we abandon the socio-political and ethnic background of the four preceding chapters and move into the area of conflicting economic and status interests. This does *not* mean that such conflicts are not just as crucially important in the ethnic, regional and historical divisions to which the previous four chapters were addressed. But in the last two chapters the historical dimension of intergroup relations, so prominent in the studies from Northern Ireland, Italy, Indonesia and Finland, becomes relatively less salient. In one case – in chapter 14 by Bourhis and Hill – we deal with the effects on reciprocal intergroup attitudes of a rivalry between the subgroups of the same profession, a rivalry which is not often openly acknowledged but quite frequently expressed in various ways. The University and Polytechnic lecturers in Britain seem to lead their lives in mutual splendid isolation, very often as if each of the groups wished to forget the existence of the other. It is interesting to see in chapter 14 what happens when each of them is reminded that the other one is also around. There could hardly be a more 'sophisticated' population of respondents; and yet it will be seen that some at least of their reactions can be subsumed within a more general pattern of group images, identities and comparisons which is usually found amongst simpler mortals.

This conflict – if conflict there is – between the two categories of lecturers is usually not an 'open' one. It is the *need* for this openness in some conditions of industrial relations that Louche tackles in chapter 15. Editorial freedom enables me to write that his data – as presented in the chapter – are practically non-existent. But the ideas may turn out to be crucially important if more data are collected in the future to support them. The major questions underlying the discussion can be formulated as follows: Is it the case that when the representatives of a politically conscious and unionized labour force negotiate with the management, it is easier for them to engage in 'give and take' from the background of an open conflict, such as a strike, than when the conflict is latent or subterranean? And could this be so because in an open conflict the *distinctive* group identity of the negotiators is more easily and clearly preserved and perceived as such, and therefore they need not keep accentuating it? Louche argues that this is the situation, at least in the context of industrial relations in France. The reader will notice that convergent evidence is mentioned in chapter 6 by Brown and Ross.

One additional point needs to be made in concluding this Introduction. In the view of this editor (which is not unbiased) the contribution that this book can make is due to the underlying and fruitful tension between the two main characteristics it presents: its unity and its diversity. The unity is in the common denominator of the underlying major issue confronted by the book: the relation between group or social identity and conflicts between groups; and also, in the common general perspective adopted by most of the contributors. The diversity is in the variety of empirical and theoretical problems attacked and methods used, of the location and populations of the field studies, and of the perspectives from which critical attacks are made upon various past and present approaches to the study of intergroup relations in social psychology. As has been said at the beginning of this Introduction, this is a 'working book'. In very few cases could one conclude that 'closure' has been achieved by the authors of the various chapters. They are all dealing with an area of social inquiry which is as wide open as it is crucial for our times. There is little doubt that more questions are left open in the book than definite answers provided. In my view, this is the mark of an honest piece of work which can and should be useful to other people.

Note

[1] This is a reference to a collection of theoretical articles and empirical studies revised and edited as one volume.

References

Brown, R.J. and Turner, J.C. 1981. Interpersonal and intergroup behaviour. In J.C. Turner and H. Giles (eds.): *Intergroup behaviour*. Oxford: Blackwell.
Sherif, M. 1966. *In common predicament: Social psychology of intergroup conflict and cooperation*. Boston: Houghton Mifflin.
Tajfel, H. 1981. *Human groups and social categories: Studies in social psychology*. Cambridge: Cambridge University Press.

Part I
The cognitive construction
of groups

1. Towards a cognitive redefinition of the social group[1]

JOHN C. TURNER

1. Introduction

This chapter is a contribution towards redefining the concept of the social group in cognitive terms. It proposes that a social group can be defined as two or more individuals who share a common social identification of themselves or, which is nearly the same thing, perceive themselves to be members of the same social category. This definition stresses that members of a social group seem often to share no more than a collective perception of their own social unity and yet this seems to be sufficient for them to act as a group. It derives from recent research on intergroup relations (cf. Doise, 1978; Tajfel, 1972, 1978; Tajfel and Turner, 1979; Turner, 1975). The theory of the social group which it represents can be described as the *Social Identification* model.

Traditionally, experimental social psychology has been preoccupied with group behaviour as the expression of cohesive or solidary social relationships between individuals. It has been assumed that individuals affiliate with each other for a variety of reasons and that a group emerges where this takes a stabilized reciprocal form. At minimum, a group has been defined as two or more persons who are in some way socially or psychologically interdependent: for the satisfaction of needs, attainment of goals or consensual validation of attitudes and values. It is considered that such interdependence leads to cooperative social interaction, communication, mutual attraction and influence between individuals. Shaw (1976), for example, defines a group as 'two or more persons who are interacting with one another in such a manner that each person influences and is influenced by each other person' (p11). An additional, but dependent, criterion has sometimes been that individuals should develop an organized system of status and role relationships and shared social norms and values which regulate their opinions and conduct in matters of common interest.

A group structure should evolve as a product of mutual interaction and influence. In general, therefore, a group has been conceptualized as some (usually small) collection of individuals in face-to-face relations of inter-action, attraction and influence who may or may not stand in differentiated, structural positions with respect to each other. This theory can be referred to as the *Social Cohesion* model.

There is no doubt that members of social groups do tend to define themselves as a group, interact with each other and develop a social struc-ture. The important disagreement between the concepts of social cohesion and social identification lies in their explanation of the psychological determinants of private acceptance of group membership. We are con-cerned here with group membership as a psychological and not a formal-institutional state, with the subjective sense of togetherness, we-ness, or belongingness which indicates the formation of a psychological group. What are the necessary and sufficient conditions for some aggregate of individuals to feel themselves to be a group and to act accordingly?

The Social Cohesion model tends to assert that group-belongingness has an affective basis. As the name implies, it considers that individuals are bound together by their cohesiveness. The latter reflects the members' attraction to each other, to the group as a whole and to group activities. However, as Lott and Lott (1965) have argued, it is most simply and prob-ably best understood as interpersonal attraction based on the direct or indirect rewards which members mediate for each other. They define it as that group property which is inferred from the number and strength of mutual positive attitudes among the members of a group. Thus the concept implies that individuals become a group insofar as they develop mutual and positive emotional bonds: what matters for group-belonging-ness is how individuals feel about each other and in particular whether they like each other.

The Social Identification model, on the other hand, assumes that psy-chological group membership has primarily a perceptual or cognitive basis. As we shall see, it considers that individuals structure their perception of themselves and others by means of abstract social categories, that they internalize these categories as aspects of their self-concepts, and that social-cognitive processes relating to these forms of self-conception produce group behaviour. The first question determining group-belongingness is not 'Do I like these other individuals?', but 'Who am I?'. What matters is how we perceive and define ourselves and not how we feel about others.

There seem to be, in fact, at least four good reasons which make it timely to distinguish between Social Cohesion and Social Identification and for preferring the latter model to the former. Firstly, the cognitive definition appears to be consistent with more empirical data. Despite traditional assumptions, for example, it is no longer certain that social cohesion is either necessary or sufficient for group formation – whereas the mere perception of common category membership may be both. We may not, after all, tend to join people we like so much as like people that we perceive ourselves joined to. This issue will be discussed presently.

Secondly, the concept of social identification seems to provide an heuristic, explanatory integration of several characteristics of intra- and intergroup behaviour in terms of two causal processes which follow directly from it. One has to do with the cognitive functioning of social categorizations. The other derives from the fact that, in extending the self-concept, social identification also extends the sphere of operation of motives associated with it. Specifically, the need for positive self-esteem motivates social comparisons to differentiate oneself from others in terms of positively valued group characteristics and to differentiate one's own group from other groups and thus plays a role in both intra- and intergroup behaviour.

Thirdly, the cognitive definition has novel theoretical and research implications for some very basic problems in social psychology, such as group formation, the distinction between interpersonal and intergroup behaviour, cooperative altruism and social influence. It also, as we shall see, creates new research issues of its own.

Fourthly, of course, there is some polemical value in stressing single-mindedly the virtues of a new idea and playing down those of the old. It may well be, indeed it is almost certain, that at some stage a theoretical conception of the social group will emerge which integrates the truth contained in both definitions. A pendulum, however, must swing in both directions before it can come to rest.

This chapter will concentrate on the explanatory power of the cognitive processes associated with social identifications. For the sake of completeness, the motivational factors at work will also be noted, but extremely briefly. To begin with, we shall outline the relationship of social identity to the self-concept and then describe some results of research on intergroup behaviour which seem to argue for the Social Identification model.

2. Social identity and the self-concept

Social categorizations are discontinuous divisions of the social world into distinct classes or categories (Tajfel, 1972). Social identification can refer to the process of locating oneself, or another person, within a system of social categorizations or, as a noun, to any social categorization used by a person to define him- or herself and others. It will be used primarily in the latter sense here and thus denotes an element of cognitive structure in self-perception and person-perception. It will also sometimes be used to indicate the process whereby an individual internalizes some form of social categorization so that it becomes a component of the self-concept, whether long-lasting or ephemeral. The sum total of the social identifications used by a person to define him- or herself will be described as his or her *social identity*. Social categorizations define a person by systematically including them within some, and excluding them from other related categories. They state at the same time what a person is and is not. This concept of social identity is descended from Tajfel's definition of it as 'the individual's knowledge that he belongs to certain social groups together with some emotional and value significance to him of the group membership' (1972, p31).

We shall hypothesize that it represents one of the two major subsystems of the self-concept. Gergen (1971) distinguishes between the self-concept as a set of psychological processes and the self-concept as a cognitive structure. The latter he defines as 'the system of concepts available to a person in attempting to define himself' (1971, p23). He further reports that these concepts fall into two main classes (basing himself on Gordon's, 1968, research). Firstly, there are terms that denote one's membership of various formal and informal social groups, i.e. social categories such as sex, nationality, political affiliation, religion and so on. Secondly, there are terms 'that are more personal in nature and that usually denote specific attributes of the individual' (p62) such as feelings of competence, bodily attributes, ways of relating to others, psychological characteristics, intellectual concerns, personal tastes and so on. It is evident that the first set of self-descriptions corresponds as a whole to our concept of social identity; the second set, similarly, we shall equate with and define as *personal identity*. Thus, social and personal identity are conceptualized as hypothetical, cognitive structures which together account for most of the self-concept. Each component, in turn, is made up of more restricted cognitive elements such as particular social categorizations or personal characteristics.

There has long been a debate over the nature of the self-concept (cf. Gergen, 1971; Mischel, 1976, p486). The controversy can be summarized as concerned with the question of whether the self-concept possesses unity, continuity and consistency across situations or whether it is multidimensional, transient, inconsistent and situation-specific. On the one hand, the self-concept as subjectively experienced at any given moment (which can be called the self-image) varies directly with the contemporary environment and immediate social context (e.g. Block, 1952). On the other, people's self-descriptions are remarkably stable over time under constant testing conditions (see Mischel, 1976, pp486–8) and measures of global self-esteem, for instance, undoubtedly have some psychological validity (see Wylie, 1974).

Part of the confusion seems to derive from a failure to distinguish between the self-concept as a cognitive structure and the self-images which are produced by the actual functioning of that structure at any given moment. We shall hypothesize that the self-concept is a relatively enduring, multifaceted system which is carried about in the head from situation to situation. It has the overall coherence and organization which produces a sense of unity and consistency and yet structurally and functionally its parts are highly differentiated. They are apparently able to operate relatively independently of each other. Thus in any given situation a different part or combination of parts of the self-concept could be at work with the subjective consequence that different self-images are produced. By analogy with an orchestra we can think of its musical technology and basic instrumentation as the cognitive structure and the actual sounds it makes as the varying self-images.

If this hypothesis is correct, then the possibility arises that social identity may on occasions function nearly to the exclusion of personal identity, i.e. that at certain times our salient self-images may be based solely or primarily on our group memberships.

There is anecdotal evidence for this viewpoint. There is also experimental evidence that our perception of ourselves and others is more influenced by group memberships in some contexts than others (e.g. Bruner and Perlmutter, 1957; Dion, 1975; Dion and Earn, 1975; Doise and Weinberger, 1973; Sherif, 1966). Particularly is this so, apparently, in situations of intergroup conflict or discrimination. Also relevant are the extremely important studies which demonstrate sharp changes in social norms according to the situational salience of people's different group memberships (Boyanowsky and Allen, 1973; Burnstein and McRae, 1962; Feshbach and Singer, 1957; Malof and Lott, 1962; Minard, 1952). Finally, there are several studies which make the point indirectly by manipulating the cognitive salience of group membership as their independent variable. These experiments will be cited presently.

It is a well-founded assumption in social psychology (e.g. Smith, Giles and Hewstone, 1980) that the adaptive function of cognitive structure is to mediate between the environment and behaviour. As part of cognitive structure, the self-concept can be presumed to play the same role. In appropriate circumstances it processes incoming information from the environment and regulates behaviour on the basis of the corresponding cognitive output. The evidence for the situational specificity of self-images, therefore, suggests the interesting conclusion that people have learnt to regulate their social behaviour in terms of different self-conceptions in different situations. Different situations tend to 'switch on' different conceptions of self so that social stimuli are construed and social behaviour controlled in the appropriately adaptive manner.

Social behaviour, therefore, should presumably tend to display some characteristic variation as the locus of cognitive control is switched from personal to social identity. Social situations which switch on or increase the prepotency of social identity should tend to produce their very own behavioural effects. This question has almost never been investigated in its own right. The general *a priori* outlines of an answer, however, have already been provided by Tajfel's (1974) proposition that social behaviour has two theoretical extremes which correspond to the poles of a continuum describing a transition from interpersonal to intergroup behaviour:

At one extreme . . . is the interaction between two or more individuals which is *fully* determined by their interpersonal relationships and individual characteristics and not at all affected by various social groups or categories to which they respectively belong. The other extreme consists of interactions between two or more individuals (or groups of individuals) which are *fully* determined by their respective memberships of various social groups or categories, and not at all affected by the interindividual personal relationships between the people involved . . . (Tajfel and Turner, 1979, p34)

It seems likely that the transition in cognitive functioning from personal to social identity corresponds to and underpins a shift from interpersonal to intergroup behaviour. Ultimately the empirical support for this proposition will depend on the extent to which plausible, causal theories of the links between social identity and intergroup behaviour are verified.

Two studies by Turner (1975; reported more fully in Turner, 1978a) provide some illustrative data. Subjects distributed sums of money between themselves and others, where half of the others were ingroup and half outgroup members. Group membership was salient in some conditions but not in others. In the latter conditions subjects discriminated in favour of themselves and against both ingroup and outgroup members. In the former, in contrast, subjects were altruistic towards ingroup and even more discriminatory towards outgroup members. The increased salience of a social identification transformed interpersonal discrimination into differential intergroup behaviour. The data also show that social identity influences intra- as well as intergroup relations. As we shall discuss presently there are good reasons for thinking that similar processes underlie reactions to both ingroup and outgroup members. The interpersonal *vs* intergroup dimension, therefore, runs more properly from interpersonal to intra- and intergroup behaviour.

Some other evidence that this continuum is genuinely empirical and not just conceptual comes from the consistent finding that social groups tend to be more competitive or at least differentiate themselves more than individuals under the same conditions (Doise and Sinclair, 1973; Doise and Weinberger, 1973; Dustin and Davis, 1970; Janssens and Nuttin, 1976; Wilson and Kayatani, 1968; cf. Turner, 1980). The implication is that there is some characteristic generic difference between interpersonal and intergroup relations (although some studies are more persuasive in this respect than others – see, for example, the discussions of how interpersonal processes can produce intergroup differentials in Turner, 1978*b*, and Turner *et al.*, 1979). The distinction between interpersonal and intergroup behaviour is discussed in more detail in Brown and Turner (1981).

We can summarize this section in the following terms. Social identity is a subsystem of the self-concept. The self-concept is a hypothetical cognitive structure which mediates under appropriate circumstances between the social environment and social behaviour. Social identity seems to be 'switched on' by certain situations in ways that we do not as yet fully understand. Once functioning, social identity monitors and construes social stimuli and provides a basis for regulating behaviour. Its cognitive output seems to be uniquely implicated in intra- and intergroup behaviour. In other words, we are hypothesizing that social identity is the cognitive mechanism which makes group behaviour possible.

The next problem, necessarily, is to specify the causal processes by which social identity produces this outcome. There are at least two general principles at work. Firstly, there are the relatively automatic cognitive processes associated with social categorizations and, secondly, there are the motivational processes which seem to characterize self-description. However, before discussing these processes, we shall consider some evidence relevant to whether social identification is necessary or sufficient for group behaviour.

3. The necessary and sufficient conditions for group formation

By and large, the Social Cohesion model has been developed and has been productive in investigating the dynamics of small, face-to-face groups. Research on intergroup relations, in contrast, naturally tends to favour the Social Identification model, since its subject matter is large-scale social category memberships such as nationality, class, sex, race or religion. These groups do not in the first instance seem to be based on, but seem to precede and encourage social and psychological interdependence between individuals. They are not emergent products of interpersonal interaction so much as historical and cultural givens into which people are directly socialized. Perhaps not surprisingly, therefore, it was experimental research on intergroup behaviour which produced problems for the traditional assumptions of the Social Cohesion model.

The relevant studies are as yet few, but nonetheless persuasive. They suggest that social cohesion may be neither necessary nor sufficient for group formation, whereas social identification, the perception by individuals that they are joined in common category membership, seems to be both necessary and sufficient. The studies have looked at interpersonal attraction and/or common category membership as independent variables for group behaviour as measured by intergroup discrimination in social perception and behaviour or intragroup altruism. They usually manipulate interpersonal attraction indirectly through some variable such as attitudinal similarity which, as it has been reliably demonstrated, increases liking between individuals.

The paradigmatic experiments were conducted by Tajfel, Flament, Billig and Bundy (1971); the question was whether social categorization *per se* was sufficient to cause intergroup discrimination. These investigators randomly classified their subjects into two distinct categories (e.g. Group X or Y) in isolation from all the other variables normally associated with group membership. Group membership was anonymous and there was no goal interdependence, social interaction or other basis for cohesive relations between members. Nevertheless, subjects discriminated against anonymous outgroup and in favour of anonymous ingroup members in the distribution of monetary rewards – under conditions where they could not benefit from this strategy. They demonstrated group behaviour in the form of uniformities in their reactions to others which were consistently related to their own and the others' group memberships. These results have been extensively replicated at the level of both behavioural discrimination and social evaluation (cf. Brown *et al.*, 1980; Tajfel, 1982;

Turner, 1980). It appears, therefore, that the mere perception of belonging to a social category is sufficient for group behaviour. The minimal conditions for group-belongingness do not seem to include cohesive interpersonal relations.

Some of the earlier studies, however, confounded common category membership with perceived interpersonal similarity, since subjects were ostensibly divided into groups on the basis of some trivial criterion such as their aesthetic preferences for paintings. Thus, there could have been cohesiveness between group members, as it is known that similarity is a powerful determinant of attraction. Other studies have controlled for this factor and disconfirmed its importance.

A study by Billig and Tajfel (1973) shows that perceived interpersonal similarity between members of the same category is not a necessary condition for intergroup discrimination. Subjects were divided into two minimal groups on an explicitly random basis. There was no reason at all for them to like members of their own group more than members of the other group. Yet they still demonstrated ingroup favouritism in the awards they made to ingroup and outgroup members. Similarly, Brewer and Silver (1978) worked with subjects who were either assigned to groups explicitly on the basis of similarities and differences in performance on a criterial task, or randomly. There were no significant differences between the two conditions: both criterial and arbitrary social categorization caused a more positive evaluation of ingroup than outgroup members.

Other experiments demonstrate that perceived interpersonal similarity is not always a sufficient condition for group formation in that subjects do not favour similar over dissimilar others where they have not been explicitly divided into groups on this basis (Deutsch *et al.*, 1969; Chase, 1971; Turner, 1978*a*, experiment 1). Two studies have manipulated social category membership and interpersonal similarity as independent variables in a factorial design. As mentioned above, Billig and Tajfel (1973) divided subjects into groups either on an explicitly random basis or on the basis of similarities and differences (the categorization: non-similarity and categorization: similarity conditions); in other conditions, the subjects were assigned arbitrary or criterial numbers without being explicitly divided into groups (the non-categorization: non-similarity and non-categorization: similarity conditions). It was found that categorization was more important than similarity in determining group formation: there was significant ingroup favouritism in the two categorization conditions but subjects did not significantly favour similar others or others with arbitrarily similar code numbers over dissimilar others in the non-categorization conditions. There was some evidence, however, that members of the criterial groups were more discriminatory than members of the arbitrary groups.

Allen and Wilder (1975) divided their subjects into two groups where the ingroup was perceived as either similar or different in beliefs to the subject and, independently, the outgroup was also perceived as either similar or different. There was ingroup favouritism in all conditions. Subjects even favoured dissimilar ingroup members over similar outgroup members. Outgroup similarity had no impact on intergroup discrimination, but ingroup similarity significantly increased it. Thus, both these studies tend to suggest that individuals do tend to favour similar others significantly more than dissimilar others when the former are members of the same social category as themselves.

Dion (1973) and Kennedy and Stephan (1977) investigated whether cohesiveness increased ingroup–outgroup discrimination. The latter hypothesized that successful cooperation should increase cohesiveness between individuals, but found that cooperative failure in a dyad produced more ingroup favouritism than cooperative success. Dion, also using two-person groups, directly manipulated the group members' perception of themselves as similar and compatible or not. He found that members of high-cohesive dyads were more cooperative towards their partners than towards outgroup members and rated them more favourably on sociometric traits. However, there was no difference in intergroup discrimination between high- and low-cohesive dyads on ratings of the groups as a whole and of their individual members on ability and motive traits: subjects evaluated the ingroup more favourably than the outgroup. Thus, cohesiveness influenced an individual's actions and attitudes towards his partner but group membership was more important in determining attitudes towards the ingroup and outgroup as collective entities. Both these studies suggest that cohesiveness in the form of interpersonal attraction is not necessary for group formation and not sufficient to increase intergroup discrimination.

Three field experiments conducted by Sole et al. (1975) add to the evidence from the laboratory. These researchers hypothesized that altruistic behaviour is based on common category membership. They manipulated the degree of opinion-similarity (on important and unimportant issues) between subjects and a stranger who needed help. With important issues (experiment 1), attraction to the stranger increased proportionately with his similarity to the subject, but helping increased only with 100 % or total similarity. With unimportant issues (experiment 2), helping increased with similarity, but attraction did not. With mixed important and unimportant issues (experiment 3), both helping and attraction increased significantly only in the condition of total similarity on important issues. Sole *et al.* conclude that the formation of altruistic social relationships is primarily determined by opinion similarity and subsequent social categorization, and not attraction. Similarity is only important as a determinant of attraction insofar as it allows the subjects to classify the stranger unambiguously as a member of the 'we-group'.

In toto, the above experiments suggest that cohesiveness *per se* may not be fundamental in psychological group membership. However, there is no doubt that social groups do tend to be cohesive in some sense: we are normally attracted to our fellow ingroup members. There seem to be at least four important considerations which can explain this.

Firstly, as in the studies of Sole *et al.*, there seem to be several variables which may function independently both as cognitive criteria for social categorization and as determinants of interpersonal attraction. The obvious examples are total or extreme similarities between people (Hensley and Duval, 1976; Sole *et al.*, 1975), common fate (Rabbie and Horwitz, 1969), shared threat (Burnstein and McRae, 1962; Feshbach and Singer, 1957) and physical proximity. Thus, social categorization and interpersonal attraction may sometimes be correlated effects of the same variables. Correspondingly, many variables which are assumed to contribute to group formation by creating cohesiveness may actually work by defining individuals as members of a common social category.

Secondly, there is plenty of evidence that variables determining interpersonal attraction seem to contribute to group-belongingness once a common category membership has already been established. This seems to be the case with social or verbal interaction (Janssens and Nuttin, 1976; Rabbie and Huygen, 1974; Rabbie and Wilkens, 1971; Stephenson *et al.*, 1976), 'collective encounter' (Doise and Weinberger, 1973), and belief similarity (Allen and Wilder, 1975). It is not clear whether these effects are produced by increases in cohesiveness, the cognitive or emotional salience of group membership, or some other process. One possible mechanism is discussed below.

Thirdly, social cohesion may arise as a direct product of social identification. We may not form a group with individuals we like so much as like people because they belong to our group. This is explicable in terms of self- and intragroup-stereotyping processes to be discussed in the next section. The basic hypothesis is that social categorizations are subjectively associated with or defined by correlated dimensions: some cluster of descriptive, evaluative or normative attributes which characterize what members of the same category are supposed to have in common and how they differ from members of other categories. Under conditions where group membership is salient, we perceive or stereotype ourselves and others in terms of the common or criterial attributes of the categories to which we and they belong. Since individuals within the same category stereotype themselves in terms of the same group characteristics, there is a perceptual enhancement of their mutual similarity which should increase intragroup attraction. Thus, social identification could create social cohesion on the basis of the stereotypical similarities perceived between oneself and fellow ingroup members. This would be *intragroup* rather than *interpersonal* attraction since it would not arise from the idiosyncratic similarities between individual persons.

It seems likely that even arbitrary social categorizations can create intragroup attraction in this manner. Individuals assigned to groups on a random basis probably tend to assume that they must have something in common or automatically invent or infer common group characteristics from the available information. At the very least, they would have information about one exemplary group member, themselves, from which to derive inferences about the characteristics of the group as a whole. This does not mean that even arbitrary social categorizations always confound social identification and cohesiveness. Self-perception in terms of common category membership is the basis for, and causes, assumed intermember similarity and the similarity in question is intragroup and not interpersonal, since it is mediated by prior acceptance of the assigned category membership.

Fourthly, and related to the above, we need to distinguish between group formation based on interpersonal attraction, liking for individuals as differentiated unique persons, and that based on attraction to individuals as exemplars of positively valued group characteristics. There seems little doubt that since we evaluate ourselves in terms of our group memberships, we are more willing to identify with categories defined by positive rather than negative characteristics. Hence, we should be more willing to form a group with individuals who share some positive common attribute. In this sense, attraction should facilitate group formation. However, the important point is that in order to perceive the likeable qualities of individuals as reflecting some shared attribute we already need some minimal cognitive basis for construing them as a social unit. Thus, attraction to *individuals as individuals* does not create a group, but attraction to *individuals as group members*, which presupposes social categorization, reinforces

social identification by defining the common attributes of group membership as positive. This is so not despite, but precisely because, group formation has to do with self-conception and so is influenced by motives
for positive self-esteem.

Some such process may well explain why variables normally determining interpersonal attraction do tend to increase attachment to a group
where individuals are already perceived as group members. Presumably in
this case there is a strong motive to generalize the positive attributes of
specific individuals to the group as a whole, to assume that we like each
other because of the common qualities of our group and hence to attribute these virtues to ourselves by affirming our identification with the
group.

To conclude this section, we can hypothesize that awareness of common
category membership is the necessary and sufficient condition for individuals to feel themselves to be, and act as, a group. This hypothesis suggests
that to understand how social groups are formed, research should focus
less on the determinants of interpersonal attraction and more on: (i) those
variables such as similarity, common fate, proximity, shared threat and
other unit-forming factors which function as cognitive criteria for the
segmentation of the social world into discontinuous social categories;
(ii) social influence processes whereby individuals are persuaded by significant others to define themselves in terms of specific social categorizations;
and (iii) other processes whereby social categories are internalized as
aspects of the self-concept such as, for example, self-attitude change on the
basis of overt compliance with distinctive group norms. If one agrees with
Lott and Lott (1965) that there is no difference between attraction to a
group and attraction to the individual persons within the group and that,
consequently, cohesiveness can be equated with interpersonal attraction,
then cohesiveness seems to be an inadequate theory of group formation.
If, however, one employs the concept of social cohesion in a more catholic
sense to include attraction to individuals as group members (exemplars or
representatives of common attributes of the group as a whole), then it does
seem to be sufficient to increase group-belongingness; but in this sense, it
always presupposes social categorization, and, thus, strictly speaking,
contributes to social identification. The most powerful determinants of
group formation, therefore, are likely to be variables which at one and the
same time define individuals as members of a common social category and
indicate that its criterial attributes are positive rather than negative. It
should be remembered, however, that once individuals define themselves
or are defined by others as members of a category, there will be strong

motivational pressures for them to assume that its characteristics are positive and even reinterpret as positive those designated as negative by outsiders. Hence, attractive group properties are not, at least in the first instance, a necessary condition for group formation.

4. Social categorization processes and group behaviour

Tajfel's categorization theory (1959, 1972; also cf. Doise, 1978) asserts that categorizing activity has both an inductive and deductive aspect. Deduction refers to the process by which a person is assigned some attribute on the basis of his category membership. Induction, for Tajfel, refers to the identification of a person as a member of a category, but we shall use it to mean the assignment to a category of some attribute perceived to characterize an exemplary member. Thus, induction is the means by which the criterial attributes of some category are inferred from one or more individual members and deduction is the process of assigning them to all members of the category. A criterial attribute or common category characteristic is any property whose continuous distribution amongst individuals is to some degree correlated with or perceived to be correlated with their discontinuous classification as members of different social groups. Under conditions where individuals' social category memberships are salient, they tend to be assigned all the characteristics perceived to define their category. This fact is the basis for what we can call Tajfel's (categorization) law that, as category memberships become salient, there will be a tendency to exaggerate the differences on criterial dimensions between individuals falling into distinct categories, and to minimize these differences within each of these categories. The accentuation of intraclass similarities and interclass differences is further enhanced by the value significance of the classification. Empirical support for the law can be found in the publications cited above.

Tajfel's law provides such a good account of stereotyping (e.g. Tajfel, 1969; Hamilton, 1976) that the latter can be considered to a large extent as simply the operation of the law in the perception of social groups. It is well known (e.g. Ehrlich, 1973) that stereotyping leads to the homogenization and depersonalization of outgroup members. These individuals become perceptually interchangeable because they are perceived in terms of their shared category characteristics and not their personal idiosyncratic natures. Several distinctively intragroup phenomena also seem to be marked by depersonalization and there is now some evidence that they, too, are influenced by the cognitive salience of group membership. The clear implication is that the same processes are also at work in intragroup behaviour.

Intragroup relations tend to be characterized by: (1) the perceived similarity of members; (2) mutual attraction between members or social cohesion; (3) mutual esteem; (4) emotional empathy or contagion; (5) altruism and cooperation, and (6) attitudinal and behavioural uniformity. There is also evidence that, as group membership is made salient, perceived intragroup similarity and intragroup liking tend to be enhanced (e.g. Hensley and Duval, 1976; Turner, 1978*a*), self and others are evaluated favourably in terms of common group membership even when own and others' individual performances were detrimental to the group outcomes (Myers, 1962; Kalin and Marlowe, 1968; Kahn and Ryen, 1972), others' goals and needs can become motives for one's own behaviour (Horwitz, 1953; Hornstein, 1972, 1976), and conformity to group norms increases without direct social influence from others (Charters and Newcomb, 1952; Doise, 1969; Shomer and Centers, 1970; Skinner and Stephenson, 1976; White, 1977). The above papers are cited because they focus more or less on the cognitive salience of group membership as their independent variable and because they report data inexplicable in terms of interpersonal relations operating within groups.

The (not necessarily exclusive) explanation for these phenomena proposed here is that once individuals' common social identification of themselves is 'switched on', they tend to perceive themselves and others in terms of that category membership. Common category characteristics are inferred from the available exemplars of the category, including oneself, and then automatically assigned, along with long-term criterial traits, to all members, again including oneself. The cognitive output of a functioning social identification is, in a nutshell, stereotypic perception. This regulates social behaviour in two main ways. Firstly, assigning oneself criterial attributes such as emotions, motives and norms can instigate and control behaviour directly. Secondly, the way we perceive others will influence indirectly how we act towards them.

This explanation modifies the normal usage of stereotyping in three ways: we are suggesting that stereotyping is as applicable to ingroups (and the self) as outgroups (e.g. Stephan, 1977*a*), that stereotypic characteristics include evaluative status or prestige, emotional experiences, needs and goals and attitudinal and behavioural norms as well as the well-studied personality or behavioural traits, and that the inductive and deductive aspects of categorizing may operate rapidly and transitorily as well as relatively slowly and stably.

Tajfel's law itself specifies that stereotyping creates or enhances per-ceived intragroup similarity. We infer the common characteristics of our category from individual exemplars and then assign them to all members. This suggests, as we have seen, that social cohesion can arise as a direct product of social identification. Intragroup liking would be created by the perceived stereotypic similarity of ingroup members as much as by their actual personal similarities. This hypothesis seems never to have been looked at directly, but some data tend to favour it (Allen and Wilder, 1975, p972; Hensley and Duval, 1976; Stephan, 1977*b*; Turner, 1978*a*). It makes the prediction that face-to-face interaction could sometimes *decrease* intragroup cohesion by providing information which disconfirmed stereotypic similarity.

Mutual esteem within groups, too, is explained simply by the idea that individuals tend to evaluate themselves and others in terms of their com-mon category membership. Prestige would be assigned to group members in the same way as any other criterial attribute. Evidence that the desire for positive self-esteem is as important in social as personal identity (see Tajfel, 1978; Tajfel and Turner, 1979) suggests that this is so. There are also more specific data indicating that the inductive and deductive aspects of intragroup stereotyping are strongly biased towards a favourable self-evaluation. Positive characteristics are more likely than negative charac-teristics to be perceived as ingroup attributes (Stephan, 1977*b*; Taylor and Jaggi, 1974) and also more likely to be assigned to oneself when group membership is salient (Dion, 1975; Dion and Earn, 1975).

The author is aware of no evidence relating directly to emotional empathy or contagion, although the role of cognitive factors in emotional states is generally accepted (see Harvey and Smith, 1977, pp107–27, for a review). A hypothetical example would be a racial incident in which one black person was assaulted by one white person. We can imagine that one possible result might be that the local black community as a whole would react angrily and seek revenge on all available whites. Each black person might respond emotionally as if he himself had been attacked. He would be assigning to himself the experience of his social category, which, in turn, he had inferred from the experience of one representative member. We need assume no friendship or acquaintance between the victim and other blacks for empathy and contagion to occur, nor any group pressure for emotional conformity. We need assume only that individuals act on the basis of their shared self-stereotype as circumstances make their category membership salient or relevant.

Hornstein (1972, 1976) and his colleagues have produced much evidence that altruism and cooperative behaviour between individuals are mediated by the perception of common category membership. Here we need only note that his independent analysis is similar to ours in its tenets that altruism is primarily an intragroup rather than an interpersonal phenomenon, that its main necessary condition is the perception of 'we-group ties' between individuals (which we would argue is dependent on a common social identification) and that it represents behaviour based on the cognitive extension of the self, not its abolition. We help others, apparently selflessly, because we perceive their needs and goals as those of our social category and hence as our very own. Social categorizations which extend self-definition beyond the individual person provide a simple and elegant mechanism for bypassing the supposed 'egotism' of human beings.

The studies cited above which demonstrate conformity without direct interpersonal influence from others pose, in microcosm, the problem of how attitudinal and behavioural uniformity is created amongst members of large-scale social categories. Our solution is to postulate a distinct form of social influence produced by the cognitive processes associated with self-stereotyping. We shall term it *Referent Informational Influence* (RII) since it is similar to, but still not identical with, an amalgam of Deutsch and Gerard's (1955) *informational influence* with Kelman's (1961) process of *identification* or French and Raven's (1959) *referent power*. RII takes place in three stages:

  (i)   Individuals define themselves as members of a distinct social category.
  (ii) Individuals form or learn the stereotypic norms of that category. They ascertain that certain ways of behaving are criterial attributes of category membership. Certain appropriate, expected or desirable behaviours are used to define the category as different from other categories.
  (iii) Individuals assign these norms to themselves in the same way that they assign other stereotypic characteristics of the category to themselves when their category membership becomes psychologically salient. Thus their behaviour becomes more normative (conformist) as their category membership becomes salient.

The main differences between RII and Normative Influence (NI) and Informational Influence (II) as usually understood can be described as follows:
(i) *Who is one influenced by?*
  NI: People with power to reward conformity and punish deviation (usually attractive others).

II: Similar people who provide information about physical or social reality.

RII: People who provide information about the criterial norms of one's social category. These will usually be common category members (who need not be attractive or similar), but in some instances where ingroup members are not available, they may be persuasive outgroup members (e.g. the mass media, school, etc.).

(ii) *What is the vehicle of social influence?*

NI: Social communication from group members or 'group pressure'.

II: Social comparisons with group members.

RII: Social identification – the processes by which one defines oneself as a category member, forms a group stereotype on the basis of other category members' behaviour, and applies the stereotype to oneself. Interpersonal communication and comparison may be important for elaborating the stereotype, but they are not the vehicle of influence, since they are not necessary for increased conformity.

(iii) *Under what conditions does conformity increase?*

NI: When one's behaviour is under surveillance by fellow group members.

II: When physical or social reality is ambiguous, complex or problematic in some way.

RII: When one's group membership (self-definition as a group member) is salient.

(iv) *What does one conform to?*

NI: The observable behaviour of other group members.

II: Ditto.

RII: One's own beliefs about the appropriate behaviour for all category members (the cognitive aspects of one's attitudes towards the ingroup, or one's stereotype of the ingroup). Own behaviour may become more normative at the same time as it differs from the observable behaviour of other group members.

Empirical evidence for RII comes so far from three sources. There are the above studies which demonstrate increased conformity or more normative behaviour simply as a function of reference group salience. There are the related studies, also cited above, which illustrate or at least suggest that people's normative attitudes and behaviours are highly situation-specific, varying according to which of their group memberships is salient in a given context (e.g. Boyanowsky and Allen, 1973; Burnstein and McRae, 1962; Feshbach and Singer, 1957; Malof and Lott, 1962; Minard, 1952).

Finally, there is the almost platitudinous fact that social roles can often have an immediate and dramatic impact on social behaviour because people tend to enact their stereotype of the social role in which they find themselves. Zimbardo's (1975) 'simulated prison' experiment provides the most significant, recent example of this process. Although many different factors were undoubtedly at work in this complex study, it seems probable that the obtained uniformities in intra- and intergroup behaviour were at least partly due to the subjects' stereotypes of what were the appropriate ways for prisoners and guards to behave (cf. Banuazizi and Movahedi, 1975).

Overall, therefore, the idea that some of the distinctive characteristics of intragroup behaviour may reflect cognitive progress associated with social categorizations that define the self-concept seems to have heuristic value. We can conclude this section by noting that perhaps its most exciting implication is that it suggests a way of accepting that group behaviour has superordinate or suprapersonal properties which cannot be reduced to interpersonal relationships whilst explaining such properties in terms of individual psychological processes. We need not posit any metaphysical entity such as a 'group mind' to argue that group behaviour is more than a summation of individual actions. There is an important discontinuity at the level of psychological processes between an individual acting as a differentiated, unique person and an individual acting as a group member, as a relatively interchangeable representative of a social category (cf. Sherif, 1966, ch.1). The fundamental difference is that the individual's very conception of self changes to partake of the common attributes of an historically originated, socially determined and culturally and situationally constructed social group.

5. Self-esteem and group behaviour

The other major way (so far researched) in which social identity regulates social behaviour is through extending the sphere of operation of motivational processes associated with self-conception. Perhaps the most important and obvious example is provided by the effects of the need for positive self-esteem on group behaviour. We have touched upon some of these effects already earlier in the chapter. In this section, we shall attempt to do no more than reintroduce the issue in an extremely cursory form.

The most immediate point is that where some social category contributes to defining the self, the need for positive self-esteem should motivate a desire to evaluate that category positively. Tajfel and Turner (1979) describe this as a need for positive social identity and have made it the basis for an extensive theoretical analysis of intergroup relations (see also Tajfel, 1978; Turner, 1975, 1981). We shall not reiterate their analyses but merely describe their basic hypothesis.

They argue that social categories are evaluated through social comparisons with other categories on relevant value dimensions. Positively discrepant or favourable comparisons between the ingroup and an outgroup provide ingroup members with high subjective status or prestige and thus positive social identity, whereas negatively discrepant or unfavourable comparisons provide low prestige and negative social identity. Thus, the need for positive social identity motivates a search for, and the creation and enhancement of, positive distinctiveness for one's own group in comparison with other groups. Where the ingroup lacks positive distinctiveness, members will be motivated either to leave that group physically or dissociate themselves from it psychologically and aspire to membership of a higher status group or to adopt creative and/or competitive strategies to restore its positive distinctiveness. These ideas have inspired a good deal of research (e.g. Tajfel, 1978).

One fundamental application is in the analysis of intergroup discrimination and ingroup biases in social perception. We have already seen that there is evidence both that social categorization *per se*, a simple ingroup–outgroup distinction, is sufficient for intergroup discrimination, and that intergroup behaviour tends to be more discriminatory or competitive than interpersonal behaviour (cf. Turner, 1980). There is also, in fact, much other evidence that perceptual and attitudinal biases favouring the ingroup over the outgroup are extremely common in intergroup relations (Brewer, 1979; Doise, 1978; Tajfel, 1978; Turner, 1981). The positive distinctiveness principle helps to explain why this should be the case. Ingroups may discriminate or compete against outgroups not because there is any realistic conflict of group interests but simply to differentiate themselves and maintain a positive social identity for their members (Tajfel, 1974; Turner, 1975, 1981). A small study by Oakes and Turner (1980) has in fact shown directly that intergroup discrimination on the basis of social categorization *per se* does seem to be associated with increased self-esteem amongst subjects.

Another, as yet untested, implication of the positive distinctiveness principle, is that there should be a motivational bias to make any descriptive group characteristic prescriptive or normative. Presumably, members will be motivated to evaluate distinctive group characteristics or criterial attributes as positive or socially desirable, and perhaps to a greater degree, the more distinctive the attribute. Thus, any characteristic which defines the ingroup as different from other groups will tend to be evaluated positively, (i.e. it will become perceived as socially desirable and expected), and so it will be transformed into a social norm which members strive to enact. This implies that to define oneself in terms of a social category is inherently to accept its common attributes as prescriptions for behaviour. It also indicates that the need for positive self-esteem has implications for intragroup behaviour as well as the forms of intergroup behaviour with which Tajfel and Turner have been concerned.

It can be hypothesized, for example, that just as individuals seek to differentiate their own from other groups, so they may also, for the same reason, seek to differentiate themselves from fellow group members in terms of their common attributes. They may tend to assign positive group characteristics to themselves and any negative characteristics to other members or, in assigning positive attributes of group membership to all members, they may nonetheless assume that they are still closer to the normative ideal.

Some evidence is provided by the phenomenon of group polarization: the discovery that uniformities in intragroup behaviour result from the members' opinions becoming more extreme in the socially favoured direction rather than from convergence on the average of their initial positions. At least one important school of thought explains polarization in terms of self-enhancing social comparisons to differentiate oneself from others (e.g. Baron and Byrne, 1977, p574). The process at work may be very similar to Codol's (1975) concept of *over-conformity*. He shows that individuals do not simply conform to group norms but compete with each other to enact the norm, each claiming that they are closer to the normative ideal than other group members. If a norm is conceptualized as a criterial attribute of category membership (as is done by Codol), then the concept of over-conformity provides a useful example of how the motivational effects of a social identification can combine with and accentuate the cognitive effects. The general rule would be that individuals tend to assign the positive aspects of the ingroup stereotype to themselves to a greater degree than they assign them to fellow ingroup members and also strive to enact them to a greater degree than others. By the same token, the fact that individuals compete to enact the same criterial attributes, that they compete to be the first amongst equals on those dimensions which describe what they have in common as group members, may explain how social differentiation serves to unify relations within groups as opposed to disrupting them as it often seems to do between groups.

To summarize: the need for positive self-esteem probably helps to regulate both intra- and intergroup behaviour; individuals do not simply perceive themselves as similar within and different between groups, but also compare and differentiate themselves from each other in terms of these similarities and differences.

6. Conclusion

This chapter has attempted to argue that, from a social psychological perspective, a social group can be usefully conceptualized as a number of individuals who have internalized the same social category membership as a component of their self-concept. It has argued, too, that group behaviour can be seen as causally dependent on the functioning of such shared social identifications. There are many issues which have been touched on only briefly or neglected completely. Perhaps the most important are: (i) the processes whereby social identifications or social categorizations are formed and internalized; (ii) the conditions under which a social identification is 'switched on' to become a salient basis for cognition and behaviour; and (iii) the implications of the Social Identification model for the distinction, theoretical and empirical, between interpersonal and group behaviour. There are doubtless others. Such omissions should be seen not merely as limitations in the present argument but also as deficiencies in the current state of empirical knowledge and as directions for future research. If the present argument helps to stimulate that research, as well as empirical work and theoretical discussion on those hypotheses which it has included, it will have served its purpose. The Social Identification model is advanced as a first approximation which will doubtless have to be revised, but which in the course of revision may contribute to renewed research interest in the social group in social psychology.

Note

[1] This chapter is a revised version of a paper first presented to the Research Colloquium on Social Identity of the European Laboratory of Social Psychology (LEPS), at the Université de Haute Bretagne, Rennes, France, 3–6 December 1978.

References

Allen, V.L. and Wilder, D.A. 1975. Categorization, belief-similarity and inter-group discrimination. *Journal of Personality and Social Psychology*, **32**, 971–7.
Banuazizi, A. and Movahedi, J. 1975. Interpersonal dynamics in a simulated prison: A methodological analysis. *American Psychologist*, **30**, 152–60.

Baron, R.A. and Byrne, D. 1977. *Social psychology*. Boston, Mass.: Allyn and Bacon, 2nd Edition.

Billig, M.G. 1973. Normative communication in a minimal intergroup situation. *European Journal of Social Psychology*, **3**, 339–43.

Billig, M.G. and Tajfel, H. 1973. Social categorization and similarity in intergroup behaviour. *European Journal of Social Psychology*, **3**, 27–52.

Block, J. 1952. The assessment of communication: Role variations as a function of interactional context. *Journal of Personality*, **21**, 272–86.

Boyanowsky, E.O. and Allen, V.L. 1973. Ingroup norms and self-identity as determinants of discriminatory behaviour. *Journal of Personality and Social Psychology*, **25**, 408–18.

Brewer, M.B. 1979. Ingroup bias in the minimal intergroup situation: A cognitive–motivational analysis. *Psychological Bulletin*, **86**, 307–24.

Brewer, M.B. and Silver, M. 1978. Ingroup bias as a function of task characteristics. *European Journal of Social Psychology*, **8**, 393–400.

Brown, R.J., Tajfel, H. and Turner, J.C. 1980. Minimal group situations and intergroup discrimination: Comments on the paper by Aschenbrenner and Schaefer. *European Journal of Social Psychology*, **10**, 399–414.

Brown, R.J. and Turner, J.C. in press. Interpersonal and intergroup behaviour. In J.C. Turner and H. Giles (eds.): *Intergroup behaviour*. Oxford: Blackwell.

Bruner, J.S. and Perlmutter, H.V. 1957. Compatriot and foreigner: A study of impression formation in three countries. *Journal of Abnormal and Social Psychology*, **55**, 253–260.

Burnstein, E. and McRae, A.V. 1962. Some effects of shared threat and prejudice in racially mixed groups. *Journal of Abnormal and Social Psychology*, **64**, 257–263.

Charters, W.W. and Newcomb, T.M. 1952. Some attitudinal effects of experimentally increased salience of a membership group. In G.E. Swanson *et al.* (eds.): *Readings in social psychology*. New York: Holt, Rinehart and Winston.

Chase, M. 1971. Categorization and affective arousal: Some behavioural and affective consequences. *Dissertation Abstracts International*, (Dec.), **32**, 6-A, 3420.

Codol, J.-P. 1975. On the so-called "superior conformity of the self" behaviour: Twenty experimental investigations. *European Journal of Social Psychology*, **5**, 457–501.

Deutsch, M., Chase, M., Garner, R. and Thomas, J.R.H. 1969. Social perception of similarity and dissimilarity and preferential treatment of a similar person in money allocation. Unpublished paper, Teachers College, Columbia University.

Deutsch, M. and Gerard, H.G. 1955. A study of normative and informational social influence upon individual judgement. *Journal of Abnormal and Social Psychology*, **51**, 629–36.

Dion, K.L. 1973. Cohesiveness as a determinant of ingroup–outgroup bias. *Journal of Personality and Social Psychology*, **28**, 163–71.

Dion, K.L. 1975. Women's reactions to discrimination from members of the same or opposite sex. *Journal of Research in Personality*, **9**, 294–306.

Dion, K.L. and Earn, B.M. 1975. The phenomenology of being a target of prejudice. *Journal of Personality and Social Psychology*, **32**, 944–50.

Doise, W. 1969. Intergroup relations and polarization of individual and collective judgements. *Journal of Personality and Social Psychology*, **12**, 136–43.

Doise, W. 1978. *Groups and individuals: Explanations in social psychology*. Cambridge: Cambridge University Press.

Doise, W. and Sinclair, A. 1973. The categorization process in intergroup relations. *European Journal of Social Psychology*, **3**, 145–57.

Doise, W. and Weinberger, M. 1973. Représentations masculines dans différentes situations de rencontres mixtes. *Bulletin de Psychologie*, **26**, 649–57.

Dustin, D.S. and Davis, H.P. 1970. Evaluative bias in group and individual competition. *Journal of Social Psychology*, **80**, 103–8.

Ehrlich, H.J. 1973. *The social psychology of prejudice*. New York: Wiley.

Feshbach, S. and Singer, R. 1957. The effects of personal and shared threats upon social prejudice. *Journal of Abnormal and Social Psychology*, **54**, 411–16.

French, J.R.P. (Jr) and Raven, B. 1959. The bases of social power. In D. Cartwright (ed.): *Studies in social power*. Ann Arbor, Michigan: Institute for Social Research.

Gergen, K.J. 1971. *The concept of self*. New York: Holt, Rinehart and Winston.

Gordon, C. 1968. Self-conceptions: Configurations of content. In C. Gordon and K.J. Gergen (eds): *The self in social interaction*, Vol. I. New York: Wiley.

Hamilton, D.L. 1976. Cognitive biases in the perception of social groups. In J.S. Carroll and J.W. Payne (eds): *Cognition and social behaviour*. Hillsdale, N.J.: Erlbaum.

Harvey, J.H. and Smith, W.P. 1977. *Social psychology*. Saint Louis: C.V. Mosby.

Hensley, V. and Duval, S. 1976. Some perceptual determinants of perceived similarity, liking and correctness. *Journal of Personality and Social Psychology*, **34**, 159–68.

Hornstein, H.A. 1972. Promotive tension: The basis of prosocial behaviour from a Lewinian perspective. *Journal of Social Issues*, **28**, 191–218.

Hornstein, H.A. 1976. *Cruelty and kindness: A new look at aggression and altruism*. Englewood Cliffs, N.J.: Prentice-Hall.

Horwitz, M. 1953. The recall of interrupted group tasks: An experimental study of individual motivation in relation to group goals. *Human Relations*, **7**, 107–12.

Janssens, L. and Nuttin, J.R. 1976. Frequency perception of individual and group successes as a function of competition, coaction and isolation. *Journal of Personality and Social Psychology*, **34**, 830–6.

Kahn, R. and Ryen, A.H. 1972. Factors influencing the bias towards one's own group. *International Journal of Group Tensions*, **2**, 33–50.

Kaliň, R. and Marlowe, D. 1968. The effects of intergroup competition, personal drinking habits and frustration in intra-group cooperation. *Proceedings of the 76th Annual Conference of the A.P.A.*, **3**, 405–6.

Kelman, H.C. 1961. Three processes of social influence. *Public Opinion Quarterly*, **25**, 57–78.

Kennedy, J. and Stephan, W.G. 1977. The effects of cooperation and competition on ingroup–outgroup bias. *Journal of Applied Social Psychology*, **7**, (2), 115–30.

Lott, A.J. and Lott, B.E. 1965. Group cohesiveness as interpersonal attraction: A review of relationships with antecedent and consequent variables. *Psychological Bulletin*, **64**, 259–309.

Malof, M. and Lott, A. 1962. Ethnocentrism and the acceptance of Negro support in a group pressure situation. *Journal of Abnormal and Social Psychology*, **65**, 254–8.

Minard, R.D. 1952. Race relationships in the Pocahontas coalfield. *Journal of Social Issues*, **8**, 29–44.

Mischel, W. 1976. *Introduction to personality*. New York: Holt, Rinehart and Winston. 2nd Edition.

Myers, A. 1962. Team competition, success and the adjustment of group members. *Journal of Abnormal and Social Psychology*, **65**, 325–32.

Oakes, P.J. and Turner, J.C. 1980. Social categorization and intergroup behaviour: Does minimal intergroup discrimination make social identity more positive? *European Journal of Social Psychology*, **10**, 295–301.

Rabbie, J.M. and Horwitz, M. 1969. Arousal of ingroup–outgroup bias by a chance win or loss. *Journal of Personality and Social Psychology*, **13**, 269–77.

Rabbie, J.M. and Huygen, K. 1974. Internal disagreements and their effects on attitudes towards in- and outgroup. *International Journal of Group Tensions*, **4**, (2), 222–46.

Rabbie, J.M. and Wilkens, G. 1971. Intergroup competition and its effects on intra-group and intergroup relations. *European Journal of Social Psychology*, **1**, 215–34.

Shaw, M.E. 1976. *Group dynamics*. New Delhi: Tata McGraw Hill, 2nd Edition.

Sherif, M. 1966. *Group conflict and cooperation: Their social psychology*. London: Routledge and Kegan Paul.

Shomer, R.W. and Centers, R. 1970. Differences in attitudinal responses under conditions of implicitly manipulated group salience. *Journal of Personality and Social Psychology*, **15**, 125–32.

Skinner, M. and Stephenson, G.M. 1976. Group categorization, group identity and the polarization of opinions. Unpublished MS, University of Nottingham.

Smith, P.M., Giles, H. and Hewstone, M. 1980. Sociolinguistics: A social psychological perspective. In R. St. Clair and H. Giles (eds.): *The social and psychological contexts of language*. Hillsdale, N.J.: Erlbaum.

Sole, K., Marton, J. and Hornstein, H.A. 1975. Opinion similarity and helping: Three field experiments investigating the bases of promotive tension. *Journal of Experimental Social Psychology*, **11**, 1–13.

Stephan, W.G. 1977a. Cognitive differentiation in intergroup perception. *Sociometry*, **40**, 50–8.

Stephan, W.G. 1977b. Stereotyping: The role of ingroup–outgroup differences in causal attribution for behaviour. *Journal of Social Psychology*, **101**, 255–66.

Stephenson, G.M., Skinner, M. and Brotherton, C.J. 1976. Group participation and intergroup relations: An experimental study of negotiation groups. *European Journal of Social Psychology*, **6**, 51–70.

Tajfel, H. 1959. Quantitative judgement in social perception. *British Journal of Psychology*, **50**, 16–29.

Tajfel, H. 1969. Cognitive aspects of prejudice. *Journal of Social Issues*, **25**, 79–97.

Tajfel, H. 1972. Social categorization. English MS. of La catégorisation sociale.
    In S. Moscovici (ed.): *Introduction à la psychologie sociale*, Vol. I Paris:
    Larousse.
Tajfel, H. 1974. Intergroup behaviour, social comparison and social change.
    Unpublished Katz-Newcomb lectures at University of Michigan, Ann
    Arbor.
Tajfel, H. (ed.) 1978. *Differentiation between social groups: Studies in the social
    psychology of intergroup relations.* European Monographs in Social Psychology,
    No. 14. London: Academic Press.
Tajfel, H. in press, 1982. Social psychology of intergroup relations. In *Annual
    Review of Psychology*, Vol. 33. Palo Alto, Calif.: Annual Reviews.
Tajfel, H., Flament, C., Billig, M.G. and Bundy, R.P. 1971. Social categoriza-
    tion and intergroup behaviour. *European Journal of Social Psychology*, **1**,
    149–75.
Tajfel, H. and Turner, J.C. 1979. An integrative theory of intergroup conflict.
    In W.G. Austin and S. Worchel (eds): *The social psychology of intergroup
    relations.* Monterey, Calif.: Brooks/Cole.
Taylor, D.M. and Jaggi, V. 1974. Ethnocentrism and causal attribution in a
    South Indian context. *Journal of Cross-Cultural Psychology*, **5**, 162–72.
Turner, J.C. 1975. Social comparison and social identity: Some prospects for
    intergroup behaviour. *European Journal of Social Psychology*, **5**, 5–34.
Turner, J.C. 1978*a*. Social categorization and social discrimination in the minimal
    group paradigm. In H. Tajfel (ed.), *op. cit.*
Turner, J.C. 1978*b*. Social comparison, similarity and ingroup favouritism. In
    H. Tajfel (ed.), *op. cit.*
Turner, J.C. 1980. Fairness or discrimination in intergroup behaviour? A reply
    to Branthwaite, Doyle and Lightbown. *European Journal of Social Psychology*,
    10, 131–47.
Turner, J.C. 1981. The experimental social psychology of intergroup behaviour.
    In J.C. Turner and H. Giles (eds): *Intergroup behaviour.* Oxford: Blackwell.
Turner, J.C., Brown, R.J. and Tajfel, H. 1979. Social comparison and group
    interest in ingroup favouritism. *European Journal of Social Psychology*, **9**, **2**,
    187–204.
White, M.J. 1977. Counternormative behaviour as influenced by de-individuat-
    ing conditions and reference group salience. *Journal of Social Psychology*,
    103, 75–90.
Wilson, W. and Kayatani, M. 1968. Intergroup attitudes and strategies in games
    between opponents of the same or of a different race. *Journal of Personality
    and Social Psychology*, **9**, 24–30.
Wylie, R.C. 1974. *The self-concept. Vol. I: A review of methodological considerations
    and measuring instruments.* University of Nebraska Press.
Zimbardo, P.G. 1975. Transforming experimental research into advocacy for
    social change. In M. Deutsch and H.A. Hornstein (eds): *Applying social
    psychology.* Hillsdale, N.J.: Erlbaum.

2. The determination of collective behaviour

STEPHEN REICHER

1. Introduction

This chapter has as its aim to account for the particular forms of behaviour that occur as soon as individuals act as members of a crowd. One of the major difficulties of both classic and modern work on crowd behaviour has been its inability to define adequately what actually constitutes a crowd in psychological terms. Le Bon (1895, translated 1947) in his seminal work on crowd psychology could only suggest that 'the primary characteristics of a crowd ... do not always involve the simultaneous presence of a number of individuals on one spot ... at certain moments half a dozen men might constitute a psychological crowd which may not happen in the case of hundreds of men gathered together by accident' (p24).

This definitional impotence pervades the early work, with the notable exception of Freud, who will be discussed below. If the modern literature is surveyed, one finds, as Turner notes (1978c), that 'Experimental social psychology has tended to be preoccupied with the affiliative–interactive aspects of group membership ... At minimum a group is defined as two or more individuals who are physically and psychologically interdependent in some way – for the satisfaction of needs or the locomotion towards a goal, for example, or in terms of common fate or social influence. An additional criterion is sometimes that these same individuals should have evolved a social structure as the product of their mutual social influence.'

It is clear, however, that crowds do not fit easily into this framework, given their immediate, and seemingly goal independent, formation, as well as their obvious lack of structure. There have been various attempts to overcome this problem: the reality of the crowd as a homogeneous entity has been challenged (Turner and Killian, 1957), crowd psychology has been approached as an asocial phenomenon (cf. Zajonc, 1965; Geen and Gange, 1977), notions of accelerated interactive process have been advanced (Berkowitz, 1970; Walters, 1968; Wheeler, 1966). Generally, the major theme has been to set the crowd aside as some sort of abnormality. As Milgram and Toch (1969) put it: 'the crowd was first presented to psychology in its pathological forms and this focus has remained fixed for historical rather than scientific reasons. Mass media reinforce this bias' (p570). But despite their awareness of the problem, these authors commit exactly the same error when they ask: 'why do the restraints that lead to conventional decent behaviour in the average man break down when he is in the crowd?' (p517).

Not only does this imply that crowd behaviour is in some way 'indecent', but, more interestingly, it appears to separate out the crowd as being not bound by convention, as being without restraints, formless and anarchic. This notion has a long history, from Le Bon's explanation of crowd behaviour as the manifestation of a 'racial unconscious' to the most recent experimental research (cf. Dipboye, 1977). Moreover, the quasi-universality of this notion suggests that Milgram and Toch's explanation of it as a historical accident perpetuated by the media is something of an over-simplification. One reason for this thesis of crowd abnormality is the difficulty of fitting the crowd to the orthodox treatment of the social group. There is, however, another, and more basic, reason for this bias.

It is a striking fact that nearly all the work on crowd psychology has occurred at times when the crowd was seen as a threat to the stability of society; thus, the early work has an obsession with the rise of socialism, and the recent work arose out of the student protests and the civil rights demonstrations of the sixties. The concern has been not so much with the processes of collective psychology as with the crowd as a social problem and, in line with this concern, the crowd was characterized as a set of undesirable behaviours. This 'social problem' orientation led in this direct way not only to the classification of the crowd as 'abnormal' but it also dictated an approach to the research that reinforced that classification.

This perspective viewed the group from outside, in terms of those features which determine it as a distinct entity displaying certain forms of behaviour of interest to the observer. Thus, to take a definition that may be considered as typical of modern experimental social psychology, '[a group is] two or more persons who are interacting with one another in such a manner that each person influences and is influenced by each other person' (Shaw, 1976, p11).

What is apparent here is a pattern of behaviour as apprehended by an outsider; what is not apparent is what it means to be in a group for the members of that group. Since the psychological consequences of membership for the group member are not the focus of explanation for this objectivist psychology, the result is that the psychological processes that are consequent upon becoming a member of the group remain refractory to explanation. Since the processes cannot be understood, the actual behaviours, instead of being seen as the result of those processes, must be seen as 'primary', and since the behaviours of interest are, to the observer, abnormal, the crowd itself is seen as abnormal. This fixity of the crowd, in terms of a limited repertoire of behaviours, was then often given a theoretical underpinning in terms of human universals, such as 'race', 'instinct' or whatever.

Since the earliest work, it has been apparent that crowds are not as inflexible as these theoretical explanations might suggest; more recently, the work on de-individuation has demonstrated this plasticity to a much greater extent (cf. Carver, 1974; Milgram, 1974; White, 1977). Indeed, it would seem that any attempt to account for collective behaviour in terms of certain alleged 'fixed patterns of mind' is, at best, unhelpful. Instead, the notion of crowd behaviour as formless and devoid of psychological process must be rejected; in order to do this, it is necessary to adopt a perspective that considers a social group from the position of the individuals who form it.

The theoretical framework that will be used in order to explain crowd behaviour is the Social Identification hypothesis of the group derived by Turner (cf. Turner, 1978a, and 1978c) from earlier work by Tajfel on the concept of social identity (cf. Tajfel, 1972, 1974). The Social Identification hypothesis proposes that a social group may be defined as: 'two or more people who share a common social identification of themselves, or, which is nearly the same thing, perceive themselves to be members of the same social category' (see chapter 1). This self-identification in terms of group forms part of the individual's social identity, which, in turn, is defined as: 'that part of an individual's self-concept which derives from his knowledge of his membership of a social group (or groups) together with the emotional significance attached to that membership' (Tajfel, 1974, p9).

Tajfel goes on to argue that, in certain situations involving high group salience, it is possible for an individual to act *purely* in terms of his social identity (cf. Tajfel, 1978a, p42). In other words, in acting towards a member of another group, the individual considers himself and the other only in terms of their group membership and the attributes implied by that membership. Similarly, it will be argued, when an individual's group membership becomes highly salient, his behaviour, whatever its object, will be guided by these attributes implied by that membership, rather than in terms of his so-called individual personality characteristics. Thus, the particularities of crowd behaviour will be characterized as the results of a collection of people acting on the basis of a common social identification, which, in replacing the previously disparate identities of those people, acts as a common basis for behaviour.

This approach has a number of implications, of which perhaps the most crucial is its assertion of the primacy of social factors in the determination of the behaviour of individuals. What is meant by this is that the theory proposes that the effects of an individual's social identifications cannot be seen as subsequent to his interpersonal interactions (as determined by intrapersonal characteristics) but may, in fact, be determining of those inter- and even intrapersonal variables. This idea is in no way novel; it is to be found in a most coherent form in Vygotsky's (1962) polemic against the Piagetian notion of egocentrism. Furthermore, it is not to be taken as an exclusive argument; by affirming the effects of socially determined factors upon the individual, the reverse determination is not ruled out of court. In the field considered here, the two factors obviously affect each other in a dialectical fashion; but the notion of the social determination of individuality runs counter to much of the mainstream psychology of the last hundred years.

As Allport (1969) wrote: 'the theories of social psychology are rarely, if ever, chaste scientific productions. They usually gear into the prevailing political and social atmosphere' (p13). Nowhere is this statement more dramatically borne out than in the early works on crowd psychology. In nearly all of them one finds elaborate statements on the mental inferiority of the 'mass', and each draws his own conclusions. For example, Sighele (1895) argued that democracy, because of its 'crowdish tendencies', is bad; Le Bon (1947) stated that, because society is founded on the fundamental ideas of race, social revolutions can be of no consequence; Le Dantec (1918) demolished socialism by stating that the only basis for the group is egotism and that therefore societies can only exist in response to a common enemy; Freud maligned the 'gentlemen socialists' on the grounds that they ignored the fundamental aggressive instincts of man; Trotter (1916) managed to construct a theory of instinct in which the German nation of the First World War could be characterized as (almost literally) lupine, and therefore the only way to teach it a lesson was through a sound thrashing administered to its entire populace. These ideological distortions can be seen most clearly in the work of McDougall, whose bias can be gauged from the following quotation: 'Even cultured minds are not immune to the fascination of the herd ... we cultivated persons usually say to ourselves when we yield to this fascination that we are taking an intelligent interest in the life of the people. But such intellectual interest plays but a small part and beneath works the powerful impulse of this ancient instinct' (of gregariousness) (1908, p74). In one breathtaking chapter in his book *The group mind* (1927), McDougall managed to account for the First World War, the Irish question, the 'inferiority' of Jews, southern Europeans and Negroes, the warring nature of Turks and Arabs and a lot more besides, in terms of unchangeable racial features. The result of his comprehensive racial typification was to conclude: 'the English represent in greatest purity the most independent branch of the northern race' (1927, p115).

Ideology has led many theorists to manipulate their theories in order to fit their social prejudices rather than the observed world. What is explicit in the early work is useful in alerting us to some of the more implicit aspects of modern theories. The fundamental premise that unites all the examples given above and also links it with most of the modern work, has been an irreducible individualism which is consonant with the dominant conception of man within our culture. In the field of collective psychology, this individualism has been expressed in three distinct ways. The first is the denial of anything social about social behaviour; the classic means of doing this was through instinct theories which locate a 'herd instinct' within the individual which then is invoked to explain all the distinctive properties of the crowd (cf. Trotter, 1916; Lorenz, 1970). Since instinct theories have gone out of vogue in recent years, alternative explanations in this tradition have been advanced using the idea that the collectivity is distinguished by the arousal of its members due to the presence of others (cf. Geen and Gange, 1977). The second way has been to separate the social from the individual and, often, to explain the social as an expression of repressed and fixed individual tendencies. There are many examples of this approach. One type uses the notion of group mind of which Allport (1969) identified seven variants; another assumes that the group allows the expression of what is repressed in the individual unconscious. This approach stemmed from the work of Freud (cf. 1922) and has been clearly expressed by Martin (1920) who maintained that: 'the crowd mind is a phenomenon which should best be classed with dreams, delusions and the various forms of automatic behaviour' (p19).

Recently, this idea has re-emerged in the work on de-individuation; it is interesting that one of the authors of the original work in the field (Festinger, Pepitone and Newcomb, 1952) acknowledged in a later paper (Cannavale, Scarr and Pepitone, 1970) that the original idea came straight from the pages of Le Bon. The third manner in which individualism has permeated psychology is probably the most common in recent years. This approach presents the social as subsequent to, and arising out of, the individual. It is the approach which defines groups as the consequence of previous interpersonal interactions.

The aim of this chapter is not to argue in favour of a simplistic social determinism, but for the need to redress the scales towards a more complete view of human behaviour. In order to do so, the existing explanations of crowd psychology will be reviewed and critically considered and the advantages of a reconceptualization in terms of the Social Identification theory (SIT) will be put forward.

2. The classic work on crowd psychology

The reason for a review of the classic works in this field is that they throw light on the modern work in a number of ways. A cursory glance at almost any early study reveals the strength of 'anti-crowd' prejudice which, in its determination of the direction of subsequent research, must be seen as a fundamental influence in the field. The following description by McDougall (1927) is typical of the general approach to collective phenomena. He contended that:

> We may sum up the psychological character of the unorganized crowd by saying that it is excessively emotional, impulsive, violent, fickle, inconsistent, irresolute and extreme in action, displaying only the coarser emotions and the less refined sentiments, extremely suggestible, careless in deliberation, hasty in judgement, incapable of any but the simpler and imperfect forms of reasoning, easily swayed and led, lacking in self-consciousness, devoid of self-respect and of sense of responsibility and apt to be carried away by the consciousness of its own force, so that it tends to produce all the manifestations we have learnt to expect from any irresponsible and absolute power. Hence its behaviour is like that of an unruly child or an untutored, passionate savage in a strange situation, rather than like that of its average member, and in the worst cases it is like that of a wild beast rather than like that of human beings. (p45)

It is less than surprising, given these unflattering beginnings, that the crowd has been seen as an undesirable phenomenon and that the main focus of research, until the present day, has been directed towards attempts to 'cure' humanity of the existence of collective behaviour (e.g. Brown, 1965; Wilder, 1978; Zimbardo, 1969). This approach has served to obscure the question of what processes determine the phenomenon of mass behaviour – whatever the crowd may be, psychology, it seems, is only interested in how to get rid of it.

The second advantage of a study of the classics in the field is that they contain, albeit often in a crude and extreme form, nearly all the ideas that inform contemporary research. In some cases, those ideas are directly imported from the work of some early theorist – this is true of 'de-individuation' which, as noted above, is a translation of Le Bon's notion of 'submergence' of the individual into the group. In other cases, the influence is more one of a tradition of thought than of any specific instance. An illustration of this is the relationship of the modern work on the mechanisms underlying the spread of ideas in crowds (cf. Berkowitz, 1970; Bandura, 1965) to early ideas about imitation as a fundamental process of social existence (cf. James, 1890; Tarde, 1903, 1912).

Finally, however naive the overall theoretical syntheses may seem today, there is no doubt that the original investigations of crowd behaviour display an astonishing descriptive richness and accuracy. Indeed, many of the theoretical contortions may be seen as the result of an unwillingness to confine oneself to a narrow range of phenomena that may more easily be fitted to a consistent explanatory framework; while this breadth of scope may serve to expose their theoretical inadequacy, it also adds greatly to the value of these pioneering studies of the crowd.

With little doubt, the most influential of these early works is that of Le Bon. His major book, *The crowd: A study of the popular mind*, has served as the point of departure of nearly every researcher into collective psychology; it is quoted, in some cases as the only reference, in every modern introductory text in social psychology that mentions the crowd; it contains almost every idea that is developed in contemporary studies – in short, it is indispensable for an understanding of this field. Nor has its influence been limited to the academic study of crowd behaviour; as Billig (1978) relates, it certainly had a profound effect on Mussolini and may well have been formative of Hitler's ideas on the mass.

Le Bon himself first became interested in the crowd through his concern with the French revolution of 1797. Through his experience as chief of ambulance services in the Paris commune of 1871, his anti-crowd prejudice became hardened. This, and his medical background are important factors to bear in mind when considering his ideas. The easiest way to describe those ideas about the crowd is to quote Le Bon directly since his exposition is both clear and concise. His basic characterization of the crowd is as follows:

> Whoever be the individuals that compose it, however like or unlike be their mode of life, their occupation, their character, or their intelligence, the fact that they have been transformed into a group puts them in possession of a sort of collective mind which makes them feel, think

and act in a manner quite different from that in which each individual of them would feel, think and act were he in a state of isolation. There are certain feelings and ideas which do not come into being, or do not transform themselves into acts, except in the case of individuals forming a group. The psychological group is a provisional being formed of heterogeneous elements which for a moment are combined, exactly as the cells that form a living body form by their reunion a new being which displays characteristics very different from those possessed by each of the cells singly. (1947, p27)

The explanation of the emergent properties of the crowd is in terms of three mechanisms: anonymity, contagion and suggestibility. Le Bon wrote of anonymity: 'The individual forming part of a group acquires, solely from numerical considerations, a sentiment of invincible power which allows him to yield to instincts which, had he been alone, he would perforce have kept under restraint. He will be the less disposed to check himself, from the consideration that a group being anonymous and in consequence irresponsible, the sentiment of responsibility which always controls individuals disappears entirely' (p30).

As to contagion, it 'is a phenomenon of which it is easy to establish the presence but which it is not easy to explain. It must be classed among those phenomena of a hypnotic order, which we shall shortly study. In a group every sentiment and act is contagious, and contagious to such a degree that an individual readily sacrifices his personal interest to the collective interest. This is an aptitude very contrary to his nature, and of which man is scarcely capable except when he makes part of a group' (p30).

And finally suggestibility: 'A third cause, and by far the most important, determines in the individuals of a group special characteristics which are quite contrary at times to those presented by the isolated individual. I allude to that suggestibility of which, moreover, the contagion mentioned above is only an effect' (p31).

The effects of suggestion are accounted for by arguing that in the group 'the conscious personality has entirely vanished' (p31) and that the individual is as prone to suggestion as in the hypnotic state. The homogeneity of the crowd is then explained as the result of the fact that the suggestion is the same for all members of the group, coming as it does from the racial unconscious. Le Bon does allow for secondary suggestions that are not the result of a racial heritage, yet the relationship of these transitory ideas to the fundamental racial ideas is as follows: 'these fundamental ideas resemble the volume of the water of a stream slowly pursuing its course. The transitory ideas are like the small waves, forever changing, which agitate its surface and are more visible than the progress of the stream itself although without real importance' (p61).

Le Bon's characterization of the group mind can be most simply illustrated by listing the section headings in the chapter dealing with this subject. They run: (1) Impulsiveness, mobility and irritability of crowds; (2) The suggestibility and credulity of crowds; (3) The exaggeration and ingenuousness of the sentiments of crowds; (4) The intolerance, dictatorship and conservatism of crowds. Furthermore, the intellectual level of the crowd is described as follows: 'the arguments [crowds] employ and those which are capable of influencing them are, from a logical point of view, of such an inferior kind that it is only by way of analogy that they can be described as reasoning' (p65). Whatever else may have disappeared in present day renderings of Le Bon's account, his damning tone has not; the consideration of the crowd as a positive and a creative phenomenon has not, as yet, been considered as a viable prospect.

Traugott (1978) identified within Le Bon's work two distinct types of explanation. The first is sociological, dealing with such factors as the objective size and strength of a crowd and their effect on collective behaviour; the second is psychological, dealing with the mechanisms of the unconscious mind. He goes on to claim that Le Bon's error was in adopting a psychological account of the crowd instead of, what Traugott suggests would be more fruitful, a sociological approach. While Traugott is correct in identifying Le Bon with psychological as opposed to sociological theory, the dichotomy he proposes between the two is a false one. The one in no way excludes the other. Indeed, this point is crucial; any account on one level (e.g. psychological) must allow for accounts on different levels (e.g. sociological, historical, economic) and it is precisely here that Le Bon is in error. He tries to reduce history and culture to manifestations of innate psychological characteristics, he is in fault not in being a psychologist but in being a psychological reductionist.

This can be seen as a result of a reification that lies at the heart of all Le Bon's work. It will be recalled that Le Bon's original interest in the crowd stems from the revolution of 1797. His book is written from the perspective of a bourgeois intellectual during a period that was witnessing the rise of French syndicalism and socialism; little wonder, then, that he considered that 'crowds are only powerful for destruction' (p18). From a different perspective one could arrive at a radically different conclusion. The point is not to pit the one against the other, but rather that it is impossible to gain an understanding of social behaviour if it is abstracted from its social context (cf. Israel and Tajfel, 1972). What Le Bon has done is to take a set of phenomena that are particular to given historical situations and, by discounting the ways in which those specific situations have affected the precise appearance of these phenomena of collective behaviour, to reify that appearance in terms of the emergence of fixed racial characteristics. This postulation of innate conditions that limit the range of behaviours has considerable attraction in terms of conceptual simplicity, and for that reason is extremely common. In the words of Dewey (1917): 'The ultimate refuge of the standpatter in every field: education, religion, politics, industrial and domestic life, has been the notion of an alleged fixed structure of mind' (p273).

This inflexibility manifests itself in a number of ways in Le Bon's work. The first and most obvious way in which Le Bon's racial unconscious leads to false constraints concerns the actual range of behaviours that different crowds, or else the same crowd at different times, may display. It is patently obvious that a crowd is not always violent, nor is it always peaceful; it is neither always fickle nor always loyal; indeed, there are as many forms of crowd behaviour as there are crowds, and, unless one wishes to extend the notion indefinitely (and in so doing make it meaningless), it is hard to see how those behaviours could be conceptualized as the result of a fixed racial heritage of mind.

Another source of inflexibility within Le Bon's account is his neglect of the limits of influence of the crowd. As Milgram and Toch (1969) observed: 'The riot police sent to break up a political rally rarely find themselves cheering for the demagogue' (p551). Given that a body of people who are racially similar are exposed to the same suggestions, there is no reason to predict that some will be prone to suggestion while others will not. This problem for Le Bon's theory can, in fact, be reduced to the more basic question of what makes a social group, for it is logical to assume that the mechanisms of the spread of the group's ideas will be limited to the members of the group. Milgram and Toch's example, then, results in the question: In what way are the riot police not members of the group of participants at the rally? Le Bon's account is unable to answer questions concerning the definition of a crowd. The crowd acts for him as a gateway to the racial unconscious and yet the conditions of that transition from individuality to homogeneity remain totally opaque.

This opacity flows inevitably from Le Bon's original reification of crowd behaviour; this point has been made before, yet it is worth reiterating given its paramount importance to the whole of collective psychology. He characterizes the crowd, essentially, in terms of the emergence of a set of behaviours, which are listed at great length in his book. Someone is then defined as a member of the crowd on the basis of exhibiting those behaviours; but this, of course, can only be a *post hoc* definition. The conditions that determine the emergence of the behaviours cannot be analysed since those behaviours are the starting point of the whole analysis. To put it in another way, since the essence of this approach is to isolate crowd behaviour from its social context, then there is no way of understanding why this should occur in one situation and not in another; and, since group membership is determined on the basis of these behaviours, there is no way of determining group membership.

Apart from rendering the basis of group membership unavailable to analysis, this way of looking at the group in terms of the way it appears to the observer leads to two further distortions in Le Bon's work. This applies to anonymity considered as the prime mechanism of crowd behaviour. Le Bon claims that the individual will shed the normal restraints on his behaviour to the extent that the group of which he forms part is anonymous. However, the individuals who make up the group will only be anonymous with respect to an outsider; with respect to other members of the crowd, the individual is not at all likely to be anonymous. For this reason, it is invalid to assume that the individual in the crowd loses all sense of responsibility because, being anonymous, there can be no repercussions to his behaviour; the influence of the outside world may be reduced, but the effects of crowd norms should be greatly increased. Le Bon believes that crowds can only release behaviours; they cannot construct them.

The second distortion that can be put down to a perspective that fails to consider crowd behaviours in terms of their significance from the point of view of the actors themselves concerns Le Bon's contrasting of the rational individual with the irrational crowd. The first point is that even within his own criteria of self-interest, the lone individual cannot be described as rational (cf. Hofstätter, 1957). More importantly, to quote Tajfel (1978a): 'The dichotomy in the explanations of mass intergroup phenomena is not, as Berkowitz (1972) wrote, between the irrational and the rational, but between the irrational and the social–cognitive. The social–cognitive causation need not be rational as seen by an outside observer; as a matter of fact, it often may, and does, appear to be highly irrational. But this kind of "irrationality" is fundamentally different from the irrationality assumed in an approach to intergroup behaviour which extrapolates from a collection of individual motivational states' (p420).

The point being made here is that, simply because the behaviour of individuals in a crowd seems to run contrary to the commonly agreed criteria of rationality (cf. Le Bon's quotation on contagion: in a group 'an individual readily sacrifices his personal interest'), it is invalid to assume that the behaviour is an automatic and fixed response to a given situation or internal state. It may be that it is the outcome of processes that mediate between the situation and the resultant behaviours in a highly meaningful way, for the individual, but that might appear arbitrary as seen from the outside. An example comes from the work of Tajfel himself; he found that (cf. Tajfel, 1970), when divided into groups on wholly minimal grounds, individuals who were asked to distribute monetary rewards between ingroup and outgroup members, were prepared to sacrifice the absolute level of reward in order to discriminate against the outgroup. While, on the surface, this may seem to go against the criteria of rationality, it is possible to make sense of this and a whole series of other findings (cf. Brewer, 1979) using a set of processes that are sensitive both to the environment and to the state of the individual (cf. Tajfel, 1974).

Apart from Le Bon, the other major attempt to elaborate an exhaustive theory of crowd behaviour is contained in McDougall's book, *The group mind*, first published in 1921. In its essentials, this account does not differ widely from that of Le Bon, for both the fundamental cause of the homogeneity and distinctiveness of the crowd are racial; but the means by which 'race' is assumed to display itself in crowd behaviour is radically different. For McDougall, the essence of a crowd is that: 'the attention of all is directed to the same object, all experience in some degree the same emotion, and the state of mind in each person is in some degree affected by the mental processes of all those around him . . . It follows that not every aggregation of individuals is capable of becoming a psychological crowd and of enjoying a collective life. For the individuals must be capable of being interested in the same object and of being affected in a similar way by them – there must be a certain degree of similarity of mental constitution among the individuals' (pp22–23, 1927 edition). This similarity of mental constitution is said to be a function of race. If race predisposes people to a common outlook on the world, then the actual mechanism of mutual influence is that of the 'principle of direct induction of emotion by way of the primitive sympathetic response'.

In plain English, this means that the perception of an emotion is said to arouse automatically the same emotion in the perceiver; the idea is reminiscent of the ideomotor theory of Cooley (1902). It also bears more than a passing resemblance to the notion of contagion and indeed, it has all the same problems. McDougall is at least aware of the problem surrounding the limits to contagion. In the end, however, despite the divergences between the two accounts, McDougall's theory is open to all the criticisms

made of Le Bon: his reification of a set of negative behaviours, his justification in terms of race, his objectivist perspective, all these he shares with
the earlier theorist. As Freud puts it: 'The problem consists in how to
procure for the group precisely those features which were characteristic
of the individual and which are extinguished in him by the formation of
the group' (1922, p18).

The tendency to underemphasize the context of crowd behaviour is
taken to an exteme in the work of Trotter, who is of interest only insofar
as his brand of reductionism is still to be found (cf. Lorenz, 1970). He
starts from the premise that: 'the two fields, the social and the individual,
are regarded here as absolutely continuous' (p12). The basis for this continuity is, according to Trotter, gregariousness, which is seen as 'a fundamental quality of man' (p26); it is through an investigation of this quality
that crowd psychology will, in his opinion, advance. All the distinctive
properties of the herd, such as homogeneity, suggestibility, contagion and
so on are seen as the manifestations of this instinct of gregariousness;
however, they are also seen as the characteristics of the human mind in
any situation. Indeed, the only factor that distinguishes the crowd from
the individual and leads to its inferior mental characteristics is the lack of
intercommunication between its members.

When Trotter talks of the continuity between the individual and the
social, he simply reduces all social events to intra-individual processes,
given that, as he asserts, the herd instinct is a product of race. The basic
point is that it is necessary to go beyond the postulation of global processes
that predict certain differences in kind between individual and group
behaviour. What an adequate psychology of the crowd must achieve is
the determination of when those differences will arise and what form they
are likely to take.

Finally, in this section, the work of Freud must be considered. Mention
will only be made here of those ideas that are of direct interest to the
account to be given later of the characteristics of crowd behaviour. There
are a number of adequate critiques available for anyone interested in his
ideas in this area *per se* (cf. Billig, 1976; Tajfel, 1978a). However, to set
the points that are of concern here in context, it is necessary to give a very
brief description of Freud's theoretical account of the social group.

A considerable part of Freud's major work on collective psychology,
Group psychology and the analysis of the ego (1922), is taken up by an approving
description of the work of Le Bon. However, in quoting the description
of the crowd member as being in a hypnotic state, he asks: 'Who is to
replace the hypnotist in the case of the group?' (p9). The answer he gives

is that it is the leader of the group. He proposes that the reason for the special nature of the crowd is that all the members have put the leader in the place of their ego-ideal and hence are bound not only to the leader but also to each other by virtue of the fact that they all share the same ego-ideal: 'A primary group ... is a number of individuals who have put one and the same object in the place of their ego-ideal and have consequently identified themselves with one-another in their ego' (p48).

He goes on to account for crowd behaviour as: 'a state of regression to a primitive mental activity of just such a sort as we should be inclined to ascribe to the primal horde ... Thus the group appears to us as a revival of the primal horde' (pp54–5). This is so because: 'The leader of the group is still the dreaded primal father ... The primal father is the group ideal which governs the ego in the place of the ego-ideal' (p59).

Many authors have noted the tension between Freud's basic psycho-dynamic ideas and his attempt at a phylogenetic fixation of the ego using the primal horde theory. A number of later analysts have found it useful to abandon this theory and to concentrate on the historical and social determination of the intrapsychic structures (cf. Becker, 1976; Billig, 1976). For this reason, Freud's biologism is less central to his account of the crowd than was the case in any of the works already considered; indeed, at times, it seems to be totally irrelevant. This is so in his approach to the definition of a social group. It has been argued previously that theories of crowd behaviour have been either incapable of defining the crowd, or else they defined it in objectivist terms which made them incapable of understanding the psychological processes that result for the individual upon his joining the crowd. Freud, however, constitutes a notable exception to this; he defines the crowd from the perspective of the individuals that form it. For him, a group consists of those people who identify with a given leader, and all the psychological effects described by earlier theorists are dependent upon that identification. Thus, for instance, he puts forward 'a definition for suggestion: a conviction which is not based upon perception but upon an erotic tie' (pp59–60). In other words, the limits to the spread of ideas and affects that Le Bon, McDougall and others sought and failed to find, are determined by a common identification. Another comment lends this notion considerably more power: 'We should consider whether an idea, an abstraction, may not take the place of the leader' (p32). Not only does this add vastly to the scope of the argument – the effects of the crowd appertaining to, and being limited to, any group of individuals who share an identification with any concept or thing – it also contradicts the primal horde theory as a basis for the understanding of common identification.

Because of his general reductionism, Freud was unable to develop this idea, and its implications concerning the social structuration of the ego. And yet, it represents a remarkable new direction in this field, a direction that will be followed in an attempt to provide an alternative to the present theories of crowd psychology.

3. Modern research relating to crowd psychology

For a period of about forty years after Freud very little work was done in the field of crowd psychology. In 1961 Rapoport was able to write: 'the mob has disappeared from the American scene and has carried with it into seeming oblivion the phenomenon of overt mob violence' (pp 50–1). The mass movements of the sixties and early seventies somewhat confounded this peaceful picture, and with them came a renewed interest in the phenomena of collective behaviour. Much of the work was concerned with the elucidation of certain specific processes that were hypothesized to lie at the heart of crowd psychology. As noted above, there are clear links between this work and the earlier ideas, and some of the same difficulties persist. The three main areas of research have been: (*a*) social facilitation; (*b*) de-individuation; and (*c*) contagion. Each one will be reviewed in turn, and finally the only serious attempt at a comprehensive *psychological* theory of crowd behaviour, that of Turner and Killian, will be considered. (There exist various non-psychological accounts of the crowd, most notably the sociological theory of Smelser (1963), but these lie outside the scope of this review.)

(a) Social facilitation

The notion of social facilitation, which, put at its simplest, asserts that the mere presence of others has an arousing effect upon an individual's performance that may in part account for the differences between individual and collective behaviour, has a history as old as that of experimental social psychology itself. In 1897 Triplett carried out a study in which he found that the average speed of a cyclist was considerably increased by the presence of another person cycling with him, and that this effect was produced even without the induction of overt competition. It is possible, of course, that the experimental manipulation may not have corresponded to the subjects' perception of the task, and that even in the 'non-competitive' condition, subjects might have seen the situation as competitive. Nevertheless, the idea was taken up by Allport (1920) who demonstrated that performance on either simple or difficult tasks was facilitated by the presence of others in the room. It was he who coined the term 'social facilitation' (cf. Allport, 1924). The exact operation of this process was, however, unclear; presence of others certainly did not always lead to improved performance, as Allport (1924) himself found in the case of the quality of subjects' refutations of logical arguments. Similarly, Pessin (1933) found that the presence of an audience led to a decrease in memory performance.

Owing to these difficulties of predicting the effects of the presence of others, research in the area of social facilitation stagnated until Zajonc (1965) found a means of reconciling the seemingly contradictory findings by using the behaviouristic notion of drive. The drive theory approach to social facilitation states that: 'the presence of conspecific organisms, as either coactors or a passive audience, produces an increment in general arousal, which in turn serves as a drive that energizes dominant responses at the expense of subordinate ones in accordance with the familiar Hull–Spence equation, $E = D \times H$' (Geen and Gange, 1977, p1268). Thus, the earlier findings were explained by saying that in those cases where the presence of others led to improved performance, the required behaviour was a dominant response and in those cases where a deterioration was observed, the behaviour was said to be a subordinate one.

A certain amount of initial confirming evidence was found for this theory. Zajonc and Sales (1966) showed that in a recognition task the presence of an audience led to increased reporting of stimuli that had been shown beforehand, and were thus assumed to be dominant responses. However, quite soon a body of discrepant evidence was accumulated. Cottrell et al. (1968) showed that facilitation effects were only obtained when the subjects thought that they were being evaluated. As a result, Cottrell (1972) proposed that the presence of others is a learned source of drive which acquires its arousal potential by serving as a stimulus for the anticipation of positive and negative outcomes. A number of studies sought to clarify the question as to whether facilitation effects were the result of arousal of Cottrell's 'evaluation apprehension'. The latter explanation was favoured by Henchy and Glass (1968) who directly measured arousal and whose results did not support a drive theory approach. They concluded: 'The implied threat of evaluation associated with the presence of others during task performance enhances the emission of dominant responses at the expense of subordinate responses' (p452).

They also noted a conceptual difficulty for the arousal theorists, namely that it is unclear as to whether there exists such a thing as general arousal.

They quote Lacey (1967) who lists three types of arousal: electro–cortical; autonomic; and behavioural; the presence of any one type depending upon the precise conditions of elicitation. If this is so, then a theory, such as Zajonc's, of general arousal is inadequate. Instead, if the theory is to be capable of empirical verification, one must specify the type, or types, of arousal that will be produced by the presence of others.

There exists more evidence on either side of the arousal/evaluation apprehension controversy (cf. Geen and Gange, 1977); but it must be noted that there exists a fundamental asymmetry when it comes to evaluating the empirical evidence relating to this controversy. The arousal hypothesis states that the presence of others *automatically* leads to facilitation effects. Therefore, any study that does not find facilitation effects, given the presence of others (assuming that the subject is aware of that presence), can be said to be disconfirming evidence for the hypothesis. On the other hand, an experiment that does find facilitation effects in the presence of others without the subjects also being told explicitly that they are being evaluated cannot be said to be disconfirming evidence for the evaluation apprehension hypothesis – unless it can further be shown that the subject himself does not consider that he is being in any way evaluated. Given the existence of a number of studies that have found that the mere presence of others does not necessarily lead to facilitation effects, it is possible to conclude that a simple arousal hypothesis explanation of social facilitation is inadequate (cf. Innes and Young, 1975; Paulus and Murdoch, 1971; Sasfy and Okun, 1974).

A totally different explanation for social facilitation comes from the theory of objective self-awareness (OSA) of Duval and Wicklund (1972). This theory states that the inward focusing that characterizes a state of OSA most often leads to an awareness of the discrepancy between the ideal and the actual self, which, in turn, leads to striving to reduce the discrepancy. Since one of the postulated antecedents of a state of OSA is the presence of others, then this constitutes a framework for reinterpreting social facilitation effects. There has been little direct empirical research relating to this theory, and furthermore, as Geen and Gange (1977) point out, since OSA is associated with negative affect which may in turn be a source of arousal, it may in practice prove impossible to distinguish the two approaches. Nevertheless, this theory does suggest a new *perspective* from which to consider social facilitation; that is, the subject's behaviour is dependent not directly upon external stimuli, of whatever nature they may be, but rather upon the internal demands of constructing an adequate identity. It is clear from some of the research that has considered the nature of the self-concept that, as subjectively experienced at any given time, it is highly dependent upon the individual's immediate social environment (cf. Oakes and Turner, 1980). Therefore, the effects of an audience should depend on which aspects of the individual's identity it makes salient along with the motivational consequences of the salience of that identity. This may provide a means for explaining the seemingly contradictory evidence noted above with respect to the effects of mere presence of others on social facilitation.

Given the present confused state of both research and theory in this field, it is impossible to draw any hard and fast conclusions. Whatever may be the explanation and limiting conditions of social facilitation, it seems clear that, contrary to the belief of Allport, this process cannot serve as an exclusive account of crowd behaviour.

(b) De-individuation

In Zimbardo's (1969) somewhat purple prose: 'Mythically, de-individuation is the ageless life force, the cycle of nature, the blood ties, the tribe, the female principle, the irrational, the impulsive, the anonymous chorus, the vengeful furies' (p249). From these mythical beginnings the idea of the individual being submerged within some common human cauldron has been used by nearly every theorist who has considered collective psychology. In many cases, it is argued that the individual developed out of the homogeneous mass and that somehow the crowd is a means of returning to that mass. An illustration of this approach can be found in the work of Jung, who defined individuation as: 'the development of the psychological individual as a differentiated individual from the general collective psychology' (1946, p561). He argued that being in a crowd leads to the loss of one's individual identity, to an unleashing of the violent side of human nature in a 'frenzy of unmeasured instinct'.

As Dipboye (1977) noted, there have been several conceptions of de-individuation. For some, as in the case of much of the recent experimental work, it is a positive affective event; for others it is negatively affective and results in attempts to reassert one's individuality (cf. Klapp, 1969); for yet others, there is a dialectic between the desire to be anonymous and the desire to be a unique person (e.g. Fromm, 1956; Laing, 1960). Whichever approach is taken, there remains the conception of a simple dichotomy between individual identity and de-individuation, or non-identity, the latter tending to be a feature of collective behaviour.

The first modern experimental study using the concept of de-individuation was that of Festinger, Pepitone and Newcomb (1952), who found that under conditions of anonymity male subjects were much more likely to express hostility towards their parents than when they were identifiable. Singer, Brush and Lublin (1965) found that females were much freer in discussing pornography anonymously than if their identities were made known to the entire group.

These results led Zimbardo (1969) to provide a theoretical framework in which de-individuation is: 'a complex hypothesized process in which a series of antecedent social conditions lead to changes in the perception of self and others' (p251). He suggested that a number of input variables lead to changes in subjective state and hence change output behaviour. Schematically, the process is as follows:

Inferred subjective changes:

Minimization of (1) Self-Observation–Evaluation;

(2) concern for social evaluation.

(leading to)

Weakening of controls based on guilt, shame, fear and commitment.

(leading to)

Lowered threshold for exhibiting inhibited behaviours.

(from Zimbardo, 1969)

One important corollary to this schema is that, as Shaver (1977) points out: 'the behaviours that follow de-individuation are not only irrational, impulsive and atypical for the person involved, they must also be self-reinforcing in the sense that they are not under the control of discriminative stimuli in the environment' (p336). Furthermore, given its insensibility to stimuli in the environment, once initiated, de-individuated behaviour can only be halted by a marked change in existing conditions.

In support for the view of the crowd as a means for rendering the individual anonymous and thus allowing him to release hidden aggressive behaviours that are normally blocked by cultural norms, a large amount of evidence can be mustered. Zimbardo (1969) reports that de-individuated women gave electric shocks of an average length of 0.90 s to a victim as opposed to 0.47 s for the identifiable subjects; Donnerstein *et al.* (1972) found that white students gave higher intensity electric shocks to a black victim if that victim could neither see nor identify them; Watson (1973) relates that warriors who de-individuate themselves when going into battle are far more likely to indulge in violent killings than those who do not; and Milgram (1974) found that subjects who were less identifiable were considerably more prone to give a high level of shock to their victims.

Perhaps the most graphic account for the effects of 'de-individuation' comes from one of Zimbardo's own studies, the simulated prison experiment (cf. Zimbardo *et al.*, 1973). In this experiment, subjects were randomly assigned to play the role of either a prisoner or a prison guard. They were then put in a situation that resembled real life as closely as possible; the guards had real control over the prisoners, such as permission to go to the toilet, deciding about privileges and necessities; unusual and humiliating behaviours could be demanded at whim and frequently were; in fact, the situation became so extreme, in terms of the participants' behaviour, that the experiment had to be ended after only six days instead of going on for two weeks as scheduled. The guards' cruelty to the prisoners had become excessive and the prisoners themselves began to display psychosomatic disorders. Yet even this study, which is probably the most remarkable in de-individuation research, contains some fundamental difficulties for the theoretical account. Raven and Rubin (1976) noted that: 'de-individuation led to reduced restraints on the part of the guards, allowing them to engage in vicious behaviour which they probably would not have done otherwise. For the prisoners, de-individuation seems to have brought about a totally different effect – the loss of independence and a sense of powerlessness, which led to passive compliance'. If de-individuation is a process which involves the simple release of restraints leading to uninhibited behaviours that are not under the control of the environment, then how could it have led to such divergent results amongst the two groups of subjects?

This dependence of 'de-individuation' on particular features of each experimental design was demonstrated in a number of studies. Both Carver (1974) and Scheir *et al.* (1974) have shown that the effects of lowered self-awareness on overt behaviour depend on the norms operating in the situation. Paloutzian (1972) found that subjects who were isolated in booths increased their level of aggression against an innocent victim if they believed that there were others acting in the same way. On the other hand, Zabrick and Miller (1972) found that for their subjects anonymity led to a lower average level of shock being used against the victim. Zimbardo himself found the same for a group of Belgian soldiers (cf. Zimbardo, 1969). It is worth following through his explanation of this, for it clearly exposes the limitations of his approach.

Zimbardo sums up his results for these subjects by saying that: 'the supposedly de-individuated subjects were behaving in a most individuated manner' (p257). He goes on to argue that those soldiers who were simply left alone, being in uniform, were de-individuated, whereas those whom he supposedly de-individuated by putting them in hoods, without name tags, in a strange lab., displayed on a television screen were made to feel 'self-conscious, suspicious and anxious' (p276). However, this raises the all-important question already raised in the discussion on Le Bon: with respect to whom are the subjects de-individuated? The soldiers left alone in uniform may have been de-individuated with respect to the experimenter but they clearly were not with respect to each other. Conversely, the hooded soldiers may have been self-conscious with respect to the experimenter but they clearly were not with respect to each other. What is changing is not *the level* of individuation but rather *the focus* of individuation. Thus, the results can be explained by saying that for the left-alone soldiers, the focus was on the ingroup, whose norm in the situation one could expect to be highly aggressive: hence their behaviour was aggressive. For the hooded soldiers, the focus of individuation was on the individuals as experimental subjects, whose norm of aggression one would expect to be below that of a group of soldiers: hence their behaviour was less aggressive than that of the left-alone group.

This notion of focus of individuation is totally alien to the basic concept underlying de-individuation theory, which allows for only two states for the subject: identity or non-identity. Identity is seen as that which renders the individual unique, which allows him to answer 'with certainty the question, Who am I?' (Dipboye, 1977, p1066). The idea of a social identity does not enter into this context; the assumption is that if one takes from the individual his 'personal' identity, one can only be left with that primitive residue that characterizes the de-individuated state. The subject is then the helpless victim of a group mind, and as Cannavale *et al.* (1970) believe: 'The group mind leads to primitivization or regression' (p142).

This theoretical position has methodological repercussions; if all that matters is robbing the person of his personal identity, then the context within which that takes place should be of no importance, therefore in some experiments subjects are de-individuated in groups, in others they are isolated and de-individuated, and all the results are treated identically. If, however, one allows that the subjects' behaviour may be determined by varying identifications, some of which may be on the basis of social groups, then the social context should be of considerable importance in determining the actual object of identification. As Milgram (1974) wrote of his subjects: 'the act of shocking the victim does not stem from destructive urges but from the fact that subjects have become integrated in a social structure and are unable to get out of it' (p66).

Two further studies by Zimbardo serve to illustrate this point (cf.

Zimbardo, 1969). In the first study, he tested girls in groups and measured their level of aggression against an innocent victim either when the subjects were or were not anonymous. The second study was identical to the first except that the girls were tested on their own. It was found that for the girls in groups the anonymity condition led to higher levels of aggression; for the isolated girls the reverse was found. Zimbardo's explanation is similar to the one he proposed for the soldiers' experiment; he claims that in the case of the isolated girls those who were made anonymous were in fact more individuated than those left alone. However, not only does this explanation weaken any value de-individuation theory might have, by making the conditions for entry into a de-individuated state almost impossible to specify, it also implies a tautology: redefining situations in which anti-social behaviour is found as ones in which there is lowered self-awareness. It is possible to measure directly self-awareness, but where this has been done the findings have not been compatible with de-individuation theory. Diener *et al.* (1973, 1975) tested the effects on aggression of anonymity, diffusion of responsibility and the existence of social models, all of which are postulated to be antecedents of de-individuation, and found that, despite widely varying levels of aggression, subjects did not report varying levels of self-consciousness.

An alternative explanation of the two studies mentioned above can be made using the notion of focus of individuation. If it is assumed that the girls in the group were acting in terms of their identities as members of that group and that, it being a group of girls, there was a norm of low aggressivity operating, then anonymity in this situation should lead to the attenuation of this identity, and hence an increase in aggression towards the victim. Conversely for the isolated girls, anonymity should decrease their identity as experimental subject, an identity that may be supposed to be consonant with aggressive behaviour in this context, and hence the level of actual aggression.

This analysis is supported by an experiment performed by White (1977) in which the dependence of behaviour in the 'de-individuation' paradigm was found to be highly dependent upon identifications made by the subjects during the experiment. White looked at the frequency of taboo language in conditions of anonymity and of reference group salience; in the salient condition, subjects were told that they had been selected for the experiment on the basis of belonging to particular social groups which the experimenter was interested in studying; in other ways, the procedure was identical to the classic de-individuation experiments. He found that the incidence of taboo language in the salient condition was half of that in the non-salient condition.

Before the topic of de-individuation is left, it is necessary to consider its use as an explanation of crowd behaviour. The argument is that in the crowd the individual loses his identity and along with it all restraints that normally limit his behaviour. The counter-argument used above was essentially that an individual can never be said to have lost his identity but only to have refocused his identity. However, even if it were possible for an individual to become submerged in the 'ageless life force' of which Zimbardo speaks, it is highly doubtful whether the conditions for this submergence exist in the crowd. For instance, one of the most frequent operationalizations of de-individuation is in terms of anonymity, and yet, as has already been stressed, the individual in the crowd is, most often, easily identifiable to other crowd members. Moreover, crowd activity is often undertaken as an expression of identity – quite the opposite to that predicted by this approach. Milgram and Toch (1969) note that one participant in the Watts riots of August 1965 claimed that people burnt, stole, killed, in order to be noticed; another spoke of the way the riots gave rise to feelings of identity. He said: 'for the first time in Watts people feel a real pride in being black. I remember when I first went to Whittier I worried that if I didn't make it there, if I was rejected, I wouldn't have a place to go back to. Now I can say: "I'm from Watts"' (p576).

If it is impossible to characterize crowd behaviour as behaviour free from identity, the question still remains: What identity does constrain collective behaviour? It is clearly not personal identity, and yet the crowd seems so unstructured, so immediate in the manifestation of its particular characteristics, that it seems hard to reconcile its behaviour with the usual notions in social psychology of group norms and group identity as arising out of individual interactions.

(c) Contagion

The mechanisms of contagion can be seen as an attempt to account for the levels of homogeneity in a crowd in terms of accelerated processes of interaction or interpersonal influence. In this way, the central theoretical notion that social structure is subsequent to individual action can be kept intact. For many theorists, some kind of mechanism of contagion has been seen as the fundamental difference between social and individual behaviour. Thus, Ribot (1897) saw sympathy as 'the foundation of all social existence'. Tarde (1903) termed imitation the 'key to the social mystery' and went on to propose that 'society is imitation'. Ross (1908) whose text is the first to use the term 'social psychology', similarly placed the burden of explanation for social behaviour on imitation. But there was very little clarity as to what 'sympathy', 'imitation', or whatever, actually were, let alone how they operated. Allport (1924) described contagion as a process in which (A) affects (B) and he proposed instead a 'circular reaction' in which (A) affects (B) affects (A) and so on, leading not only to diffusion, but also to increase in intensity. This was elevated by Blumer (1946) to the fundamental process of collective behaviour. Whether circular or linear, however, the process of contagion seems to imply some form of physical interaction between the agent of spread and the recipient, be it as minimal as mere observation of the one by the other. Thus, Rapoport (1963) can speak of: 'the underlying similarity between social diffusion and other chain reaction processes such as epidemics, the spread of solvents through solutes, crystallization'.

The modern approach to contagion mainly used conditioning concepts such as those discussed by Bandura (1965) and Walters (1968). Both considered media violence and concluded that it operated by influencing the strength of inhibitions against aggression; if the model is rewarded for aggressing, the viewer is informed that the expected negative outcomes of aggression may not occur. Aronfreed (1969) used a similar logic in suggesting that the observer behaves aggressively due to the gratifications he expects as a consequence of his actions. Wheeler (1966) has elaborated a general behavioural theory of contagion which used exactly the same notions as those of Bandura (1965); in other words, lowered inhibitions due to the existence of models leads to the release of antisocial behaviours in the crowd. This model contains all the difficulties already discussed, confronted by a conception of social behaviour as a release of normally proscribed behaviours. Berkowitz (1970) provided an alternative in which contagion is not seen as operating through a reduction of inhibitions. Instead, he argued: 'a classical conditioning model appears to be better than the more popular operant notions used in this area. On these occasions the observer reacts impulsively to particular stimuli in his environment, not because his inhibitions have been weakened or because he anticipates the pleasures arising from his actions, but because situational stimuli have evoked the responses he is predisposed or set to make in that setting. Contagious violence often comes about in this way' (p104).

Berkowitz underlined the automatic nature of this process when he wrote that: 'The role of thinking must not be exaggerated . . . Impulsive behaviour is not carried out with deliberation and forethought. It bursts forth relatively free of control by intellect and cognitive processes' (p133).

However, if contagion is as uncontrolled a process as is being suggested, then the old problem returns: how can one account for the limits of spread of ideas and emotions in the crowd? To use again the example of the riot police at a political rally, they are subject to exactly the same stimuli as the supporters and yet the behaviour that 'bursts forth' from them is of a decidedly different nature. Historically, there have been several attempts to explain these limits on contagion. As shown in the previous section, both Le Bon and McDougall proposed that these limits were, essentially, the product of racial factors. Ross (1908) concurred but added sex as a factor in the limitation on the propagation of idea and affect. These intra-individual limits are, however, too inflexible to account for the complexity of crowd behaviour. The same individual may, at different times, react in totally different ways to exactly the same contagious stimulus; the police-man who, say, found the National Front to be a repulsive organization would react differently according to whether he was taking part in an anti-Front demonstration (were that allowed) or stopping a similar demon-stration from clashing with the Front, in his official capacity.

Hovland and Janis (1959) suggested that contagion is content-bound in its effects. While this is quite fair as an empirical observation, it has little explanatory value. What is of interest is the why and the how of these content boundaries. One interesting such explanation is that of Cantril (1941) who argued that information will be accepted either when an individual's mental organization is unstructured or when it is rigidly structured in order to accept the information.

(d) Emergent norm theory

Emergent norm theory is the name given by Turner and Killian (1957) to their attempt to bring the crowd into line with the orthodox treatment of the social group. They consider that Le Bon's description of the crowd is 'graphic and highly accurate', but that he overestimates its homogeneity. The illusion of homogeneity arises, they believe, because bystanders refer to the norm (i.e. the consensus on appropriate conduct) rather than to actual social behaviour in their characterization of the crowd. This norm itself is the product of the actions of a few active and conspicuous members, which, being perceived as the dominant mode of behaviour, constrains the activity of the other members. Thus, a person behaves as he does in the crowd because that behaviour is seen as appropriate or as required.

Collective behaviour itself is seen as an attempt to define an ambiguous situation: the search for leadership is therefore the attempt to have others take responsibility for actions that are originally of questionable legitimacy.

It is clear that this theory is little more than a redescription of the crowd in terms of the commonly held notions of group theory. This is made clear when the authors claim that: 'Norm theory states that a person must have a social identity if group norms are to be effective over him. Therefore, the control of a crowd is greatest among people who are known to each other.'

In other words, what is being implied here is that social identity is the product of interpersonal interactions based on such factors as liking, proximity, and a number of similar factors (cf. Hogg, 1979). Recently this view of the social group has come under attack (cf. Turner, 1978*b*, and chapter 1 in this book) for, amongst other things, its empirical inadequacy.

First of all, Turner and Killian's account contains at its centre a major contradiction. They claim that the crowd is not in fact homogeneous, but merely appears to be so due to the fact that observers are blinded by the prevalent norms. However, these norms are supposed to be the product of activity by a number of conspicuous militants. Therefore, presumably, at first no norms exist and therefore there should be a period before the illusion of homogeneity arises. However, the whole point about crowd behaviour is the immediacy with which its unique characteristics manifest themselves. It is possible to maintain that this is an illusion; but contrary to its claims, emergent norm theory gives us no understanding of the immediacy of that illusion – unless, of course, it postulates the immediate formation of group norms, in which case it contains an important internal contradiction. The other premises of Turner and Killian's, such as norms coming from active members, crowd behaviour as an attempt to disambiguate situations, crowd control as a function of the interacquaintance of its members, all remain without empirical confirmation.

4. Social identity and crowd behaviour

The explanation of crowd behaviour to be outlined here is based on the Social Identification hypothesis (SIH) of Turner (cf. Turner, 1978*a*, *c*, and chapter 1) which grew out of Tajfel's work using the notion of social identity (cf. Tajfel, 1972, 1974, 1978*a*, *b*). This concept of social identity, which forms a crucial dimension of the early work on intergroup relations, has been elaborated by Turner to apply also to processes occurring *within* groups. As he argued in 1978*c*:

Social identification can refer to the process of locating a person within a system of social categorizations or to any social categorization used by a person to define himself or others. It will be used in the latter sense here and thus denotes an element of cognitive structure. The sum total of the social identifications used by a person to define himself will be described as his *social identity*. Social categorizations describe a person by systematically including him within some and excluding him from other related categories. This concept of social identity is descended from Tajfel's definition of it as 'the individual's knowledge that he belongs to certain social groups together with some emotional and value significance to him of the group membership'. (1972, p31)

Turner goes on to argue that the self-concept, of which social identity forms a part, is highly structurally differentiated with the parts able to operate independently of each other: 'If this hypothesis is correct, then the possibility arises that social identity may on occasions function more or less to the exclusion of personal identity, i.e. that at certain times our salient self-images may be based solely or primarily on our group memberships.' In other words, what is being postulated is that an individual's cognitive functioning shifts along a continuum from the domination of personal identity to that of social identity. This shift is seen to underlie the transition from interpersonal to intergroup behaviour, following Tajfel's (1978a) reference to 'a continuum that goes from the probably fictitious extreme of "pure" interpersonal behaviour to the rarely encountered extreme of purely intergroup behaviour' (p42). The exact manner in which identity shifts are reflected in behaviour is unclear. It seems, however, that the identity construct is involved in the processing of incoming information, such that: 'Once functioning, social identity monitors and construes social stimuli and provides a basis for regulating behaviour. Its cognitive output seems to be uniquely implicated in intra- and intergroup behaviour. In other words, we are hypothesizing that social identity is the cognitive mechanism that makes group behaviour possible.' The relevance of this theoretical framework to the explanation of crowd psychology can best be illustrated by considering, in turn, those problems that have preoccupied the research in this field since it began. These problems will be posed as a set of questions to which a coherent set of answers in terms of SIH will be given. The questions are:

(a) What is a crowd?
(b) What is the basis of the behavioural homogeneity of individuals in a crowd?
(c) How can one explain the genesis and nature of the ideas and emotions that characterize the behaviours of individuals in a crowd?

(d) What is the mechanism whereby these ideas and emotions are spread to members of the crowd?

(e) How can one account for exactly who will and who will not accept these ideas and emotions?

(f) How can one account for exactly which ideas will and which will not be liable to this process of spread?

(g) Why are individuals more confident in their ideas and more extreme in their emotions when they form part of a crowd?

(h) Why are individuals more likely to convert their ideas and emotions into actions when they form part of a crowd?

(a) Definition of the crowd

It will be recalled from the Introduction that, for SIT, a group is defined in terms of those individuals who identify themselves as members of the group. Unlike nearly all previous theoretical accounts, the crowd will be treated here in exactly the same manner as all other social groups; that is, a crowd will be defined as that set of individuals who share a common social identification of themselves in terms of that crowd.

It may be argued that the very reason why the crowd is of such interest is because it exhibits features that are not to be found in most social groups and that therefore it ought to be differentiated from them in some way. While it is true that the crowd does display some very special characteristics – both 'physical' (lack of structure, lack of history and culture) and behavioural (instability, extremity, dogmatism, and so on) – this does not necessarily mean that the *psychological* processes at play are any different in the case of collective behaviour.

Tajfel (1974) argued that the function of social categorization into groups is to serve 'as a system of orientation which creates and defines the individual's own place in society' (p11). The situation in which a crowd is generated is usually marked by uncertainty and lack of structure. If the individual identifies with the crowd as a means of locating himself within a confused social situation, then, initially at least, the crowd can only be said to have a reality in terms of a set of social identifications. However, it is evident that as long as the crowd remains a set of idiosyncratic definitions, it is of little use in stratifying the situation, and hence as a guide to action. What is necessary is a common definition of the social identity of the crowd in terms of a set of criterial attributes that determine those behaviours and perceptions appropriate to a group member in the given situation. It is precisely this problem of identity construction that constitutes the crux of the problem of crowd behaviour. It must be stressed, however, that this process of construal is not unique to crowds but can be found in all social groups. The crowd differs only as a matter of degree. This can be put down to two factors: firstly, crowd situations are characterized by uncertainty in which no pre-existing norms can be automatically applied whereas most other social groups act in a relatively well-defined social environment; and secondly, unlike the crowd, long-standing groups tend to have evolved structures to deal with the problems of adapting to novel situations. Nonetheless, these established groups must, over a period of time, construct new identities to deal with an ever-changing social reality; the social identity of a student in 1979, for instance, has little in common with that of the student of the 1920s.

(b) Homogeneity of the crowd

The basis for the behavioural homogeneity of individuals in a crowd is the fact that they are all acting on the basis of a common social identity. In other words, the cognitive structure mediating between the incoming stimuli and behaviour will be identical for all the members of the crowd and therefore, to the extent that they are all exposed to the same stimuli, they will exhibit the same behaviours. It is interesting to note that this hypothesized similarity in terms of cognitive structure is identical to the 'similarity of mental constitution' posited by McDougall to be the prerequisite condition for behavioural homogeneity in the crowd (cf. above). But, for McDougall, this similarity was a function of racially determined mental structures. The basis of cognitive similarity is the act of identifying with the group. While, as Turner admits, the factors that determine the 'switching on' of social identity are not clear, it is nevertheless clear that the same person may change his identification (and hence the operation of his 'mental structure') according to the situation. To return to an illustration used earlier, the same person, watching a National Front rally, might, when in uniform and acting in an official capacity, identify himself as a policeman but when out of uniform he might act as an anti-fascist – leading to radically different behaviours.

A possible objection might be that, for homogeneity to arise, there must be a social identity corresponding to crowd membership that defines appropriate behaviours in the given situation; and, as already admitted, that specific identity does not exist from the beginning but has to undergo a process of construction. Therefore, the cognitive basis for homogeneity only appears after a period of time and, consequently, during that period there can be no behavioural homogeneity amongst crowd members. It is, however, fully possible that the duration of this period is so short in crowd situations as to pose no real problem for the theoretical framework being proposed here.

(c) Genesis and nature of the social identity of a crowd

The argument used so far to explain crowd behaviour has been that it is due to individuals identifying with the crowd and acting in terms of the resultant social identity. The question that arises is: 'What identity?' The very nature of the crowd as an immediate creation in a confused situation precludes the existence of a completely preformed identity, hence the validity of this account relies on its ability to specify the means by which an initially amorphous body of individuals can come, with great rapidity, to be defined in terms of a set of ideas and emotions that regulate their conduct; in other words, it is necessary to explain the creation of a social identity for the members of the crowd.

The answer to this problem has already been sketched out by Turner (1978c). It corresponds for him to the inductive aspect of categorization. He describes the process as follows: 'Tajfel's categorization theory (1959, 1969, 1972; cf. also Doise, 1976) asserts that categorizing activity has both an inductive and deductive aspect. Deduction refers to the process by which a person is assigned some attribute on the basis of his category membership. Induction for Tajfel is similar to the process of social identification but we shall use it to mean the assignment to a category of some attribute perceived to characterize the exemplary member. Thus, induction is the means by which the criterial attributes are inferred from one or more individual members.' What is proposed here is a kind of self-fulfilling prophecy with respect to identity creation; the act of identifying with a group implies, for the subject, that there is some specific identity that corresponds to group membership. Since being a member of the group implies 'possession' of its criterial attributes (Tajfel's 'deductive law'), then the behaviour of any member, when acting in terms of that membership, will display those attributes. Therefore, using this logic, it is valid to infer the criterial attributes of the crowd's social identity from the actions of its members. How might this work in practice?

Consider, once more, a crowd of people watching a fascist rally. To the extent that they identify themselves as anti-fascist, they must then clarify for themselves what it means to be an anti-fascist in that situation. Suppose then that an individual who is seen to fulfil the criteria of being an anti-fascist, perhaps by a badge that he wears or by a slogan that he shouts, picks up a stone and flings it at the rally. That act, or rather the idea that it represents, that of disrupting the fascist rally, can come to be definitional of that particular crowd, resulting in a hail of stones, bricks and slogans upon the members of the fascist gathering.

It is clear that while crowd members are faced with the problem of identity construction, that construction does not take place in a void. The act of social identification on the part of an individual always occurs in a specific social situation and it corresponds to particular needs on the part of that individual. Thus, while it was stated earlier that one of the functions of identifying with a social group was to clarify a social situation, that clarification can only occur if the individual takes up a specific social location from which he can determine his relationship to other participants in the situation and hence know how to behave towards them. This means that identification does not occur towards the neutral category 'crowd' (which does not locate the individual but merely redescribes him), but rather towards some particular type of crowd – a crowd of anti-fascists, of trade unionists, of civil rights demonstrators, or whatever.

Given that the identification is towards some particular category, then the construction of an identity will be constrained by the historical and cultural continuity that the category represents; hence, for example, the physical disruption of a fascist rally may become a criterial attribute for a crowd of anti-fascists, but racist provocation may not. Hence, the identity process that occurs for members of a crowd may be described as follows: there is an immediate identification with a superordinate category which defines a field of possible identities; crowd members must then construct a *specific identity* which corresponds to the concrete situation. The means by which they do this is the 'inductive' aspect of categorization.

(d) The spread of ideas and emotions in the crowd

The process by which ideas and emotions are diffused amongst the members of a crowd has been, under the name of contagion, perhaps the prime concern of previous theories of collective behaviour. As has been shown, nearly all of these theories have proposed mechanisms of contagion that are premised upon some level of physical interaction between crowd members. The process to be described here is radically different in being a *cognitive* one. It follows logically from the identification of an individual with the crowd. Turner (see the previous chapter) terms this process 'Referent Informational Influence' (RII) and described it in the following way:

RII takes place in three stages:

(i) Individuals define themselves as members of a distinct social category.

(ii) Individuals form or learn the stereotypic norms of that category. They ascertain that certain ways of behaving are common criterial attributes of category membership. Certain appropriate, expected or desirable behaviours are used to define the category as different from other categories.

(iii) Individuals assign these norms to themselves in the same way that they assign other stereotypic characteristics of the category to themselves when their category membership becomes psychologically salient. Thus, their behaviour becomes more normative (conformist) as their category membership becomes salient (see p32)

In the case of individuals in a crowd condition (i) is upheld as a matter of definition; condition (ii) has been discussed above, which leaves condition (iii). In the absence of any well-formulated theory of group salience, intuition and anecdote will have to be relied upon. It seems fair to assert that in the case of the individual in a crowd, group salience is extremely high. Therefore, the act of identification with the crowd will lead to an instantaneous assimilation of its criterial attributes relating to specific ideas, emotions, behaviours and so on. Furthermore, to the extent that any new idea, emotion or behaviour becomes a criterial attribute of the crowd, it too will be assimilated by the crowd members.

(e) Specification of individuals liable to contagion

If the process of contagion was the major concern of previous accounts of the crowd, then their major problem was that of specifying the limits of that process. Their inability to do so, or else their postulation of limits too inflexible to account for the observed complexity of the problem, constitutes a fundamental objection to this body of work.

Consider the following example: a football match between two rival teams, with the scores equal. A goal is disallowed due to a disputed off-side decision. At this point one would be able to distinguish at least three different bodies of individuals, each homogeneous, each subject to a different set of 'contagious' attributes and resistant to all others. Those three groups would be the supporters of the team that had its goal disallowed, the supporters of the team that conceded the disallowed goal and a group of neutrals. This is an exceptionally simple situation: there would be little difficulty in thinking of many similar ones. And yet, with one exception, there exists no theory of crowd behaviour that can explain how it comes about that different individuals react differently to each set of 'contagious' attributes.

The answer to this problem of limitations is contained within the present account of the process of contagion. The effects of contagion will be limited to those individuals who have identified with the crowd. Furthermore, on this basis, there will be as many *psychological* crowds as there are different groups of individuals identifying with different categories. In the example cited above, there will be one crowd who identify with the first side, one crowd who identify with the second and a last crowd who identify themselves as neutrals. The differing behaviours of the three groups can be readily understood from this perspective.

(f) Specification of the possible content of contagion

This second area of limitation upon the process of contagion is important for the present argument. It is here that it becomes clear that, in order to understand the behaviours of individuals in the crowd, the crowd itself must be situated in its wider historical, cultural and political context.

Crowd members must construct an identity that determines the behaviours that are appropriate to the given situation; but they will be limited in so doing by those higher order (i.e. more general) attributes that define the category under which the crowd is subsumed. In the course of identity formation, certain behaviours will come to be criterial attributes of the crowd and these will be contagious in the sense that they will be assimilated by all those who have identified themselves as members of the crowd. However, it is clear that only criterial attributes of the crowd can be contagious; therefore, since the range of these attributes which constitute the identity of the crowd is limited by the dimensions of the category under which the crowd is formed, the content of the contagious process will be limited by the pre-existing attributes of this category.

For this reason, the behaviour of crowd members will not be random. It will represent the adaptation to a novel situation of an historical tradition. The crowds that have inspired various theorists over the last century to a study of collective psychology ranged from the popular crowds that so fascinated Le Bon and McDougall, to the civil rights, student activist and black crowds of latter-day American social psychology. Their behaviours will necessarily remain mysterious until one considers each crowd in the light of the social movement that it represents. The popular crowds of the turn of the century of which such an unfriendly picture has been painted, and which consisted of working men, were violent, dangerous and destructive; but to go on from this to making violence, danger and destruction constitutive elements of every crowd gives one little help in explaining, say, the behaviour of a crowd of Hindus at a religious festival. The violence of these popular crowds could be understood in terms of their ideology which included the conception of the destruction of a social order. A similar ideology was underlying the destructive behaviours of the civil rights, student activist and black crowds.

This question of the ideology associated with particular social categories (ideology being conceptualized here as that set of attributes that define the category and hence constrain the field of possible identities of any given crowd subsumed under this category) is one whose elucidation is beyond the competence of the psychologist. It requires other levels of analysis: sociological, historical and political. The task of the psychologist is to explain the *processes* that mediate between social reality and the behaviour of the individual in the crowd, and hence to show which parameters are of importance in determining the form of those behaviours; it is not for him to determine the levels of those parameters. To do so would imply, as indeed many theorists propose, that behaviours of crowd members are somehow the pure expression of autistically expressed fixed tendencies.

(g) Confidence and extremity in the crowd

The traditional studies concerning those characteristics of a communicator that make his message more persuasive have yielded a number of factors. The most commonly mentioned is that of the prestige of the communicator. It is a notion with a pedigree stretching back to Aristotle who maintained that: 'Persuasion is achieved by the speaker's personal character when the speech is so spoken as to make us think him credible. We believe good men more readily than others.'

Hovland et al. (1953) distinguished two factors in this notion of prestige, expertness and trustworthiness, and proposed that an increase in either will increase the credibility of the communicator's message. A similar role has been assigned to the attractiveness of the communicator to the recipient (Newcomb, 1961; Schachter et al., 1951) and also to his similarity to the recipient (Dabbs, 1964).

In the case of the crowd, these interpersonal explanations of confidence seem to be little use, the personal qualities of the communicator having little effect on the way in which the message is received. One example might be the anonymous creature whose cry of 'fire' inspires total confidence (and total panic) to a crowd in an enclosed space. The reason for the irrelevance of interindividual research is that a piece of information is seen as constitutive of the social identity of the group, as opposed to it, or as irrelevant to it.

As an illustration of this, imagine a crowd at a rally opposing apartheid in South Africa. To the communication that a black leader who had recently died in captivity had been a victim of police assassination, total confidence would be given; to a counter-communication that he died from voluntarily banging his head against a brick wall in order to discredit the South African security forces, no credence would be given at all; to a third communication, that the day he died it was warm and windy, no regulated response would be given, since the information would be orthogonal to those dimensions by which the category 'opponents of apartheid' was defined.

Two criteria will primarily affect the confidence of crowd members in the information given to them. The first is that the information is seen to accord with those prior attributes by which the category, of which the crowd is one exemplar, is defined. The second condition is that the individual who communicates the information is seen to be a member of the group, since the logic of the inductive aspect of categorization, by which the given crowd acquires its identity, is dependent upon the membership of the observed person.

Two different processes are implicated for the individual when acting in terms of his two modes of identity: personal and social. For the individual *qua* individual confidence in a communication is a matter of trying to ascertain the correspondence between that communication and 'objective reality' as he sees it. For the individual *qua* crowd member, this question of correspondence is shifted to that between the communication and the social identity of the crowd. The crowd's identity represents the common reconstruction of a confused social reality on the part of the individuals who identify with the crowd. For an individual acting as such, confidence must be based on probabilistic factors such as the personal character of the communicator, etc. The confidence of crowd members in a piece of information is not probabilistic; it is all-or-none. Those communications that do not accord with social identity will be unreservedly rejected and those that do will be received with complete confidence.

A similar explanation can be used to account for the extremity of emotions amongst crowd members. An emotion, just like any other attribute, can become part of the crowd's social identity and, to the extent that it does so, it will be accepted by every individual who behaves in terms of that identity. Crowd members acting in terms of their own social identity will treat others in terms of the others' social identity. Action towards anyone who is a member of a group which is seen as a target will not be emotionally constrained by his personal characteristics. An awe-inspiring example of this is provided by Trotsky's account of a pogrom in the Russia of 1905. He described the way in which an overwhelming anti-Jewish identity was built up through the use of symbols of Christianity, of icons, crosses and chants to reiterate the central message of hatred and revulsion against all those cast as Jews. This resulted in the indiscriminate torture and butchery of women, children and even babies – as long as they were members of the target outgroup.

One factor that serves to accentuate this extremity is the 'prima inter pares' (PIP) effect described by Codol (1975). According to this notion, once a norm is established for a particular group then individuals who are of the group compete to conform to the norm more than the other group members. This idea adapted to an emotional attribute, such as 'aggression', for example, would predict that each individual would strive to be more aggressive than the next, with a resultant shift in the general level of aggression towards an increase in intensity.

(h) Idea and action in the crowd

In order to explain the tendency of crowd members to convert their ideas and emotions into actions it is necessary to use two further notions. The first is a concept used by Bandura (1977) to which he refers as 'self-efficacy'. This asserts that an individual will perform a behaviour to the extent that he believes that he will be able to carry it successfully to completion. The second idea comes from the research into aggression: it has been found that one factor of considerable importance in determining the elicitation of an aggressive response is the perceived legitimacy of that response in the given situation (cf. Burnstein and Worchel, 1962; Taylor and Epstein, 1967; Billig, 1976; Tajfel, 1978b for summaries).

Considering these two variables, expectation of success and legitimacy, as factors that mediate between an idea and its expression in behaviour, it is possible to understand why individuals in the crowd express ideas which might normally be restrained. It has often been noted, from Le Bon onwards, that crowd members display feelings of almost infinite power. What an individual cannot achieve alone, a crowd of hundreds or thousands may find as no difficulty at all. Expectation of success has a greater likelihood of being found for individuals in a crowd than for individuals alone, acting as individuals.

The explanation of the belief of crowd members in the legitimacy of their projected behaviours can be related to the fact that the acceptance of the ideas on which these behaviours are based is premised on their accordance with the identity of the crowd. This is the arbiter of all aspects of the social reality in which crowd members find themselves, including the determination of what is and what is not legitimate. Any behaviours implicated by ideas acceptable to the crowd will also be seen by the crowd as legitimate.

A large amount of space has been taken up with a critique of the pre-existing notions for explaining collective behaviour, and new conceptions have been used in the present account, based on the SIT. The explanatory and heuristic value of these ideas has been the theme of a number of articles (e.g. Brewer, 1979; Tajfel, 1978b; see the previous chapter); their application to crowd behaviour reveals at one a number of problems, and a number of exciting implications.

5. Conclusion

The entire project of the previous four sections has been to show that large-scale social behaviour cannot be seen as arising out of, and hence as being constrained by, intra- and interpersonal events. Rather, it displays the primacy of social factors in the determination of the behaviour of individuals in groups. The core of the argument has been that those theories which present crowd behaviour as the release of behavioural predispositions are unable to account for the creativity of the crowd, whereas those which seek to account for this creativity in terms of structures arising out of interactions between crowd members cannot explain the immediate homogeneity of the collectivity. The only way to reconcile these two characteristics, creativity and immediate homogeneity, is to regard crowd behaviour as the expression of a social identity, the analysis of which cannot be understood without recourse to the examination of cultural, political and historical factors.

The effect of social factors is to place the individual in situations that demand certain forms of behaviour. The self arises as a reflection of those behaviours and prolongs them even when the situational restraints are removed. The fundamental point is that any behaviour which involves the manipulation of an object that is exterior to the individual will depend upon that individual's location relative to the object, in other words, his identity, and that the location will always have a social dimension. In interpersonal interaction, as Tajfel (1978a) suggested, behaviour is never solely in terms of personal identity, but always involves some measure of social identity. Behaviour towards inanimate objects, as Leontiev (1976) argued at length, is governed by the meaning of the object, which in turn depends upon the social use of that object. Therefore the individual's relationship to that object will be socially determined. The self that arises out of these behaviours will necessarily bear the mark of social structure.

The exciting point about the crowd is that, given that it is a response to social uncertainty, it can force an individual into a novel social location, and evoke from him novel behaviours that correspond to that location. In this way, a process of social construction that probably ended in early childhood, and which adequately directed the individual in times of calm, re-emerges when the social structure itself undergoes a temporary destabilization.

It is not, as Le Bon originally suggested, that man in the crowd displays the beast in man, but rather that the crowd in society displays the beast in society. If the crowd has tended to be a violent phenomenon, it is not due to a mysterious human nature but rather to the fact that 'hatred and intolerance can never be banished together with all the wanton miseries they provoke, until we can distinguish between men and their environment, until we can understand that the real enemies of humanity are not human beings – not members of sects, races or nations – but social systems which breed and perpetuate injustice and exploitation' (Lowenthal, 1936, px).

References

Allport, F. 1920. The influence of the group upon association and thought. *Journal of Experimental Psychology*, **3**, 159–82.

Allport, F. 1924. *Social psychology*. Boston: Houghton Mifflin.

Allport, G.W. 1969. The historical background of modern social psychology. In G. Lindzey and E. Aronson (eds): *Handbook of social psychology*, 2nd Edition, Vol. 1. Reading, Mass.: Addison-Wesley.

Aronfreed, J. 1969. The problem of imitation. In L.P. Lipset and H.W. Reese (eds): *Advances in child development and behaviour*, Vol. 4. New York: Academic Press.

Bandura, A. 1965. Influence of model's reinforcement contingencies on the acquisition of imitative responses. *Journal of Personality and Social Psychology*, **1**, 589–95.

Bandura, A. 1977. Self-efficacy: Toward a unifying theory of behavioral change. *Psychological Review*, **84**, 191–215.

Becker, E. 1976. *The birth and death of meaning.* Harmondsworth: Penguin Books.

Berkowitz, L. 1970. The contagion of violence: An S–R mediational analysis of some effects of observed aggression. In W.J. Arnold and M.M. Page (eds): *Nebraska Symposium on motivation,* Vol. 18. Lincoln: University of Nebraska Press.

Berkowitz, L. 1972. Frustrations, comparison and other sources of emotion arousal as contributors to social unrest. *Journal of Social Issues,* **28**, 77–91.

Billig, M. 1976. *Social psychology and intergroup relations.* European Monographs in Social Psychology, No. 9. London: Academic Press.

Billig, M. 1978. *Fascists: A social psychological view of the National Front.* European Monographs in Social Psychology, No. 15. London: Academic Press.

Blumer, H. 1946. Elementary collective groupings. In A. McLung Lee (ed.): *Principles of sociology.* New York: Barnes and Noble.

Brewer, M.B. 1979. Ingroup bias in the minimal intergroup situation: A cognitive-motivational analysis. *Psychological Bulletin,* **86**, (2), 307–24.

Brown, R. 1965. *Social psychology.* London: Collier Macmillan.

Burnstein, E. and Worchel, P. 1962. Arbitrariness of frustration and its consequences for aggression in a social situation. *Journal of Personality,* **30**, 528–40.

Cannavale, F.J., Scarr, H.A. and Pepitone, A. 1970. De-individuation in the small group: Further evidence. *Journal of Personality and Social Psychology,* **16**, 141–7.

Cantril, H. 1941. *The psychology of social movements.* New York: Wiley.

Carver, C.S. 1974. Facilitation of physical aggression through objective self-awareness. *Journal of Experimental Social Psychology,* **10**, 365–70.

Codol, J.P. 1975. On the so-called 'superior conformity of the self' behaviour: Twenty experimental investigations. *European Journal of Social Psychology,* **5**, 457–501.

Cooley, C.H. 1902. *Human nature and the social order.* New York: Scribner.

Cottrell, N.B. 1972. Social facilitation. In C. McClintock (ed.): *Experimental social psychology.* New York: Holt, Rinehart and Winston.

Cottrell, N.B., Wack, D.L., Sekerak, G.J. and Rittle, R.H. 1968. Social facilitation of dominant responses by presence of an audience and the mere presence of others. *Journal of Personality and Social Psychology,* **9**, 245–50.

Dabbs, J.M. 1964. Self-esteem, communicator characteristics and attitude change. *Journal of Abnormal and Social Psychology,* **69**, 173–81.

Dewey, J. 1917. The need for social psychology. *Psychological Review,* **24**, 266–77.

Diener, E., Westford, K.L., Dineen, J. and Fraser, S.C. 1973. Beat the pacifist: The de-individuation effects of anonymity and group presence. *Proceedings of the American Psychological Association,* 81st Annual Convention, **8**, 221–2.

Diener, E., Dineen, J., Endresen, K., Beamon, A.L. and Fraser, S.C. 1975. Effects of altered responsibility, cognitive set and modelling on physical aggression and de-individuation. *Journal of Personality and Social Psychology,* **31**, 328–37.

Dipboye, R.L. 1977. Alternative approaches to de-individuation. *Psychological Bulletin,* **84**, 1057–75.

Doise, W. 1976. *L'articulation psychosociologique et relations entre groupes.* Brussels: De Boeck.

80   Stephen Reicher

Donnerstein, E., Donnerstein, M. and Evans, R. 1972. Variables in inter-racial aggression: Anonymity, expected retaliation and a riot. *Journal of Personality and Social Psychology*, **22**, 236–45.

Duval, S. and Wicklund, R.A. 1972. *A theory of objective self-awareness*. New York: Academic Press.

Festinger, L., Pepitone, A. and Newcomb, T. 1952. Some consequences of de-individuation in a group. *Journal of Abnormal and Social Psychology*, **47**, 382–9.

Freud, S. 1922. *Group psychology and the analysis of the ego*. London: Hogarth Press.

Fromm, E. 1956. *The art of loving*. New York: Harper and Row.

Geen, R.G. and Gange, J.J. 1977. Drive theory of social facilitation: Twelve years of theory and research. *Psychological Bulletin*, **84**, 1267–88.

Haney, C., Banks, W. and Zimbardo, P.G. 1964. Interpersonal dynamics in a simulated prison. *International Journal of Criminology and Penology*, **1**, 69–97.

Henchy, T. and Glass, D.C. 1968. Evaluation apprehension and the social facilitation of dominant and subordinate responses. *Journal of Personality and Social Psychology*, **10**, 446–54.

Hofstätter, P.R. 1957. *Gruppendynamik: Kritik der Massenpsychologie*. Hamburg: Rowohlt Taschenbuch.

Hogg, M. 1979. Group formation and cohesiveness: A review. Unpublished MS, University of Bristol.

Hovland, C.I. and Janis, I.L. 1959. *Personality and persuasability*. New Haven: Yale University Press.

Hovland, C.I., Janis, I.L. and Kelley, H.H. 1953. *Communication and persuasion*. New Haven: Yale University Press.

Innes, J.M. and Young, R.F. 1975. The effect of presence of an audience on evaluation apprehension and objective self-awareness. *Journal of Experimental Social Psychology*, **11**, 35–42.

Israel, J. and Tajfel, H. (eds) 1972. *The context of social psychology: A critical assessment*. European Monographs in Social Psychology, No. 2. London: Academic Press.

James, W. 1890. *The principles of psychology*. New York: Holt, Rinehart and Winston.

Jung, C. 1946. *Psychological types or the psychology of individuation*. New York: Harcourt Brace.

Klapp, O.E. 1969. *Collective search for identity*. New York: Holt, Rinehart and Winston.

Lacey, J.I. 1967. Somatic response patterning and stress: Some revisions of activation theory. In R.H. Appley and R. Trumbull (eds): *Psychological stress*. New York: Appleton Century Croft.

Laing, R.D. 1960. *The divided self*. London: Tavistock.

Le Bon, C. 1947. *The crowd: A study of the popular mind*. London: Ernest Benn.

Le Dantec, F. 1918. *L'égoisme: Seule base de toute société*. Paris: Flammarion.

Leontiev, A. 1976. *Le développement du psychisme*. Paris: Éditions Sociales.

Lorenz, K. 1970. *On aggression*. London: Methuen.

Lowenthal, M. 1936. *The Jews of Germany*. London: Russell.

Martin, E.D. 1920. *The behaviour of crowds.* New York: Harper and Row.

McDougall, W. 1908. *Introduction to social psychology.* London: Methuen.

McDougall, W. 1927. *The group mind*, 2nd Edition. Cambridge: Cambridge University Press.

McDougall, W. 1933. *The energies of men.* London: Methuen

Milgram, S. 1974. *Obedience to authority: An experimental view.* New York: Harper and Row.

Milgram, S. and Toch, H. 1969. Collective behaviour: Crowds and social movements. In G. Lindzey and E. Aronson (eds): *Handbook of social psychology*, 2nd Edition, Vol. 4. Reading, Mass.: Addison-Wesley.

Newcomb, T.M. 1961. *The acquaintance process.* New York: Holt, Rinehart and Winston.

Oakes, P. and Turner, J.C. 1980. Social categorization and intergroup behaviour: Does minimal intergroup discrimination make social identity more positive? *European Journal of Social Psychology*, **10**, 295–301.

Paloutzian, R.F. 1972. Some components of de-individuation and their effects. *Dissertation Abstracts International*, **33**, 2496A–7A.

Paulus, P.B. and Murdoch, P. 1971. Anticipated evaluation and audience presence in the enhancement of positive responses. *Journal of Experimental Social Psychology*, **1**, 280–91.

Pessin, J. 1933. The comparative effects of social and mechanical stimulation on memorizing. *American Journal of Psychology*, **45**, 262–70.

Rapoport, A. 1961. *Fights, games and debates.* Ann Arbor: Michigan University Press.

Rapoport, A. 1963. Mathematical models of social interaction. In R.D. Luce, R.R. Bush and E. Galanter (eds): *Handbook of mathematical psychology.* New York: Wiley.

Raven, B. H. and Rubin, J. Z. 1976. *Social psychology.* New York: Wiley.

Ribot, T. 1897. *The psychology of the emotions.* London: Scott.

Ross, E.A. 1908. *Social psychology: An outline and source book.* New York: Macmillan.

Sasfy, J. and Okun, M. 1974. Form of evaluation and audience expertness as joint determinants of audience effects. *Journal of Experimental Social Psychology*, **10**, 461–7.

Schachter, S., Ellerston, N., McBride, D. and Gregory, D. 1951. An experimental study of cohesiveness and productivity. *Human Relations*, **4**, 229–38.

Scheir, M.F., Fenigstein, A. and Buss, A.H. 1974. Self-awareness and physical aggression. *Journal of Experimental Social Psychology*, **10**, 264–73.

Shaver, K.G. 1977. *Principles of social psychology.* Cambridge, Mass.: Winthrop.

Shaw, M.E. 1976. *Group dynamics: The psychology of small group behaviour.* New Delhi: Tata McGraw-Hill.

Sighele, S. 1895. *Psychologie des sectes.* Paris: Girard and Brière.

Singer, J.E., Brush, C.A. and Lublin, S.C. 1965. Some aspects of de-individuation: Identification and conformity. *Journal of Experimental Social Psychology*, **1**, 356–78.

Smelser, N.J. 1963. *Theory of collective behaviour.* London: Routledge and Kegan Paul.

Stotland, E. and Cottrell, N. 1961. Self-esteem, group interaction and group influence on performance. *Journal of Personality*, **29**, 273–84.

Tajfel, H. 1959. Quantitative judgment in social perception. *British Journal of Psychology*, **50**, 16–29.

Tajfel, H. 1969. Social and cultural factors in perception. In G. Lindzey and E. Aronson (eds): *Handbook of social psychology*, 2nd Edition, Vol. 3. Reading, Mass.: Addison-Wesley.

Tajfel, H. 1970. Experiments in intergroup discrimination. *Scientific American*, **223**, 96–102.

Tajfel, H. 1972. La catégorisation sociale. In S. Moscovici (ed.): *Introduction à la psychologie sociale*. Paris: Larousse.

Tajfel, H. 1974. Intergroup behaviour, social comparison and social change. Unpublished Katz-Newcomb lectures, Ann Arbor: University of Michigan.

Tajfel, H. (ed.) 1978a. *Differentiation between social groups: Studies in the social psychology of intergroup relations*. European Monographs in Social Psychology, No. 14. London: Academic Press.

Tajfel, H. 1978b. Intergroup behaviour: Individualistic perspectives. In H. Tajfel and C. Fraser (eds): *op. cit.*

Tajfel, H. and Fraser, C. (eds) 1978. *Introducing social psychology*. Harmondsworth: Penguin Books.

Tarde, G. 1903. *The laws of imitation*. New York: Henry Holt.

Tarde, G. 1912. *Penal philosophy*. Boston: Little and Brown.

Taylor, S.P. and Epstein, S. 1967. Aggression as a function of the interaction of the sex of the aggressor and the sex of the victim. *Journal of Personality*, **35**, 474–86.

Traugott, M. 1978. Reconceiving social movements. *Social Problems*, **26**, 38–49.

Triplett, N. 1897. The dynamogenic factors in pacemaking and competition. *American Journal of Psychology*, **9**, 507–33.

Trotter, W. 1916. *Instincts of the herd in peace and war*. London: Ernest Benn.

Turner, J.C. 1978a. Social identification and intergroup behaviour: Some emerging issues in the social psychology of intergroup relations. Research proposal to the SSRC. (UK), October, 1978.

Turner, J.C. 1978b. Social categorization and social discrimination in the minimal group paradigm. In H. Tajfel (ed.), *op. cit.*

Turner, J.C. 1978c. Towards a cognitive re-definition of the social group. Paper presented to the Research Colloquium on Social Identity of the European Laboratory of Social Psychology (LEPS), at the Université de Haute Bretagne, Rennes, France, 3–6 December 1978. (Rewritten for chapter 1 of this book.)

Turner, R.H. and Killian, L. 1957. *Collective behaviour*. Englewood Cliffs, N.J.: Prentice Hall.

Vygotsky, L.S. 1962. *Thought and language*. Cambridge, Mass.: MIT Press.

Walters, R.H. 1968. Some conditions facilitating the occurrence of imitative behaviour. In E.C. Simmel, R.A. Hope and G.A. Milton (eds.): *Social facilitation and imitative behaviour*. Boston: Allyn and Bacon.

Watson, R.I. 1973. Investigation into de-individuation using a cross-cultural survey technique. *Journal of Personality and Social Psychology*, **25**, 342–5.

Wheeler, L. 1966. Motivation as a determinant of upward comparison. *Journal of Experimental Social Psychology*, suppl. 1, 27–31.

White, M.J. 1977. Counter-normative behaviour as influenced by de-individuating conditions and reference group salience. *Journal of Social Psychology*, **13**, 75–90.

Wilder, D.A. 1978. Perceiving persons as a group: Effects on attributions of causality and beliefs. *Social Psychology*, **41**, 13–23.

Zabrick, M.L. and Miller, N. 1972. Group aggression: The effects of friendship ties and anonymity. *Proceedings of the 80th Annual Convention of the American Psychological Association*, **7**, 211–12.

Zajonc, R.B. 1965. Social facilitation. *Science*, **149**, 269–74.

Zajonc, R.B. and Sales, S.M. 1966. Social facilitation of dominant and subordinate responses. *Journal of Experimental Social Psychology*, **2**, 160–8.

Zimbardo, P.G. 1969. The human choice: Individuation, reason and order versus de-individuation, impulse and chaos. In W.J. Arnold and D. Levine, (eds.): *Nebraska Symposium on Motivation*, Vol. 17. Lincoln: University of Nebraska Press.

Zimbardo, P.G., Haney, C., Banks, W.C. and Jaffe, D. 1973. A Pirandellian prison: The mind is a formidable jailer. *New York Times Magazine*, April 8th, 1973.

3. Social identity and relations of power between groups[1,2]

JEAN-CLAUDE DESCHAMPS

1. Introduction

The notion of social identity presents problems which are difficult and arduous; our discussion in this chapter will be confined to only a few of them, one of which in particular will be stressed. But before this is done, and without attempting to present a full historical outline, some points of reference need to be mentioned so as to provide a perspective on the development of the notion of social identity.

William James is the first author who must be mentioned; in several chapters of his *Principles of Psychology* (1890) he was concerned with the definition of the Self. He introduced the distinction between the *I* and the *Me* which still remains important today in the work on the concept of identity. The Self is a duality: it consists of the *I*, a conscious and knowing subject, and the *Me* which is known to the *I*. This separation of the two distinct aspects of the Self does not mean, however, that they represent two separate and autonomous aspects of reality; the *I* and the *Me* cannot be dissociated within the Self. The *I* is conceived as the reference in the Self to the knowing subject, while the *Me* is the Self as it is known to the *I*. In turn, the *Me* can be subdivided into three categories as a function of the elements of which it is constituted: the material *Me*, the social *Me* and the spiritual *Me*.

Towards the beginning of the century, George Herbert Mead (1934) was also concerned with the definition of Self. For Mead, the Self is constituted by a 'sociological' component – the *Me*, which is an internalization of social roles; and by a more personal component, the *I*. Thus, Mead distinguished between two aspects of the Self: the *I* which represents the Self as a subject, and the *Me* which represents it as an object. More specifically, the *I* is the reaction of the organism to the attitudes of others, the *Me* is the organized sum total of the attitudes of others which the person takes over. The attitudes of others constitute the organized *Me* to which one reacts as *I*; the Self emerges from an interaction between the *I* and the *Me* which are its constituting elements. The *I* represents the creative aspect of the Self which responds to the attitudes of others; while the *Me* consists of an organization of the judgements of others which the Self reflects. It is this dialogue between the *I* and the *Me* which amounts to what the Self is, and this dialogue is a transposition to the level of the individual of the processes which link a person to other persons in their interactions.

The notion of identity has also been used in a 'neo-Freudian' psycho-analytic perspective, particularly by Erikson (e.g. 1963) in the wake of the psychoanalytic 'culturalist' tradition. He developed the concept of 'basic personality' first formulated by Kardiner (1939, 1945) and Linton (1945), and also of social or national character introduced by Fromm (1941, 1956). Erikson's aim was to describe personality patterns shared by the members of a society and resulting from experiences which are common to them. In this perspective, identity is, as for Mead, an articulation of its individual and collective components, of what is personal and what derives from a shared culture.

More recently, social identity has been the focus of attention in the work of some sociologists (e.g. Berger and Luckmann, 1966) and cultural identity was the subject of ethnological research, as for example in the seminar directed by Lévi-Strauss and published in 1977.

In social psychology, the notion of identity has been related to research on social roles, on the positions occupied by individuals in a social struc-ture. Social identity has been mainly conceptualized as a variable dependent upon these positions of individuals in society. This is particularly clear in the work of Sarbin and Allen (1968) who consider that 'social identity would be a part process of the self, representing ... cognitions arising from placements in the social ecology' (p550). More recently, Zavalloni (1973) expressed the view that her 'Social Identity Inventory' would enable us 'to conceive how membership of certain groups (such as nation, social class, sex, etc.) can affect the perception of Self and personal values, and vice versa' (p253). For Tajfel (1972, p292) 'social identity of individuals is linked to their awareness of membership of certain social groups, and to the emotional and evaluative significance of that membership'. Many other authors, including Sherif, insisted that social identity of individuals cannot remain independent of their membership groups. We shall therefore consider, following these authors, that social identity has 'something to do' with group membership.

If it is true that social identity is linked to group membership, we still have the task of defining what is meant by a 'group'. The next section of this chapter will specify – in a schematic manner – how power structures inherent in some relations between groups may induce certain types of identity which can be conceived in terms of 'subject' or 'object'. It will then be shown that results of some studies in social psychology can provide illustrations of our argument; and that – although the aims of these studies may appear remote from the problems raised here – the link between them and the present argument suggests that this is one of the research directions which needs to be taken up in social psychology.

2. The group

What is meant by the term 'group' *in the present context*?

In the definition suggested by Zavalloni (1973, p245) 'the notion of "group" includes several elements which, at different levels, *identify* an individual; this applies to social categories as general as those of age, sex or nationality, but it may also refer to roles or social positions such as the membership of a profession, a political affiliation, etc.'

This is not, however, sufficient to define a group, since a group has no existence but in its relation to other groups. As Tajfel wrote (1972, p295), 'the characteristics of one's own group (such as its status, its richness or poverty, the colour of its skin) acquire their significance only in relation to the perceived differences from other groups and the evaluation of these differences ... the definition of a group (national, racial, or any other) makes sense only in relation to other groups. A group becomes a group in the sense that it is perceived as having common characteristics or a common fate only because other groups are present in its environment.'

But even this further specification does not seem sufficient. The relations between groups are not only those of co-existence or juxtaposition; if that was the case, the definition quoted above would have been sufficient. Groups exist within a system of mutual dependence; they acquire a reality which is defined in and through their interdependence. They are not pre-existing closed spheres each of which would be able to engender its own specific system of meanings. It cannot therefore be said that each group has its own interpretations and values; groups exist as something which is concrete and 'objective' only in the context of some values which are common to the society as a whole. Therefore, it is not the difference between systems of values which determines the existence of specific groups but – on the contrary – a common system of values and its homogeneity.

The existence of concrete and 'objective' differences between individuals is not sufficient for the emergence of a group or the formation of several groups. These differences will remain unnoticed if they do not acquire their significance in relation to shared values. In other words, they can become 'legible' only if they relate to a shared and common symbolic universe of values which makes it possible for different groups to exist.

We stressed a definition of groups as existing in and through their relations of interdependence but one must beware of a trap which consists of reducing the relations between groups to an interaction between interchangeable and equivalent elements of a system to which they all belong. In fact, the relations of interdependence between groups, in their concrete reality as well as at a symbolic level, often remain asymmetrical. The groups of 'children', 'old men', 'women', 'blacks', 'unskilled labourers' or 'workers' are not equivalent to, and interchangeable with, those of 'adults', 'males', 'whites' or 'middle-class'. Age, sex, 'race', social position assign to them all a specific location in the social relationships based on production. Differences in power will then be reflected in the relations of interdependence between the groups. The 'dominant' groups can retain their position only because of the existence of other groups.

But – and this is the problem we shall now consider – the world order, created and conceptually constructed, as it is, by those who dominate it, implies the fact that membership of groups is not equally salient for all. Its salience varies for individuals considered as social actors depending upon their possession of power or the lack of it; and upon their distance from a point of reference in relation to which everyone is *supposed* to be able to define himself (in a society of citizens who are free and equal in their rights) but which, in reality, only tends to define those who are the owners of material or symbolic capital.

3. Social identity and relationships of domination

According to the analysis of the language of the contemporary press conducted by Guillaumin (1972), the dominant discourse assigns their place to individuals through defining, locating and ordering each of them in relation to others. But only those who dominate are each clearly defined as an entity, as a collection of individuals each occupying 'his' place which is similar for all of them in the sense that they are all considered as unique and singular. Outside of this collection of 'singular' individuals of which they are all members, those who dominate only perceive entities which are composed of undifferentiated elements: the 'child', the 'woman', the 'black', the 'worker', etc. In this symbolic order which the dominant groups create and which legitimizes the economic constraints defining those who are dominated and the power of those who dominate, the former have no specificity, uniqueness, singularity or individuality as individuals. Characteristics which are attributed to their groups are sufficient to provide a full definition of what they are.

For Guillaumin (1972, p217), 'the group which is adult, white, male, of middle class, healthy in ideas and customs, is thus the category which ... imposes upon others ... their own definition as a norm ... The group which, in this way, refers to itself as *I*, in the language as well as in the law, in power and in general consensus, is therefore, first of all, a symbolic group which does not conceive of itself as a concrete group brought together by compulsory links. As a reflection of the distribution of power it is, in the real sense of the terms, the social subject. It constitutes the point of reference of the relationship' (between the dominant and the dominated).

In other words, one can distinguish between two kinds of individuals. On the one hand, there are those who conceive of themselves as unique, or at least as not belonging to any particular category; on the other, there are those who are particles of an entity and are not considered in terms of their personal characteristics. Once designated as a woman, a child, or a black, they are defined by these terms. Thus, all social agents are defined in relation to the 'social subject', as this term is discussed by Guillaumin, i.e. in relation to a norm which has become embodied in a concrete group. A member of this dominant group will define himself in a manner which is internally consistent; he is homogeneous with the social subject and is, by definition, included in the context which provides the general point of reference. This remains the case independently of what may be, in reality, his personal distance from the norm. The dominated have no such homogeneity with the social subject. There is in their case no similarity between their *de facto* identity which is assigned to them by those who dominate, and the symbolic and central reality which constitutes the social subject, the norm, the point of reference.

Both the dominant and the dominated[3] define themselves in relation to the same norm which is shared and unique; this is the imaginary *I* represented by the dominant. In this way, the dominant cannot be placed in opposition to, or contradiction with, this point of reference. This is not the case for the dominated. He is trapped between the *Me* to which he has been assigned by the dominant and the point of reference of *Me* also imposed by the dominant who at the same time prevents the accession to it by the dominated.

It follows from this brief outline that social identity can vary fundamentally as a function of the material and symbolic capital which is owned by the individual. This can be stated as the proposition that the social identity of those who dominate will be defined in terms of 'subjects' and of those who are dominated in terms of 'objects'. The former do not think of themselves as being determined by their group membership or their social affiliation. They see themselves above all as individualized human beings who are singular, 'subjects', voluntary actors, free and autonomous. Their group is first and foremost a collection of persons. This is not the case for the dominated who are defined as undifferentiated elements in a collection of impersonal particles, and are thought of as 'objects' rather than 'subjects'.

But this is not quite sufficient when we consider that, at the same time, all social beings live in a common symbolic universe. The dominated, while he is assigned by the dominant to the 'object' category, cannot escape the general norm which defines all human beings as subjects, as citizens who are free and equal before the law. This inherent contradiction results in uncertainty about themselves and their identity.

The traditional notion of social identity attempts to achieve a definition of the individual as located at the point of convergence between the social and the psychological; this notion aims to deal with questions concerning the extent to which individuals are defined through their membership of certain social groups and what is the part played in that definition by their individual, personal and idiosyncratic characteristics. In contrast, the model proposed here, which is no more than a rough outline, does not take as its point of departure a distinction between personal (or individual) identity and social identity. We shall distinguish instead between what will be referred to as 'de facto identity' and 'imaginary identity'. In this perspective, the former is the definition of self attributed to individuals in and through their social relations. In the case of those who are dominant, these definitions are made in terms of persons or subjects; for the dominated, they are a part of a collective object. As a result, the de facto identity is, for the dominants, homologous with their imaginary identity which was defined earlier as the social subject or the referent, the norm describing a 'subject'. In contrast, the de facto and the imaginary identities lack congruence in the case of those who are dominated. In the following section of this chapter, an attempt will be made to ascertain whether this distinction can find its equivalent in some of the results of research in social psychology and related fields.

4. Empirical examples

(a) Relations of domination and self-identity

The technique which was, until recently, most frequently used in social psychology in order to elicit the social identity of an individual is due to Kuhn and McPartland (1954): it is the Twenty Statements Test (TST). Their hypothesis was closely related to the position of Sarbin and Allen (1968) mentioned earlier in this chapter: the behaviour of an individual derives from his identity, and his identity derives from the position he occupies in society. The technique is very simple: the respondent is requested to give successively twenty different answers to the question: 'Who am I?' The results showed that the subjects responded first in terms of social categories designating roles, status or the membership of a group (e.g. a man, a student, a Catholic, etc.). After having provided these 'consensual'[4], sociological or positional responses, i.e. after the respondents had exhausted the 'social labels', other responses made their appearance which were referred to by the authors as 'sub-consensual', in the sense of being subjective or idiosyncratic (e.g. happy, worried, intelligent, etc.).

Employing the same technique, Gordon (1968) asked 156 students (men and women) to reply fifteen times to the question: 'Who am I?' The most frequent responses concerned age (82 %) and sex (74 %). It appears therefore that categories of social identity such as age, sex or occupation form a part of the self-concept of an individual. But at the same time, this research shows that the self-concept varies with the social categories to which an individual belongs: i.e. subjective social identity varies as a function of objective social identity. For example, it has been noticed that women mentioned their sexual category membership more often than men, blacks referred more frequently to their ethnic affiliation than whites, Jews to their religious affiliation more often than Christians. It would appear that being placed in a position of minority or of being dominated produces in the individuals involved a heightened awareness of the social categories which determine their minority status.

In a study concerned with the attitudes of pupils reaching the end of their compulsory schooling, Doise, Meyer and Perret-Clermont (1976) also employed the TST amongst other measures. In this study, the authors tried to show 'how a social dynamic is reflected in the shaping of the individuals who participate in it' (p26). The study used a questionnaire which was given to a sample of Swiss teenagers (male and female), all of the same age, who were enrolled in secondary education leading to the diploma of secondary studies (the *maturité*) or in pre-professional (*Pré-professionnel*) training leading to apprenticeship. Each respondent was requested to reply seven times to the question: 'Who am I?' The data showed that the pre-professionals, who are of a lower status (*'dominé'*) in our society gave a significantly greater proportion of 'consensual' responses (53 % gave more than two such responses out of the possible total of seven) than the pupils of the secondary education establishment (of whom only 33 % gave more than two 'consensual' responses). These data confirmed once again that the 'dominated' define themselves more in terms of their social position and their group membership – i.e. as elements of a collective entity – than the 'dominant' who conceive of themselves relatively less in terms of 'groups' and more in terms of their personal characteristics.

But there is more: the respondents who are in secondary education, and particularly those in the 'prestigious' streams (*Classiques* and *Scientifiques* as distinct from *Modernes*) see themselves more clearly as masters of their fate and relatively autonomous; they have a view of themselves which stresses internal causality. In contrast, the pre-professionals (*Préprofessionnels*) show more of a tendency to perceive themselves as dependent upon outside contingencies, as determined by factors which are external to them. They have a perspective which is more 'social' in the sense that it relates to external causality as compared with the secondary pupils who adopt a more 'individual' approach. For example, in response to a question about the streaming of the pupils ('Who decides which stream the pupils will enter?'), there are no differences between the pre-professionals on the one hand, and the *Classiques* and *Scientifiques* on the other in those of their answers which concern the 'marks' and the 'teachers'. In contrast, the pre-professionals are the only ones who mention the 'management' (of the institution) and generally they provide more often answers which are 'institutional'. The answers of the *Classiques* and the *Scientifiques* are more 'individual'; for example, they mention more frequently the 'pupil' or the 'parents'. In brief, the dominants define themselves more as subjects and perceive their actions as voluntary while the dominated see themselves much more as objects acted upon by outside forces.

In a recent study by Deschamps and Lorenzi-Cioldi (unpublished) we attempted to operationalize the relations of domination – or rather to provide *one* possible form of their operationalization. This was done through creating an asymmetrical relationship which located the social actors along an axis of 'dominant'/'dominated'. In an experiment, one group of subjects were given the opportunity of making the choice of the locus they wished to occupy in the situation (the group of the 'choosers',

C); the remaining group of subjects (the group of the 'chosen', $\bar{C}$) did not have such a choice, since their position was defined in advance through the choice made by the first group.[5] As a result of this experimental induction, some individuals could see themselves as autonomous (i.e. they had the illusion that they controlled the situation), while others were heteronomous or externally determined in their choices. Amongst the various dependent measures which followed, the question 'Who am I?' was particularly relevant in the present context. The first results of the study seem congruent with the theoretical outline presented earlier. The responses depended upon the individuals' positions in the social situation, or – in other words – upon the conditions of production and functioning of the 'subject' form of identity. The responses of the 'choosers' and the 'chosen' were roughly categorized with the following results: the C subjects showed a tendency to make reference to groups, entities or objects which were generic (e.g. 'a woman', 'a girl', etc.); the $\bar{C}$ subjects referred to groups, entities or objects which were more concrete and 'positioned' (e.g. 'a woman in a world of men'; 'I am a girl of nineteen'; etc.). As distinct from the C, the $\bar{C}$ fell back upon the imaginary, dreams, or artistic talents (e.g. 'a small planet in the universe'; 'a kitten strolling in the countryside'; 'an imaginary musician') and introduced more notions which had a connotation of anxiety (e.g. 'ephemeral', 'need for security', 'doubt', 'escape', 'pessimistic', 'fear', 'worried'). Finally, the responses of the C did not make reference to other people while the $\bar{C}$ seemed to define themselves in relation to others taken as a point of reference, a norm, a mode of comparison (as, for example, in the answer 'a woman in a world of men').

(b) Relations of domination and the identity of the *alter*

In the reference made above to the study by Doise *et al.* (1976), we used the notions of internal and external causality which are directly related to research in social psychology on the processes of attribution. One of the earliest studies on attribution, conducted by Thibaut and Riecken (1955), employed the same distinction between internal and external causality attributions. The authors hypothesized that an individual perceives the source of 'consenting' or 'conforming' behaviour of another person as internal when that person has some degree of power and is of high status; and as external in the case of people who have no power and are of low status. In the study, a subject was requested to obtain from two other people their consent to become blood donors in a collection organized by the Red Cross. In fact, these two people were collaborators of the experimenters: one of them was presented as someone having a higher status, and the other a lower status, than that of the subject. In each case, the two confederates of the experimenter gave their agreement to the subject's request; at the end of the experiment the subjects completed a questionnaire in which they assessed the two confederates.

The results showed that the status manipulation was effective: the subjects assumed that the low-status confederate was convinced by their arguments and that the high-status confederate, considered to be more autonomous, acted as he did for his own independent reasons. In other words, they considered the behaviour of the low-status subject to be heteronomous and externally determined, while the high-status subject acted autonomously and independently of the influence which had been exerted upon him.

In the same area of research on attribution, some authors studied the influence of the relative status of interacting social categories on the internal or external attributions of causality. In a study concerned with explanations of success and failure, Deaux and Emswiller (1974) were able to show that what was attributed for a man to his competence was attributed for a woman to the working of chance. The subjects were 130 students, 55 men and 75 women; they were requested to evaluate the performance of a stimulus person, man or woman, in the same tasks, one of which was 'masculine' and one 'feminine'. It was ascertained in advance that those tasks were consensually perceived by the subjects of both sexes as being respectively 'masculine' and 'feminine'. The performance of the stimulus persons, man and woman, was perceived by the subjects as being of a similar level. The study showed that, as predicted, the performance of the male stimulus person was attributed to internal causality (competence) when the task was masculine, and that, in the same task, an identical performance by the female stimulus person was attributed to external causality (chance). There were no differences in these attributions between the subjects of the two sexes. In contrast, the inverse pattern did not appear for a feminine task in which the male stimulus person was perceived to be as competent as the female stimulus person; here again, there were no sex differences in the attributions made by the subjects. If we consider the stimulus persons in this study to be representative of their sex categories, the data show that the location of social groups or categories in a social system, just as the respective positions of individuals in the experiment of Thibaut and Riecken (1955), can play a part in the internal or external attributions of causality; and, by the same token, in the perception of social beings as subjects or as objects.

(c) **Language and social identity**

The social class differences in the use of language have been for some years a subject of study by sociolinguists. Bernstein was one of the early workers in this field. His principal thesis can be summarized as follows: in different social situations, individuals elaborate different linguistic codes. The more a group of social actors have in common in their characteristics or in their interests, the more likely it is that they will often use a domain of meanings which they share and which need not be repeatedly made explicit. This results in particularized language practices, or a linguistic code which is 'restricted' in the sense that it presents difficulties of comprehension outside of its specific situation. There are other situations which are characterized by differences between the social agents who participate in them. In such cases, meanings must be made more explicit and individualized, and the linguistic code will be more universalist or 'elaborated' so that it can serve to express the particularity of personal experiences. But there are certain types of interaction which predominate in certain social groups; the result of this is the elaboration and utilization of specific codes, and in this way the social class system has the effect of limiting the access of some people to the elaborated codes.

It is well known that Bernstein's thesis has been strongly attacked: Labov (1969) was one of the critics who argued that different linguistic practices have the same intralinguistic 'value'. Without entering this controversy, it is still possible to take the view that Bernstein has been able to collect data which are important and worthy of interest even if his interpretation of them can be criticized.

One of the points Bernstein (1975) made is that 'in a group of high social status, the proportion of use of the pronoun "I" as compared with all other personal pronouns is higher than in a working class group' (p 105, in the French edition), and that the 'relative frequency of the pronoun "I" is the greatest in the upper class' (p109, *ibid.*). In contrast, 'subjects from the working class ... use a form of discourse which is relatively non-individualized' (pp108–9, *ibid.*). In spite of the warmth and vitality which is often associated with it, the restricted code remains 'a language which is impersonal in the literal sense of the term' (p47, *ibid.*) and it does not elicit 'the appearance of a differentiated "me" in the discourse' (pp196–7, *ibid.*). Bernstein noted the presence of 'I' in the discourse of some people, and its absence in the discourse of others. The elaborated code which is used by the dominants is a mark of the perception of self in terms of a person, of an individual who says 'I'. In contrast, the use of the restricted code in linguistic practices is a mark of the dominated perceiving them-selves as, above all, the elements of an entity. If it is true that 'the elaborated code presupposes, in principle, the existence of a frontier set between the "me" and others, . . . in the case of the restricted code which presupposes, in contrast, an *alter* which is generalized and undifferentiated, a frontier or a break is created between those who participate in this code and the others' (p198, *ibid.*).

The dominated are thus defining themselves as belonging to a collection, a plurality. But this plurality is not a collective *subject*, as Bernstein seemed to indicate when he wrote that 'the restricted code appears . . . in the milieux whose culture favours the "us" as compared with the "me"' (p196, *ibid.*). Such a plurality is much more of a collective object than Bernstein assumed. As Bisseret (1974) remarked, in the language of the dominated one counters more often the indefinite '*on*' than the '*nous*' (we).[6] 'In the popular language, one hears more often "*on est*", "*on aime*" than "*nous sommes*", "*nous aimons*" ("*Nous on aime pas ça*", "*Nous autres, on s'en fout*", "*On est parti, ma soeur et moi*")' (Bauché, 1920, as quoted by Bisseret, 1974, p252).

In these conditions, 'in order to be expressed and acted upon, the "we" as a collection of "I"'s, as a totality of "subjects", needs a social situation which makes it possible to exert a certain degree of control upon the dominant customs or practices. An active solidarity, a feeling of 'we' does not necessarily arise just because the powerless are subjected in common to conditions in which they are oppressed. The discourse of the powerless usually reflects their membership of a collective *object*, of an *impersonal* plurality. In contrast, the fact that the linguistic expressions of the members of the dominant class reflect the self-concept of each of them as an individ-uality does not mean that they do not at the same time display an objective solidarity in their exercise of power and in the defence of their class interests' (Bisseret, 1975, p269).

It will be clear that the present chapter is intended to be a collection of questions and a basis for discussion rather than an attempt to provide a series of answers. We have not been able to help in providing a more explicit definition of the notion of social identity, nor did we claim that this is what we were attempting to do. On the contrary, the chapter contains a number of presuppositions which need a good deal of further support, and several notions which are – to say the least – vaguely defined; these notions create a number of problems which are as difficult to deal with as those deriving from the earlier notions about social identity. It could be said that – far from having clarified the issues – we have managed to make them even more obscure. But it seemed necessary to insert into social psychology a concern with problems of power – or, more precisely, with relationships of power. If this is not done, particularly with regard to relationships of domination between social groups, we risk skirting around a number of phenomena the study of which is indispensable for our understanding of certain forms of social behaviour.

Notes

[1] This chapter was written within the framework of the research project No.1.707.0.78 sponsored by the *Fonds National Suisse de la Recherche Scientifique* (FNRS). It is an extended version of a contribution to the colloquium on 'Social identity' organized by the *Laboratoire Européen de Psychologie Sociale* (LEPS) in Rennes in December, 1978. The earlier version was published in the *Revue Suisse de Sociologie*, 1980.

[2] Translated from the French by Henri Tajfel

[3] The terms 'dominant' and 'dominated', a literal translation of *dominant* and *dominé* used by Deschamps in the French text, have been retained here because they are closer to the sense of his argument than would have been some more usual English approximations, such as, for example, 'powerful' and 'powerless' (Translator's note).

[4] Kuhn and McPartland define consensual responses as propositions referring to groups or classes which are based on common sense in their boundaries and conditions of membership, in distinction from propositions referring to groups, classes, attributes, traits or anything else which needs a further interpretation in order to be made more precise or to be situated in relation to other persons.

[5] One group of subjects were able to formulate their self-definition in the situation, since they were allowed to choose between two tasks of the same kind but which presumably differed in their attractiveness (to view a film which was presented as very interesting as compared with reading a text on the same theme which was presented as being 'in English and very technical'). The remainder of the subjects had no choice, as their task was defined by the others; they occupied the 'position' left vacant after the others had made their choice.

[6] The French indefinite *on* is untranslatable into English in the sense in which it is used here. The nearest translation would be 'one' (such as in 'one likes to go on holidays') but this does not reflect the more impersonal (and, according to Deschamps, socially more significant) use of *on* which is referred to in the text. This is why the subsequent examples in the text were left in their French original. (Translator's note).

References

Bauché, H. (1920). *Le langage populaire: Grammaire, syntaxe et dictionnaire du français tel qu'on le parle dans le peuple avec tous les termes d'argot usuel.* Payot: Paris.

Berger, E. and Luckmann, T. (1966). *The social construction of reality.* Doubleday: New York.

Bernstein, B. (1975). *Langage et classes sociales.* Éditions de Minuit: Paris.

Bisseret, N. (1974). Langage et identité de classe: Les classes sociales 'se' parlent, *L'Année Sociologique*, **25**, 237–64.

Bisseret, N. (1975). Classes sociales et langage: Au-delà de la problématique privilège/handicap, *L'Homme et la Société*, **37–38**, 247–70.

Deaux, K. and Emswiller, T. (1974). Explanations of successful performance on sex-linked tasks: What is skill for the male is luck for the female, *Journal of Personality and Social Psychology*, **29**, 80–5.

Doise, W., Meyer, G. and Perret-Clermont, A.–N. (1976). Étude psycho-sociologique des représentations d'élèves en fin de scolarité obligatoire, *Pratique et Théorie* (Cahiers de la Section des Sciences de l'Éducation de l'Université de Genève, Genève), **2**, 15–27.

Erikson, E.H. (1963). The problem of ego identity. In M. Stein, A.J. Vidich and D.N. White (eds): *Identity and anxiety*. Free Press: Glencoe.

Fromm, E. (1941). *Escape from freedom*. Farrar and Rinehart: New York.

Fromm, E. (1956). *The sane society*. Routledge and Kegan Paul: London.

Gordon, C. (1968). Self-conceptions: Configurations of content. In C. Gordon and K. Gergen (eds): *The self in social interaction*. Wiley: New York.

Guillaumin, C. (1972). *L'Idéologie raciste: Genèse et langage actuel*. Mouton: Paris.

James, W. (1890). *Principles of Psychology*. Holt: New York.

Kardiner, A. (1939). *The individual and his society*. Columbia University Press: New York.

Kardiner, A., Linton, R., Dubois, C. and West, J. (1945). *The psychological frontiers of society*. Columbia University Press: New York.

Kuhn, M.H. and McPartland, T.S. (1954). An empirical investigation of self-attitudes, *American Sociological Review*, **19**, 68–76.

Labov, W. (1969). The logic of nonstandard English, *Georgetown Monographs on Language and Linguistics*, **22**, 1–22.

Lévi-Strauss, C. (1977). *L'Identité: Séminaire dirigé par Claude Lévi-Strauss*. Bernard Grasset: Paris.

Linton, R. (1945). *The cultural background of personality*. Appleton Century: New York.

Mead, G.H. (1934). *Mind, self and society from the standpoint of a social behaviorist*. University of Chicago Press: Chicago.

Sarbin, T.R. and Allen, V.L. (1968). Role theory. In G. Lindzey and E. Aronson, (eds): *Handbook of social psychology*, Vol. I. Addison-Wesley: Reading, Mass.

Tajfel, H. (1972). La catégorisation sociale. In S. Moscovici (ed.): *Introduction à la psychologie sociale*, Vol. I. Larousse: Paris.

Thibaut, J.W. and Riecken, H.W. (1955). Some determinants and consequences of the perception of social causality, *Journal of Personality*, **24**, 272–302.

Zavalloni, M. (1973). L'Identité psychosociale: Un concept à la recherche d'une science. In S. Moscovici, (ed.): *Introduction à la psychologie sociale*, Vol. 2. Larousse: Paris.

4. Intergroup relations and attribution processes[1]

MILES HEWSTONE AND J.M.F. JASPARS

1. Introduction

It is the view of several contemporary social psychologists (e.g. Billig, 1976; Doise, 1978; Moscovici, 1972; Tajfel, 1972a, 1978) that the 'individual' approach to social psychology has been too prevalent. Specifically, these critics are concerned that the individualistic approach fails to give an adequate account of complex intergroup phenomena. It would seem to be asking a lot of a theory, that it should parsimoniously and simultaneously account for social phenomena at both interpersonal and intergroup levels. However, some theories aspire to do just this (e.g. Frustration–Aggression theory as applied to intergroup relations by Berkowitz, 1971, 1972) and some scholars still argue that a new level of theory is not necessary in the shift from one level of analysis to another (e.g. Taylor and Brown, 1979).

In opposition to this defence of the scientific *status quo*, critiques have been made of a number of these 'reductionist' approaches – for example, Tajfel's (1979) critique of 'belief similarity' as applied to prejudice (Rokeach, 1960) and criticisms of Festinger's (1954) theory of social comparison processes by Tajfel (1978) and Turner (1975). This chapter plans to apply these same criticisms to *attribution theory*, in an attempt to 'socialize' it.

Attribution theory (Heider, 1958; Jones and Davis, 1965; Kelley, 1967, 1973) has been concerned with the processes by which individuals explain and interpret events they encounter. In particular it has dealt with the *causal* explanations that individuals construct for their own behaviour and that of others. This traditional perspective, we argue, has been too individualistic – explaining the behaviour of an individual *qua* individual. The examination of attribution processes at the intergroup level has been neglected. At this level we are interested in how members of different social groups explain the behaviour (and the consequences of the behaviour) of members of their own and other social groups. In other words we are not interested in the explanation of the behaviour of individuals as such, but in the explanation of the behaviour of individuals who act as members or representatives of social groups.

In exploring attribution at this level we are not setting out across a barren landscape, and in this chapter a number of empirical studies in this area will be presented and related to a theory of intergroup attribution. As this work is based on social categorization and social representations, these areas will be discussed in some detail. In addition, current research will be outlined, which illustrates how the study of attribution at this level can contribute to the areas of both attribution theory and research on intergroup relations.

To explain the behaviour of members of one's own and other groups is an activity that is required of all members of a complex society, as the following quotation from Tajfel makes clear:

> We live in a social environment which is in constant flux. Much of what happens to us is related to the activities of groups to which we do or do not belong; and the changing relations between these groups require constant readjustments of what happens and constant *causal attributions* about the why and the how of the changing conditions of our life. (Tajfel, 1973, p80; emphasis added)

2. Social attribution

The *social* nature of attributional phenomena has been well discussed by Deschamps (1973–4, 1977, 1978, in press). He is critical of the fact that previous work in this area has been explicitly and unapologetically interpersonal or individualistic (e.g. Kelley, 1967; Jones and Davis, 1965). His aim is to show that the processes of social categorization are at the heart of attribution – at least in the case of intergroup relations. This is what he calls *social attribution*, and by intergroup relations he means the fact that individuals define themselves in a given situation as belonging to different social groups or social categories.

Let us take, as an example of traditional attribution theory, the attempt to clarify the observer's understanding of the social environment. According to Heider (1958, p297) this understanding is achieved by a causal analysis bearing some resemblance to experimental methods. Kelley (1967) extends the experimental analogy in his analysis of variance model of the four factors which permit an observer to attribute a cause to an effect. He proposes that the individual interprets a given effect in the context of various types of information. Variations in effects are examined over:

(a) *entities*, from which *distinctiveness* information is obtained;

(b) *persons*, from which *consensus* information is obtained;

(c) *time/modalities*, from which *consistency* information is obtained.

It is on the basis of these informational criteria that the individual performs a 'mental analysis of variance' and then makes inferences. Both Deschamps (1973-4) and Apfelbaum and Herzlich (1970-1) argue that the attributing observer is assumed to behave like a statistician – treating all information objectively.

The criticisms of traditional attribution theory start, in essence, from the question of *what* for the subject is 'reality' (Apfelbaum and Herzlich, 1970-1). Kelley introduces the matter when he writes as follows: 'It is one of the well documented hypotheses of social psychology that the pressures toward uniformity which are based in social reality are most effective when the physical reality checks are absent or meagre' (Kelley, 1967, p207). Kelley goes on to refer to, and implicitly support, Festinger's (1954) postulate that: 'physical reality tests take precedence over social reality information' (*ibid.*). Thus social reality is relegated to a position in which it assumes importance only in the absence, or impoverished nature, of physical reality checks.

This matter has been hotly contested by other researchers. For example, Apfelbaum and Herzlich (1970-1) contend that Kelley's ideal of objective knowledge of the environment would be gained only by withdrawing from the social world, by not being part of it. Deschamps (1973-4) reiterates these criticisms and insists that:

> cette théorie de l'attribution semble s'appliquer à un sujet isolé, detaché de tout contexte social, passif vis-à-vis du monde qui l'entoure. La dimension sociale de l'attribution n'est pas envisagée. (Deschamps, 1973-4, p713)[2]

and in later work, citing Lemaine *et al.* (1969) he argues that it is:

> ... une erreur épistémologique de croire qu'un agent social, dans la vie quotidienne, *cherche* à avoir une vue 'objective' ou 'scientifique' du monde dans lequel il doit se comporter ... (Lemaine, Desportes and Louarn, 1969, cited in Deschamps, 1977, p35)[3]

Finally, with regard to this matter, we may challenge the very postulate from which Kelley started. Thus Tajfel (1974, 1978) challenges Festinger's (1954) assertion that *social* comparisons only take place 'to the extent that objective non-social means are not available' (Hypothesis 1 in Festinger, 1954). Tajfel points out that the 'objective non-social means' (of making comparisons) can often lack validity unless they are used in conjunction with the significance they acquire in the social setting. Thus, he continues, social reality can be as objective as is non-social reality and conversely 'objectivity' can be as social as it is physical.

Some time has been spent on what may seem to be a philosophical question, that of objectivity versus subjectivity. We should now attempt to translate these ideas and arguments into empirical propositions, as did Kelley himself. Firstly, we should state that our critique of Kelley is not as strong as either Deschamps's or Apfelbaum and Herzlich's. We would argue that the consensus criterion (variation in effects over other persons) does allow for some degree of social integration. Kelley's statement as to the pre-eminence of physical reality is translated into the proposition that the consistency criteria may be more important than the consensus criterion. This is indeed what McArthur (1972) found to be the case. However, there are methodological problems with this study (see Ruble and Feldman, 1976) which question its validity, and there is the very asocial context within which the study was carried out. The experiment should therefore be replicated with some changes (see 'Current research', section 6, below).

For the purposes of this section we will not be side-tracked into such issues. The major consequence of attribution theory's emphasis on physical rather than social reality is its failure to underline the fact that *individuals* may belong to different social *groups*. Furthermore, these individuals may act in terms of that group membership and achieve social identity through that membership (see Tajfel, 1974; 1978; Tajfel and Turner, 1979; Turner, 1975). In this alternative perspective (what Deschamps calls *social attribution*) an observer attributes the behaviour of an actor, not simply on the basis of individual characteristics, but on the basis of the group or social category to which the actor belongs and to which the observer belongs. The importance of this extension of attribution theory is indicated with reference to Thibaut and Riecken's (1955) experiment on the locus of causality imputed to persons of high and low status when they volunteer as blood donors. As Deschamps (1978) points out, the results of this study seem to hinge on the fact that stimulus persons are defined by their belonging to different social categories, by their occupation of different rungs on the social ladder (see chapter 3).

Traditional attribution theory has not, however, completely ignored the importance of social categories. Thus Jones and McGillis (1976) draw a distinction between *category-based* expectancies and *target-based* expectancies.[4] Jones and McGillis define the former in the following manner: 'A category-based expectancy derives from the perceiver's knowledge that the target person is a member of a particular class, category or reference group' (1976, p393). It is clear that this type of expectancy serves a similar role to that which Deschamps outlines for social categorization; the individual is thus located in a 'socio-cultural network'. Target-based expectancies are quite different; they are utilized in the case of interpersonal attribution, and are obviously closely related to Kelley's (1967) notion of consistency: 'Target-based expectancies are derived from prior information about the specific individual actor' (Jones and McGillis, *op. cit.*, p394). Which expectancies are utilized by an observer will obviously depend on a number of factors – for example, whether the situation is seen in interpersonal or intergroup terms – but Deschamps (1977) has noted a number of attribution experiments which seem to demand an explanation in terms of social categories (e.g. Gergen and Jones, 1963; Jones, Davis and Gergen, 1961; Jones and DeCharms, 1957; Steiner and Field, 1960).

The emphasis on social categories, as contained in the European critiques, may be integrated with Hamilton's (1978, p323) assertion that social psychological studies of the attribution of responsibility have been relatively sociologically "naked". He argues that these studies have overlooked the simple fact that society acts in each of us (see the discussion of social representations, below). His suggestions for the incorporation of the notion of role in these studies, particularly as this links up with the rules in a society for attributing responsibility, are noteworthy. Hamilton views roles as 'normative contexts' which determine the extent to which an actor is held accountable, rather than forces which compel him or her to act. Thus occupational status is positively correlated with standards of accountability, more severe rules for the attribution of responsibility being applied to high-prestige actors.

What both these approaches, the European one and that of Hamilton, have in common is a dissatisfaction with attribution theory as applied in the narrow sense. We will now look at the relevant empirical evidence.

3. Empirical evidence for social attribution

That there is such a phenomenon as social attribution is demonstrated by a number of studies, the first of which is perhaps the famous study of rumour by Allport and Postman (1947).[5] The evidence is not, however, available in profusion.[6] We have felt it important in this chapter to draw together the strands of research from both sides of the Atlantic.

Experiments on intergroup attribution appear to be connected with experiments in social perception, such as the study by Hastorf and Cantril (1954). In this experiment subjects were asked to watch a football game between the colleges of Dartmouth and Princeton and to record the number of fouls committed by each team. Subjects were students from both colleges and their reports were found to be biased in favour of their own group (i.e. they saw more fouls committed by the opposing team). This finding was discussed in terms of Bruner's (1957) work on motivational biases in perception. Bruner's work was also used in a neat study by Duncan (1976). Duncan's study is exemplary in the manner in which his research interests are carefully integrated with a solid theoretical background. He provides a useful review of early perceptual and cognitive work in social psychology (e.g. Allport, 1954; Bruner, 1957, 1958; Heider, 1958; Tajfel, 1969), linking this with the non-social cognitive work of Kelly (1955) and Brunswik (1956). Most importantly, he underlines the continuity between contemporary attribution theory and early work in social perception; both have in common the acceptance that systems of values and beliefs are important determinants of behaviour. This is most clearly expressed in Bruner's (1957) statement: 'Perception involves an act of categorization' (Bruner, 1957, p123). The problem examined by Duncan grows out of a re-examination of Tajfel's (1969) definition of stereotyping and the example of this process that Duncan chooses to examine is the stereotype of the black as 'impulsive and given to violence'. That is, the concept of violence is more 'accessible' (see Bruner, 1957) when viewing a black than a white. Duncan examined the perception of intergroup violence by asking subjects (white American college students) to view a videotaped interaction between a black and a white, and to give behaviour ratings of an increasingly more violent situation in which, finally, one participant pushed the other. Descriptions available to the subjects consisted of a modified Bales (1970) category-system for coding behaviour; the categories varied from 'dramatizes' to 'ask for information', 'aggressive behaviour' and 'violent behaviour'. In addition, subjects were asked to attribute the observed behaviour to Kelley's (1967) stimulus-, situation- and person-attribution choices. The results were clear-cut. When the videotape contained a black protagonist and a white victim, 75 % of the subjects chose 'violent behaviour' as the appropriate category. When these roles were reversed only 17 % of the subjects labelled the act in this manner. Certainly these results suggest that the threshold for labelling an act as violent is lower when the actor is black, than when he is white. This is even the case when both protagonist and victim are of the same race. The most important results, from the point of view of a social attribution theory were, however, that when the harm-doer was black, subjects perceived the violent behaviour to be due to stable personality dispositions of the harm-doer; when the harm-doer was white, subjects attributed the behaviour to external, situational constraints.

Another example is the study by Taylor and Jaggi (1974), carried out in Southern India, on ethnocentrism and causal attribution. By ethnocentrism is meant here the tendency of group members to favour members of their own group, rather than members of outgroups (see LeVine and Campbell, 1972; Sumner, 1906). The notion that such a bias may be at work in causal attribution was developed from Kelley's (1973) discussion of an 'egocentric assumption' at work in attribution; by this is meant the tendency for an individual to attribute to the self causes of events with positive outcomes and to attribute to others causes of events with negative outcomes. Taylor and Jaggi's basic hypothesis was that observers (Hindu adults) should make internal attributions to other Hindus (i.e. ingroup members) performing socially desirable acts and external attributions for undesirable acts. The reverse was predicted for attributions to Muslims (i.e. outgroup members). Subjects (Hindu adults) read a series of one-paragraph descriptions. They were asked to imagine themselves in a certain situation, being acted toward in a certain manner by another Hindu (ingroup member) or Muslim (outgroup member). Some situations described involved socially desirable behaviour – for example, the subject is sheltered from the rain or praised by a teacher. Other situations are socially undesirable – for example, the subject is refused shelter or scolded by a teacher. Subjects had to explain the behaviour of the other person involved by choosing one of a number of explanations. In each case one explanation was 'internal', the remainder were 'external'. The above predictions were clearly borne out by the data. Unfortunately Taylor and Jaggi do not report data for Muslim subjects. However, this deficiency was remedied in a study which we now review.

Mann and Taylor (1974) performed a similar study using members of French Canadian and English Canadian ethnic groups and superimposing a social class variable onto that of ethnic categorization. Subjects read a questionnaire enumerating ten common actions, five positive and five negative, and were asked to judge, as a percentage rating, the degree to which the behaviour was caused by relatively stable personality traits of the actor. Each subject was presented with three questionnaires identifying, respectively, (a) the ethnic group of the actor; (b) the social class of the actor; and (c) the ethnic group and social class of the actor. In this study both ethnocentric attitudes and stereotypes seemed to influence attribution. French Canadian subjects were found to be more ethnocentric than English

Canadians, but the type of behaviour (e.g. sociable – unsociable, considerate – inconsiderate) and its relation to social stereotypes was also important. In contrast to the French Canadians, English Canadians placed less emphasis on ethnic differences and more on the social class of the actors. These differences are explained in terms of the 'ethnic distinctiveness' of the French Canadian minority and the context of intergroup relations in Quebec. Thus it appears that different factors will influence the causal attributions of members of different cultural and subcultural groups, depending on both groups' relative socio-structural positions. An earlier study by Aboud and Taylor (1971) also bears on this question of what information different groups incorporate into their attributions and in what manner. Aboud and Taylor were specifically interested in the differential utilization of ethnic and role stereotypes in the process of cross-cultural person perception. They found that ingroup perception was characterized by the use of role stereotypes, arguably resulting in 'relatively accurate' interaction. For outgroup perception, however, predominantly ethnic stereotypes were used and it was suggested that this could lead to less efficient interaction in cross-cultural settings.

Another intergroup attribution study carried out in Canada is that of Guimond and Simard (1979). This study stands apart from the others in that it starts from Lerner's (1970, 1977; Lerner, Miller and Holmes, 1976; Lerner and Miller, 1978) 'just-world hypothesis' version of attribution, rather than the expositions of Kelley and Jones and Davis. Lerner contends that the attributing subject has a desire to avoid misfortune experienced by the actor he or she observes. This results in an attribution to the actor, rather than to chance, and is based on the premise that 'people get what they deserve'.

Arguing from Rubin and Peplau (1973), Guimond and Simard suggest that the just-world hypothesis has important implications for the way in which people react to 'inferior' groups. Lerner's hypothesis would indicate that the individuals within these groups are themselves to blame. Indeed, this is exactly the pattern of attributions a number of researchers have found. For example, Campbell (1971) and Erskine (1968) demonstrated that the majority of American whites blamed the blacks for the unfavourable situation in which they found themselves. There has also been some interesting work on how people *explain* poverty. Feagin (1972) proposed three types of explanation – *individualistic, structural* and *fatalistic* – and his results indicate that individualistic causes are considered as the most important.

Guimond and Simard spell out the ideological implications of this research, posing the question: do the victims (of poverty) espouse an individualistic ideology and blame themselves for their lot? Guimond and Simard suggest that, for the most part, the 'victims' do not make attributions in line with Lerner's theorizing. Thus black people in Feagin's study blamed the 'system', rather than themselves, for their poverty.[7]

Guimond and Simard took up this question of differing explanations offered by dominant and subordinate groups in the context of Quebec. They hypothesized that the intergroup inequality between French Canadians and English Canadians would be explained differently by the two groups. It was predicted that (in line with Lerner's formulation) the English Canadians would tend to blame the French Canadians and accept individualistic explanations. On the other hand, French Canadians were expected to blame the English Canadians and offer explanations in terms of structural causes, thus differing from Lerner's formulation.

In a straightforward design, Guimond and Simard asked French Canadian and English Canadian students to choose between five structural and five individualistic causes of economic inequality between the two groups. Here we shall just draw attention to one set of results. Firstly, the English Canadian subjects blamed the French Canadians (the 'victims') and explained the phenomenon in terms of individualistic causes. The inverse was true for French Canadian subjects who blamed the English Canadians and attributed the inequality to structural causes.

The experiment demonstrates that different causal explanations are espoused by different social groups. In addition, it relates the phenomenon of intergroup attribution to Lerner's work and comes up with an interesting finding: majority (or dominant) groups in a society seem to make attributions in line with Lerner's predictions – whereas minority (or subordinate) groups do not. The explanation for this finding would appear to lie at the ideological level. Whereas the English Canadians espouse a type of 'Protestant individualism' ideology, the French Canadians' attributions indicate a more dialectical conception of society. In fact Guimond and Simard's finding is unlikely to generalize to all majority–minority intergroup relations. What undoubtedly mediates attributions is the level of consciousness attained by the group. In this study the French Canadians appear to have achieved a causal understanding of society which is distinct from that of the majority group. They are a 'group for themselves' in Billig's (1976, p263) terms. However, in another context the explanations of the minority group might still be a function of the 'false consciousness' imposed by the dominant group[8]; in this case it is more likely that they would make attributions in line with Lerner's formulation.

Table 1. *Experimental design (see Deschamps, 1977)*

	Same town	Different town
Same six	ST	S$\bar{\text{T}}$
Different six	$\bar{\text{S}}$T	$\bar{\text{S}}\bar{\text{T}}$

These studies clearly demonstrate the importance of an actor's social group or category-membership for attribution. However, they represent only a beginning. One of the ways in which Deschamps (1977, experiment 1) has tried to extend attribution theory along intergroup lines is by examining the effects of 'crossed' and 'simple' categorizations on attributions of competence. By crossed categorization is meant the overlapping of categories, rather than a simple dichotomization of ingroup and outgroup. For example, a distinction between *males* and *females* might be crossed with a distinction between *working class* and *middle class*. Deschamps was interested in whether simultaneous membership of two groups would decrease ethnocentric bias in attribution (i.e. making attributions which favour the ingroup). He had members of different groups working, individually but in 'co-presence', at a problem-solving task and then asked each subject to estimate the performance of all individuals in his group.

The subjects were 'wolf-cubs' (junior members of the boy scout movement) at a camp. They were drawn from two towns; within each town the subjects knew each other, but between towns they did not. The first category was, therefore: same town (T)/different town ($\bar{\text{T}}$). Groups of twelve boys were then made up (six from each town) and divided into 'sixes', the basic wolf-cub unit. This category was established on the first day of the camp: same six (S)/different six ($\bar{\text{S}}$). The basic design is shown in a 2 × 2 table (see Table 1). Subjects have to estimate the number of successful problem-solving games other members will complete and to attribute this externally or internally.

There are two main experimental findings. Firstly, subjects biased their attributions in favour of members of the same group as themselves (this was true for both 'T' and 'S' variables). In the case of 'failure' on the tasks, internal causality is attributed to members of the categories to which the subjects do not belong. External causality is attributed to members of the categories to which the subjects do belong. The inverse is true in the case of 'success' on the tasks. The 'S' category was in fact more important than the 'T' category. Deschamps suggests that subjects saw their task as confined within the duration of the camp and thus emphasized the 'S' category. Secondly, there was no difference between attributions of competence to self (i.e. estimation of own performance) and to members of the same category. Further analysis demonstrated a difference between attributions to another in the same 'T' category and to the self, but not between attributions to another in the same 'S' category and the self. Deschamps contends that this is due to the heightened *salience* of the 'S' category.[9]

Deschamps (1977, experiment 2) further extends intergroup attribution in an experiment which throws light on the question of group *versus* self attributions. This study examined crossed and simple categorization, this time in the case of male/female and blue/red (experimentally established) groups. The tasks were the same as those in experiment 1. Summarizing the results, boys established a stronger attributional bias in favour of the ingroup than did girls; this preference for the ingroup was confined to the 'simple' categorization condition (the introduction of crossed categorization eliminated intersex discrimination) and to one category only (the 'natural and strong' category, male/female, had a significant impact, whereas the 'artificial and weak', red/blue, category did not). Of particular interest to the group *versus* self attribution question are the following results. For girls, there is no difference between self- and other-attribution in the simple categorization condition. They attribute to the self as they do to others of the same sex. Boys, however, favour the self in relation to the ingroup (same sex) in this simple condition. The results are different in the crossed categorization condition. It seems that crossed categorization diminishes an *ethnocentric* tendency and an *egocentric* tendency; but this finding is qualified by the status of the group to which an individual belongs. The girls devalue the category 'self' in relation to the ingroup, although they do not establish a distinction between the ingroup and the outgroup. The boys' overevaluation of self diminishes in this condition; their self-attributions are the same as their same-sex attributions.

Deschamps's explanation for these results runs as follows. It is suggested that the 'egocentric tendency' may be less strong than the 'ethnocentric tendency' in the case of socially 'inferior' categories (in this case, girls). The social status dimension (in addition to curbing ethnocentric overevaluation) also curbs egocentric overevaluation, which is why girls' self-attributions are not more favourable than their ingroup attributions in the simple categorization condition. In the crossed categorization condition ethnocentric overevaluation of the ingroup is eliminated; but because the social status dimension is still salient the social inferiority of the group categorization is manifested at the individual level. Attributions to the self are less favourable than attributions to both the ingroup and the out-group.

Thus Deschamps shows that the relationship between group and self attributions is a complex one. At the very least it is affected by two variables: the nature of the social categorization (simple/crossed) and the social status of the relevant groups (superior/inferior).

Taylor and Doria (1979) have also been concerned with the relation between group- and self-attribution. They address the issue of 'group-serving' biases in attribution, as distinct from 'self-serving' biases discussed in traditional attribution theory (Bradley, 1978; Miller and Ross, 1975). Discussing the Taylor and Jaggi (1974) study, these authors have no illusions as to what it did, and did not, demonstrate. Moving on from the demonstration of group-serving biases *per se* Taylor and Doria aim to study the simultaneous operation of self- and group-serving biases. As they point out, pitting these two biases against each other will be particularly important in conditions of group failure. In this case the individual can blame the other group members for the failure (i.e. make an external attribution) and thus operate a self-serving bias. However, such a bias would necessitate derogating the group. Alternatively, the individual may accept blame for group failure; in this case the group-serving bias subordinates the self-serving bias.

Taylor and Doria examined self- and group-serving biases under condi-tions of individual and group success and failure. The subjects used were Canadian college athletes, to whom questionnaires were administered before and after a number of games.

To summarize the results, Taylor and Doria found, firstly, a self-serving bias: players made more self-attributions for individual and team success, than they did for individual and team failure. Secondly, a team-bias in attribution was found: players attributed team success to the good play of the team, more than they attributed team failure to the poor play of the team. However, when self- and team-serving attributions were pitted against each other, the latter predominated: individuals who enjoyed success attributed this to the help of team-mates; individuals who failed, however, protected the team's image and did not attribute this failure to their team-mates.

These last two studies have clearly gone beyond the initial brief of intergroup attribution and have used an attributional framework to explore the relationship between personal and social identity. Taken as a whole, however, we feel that all these studies clearly state the case for a more social approach to attributional phenomena. They empirically validate the be-haviour of an actor in terms of his or her group membership. The evidence may also be used to make a theoretical point about the attention that should be paid to the person or the situation when making attributions. The tendency to *under*estimate the role of context, or *over*estimate the role of personal or dispositional factors (see Jones and Harris, 1967), has been referred to as 'the fundamental attribution error' (Ross, 1977, p184). Jones (1979) traces this finding back to Heider's notion that 'behaviour engulfs the field' (Heider, 1958, p54). It is not our intention to question the validity of this notion for *interpersonal* attribution, but we would argue that the studies on intergroup attribution show that behaviour does not *always* engulf the field. Rather, the strength and content of the prior beliefs about the other group may be dominant. Indeed, if we take these beliefs to be part of the Gestalt 'field', we might say that 'the field engulfs the behaviour'.

Thus we are considering the effect of preconceptions on attribution processes, a matter with which Kelley himself has been concerned. He refers (Kelley, 1973) to causal preconceptions and stereotypes as *causal schemata* (see also Kelley, 1972) and he has posed the question which is at the heart of all these studies on intergroup attribution: 'How do *a priori* beliefs affect the intake and processing of further information bearing on the attribution problem?' (Kelley, 1973, p119). He goes on, in the same paper, to argue that prior beliefs about causation do have an effect on information-intake concerning cause–effect covariation. He is adamant that a model of the attribution process must take cognizance of prior beliefs and suggests the study of how perceivers resolve conflicts between existing cognitive structures and new data. These ideas form a strong link, notwithstanding Kelley's concentration on interpersonal attribution, with the emphasis we place on social representations in the following theory of social attribution.

4. A theory of social attribution

A tentative theory of social attribution has been advanced by Deschamps (1973–4) on the basis of early perceptual and cognitive studies in social psychology (e.g., the contributions of Tajfel, 1959, 1972; Tajfel and Wilkes, 1963). Deschamps's theoretical framework is constructed from research in two areas, these being: social categorization, and social representations.

(a) Social categorization

In this chapter we will make no attempt to cover all aspects of research on social categorization, primarily because it has been more than adequately done elsewhere (e.g. Billig, 1976, chapter 9; Tajfel, 1972*b*; 1978, chapter 3;

Tajfel and Turner, 1979). Here we will make just four brief points, which are relevant to the present discussion:

(1) Categorization of the social environment is essential, in cognitive organizational terms (Allport, 1954), allowing for more efficient interaction and guiding behaviour (Triandis, 1971). Although important information regarding individual differences within a category may be lost (e.g. Tajfel and Wilkes, 1963), the complex social environment must be reduced to manageable units. This is achieved in particular by the use of stereotypes – the attribution of general psychological characteristics to large human groups (see Tajfel, 1972*b*, 1973).

(2) Research on social categorization using the 'minimal group' paradigm (Tajfel, 1970; Tajfel, Flament, Billig and Bundy, 1971) has shown quite clearly that the very act of social categorization leads to intergroup behaviour in which the ingroup is favoured and the outgroup is discriminated against (see Tajfel and Turner, 1979 for an up-to-date review).

(3) The study of social categorization drew the attention of social psychology to the role that large-scale categories play in influencing individual behaviour (see Tajfel, 1978 for a review of recent work in this tradition).

(4) Finally, recent work in this area has conceived of social categorizations in a precise way, and one which we feel to be most useful in interpreting the results of studies in the area of intergroup attribution. Social categorizations are defined as: 'cognitive tools that segment, classify and order the social environment, and thus enable the individual to undertake many forms of social action. But they do not merely systematize the social world; they also provide a system of orientation for self-reference: they create and define the individual's place in society' (Tajfel and Turner, 1979, p40).

(b) Social representations

By way of introducing social representations, Deschamps acknowledges their evolution from early work on stereotypes (e.g. Katz and Braly, 1933; Lippman, 1922). However, the notion of social representations, as introduced and utilized predominantly by French researchers (e.g. Herzlich, 1972; Moscovici, 1961), is sufficiently innovative to require elaboration.

There are now many different definitions of the concept, which grew out of Durkheim's (1967 edn) *'représentation collective'*, the most complete of which has been supplied by Moscovici:

> [Social representations are] cognitive systems with a logic and language of their own ... They do not represent simply 'opinions about', 'images

of' or 'attitudes towards' but 'theories' or 'branches of knowledge'
in their own right, for the discovery and organization of reality ...
systems of values, ideas and practices with a two-fold function; first,
to establish an order which will enable individuals to orient themselves
in their material social world and to master it; and secondly, to enable
communication to take place among members of a community by
providing them with a code for naming and classifying unambiguously
the various aspects of their world and their individual and group history.
(Moscovici, pxiii in his foreword to Herzlich, 1973)

If this definition is rather cumbersome we can, for the purpose of this
chapter, define social representations simply as the shared systems of belief
that individual members of social groups hold about their own group and
other groups.[10] We use the concept in the same way that other researchers
have used complex cognitive structures, as 'bridges' between individual
and social reality. The importance of cognitive structures in this respect
is exemplified by Moscovici's conclusion that: 'the contact point between
psychological and sociological is to be found at the level of cognitive
structures' (Moscovici, pxiv in his preface to Doise, 1978). Thus these
representations mediate an individual's 'social construction of reality'
(Berger and Luckmann, 1967).

Many other workers have added their own ideas to these basic features
of the social representation, some earlier (e.g. Flament, 1972) and some
more recent (e.g. Abric, 1979; Codol, 1979), but we shall now address
the more pertinent question of why these structures are important. Here
we can do no better than quote again, this time from Doise:

Social representations are of particular significance in group interaction.
Their content may be modified by the nature of intergroup relations,
but they themselves also influence the development of these relations,
by anticipating their development and justifying their nature. Although
representations are determined by interaction, they in turn also influence
the course of interaction. (Doise, 1978, p114)

It is important to note the dialectical orientation of this argument and to
notice why it is necessary to examine the representations of all the groups
involved. This approach encompasses Berger and Luckmann's (1967) insistence that there is not 'a reality', but that society is made up of many
subjective realities, each reflecting the objective and subjective positions
of groups in the social system.

On the basis of the foregoing arguments for the relevance of social
representations for all intergroup behaviour, we agree with Deschamps
that they should form an essential part of a theory of social attribution.

There is also evidence from the study of the functions of stereotypes (e.g. Tajfel, 1973; 1981) that these social beliefs have a role to play in attributions. Thus Tajfel (1973) emphasizes the role of stereotypes in the construction of a 'system of causes' by which we achieve social understanding. Furthermore, in the case of attributions to groups, Tajfel underlines the fact that this system of causes functions so as to preserve the individual's or the group's self-image and integrity. It is clear then that the importance of social representations for intergroup attribution lies, at least in part, in their constituting *a priori* causal schemata (to use Kelley's 1972, 1973, terms), thus influencing information integration and information processing.

Thus the *content* of the social representation may serve to suggest possible causes, to make them more 'accessible'. Earlier in this chapter we noted in passing Bruner's (1957) concept of category accessibility, let us now say more about it. Bruner makes three points concerning the accessibility of categories for use in social perception:

The greater the accessibility of a category,

(a) the less the input necessary for categorization to occur in terms of this category,

(b) the wider the range of input characteristics that will be 'accepted' as fitting the category in question,

(c) the more likely that categories that provide a better or equally good fit for the input will be masked.

(Bruner, 1957, pp129–30).

Thus 'accessible' categories would tend to preclude the operation of other causal categories, which is exactly what seems to be happening in many of the experiments reviewed earlier. The link between these simplifying categories and social representations is clear from the following quotation: 'the potentially "accessible categories" are part of the pattern of beliefs, myths, traditions and images of a culture' (Tajfel, 1980).

In this way social categories and social representations serve to enhance the simplification and predictability of causal attributions. As Tajfel (1973) argues, the need for both these factors is just as great in causal attributions to groups, as to persons. Tajfel suggests that attributions to groups *are* different from attributions to persons to the extent that they involve 'personalizing' large groups of people (or stereotyping individuals) and to the extent that 'needs, biases, interests and preconceived ideas' (p91) tend to be the perceiver's response to the complexity of intergroup attribution.

Thus far our argument may have implied a rather static view of the role of social representations, i.e. that they are used only for understanding behaviour. Such a view is quite wrong. Indeed Doise is at pains to underline the active nature of these cognitive structures: 'Representations, by providing a certain image of the other group, *attributing* certain kinds of motive to it, pave the way for action with respect to that group' (Doise, 1978, p120; emphasis added). Thus the act of intergroup attribution is seen as an initial form of social action. Indeed, such a form of attribution may constitute a type of *social competition* in Turner's (1975) sense of striving for positive social identity.

In the same sense that our view of social representations is a dynamic one, we wish to emphasize the dialectical relationship between representations and attributions. Thus Moscovici (1979) has argued that how an individual makes attributions determines his vision of the social world and, furthermore, this vision itself determines his or her behaviour (including the making of attributions).[11]

Thus social representations are seen to be crucial to the type of attribution we are interested in. Let us now look at the predictions and explanations this theory of social attribution can provide.

(c) An integration

Working from these two viewpoints, of social categorization and social representations, Deschamps (1973–4) makes the point that in a situation of less than complete information observers infer the characteristics of a social object on the basis of the category to which it belongs. The thrust of this argument is that typical intergroup biases are at work in attribution processes. These may operate in two main ways:

(1) *Ethnocentric responses.* As in the Taylor and Jaggi (1974) study we take this term to mean that people will share positive attitudes and stereotypes about the ingroup in comparison with the outgroup. In attributional terms this leads to the prediction that group members will show a more favourable pattern of attributions for ingroup members, than for outgroup members.

(2) *Minority group responses.* Despite the popularity of the concept of ethnocentrism, there are problems associated with it (see Billig, 1976, pp292–301; van Knippenberg, 1978; Tajfel and Turner, 1979). The core of this criticism is that the doctrine of ethnocentrism is not applicable to many of the members of a society's 'lower depths'. In many studies such minority group members as blacks, working class adolescents, etc., have been found to devalue their own group (e.g. Doise and Sinclair, 1973;

Milner, 1975; Vaughan, 1964) and their own language (e.g. Cheyne, 1970; Lambert, Hodgson, Gardner and Fillenbaum, 1960). In attributional terms this leads to the prediction that members of such objectively 'inferior' groups will show a more favourable pattern of attributions for outgroup members, than for ingroup members.[12]

As Deschamps (1973–4) points out, the ethnocentric hypothesis tends to assume that groups are in the presence of other 'equal' groups and fails to take account of the fact that at any given moment some social categories or groups are ideologically dominant in society (see chapter 3). Deschamps and Doise (1978) further account for this finding by explaining that groups of high status find it easy to establish their differentiation from groups of lower status. In contrast, a conflict is created in lower status groups between social differentiation and a tendency to reduce their distance from a privileged group on those dimensions which are salient in the social situation.

Thus Deschamps's focus on social categorization and social representations is seen to have made a number of worthwhile points about social attribution and to have generated some concrete predictions.

5. Additions to the theory of social attribution

A few supplementary points need to be added to this outline of a theory of social attribution. The most important addition is the analogy between actor–observer differences in attributional tendencies and ingroup–outgroup differences in such tendencies (Stephan, 1977; Triandis, 1977). Much of the recent literature on attribution theory has been concerned with the differences between actors and observers in the types of attributions they make (Eisen, 1979; Jones and Nisbett, 1971; Monson and Snyder, 1977; Nisbett et al., 1973; Storms, 1973). Jones and Nisbett argue that observers make more dispositional and less situational attributions than actors. Among the reasons for this difference are two main ones:

(a) The first is *perceptual*; that is, the actor's attention is focused on situational cues, whereas the observer's attention is focused on the actor.

(b) The second reason is *informational*; that is, the actor knows more about his past and present experiences than the observer.

Extrapolating these propositions to the level of intergroup perception Stephan (1977) argues that there are four differences between observing the behaviour of an ingroup and an outgroup member (particularly in the case of culturally defined groups):

Table 2. *Locus of attribution as a function of type of*
behaviour and type of actor

Type of Behaviour	Type of Actor	
	Ingroup	Outgroup
Positive	Dispositional	Situational
Negative	Situational	Dispositional

(1) You have more information on the antecedents of the observed behaviour.
(2) You possess more detailed 'experiential accompaniments'.
(3) You are more likely to empathize.
(4) You are more likely to analyse the situation in terms which are similar to those of the actor.

As Stephan correctly deduces, the logical extension of this reasoning for intergroup attribution is the prediction that observers should make more dispositional and less situational attributions to account for the positive behaviour of ingroup than of outgroup members. In the case of negative behaviour, observers should make more situational and less dispositional attributions to account for the behaviour of ingroup than of outgroup members. This predicted pattern of attributions is shown in Table 2. This is, of course, exactly the pattern of attribution found by Taylor and Jaggi (1974).

Whilst this extension of Jones and Nisbett may seem useful, Stephan indicates that it does *not* permit differential predictions to be made for different outgroups. This is a crucial flaw, given that the whole point of a theory of social attribution is that (in our case, by incorporating social representations and other sociostructural variables) it should predict and explain results for attributions made to *different* outgroups. In Stephan's case this is achieved by discerning the nature of intergroup attitudes. However, we would argue that this analysis is still rooted in interpersonal concepts, such as 'empathy', and that it fails to acknowledge the fact that intergroup biases in attribution may be part of a much wider process – the search for positive social identity. In our case, having started out from Deschamps' (1973–4) theorizing (with its emphasis on social categorization and social representations) we already have a framework capable of making differential predictions for different outgroups.[13]

This criticism does not, of course, imply that the actor–observer, ingroup–outgroup analogy is theoretically useless. What it contributes, in our analysis, is a focus on the types of explanation offered by ingroup and outgroup members. We have attempted to elaborate this aspect of the theory by speculating on what Buss's (1978) conceptual critique of attribution theory could add to this work. Contrary to Jones and Nisbett's (1971) assumption that both actors and observers use causal attributions, Buss suggests that they may be offering logically different *kinds* of explanations. He shows that Jones and Nisbett's actors are all engaged in attempting to justify their actions, provide a rationale for their behaviour and so on; their explanation is *not* simply causal.[14] Buss calls such explanations *reason* explanations and argues that they are characteristic of actors, whereas observers use more simple *causal* explanations.[15] Buss defines causes as 'that which brings about a change' (p1311) and reasons as 'that for which a change is brought about (e.g. goals, purposes, etc.)' (*ibid.*). If we tentatively extrapolate this argument to the level of intergroup attribution, we might predict that observers would generate reason explanations for ingroup members, but causal explanations for outgroup members. This point certainly requires empirical validation.

Finally, we may extend Deschamps's theory of social attribution by looking at a different *type* of attribution. Thus far, the discussion has focused on social perception or the attribution of others' behaviour. However, attribution theory has always been concerned with self-attribution – how an individual explains his or her behaviour or the treatment he or she receives from another (see, e.g. Bem, 1967, 1972; Jones and Nisbett, 1971). Deschamps (1977, experiment 2) and Taylor and Doria (1979) also investigate self-attributions in the course of their experiments, but not in quite the same way as the experiments described below. Recent work by Dion and colleagues (Dion, 1975; Dion and Earn, 1975; Dion, Earn and Yee, 1978) provides a very social example of self-attribution. These researchers have been concerned with aspects of prejudice in the sense of victimization, rather than with the phenomenon more usually studied – bigotry. In their studies they have looked at minority group members' (Jews, women, American ethnic Chinese) feelings when they are discriminated against. The member of a minority group takes part in a group ticket-passing task, in which he or she is the only minority–group member. The subject is made to fail at the test as a result of negative evaluative feedback provided by the other group members.

The subject is then asked to complete a number of self- and other-ratings, affect measures and so on. The dependent variable of interest to us is the subjects' responses to an open-ended question in the post-experimental questionnaire, which asked them to give possible *reasons* for their performance on the ticket-passing task. In a study in which Jews constituted the minority, and gentiles the majority, Dion and Earn (1975) found that 17 of the 24 subjects in the 'prejudice' condition gave a causal explanation in terms of their 'discrepant, religious affiliation or "being Jewish"' (Dion and Earn, *op. cit.*, p947). Subjects in the 'no prejudice' condition attributed their failure to the others' dislike of their physical appearance and personal interests, or did not know.[16]

Although this experiment was primarily concerned with the 'phenomenology of prejudice' and not with attribution (there is no discussion of the attribution literature on success and failure, for example) it yields results of some interest to our perspective. It demonstrates that individuals not only make attributions about others based on their membership of certain social categories, but that they may also make self-attributions in a similar manner. Thus we have here a 'self-stereotyping' process, in which the minority-group members perceive themselves primarily in intergroup terms (as members of the social category – Jews) and make attributions in accordance with this. This is exactly what Turner has in mind when putting forward his cognitive definition of a social group (see chapter 1). Turner argues that the basic processes of social categorization theory (Tajfel, 1959, 1972b, 1973; Doise, 1978) – the accentuation of intracategory similarities and intercategory differences – not only function at the *inter*-group level, thus accounting for stereotyping phenomena (see Hamilton, 1976; Tajfel, 1973; 1981), but also function at the *intra*group level.

In this section we have outlined some of the possible additions to Deschamps's original contribution. These have included the notions of actor–observer differences, causal versus reason explanations and a more social look at self-attribution. We will now outline some of our current research and suggest some future directions for work in this area.

6. Current research and future directions

In this section we will summarize a number of current studies which are intended to test some of the assumptions modifying an explicitly interpersonal attribution theory. We will also briefly discuss the links that should be made from work on intergroup aspects of attribution theory to more general work on intergroup relations.

First, we shall return to the question of *what* for the subject is 'reality'; or more precisely, to Kelley's (1967) assertion of the primacy of physical over social reality. As we noted earlier (p102), Kelley's statement that the consistency criteria may be more important than the consensus criterion is alleged to have been supported by McArthur (1972). Leaving aside the methodological critique of this study (Ruble and Feldman, 1976) we already noted that McArthur's test of Kelley's proposition was carried out in a strikingly *asocial* experiment. Questionnaire studies with student subjects have become almost *de rigueur* in attribution research, but it is the nature of McArthur's questionnaire which is debatable. Subjects were to read a paragraph describing a person's response to something, followed by information pertaining to Kelley's criteria of consensus, consistency and distinctiveness. Subjects then had to attribute the response to the person, the stimulus, the circumstance or a combination of these alternatives. The nature of the experiment is, we argue, defensible, in view of the constrained experimental hypotheses. However, of the 16 items in the questionnaire, only three used persons as 'stimuli'. That is, the vast majority of the items were asocial, insofar as the actors' responses were to objects or 'nonpersons', as opposed to 'persons'. Thus they took the form of:

'Paul is enthralled by a painting' (asocial),

rather than

'Paul is enthralled by a girl' (social).

At the very least, we feel this experiment should be replicated with more social items. If, as Kelley suggests, consensus information is the primary source of information about 'social' reality, then it may become more important as the social nature of the attribution is changed. This is precisely what one of our current experiments is examining. Given the importance attached to the social versus physical reality question, it seems crucial to examine its validity in a more social context. Apfelbaum and Herzlich (1970–1) emphasized the issue in their critique ten years ago, but there has been no empirical validation of the point. A study is required to examine, simultaneously, the importance of the various informational criteria (and their possible combinations), in Kelley's (1967) original formulation, for both asocial and social attributions.

Whereas this first experiment accepts Kelley's conception of consensus, it is possible to question the nature of what he calls consensus information. For Kelley, consensus refers to agreement among *actors*, not among *observers* (i.e. subjects in the experiment). Thus he defines consensus in the following terms: 'my response is similar to those made by other persons to the same stimulus' (Kelley, 1973, p112). For us, consensus should be thought of more as a social influence process, as observed in the studies of Asch (1951) and Sherif (1936), such as the influence of another's opinion on an observer's attributions. However, even the research we have reviewed under the rubric of 'intergroup' attribution seems to have been predominantly individualistic in emphasis. Subjects expressed their judgements alone, on a questionnaire, and never discussed their attributions with other group members. What would be the effect of studying this process in a real group context?[17]

Evidence from the social psychology of group decision-making suggests that extrapolating from the individual to the group would be inappropriate. Studies on the 'group-polarization' effect (see Doise, 1969; Moscovici and Zavalloni, 1969; Myers and Lamm, 1976; Wetherell and Turner, unpublished) validate, for the most part, the proposition that, following group discussion, individuals make more extreme decisions than the average of their individual decisions prior to group-discussion. In our experiment we do not study the effect of group discussion in this 'before and after' manner, but rather as a between-groups variable. This variable seems particularly important in terms of the way we have come to view social attribution. Rather than conceiving of the attributing subject as one who sits alone and carries out a kind of 'analysis of variance in the head', we suggest that the attributions of others will be sought. That is, consensual validation will be searched and a *social*-cognitive process will ensue. In addition, we predict that stronger intergroup effects on attribution will be found in the group discussion condition.

Our third current experiment, in collaboration with Frank Fincham, seeks a more precise examination of the influence of social categorization on attribution processes. In essence, what the studies reviewed in this chapter purport to show is that, in an intergroup context, attributions are made as a function of the social group membership of both the actor and of the observer. Thus *social categorization* is the key variable. There exist also a number of studies of a similar nature, but which claim to show attributional bias as a function of *personal similarity*. These are the studies generally said to exemplify *defensive attribution* (Shaver, 1970). This phenomenon entails decreased attributions of responsibility to an actor for an accident.

As defined by Shaver (1975) defensive attribution is a desire on the part of perceivers to make attributions that will reduce the threat posed by the situation they face. Two factors are important in inducing the feeling of threat. The first is situational possibility: the person must consider it possible that he or she could find him/herself in a similar situation to that of the actor. The second factor, which we emphasize here, is personal similarity between the actor and the observer. The threat is engendered by the implication that if the actor him/herself were in the situation, he or she would be likely to make the same mistake (which brought about the accident). In this case, to impose responsibility on the actor would set harsh standards for the future behaviour of the similar observer. The solution suggested to this observer is as follows: 'If you are faced with a threatening attribution situation, in which threat can be reduced by attributing responsibility and denying personal similarity, you will do that. If you cannot deny personal similarity, than you are more likely to attribute the negative outcome to chance' (Shaver, 1975, p110). Studies bearing on this notion of defensive attribution have been provided by a number of researchers (e.g. Chaikin and Darley, 1973; Shaver, 1970; see also Fincham and Jaspars, 1980).

Studies on intergroup attribution and defensive attribution pose an interesting question: Can we be sure that studies of the former type have satisfactorily excluded personal similarity as a variable and that studies of the latter type have satisfactorily excluded the possibility that a categorization effect is at work? As far as defensive attribution studies are concerned, the answer to this question must be 'no'. Personal similarity between actor and observer has been manipulated by such variables as marijuana use (McKillip and Posavac, 1975, experiment 1), alcohol use (Pliner and Capell, 1977), attitudinal agreement (Pliner and Capell, experiment 2) and sex of the subject (Shaw and McMartin, 1977). We argue that it is not possible to explain the results of these experiments in terms of personal similarity *per se*. The notion of categorization may be involved. The same problems exist with the research reviewed in this chapter – for example, Hindus are undoubtedly personally similar to other Hindus, in some respects, as well as being members of the same religious group.

What we need to do then is to separate conceptually personal similarity and social categorization. This is, of course, exactly the problem which was faced by Billig and Tajfel (1973) in the elucidation of discrimination in the 'minimal' group experiments. We have therefore followed their design and placed it in an attributional context. We will not detail the rather complex design here, our purpose at present is simply to indicate the necessity of examining the variables of personal similarity and social categorization, separately and in interaction, to specify more precisely the nature of attributional bias.

This last experiment, linking as it does attribution and research on minimal groups, brings us to the question of how the type of research discussed in this chapter relates to other work on intergroup relations. Whilst we have criticized attribution theory for being *a*social, we may also criticize intergroup relations theory for being *a*causal. By this we mean that insufficient attention has been paid to the role of causal attributions in the genesis of intergroup relations. As Doise argues in the case of social representations (see p113 above), we consider the relationship between intergroup attributions and intergroup relations to be a dialectical one. In our view, not only do causal attributions reflect intergroup divisions, they may actually create them. Thus Tajfel (1981) has used a discussion of intergroup attribution to emphasize the 'group function' of explanations. A plethora of experiments have drawn attention to the fact of intergroup differentiation, we now advocate a study of the attributions, or explanations, that accompany it.

This task has been commenced already, as in Tajfel's (1981) discussion of social stereotypes. He outlines four individual and social functions of stereotyping: the cognitive function; the value preservation function; the ideologizing function (explaining or justifying a variety of social actions) and the positive differentiation function. It is the third function which is directly relevant to this chapter, a part of which Tajfel calls the *social causality* function. Tajfel gives a number of examples of attribution at the social level, from the witch-hunts of the 17th century, to the explanatory function of anti-semitism. With regard to this latter example, Billig (1978) discusses the 'conspiracy theory' of international relations in attributional terms. The conspiracy theory, as Billig outlines, is crucial to the ideology of the National Front. Its aim is to attribute the ills of contemporary society to 'the conscious machinations of a few individuals' (Billig, *op. cit.*, p317). These individuals are, of course, various high-placed Jewish businessmen and politicians and, as Billig points out, the conspiracy theorist could therefore be said to be making 'personal attributions'.

The point here is not that attribution theory may constitute *the* way in which to examine the conspiracy theory, nor even that it may prove useful. Rather, our intention is to emphasize the kind of large-scale, shared explanations which go to make up social reality. Attribution theory should be integrated with intergroup psychology to elucidate further the causal nature of social stereotypes, social representations and even large-scale ideologies.

Finally, with regard to our link from attribution to intergroup relations, we want to know at what *level* of intergroup relations attributions are important. Doise (1972) distinguishes between three levels of intergroup relations:

(1) the level of *behaviour*;
(2) the level of *evaluations*;
(3) the level of *representations*.

He argues that change at one level is sufficient to bring about a change at the other two levels. For example, he argues that the work of Tajfel and his colleagues on 'minimal groups' (e.g. Tajfel *et al*, 1971) has shown that differentiation at the level of cognitive representations (introducing the representation of belonging to two different social categories) leads to an intergroup discrimination at the behavioural (i.e. matrix completion) level, as well as at the evaluative (i.e. rating of ingroup and outgroup) level. These experiments show change in the direction from representations to behaviour and evaluations. Sherif's (1966) work, in contrast, shows that differentiation at the level of behaviour (e.g. creation of superordinate goals forcing opposing groups of boys to work together) leads also to change at the other two levels. We argued above for the link between social representations and social attribution and it seems correct to slot in attributions at the same level as evaluations. Perhaps this framework will help to suggest new experiments and to emphasize the interconnection between the three levels of analysis. At the very least it should underline the importance of attributions for a general theory of intergroup relations.

In this section we have outlined a number of future directions for research on intergroup attribution. We hope that both theoretical and empirical advances will succeed in articulating the causal aspects of inter-group relations and in rendering attribution theory more social.

7. Conclusion

In this chapter we have taken issue with the individualistic bias of attribution theory. It is clear from the studies we review that in some cases attributions to individuals are made not as a function of their unique individuality, but as a function of the social group or category to which they belong. The notions of social categorization and social representation serve to support a first attempt at a theory of attribution at this intergroup level. It is interesting, in relation to our critique of attribution theory as individualistic, to allude to the place of attribution theory in the development of social psychology. Steiner (1974) appears to blame attribution theory in particular for drawing social perception away from the 'social'. He argues that, historically, research in the area of social perception was very *social* (e.g. work of Cooley, 1902; Mead, 1913) and that this trend was continued more recently, as seen in the work on stereotypes (Katz and Braly, 1933), reference groups (Newcomb, 1943) and socialization (Allport, 1954). However, Steiner continues, the reconstruction of social perception as cognitive dissonance (Festinger, 1957) and, in particular, attribution theory (Jones and Davis, 1965; Kelley, 1967) interrupted this tradition. As Steiner comments on these last two references: 'On reading these models the overworked man from Mars might conclude that earthlings never converse with one another, never listen to another's judgement, and never accept the prefabricated verdict of social reality' (Steiner, 1974, p103). He goes on to suggest, although he does not provide a programmatic statement of *how* to achieve it, in which direction we should move: 'Someday we shall have to revive the question: So what? How do attributions affect the collective enterprise that is our way of life?' (*ibid*). In this chapter we have attempted to revive this question and to provide some sort of programmatic statement of how to proceed.

In conclusion, we are arguing for an extended notion of attribution theory, to include what Steiner (1974) had in mind and what Deschamps (1973–4) has called social attribution. If, as Kelley (1967, p196; 1973, p107) has argued, attribution theory bears on the central issue of psychological epistemology (subjective validity), then it must be extended to areas other than that of interpersonal interaction. For Man 'knows' the world, not simply in terms of interpersonal encounters, but also in terms of the changing relations of large-scale social categories. These social groupings are fundamental to our social identity and to the social reality that we actively cognize. They must therefore be related to the process of social understanding – the very backbone of attribution theory. Thus attribution theory may be used to examine phenomena as diverse as the conspiracy theory of international relations (Billig, 1978) and the influence of an actor's race on the way his or her behaviour is categorized and explained (Duncan, 1976). We maintain that such a theory can be formulated and tested. Concerned, as it is, with explaining the behaviour of individuals as members of different social groups, its contribution to intergroup psychology would be unquestionable.

Notes

[1] We would like to thank John Turner and Penny Oakes for their most valuable comments on an earlier draft of this chapter; and the Social Science Research Council for supporting doctoral research by the first author. Interestingly, some ideas similar to those presented here have recently been arrived at independently by Pettigrew. This chapter was already in press at that time; the reader is referred to Pettigrew, T.F. 1979. The ultimate attribution error: Extending Allport's cognitive analysis of prejudice. *Personality and Social Psychology Bulletin*, 5, 461–76.
[2] 'This theory of attribution seems to apply to an isolated subject, detached from the social

context, passive with regard to the outside world that surrounds him. The social dimension of attribution is not envisaged.'

[3] '... an epistemological error to believe that a social agent, in everyday life, seeks to have an "objective" or "scientific" view of the world in which he behaves ...'

[4] We are grateful to Frank Fincham for drawing our attention to this work.

[5] The importance of this study was suggested to us by Henri Tajfel.

[6] In fact, we consider the number of studies on social attribution to be quite limited and have cited all the studies we know of. In addition to the studies discussed, readers might consult Campbell and Schuman (1969), Wilder (1978), Deschamps (1972–3) and Deause and Emswiller (1974).

[7] Interestingly, Townsend's (1979) recent sociological study on poverty provides some support for Lerner. In his sample of 'the poor', around 30 % blamed individuals for poverty, 22 % blamed the government and only 3 % blamed industry. This led Schott (1979) to refer to a 'poverty of political consciousness' (p625) among the poor themselves.

[8] For a discussion of ideology and consciousness in intergroup relations see Billig (1976, pp261–8).

[9] It is relevant to note Eiser and Stroebe's discussion of dimensional salience, why certain dimensions are important in certain situations. They argue that 'salient dimensions should be salient not simply for purposes of discrimination, but also *explanation*' (Eiser and Stroebe, 1972, p215, emphasis added).

[10] This definition acknowledges Jaspars's (1979) assertion that: 'what is social about social representations is not in the first place that such representations are representations of social reality, nor that they are social in origin; they are social because they are *shared* by many individuals and as such constitute a social reality which can influence individual behaviour' (p7).

[11] In the same manner, both Taylor and Jaggi (1974) and Stephan (1977) are concerned with the light that attribution theory may throw on the operation of cognitive processes such as stereotyping.

[12] Of course, the situation with regard to minority groups is changing rapidly, due to their *redefining* in positive terms aspects of their ethnicity, for example see Tajfel, 1974; 1978a; and due to their perception of *cognitive alternatives* (Turner and Brown, 1978) to the *status quo*. It would be interesting to relate both these factors to attributional behaviour.

[13] The extension of the actor – observer distinction to ingroup – outgroup differentiation in attribution could possibly be applied to the case of a number of outgroups by taking into account the relations between the ingroup and the various outgroups. The differences between in- and outgroups which are mentioned by Stephan (p117 in this text) might extend to differences between outgroups. The prediction which would follow from this is that the more an outgroup resembles the ingroup the stronger the tendency will be to treat it in a way that is similar to the ingroup.

[14] A link may be forged here with Doise's (1978) subcategory of social representations referred to as *justificatory representations*. As Doise points out, these representations function so as to justify behaviour in relation to the other group. An example given is the stereotyping of members of lower socio-economic groups so as to maintain the *status quo* in the economic and social system. See also Tajfel (1978) on the justificatory function of stereotypes.

[15] There is a vast philosophical literature on causes and reasons which cannot be summarized here. The reader is referred to Buss' (1978) paper and also to Harré and Secord (1972) and Ryan (1970) for extended discussions of the issue.

[16] Before the experiment, subjects in the 'no prejudice' condition only had to provide the experimenter with information about hobbies, pastimes etc. Subjects in the 'prejudice' condition had to provide information such as name, ethnic status and religious affiliation.

[17] This extension of attribution theory was derived, in part, from a paper by Taylor and Royer (1979).

References

Aboud, F.E. and Taylor, D.M. 1971. Ethnic and role stereotypes: their relative importance in person perception. *Journal of Social Psychology*, **85**, 17–27.

Abric, J.C. 1979. Représentations sociales et interaction conflictuelle: Etudes Experimentales. Paper presented at the colloquium on social representations, Maison des Sciences de l'Homme, Paris, January, 1979.

Allport, G.W. 1954. *The nature of prejudice*. Cambridge, Mass.: Addison-Wesley.

Allport, G.W. and Postman, L. 1947. *The psychology of rumour*. New York: Holt.

Apfelbaum, E. and Herzlich, C. 1970–1. La théorie de l'attribution en psychologie sociale. *Bulletin de Psychologie*, **24**, 961–76.

Asch, S. 1951. Effects of group pressure upon the modification and distortion of judgements. In H. Guetzkow (Ed.), *Groups, leadership and men*. Pittsburgh: Carnegie Press.

Bales, R.F. 1970. *Personality and interpersonal behaviour*. New York: Holt, Rinehart & Winston.

Bem, D.J. 1967. Self-perception: An alternative interpretation of cognitive dissonance phenomena. *Psychological Review*, **74**, 183–200.

Bem, D.J. 1972. Self-perception theory. In L. Berkowitz (Ed.), *Advances in experimental social psychology* (Vol. 6). New York: Academic Press.

Berger, P.L. and Luckmann, T. 1967. *The social construction of reality*. Harmondsworth: Penguin.

Berkowitz, L. 1971. The study of urban violence: Some implications of laboratory studies of frustration and aggression. In J.C. Davies (Ed), *When men revolt and why*. New York: The Free Press.

Berkowitz, L. 1972. Frustrations, comparisons and other sources of emotional arousal as contributors to social unrest. *Journal of Social Issues*, **28**, 77–91.

Billig, M. 1976. *Social psychology and intergroup relations*. European Monographs in Social Psychology, No. 9. London: Academic Press.

Billig, M. 1978. *Fascists: A social psychological view of the National Front*. European Monographs in Social Psychology, No. 15. London: Academic Press.

Billig, M. and Tajfel, H. 1973. Social categorisation and similarity in intergroup behaviour. *European Journal of Social Psychology*, **3**, 27–52.

Bradley, G.W. 1978. Self-serving biases in the attribution process: A re-examination of the fact or fiction question. *Journal of Personality and Social Psychology*, **36**, 56–71.

Bruner, J.S. 1957. On perceptual readiness. *Psychological Review*, **64**, 123–51.

Bruner, J.S. 1958. Social psychology and perception. In E.E. Maccoby, F.M. Newcomb and E.L. Hartley (Eds), *Readings in social psychology*. New York: Holt, Rinehart & Winston.

Brunswik, E. 1956. *Perception and the representative design of psychological experiments*. Berkeley: University of California Press.

Buss, A.R. 1978. Causes and reasons in attribution theory: A conceptual critique. *Journal of Personality and Social Psychology*, **36**, 1311–21.

Campbell, A. 1971. *White attitudes toward black people*. Ann Arbor: Institute for Social Research.

Campbell, A. and Schuman, H. 1969. *Racial attitudes in fifteen American cities.* Ann Arbor, Michigan: Institute for Social Research.
Chaikin, A.L. and Darley, J.M. 1973. Victim or perpetrator? Defensive attribution of responsibility and the need for order and justice. *Journal of Personality and Social Psychology,* **25,** 268–75.
Cheyne, W. 1970. Stereotypical reactions to speakers with Scottish and English regional accents. *British Journal of Social and Clinical Psychology,* **9,** 77–9.
Codol, J.-P. 1979. L'interdépendance des représentations dans une situation de groupe. Paper presented at a colloquium on social representations, Maison des Sciences de l'Homme, Paris, January, 1979.
Cooley, C.H. 1902. *Human nature and the social order.* New York: Scribner.
Deaux, K. and Emswiller, T. 1974. Explanations of successful performance on sex-linked tasks: What is skill for the male is luck for the female. *Journal of Personality and Social Psychology,* **29,** 80–5.
Deschamps, J.-C. 1972–3. Imputation de la responsabilité de l'échec (ou de la réussite) et catégorisation sociale. *Bulletin de Psychologie,* **26,** 794–806.
Deschamps, J.-C. 1973–4. L'attribution, la catégorisation sociale et les représentations intergroupes. *Bulletin de Psychologie,* **27,** 710–21.
Deschamps, J.-C. 1977. *L'Attribution et la catégorisation sociale.* Berne: Peter Lang.
Deschamps, J.-C. 1978. La perception des causes du comportement. In W. Doise, J.-C. Deschamps, and G. Mugny (Eds), *Psychologie sociale expérimentale.* Paris: A. Colin.
Deschamps, J.-C. in press. Social attribution. In J. Jaspars, F. Fincham, and M. Hewstone (Eds), *Attribution theory: Conceptual, developmental and social dimensions.* European Monographs in Social Psychology. London: Academic Press.
Deschamps, J.-C. and Doise, W. 1978. Crossed category memberships in intergroup relations. In H. Tajfel (Ed.), *op. cit.*
Dion, K.L. 1975. Women's reactions to discrimination from members of the same or opposite sex. *Journal of Research in Personality,* **9,** 294–306.
Dion, K.L. and Earn, B.M. 1975. The phenomenology of being a target of prejudice. *Journal of Personality and Social Psychology,* **32,** 944–50.
Dion, K.L., Earn, B.M. and Yee, P.H.N. 1978. The experience of being a victim of prejudice: An experimental approach. *International Journal of Psychology,* **13,** 197–214.
Doise, W. 1969. Intergroup relations and the polarisation of individual and collective judgements. *Journal of Personality and Social Psychology,* **12,** 136–43.
Doise, W. 1972. Relations et représentations intergroupes. In S. Moscovici (Ed.), *Introduction à la psychologie sociale.* Paris: Larousse.
Doise, W. 1978. *Groups and individuals: Explanations in social psychology.* Cambridge: Cambridge University Press.
Doise, W. and Sinclair, A. 1973. The categorisation process in intergroup relations. *European Journal of Social Psychology,* **3,** 145–57.
Duncan, B.L. 1976. Differential social perception and attribution of intergroup violence: Testing the lower limits of stereotyping of Blacks. *Journal of Personality and Social Psychology,* **34,** 590–8.
Durkheim, E. 1898. Représentations individuelles et représentations collectives.

Revue de metaphysique et de morale. In *Sociologie et philosophie*. Paris: Presses Universitaires de France, 1967.

Eisen, S.V. 1979. Actor–observer differences in information inference and causal attribution. *Journal of Personality and Social Psychology*, **37**, 261–72.

Eiser, J.R. and Stroebe, W. 1972. *Categorization and social judgement*. London: European Monographs in Social Psychology, No. 3. Academic Press.

Erskine, H. 1968. The polls: Recent opinion on racial problems. *Public Opinion Quarterly*, **32**, 696–703.

Feagin, J.P. 1972. God helps those who help themselves. *Psychology Today*, **6**, 101–29.

Festinger, L. 1954. A theory of social comparison processes. *Human Relations*, **7**, 117–40.

Festinger, L. 1957. *A theory of cognitive dissonance*. Evanston, Illinois: Row, Peterson.

Fincham, F.D. and Jaspars, J.M.F. 1980. Attribution of responsibility: From man-the-scientist to man-as-lawyer. In L. Berkowitz (Ed.), *Advances in experimental social psychology*. Vol. 13. New York: Academic Press.

Flament, C. 1972. The cognitive structures of the scientist. In J. Israel and H. Tajfel (Eds) *The context of social psychology*. London: European Monographs in Social Psychology, No. 2. Academic Press.

Gergen, K. J. and Jones, E.E. 1963. Mental illness, predictability and affective consequences as stimulus factors in person perception. *Journal of Abnormal and Social Psychology*, **67**, 95–104.

Guimond, S. and Simard, L.M. 1979. Perception et interprétation des inégalites economiques entre Francophones et Anglophones au Québec. Paper presented to the 40th Congress of the Canadian Psychological Society, Quebec. June, 1979.

Hamilton, D.L. 1976. Cognitive biases in the perception of social groups. In J.S. Carroll and J.W. Payne (Eds.), *Cognition and social behaviour*. Hillsdale, N.J.: Erlbaum.

Hamilton, V.L. 1978. Who is responsible? Toward a *social* psychology of responsibility attribution. *Social Psychology*, **41**, 316–28.

Harré, R. and Secord, P.F. 1972. *The explanation of social behaviour*. Oxford: Blackwell.

Hastorf, A.H. and Cantril, H. 1954. They saw a game: a case study. *Journal of Abnormal and Social Psychology*, **49**, 129–34.

Heider, F. 1958. *The psychology of interpersonal relations*. New York: Wiley.

Herzlich, C. 1972. La représentation sociale. In S. Moscovici (Ed.), *Introduction à la psychologie sociale*. Paris: Larousse.

Herzlich, C. 1973. *Health and illness: a social psychological analysis*. London: Academic Press.

Jaspars, J.M.F. in press. Attitudes and social representations. Paper presented at colloquium on social representations, Maison des Sciences de l'Homme, Paris, 8–10 January, 1979.

Jones, E.E. 1979. The rocky road from acts to dispositions. *American Psychologist*, **34**, 107–17.

Jones, E.E. and Davis, K.E. 1965. From acts to dispositions: The attribution process in person perception. In L. Berkowitz (Ed.), *Advances in experimental social psychology* (Vol. 2). New York: Academic Press.

Jones, E.E., Davis, K.E. and Gergen, K.J. 1961. Role playing variations and their informational value for person perception. *Journal of Abnormal and Social Psychology*, **63**, 302–10.

Jones, E.E. and De Charms, R. 1957. Changes in social perception as a function of the personal relevance of behaviour. *Sociometry*, **20**, 75–85.

Jones, E.E. and Harris, V.A. 1967. The attribution of attitudes. *Journal of Experimental Social Psychology*, **3**, 1–24.

Jones, E.E. and McGillis, D. 1976. Correspondent inferences and the attribution cube: A comparative reappraisal. In J.H. Harvey, W.J. Ickes and R.F. Kidd (Eds), *New directions in attribution research*, Vol. 1. Hillsdale, N.J.: Erlbaum.

Jones, E.E. and Nisbett, R.E. 1971. *The actor and the observer: Divergent perceptions of the causes of behaviour.* New Jersey: General Learning Press.

Katz, D. and Braly, K. 1933. Racial stereotypes of 100 college students. *Journal of Abnormal and Social Psychology*, **28**, 280–90.

Kelley, H.H. 1967. Attribution theory in social psychology. *Nebraska Symposium on Motivation*, **15**, 192–238.

Kelley, H.H. 1972. *Causal schemata and the attribution process.* New Jersey: General Learning Press.

Kelley, H.H. 1973. The processes of causal attribution. *American Psychologist*, **28**, 107–28.

Kelly, G.A. 1955. *The psychology of personal constructs* (2 Vols.) New York: Norton.

van Knippenberg, A. 1978. Status differences, comparative relevance and intergroup differentiation In H. Tajfel (Ed.), 1978, *op. cit.*

Lambert, W.E., Hodgson, R.C., Gardner, R.C. and Fillenbaum, S. 1960. Evaluational reactions to spoken languages. *Journal of Abnormal and Social Psychology*, **60**, 44–51.

Lemaine, G., Desportes, J.P., and Louarn, J.P. 1969. Rôle de la cohésion et de la différenciation hiérarchique dans le processus d'influence sociale. *Bulletin du CERP*, **28**, 237–53.

Lerner, M.J. 1970. The desire for justice and reactions to victims. In J. Macaulay and L. Berkowitz (Eds), *Altruism and helping behaviour.* New York: Academic Press.

Lerner, M.J. 1977. The justice motive: Some hypotheses as to its origins and forms. *Journal of Personality*, **45**, 1–52.

Lerner, M.J. and Miller, D.T. 1978. 'Just World' research and the attribution process: Looking back and ahead. *Psychological Bulletin*, **85**, 1030–51.

Lerner, M.J., Miller, D.T. and Holmes, J.G. 1976. Deserving and the emergence of forms of justice. In L. Berkowitz (Ed.), *Advances in experimental social psychology* (Vol. 9). New York: Academic Press.

LeVine, R.A. and Campbell, D.T. 1972. *Ethnocentrism: Theories of conflict, ethnic attitudes and group behaviour.* New York: Wiley.

Lippman, W. 1922. *Public opinion.* New York: Macmillan.

Mann, J.F. and Taylor, D.M. 1974. Attribution of causality: Role of ethnicity and social class. *Journal of Social Psychology*, **94**, 3–13.

McArthur, L.A. 1972. The how and what of why: Some determinants and consequences of causal attributions. *Journal of Personality and Social Psychology*, **22**, 171–93.

McKillip, J. and Posavac, E.J. 1975. Judgements of responsibility for an accident. *Journal of Personality*, **43**, 248–65.

Mead, G.H. 1913. The social self. *Journal of Philosophy*, 374–80.

Miller, D.T. and Ross, M. 1975. Self-serving biases in the attribution of causality: Fact or fiction? *Psychological Bulletin*, **82**, 213–25.

Milner, D. 1975. *Children and race*. Harmondsworth: Penguin Books.

Monson, T.C. and Snyder, M. 1977. Actors, observers and the attribution process. *Journal of Experimental Social Psychology*, **13**, 89–111.

Moscovici, S. 1961. *La psychanalyse, son image et son public*. Paris: Presses Universitaires de France (2nd edition, 1976).

Moscovici, S. 1972. Society and theory in social psychology. In J. Israel and H. Tajfel (Eds), *The context of social psychology*. European Monographs in Social Psychology, No. 2. London: Academic Press.

Moscovici, S. 1979. Evolution de la recherche contemporaine sur les problèmes des représentations sociales. Paper presented at a colloquium on social representations, Maison des Sciences de l'Homme, Paris, January, 1979.

Moscovici, S. and Zavalloni, M. 1969. The group as a polariser of attitudes. *Journal of Personality and Social Psychology*, **12**, 125–35.

Myers, D.G. and Lamm, H. 1976. The group polarisation phenomenon. *Psychological Bulletin*, **83**, 602–27.

Newcomb, T.M. 1943. *Personality and social change*. New York: Holt, Rinehart & Winston.

Nisbett, R.E., Caputo, C., Legant, P. and Maracek, J. 1973. Behaviour as seen by the actor and as seen by the observer. *Journal of Personality and Social Psychology*, **27**, 154–64.

Pliner, P. and Capell, H. 1977. Drinking, driving and the attribution of responsibility. *Journal of Studies on Alcohol*, **38**, 593–602.

Rokeach, M. 1960. *The open and closed mind*. New York: Basic Books.

Ross, L. 1977. The intuitive psychologist and his shortcomings: Distortions in the attribution process. In L. Berkowitz (Ed.), *Advances in experimental social psychology* (Vol. 10). New York: Academic Press.

Rubin, Z. and Peplau, A. 1973. Belief in a just world and reactions to another's lot: A study of participants in the national draft lottery. *Journal of Social Issues*, **29**, 73–93.

Ruble, D.N. and Feldman, N.S. 1976. Order of consensus, distinctiveness, and consistency information and causal attributions. *Journal of Personality and Social Psychology*, **34**, 930–37.

Ryan, A. 1970. *The Philosophy of the social sciences*. London: Macmillan.

Schott, K. 1979. The un-affluent society. *New Statesman*, **98**, 622–5.

Shaver, K.G. 1970. Defensive attribution: Effects of severity and relevance on the responsibility assigned for an accident. *Journal of Personality and Social Psychology*, **14**, 101–13.

Shaver, K.G. 1975. *An introduction to attribution processes*. Cambridge, Mass: Winthrop.

Shaw, J.I. and McMartin, J.A. 1977. Personal and situational determinants of AR for an accident. *Human Relations*, **30**, 95–107.

Sherif, M. 1936. *The psychology of social norms*. New York: Harper and Row.

Sherif, M. 1966. *Group conflict and co-operation: Their social psychology*. London: Routledge & Kegan Paul.

Steiner, I.D. 1974. Whatever happened to the group in social psychology? *Journal of Experimental Social Psychology*, **10**, 94–108.

Steiner, I.D. and Field, W.L. 1960. Role assignment and interpersonal influence. *Journal of Abnormal and Social Psychology*, **61**, 239–46.

Stephan, W. 1977. Stereotyping: role of ingroup outgroup differences in causal attribution of behaviour. *Journal of Social Psychology*, **101**, 255–66.

Storms, M.D. 1973. Videotape and the attribution process: Reversing actors' and observers' points of view. *Journal of Personality and Social Psychology*, **27**, 165–75.

Sumner, G.A. 1906. *Folkways*. New York: Ginn.

Tajfel, H. 1959. Quantitative judgement in social perception. *British Journal of Psychology*, **50**, 16–29.

Tajfel, H. 1969. Social and cultural factors in perception. In G. Lindzey and E. Aronson (Eds), *Handbook of social psychology*. Vol. 3. Reading, Mass: Addison-Wesley.

Tajfel, H. 1970. Experiments in intergroup discrimination. *Scientific American*, **223**, (5), 96–102.

Tajfel, H. 1972a. Experiments in a vacuum. In J. Israel and H. Tajfel (Eds.), *The context of social psychology*. European Monographs in Social Psychology, No. 2. London: Academic Press.

Tajfel, H. 1972b. La catégorisation sociale. In S. Moscovici (Ed.), *Introduction à la psychologie sociale*. Paris: Larousse.

Tajfel, H. 1973. The roots of prejudice. In P. Watson (Ed.), *Psychology and race*. Harmondsworth: Penguin Books.

Tajfel, H. 1974. Social identity and intergroup behaviour. *Social Science Information*, **13**, 65–93.

Tajfel, H. 1978. (Ed.) *Differentiation between social groups: Studies in intergroup behaviour*. European Monographs in Social Psychology, No. 14. London: Academic Press.

Tajfel, H. 1979. Individuals and groups in social psychology. *British Journal of Social and Clinical Psychology*, **18**, 183–91.

Tajfel, H. 1980. The 'New Look' and social differentiations: A semi-Brunerian perspective. In D. Olson (Ed.), *The social foundations of language and thought: Essays in honour of J.S. Bruner*. New York: Norton.

Tajfel, H. 1981. Social stereotypes and social groups. In H. Tajfel: *Human groups and social categories*. Cambridge: Cambridge University Press.

Tajfel, H., Flament, C., Billig, M. and Bundy, R.P. 1971. Social categorization and intergroup behaviour. *European Journal of Social Psychology*, **1**, 149–78.

Tajfel, H. and Turner, J.C. 1979. An integrative theory of intergroup conflict. In W.G. Austin and S. Worchel (Eds), *The social psychology of intergroup relations*. Monterey, California: Brooks/Cole, 1979.

Tajfel, H. and Wilkes, A.L. 1963. Classification and quantitative judgement.

British Journal of Psychology, **54**, 101–14.

Taylor, D.M. and Brown, R.J. 1979. Towards a more social psychology. *British Journal of Social and Clinical Psychology*, **18**, 173–81.

Taylor, D.M. and Doria, J.R. Self-serving and group-serving bias in attribution. McGill University, Montreal, mimeo.

Taylor, D.M. and Jaggi, V. 1974. Ethnocentrism and causal attribution in a South Indian context. *Journal of Cross-Cultural Psychology*, **5**, 162–71.

Taylor, D.M. and Royer, L. 1979. Group processes affecting language choice in intergroup relations. Paper presented at the International Conference on Social Psychology and Language, University of Bristol, (16th-20th July, 1979).

Thibaut, J.W. and Riecken, H.W. 1955. Some determinants and consequences of the perception of social causality. *Journal of Personality*, **24**, 113–33.

Townsend, P. 1979. *Poverty in the United Kingdom: A survey of household resources and standards of living*. Harmondsworth: Penguin Books.

Triandis, H.C. 1971. *Attitude and attitude change*. New York: Wiley.

Triandis, H.C. 1977. *Interpersonal behaviour*. Monterey, California: Brooks/Cole.

Turner, J.C. 1975. Social comparison and social identity: Some prospects for intergroup behaviour. *European Journal of Social Psychology*, **5**, 5–34.

Turner, J.C. and Brown, R. 1978. Social status, cognitive alternatives and intergroup relations. In H. Tajfel (Ed.), 1978, *op. cit.*

Vaughan, G.M. 1964. Ethnic awareness in relation to minority group membership. *Journal of Genetic Psychology*, **105**, 119–130.

Wetherell, M. and Turner, J.C. Group polarisation and social identification. University of Bristol, mimeo.

Wilder, D.A. 1978. Perceiving persons as a group: effects on attributions of causality and beliefs. *Social Psychology*, **41**, 13–23.

Part II
The dynamics of interaction between groups: Experimental studies

5. Perceived illegitimacy and intergroup relations

BRIAN CADDICK

1. Introduction

After a period in the social psychological wilderness, intergroup behaviour has once again begun to emerge as a respectable and deserving topic for study and research. The dramatic and widely communicated inter- and intranational events of the late 1960s and 1970s have no doubt contributed to this reawakening of interest, but the heuristic value of some recent theoretical and critical offerings (see, for example, LeVine and Campbell, 1972; Deutsch, 1973; Billig, 1976; Tajfel, 1978) should not be underestimated. Of some importance among these scholarly contributions are the efforts by Tajfel and his colleagues to formulate a theory which breaks free of the extrapolations from interpersonal to intergroup behaviour characteristic of much earlier work, and which takes greater cognizance of the social setting (the 'background of the relations, as perceived by the people concerned, between their own and other social groups' Tajfel, 1978, p50) out of which intergroup behaviour develops. One feature of these efforts has been an attempt to understand and delineate the part played by perceived illegitimacy – that is to say, group members' perceptions of unjust and unfair relations between their own and other group(s) – in the way groups view and respond to one another. What follows is a consideration of this particular aspect of Tajfel's theory and a discussion of some recent experimental evidence bearing on his argument. Some implications inherent in the findings and some suggestions for further research – particularly around the issue of improving intergroup relations – will also be presented.

Since comprehensive outlines of Tajfel's theory are already available elsewhere (Tajfel, 1974, 1978; Tajfel and Turner, 1979; Turner, 1975) its complete reiteration here is not warranted. Nevertheless, in order to give direction and coherence to the present discussion, some brief restatement will be necessary. Before that, however, we need to clear the ground somewhat by indicating which of the several ways the term 'perceived illegitimacy' has entered into the theory which will be of central interest here. The quotations which follow show why such a clarification is desirable:

> In relation to the issue of similarity in social comparison theory, it is possible to maintain that the perceived illegitimacy of the perceived intergroup relations provides a bridge from non-comparability to comparability ... perceived illegitimacy of an existing relationship in status, power, domination or any other differential implies the development of some dimensions of comparability (i.e. an underlying similarity) where none existed before. (Tajfel, 1978, p75)

> An insecure comparison is one in which 'cognitive alternatives' to the existing outcome are perceived ... what factors in a status relationship create an awareness of cognitive alternatives? Tajfel's answer is that this is based on the perceived illegitimacy of the status differences between groups, the degree to which the groups perceive their status relations to be in conflict with superordinate values of justice, fairness or equity. (Turner and Brown, 1978, pp208–9)

> It will be obvious that a combination of illegitimacy and instability [in the status relations between groups] would become a powerful incitement for attempts to change the intergroup *status quo* or to resist such changes on the part of groups which see themselves threatened by them. (Tajfel, 1978, p52)

> The perceived illegitimacy of an intergroup relationship is ... socially and psychologically the accepted and acceptable lever for social change and social action in intergroup behaviour ... it provides the basis for the shared and durable ideologizing of arousal, discontent and frustration. (Tajfel, 1978, p76)

Though obviously not perfectly distinct and separable from one another, it is possible to discern in these statements at least four ways in which perceived illegitimacy enters into Tajfel's account of the process of intergroup relations. On the one hand, it is via perceptions of illegitimacy that groups become salient to one another for comparison purposes (this might be termed its 'awareness' role). On the other, perceived illegitimacy is associated with the realization by members of a group that their group's present position is not the only one possible (an 'insight' role). Then there is a 'motivational' role in the sense that perceived illegitimacy is seen to have activity-energizing properties. And finally, there is an 'ideological' role where illegitimacy becomes something of a dialectical element in the struggle for 'justice' and 'equity'.

This variety of usage is not especially surprising. Illegitimacy is not, in any application, a connotatively simple term. Thus, in stating that it is the second and third of these 'roles' which will concern us here, no denial of the first and fourth possibilities is intended. It is simply the case that it is in relation to the insight and motivational roles that perceived illegitimacy's place in the overall theory is most thoroughly developed and also, no doubt as a consequence of this development, it is here that some relevant experimental findings have been adduced. These we wish to discuss but, first, a brief reacquaintance with certain features of the theory is useful.

(a) The relevant theoretical issues

A basic and fundamental assumption of the theory is that individuals have a need for, and are thus motivated to establish and/or maintain, a positive self-concept. The importance of this for intergroup behaviour arises out of the fact that, in intergroup settings, group membership – or a person's social identity – generally becomes a significant component of one's self-concept; as a consequence, self-concept needs, in so far as they are salient, become needs to establish or maintain a satisfactory social identity. The satisfactoriness of one's social identity, being normally a relative matter, is usually determined through comparisons, on meaningful dimensions, with other groups. Depending on the outcome of these comparisons – and assuming that neither individual mobility between groups nor the assimilation of one group by another is possible – individuals may be motivated by their social identity needs to establish or maintain ingroup distinctiveness on these or other valued dimensions. It is at this point that certain forms of intergroup behaviour begin to manifest themselves.

The major theoretical focus is on intergroup contexts where some kind of superior/inferior status differentiation already exists. Taking a step backwards momentarily, where a differentiation of this sort is seen by all concerned to be legitimate and stable, then there are no particular implications for social identity or social identity linked intergroup behaviour. In such cases – taken by Tajfel to be relatively rare or somewhat trivial – social identity is said to be 'secure'. 'Insecure' social identity results when the differentiation is perceived by members of a group to be illegitimate and unstable. Experiencing circumstances such as these, superior group members may attempt to find justifications for the maintenance of the *status quo*, either by creating new forms of psychological distinctiveness or enhancing those among the old ones which are still serviceable. Inferior group members, for their part, may reinterpret existing inferior characteristics of their group so that they now acquire a positively valued distinctiveness from the superior group and/or they may attempt to create new group characteristics with the same purpose in mind.

Possible examples of the sorts of things Tajfel is referring to spring readily to mind: 'black is beautiful' and the other black pride slogans of American Negroes during the 1960s (see Bracey, Meier and Rudwick, 1970); the claims by some white racist spokesmen at the turn of the century that American whites would and should remain dominant because of their supposedly greater cranial, and therefore intellectual, capacities (see Fishel and Quarles, 1970, pp379–81). Examples like these are, of course, rich and provocative but also somewhat bedevilled by their embeddedness within the usual welter of variables associated with social events of such magnitude; strictly speaking, then, they provide suggestive but insufficient evidence for Tajfel's proposals. For this reason, a study by Turner and Brown, included as a chapter in Tajfel's earlier book outlining his theory and related research (Tajfel, 1978) takes on a particular significance. Turner and Brown's experiment was a neat factorial design constructed so as to produce and, hopefully, monitor the impact of variations in both the legitimacy and the stability of relations between the groups. It stands as the major direct test of Tajfel's legitimacy/illegitimacy argument under controlled conditions and, for these and other reasons that will soon become apparent, merits our attention here. We need to begin with an outline of the experimental procedure.

(b) The Turner and Brown experiment

Turner and Brown's college student subjects were recruited to work as members of three-person groups in what was purported to be a study of reasoning skills. The ostensible task of these groups, which were tested one at a time, was to discuss an issue with social/philosophical overtones and then to prepare and tape-record the group's views on this issue and the reasons for holding these views. Supposedly, the taped remarks were to be used as the data to be analysed later for reasoning skills.

Before entering into their discussions, group members were also given some additional information which served to defined the conditions of the experiment. It was first pointed out, in connection with the fact that the group's members were either all Arts or all Science students, that while reasoning skills were important for all students, research suggested that there were known performance differences between the two faculty groups. This defined a status differentiation which, for half the subjects, was favourable and, for the other half, unfavourable. Following on from this, the experimenter commented that the difference was either unfair and unreasonable or fair and to be expected. Unfairness was said to derive from an inbuilt test bias not well recognized by psychologists and undoubtedly to blame for discriminatory outcomes when such tests were used in personnel selection and assessment. Subjects receiving the 'fair' message also heard about the testing bias, but this was described as legitimate, well-known, taken into account and corrected for in practice. Finally, subjects were informed either that the normal findings relating to reasoning skills differences between the two groups were almost certain to obtain in the present circumstances, or were, in fact, open to the possibility of change.

Three measures were taken to trace the effects of the manipulations. First, the groups were asked to give ratings of their taped arguments and those of another group (provided by a standard tape identified as being prepared by a group from the other faculty). Then, subjects were asked to suggest – if they wished – other methods by which reasoning skills might be assessed, and additional factors other than reasoning skills which needed to be taken into account in assessing overall intellectual ability.

Drawing from Tajfel's proposals, Turner and Brown predicted that their 'illegitimate' superiors would seek to justify and maintain their advantage and would show this by heightened ingroup bias in their ratings of the tapes, and by using the opportunity provided by the 'methods' and 'factors' questions to suggest new and alternative dimensions of comparison. 'Illegitimate' inferiors, it was expected, would also use the methods and factors questions to suggest other dimensions of comparison. Their findings, though complex, were taken to give a measure of support to Tajfel's proposals. Yet, notwithstanding the authors' intentions and interpretations, there is a methodological problem in relation to the responses of the illegitimate superiors which calls this conclusion into question and opens the way for a markedly different view.

The methodological problem is straightforward enough. Tajfel states that justification by the members of illegitimately superior groups will manifest itself as an enhancement of differences on those comparative dimensions which are still serviceable, and by the creation of ingroup-favouring differences on newly-created dimensions of comparison open to such use. For neither possibility, however, did the experimenters provide a response format suitable for the expression of these kinds of behaviours. The tape ratings were inappropriate since they referred to a dimension of comparison already identified by the experimenter as unfair and unreasonable. The methods and factors suggestions were similarly inappropriate since, if the subjects had been listening to the experimenter's comments, they could not but have concluded that what were needed were new methods and new factors to help restore justice and fairness to the whole process of assessment. The fact, then, that the illegitimate superiors seemed willing to suggest new methods and new factors implies that they were seeking to redress an unjust imbalance from which they might unfairly benefit. As for the tape ratings, the illegitimate superior data are unfortunately too variable (one high ingroup bias, one low) to permit any satisfactory conclusions. Indeed, the variation underscores a second methodological shortcoming: with only two groups in each status/legitimacy/stability combination cell, one really requires independent ratings of in- and outgroup performance before drawing the conclusion that ingroup favouring ratings demonstrate bias.

In relation to all this, it would seem appropriate to ask two questions. First, is there any other evidence which would support the arguments which Tajfel has put forward regarding illegitimate superior status and intergroup behaviour? Second, should it not be acknowledged that the responses made by all of Turner and Brown's illegitimacy conditions subjects – superiors and inferiors – are rather more in line with the idea of actual equity restoration which forms part of the equity theory view of social interaction (Walster *et al.*, 1973)? An answer to the first of these is provided by an experiment by Caddick (1978), which is described below. The second question raises wider theoretical issues which are usefully considered after Caddick's findings have been presented.

(c) Caddick's experiment

As in the previous study, Caddick's interests were in tracing the effects of perceived illegitimacy and perceived instability on intergroup behaviour. Again, however, we will limit our attention to the first of these.

Caddick's subjects were 13 and 14 year old schoolboys attending British state schools at the third form level. In their school setting they were randomly formed into three- or four-person groups and, in the crucial second session of the experiment, were tested in a two-group context, paired groups being balanced in terms of member numbers. The boys were led to believe that they were participating in a study aimed at determining how well pupils might accomplish school work if they were permitted to work together with others.

Groups came to the second session having completed two tasks in an earlier session in which all groups were present. One of the tasks was to draw a map of their schoolground, showing where an imaginary gang of robbers might have most effectively hidden some stolen money. The second was a spot-the-ball task in which members of the group viewed a set of action football photographs and recorded their collective view as to which, if either, of two paper discs affixed to each photo covered the ball. In the second session, false feedback on their performance on this latter task was conveyed to the two groups present so that a differentiation between the groups was created. At this point, a new spot-the-ball task was administered, the answers 'marked', and again feedback was given to the effect that there was still an apparent performance difference between the groups. Following on from this, the subjects rated their own and the other group on scales relevant (PR) or irrelevant (PI) to the performance difference. They also evaluated each other's previously drawn maps, and distributed rewards to in- and outgroup members using reward choice matrices similar to those employed in earlier intergroup studies (Tajfel *et al.*, 1971; Billig and Tajfel, 1973).

The critical conditions in connection with which these data were collected were as follows. Members of the control condition groups were given information which described the spot-the-ball task differentiations as legitimate and stable. Members of the illegitimacy condition groups, however, experienced procedural changes designed to create an impression of illegitimacy in the second spot-the-ball task result. Specifically, one of the two groups – the earlier low scoring group – was required to use a set of spot-the-ball photographs for which the correct answers were much more difficult to ascertain (the choice required was between three, rather than two, ball location possibilities). This set – explained as having been brought along by mistake – was assigned to this group through what was made to appear to be the outcome of a vote on the matter by the other group. The aim, then, was to produce a differentiation which was both unfair and, at least in part, a consequence of the superior group's doing.

(d) The findings as presented in Table 1

A brief explanation of what the figures represent is given below.

Table 1. *Ingroup bias and perceived illegitimacy in the status relations between two groups* (Caddick, 1978)

Status of group	Dependent measure	Conditions of legitimate status differentiation	Conditions of illegitimate status differentiation	Statistical comparisons (Dunnett's test, one-tailed)*
Superior	FAV matrices	6.77	8.41	$p > 0.05$
	PULL matrices	0.19	2.89	$p > 0.01$
	Δ matrices	1.29	3.54	$p > 0.06$
	Map scores	9.57	27.45	$p > 0.06$
	PI scores	2.50	7.50	ns
	PR scores	25.25	30.86	ns
Inferior	FAV matrices	6.80	9.36	$p > 0.01$
	PULL matrices	0.07	3.77	$p > 0.01$
	Δ matrices	2.25	3.68	ns
	Map scores	2.18	21.30	$p > 0.05$
	PI scores	4.46	11.14	ns
	PR scores	−17.32	−9.14	ns

* As noted in the text, the overall experiment included other conditions and therefore other planned comparisons. To control against the Type I error of multiple t-testing, Dunnett's test was used.

FAV, PULL and Δ matrices

The reward choice matrices used in Caddick's study were modelled after those used by Tajfel *et al.* (1971 Experiment II) and Billig and Tajfel (1973), details of which can be found in those reports. Essentially, the matrices provide a means by which the subjects can distribute rewards to members of the ingroup and/or the outgroup, adopting one or more of several alternative strategies. Among the strategies is included the possibility of creating an ingroup-favouring differentiation (without, since the respondent is advised that he is *not* making choices for himself, the involvement of instrumental self-interest). Responses of this sort are represented by scores above 6, 0 and 0 (the points of equal reward) for the FAV, PULL and Δ matrices, respectively. FAV and PULL matrices, it should be noted, are matrices requiring choices for an ingroup member – outgroup member pair (i.e. direct intergroup comparison); Δ matrices require choices either for two ingroupers or two outgroupers and the ingroup – outgroup differentiation is then calculated as the difference in pay-off awarded the two pairs.

Map scores

The subjects were asked to rate ingroup and outgroup maps on 'imaginativeness of hiding place chosen for the money' and 'chances that the money might be discovered accidentally'. These two scales were combined and the map scores noted in Table 1 are the mean difference scores for ingroup/outgroup ratings. Scores above 0 represent evaluations in the ingroup's favour.

PR and PI scores

These are again mean difference scores for ingroup-outgroup ratings. The combined scales used in calculating the PR (performance relevant) scores were 'how good each group was at thinking quickly' and 'how good each group was at working together as a team'. The combined scales used in calculating the PI (performance irrelevant) scores were 'how likeable each group was' and 'how pleasant others would find each of the two groups to work with'. Again, scores above 0 are in favour of the ingroup.

Except for the PR ratings, the responses required of the subjects afforded an opportunity to create a positively valued differentiation between in- and outgroup on new dimensions of comparison – either so as to maintain, bolster up or reassert superiority undermined by suggestions of illegitimacy, or in order to establish a more favourable ingroup position than the existing one of apparently illegitimate inferiority. The PR ratings, being linkable to performance, permitted the enhancement or minimization of performance differences according to the same needs. As Table 1 shows, all trends are in line with what Tajfel's theory relating to illegitimate status differentiations would lead one to expect, particularly in the case of the FAV, PULL and Map results. Where the trends are weaker, this is arguably the consequence of peculiarities associated with the measures themselves. For example, in their Δ matrix choices for a pair of *in*group members some subjects were inclined to assign the recipients equal rewards, presumably to retain intragroup fairness for the ingroup. Because of the way the matrices are constructed, this reduced the degree to which indirect differentiations between in- and outgroup could be made, introducing as a consequence greater overall variability in these particular data and a corresponding lessening of certainty in the statistical comparisons carried out. As for the PI and PR ratings, these of course were given in a context where all the participants knew one another relatively well as classmates. Thus, it seems likely that any impulse to create significant PI differences would have had to operate against already existing knowledge about the likeability and pleasantness of fellow pupils distributed in a random, and therefore presumably balanced, way between in- and outgroup. The PR responses were open to background influences in a similar way – influences moderated, perhaps, by the performance feedback remarks. There are plausible reasons, then, for the PI and PR and Δ matrices trends being weaker. However, the overall message is one of support for Tajfel's argument and through this we are left with an intriguing difference between Caddick's findings and the results of the previous experiment.

Why should Caddick's illegitimate superiors have striven to maintain their superiority while Turner and Brown's gave evidence of the reverse? There is one major difference in the conduct of the two studies which probably accounts for their contrasting results. In Caddick's experiment, the illegitimate superiors were made to feel at least partly responsible for the outcomes experienced by the other group. Not so the comparable subjects in the Turner and Brown study: their advantage stemmed from the questionable activities of some third party (or parties), activities condemned by no less an expert than the experimenter himself. Though given no real opportunity to do otherwise, it is hard to imagine these college students behaving other than the way they did. Caddick's subjects, on the other hand, were already committed by the rigged outcome of the secret ballot which made it appear that they had been instrumental in handicapping the other group. To acknowledge this by being more fair in their intergroup evaluations and reward disbursements would be to paint a not particularly attractive picture of the ingroup's prior behaviour. This, in itself, would be a threat to one's social identity, a threat avoided – in this case, it would seem – by denying illegitimacy with a vigorous re-emphasis of the ingroup's superiority.

As for the Turner and Brown findings, it would appear that equity theory – particularly that part concerned with actual equity restoration – would best account for the responses of the subjects (inferior and superior) in their illegitimacy conditions. Equity theory (Walster et al., 1973) asserts that the perception of injustice or unfairness in social relationships leads the perceiver to feel distressed. Such distress is uncomfortable and motivates attempts to alter the conditions which promote it. One such alteration is action aimed at redressing the injustice by restoring actual equity to the relationship. Thus, both those who are benefiting and those who are suffering from some unfair set of circumstances may act so as to eliminate the conditions which permit it – in the present case, for instance, by suggesting better and more thorough psychological assessment procedures.

To leave the matter here, however, would be to ignore an important and potentially fruitful theoretical issue. Equity theorists also argue that individuals may act so as to restore equity psychologically (Adams, 1965; Walster et al., 1973). That is to say, inequity may be converted into equity by the psychological distortion of the outcomes and inputs – one's own and the other's – which lead to the perception or accusation of inequity in the first place. Such an argument clearly encompasses Caddick's findings, just as actual equity restoration seems to explain Turner and Brown's. Thus, the question asked earlier about equity theory and the Turner and Brown data is of wider significance than its initial phrasing would imply.

In the remainder of this chapter, we shall concern ourselves with the apparant overlap of equity theory and the social identity approach to intergroup relations and some of the issues to which this overlap gives rise.

2. Equity theory, social identity and intergroup relations

There is a sense in which the heading for this section could read 'apples and oranges and intergroup relations'. This is because, while Tajfel's theory is explicitly and specifically to do with relations between groups, equity theory – in its conceptualization and in its related research – is essentially concerned with transactions between individuals or subunits of a common culture. A clear picture of this emerges from the extensive bibliography of equity theory research prepared and annotated by Adams and Freedman (1976): of the one-hundred-and-sixty-odd entries cited, not one could seriously be classified as a study of intergroup relations. This is not altogether surprising, of course, given that the definitive version of the theory (Walster *et al.*, 1973) is built on the idea that it is in the interests of a social group to develop an equity outlook *among its members* and to create conditions *within its own boundaries* which help to promote equitable behaviour. It would not do to be pedantic on this issue, however, despite Tajfel's well-founded concerns about the extrapolation of the social psychology of interpersonal relations to relations between groups (Tajfel, 1974). The generalization of *intra*group socialization effects to intergroup contexts is not beyond the bounds of possibility. Moreover, as Lerner (1975, 1977) has argued, equity as a motivational influence may be but one form of a more general justice motive which, because it derives from the 'natural, universal process whereby all people develop by learning to control their use of power for their own long term benefit' (1975, p12), is not wholly cultural in origin and thus not so constrained in its applicability. For the sake of sensibility as well as argument, then, we will regard equity theory and the social identity approach of Tajfel as 'like fruit' – if not from the same tree, then at least from the same orchard.

Having given ourselves this freedom, we are better able to acknowledge the apparent message in the material so far presented and discussed. This is that, as an explanatory tool for use in analysing and making some sense out of behaviour associated with illegitimate intergroup relationships, equity theory seems to offer more potential than does Tajfel's approach. At any rate, equity theory foresees the possibility of two distinctly different responses by members of an illegitimately superior group, while the social identity argument sees but one.[1] Having said that, however, it needs also to be said that there is no reason why Tajfel's theory could not be altered so as to become more comprehensive in this sense. This we can see if we consider, in more detail than does Tajfel himself, the kinds of interpersonal processes that could conceivably take place with the perception of illegitimacy.

It is useful to recall here two earlier ideas: perceived illegitimacy's 'insight' and 'motivational' roles. We might suppose that the perception of illegitimacy in precipitating an awareness of cognitive alternatives in the relations which currently exist between one's own and another group could have the effect of either disrupting some established cognitive set or setting up dissonant or imbalanced relations between cognitive elements associated with the ingroup, the outgroup and/or the differentiation between them. Any of these might lead to the kinds of outcomes postulated by Tajfel. That is to say: the reactions he attributes to the experiencing of an insecure social identity could be seen as attempts either to achieve some kind of cognitive reintegration or stability (Rokeach, 1960), or to reduce dissonance (Festinger, 1957), or to restore balance (Heider, 1958). But, of course, these same processes – cognitive reintegration, dissonance reduction, balance restoration – might just as well lead to other kinds of resolutions: for example, superior group members accepting, and behaving in a manner consistent with their acceptance, that their group's status should be no greater than the other group's. It should be noted, however, that if one were to insist upon the primacy of the need for a satisfactory social identity, instances of the latter sort would presumably be infrequent.

But we need not limit ourselves here to cognitive dynamics. It would not be unreasonable, for example, to argue that members of an inferior group whose inferiority had been illegitimately imposed upon them might well experience anger. Along with the newly awakened need to make more secure an insecure social identity, such anger might then be an additional spur to action. The emotional counterpart for members of a superior group aware of their group's illegitimately based ascendancy would presumably be guilt. One approach to the reduction of guilt – well known to clinicians and, in fact, the essence of Tajfel's proposals – is to deny guilt by acting so as to justify the conditions which give rise to its occurrence. Another approach is to accept the implicit or explicit accusation of injustice and act so as to change the *status quo* into a more just and equitable state of affairs (while still remaining a member of the ingroup). It is interesting to note that here, unlike the case of the cognitive dynamics possibilities mentioned above, the latter alternative would not necessarily be ruled out by an assumed primacy of a unidirectional need for a satisfactory social identity: in some circumstances, being just and fair is highly relevant to the maintenance or establishment of a satisfactory concept of self.

Before considering the implications of altering Tajfel's theory to include the possibility of pro-outgroup action by an illegitimately advantaged group, one thing needs to be made clear. This is that, by suggesting such an alteration, it is not also being suggested that the social identity approach is but an extension of equity theory into the sphere of intergroup relations. Equity theory, however broad its applicability, is nevertheless nothing more than a systematic treatment of how one particular social value affects social behaviour. Undoubtedly, that value is a powerful and important one. However, as Weick (quoted in Homans, 1976) puts it: 'Man does not live by equity alone', and this is as true of intergroup relations as it is of relations at any other level of interaction. There are two ways in which Tajfel's argument reflects this truism and, in so doing, makes itself un-incorporable within an equity theory framework. First, the social identity approach is concerned not just with illegitimate intergroup relationships but with other kinds (i.e. unstable ones) as well. Second, illegitimacy and inequity are not always one and the same thing. As mentioned earlier, Lerner (1977) has pointed out that there are several forms of justice, including equity. To give but one example, justice is involved (but not equity) when A and B agree to toss a coin to see which receives a reward and, the coin coming up in A's favour, he/she claims the prize. Illegitimacy results (but not inequity) if the coin comes up in A's favour but B makes off with the prize. Coin tossing, of course, is not a characteristic of inter-group events (except in the case of some sports matches) but the 'violation of legitimate interests' is a common enough phrase in such contexts and it is not always used to refer to some inequity. In addition to these two points, there is a third factor to be considered: Tajfel's theory is well able to handle the 'minimal group' data of the early social identity experiments (Tajfel *et al.*, 1971; Billig and Tajfel, 1973; Turner, 1975). This is something that equity theory cannot do without some excessively non-parsimonious – and therefore rather unconvincing – argument. In short, there is little to be gained by attempting to place one set of proposals within the theoretical boundaries of the other.

Placing the theories side by side may be a different matter, however. As it stands, Tajfel's theory is a 'pessimistic' one. That is to say, it provides no grounds for expecting intergroup cooperation or adjustment to a mutually more satisfying intergroup relationship as the consequence of social identity motivations. This may be a rather limited position since, whatever one might say about the frequency, importance or, indeed, functionality of intergroup conflict in human affairs, history also reveals that relations between groups are not exclusively competitive. With amendments such as those suggested above, it is possible that various patterns of co-existence, or some actions with respect to other groups which are neither attempts at blurring the boundaries (allowing the 'passing' of one group into another) nor engagements in a process of 'spiralling rivalry until some final inequity is reached' (Turner, 1975, p10) might well be seen to fall within the nexus of Tajfel's social identity argument. In any case, there would at least be some grounds for asking, in relation to social identity processes, an important and potentially fruitful research question. Specifically: under what conditions will a group which holds an illegitimately ascendant position within a web of intergroup relationships accept or actively work towards an improvement in the standing or circumstances of a group (or groups) less well placed?

Of course, there are answers to this question which would not involve social identity processes at all, except in so far as these provided some or all of the resistance against which other, more powerful influences had to operate. On the other hand, if it is true that being just and acting fairly are meaningful issues when it comes to the positivity of one's self-concept or social identity, then there is certainly some value in attempting to discover and delineate the conditions which promote actual justice and fairness as against justification and other actions aimed at maintaining a positive social identity by ingroup-favouring differentiations between groups. It is here that a sideways glance at equity theory is, in a sense, encouraging and possibly helpful. The encouraging part is that while equity theory, like social identity theory, posits a basic and unidirectional push towards self-maintaining or self-gratifying outcomes, what equity research findings suggest is that the more satisfying/less distressing outcomes – i.e. the ones for which experimental subjects tend to opt – are often those in which the welfare of others is not ignored. Now it may be that findings such as these are deeply influenced by the usual concomitants of laboratory experimentation – face-to-face interaction, explicit or implicit scrutiny of responses by a powerful figure, minimal rewards for acting selfishly, the possibility of retaliation or esteem-damaging accusations – but they are no less significant for that, especially in a world where increasing interdependence between groups is bringing with it increased opportunity for communication, scrutiny and influence. The helpful side of the coin derives from the fact that the question asked above is, if we allow for certain differences of emphasis, essentially that which has interested those equity theorists concerned with the problem of differentiating between actual and psychological equity restoration. There already exist, then, some ideas which may be exploitable.

Probably the most pertinent amongst these is the basic equity theory position on psychological equity restoration via the justification of inequitable advantages in one's favour. Walster, Berscheid and Walster's discussion of this issue (Walster *et al.*, 1973) suggests that justifications are easier to maintain the less they involve a distortion of reality and the more able is the justifier to isolate himself/herself from those who are disadvantaged, or those who sympathize with the disadvantaged. These points are easily and immediately translatable into a social identity purview and, of course, are especially meaningful because groups are often better able than individuals to create their own versions of social reality and to isolate themselves successfully from others. But it does not follow that groups are beyond moving away from their justifications. Who is to say, for example, that the relative improvement in the lot of American Negroes over the past three decades has not been assisted by a conflict of values in whites made acute, on the one hand, by a decreasing ability to argue intrinsic, ingroup-favouring differences in the face of growing evidence to the contrary and, on the other, by America's embarrassing visibility on the issue to all and sundry? Or, to employ another current example, is it not also possible that the position of women in Western society is undergoing change at least partly because earlier notions of male-favouring differences are becoming more difficult to sustain by men, who are also less able to isolate themselves within male-only enclaves and institutions? The anecdotal but nevertheless common observation that the epithet 'male chauvinist pig' conveys an identity which many men consciously act so as to avoid but others seek to cultivate suggests that the latter example is one which is particularly ripe for exploratory research. More generally, of course, the variables of isolability and degree of sustainable distortion are easily introduced into the laboratory for an investigation of their effects on the behaviour of members of illegitimately superior groups.

Equity theory provides at least one other idea which is open to being conceptualized in social identity terms: the notion of adequacy of compensation. The equity theory view is that when the compensation which a 'harm-doer' can offer a 'victim' is inadequate, it is more likely that equity restoration will be by psychological means. Inadequacy here, one imagines, may derive either from limitations in, or constraints upon, the resources available to the harmdoer, or from the enormity of the injustice suffered by the victim (as, say, in the case of the victim of a murder, or where the injustices suffered go back for generations). Translated into social identity terms, the argument becomes: where justice for, and fair treatment of, an illegitimately disadvantaged group is only partly possible, the social identity benefits to be gained by acting in this manner are reduced and members of an illegitimately superior group are more likely to act so as to justify and maintain their superiority.

It would be quite wrong, of course, to restrict our attention to equity theory for hints and suggestions about the kinds of conditions in which members of illegitimately superior groups might be motivated by social identity considerations to act in a just and fair manner (or otherwise) towards members of an outgroup. Some of the more obvious possibilities lying outside of equity theory but well worth investigating include:

(a) The extent to which the differentiation in question is the only or the major means by which a positively-valued social identity might be maintained.

(b) The presence or absence of sub-groupings within the ingroup – for example, abolitionists, feminists, political groups – who continually draw attention to the conflict of values inherent in the status quo.

(c) The presence of some third party – for example, an ombudsman, consumer protection groups, conciliation services, judiciary systems – onto which major responsibility for ensuring justice and legitimacy can be unloaded.

(d) The extent to which other forms of recognized 'justice' can be invoked to maintain or undermine the status quo (e.g. first come, first served; the rewarding of merit; the rewarding of past sacrifice; just reward for risk undertaken; etc.).

Directly or indirectly, most of these suggestions and, of course, equity theory itself as used in this context, draw attention to the centrality of value conflict within the process of maintained or escalated intergroup differentiation or mutually acceptable adjustment. Value conflict is, par excellence, a social psychological topic and one whose contribution to social conflict and to social co-existence undoubtedly needs more study. So far, research and experimentation carried out in connection with Tajfel's theory have, if anything, emphasized the former and ignored the latter – a not very surprising state of affairs given that the theory, as it stands, takes no formal accounting of the issues that have concerned us in the final part of this paper. It is, however, the single area in which the theory – with amendments such as those we have discussed – might make a pro-active contribution, as it were, to the management or resolution of conflict in some settings. Otherwise, what is left is the somewhat fanciful (or, more kindly, premature) idea, common to science fiction writers and some social philosophers, that a single, one-world-united identity remains our only hope for just and mutually acceptable co-existence. Signs that this will eventuate are not particularly auspicious.

Note

[1] It needs to be emphasized again here that we are discussing that part of Tajfel's theory in which movement between groups is not possible. In other words, we are ignoring, as irrelevant to our present concern, his comments about revolutionaries and renegades who, out of a conflict of values relating to their group's superiority, leave that group.

References

Adams, J.S. 1965. Inequity in social exchange. In L. Berkowitz (ed.): *Advances in experimental social psychology*, Vol. 2. New York: Academic Press, 267–9.

Adams, J.S. and Freedman, S. 1976. Equity theory revisited. In L. Berkowitz and E. Walster (eds.): *Advances in experimental social psychology*, Vol. 9. New York: Academic Press, 43–90.

Billig, M. 1976. *Social psychology and intergroup relations*. European Monographs in Social Psychology, No. 9. London: Academic Press.

Billig, M. and Tajfel, H. 1973. Social categorization and similarity in intergroup behaviour. *European Journal of Social Psychology*, **3**, 27–52.

Bracey, J.H. Jr., Meier, A. and Rudwick, E. (eds) 1970. *Black nationalism in America*. Indianapolis: Bobbs-Merrill.

Caddick, B.F.J. 1978. Status, legitimacy and the social identity concept in intergroup relations. Unpublished Ph.D. dissertation, University of Bristol.

Deutsch, M. 1973. *The resolution of conflict: Constructive and destructive processes*. New Haven: Yale University Press.

Festinger, L. 1957. *A theory of cognitive dissonance*. Palo Alto: Stanford University Press.

Fishel, L.H. Jr. and Quarles, B. 1970. *The Black American: A documentary history*. New York: William Morrow.

Heider, F. 1958. *The psychology of interpersonal relations*. New York: Wiley.

LeVine, R.A. and Campbell, D.T. 1972. *Ethnocentrism: Theories of conflict, ethnic attitudes and group behaviour*. New York: Wiley.

Lerner, M.J. 1975. The justice motive in social behaviour. *Journal of Social Issues*, **31**, (3), 1–19.

Lerner, M.J. 1977. The justice motive: Some hypotheses as to its origins and forms. *Journal of Personality*, **45**, 1–52.

Rokeach, M. 1960. *The open and closed mind: Investigations into the nature of belief systems and personality systems*. New York: Basic Books.

Tajfel, H. 1974. Intergroup behaviour, social comparison and social change.

Katz-Newcomb Lectures, University of Michigan, Ann Arbor.

Tajfel, H. 1975. The exit of social mobility and the voice of social change: Notes on the social psychology of intergroup relations. *Social Science Information*, **14**, (2), 101–18.

Tajfel, H. (ed.) 1978. *Differentiation between social groups: Studies in the social psychology of intergroup relations.* European Monographs in Social Psychology, No. 14. London: Academic Press.

Tajfel, H., Flament, C., Billig, M. and Bundy, R.P. 1971. Social categorization and intergroup behaviour. *European Journal of Social Psychology*, **1**, 149–177.

Tajfel, H. and Turner, J.C. 1979. An integrative theory of intergroup conflict. In W.G. Austin and S. Worchel (eds): *The social psychology of intergroup relations.* Monterey: Brooks-Cole.

Turner, J.C. 1975. Social comparison and social identity: Some prospects for intergroup behaviour. *European Journal of Social Psychology*, **5**, 5–34.

Turner, J.C. and Brown, R.J. 1978. Social status, cognitive alternatives and intergroup relations. In H. Tajfel (ed.), *op. cit.*

Walster, E., Berscheid, E. and Walster, G.W. 1973. New directions in equity research. *Journal of Personality and Social Psychology*, **25**, 151–176.

Weick, K.E. 1976. Quoted in Homans, G.C. Commentary. In L. Berkowitz and E. Walster (eds.): *Advances in experimental social psychology*, Vol. 9. New York: Academic Press, p237.

6. The battle for acceptance: An investigation into the dynamics of intergroup behaviour[1]

RUPERT J. BROWN AND GORDON F. ROSS

1. Introduction

A cursory examination of the intergroup relations literature since 1950 reveals a curious fact: apart from the pioneering work of the Sherifs and their colleagues (e.g. Sherif and Sherif, 1953; Sherif, Harvey, White, Hood, and Sherif, 1961), very little research has studied the temporal and dynamic aspects of intergroup situations. And if one confines one's search to experimental investigations this omission becomes particularly noticeable, the main exceptions coming from the area of bargaining where, since Douglas (1962), there has been a sustained interest in how intergroup negotiations proceed over time (e.g. Blake and Mouton, 1961; McGrath, 1966; Morley and Stephenson, 1977). This work aside, experimental studies of intergroup relations have typically employed simple linear designs; the effects of the independent variable, or variables, have been measured at a single moment in time and the reciprocity of intergroup behaviour has been largely ignored. This has had the consequence that we now know a little about the effects of changing the intergroup goal, status, and power relations (see Sherif, 1966; Tajfel, 1978), but still almost nothing about the way competitive or cooperative interactions *develop* over time. We have, in other words, focused on structure at the expense of process. In view of the fact that relationships between social groups outside the laboratory are not transient affairs but have a history, and a future, such an imbalance of emphasis must eventually detract from a proper understanding of the aetiology of social conflict and cohesion.

There have, of course, been sound methodological reasons for this concentration on static features of social situations. For the purposes of testing many hypotheses it has not been necessary to incorporate temporal factors into the design of experiments. Indeed, the prevailing methodological orthodoxy in psychological research holds that the most efficient design is, in fact, the 'post-test only' type where one makes only a *single* assessment of the effects of some treatment (see Campbell and Stanley, 1963).

But the nature of the research has also inevitably reflected the kinds of theories that have informed it, and dominating the study of intergroup relations since the war has been the 'realistic conflict theory' of Sherif (1966). This holds that attitudes and behaviour are mainly determined by the nature of the objective goals linking groups and hence inevitably places much emphasis on the structural features of intergroup situations. Thus, research inspired by this tradition has demonstrated reliable effects due to varying the nature of the interdependence between groups (e.g. Sherif *et al.*, 1961; Blake, Shepard and Mouton, 1964; Rabbie and de Brey, 1971). It has, however, had difficulty in explaining the occurrence of social change in the absence of corresponding changes in structural conditions (see Tajfel and Turner, 1979). A somewhat different approach, that of Gaming Theory, has had a similar preoccupation. Here, the concern has usually been to examine the effects of changing the structure of the 'pay-off matrix' on subsequent competitive behaviour (see, for example, Rapoport and Chammah, 1965).

However, recent theoretical developments promise to shed some light on the changing and dynamic aspects of intergroup relations. Foremost amongst these has been the Bristol Theory of intergroup relations proposed by Tajfel and his associates (Tajfel, 1978; Tajfel and Turner, 1979). The theory consists essentially of four elements: Categorization, Identity, Comparison, and Distinctiveness. Put at its simplest it proposes that these four concepts – 'processes' would be a more accurate word – are linked in the following manner: *Categorization*, by segmenting the world into groups, gives both a necessary order to a person's world *and* a locus of identification. The group(s) to which a person belongs provide a satisfactory *Identity* for that person to the extent that *Comparisons* of it (or them) with other groups are favourable, and result in it obtaining some *Positive Distinctiveness vis à vis* these others. A group therefore aims to differentiate itself from others in order to achieve or maintain superiority on some existing and situationally relevant dimension of comparison.

The fundamentally dynamic nature of the theory is revealed in three main ways. *First*, as Turner (1975) has maintained, the hypothesized need for a satisfactory or positive identity occurs not in the ingroup in isolation, but in a context of *mutual* comparisons and differentiations between groups. Other things being equal, this mutuality is likely to give rise to ever increasing competitiveness since one group cannot be 'better' unless another is 'worse'.

Secondly, the term 'social identity' in the theory is not meant to refer to a fixed and unchanging entity. Social relationships between groups are seldom static affairs and since any changes in status or power relations will have consequences for the outcome of intergroup comparisons, social identity, which is maintained by such comparisons, must perforce change also. And nor is the causal arrow unidirectional; changes in social identity may, in their turn, result in attempts to alter existing intergroup relationships. These changes in identity, whether as consequents or antecedents, are described in the theory by the notion of 'insecurity' (Tajfel, 1978). Insecurity is thought to arise in stratified situations whenever a change in the *status quo* is conceivable, perhaps because of some instability in the positions of the groups or because attributes of status and power in one of the groups are seen as being illegitimately acquired (Turner and Brown, 1978). The consequences of an insecure identity are thought to be a renewed search for positive distinctiveness and this search may take two quite different forms: direct competition on the existing dimensions of comparison or a redefinition or alteration of the elements of the comparative situation. The first is manifested as ingroup favouritism in behaviour and attitudes along the consensually agreed 'relevant' comparative dimensions. The second strategy, called 'social creativity' (Tajfel and Turner, 1979) can itself take two forms. It may involve comparing the ingroup to the outgroup on some *new* dimension, perhaps because the existing dimensions hold little promise of distinctiveness, or it may involve the *reinterpretation* of existing characteristics so that what was once devalued is now seen favourably.

In principle, these two strategies are equally available to both dominant and subordinate groups but, in practice, the first should be more characteristic of high-status groups since it is probably easier for them to defend an existing superiority than it is for a low-status group to reverse it. On the other hand, low-status groups may have more to gain by finding new sorts of comparison and hence will be more likely to use the second strategy. But in either case, the success of these strategies in achieving an adequate social identity involves two stages, described by Tajfel (1978) as follows: 'The first (which is a condition *sine qua non* for the success of the enterprise) is the positive evaluation by the ingroup of its newly created characteristics. The second consists of the acceptance by the outgroup of this evaluation' (Tajfel, 1978, p96).

In this *third* manner, then, the dynamic nature of the theory is once again revealed: the search for positive distinctiveness is not an autistic process but requires for its consummation some recognition from other groups in the social order. Without that recognition – and given the competitive character of many intergroup relationships, such recognition may not be conceded lightly – still more vigorous attempts at differentiation are to be expected. It is this battle for acceptance which provides the main focus for the present experiment.

However, despite these advances at the theoretical level there has been a woeful lack of empirical research to substantiate them. Take for instance Turner's (1975) proposition that 'social' competition should be an upwardly spiralling process as groups continually jockey for superiority. It is true that the early Minimal Categorization experiments (see Brewer, 1979; Turner, 1978 for reviews), which provided one of the points of departure for the Bristol Theory, established that such competition was remarkably easy to elicit and was shown by *both* the *ad hoc* groups concerned. What they did not illuminate, however, was how that initial competitiveness *develops* as each group learns of the other's behaviour.

Studies of intergroup bargaining, on the other hand, have done a little to elucidate how orientations change over time (see Stephenson, 1981 for a review) and some curious paradoxes have emerged. For instance, in the tradition established by Blake and Mouton much emphasis is placed on the avoidance of intergroup differentiation for the resolution of conflict (Blake, Shepard and Mouton, 1964). Typically, competitive negotiations, where differentiation is high, lead to completely deadlocked outcomes (Blake and Mouton, 1961). In contrast, Stephenson (1981), following Douglas (1962), has argued that an initial period of differentiation is *more* likely to lead to conflict resolution than its absence, on the grounds that only with such a competitive phase will the issues separating the sides be clearly understood by both parties. However, more research is needed to document this latter suggestion convincingly; at present the evidence is mostly correlational (e.g. Stephenson, Kniveton, and Morley, 1977) and it is not clear whether this initial 'conflict' phase is necessary, or even merely sufficient, to bring about negotiation settlements (see Tysoe, 1979). But, in any case, the implications of this work for other intergroup contexts may be limited, since it has largely assumed not only that the groups in question have already entered into a negotiation relationship, but also that a resolution of their differences within the existing institutional framework is both inevitable and desirable. Important questions about how groups come to be bargaining in the first place – itself a cooperative activity

– or about when groups will attempt to change the whole nature of the negotiation framework itself, thus remain unanswered (see chapter 15 for another discussion of this issue).

There is also, of course, a large volume of research using the gaming paradigm which has examined the effects of the 'other player's' strategy on a person's competitive behaviour (see Oskamp, 1971; Deutsch, 1973). However, as several studies have now established, the applicability of this study of dyadic interaction to intergroup situations is questionable (e.g. Wilson, Chun, and Kayatani, 1965; Rabbie and Visser, 1976). The latter research is of some interest here since it charted behaviour of individuals, dyads and triads over a number of trials in a Prisoner's Dilemma situation. However, the results were rather difficult to interpret: the size of the group and the period of the game interacted in a complex fashion to produce clear differences at some phases but not at others and it is possible that their findings may be specific to the particular paradigm used. A further difficulty lies in the interpretation of the different choices in the Prisoner's Dilemma paradigm. This is not a simple matter and thus the nature of the intergroup interaction is not always easy to ascertain. In another experiment, Sopacua and Visser (1976) studied the effects of allowing informational feedback about the other group's choices in a Minimal Categorization situation (Tajfel, Flament, Billig, and Bundy, 1971), where the meaning of a strategic option is much clearer. Consistent with the spiralling 'social competition' effects predicted by Turner (1975), there was evidence of groups showing progressively less fairness and more absolute favouritism as they became more knowledgeable about the other group's decisions. But no attempt was made to control the other group's strategy in this study and so inevitably this interpretation lacks rigour.

However, the results from another experiment employing the same paradigm were less ambiguous (Griffin, 1977). Here, information about the presumed discriminatory behaviour of 'typical' ingroup and outgroup members *was* systematically varied and fed back to the subjects in a second phase of the experiment. Their subsequent behaviour provided support for the 'social competition' notion since a significant increase in discrimination was observed in the condition in which the ingroup and outgroup models were both presumed to have shown ingroup favouritism in their previous choices.

The investigation of the dynamics of the hypothesized social identity processes has also been neglected. Experiments by Caddick (1978) and Turner and Brown (1978) (see chapter 5) have established the importance of perceived illegitimacy and instability in mediating the intergroup attitudes of different status groups, but in these studies the concepts were operationalized as ahistorical independent variables, largely by the use of instructions. It was not possible, and nor was it necessary for the purposes of the experiments, to examine, for example, how perceptions of illegitimacy might arise naturally in different social conditions and thence give rise to the use of different strategies for attaining distinctiveness. Two field studies have partially rectified this omission. In the first, conducted in New Zealand, Vaughan (1978) traced changes in ethnic identification in Pakeha and Maori children over a ten year period. The results from the subordinate Maori group were particularly interesting since they showed a clear positive correlation between ingroup identification and societal change (as indexed by increased urbanization). Vaughan convincingly argued that these social changes were instrumental in creating some status instability between the Pakeha and Maori groups whose effects were, as predicted by the Bristol Theory, to increase group identification in the subordinate group. Likewise, in an earlier study by one of us (Brown, 1978) it was possible to relate historical changes in the status relations between three groups of engineering workers to their present-day social identities and intergroup attitudes. On the dimension of wages, for instance, government economic policies had ensured that the groups had constantly interchanged positions over a five year period prior to the study. This instability had the result that two out of the three groups showed marked ingroup favouritism in the assignment of 'appropriate' wage levels to each group, even to the extent of sacrificing absolute gains for the ingroup. Even in the third group, where such favouritism was largely absent – as was also, significantly, any perception of illegitimacy about the *status quo* – there was evidence of 'social creativity' as the members asserted their superiority on new, and hitherto unconsidered, dimensions of comparison.

But such naturalistic accounts of changing social identity are necessarily somewhat interpretative and there is a clear need for the greater precision afforded by the experimental method. This, then, provided the principal rationale for the present study whose purpose was, among other things, to examine the change in superior and inferior group identities over the course of a controlled period of intergroup interaction. More specifically, it was concerned with the effects on group morale and attitudes as the ingroup's attempts to achieve or preserve positive distinctiveness were conceded, partly conceded, or thwarted by the outgroup.

In the experiment to be reported these concessions (or lack of them) were operationalized by having the ingroup receive evaluations of itself (from an outgroup) which differed in the degree to which the ingroup's identity was threatened. In one communication (Low Threat), the ingroup's claim to be *generally* better or as good as the other group was agreed to by the outgroup despite an existing, experimenter imposed, and slightly unfair status difference between the groups on just a *single* attribute. In another (Moderate Threat), the illegitimate status difference on this principal dimension was reinforced but parity between the groups on *alternative* dimensions was claimed or acknowledged. And in a third (High Threat), the ingroup's claims for distinctiveness along any dimension at all were generally rejected by the outgroup. The significance of these different communications from the point of view of the Bristol Theory should be clear from our earlier remarks on the importance of social recognition: to the extent that other groups fail to recognize the ingroup's claim to be different, then increased intergroup differentiation and outgroup rejection is predicted. Thus the principal hypothesis (Hypothesis 1) stated that:

> *Levels of ingroup bias and feelings of antipathy towards the outgroup should increase in proportion to the degree of threat to identity implied by the communication from the outgroup.*

There is already evidence from sociolinguistics to support this idea. Bourhis and Giles (1977) conducted an experiment involving a group of Welsh people for whom learning the Welsh language was an important part of their cultural identity. When these people were confronted by a very English-sounding speaker who challenged their reasons for learning what he deridingly called 'a dying language', they significantly broadened their Welsh accents and, in some cases, switched to Welsh completely. Bourhis' and Giles' plausible interpretation for this phenomenon was that the subjects felt their identity threatened by the outgroup member and consequently 'diverged' from him to make themselves more linguistically distinct. This interpretation was strengthened by the results from a study conducted in Belgium by Bourhis, Giles, Leyens, and Tajfel (1979). Using a similar methodology they found further evidence of language divergence in response to an explicit threat to the ingroup's linguistic integrity.

A second hypothesis concerned the alternative differentiation strategies that might be adopted as a reaction to a threatened identity. One way this may be done is to seek and stress the importance of *new* evaluative dimensions on which distinctiveness may be achieved. As already noted, such 'social creativity' is thought to be much more likely to occur in low-status groups since they have the most to gain by attempting to change the nature of the comparative dimensions. Thus the second hypothesis (Hypothesis 2) stated that:

Greater importance would be attached to alternative comparative dimensions amongst inferior groups than amongst superior groups.

As a corollary of both Hypotheses 1 and 2 it was also predicted that increases in differentiation along these alternative dimensions would again vary in proportion to the degree of threat to identity experienced, and that these changes would be most prominent in the lower status groups. It should also be made clear that the strategies implied in these two hypotheses were not thought to be mutually exclusive.

In addition to testing these specific hypotheses, the experiment was designed to investigate, in a more exploratory way, a further theoretical issue. This concerns the relationship between threats to identity and position on Tajfel's (1978) proposed bipolar continuum distinguishing *interpersonal* from *intergroup* modes of action. The former describes encounters in which the interaction is solely or largely determined by relationships between individuals, while the latter refers to situations in which behaviour is wholly or mostly determined by the membership of and relationship between different social categories. It seemed plausible to suppose that one consequence of the High Threat condition would be an increase in the salience of group membership, which would result in subjects shifting towards the 'intergroup' pole of the continuum, especially if they belonged to an inferior group and 'exit' from it was impossible (see Tajfel, 1975, 1978). According to Tajfel (1978) such a shift would be indicated by more stereotyped intergroup attitudes (i.e. perception of intragroup homogeneity), and a decreased desire to leave the group. It is also possible to predict that the degree of attachment to the group would be positively correlated with the level of positive intergroup differentiation since, theoretically, a decreased wish to abandon one's group implies a greater need to attain positivity via that group – i.e. through intergroup comparisons. Indeed, there is already some evidence to support this contention (Ross and Brown, 1977).

2. Method

Subjects (Ss)

95 children (47 girls, 48 boys) aged approximately 12 years attending a Bristol comprehensive school.

Procedure

There were three experimental sessions and in each the procedure adopted was identical. The session began with the experimenter (E) describing the aims of the research which was purportedly concerned with the study of 'reasoning ability'. Reference was made to other aspects of intelligence such as 'verbal ability, memory, and creativity' but it was emphasized that E was not interested in these, only in how good the children were at reasoning tasks. In this way E established the principal evaluative dimension, 'reasoning ability'.

Ss were then assigned to two minimal and anonymous groups ('X' and 'Y') by an explicitly random procedure. This anonymity was maintained throughout by the use of code numbers. The apparent rationale for this division was E's interest in trying out two different forms of a reasoning test (each group would receive a different version of the test). The test was to be administered in two parts with a rest interval in between. The nature of the different test forms was then publicly revealed. One, form 'X', was in open-ended format; the other, form 'Y', whilst having the same questions, was presented in a multiple choice format (three alternative answers per question being provided). No explicit reference was made to the latter being easier, but it was assumed that it would be seen to be so. The purpose of putting the 'X' group at a slight disadvantage in this was to introduce an element of illegitimacy when the results of the test were announced, and hence enhance the pressures to seek distinctiveness. To heighten the comparative aspect of the situation the pretest instructions concluded with the following words:

Because the questions are the same in the two forms of the text we will be able to tell from your answers how good each group is at reasoning.

Ss then answered part 1 of the test after which their answer sheets were collected by two assistants (As) for 'marking'. During this interval Ss were kept occupied with a task quite unrelated to the reasoning test.

On As' return the results of the first part of the reasoning test were given privately to each S. This was accomplished by attaching a sheet to the first booklet of dependent measures which read simply:

Your group came TOP/BOTTOM. Therefore at reasoning your group is BETTER/WORSE than the other group.

The appropriate words were deleted for members of groups 'X' (the losing or *Inferior* group) and group 'Y' (the winning or *Superior* group). After answering the thirteen questions which comprised the first set of dependent measures (see below), S was asked finally to 'summarize what you think about the abilities of the two groups' by choosing one of three alternative opinion statements which s/he agreed with most. The statements were worded differently for the two groups but in both cases varied in the degree of competitiveness expressed:

Group 'X' (losing group)

(1) *Competitive* (denial of *status quo* in direction favouring ingroup)
We are just as good as the other group in *all* aspects of intelligence, not just reasoning.

(2) *Moderately competitive* (acceptance of *status quo* but emphasis on dimensions in which ingroup superiority is likely or possible)
The other group may be better than us at reasoning, but at other things like verbal ability, memory, and creativity, which are just as important, we are as good as the other group.

(3) *Non-competitive* (denial of *status quo* in direction favouring outgroup)
The other group is better than us in *all* aspects of intelligence.

Group 'Y' (winning group)

(1) *Competitive*

We are better than the other group in *all* aspects of intelligence, not just reasoning.

(2) *Moderately competitive*

In other less important things like verbal ability, memory, and creativity, the other group may be as good as us, but at reasoning, which is the most important thing, we are better than them.

(3) *Non-competitive*

They are just as good as us at reasoning and other aspects of intelligence.

The purpose of this final question was to provide a plausible way of varying (in the second booklet) what the other group had said about the ingroup, in order to manipulate the Threat variable.

There then followed another brief interval in which the As again retired, this time supposedly to collate what people in each group had said about the other group. Ss meanwhile performed a further 'filler' task. When the As returned for the second time they brought with them a second set of dependent measure booklets to which was attached an information sheet summarizing what the other group had supposedly said about S's own group. This 'feedback' from the other group took one of three forms which were derived directly from the opinion statements at the end of the first booklet, the Inferior group Ss receiving one of the Superior group opinions and vice versa. The feedback given bore no relation to the actual opinions of the outgroup, however; each opinion was allocated equally often and randomly throughout each status group to form the three levels of the independent variable, 'Threat to Identity'. The wording of these communications from the outgroup is illustrated by the following two examples:

To the Superior Group (HIGH THREAT condition):

This is what most people in the other group thought: They think they are just as good as your group in *all* aspects of intelligence, not just reasoning.

To the Inferior Group (HIGH THREAT condition):

This is what most people in the other group thought: They think they are better than your group in *all* aspects of intelligence, not just reasoning.

In a similar way, the communications in the MODERATE and LOW THREAT conditions followed respectively the wording of statements (2) and (3) above.

It will be observed that the manipulation was not exactly equivalent in the two groups. This was because the feedback was conceptualized in terms of 'threat', and once the status difference had created an asymmetry in the situation it did not seem plausible to word the communications identically for both groups. The aim was to make equivalent the *psychological* meaning (in terms of threat to identity), rather than the literal meaning.

Ss, having been asked to read the outgroup's comment carefully, then answered another thirteen questions identical to those already asked in the first booklet. Their responses to this second set of measures could then be examined against the baseline established in the first set, before they had learned of the outgroup's evaluation.

Finally, Ss were asked to make some brief written remark on the comment they had received from the outgroup – to say how fair they thought it was and whether or not they accepted it.[2] Then, instead of proceeding to the second part of the test as expected, the experiment was terminated and Ss participated in a thorough debriefing session in which the aims of the experiment were outlined and the full nature of, and rationale for, the deceptions used were explained.

Dependent measures

All measures were Likert type rating scales using a 10 cm unmarked line, scored from 0–9. They included evaluations of own and other group at reasoning ability and 'other aspects' of intelligence, measures of affective orientation towards own and other group, and measures assessing the importance attached to various intellectual attributes, the perceived homogeneity of each group, and the degree of attachment to the ingroup.

Experimental design

The two independent variables, *Threat* and *Status*, formed a 3 × 2 complete factorial design with independent groups. To facilitate analysis of the data by ANOVA, observations from five randomly selected Ss were discarded to produce a balanced design with $n = 15$. An additional 'within-subjects' factor, *Before/After* feedback, was incorporated into the design to examine *changes* in ratings in response to the outgroup evaluation.

3. Results[3]

(a) Ss' initial perceptions of the situation and subsequent reactions to the outgroup communications

In order to understand properly the impact of the Threat variable it is necessary to appreciate how Ss viewed the intergroup relationship *prior* to receipt of the outgroup evaluation. Later sections will describe the results of various analyses in detail but a preliminary indication was obtained from the summary evaluations of the outgroup that Ss were asked to provide at the end of the first booklet (see 'Method', section 2 above). From the frequency of choice for the three alternatives it was clear that for both Superior and Inferior groups the clear majority of choices were for the *moderately* competitive statement in which E's definition of the situation was largely concurred with, but where there was also some possibility for ingroup enhancement. There were, however, a number of Ss in the Superior group (some 22 %) who diverged from this consensual view and denied that their group was superior (i.e. they opted for statement 3).

It was against this background, then, that the Threat variable, in the shape of different evaluations apparently emanating from the outgroup, was

Table 1. *Content analysis of reactions to outgroup communication*[2]

	Coding category				
	favourable ——————————————————— unfavourable				
	(1)	(2)	(3)	(4)	(5)
High Threat	0	3	4	14	0
Moderate Threat	0	11	5	4	1
Low Threat	4	9	1	1	5

Key:
(1) Disagreement implying favourable orientation towards outgroup.
(2) Complete agreement.
(3) Qualified agreement.
(4) Complete rejection implying unfavourable orientation towards outgroup.
(5) Meaning ambiguous.
(Cell frequencies arrived at by consensus of three judges' independent codings.)

manipulated. To assess the effectiveness of this manipulation Ss' unstructured comments at the end of the second booklet of measures were content analysed. Three judges coded each comment for the extent to which it expressed agreement with the outgroup's evaluation or, if it disagreed, the nature of the disagreement in terms of implied favourable or unfavourable orientation towards the outgroup. Five coding categories were employed and the mean interjudge agreement was better than 80 %. Table 1 gives the frequencies with which the comments were assigned to these categories, broken down by level of Threat.

It is clear that the Threat manipulation set off the expected reaction. The comments are largely unfavourable in the *High* condition, become more favourable in the *Moderate* condition, and are almost completely favourable in the *Low* condition. Collapsing (1) and (2) (the two unambiguously favourable categories), and ignoring (5), produces a highly significant χ^2 statistic ($\chi^2 = 22.5$, df $= 4$, $p < 0.001$). To illustrate the coding system, as well as to give a flavour of the kind of remarks made by Ss, some typical comments are given verbatim below:

High Threat

I think they are disgusting. They are wrong – our group are ace kings (Superior group comment, coded (4)).

I think they are big headed and it is false (Inferior group comment, coded (4)).

Moderate Threat

I accept the statement but I think we should of [*sic*] had more time (Inferior group comment, coded (3)).

Low Threat

    I think that they were just being modest but I think most of it's true except when they said we were as good as them at reasoning (Inferior group comment, coded (1)).

    I think they were right in each way (Superior group comment, coded (2)).

Already it can be seen from some of these comments how quickly and strongly the children developed loyalties to, and identification with, what were quite trivial and anonymous groups.

(b) Effects of threat on intergroup attitudes

(i) Ingroup bias in evaluations on existing dimension   Table 2 records the mean ingroup bias in evaluations of reasoning ability in the six experimental conditions. The most striking feature of the data was the large difference between the two status groups in the level of bias displayed (overall means: $\bar{X}_{\mathrm{Sup}} = +4.6$, $\bar{X}_{\mathrm{Inf}} = -1.1$), an effect accounting for over a third of the variance. In itself, however, this difference is unsurprising since Ss, when confronted with a seemingly 'objective' status difference, should be expected to reflect this in their evaluations. What is more interesting is that the evaluations were not consensual; that is, the level of *out*group bias in the subordinate groups nowhere near matched the high level of ingroup bias shown by the Superior groups. This suggests that the status relations were, as intended, seen as somewhat illegitimate. The effects of providing Ss with an outgroup evaluation of their ingroup can be seen in the two significant interactions observed in the 'within-subjects' stratum. Overall, there was an increase in the amount of bias shown after receipt of the feedback ($\bar{X}_{\mathrm{Before}} = +1.1$, $\bar{X}_{\mathrm{After}} = +2.3$), but essentially this increase occurred only in the lower status groups. The effects of the Threat variable were not very noticeable overall, but one interaction did approach significance. Examination of this interaction revealed that the effects of Threat on the Inferior groups were precisely as predicted by Hypothesis 1, but that the Superior groups showed little or no reaction. The interaction is depicted in Figure 1, and from this it can be seen that the increases in bias observed in the Inferior groups were directly proportional to the level of threat. Clearly, though, the data from the Superior groups offered little support for the hypothesis.

(ii) Affective reactions   Hypothesis 1 also predicted that feelings of antipathy towards the outgroup should vary according to the degree of threat

Table 2. *Ingroup bias in reasoning evaluations*

Threat	Status	Before	After	Change
High	Superior	+3.7	+3.5	—0.2, ns
	Inferior	—2.1	+1.8	+3.9, $p < 0.001$
Moderate	Superior	+5.1	+4.3	—0.8, ns
	Inferior	—3.4	—1.2	+2.2, $p < 0.05$
Low	Superior	+4.8	+6.2	+1.4, ns
	Inferior	—1.3	—0.5	+0.8, ns

ANOVA
Status, $F(1, 84) = 70.7$, $p < 0.005$; variance = 34 %.
Before/After, $F(1, 84) = 7.2$, $p < 0.01$; variance = 1 %.
Status × Before/After, $F(1, 84) = 6.0$, $p < 0.025$; variance = 1 %.
Threat × Status × Before/After, $F(2, 84) = 2.7$, $p < 0.1$; variance = 1 %.
$MS_{\text{error between}} = 20.7$.
$MS_{\text{error within}} = 8.8$.

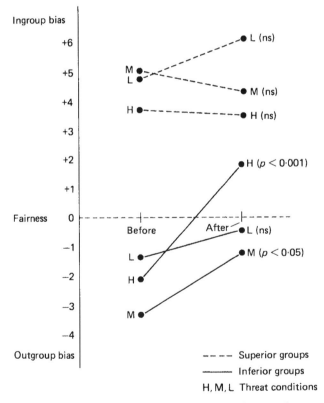

Figure 1. Changes in bias in reasoning evaluations as a function of Status and Threat

Table 3. *Affective reactions toward outgroup*

| (a) Liking for outgroup members | | | | |
Threat	Status	Before	After	Change
High	Superior	5.1	4.6	} − 0.6, ns
	Inferior	5.2	4.4	
Moderate	Superior	4.1	5.0	} + 0.3, ns
	Inferior	5.4	5.1	
Low	Superior	3.7	4.4	} + 1.4, $p < 0.01$
	Inferior	4.8	6.9	

ANOVA
Threat × Before/After $F(2, 84) = 4.8$, $p < 0.025$; variance = 2 %
$MS_{\text{error between}} = 9.3$
$MS_{\text{error within}} = 3.1$.

| (b) Feelings of annoyance towards outgroup | | | | |
Threat	Status	Before	After	Change
High	Superior	0.1	2.3	} + 1.6, $p < 0.01$
	Inferior	2.3	3.2	
Moderate	Superior	0.4	0.9	} + 1.1, $p < 0.05$
	Inferior	2.0	3.7	
Low	Superior	0.9	0.8	} − 0.8, ns
	Inferior	3.5	1.9	

ANOVA
Status $F(1, 84) = 16.3$, $p < 0.005$; variance = 10 %
Before/After $F(1, 84) = 4.5$, $p < 0.05$; variance = 1 %
Threat × Before/After $F(2, 84) = 6.0$, $p < 0.005$; variance = 3 %
$MS_{\text{error between}} = 9.75$
$MS_{\text{error within}} = 4.04$.

experienced. The results from the two relevant measures – liking for out-group members and feelings of annoyance towards them – provided unequivocal support for the hypothesis. On both there was a significant Threat × Before/After interaction and inspection of Tables 3(a) and 3(b) reveal that in each case friendliness towards the outgroup decreased as the level of threat increased, regardless of the status of the group. In the case of annoyance the support is particularly impressive with significant *increases* in annoyance in the *High* and *Moderate* conditions, but a nonsignificant *decrease* in the *Low* Threat condition. On this measure there was also an effect due to the Status variable, with Inferior group Ss expressing considerably more annoyance than their higher status counterparts. Again, this may reflect the illegitimate character of the status difference.

Table 4. *Perceived importance of reasoning and 'other aspects' of intelligence*

		Before		After	
Threat	Status	(e.d.) Reasoning	(a.d.) Other	(e.d.) Reasoning	(a.d.) Other
High	Superior	5.4	6.7	7.1	6.3
	Inferior	7.3	7.1	6.5	6.5
Moderate	Superior	5.9	7.3	6.6	7.3
	Inferior	7.5	6.6	7.3	6.9
Low	Superior	5.8	6.5	5.7	7.3
	Inferior	4.5	5.9	4.8	4.8

ANOVA
Status × Before/After $F(1, 84) = 4.8$, $p < 0.05$; variance $= 0.5\%$
Status × Threat × Before/After × (e.d.)/(a.d.) $F(2, 84) = 5.3$, $p < 0.01$; variance $= 1\%$
$MS_{error\ between} = 19.1$
(i) $MS_{error\ within} = 3.1$ (Before/After stratum)
(ii) $MS_{error\ within} = 6.3$ ((e.d.)/(a.d.) stratum)
(iii) $MS_{error\ within} = 2.2$ ((i) × (ii) stratum)

(c) Social creativity as a response to threat

Contrary to Hypothesis 2, there was no evidence that Inferior group members wanted to attach greater importance to alternative value dimensions (a.d.), either before or after the manipulation of the Threat variable. Indeed, if anything, it was the Superior groups who tended to upgrade the importance of 'other aspects' of intelligence, as Table 4 shows. The major changes in response to the feedback appeared in the *High* and *Low* Threat conditions. In the former, the Superior groups switched from attaching greater importance to a.d. before the feedback, to perceiving the *existing* dimension (e.d.) to be more important *after* it. The Inferior group in this condition, by contrast, seemed to downgrade the importance of both. In the *Low* condition, the major changes were in the perceived importance of a.d. – the Superior group tended to increase and the Inferior group to decrease, the importance of 'other aspects'.

If the importance attached to the other aspects of intelligence by the Inferior groups was no greater than that attached to reasoning ability, the levels of differentiation along these new dimensions suggested that they were far from being irrelevant for them. Table 5 shows the means and reveals that the one significant effect was a general increase from Before to After in the amount of ingroup bias shown. And it should be noticed that the absolute values for the Inferior groups were markedly higher than those shown by them in the reasoning evaluations; all cells except one are

Table 5. *Ingroup bias in evaluations along alternative comparative dimensions*

Threat	Status	Before	After	Change
High	Superior	+3.3	+3.4	+0.1, ns
	Inferior	+0.1	+3.2	+3.1, $p < 0.01$.
Moderate	Superior	+0.3	+2.1	+1.8, $p < 0.1$
	Inferior	−0.1	+1.7	+1.8, $p < 0.1$
Low	Superior	+2.1	+2.2	+0.1, ns
	Inferior	+0.3	+1.4	+1.1, ns

ANOVA
Before/After $F(1, 84) = 9.4$, $p < 0.005$; variance = 3 %
$MS_{error\ between} = 15.2$
$MS_{error\ within} = 8.6$

displaying positive differentiation, and after the feedback the levels are virtually indistinguishable from those of the Superior groups. Lastly, although there were no significant effects due to the Threat variable, the increases in bias in these Inferior groups were again proportional to the degree of threat experienced.

(d) Social identity and the Interpersonal – Intergroup continuum

It had been predicted that threats to the Inferior group's distinctiveness would result in a shift towards a more group-like social orientation. On a combined measure of perceived intragroup homogeneity in both groups, designed to assess the stereotypy of Ss' attitudes, there was only limited support for this idea. Those in the High Threat condition did show a slight increase in the degree to which the groups were seen as internally homo-geneous in their level of reasoning ability, but ANOVA revealed that these changes were not statistically significant. In fact, no significant effects at all were observed on this measure. On the other hand, the measure of group attachment gave clear support for the prediction. The means are given in Table 6 from which it can be seen immediately that the Inferior group members show, not surprisingly, a greater readiness to move into the Superior group than vice versa. However, more pertinent are the Before/After effects. There was, first of all, a general decrease in the desire to leave the group between phase 1 and phase 2, but this decline was significantly moderated by the Threat and Status variables. From the changes scores it is clear that the Inferior group Ss in the High Threat condition reacted to the outgroup communication with an *increased* iden-tification with the group (the desire to leave the group declined signif-

Table 6. *Desire for mobility into other group*

Threat	Status	Before	After	Change
High	Superior	0.6	0.7	+0.1, ns
	Inferior	3.9	2.9	−1.0, $p < 0.02$
Moderate	Superior	1.1	1.7	+0.6, ns
	Inferior	3.0	2.4	−0.6, ns
Low	Superior	1.9	1.0	−0.9, $p < 0.05$
	Inferior	4.2	2.6	−1.6, $p < 0.001$

ANOVA
Status, $F(1, 84) = 15.3$, $p < 0.005$; variance = 13 %.
Before/After, $F(1, 84) = 11.3$, $p < 0.005$; variance = 1 %.
Threat × Before/After, $F(2, 84) = 4.2$, $p < 0.025$; variance = 1 %.
Status × Before/After, $F(1, 84) = 8.1$, $p < 0.01$; variance = 1 %.
$MS_{error\ between} = 12.0$
$MS_{error\ within} = 1.3$

Table 7. *Perceived unfairness of the test*

Threat	Status	Before	After	Change
High	Superior	3.7	2.5	−1.2, $p < 0.05$
	Inferior	1.7	3.3	+1.6, $p < 0.01$
Moderate	Superior	2.9	3.5	+0.7, ns
	Inferior	0.9	1.2	+0.3, ns
Low	Superior	2.7	2.2	−0.5, ns
	Inferior	3.8	2.9	−0.9, ns

ANOVA
Threat × Status × Before/After, $F(2, 84) = 5.75$, $p < 0.005$; variance = 1 %.
$MS_{error\ between} = 19.1$
$MS_{error\ within} = 2.2$

icantly). Also, and interestingly, significant decreases in the wish for mobility were observed in the Low Threat condition for both Status groups, although the Inferior group members showed the sharpest decline.

Associated with these changes were alterations in the levels of perceived illegitimacy which again, in the case of Inferior groups, were directly related to the Threat variable, as can be seen in Table 7. The means from the High Threat condition were particularly interesting: Inferior group Ss, as expected, show a sharp increase in their feelings of injustice; but the Superior group's reaction was quite the reverse – their response to the threat posed by the Inferior group was to claim that the reasoning test was actually *fairer* than they had previously stated it to be. Finally, the relationship between ingroup attachment and intergroup differentiation was examined by factor analysis of all measures. Eight factors emerged all of which, with two important exceptions, proved to be orthogonal to one another even with rotation for oblique factors. The exceptions were factors clearly identifiable as 'Desire for Mobility' and 'Ingroup Bias' which were, as predicted, substantially and *negatively* correlated with each other ($r = -0.41$).

4. Discussion

Theoretically, the starting point for this experiment was the assumption that people prefer to have some means of defining themselves positively through their membership of social groups. From this premise, as we saw in the Introduction, a number of predictions can be made concerning the effects of depriving or providing group members with such means to a positive social identity. How far were these predictions borne out by our results?

Hypothesis 1 received substantial support. Both from their unstructured comments at the end of the experiment and their responses to the affective measures, it was clear that both the Superior and Inferior groups in the High Threat condition reacted sharply and negatively to the apparent attempt by the outgroup to prevent them gaining positive distinctiveness. For the Superior group the threat was constituted by the message from the outgroup which denied them recognition of superiority on existing, or any other, dimensions. For the Inferior group members, on the other hand, the threat merely came from denying them parity on the other untested dimensions where, given the social pressures to accept the experimenter's definition of the situation, their main hope for distinctiveness lay. As predicted, the moderately threatening messages, where at least some possibility for ingroup enhancement was recognized, produced a weaker negative reaction, while the Low Threat condition actually resulted in an improvement in the affective relations between the groups.

At the evaluative level this same pattern emerged, but only from members of Inferior groups. On both existing and new dimensions their increases in ingroup bias varied directly with the levels of threat. The results from the High Threat condition were particularly interesting; from showing significant ingroup *derogation* before receiving the outgroup communication, these subjects' image of themselves changed to one of *positive* regard in relation to the other group. Thus we seem to have discovered further conditions in which a low status group will positively differentiate itself from a dominant group. Previous work (e.g. Caddick,

1978; Turner and Brown, 1978) had shown the importance of variables like perceived illegitimacy and instability in achieving this, but was not able to demonstrate how or when these perceptions would arise. Here, perhaps, is one answer – when an 'inferior' group's attempts to attain distinctiveness on new value dimensions are rejected by the 'superior' group.

It should also be noted that the results from the affective measures and, less strongly, those from the evaluative scales give clear support to the distinction between 'realistic' and 'social' competition proposed by Turner (1975). Between the two phases of the study the objective goal relations between the groups were constant. Hence, according to Sherif's (1966) 'Realistic Conflict' model, so also should the intergroup attitudes have remained unaltered. Yet there was clear evidence that the 'Threat to Identity' variable elicited changes in the intergroup representations consistent with the 'social' competition effects predicted by the Bristol Theory. And it is worth just remarking that these changes occurred in what was essentially a 'Minimal Categorization' situation (see Tajfel et al., 1971; Turner, 1978) – i.e. complete absence of inter- and intragroup face-to-face interaction – and thus further illustrate the highly cognitive nature of the group identification process and its importance for intergroup relations (see chapter 1). This may be contrasted with Sherif's (1966) view that the existence of a group presupposes some degree of intragroup interaction and organization.

There remains, however, the problem of why the differentiation of the Superior groups proved so resistant to the Threat manipulation. It seems likely that a contributing factor may have been the presence of the sizeable minority within these groups who did not accept the experimenter's initial definition of the situation and were prepared to deny that the groups differed in reasoning ability. For these subjects, all but one of whom happened to be assigned to the High and Moderate conditions, the Threat manipulation, which assumed a consensual status difference, may have been inappropriate. Another possibility is that the Superior groups as a whole may have felt sufficiently secure not to feel troubled by the other group's view of them. However, these interpretations cannot be the whole story since, on the affective measures, the Threat variable clearly *was* effective for them, and, also, analyses excluding the deviant minority did not change the overall picture very markedly.

The second hypothesis received little support from the data. Contrary to prediction, it was the Superior groups who attached more importance to the alternative dimensions than to the existing one (except in the High Threat condition), and the Inferior groups who seemed hardly to differentiate between the dimensions. One reason for the latter result could be that the alternative dimensions may have been seen as being correlated with the existing one, and hence offered little scope for differentiation. Nevertheless, the unexpected finding of greater 'creativity' in the Superior groups is somewhat problematic for the Bristol Theory. Although the use of such a strategy by high-status groups has been documented before (Turner and Brown, 1978) and is certainly not excluded by the theory, the emphasis has always been on the greater likelihood of observing such novel differentiation strategies among *subordinate* groups (see Lemaine, 1974; Tajfel, 1978). The difficulty raised by our data is that they suggest an inability to predict which strategies are most probable in any particular situation. Without this predictive power the theory is reduced to making *ad hoc* interpretations of each set of anomalous findings and its explanatory value is correspondingly lessened.

Consistent with Tajfel's (1978) proposed bipolar continuum, the results of the factor analysis showed a clear negative correlation between the 'individualist' factor identified as 'social mobility' and the 'collectivist' factor of positive intergroup differentiation. Less convincing, however, were the results from the perceived homogeneity measure which proved unrelated to either of these factors and relatively insensitive to the experimental manipulations. Even in the High Threat situation, where group membership should have been quite salient, there were only non-significant increases in perceived intragroup similarity. But this null result should be set against other experiments which have used more direct and sensitive measures of similarity. Both Philo (1979) and Doise, Deschamps, and Meyer (1978), using variance measures derived from several intragroup ratings, *have* been able to demonstrate that increased group salience results in more stereotyped perceptions.

In conclusion, it is clear from this exploratory study that, as we had surmised, the dynamics of intergroup relations play an important part in their subsequent determination. Merely learning what another group thinks of your own group can, as we have shown, have important consequences for the way the two groups are later viewed. But this experiment is only the beginning. For pragmatic reasons we chose to limit ourselves to one-way communication between the groups and prevented any possibility at all of intragroup interaction. Such constraints inevitably inhibited the operation of important processes such as the development of an intergroup dialogue, and the formation and change of ingroup ideology in the face of more or less intractable outgroups. The study of these dynamics is an obvious direction in which the research begun here might continue.

Notes

[1] This experiment was conducted as part of an SSRC research programme, 'Social Categorization, Social Identity, and Intergroup Behaviour' directed by Henri Tajfel at the University of Bristol.

[2] Due to an administrative oversight these comments were collected in only two of the three sessions.

[3] All significance levels are for two tailed tests, unless stated otherwise. The significance of Before/After changes was assessed via t-tests for simple effects.

[4] The authors are grateful to Maryon Tysoe and Jennifer Williams for their comments on an earlier version of this chapter.

References

Blake, R.R. and Mouton, J.S. 1961. Loyalty of representatives to ingroup positions during intergroup competition. *Sociometry*, **24**, 177–83.

Blake, R.R., Shepard, H.A. and Mouton, J.S. 1964. *Managing intergroup conflict in industry*. Texas: Gulf Publishing Co.

Bourhis, R.Y. and Giles, H. 1977. The language of intergroup distinctiveness. In H. Giles (ed.): *Language, ethnicity and intergroup relations*. European Monographs in Social Psychology, No. 13. London: Academic Press.

Bourhis, R.Y., Giles, H., Leyens, J.-P. and Tajfel, H. 1979. Psycholinguistic distinctiveness: Language divergence in Belgium. In H. Giles and R.N. St Clair (eds). *Language and social psychology*. Oxford: Blackwell.

Brewer, M.B. 1979. Ingroup bias in the minimal intergroup situation: A cognitive–motivational analysis. *Psychological Bulletin*, **86**, (2), 307–24.

Brown, R.J. 1978. Divided we fall: An analysis of relations between sections of a factory workforce. In H. Tajfel (ed.), *op. cit.*

Caddick, B. 1978. Status, legitimacy and the social identity concept in intergroup relations. Unpublished Ph.D. thesis, University of Bristol.

Campbell, D.T. and Stanley, J.C. 1963. Experimental and quasi-experimental designs for research on teaching. In N.C. Gage (ed.): *Handbook of research on teaching*. Chicago: Rand McNally.

Deutsch, M. 1973. *The resolution of conflict*. New Haven: Yale University Press.

Doise, W., Deschamps, J.C. and Meyer, G. 1978. The accentuation of intra-category similarities. In H. Tajfel (ed.), *op. cit.*

Douglas, A. 1962. *Industrial peacemaking*. New York: Columbia University Press.

Griffin, C. 1977. The effects of informational feedback on intergroup discrimination. Paper presented to BPS Conference, Durham, 1977.

Lemaine, G. 1974. Social differentiation and social originality. *European Journal of Social Psychology*, **4**, 17–52.

McGrath, J.E. 1966. A social psychological approach to the study of negotiations. In R. Bowers (ed.): *Studies on behaviour in organizations: A research symposium*. Allens, Georgia: University of Georgia Press.

Morley, I.E. and Stephenson, G.M. 1977. *The social psychology of bargaining*. London: Allen & Unwin.

Oskamp, S. 1971. Effects of programmed strategies on cooperation in the Prisoner's Dilemma and other mixed-motive games. *Journal of Conflict Resolution*, **15**, 225–59.

Philo, N. 1979. Social categorization and the accentuation of intragroup similarities. Unpublished Ph.D. thesis, University of Bristol.

Rabbie, J.M. and de Brey, J.H.C. 1971. The anticipation of intergroup cooperation and competition under private and public conditions. *International Journal of Group Tensions*, **1**, 230–51.

Rabbie, J.M. and Visser, L. 1976. Competitive and defensive orientations in interpersonal and intergroup conflict. Paper presented to the XXI International Congress of Psychology, Paris, 1976.

Rapoport, A. and Chammah, A.M. 1965. *Prisoner's Dilemma: A study in conflict and cooperation.* Ann Arbor: University of Michigan Press.

Ross, G.F. and Brown, R.J. 1977. Mobility experiment: Preliminary report. Unpublished MS, University of Bristol.

Sherif, M. 1966. *Group conflict and cooperation: Their social psychology* London: Routledge & Kegan Paul.

Sherif, M., Harvey, O.J., White, B.J., Hood, W.R. and Sherif, C.W. 1961. *Intergroup conflict and cooperation. The Robber's Cave experiment.* University of Oklahoma Press.

Sherif, M. and Sherif, C.W. 1953. *Groups in harmony and tension: An integration of studies on intergroup relations.* New York: Octagon Books.

Sopacua, M. and Visser, L. 1976. Uncertainty in interpersonal and intergroup relations. Unpublished MS, University of Utrecht.

Stephenson, G.M. 1981. Intergroup bargaining and negotiation. In J.C. Turner and H. Giles (eds): *Intergroup behaviour.* Oxford: Blackwell.

Stephenson, G.M., Kniveton, B.H. and Morley, I.E. 1977. Interaction analysis of an industrial wage negotiation. *Journal of Occupational Psychology*, **50**, 231–41.

Tajfel, H. 1975. The exit of social mobility and the voice of social change: Notes on the social psychology of intergroup relations. *Social Science Information*, **14**, 101–18.

Tajfel, H. (ed.) 1978. *Differentiation between social groups: Studies in the social psychology of intergroup relations.* European Monographs in Social Psychology, No. 14. London: Academic Press.

Tajfel, H., Flament, C., Billig, M.G. and Bundy, R.P. 1971. Social categorization and intergroup behaviour. *European Journal of Social Psychology*, **1**, 149–78.

Tajfel, H. and Turner, J.C. 1979. An integrative theory of intergroup conflict. In W.G. Austin and S. Worchel (eds): *The social psychology of intergroup relations.* Monterey, Calif.: Brooks/Cole.

Turner, J.C. 1975. Social comparison and social identity: Some prospects for intergroup behaviour. *European Journal of Social Psychology*, **5**, 5–34.

Turner, J.C. 1978. Social categorization and social discrimination in the minimal group paradigm. In H. Tajfel (ed.), *op. cit.*

Turner, J.C. and Brown, R.J. 1978. Social status, cognitive alternatives and intergroup relations. In H. Tajfel (ed.), *op. cit.*

Tysoe, M. 1979. An experimental investigation of the efficacy of some procedural role requirements in simulated negotiations. Unpublished Ph.D. thesis, University of Nottingham.

Vaughan, G.M. 1978. Social change and intergroup preferences in New Zealand. *European Journal of Social Psychology*, **8**, 297–314.

Wilson, W., Chun, N. and Kayatani, M. 1965. Projection, attraction and strategy choices in intergroup competition. *Journal of Personality and Social Psychology*, **2**, 432–5.

7. Power and intergroup discrimination[1]

SIK HUNG NG

1. The problem

Discrimination can be meaningfully described only in relation to some notion of fairness, usually in the nature of equality. What is not equality is discrimination in fact. When equality and discrimination are viewed in the *abstract*, people are morally, or at least idealistically, more inclined towards equality than discrimination. Once equality and discrimination are connected to the concrete situation, our moral stance begins to sway. One type of concrete situation is the relation between groups. A large number of intergroup experiments carried out since the early 1970s have shown how readily discrimination against the outgroup can be elicited by the simple act of categorizing people into groups (e.g. Tajfel, 1970 and 1978a). While the evidence from these studies clearly shows the direct relationship between the experimental manipulation of social categorization on the one hand, and the occurrence of outgroup discrimination on the other, there are at least two aspects which still remain problematic and unexplored. Both aspects are related to power. They concern firstly the nature of the intergroup power relation within which discrimination or equality occurs; and secondly, the nature of the property over which discrimination or equality occurs, that is, whether the property at issue is a property for power (e.g. a resource which will critically determine the outcome of a competition) or for use (e.g. monetary reward). Together they constitute the problem of the present chapter. In the following pages, an attempt will be made to put forth a preliminary formulation of the problem, to be followed by a report of two experiments which were conducted under the guidance of the formulation.

2. A preliminary formulation of the problem

(a) Intergroup power relations

Instead of asking what causes intergroup discrimination, we ask what makes it possible. The literature on racial discrimination has an instructive bearing on the delineation of these two questions. Theories of frustration and aggression, prejudice, ethnocentrism, and authoritarianism are all addressed to the question of what causes discrimination. By themselves, they are insufficient for the understanding of the occurrence of racial discrimination because they have not provided any answer to the question of what makes discrimination possible. They have excluded from their formulation the basic fact that whatever the psychological antecedent to discrimination may be, there must be at the same time a usable power such that the antecedent can be translated into discrimination. (An analogous rationale underlies Campbell's (1963) discussion of the relation between attitude and behaviour.) This usable power is derived from the power relation between the groups such that one or both groups are placed in a position to discriminate, if they so wish, without fear of reprisal; while the group or groups which are being discriminated against would not engage in disruptive rebellion. The role of the power relation in discrimination has been explicitly recognized by students of race relations (e.g. Myrdal, 1944; Cox, 1948; Blalock, 1967; and Wilson, 1973).

The question of what makes discrimination possible calls for, amongst other things, an analysis of the power relation between the groups in question, as well as the power relation between them and whatever other party may be significantly involved. At the societal level, and where discrimination acquires a coercive flavour, the power element and the justifying ideology which sustain the discrimination are obvious enough. At the experimental level where discrimination occurs as a result of social categorization, the relevance of a power analysis is less obvious but is nevertheless real.

In the traditional social categorization experiments, the induction of social categorization is followed by a procedure which asks all the experimental subjects to divide a property (usually pecuniary points) between members of the ingroup and/or the outgroup. This procedure must necessarily result in a bilateral and equal power relation between the groups since the members of both groups are now given the same power to distribute the property; and the experimenter, while in the background of the scene, would enforce the distributions made by the group members. It is within this particular type of intergroup power relation that the data on discrimination have been generated. Not only the induction of social categorization, but also the creation of this *tacit, bilateral and equal power relation*, are the constant elements throughout the experiments. The power element is inherent in the social categorization paradigm even though it has not been mentioned in the design of the experiment and the interpretation of the data.

This bilateral equal power relation would lead to a kind of Hobbesian state of nature wherein there is a general war of all against all between the groups. As pointed out by Ng (1978), prior to the formation of this power relation (that is, before the experimenter asks the subjects to distribute the property), the two groups are not confronting one another and the relation between them is completely unstratified. Members of both groups are supposed to be equal to one another. The onset of this power relation confronts one group with the other on an equal power footing in a *laissez-faire* situation. This effectively renders the previous state of equality very vulnerable to change, for each member is now in a position to make an outgroup member look inferior by giving the latter less of the property, unless this exploitative use of power is counteracted by a reciprocal act. It would appear that the bilateral equal power relation not only makes discrimination possible, but also makes it necessary for the preservation or achievement of a positive social identity.

Note that the above analysis in terms of the power relation cannot answer the question of what *causes* discrimination, and hence it would not replace the existing analysis which is based on social categorization, social identity, and social comparison (see Tajfel, 1978b). Our aim is to make the implicit power element more explicit, and in doing so, to introduce into the discussion a 'new' and what seems to us to be an important dimension.

Now supposing that the induction of social categorization is followed by the creation of a power relation which is different from the tacit bilateral equal power relation. Two alternative kinds of power relation have been examined in the present experiments. Experiment 1 looked into a *unilateral* direct power relation in which only members of *one* group were in the position to distribute the property. Two variants of the unilateral power relation were set up. In one, the unilateral power was *secure*, i.e. the decisions made by the members of the empowered group were binding on the other, 'subordinate' group. In the *insecure* variant, the decisions were not binding.

The critical difference between a secure and an insecure power lay in the absence or presence of an effective counter-power on the part of the subordinate group. Following Thibaut and Kelley (1959), and Thibaut and Faucheux (1965), a counter-power was implemented by providing the subordinate group with an *exit* into a viable *external alternative* such that the subordinate group was in a position to divorce itself from the 'superordinate' group. It was hypothesized, and later found, in Experiment 1 that outgroup discrimination occurred to a significantly greater extent in the secure than insecure condition. In fact, there was a slight tendency towards *outgroup favouritism* in the insecure condition.

A more complex unilateral power relation was set up and examined in the first stage of Experiment 2. As in Experiment 1, only the members of one group were in a position to distribute the property. What follows was unique to Experiment 2. The distributions proposed by the members of one group (Group A) would then be judged by a select voting Committee who would either pass or veto the members' proposals, on the basis of a majority vote. Membership in the Committee was drawn from Group A and the other group (Group B), and by varying the numerical ratio of the Group A and Group B members in the Committee, Group A would have either more power (Majority condition), equal power (Equal Power condition), or less power (Minority condition) than Group B. The hypothesis was that the extent of outgroup discrimination would be greatest in the Majority condition, less so in the Equal Power condition, and least in the Minority condition. The results were in the predicted direction, but only one significant difference was found, namely, that between the Majority condition on the one hand, and the Equal Power and Minority conditions on the other.

Both Experiments 1 and 2 were in fact more complex than has just been implied. The above highlights only those parts of the experiments which have a direct and immediate bearing on the two kinds of power relations which offer alternatives to the conventional bilateral equal power relation within which intergroup discrimination has been traditionally examined. Experiment 2 will also examine the extent to which discrimination varies according to the nature of the property at issue.

(b) Property for power and property for use

The second aspect of the problem concerns the nature of the property to be distributed to the ingroup and the outgroup. Our focus will be on tangible properties, and we will exclude from our discussion such intangibles as intergroup perception and sociometric preferences.

In line with Westergaard and Resler (1975), a crude but important distinction can be made between a property for use and a property for power. A property for use has only consumption value, whereas a property for power has the value of enabling its owner to realize his will, despite resistance, such as in prevailing over the opponents in a competitive situation. Although the distinction is unambiguous on the conceptual level, it becomes blurred when it is applied to the on-going situation because almost any property can be transformed into a property for power. Air, for instance, is for breathing: once it becomes controllable, it can turn into a property for power. And so can water, money, land, labour, and technology. The ambiguity of the distinction is inherent in the Proteus-like nature of power, which makes it impossible to classify a property permanently into either one of the two categories. An application of this distinction must be circumscribed and used only in relation to the concrete situation. This limitation, however, does not diminish the conceptual importance of the distinction.

In a typical social categorization experiment, the property to be distributed consisted of pecuniary points (in the form of point matrices). The experiment ends as soon as the distribution has been completed, and the monetary worth of the points represents a terminal reward which under the present experimental circumstances would have only consumption value. Hence, the existing social categorization experiments have been confined to the study of intergroup discrimination over a property for use, and have rarely studied the discrimination over a property for power.

It is the primary aim of both Experiments 1 and 2 to generate empirical observations of the discriminatory distribution of a property for power. The general theoretical expectation was that there would be a main social categorization effect leading to outgroup discrimination. From this general pattern, there would be variations in accordance with the specific nature of the intergroup power relation as noted in the preceding section.

Experiment 2 has also examined the discriminatory distribution of a property for use. This makes it possible to compare the two types of discrimination. The comparison was made under the guidance of the following preliminary theoretical expectation which was developed through a consideration of the respective social and psychological consequences of the two properties. A property for power enables its owner to have greater *control* of the competitive situation and to prevail over the opponent, leading to *victory*, and as a result, the capturing of the tangible *prize*. A property for use, by contrast, contains only a value which is analogous to the prize, even though it may also confer on its owner a sense of victory. While the utilities of control, victory, and prize may vary with different cultures, we may assume they are all desirable to people who are enculturated by 'Western' civilization. From this, it may be concluded that a property for power is at least *qualitatively* more attractive than a property for use. That is to say, where their prize values are at par, a property for power excels firstly by virtue of its unique control value, and secondly by reason of its more salient victory value. The two properties examined in Experiment 2 were related to one another in such a way that the prize value of power constituted the totality of the value of the property for use. (This was necessary for the purpose of comparison because if the prize value of a property for use exceeded, or was not comparable to that of a property for power, the properties could not be ranked and no meaningful comparison could be made.) As expected, there was a greater outgroup discrimination over a property for power than over a property for use.

The form in which a property for power was expressed varied from one experiment to another; its defining characteristic, however, remained invariant, and was operationalized as the resource which would critically determine the outcome of a competition. Such an operationalization was derived directly from the general definitions of power given by Hobbes (1651), and Russell (1938), and was in accordance with Weber's (1947) definition of *Macht*. As for the property for use, it took the form of bonus grade points which would enhance the assessment received by the student subjects.

It should be noted that in the present set of experiments, the procedure whereby the experimental subjects divided the properties between the ingroup and the outgroup was different from that normally used in social categorization experiments. The latter employed a multiple set of point matrices to allow the subjects to choose between four types of distribution (maximum intergroup difference in favour of ingroup, maximum ingroup profit, maximum joint profit, and equality. See chapter 8 in this volume). In the present experiments, the subjects divided the properties in an open-ended manner, either equally between the ingroup and the outgroup, or in a way which was discriminatory in varying degrees.

3. Experiment 1

Hypotheses

Discrimination against the outgroup in the distribution of a property for power will be greater when the unilateral power relation is secure than when it is insecure. From this primary hypothesis, a secondary hypothesis can be derived. The degree of security of a unilateral power relation can be enhanced by the availability of a resource which the superordinate group can use to appease the subordinate group. It would follow that outgroup discrimination would become more possible, and hence greater, when appeasement is possible than when appeasement is impossible. The main effect due to the appeasement factor will be more pronounced in the insecure than the secure power relation condition, since it is in the former condition that appeasement will make the most difference.

Method

Subjects and Design

Eighty male pupils aged 10 to 13 from an intermediate school at Dunedin served as subjects. Four boys were tested in one experimental session and were assigned randomly to one of the four experimental conditions. The four conditions were created by a 2 (Secure v Insecure power relation) × 2 (Appeasement v No Appeasement) factorial design, each with 20 subjects.

Procedure

Each experimental session followed the same basic procedure. As soon as the four boys were led into the experimental room (a spare room at the school), they were given a demonstration of a TV soccer game. The game invariably fostered a great deal of enthusiasm amongst them and allowed the experimenter (who had been introduced to them by their teacher) to explain that if they wanted to play TV soccer, they as a team would have to compete successfully with another team from their class in a game of quoits. A demonstration of the quoits game was then given. After explaining the scoring convention (1 point for each quoit thrown on the target), the experimenter let the boys practise with the quoits to ensure they were familiar with the quoits game. The quoits were of two sizes, and the boys soon realized that while it was almost impossible to score points with the small quoits, it was easy to gain points with the large quoits. Under the circumstances, the large quoits would constitute the property for power. The manner in which the large quoits were divided between the ingroup and the outgroup would indicate the extent of outgroup discrimination, as will be explained below.

Each team member would make four throws. The team with the higher total score would be allowed to play TV soccer. To play the quoits game, each member would first divide a set of eight quoits (four large and four small) between another (unspecified) ingroup member and an outgroup member. He could divide the quoits either fairly (two large and two small quoits to each member) or unfairly to favour either the ingroup member (e.g. three large and one small quoits to the ingroup member, and one large and three small quoits to the outgroup member) or the outgroup member (e.g. four large quoits to the outgroup member and four small quoits to the ingroup member). The division would indicate the extent of discrimination over a property for power.

In the *Insecure* power condition, the team members understood that the experimenter would later inform the opposing team of their divisions of the quoits (and in the Appeasement condition, also their divisions of sweet gums – see below) and it would be up to the opposing team to decide whether to play with them or with another team. In the latter event, the subjects' team would be disqualified and would automatically lose the chance to compete at quoits to win a game of TV soccer. In the *Secure* power condition, the team members were told that the opposing team would either accept their divisions of the quoits (and also their divisions of sweet gums in the Appeasement condition) or else would be disqualified, in which case the subjects' team would automatically be allowed to play TV soccer.

Within each of the power conditions, half of the teams (i.e. five teams) were assigned to the Appeasement condition and the other half to the No Appeasement condition. In the *Appeasement* condition, apart from dividing the quoits, each team member would also divide four sweet gums in any combination between the ingroup member and the outgroup member (e.g. four sweets to the ingroup member and none to the other member). The sweets were presented as a personal gift from the experimenter and were unrelated to the quoits game. In the *No Appeasement* condition, no sweets were given to be divided.

The division of the quoits (and sweets in the Appeasement condition) was indicated privately to each subject on a questionnaire which presented the question(s) diagrammatically in such a way as to make the question(s) readily intelligible.

Results

The results were analysed to find out firstly the generality of outgroup discrimination, and then the variation of outgroup discrimination in relation to those factors as stated in the hypotheses. Table 1 gives the means of large quoits and sweets allocated to the ingroup. A mean of 2, it will be recalled, indicates equality; while a larger score would indicate ingroup favouritism (i.e. outgroup discrimination), and conversely, a smaller score would mean outgroup favouritism.

As can be seen in Table 1, outgroup discrimination over the quoits occurred only in the two Secure conditions, while there was a slight outgroup favouritism in the Insecure conditions. For each of the four conditions, the subjects' responses were classified into either outgroup discrimination, equality, or outgroup favouritism. The resulting frequency distributions are summarized in Table 2. The numbers of quoits given to the ingroup and outgroup were compared to assess the significance level of the bias. The Wilcoxon test indicated that the outgroup discrimination in the Secure/Appeasement condition ($T = 0$, $N = 17$, $p < 0.005$) and

Table 1. *Mean number of large quoits and sweets given to the ingroup*

	Secure Power		Insecure Power	
	Appeasement	No Appeasement	Appeasement	No Appeasement
Large quoits	3.10 (0.64)[a]	3.50 (0.69)	1.95 (0.22)	1.90 (0.31)
Sweets	2.45 (0.60)	—	1.45 (0.89)	—

[a] Standard deviation

Table 2. *Number of subjects showing outgroup discrimination, equality, or outgroup favouritism in their allocations of quoits and sweet gums*

	Secure Power			Insecure Power		
	Appeasement		No Appeasement	Appeasement		No Appeasement
	LQ	S	LQ	LQ	S	LQ
Outgroup discrimination	17	8	18	0	2	0
Equality	3	12	2	19	8	18
Outgroup favouritism	0	0	0	1	10	2

Note: LQ = Large quoit; S = Sweet gum. No allocation of sweet gums was made in the No Appeasement conditions.

the Secure/No Appeasement condition ($T = 0$, $N = 18$, $p < 0.005$) were both highly significant. It is obvious that the outgroup favouritism in the two Insecure conditions was too minute to be significant.

A 2 (Secure v Insecure) × 2 (Appeasement v No Appeasement) ANOVA was carried out to assess the effects of the independent variables on the variation in the amounts of large quoits given to the ingroup. There was one significant main effect due to the Secure/Insecure factor in the hypothesized direction ($F = 146.99$, df $= 1, 76$, $p < 0.001$) and an interaction effect ($F = 3.94$, df $= 1, 76$, $p = 0.05$). The latter reflects the uneven operation of the appeasement factor which became effective only in the *Secure* condition and led to significantly *less* outgroup discrimination when appeasement was possible ($F = 6.15$, df $= 1, 76$, $p < 0.05$). Thus while the primary hypothesis was confirmed, the secondary hypothesis was totally contradicted.

The sweet gums were intended as a means of appeasement. There was no *a priori* theoretical expectation as to how the sweets would be divided. The following analyses were carried out on a *post hoc* basis in order to provide a full perspective for the discussion of the results. As can be seen in Table 2, not a single subject in the Secure condition gave more than half of the sweets to the outgroup, while as many as 10 subjects did so in the Insecure condition. When the group means are considered (Table 1), it can be seen that there was an overall tendency of outgroup *discrimination* in the Secure condition whereas there was an overall tendency of outgroup *favouritism* in the Insecure condition. t-tests (for correlated pairs)[2] showed that both tendencies were significant ($t = 3.33$, df $= 19$, $p < 0.01$; $t = 2.77$, df $= 19$, $p < 0.05$, respectively). A t-test (between uncorrelated means) showed that significantly fewer sweets were given to the outgroup in the Secure than Insecure condition ($t = 4.17$, df $= 38$, $p < 0.005$).

An inspection of Table 1 also shows a consistently greater outgroup discrimination in the allocation of large quoits than sweets. To assess the significance level of this difference, the results were first analysed by means of a 2 (Secure v Insecure) × 2 (Large quoits v Sweet gums) ANOVA with the second, repeated measurements factor treated at the subplot level. A significant main effect for each factor was found ($F = 46.53$, df $= 1, 38$, $p < 0.001$; $F = 21.34$, df $= 1, 38$, $p < 0.001$, respectively for the first and second factor). The means of quoits and sweets in the Secure/Appeasement condition were then compared, using the error term at the subplot level. The difference of the means was significant ($F = 13.63$, df $= 1,38$, $p < 0.001$). By the same test, the mean number of large quoits given to the ingroup in the Insecure/Appeasement condition was also significantly larger than that of sweets ($F = 8.06$, df $= 1,38$, $p < 0.01$).

Discussion

The secure and insecure unilateral direct power relations were posited as two alternatives to the conventional tacit bilateral equal power relation for further study of intergroup discrimination. In line with the primary hypothesis, they did affect significantly the allocation of large quoits. In addition, a similar significant main effect was found in the allocation of sweets. Contrary to the secondary hypothesis, there was no main effect due to the appeasement factor. When the allocations of large quoits and sweets to the ingroup were compared, it was found that significantly more quoits than sweets were assigned to the ingroup.

It should be noted that the division of the large quoits was not made under the same minimal intergroup conditions as the traditional social categorization experiments. In the latter, self-interest was unrelated to how much one gave to the ingroup member. In the present experiment, however, ingroup members were bound by a common fate in that their chance of being allowed to play TV soccer was determined by the aggregate performance of all the members at the quoits match. Therefore, self-interest was involved in the allocation of the large quoits. The possible confounding effect due to self-interest must then be discussed.

One would expect self-interest to accentuate the extent of outgroup discrimination produced by social categorization. This would have the effect of inflating the absolute level of outgroup discrimination in the allocation of the large quoits. It is possible that had self-interest not been involved, there would have been less outgroup discrimination in the Secure power condition; and that by the same token, there would have been more equality and/or outgroup *favouritism* in the Insecure power condition. Even then, the highly significant *difference* found between the Secure and Insecure conditions remains intact – it cannot be attributed to self-interest.

One may conclude that the type of power relation has a significant bearing on discrimination. Outgroup discrimination cannot be interpreted as the direct consequence of social categorization alone – power is also involved. Furthermore, it appears that outgroup discrimination is confined to those situations where the power relations are functionally capable of sustaining discrimination. Where the power relation is insecure, equality is the modal response and there is even a slight tendency towards outgroup favouritism.

The occurrence of outgroup favouritism in the Insecure condition confirms our central argument about the role of the intergroup power relation much more strongly than we had anticipated. The provision of a viable external alternative had indeed created a powerful counter-power to the exploitative use of a unilateral power advantage. This idea of a counter-power being embodied in the availability of an external alternative and the possibility of exit is, as will be discussed in the concluding section of the present chapter, a dominant line of thought in the contemporary social psychology of power.

The inclusion of an appeasement factor in the present experiment throws some light on the dynamics generated by the Insecure power condition, even though no main appeasement effect was found. In the Insecure power condition, the unilateral decision-making power given to the subjects' team was counteracted by the fact that it was possible for the opposing team to divorce itself from the subjects' team, in which event, the subjects' team would be a dead loser. Under such circumstances, the subjects were therefore confronted with the problem of how to entice the opposing team to accept the relationship and to enter into competition with them. It would appear that the subjects attempted to solve this problem by conceding the sweets and by offering equality with respect to the large quoits. In the Secure power condition, such a problem did not exist and hence it was unnecessary either to give the sweets away or to offer the opponent an equal basis for competing in the quoits match.

The remaining observation requiring further discussion is the significantly higher level of outgroup discrimination over the large quoits than sweets. Two of the possible factors leading to this observation may be noted. It will be recalled that self-interest was involved in the allocation of quoits. The allocation of sweets, on the other hand, was relatively unrelated to self-interest; and this might be one reason why the subjects were willing to give more sweets than quoits to the outgroup. Another factor might have been the relatively greater utility or functional importance of the large quoits in that it was the large quoits, rather than the sweets, which would critically and directly determine the subjects' chance of playing TV soccer. It is impossible to tell from the present experiment how important the latter factor might have been. In the next experiment, one of the aims will be to test the utility argument by comparing a property for power with a property for use under more rigorously controlled experimental conditions.

4. Experiment 2

Hypotheses

This experiment examines the occurrence of intergroup discrimination in a more complicated kind of intergroup power relation. As in the first experiment, a property is to be allocated by the members of one group only, and because of this, they have unilateral power over the other, respondent group. This power, however, is indirect. It has to be mediated by a select Committee which, by means of a majority vote, can either pass or veto the allocations. When an allocation is vetoed, neither the ingroup member nor the outgroup member will receive the property and they will have to compete against one another without it. The most that the Committee can do to counteract discrimination is to change an unfair competition into a fair competition. It can neither reverse the direction of discrimination, nor can it liberate the respondent group from the competitive relation (that is, it cannot create a counterpower for the respondent group which is equivalent to that created by the Insecure condition in the first experiment). That is to say, the unilateral indirect power which one group has will never become a liability, and because of this, outgroup discrimination is permissible within this type of power relation. This leads to the general expectation (*Hypothesis 1*) that, within a unilateral indirect power relation, there will be always outgroup discrimination over a property for power, regardless of the following variations of the power relation.

Within the unilateral indirect power relation, the magnitude of outgroup discrimination will vary directly with the amount of control which the group has over the Committee (*Hypothesis 2*). As will be described shortly, the amount of control is to be manipulated simply by varying the composition of the Committee to give a Majority, Equal Power, and Minority condition. If both Hypotheses 1 and 2 were true, then there would be outgroup discrimination in all the three power conditions and the magnitude of this discrimination would decrease in that order.

The present experiment also compares the magnitude of outgroup discrimination over a property for power and a property for use. In line with the theoretical formulation of the problem stated at the beginning of this chapter, the value of the property for use will constitute the totality of the 'prize' value of the property for power. That is to say, the property for use will coincide with the tangible prize of the property for power. The theoretical expectation is that the subjects will discriminate against the outgroup in the allocation of the property for power in order to control the competition, even though they may be less discriminatory in the allocation of the actual prize of the competition (i.e. the property for use). The hypothesis is that outgroup discrimination will be greater in the allocation of a property for power than in the case of property for use (*Hypothesis 3*). Since the division of the prize is obviously related to the members' performance in the competition as well as the comparability of the conditions under which they compete (whether one is more advantaged than another), these two factors have also to be examined before Hypothesis 3 can be tested. This is part of the reason why the present experiment has adopted a rather complex design and procedure.

Method

Subjects

Students in nine Introductory Psychology laboratory classes participated in the experiment as part of their scheduled laboratory work. The size of a class varied from 28 to 32 and the total number of subjects was 263.

Design

The whole experiment consisted of nine sessions, one for each laboratory class. Each session began with the subjects divided into two groups, A and B. Thereafter, it passed through two phases. The *Power* variable was introduced in the first phase to set up the *Majority, Equal Power*, and *Minority* conditions, with three sessions per condition. When the power condition was established, each Group A subject divided the use of a calculator between another Group A member and a Group B member. In the second phase, the experimenter set up the *Privilege* factor by manipulating the Committee's voting such that each Group A member in the same session would be allowed to use the calculator for either seven minutes (*Advantaged* condition), five minutes (*Equal Advantage* condition), or three minutes (*Disadvantaged* condition). The three conditions were set up within each of the power conditions, resulting in a 3 × 3 factorial design for this stage of the experiment. Both the Group A and Group B subjects were then asked to divide 10 grade points between a Group A member and a Group B member (other than themselves). Because of their functional values, which are to be described below, the calculator and the grade points served respectively as a property for power and a property for use. Table 3 exhibits the overall experimental design and the number of subjects in each condition.

Table 3. *Design of experiment showing the numbers of subjects in the Power and Privilege conditions*

	Power conditions			
	Majority	Equal Power	Minority	N
First phase of experiment	45[a]	44	45	134
Second phase of experiment Privilege conditions				
Advantaged	16[a] (16)[b]	15 (15)	15 (13)	46 (44)
Disadvantaged	14 (15)	15 (14)	16 (13)	45 (42)
Equal Advantage	15 (15)	14 (14)	14 (14)	43 (43)

[a]Subjects belonging to Group A; [b]Subjects belonging to Group B. Note that in the first phase of the experiment, the allocation of calculator time was made by Group A subjects only; in the second phase, the allocation of grade points was made by both Group A and Group B subjects.

Procedure

The stated purpose of the scheduled laboratory class in which this experiment took place was to generate data on the performance of arithmetic problems under the following contrived conditions, with the students themselves serving as their own subjects. It was emphasized to them that although the contrived conditions might appear arbitrary, they represented attempts to simulate certain real-life situations.

The subjects in the same session were first divided into Group A and Group B on a chance basis. Each subject pulled out from a box a paper on which was marked either 'Group A' or 'Group B', together with a membership number. They were explicitly instructed to conceal their group identity and membership number in order to ensure anonymity. It was related to them that each member in Group A would be paired with a Group B member by means of their identical membership number. The two persons in the pair would later work separately on an identical set of arithmetic problems for 10 minutes and the person who did better would receive 10 bonus points toward his/her grade. The competition would be conducted with the aid of calculators. Only one calculator was available to each pair of competitors. (The experimenter explained this deliberate procedure in terms of the fact that in many real-life competitions, a scarce resource, which was represented by the calculator in the present experiment, was available to some people but not to all.) In these circumstances, the calculator would serve as the critical means of prevailing over the competitor, that is, as a property for power.

To decide which one of the two competitions could use the calculator, and for how long during the 10 minutes' time, each Group A subject would first propose for how much of the 10 minutes' time *another* Group A member should be allowed to use the calculator. This could vary from zero to 10 minutes, and the balance would be given to the other, Group B, member. The data on the proposed allocations would indicate the extent of outgroup discrimination over a property for power. Each proposed allocation would then be voted on by a six-member Voting Committee who either passed or vetoed it by a majority decision. If a proposed allocation were vetoed, then neither of the two persons in question would be allowed to use the calculator at all. By varying the composition of the Voting Committee, the power variable was set up to produce three power conditions. In the *Majority* condition, four of the six committee members were drawn (randomly) from Group A and two from Group B, thus enabling Group A to have majority control over the voting. In the *Minority* condition, the above ratio was reversed. Finally, in the *Equal Power* condition, there were three members from each group. The power condition was established *before* the Group A subjects made their proposed allocations.

In this way, Group A subjects divided a property for power (calculator time) between an anonymous ingroup member and an outgroup member under one of the three power conditions. The next stage of the experimental procedure consisted in observing how the 10 bonus grade points were divided between an anonymous ingroup member and an outgroup member. The essential feature of this stage was the standardization of the duration of using the calculator, and through this, the introduction of the Privilege variable.

Upon collection of the proposal papers (on which each Group A subject has indicated how much of the calculator time was to be given to an ingroup and an outgroup member), the Voting Committee members were called away to an adjoining room to vote on the individual proposals by secret ballot. It usually took a long time to ascertain the majority decision on each of the proposals. The experimenter seized this fact and suggested to the Committee that to save the rest of the class from waiting for too long, maybe they should reach a *general* decision on how much use of the calculator should be given to the Group A and Group B members in each pair. This manipulation was necessary in order to standardize the use of the calculator by subjects in the same session such that when they later divided the grade points, they would be doing this under a uniform condition. Otherwise they would be dividing the points between pairs of competitors whose use of the calculator would have varied considerably, which would then compound the analysis since the relative use of the calculator must be considered as a possible factor affecting the division. In fact, such a factor was precisely the Privilege variable which we sought to create. Regardless of the actual general decisions made by the Committee members, the experimenter announced to the Committee a predetermined result which allowed the Group A member in each dyad to use the calculator for either seven minutes (the *Advantaged* condition), three minutes (*Disadvantaged* condition), or five minutes (*Equal Advantage* condition). In three of the sessions,[3] the experimenter detected signs of disbelief at the procedure, and in order to prevent its amplification, had to reveal the manipulation to the Committee and gained their acquiescence during the rest of the experiment. The voting result was then announced to all the subjects, and the experimenter reiterated the reason as to why a general decision had been made.

Before they worked on the arithmetic problems, the subjects of both groups were given a questionnaire on which each would indicate how many grade points he/she would prefer to give to an ingroup member (other than oneself) and an outgroup member under the following occasions, (a) when the ingroup member performed better than the outgroup member (*Better* performance condition), (b) when the ingroup member performed worse (*Worse* condition), and (c) when both produced the same performance (*Same* condition). Three measurements of the allocation of a property for use (i.e. grade points) were deemed necessary in the present context because the allocation was inevitably linked to performance.

Dependent Measures

Apart from the allocations of calculator and grade points as described above, the two manipulation checks described below were included. Since the power variable was operationalized by varying the numerical ratio of ingroup/outgroup members of the Voting Committee, objectively, the amount of control by the ingroup members over the voting would increase progressively from the Minority to the Equal Power and then the Majority condition. Not all the subjects would expect the Voting Committee to discriminate against one group in favour of another group, but when they did so, the amount of discrimination favouring the ingroup should be realistically proportional to the amount of control by the ingroup over the voting. That is, the number of Group A subjects who expected the voting to favour their own group should increase from the Minority condition to the Equal condition and then the Majority condition.

Immediately following the question on the allocation of the calculator, another question asked the Group A subjects to indicate whether they thought the Voting Committee would favour the Group A member more, or less than, or equally to the Group B member. If the power variable were successfully manipulated, the proportion of subjects choosing the 'more' response should increase from the Minority to the Equal Power and then the Majority condition.

The Privilege variable was checked by asking both the Group A and Group B subjects whether they had felt being advantaged, disadvantaged, or equal to their competitors during the arithmetic exercise.

Under the Procedure section, the Advantaged and Disadvantaged conditions were designated from the point of view of Group A. Henceforth they will pertain to Group B subjects as well. That is, Group B subjects who were given seven minutes of the calculator would be Advantaged, and those given three minutes, Disadvantaged. Similarly, insofar as the Majority and Minority power conditions also relate the Group B subjects, they will refer respectively to B group's having four and two members on the Voting Committee.

Results

Manipulation Checks The results pertaining to the *Power* variable are shown in Table 4, which gives the actual numbers of subjects in the three power conditions who expected the outcome of the voting to be fair or to favour either the ingroup or the outgroup. The modal expectation in the three conditions was a fair vote. This response varied from 53 % in the Majority condition to 66 % in the Equal Power condition and 68 % in the Minority condition. The remaining responses were distributed in a manner consistent with the operationalization. Thus, in the Majority condition, all except one of the remaining 21 responses expected the voting to favour the ingroup. In the Equal Power condition, nine expected the voting to favour the ingroup while five were in the opposite direction. Only in the Minority condition were there more responses expecting the vote to favour the outgroup than the ingroup (nine v five).

The 'Fair' and 'Favour Outgroup' responses were collapsed and the resulting 2 (Favour Ingroup v Fair/Favour Outgroup) × 3 (Majority vs Equal Power vs Minority) contingency table was subjected to chi-square test, which yielded a significant overall difference ($\chi^2 = 13.15$, df = 2, $p < 0.005$). Each of the three power conditions was then compared with one another. The Majority condition was significantly different from both the Equal Power ($\chi^2 = 4.86$, df = 1, $p < 0.05$), and Minority ($\chi^2 = 12.05$, $p < 0.005$) conditions, while the latter two conditions were not significantly different from one another ($\chi^2 = 1.73$). Thus the manipulation of the Power variable was only partially successful. Instead of setting up three different levels of the Power variable, as originally intended, only two levels (Majority v Equal Power and Minority) were actually created. Furthermore, we noted that even in the Majority condition, more than half of the subjects expected a fair vote.

Table 4. *Expectation of the outcome of the Committee's voting*

	Favour Ingroup	Fair	Favour Outgroup	N
Majority	20	24	1	45
Equal Power	9	27	5	41
Minority	5	30	9	44

Note: No answer was given by three subjects in the Equal Power condition and by one subject in the Minority condition.

Table 5. *Feeling induced by the Privilege variable*

	Feel			
	Advantaged	Disadvantaged	Equal	N
Advantaged	23^a $(22)^b$	14 (10)	8 (11)	45 (43)
Disadvantaged	2 (1)	35 (32)	7 (9)	44 (42)
Equal Advantage	3 (3)	12 (15)	27 (25)	42 (43)

[a] Subjects belonging to Group A; [b] Subjects belonging to Group B.
Note: No answer was given by one Group A subject in each of the Privilege conditions, and one Group B subject in the Advantaged condition.

The *Privilege variable*, operationalized in terms of the length of time allowed for using the calculator, was checked by asking the subjects whether they had felt advantaged, disadvantaged, or equal to their competitors. The frequency distributions for Group A and Group B subjects are shown in Table 5 above. For Group A (and Group B), the modal response in each of the Privilege conditions was as intended and varied from 51 % (51 % for Group B) in the Advantaged condition, to 64 % (58 %) in the Equal Advantage condition and 79 % (76 %) in the Disadvantaged condition. A 3 × 3 chi-square test revealed a highly significant overall difference in Group A ($\chi^2 = 63.98$, df = 4, $p < 0.001$) as well as in Group B ($\chi^2 = 50.17$, $p < 0.001$). In Group A, the Advantaged condition was significantly different from both the Equal Advantage ($\chi^2 = 25.77$, df = 2, $p < 0.001$) and Disadvantaged conditions ($\chi^2 = 26.70$, df = 2, $p < 0.001$). Comparison between the Disadvantaged and Equal Advantage conditions presented a problem because the expected frequencies in the 'Advantaged' response category were too small for a chi-square to be applied to the 2 × 3 con-

Table 6. *Allocation of calculator time expressed in average number of minutes and frequency distribution*

	Minutes allocated to ingroup member	Frequency distribution		
		Outgroup discrimination	Equality	Outgroup favouritism
Majority	6.2^a $(1.6)^b$	24	21	0
Equal Power	5.5 (1.6)	12	26	6
Minority	5.5 (1.5)	13	29	3

^{a} Mean; ^{b} Standard deviation.

tingency table. Instead, the comparison was confined to the 'Disadvantaged' and 'Equal Advantage' categories and the highly significant result ($\chi^2 = 21.59$, df = 1, $p < 0.001$) was interpreted as indicating a significant difference between the Disadvantaged and Equal Advantage conditions. The same pattern of significant comparisons was obtained in Group B ($\chi^2 = 20.88$, 30.87, and 13.67 respectively).

The above results indicate a high degree of success in the manipulation of the Privilege variable. The extent to which the privilege variable was confounded by the power variable was slight, since a chi-square test of the power variable revealed no significant overall difference either in Group A ($\chi^2 = 2.67$, df = 4, ns) or Group B ($\chi^2 = 6.63$, df = 4, ns). The feelings of advantage, etc., were quite uniform across the three power conditions.

Distribution of calculator time Analysis of the results followed the same strategy as in the first experiment. Firstly, the lengths of time allocated to the ingroup and outgroup were compared to find out the extent and significance level of outgroup discrimination. Then, the variations in outgroup discrimination across the power conditions were analysed. (For the sake of presentation, the above order will be reversed when the results on grade points are analysed in the next section.) Table 6 summarizes the results in means and frequencies. The latter gives the number of subjects whose allocations were either for *equality* (five minutes to each member), *outgroup discrimination* (six or more minutes to the ingroup), or *outgroup favouritism* (four or less minutes to the ingroup).

The mean lengths of time allocated by the subjects in the three power conditions all showed outgroup discrimination. A *t*-test (for correlated pairs) showed that the discrimination was significant in all the three conditions (Majority: $t = 5.03$, df $= 44$, $p < 0.01$; Equal Power: $t = 2.08$, df $= 43$, $p < 0.05$; Minority: $t = 2.26$, df $= 44$, $p < 0.05$). Hypothesis 1 was supported.

A one-way analysis of variance showed that the main effect due to the power variable was approaching significance ($F = 2.92$, df $= 2, 131$, $p = 0.057$). Duncan's multiple range test showed that the mean length of time in the Majority condition was greater than that in the other two conditions ($p < 0.05$), whereas there was no significant difference between the latter two conditions.

A similar but fuller picture is given by the frequency distribution results. The responses in the Majority condition showed either outgroup discrimination (53 %) or equality (47 %), with none favouring the outgroup. In the Minority condition, responses discriminating against the outgroup became less frequent (29 %) while those favouring the outgroup and for equality were more frequent (7 % and 64 % respectively). The Equal Power condition exhibited a pattern similar to that in the Minority condition (the corresponding figures were 27 %, 14 % and 59 %). 'Equality' and 'outgroup favouritism' responses were collapsed for comparison with the 'outgroup discrimination' responses by chi-square test. An overall significant difference was found across the power conditions ($\chi^2 = 8.23$, df $= 2, p < 0.025$). The Majority condition was significantly different from both the Minority ($\chi^2 = 5.55$, df $= 1$, $p < 0.025$) and Equal Power conditions ($\chi^2 = 6.34$, df $= 1, p < 0.025$), while the latter two conditions were not significantly different from one another ($\chi^2 = 0.03$).

In terms of both frequencies and means, the results indicate a significantly greater outgroup discrimination in the Majority condition than in the two other conditions. This finding is an exact replica of the perception of greater relative power by subjects in the Majority condition, and provides partial support for Hypothesis 2.

Allocation of grade points   Allocation of grade points was made by both Group A and Group B subjects. Each subject divided ten points between an ingroup and an outgroup member on three occasions: when the ingroup member performed (*a*) better, (*b*) worse than, or (*c*) the same as the outgroup member. Two of the 263 subjects had incomplete data. The amounts given to the ingroup member by the remaining 261 subjects on the three occasions were treated as repeated measurements and subjected to a $2 \times 3 \times 3 \times (3)$ analysis of variance. The first three factors (namely, Group A v Group B; Majority v Equal Power v Minority; Advantaged v Disadvantaged v

Table 7. *Summary of major ANOVA results on the allocation of grade points to ingroup members*

Plot	Ss	df	F	$p \leqslant$
G	1.02	1	0.32	0.574
X	5.58	2	0.86	0.422
Y	197.57	2	30.54	0.001
GX	24.11	2	3.73	0.026
Error 1	786.10	243		
Total 1	1055.60	260		
Sub-plot				
Z	1324.95	2	231.05	0.001
ZX	34.27	4	2.99	0.019
ZXY	54.69	8	2.38	0.016
Error 2	1393.48	486		
Total 2	2850.66	522		

Note: G = Group A v Group B; X = Majority v Equal Power v Minority; Y = Advantaged v Disadvantaged v Equal Advantage; Z = Ingroup member performs better than v Worse than v Same as the Outgroup member.

Equal Advantage) were orthogonal factors and were analysed at the plot level, while the fourth factor (repeated measurements) was analysed at the subplot level. Table 7 summarizes the major ANOVA results pertaining to the four factors and their significant interactions.

As expected, no significant main effect was found for the Group (G) and Power (X) factors, whereas the Privilege (Y) and Performance (Z) factors were found to have highly significant main effects. The YZ means are shown in Table 8 under the 'Ingroup' columns. More than half of the ten grade points were given to ingroup members in the Disadvantaged (5.8) and Equal Advantage (5.2) conditions, while less than half was given in the Advantaged condition (4.6). Duncan's multiple range test revealed that the differences amongst the three conditions were all significant at the 0.01 level. The performance factor produced a similar and even more clear-cut pattern of results. More than half of the points were assigned to ingroup members in the Better (6.8) and Same (5.2) conditions, and less than half in the Worse (3.6) condition. All the three differences were significant at the 0.01 level. Relative to the Privilege factor, the Performance factor had an overriding effect, as indicated by the uniformly greater individual means in the top row than those in the second row, which in turn were uniformly greater than that in the third row.

A comparison of the ingroup and outgroup means in Table 8 reveals a perfectly consistent outgroup discrimination. That is, when the Privilege

Table 8. *Mean grade points given to ingroup and outgroup members as a function of the Privilege and Performance factors*

	Advantaged		Equal Advantage		Disadvantaged	
	Ingroup	Outgroup	Ingroup	Outgroup	Ingroup	Outgroup
Perform Better	6.0	5.8	6.9	6.4	7.4	6.9
Perform Same	4.6	4.2	5.2	4.8	5.8	5.4
Perform Worse	3.1	2.6	3.6	3.1	4.2	4.0

condition and performance of the ingroup and outgroup members were identical, fewer grade points were allocated to the outgroup member than the ingroup member. This happened in all the nine comparisons, even though the bias was small. To assess the significance level of this bias, the total amount given by each subject to the ingroup member on the three occasions was compared to that given to the outgroup member by means of a t-test (for correlated pairs). The bias was significant ($t = 2.86$, df $= 260$, $p < 0.01$).

As shown in Table 7, the three significant interactions all involved the Power (X) variable. These are graphically shown in Figure 1 below. All the three graphs portray a convergence around the Equal Power condition. This seems to indicate that in an intergroup relation of equal power, the effects on the allocation of grade points due to the Group (G), Performance (Z), and Privilege (Y) factors were less than those in the other unequal power relation conditions.

A Comparison of the discriminations over a Property for Power and a Property for Use   A greater overall outgroup discrimination occurred in the allocation of calculator time *vis-à-vis* grade points (5.8 v 5.2), as hypothesized. A comparison of the two types of discrimination was problematic however because the experimental conditions under which they occurred were not identical. The allocation of calculator time was made by the subjects without any reference to the privilege or performance factor. In order for the allocation of grade points to be meaningfully compared with the allocation of calculator time, the privilege and performance factors should be minimal. The closest approximation to such a requirement is provided by the grade points which the subjects in the Equal Advantage condition allocated to ingroup members who performed equally as the outgroup members. When the data of these 43 Group A subjects were compared by a t-test (for correlated pairs), a significant difference was found ($t = 3.29$, df $= 42$,

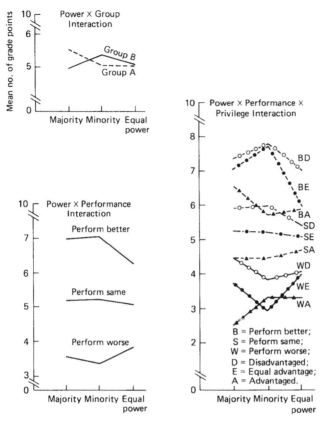

Figure 1. Allocation of grade points as a function of the interaction among the Power, Group, Privilege and Performance factors

$p < 0.01$). The same conclusion was reached when the t-test was applied to all the Group A subjects ($t = 3.62$, df $= 131$, $p < 0.01$, two subjects with missing data were excluded). Thus there is some support for Hypothesis 3.

Discussion

All the three hypotheses received some empirical support. There was a small but unmistakable tendency towards outgroup discrimination in the allocation of both types of properties. The discrimination over the property for power increased when control over the Committee was perceived to be decisive (the Majority condition vs the Equal Power and Minority conditions). The property for power elicited a greater discrimination than the property for use. This difference, however small, was significant. In a small but subtle way, it illustrates the theoretical relevance of the conceptual distinction made between the two kinds of properties.

The finding concerning the occurrence of outgroup discrimination in all the Performance and Privilege conditions offers a pivotal case for comparing social categorization with equity theory (e.g. Walster, Berscheid and Walster, 1976). On the one hand, the highly significant main effects due to the Performance and Privilege factors give strong support to equity theory. And yet when these two factors were held constant, there was always outgroup discrimination in the division of the property, and this occurred persistently in all the different levels of the two factors. It would be difficult, even conceptually, to accommodate the social categorization effect into the equity model. Both ideas need to be considered in the study of how properties are distributed. A synthesis of the two ideas would be an interesting problem for future research.

5. Conclusion

This chapter examines two aspects of power in relation to intergroup discrimination. Discrimination, like any other social behaviour, does not occur in a social vacuum. The social context in which groups discriminate against one another partly consists of the power relation between the groups. The very fact that one group, or both groups, are in a position to discriminate is an important fact of social arrangement which should be investigated. There may be diverse causes of discrimination, some of which are more minimal than others. Yet there can be no minimal and sufficient cause apart from one which is embedded in, and mediated by, the social arrangement of power. As already pointed out in the theoretical part of this chapter, a certain tacit bilateral equal power relation is inherent in the experimental design of the social categorization studies of discrimination, even though this element of power has not been explicitly formulated as a part of the problem.

Some of the possible effects of the intergroup power relation on discrimination are examined by creating experimentally two 'new' kinds of power relation, namely, a unilateral direct power relation and a unilateral indirect power relation. A unilateral direct power relation that is secure enough is found to sustain a high level of outgroup discrimination. When it is insecure, equality becomes the modal response. The insecurity has its source in the open nature of the power relation, from which exit is possible on the part of the respondent group. In the presence of a viable external alternative, exit will become a reality. Being confronted by this reality, the apparently more powerful group finds that the power they have is illusory, in fact, a deficit. In the absence of a secure power relation which would be capable of sustaining discriminatory behaviour, discrimination gives way to equality.

Exit from the relation and the presence of an external alternative are hence ingredients of an effective counter-power. They play an important part in the social psychological formulation of the power relation between people, particularly within the social exchange theoretical framework. A full discussion of this connection is presented elsewhere (Ng, 1980), and it will be sufficient for the present purpose to highlight the following point. In many real-life situations, as Apfelbaum (1974) has pointed out, the correct identification and creative formulation of an alternative to the existing relationship is the only option open to the subordinate group for the betterment of the members' interests. However, one should not be unduly hopeful about the use of the alternative as a power balancing mechanism. The reason for this caution is not only that viable alternatives may in fact be limited in supply, and a *laissez-faire* type of market situation offers only a limited set of choices which amount to no real choice at all; but also a more important reason is that exit from a power relation may be more problematic than what can be envisaged from an abstract, liberal democratic point of view. If that were not the case, then the path would be less thorny for the French Canadian, Welsh, Irish, and Scottish nationalists. It would be hard to explain, too, why disloyalty is such a socially disapproved mode of response. Exit is at once promising and problematic for those who wish to practise it. It is precisely because of the ambivalent nature of exit that it should be treated as an important research problem. An important development in the further study of the connection between intergroup power relation and discrimination lies in uncovering the use and counter-use of exit, and not in treating exit just as an independent variable to be contrived in the laboratory. An interesting discussion of exit can be found in Tajfel (1975) and Hirschman (1970).

The second kind of power relation examined in this chapter is a unilateral indirect power relation from which exit by the respondent group is impossible. Such a power relation is permissive of outgroup discrimination, which increases when control over the respondent group is more assured. The indirect nature of the power relation (as represented by the select Voting Committee in Experiment 2) is reminiscent of a situation in which an act of discrimination is dissociated from the actor, and filters through an intermediary body before it takes effect. In such a situation, responsibility becomes diffuse, discrimination is delayed, and the groups do not confront one another directly.

When the results of the two power relations are taken together, they point to the following conclusion. *Outgroup discrimination is not a necessary outcome of social categorization, but is contingent upon a permissive intergroup power relation. In the presence of such a power relation, the magnitude of discrimination increases when the power advantage becomes decisive.*

The second aspect of power examined in this chapter concerns the nature of the property over which discrimination occurs. *The results show a tendency towards outgroup discrimination* (in the presence of a permissive power relation) *over a property for use* (grade points), *and an even greater tendency over the means (i.e. a property for power) of capturing that property.* As already noted, the theoretical prediction that a property for power elicits a greater discrimination than a property for use must be circumscribed by the stipulation that the latter's tangible prize value does not exceed those promised by the former. Otherwise, one would be forced to admit absurd statements such as that the large quoits or the calculators would lead to more discrimination than, say, a hundred dollars. A theory of utility would be required in order to reformulate the prediction at a more general level. Such a theory must articulate not only the general psychological principles of human motivation and learning, as well as cognitive processes on the intergroup level, but also factors which are culturally more specific. We are not aware of a theory of this kind, although there are interesting attempts (e.g. Tedeschi, Schlenker and Bonoma, 1973).

The experimental investigation of discrimination over a property for power need not be regarded as merely an adjunct to the conventional study of discrimination over a property for use. It constitutes a problem area of its own of no less importance. Notwithstanding the relative neglect of this problem area by social psychologists, there are signs that social psychology will increasingly address the problems of classical political economy (Davis, Laughlin and Komorita, 1976; Ng, 1980). Moreover, if we are not only concerned with the question of discrimination, but also with equality, then a meaningful answer should deal seriously with the equality of power, whatever else it may also deal with. In this regard, the study by Branthwaite and Jones (1975) provides an interesting point of departure. It was found that the English subjects manifested a much higher level of equality than their Welsh counterparts, and the authors attributed this to the former's more advantaged position in society relative to the latter. As an index of discrimination and equality, they used pecuniary points.

The interesting question is, if the points were to represent the power on which their advantaged position is based, would the English subjects (or for that matter, subjects of any other social category) still be as equality-minded as before?

Notes

[1] The first experiment in this study was supported by a grant from the Otago Research Committee (Grant No. 36–650). The author wishes to thank: the Committee; Barry Longmore and Roxane Smith for their assistance in the execution of the experiments; and Carol Hunter for typing the manuscript.
[2] A Wilcoxon test was not used because of the large proportion of identical pairs, i.e. equal allocations to ingroup and outgroup.
[3] These happened in the Minority/Advantaged, Majority/Equal Advantage, and Equal power/Disadvantaged sessions.

References

Apfelbaum, E. 1974. On conflict and bargaining. In: *Advances in Experimental Social Psychology*, Vol. 7 (Ed. L. Berkowitz), pp103–56. Academic Press, New York.

Blalock, H.M. Jr. 1967. *Toward a theory of minority-group relations.* John Wiley and Sons, New York.

Branthwaite, A. and Jones, J.E. 1975. Fairness and discrimination: English versus Welsh. *European Journal of Social Psychology*, **5**, 323–38.

Campbell, D.T. 1963. Social attitudes and other acquired behavioural dispositions. In: *Psychology: A study of a science*, Vol. 6 (Ed. S. Koch), pp94–173. McGraw-Hill, New York.

Cox, O.C. 1948. *Caste, class and race: A study in social dynamics.* Modern Reader Paperbacks, New York.

Davis, J.H., Laughlin, P.R. and Komorita, S.S. 1976. The social psychology of small groups: co-operative and mixed-motive interaction. *Annual Review of Psychology*, **27**, 501–41.

Hirschman, A.O. 1970. *Exit, Voice and Loyalty.* Cambridge, Mass.: Harvard University Press.

Hobbes, T. 1651. *Leviathan.* Edited with an introduction by C.B. Macpherson. Penguin, Middlesex, 1968.

Myrdal, G. 1944. *An American dilemma: The Negro problem and modern democracy.* Harper, New York.

Ng, S.H. 1978. Minimal social categorization, political categorization, and power change. *Human Relations*, **31**, 765–79.

Ng, S.H. 1980. *The social psychology of power.* London: Academic Press.

Russell, B. 1938. *Power: A new social analysis.* London: George Allen and Unwin.

Tajfel, H. 1970. Experiments in intergroup discrimination. *Scientific American*, **223**, 96–102.

Tajfel, H. 1975. The exit of social mobility and the voice of social change: Notes on the social psychology of intergroup relations. *Social Science Information*, **14**, 101–18.

Tajfel, H. (Ed.) 1978*a*. *Differentiation between Social Groups: Studies in the Social Psychology of Intergroup Relations*. London: Academic Press.

Tajfel, H. 1978*b*. Social categorization, social identity and social comparison. In H. Tajfel (ed.), 1978*a*, *op. cit.*

Tedeschi, J.T., Schlenker, B.R. and Bonoma, T.V. 1973. *Conflict, Power, and Games*. Chicago: Aldine.

Thibaut, J.W. and Faucheux, C. 1965. The development of contractual norms in a bargaining situation under two types of stress. *Journal of Experimental Social Psychology*, **1**, 89–102.

Thibaut, J.W. and Kelley, H.H. 1959. *The Social Psychology of Groups*. New York: Wiley.

Walster, E., Berscheid, E. and Walster, G.W. 1976. New directions in equity research. In Equity Theory: Toward a General Theory of Social Interaction. *Advances in Experimental Social Psychology*, Vol. 9. (Ed. L. Berkowitz and E. Walster), pp1–42. New York: Academic Press.

Weber, M. 1947. *The theory of social and economic organization*. (Translated by A.M. Anderson and T. Parsons). New York: Oxford University Press.

Westergaard, J. and Resler, H. 1975. *Class in a capitalist society*. London: Heinemann.

Wilson, W.J. 1973. *Power, racism and privilege*. New York: Macmillan.

8. Cross-cultural studies of minimal groups: Implications for the social identity theory of intergroup relations

MARGARET WETHERELL

1. Introduction

Intergroup relations has always been something of a 'poor relation' in social psychology: seldom studied and often disregarded in the textbooks. There was one burst of interest in the late forties and fifties stimulated by Sherif's classic experiments and fuelled in general by the Gestaltist tradition in social psychology. Since then, there was decline and stagnation, paralleled by the overall lack of interest in group phenomena evident in mainstream social psychology in the last decade or so (Steiner, 1974). The revival of interest in the psychology of intergroup behaviour witnessed recently is thus long overdue.

The resurgence of intergroup relations as a socio-psychological topic was mainly engendered by the experiments and theories of several European social psychologists, notably Tajfel (1972a; 1974a; 1978) and Turner (1975a) at the University of Bristol and Doise and his colleagues (Doise, 1978; Doise and Dann, 1976, Doise and Sinclair, 1973) at the University of Geneva. This work has taken as its background assumption Sherif's (1966) dictum that group interaction must not be reduced to the cumulative effects of members' different personal identities. Tajfel (1974a) and Turner (1978) in fact assert that a truly social psychological account of intergroup relations should be based upon an analysis of the effects of social identification or the qualitatively different results of defining oneself as a group member.

Rejection of psychological reductionism led the Sherifs (1953) to study the impact of different goal relationships (competition for scarce resources, superordinate goals) upon intergroup relations. In contrast, Tajfel (1970) and his colleagues (Tajfel et al., 1971) speculated about the *necessary* conditions for intergroup discrimination – could it be that merely dividing people into two groups was a strong enough stimulus? It was the experiment they designed to test this supposition which established the 'minimal group' procedure.

The results Tajfel *et al.* obtained in their study are well-known. It was discovered that minimal categorization was sufficient to induce intergroup discrimination and competition. Thus, it appeared that some process intrinsically associated with categorization/identification was responsible for the ingroup favouritism and outgroup depreciation. A review of related research and consideration of other possible interpretations of the data (Turner, 1975*b*) has demonstrated that alternative explanations in terms of demand characteristics, anticipation of future interaction, common fate and beliefs about reciprocation can be ruled out. Furthermore, Billig and Tajfel (1973) have shown that the effects of categorization are not mediated by the perception of interpersonal similarity. It seems that categorization *per se* can be both a sufficient and necessary condition for intergroup discrimination. This finding has stimulated new theoretical developments, two of which will be described below, and it has also sparked off a great deal of research including the cross-cultural experiments described in this chapter.

In his 1970 article, Tajfel set out the first version of a theory of intergroup psychology based on the minimal group findings. It was essentially a normative theory. He argued that the regularity across cultures of discrimination against outgroups implied that there was some underlying psychological factor in this behaviour, *viz*, the individual's internalization of specific social norms or expectations. During socialization the child finds a location in the established 'social construction of reality'. The child's categorization of the social environment into groups is overlaid by society's definition of these groups as 'we' or 'they'. Value judgements inevitably come to be associated with the group categorizations. In other words, the child internalizes a 'generic' norm of behaviour towards outgroups. Consequently, whenever a child is faced with a situation which contains an explicit group categorization, he is likely to behave in a partisan way. Seen in these terms, the minimal categorization experiment provides a situation where the generic norm of discriminatory behaviour against outgroups can operate. If a generic norm has been internalized, then all that is necessary for discrimination to occur is to create a situation in which the individual can perceive an ingroup and an outgroup.

Tajfel was to modify this theory considerably, rejecting the earlier normative account on the grounds that it was not genuinely heuristic. If the subjects had chosen fairness or maximum joint profit strategies rather than the discriminatory choices, their behaviour could also be explained in terms of norms (Tajfel, 1974*b*). There are many examples of groups that are not ethnocentric (i.e. they do not act in terms of a generic norm of outgroup discrimination) and so the norm is not universal. This being the case, a normative explanation of the minimal group experiments risks becoming circular. Competitive behaviour in the minimal categorization experiment becomes the criterion for deciding that the subjects are responding to the generic norm of competition. The experiment merely discriminates between ethnocentric and non-ethnocentric subjects (between those responding to the norm and those who are not) and thus the predictive utility of normative theories would seem to be negligible. As Turner (1975a) pointed out, specification of the *process* involved is required.

For these reasons, social identity theory (Tajfel, 1972a, 1974a, b; Turner, 1975a, b) is to be preferred. It is now maintained that analysis of the processes of social identity and its effects can explain minimal group behaviour. The sequence is as follows: as a result of the cognitive processes associated with categorization of the social environment into groups, individuals come to identify with particular groups. To achieve a positive social identity a group must appear to be different from other groups on positively valued dimensions. The group member must constantly maximize the difference between his group and other groups if he or she is to retain a positive self-evaluation. Thus, ingroup members discriminate against the outgroup in the minimal group experiments because the discriminatory strategies establish a distinction between the two groups and enhance the positive value of the ingroup, engendering a positive social identity.

A question arises as to the universality of this model. Tajfel certainly maintains that normative explanations of intergroup psychology cannot claim universal status: 'The answer to these (intergroup) questions cannot be assumed *a priori* to be "universal"; they can acquire meaning only against the social background which provides the canvas for their study' (Tajfel *et al.*, 1971, p151).

However, with the introduction of social identity and social comparison into the theory of the social categorization process, there seems to be a suggestion that self-evaluation via intergroup comparison and the resultant desire to maximize group distinctiveness are widespread if not universal phenomena. Normative explanations depend on an analysis of the behavioural codes within a society, as it is the internalization of these which produces discriminatory or cooperative behaviour. Social identity theory, however, goes beyond such an analysis postulating a universal 'value', a desire for a positive social identity, which in itself motivates group members to differentiate the ingroup from the outgroup on some positively valued dimension. Thus, the theory of social comparison and social identity is in some sense *independent* of the social context. The assertion is that the content of social identity and the choice of dimensions for comparison are socially determined; but the theory implies that the comparative, self-evaluational processes associated with social categorization of the environment are not a product of one kind of culture.

This brings us to the cross-cultural research which is the subject of this chapter. According to various commentators (Jahoda, 1978; Whiting, 1968), the benefits of cross-cultural social psychology are threefold. First, it can provide information about the influence of different social environments upon psychological structures emphasizing the variety of social behaviour. Second, by means of cross-cultural surveys, the universality of different phenomena can be ascertained giving hints about common human attributes. Third, it can be used as a tool for theory evaluation, helping to assess the culture-bound nature of specific theories, suggesting fruitful modifications and new directions for research. Research using the minimal group procedure in different cultures should inform about all three of these aspects: allowing evaluation of the theory in relation to the more flexible normative accounts and at the same time giving information about the universality of the intergroup discrimination produced by minimal categorization. This chapter describes two cross-cultural studies carried out with these intentions.

To a certain extent, the generality of the minimal group findings across different subject samples has already been examined. Vaughan (1978), for example, discusses one study (Vaughan, Tajfel and Williams, published in 1981) which found intergroup discrimination in children as young as seven, while Doise et al. (1972) have found the same pattern of results with adults. Thus, the phenomenon does not seem to be confined to the adolescent schoolboys used as subjects in the initial minimal group experiments. The sex of the subjects also has no effect (Vaughan et al., 1981; Wetherell and Vaughan, 1979). Several studies have now been carried out in different Western societies. Doise et al., for example, used German soldiers as subjects and Wetherell and Vaughan have found that New Zealand European children of both low and high socio-economic status will discriminate in the minimal group situation. The latter study did, however, demonstrate that New Zealand children used the fairness strategy significantly more than a comparable sample of English children. This may have resulted from the emphasis on an egalitarian norm in New Zealand society. We also noted a consistent but non-significant trend for children of higher socio-economic status to be less discriminatory in their allocation of money to the groups. This finding is perhaps not surprising in the light of another New Zealand study (Thomas, 1975) which found the same kind of class difference in competitiveness in interpersonal coin games. It is probable that the minority position of low socio-economic status children in New Zealand would expose them to more instances of discriminatory behaviour, encouraging modelling and thus greater intergroup discrimination. It is also possible that since upward social mobility is not normative for this social class, they feel more bound and defined by their social groups, however minimal, and are more concerned with obtaining positive social identity from these groups than from their individual status (cf. Tajfel, 1974*a* on the 'social change belief structure'). Whatever the case, more research needs to be done on social class differences in this respect. (Also, see the discussion of social status and identity in chapter 3.)

Our cross-cultural research continues and extends this tradition of attempts to investigate the generality and replicability of the discriminatory behaviour found in the minimal group experiments. Two experiments were carried out in New Zealand, taking advantage of the opportunities presented by the pluralistic nature of this society to compare the responses of children from two radically different cultural backgrounds – Polynesian and Western. The first experiment merely contrasted these two cultural groups, exploring the feasibility of using the minimal categorization experiment with young Polynesian children and the possible direction of any differences. Once the viability of this type of cross-cultural study was established, the second experiment made a more detailed comparison among Europeans (New Zealand whites), Samoans (the largest group of immigrants from the Pacific Islands) and urban Maoris (the native Polynesian race, now virtually enculturated into New Zealand society).

All the children in the Polynesian category in the first experiment (except for the few Maoris) and the Samoan children in the second experiment were immigrants, most in fact were second generation immigrants. Despite this, the experiments can be seen as a valid cross-cultural exercise. The recency of the large increase in the Polynesian population in New Zealand, the tendency for Pacific Islanders to live in certain inner-city suburbs and the size and relative social isolation of these groups have ensured that their cultural distinctiveness is preserved. The Samoans, in particular, have retained strong economic and cultural ties with their place of origin. Unlike the smaller groups of Tongans, Cook Islanders and Niueans, the Samoans in Auckland have maintained their traditional social structures, notably the extended family network (the *'āiga*), their language and their church (cf. Ablon, 1971). New Zealand sociologists (Pitt and MacPherson, 1971; 1974) assert that this has occurred to such an extent that there is a separate Samoan subculture in inner-city Auckland.

Cross-cultural comparison was not the only aim of the second experiment reported below. It was also designed to test the effects of the response condition (the dependent measure) typically used in the minimal group experiments. Two previous experiments have directly examined the 'strength' of the minimal group behaviour, comparing the responses obtained in the typical methodology with those obtained in a different situation. Vaughan *et al.* (1981) compared minimal categorization with an interindividual task where the children were asked to allocate money to a friend and an enemy. They found no significant differences between these two conditions implying that minimal group categorization taps behaviour which is as discriminatory as that found in clear-cut interpersonal conflict situations. Wetherell and Vaughan (1978) compared minimal categorization with a more realistic group division, based not on the usual trivial criteria but on groupings familiar to the children (school classes). In this condition, group membership was no longer anonymous and the groups had interacted in the past; however, self-interest was ruled out as a motive. Again, it was found that the 'minimal' categorization was as effective in producing intergroup discrimination as categorization combined with the other factors normally associated with group interaction. However, these studies were not designed to test the possibility that the discrimination observed in the minimal group situation is an artifact produced by a certain kind of methodology. It could be that the presentation of strategies for money division encourages the subjects to act competitively. This possibility was investigated in the second experiment which contrasted a condition in which response strategies were defined in advance with a free-choice response condition. This manipulation will be described in more detail in the introduction to the second experiment.

The aims of the two experiments can be summarized in a question: Does the discriminatory behaviour displayed in the minimal group situation reflect a basic and universal socio-psychological process or is it the product of a certain type of methodology and a particular cultural background?

2. Experiment 1: Comparison of Polynesian and European children

As noted above, this experiment was exploratory since it assessed the feasibility of using the minimal group procedure with young immigrant children. Besides cultural group, the other variable examined was the sex of the subjects.

The experiment was part of a larger study with different New Zealand groups (Wetherell and Vaughan, 1979). The larger study included the manipulation designed to compare minimal categorization and a more realistic but still minimal categorization; this manipulation was also applied to the cross-cultural study. As this variable had no effect upon the responses of any of the subjects, it will not be analysed here, although the two different methods of categorization are described in the Method section.

Method

Subjects

The responses of 38 Polynesian children, 20 girls and 18 boys, were compared with those of 75 European children, 46 girls and 29 boys.[2] All the children came from a low socio-economic status area and had an average age of eight years. School records were used to determine the child's ethnic group and the Polynesian category included Samoans, Maoris, Cook Islanders and Niueans. In the school as a whole, approximately half the children were Polynesian and half white Europeans.

Procedure

As in other minimal categorization experiments, this study was divided into two parts. The first part established the group categorization and the second assessed its effects.

Part One

The categorization was effected in two different ways. For most of the subjects it was established on a nearly arbitrary basis (picture preferences) but for others it was grounded in an already familiar division (school classes). In the latter case, group membership was not anonymous and there was a previous history of group interaction; but there was no institutionalized conflict of interests.

The children in the minimal categorization condition were told that the experimenters were interested in their preferences for different paintings drawn by children about the same age as themselves. The experimenter then showed six pairs of pictures to the children and the children were asked to indicate their preferences by marking prepared sheets. Once this was finished, one experimenter pretended to mark the sheets while another experimenter kept the class occupied.

Next, the class was told that the pictures had come from two schools in Auckland, simply referred to as the blue and red schools. They were further told that by coincidence half of them had preferred the pictures from the blue school while the other half had chosen the pictures from the red school. It was explained that their class was now divided into two groups, blue and red, and that they would discover their group membership later in the course of another task. The subjects were then taken out of the classroom in small groups to another room for the second part of the experiment.

In the more realistic categorization condition, the experimenters did not show the pictures but instead alluded to the existence of another real group,

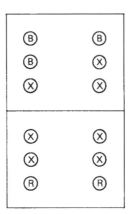

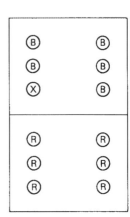

(B) ≡ Blue disc   (R) ≡ Red disc   (X) ≡ Coin

Figure 1. The three cards constituting a 3 × 2 coin matrix. Note: The author is indebted to G.M. Vaughan for his suggestions concerning the structure of this figure, Table 3 and Table 4.

another class in the same school. Thus, group categorization was effected on lines familiar to the subjects. The experimenter discussed with the children the activities they had engaged in with the other group to establish firmly the existence of the outgroup. The class was then informed that the experimenter was not only interested in their various activities but she also had a task for them which required giving the two groups colour codes, their own class being the blue group and the other class the red group. The children were then taken away in small groups to a separate room for the second part of the experiment.

Part Two

This part of the experiment measured the effect of the group categorization upon the subjects' allocation of two-cent coins to the two groups. Each child was tested individually by the experimenter. First, the children in the minimal categorization condition were told which pictures they had preferred and consequently whether they belonged to the red or the blue group. In reality, the subjects (unknown to them) were randomly assigned to blue or red. Subjects in the more 'realistic' condition were reminded of their colour code. After re-establishing the categorization, subjects were instructed that they were to divide some two-cent coins between people in their group and the people in the other group. It was stressed that self-interest was not involved because the money would always be divided between *other* people in the two groups. The subjects were informed that they would get a fixed amount of money at the end of the day. (This instruction should have minimized the influence of a reciprocation belief).[3] These instructions were repeated until the subject acknowledged comprehension.

The subjects were then asked to carry out their task by choosing one card

Table 1. *Intergroup strategies and choices*

Strategy	Abbreviation	Definition
Maximum joint profit	MJP	That choice in a matrix which results in the greatest possible common benefit to the two groups i.e. that column in the matrix which corresponds to highest total number of points that can be awarded.
Maximum ingroup profit or absolute ingroup favouritism	MIP	That choice in a matrix which corresponds to the highest number of points that can be awarded to the ingroup.
Maximum difference in favour of the ingroup of relative ingroup favouritism	MD	That choice in a matrix which results in the greatest possible difference between the number of points awarded to the two groups, this difference being in favour of the ingroup.
Parity	P	That choice in a matrix which awards equal number of points to the two groups.

Note: This table was taken from *Social categorisation and social comparison in intergroup relations* by J. Turner. Unpublished Ph.D. Thesis, University of Bristol, 1975b. Reprinted by permission. (Slight modifications were made to the table because of a different experimental design.)

out of three displayed in front of them where each card had several two-cent coins arranged on it. The subject was to choose the card with the arrangement of money which seemed to be the best way of allocating rewards to the two groups. Each card was divided in the middle by a black line. On one side of the line were six red dots, the size of two-cent coins, and on the other side six blue dots of the same size. A pictorial representation of the cards is given in Figure 1. The ingroup colour was always nearest to the subject. To make the principles involved even more salient to the child, after each choice he or she was required to place the coins into two money boxes painted blue and red respectively. This made it clear that every choice involved making a decision for both groups. The two-cent coins were set out each time on the card by the experimenter in a prearranged matrix pattern which will now be described.

The matrix arrangement was designed so that each card presented one strategy for dividing up the money or one strategy combination. Table 1 gives a list of the different strategies, their abbreviations and a definition of each. Five avenues were open to the child – the three strategies P, MD, MJP and the two strategy combinations MD/MP and MJP/MIP – although not all these alternatives were isolated on any one trial. These strategies were encapsulated in two types of matrix form, a maximum difference matrix isolating MD, and a maximum

Table 2. *Examples of an MD-type and an MJP-type matrix and their baselines showing the location of strategies*

MD-type Matrix

	Parity	MJP/MIP	MD
Ingroup	2	3	1
Outgroup	2	4	0

Baseline for MD-type

	Parity		MD/MIP/MJP
Ingroup	2	0	4
Outgroup	2	1	3

MJP-type Matrix

	Parity	MJP	MD/MIP
Ingroup	2	1	3
Outgroup	2	4	0

Baseline for MJP-type

	MD/MIP/MJP		Parity
Ingroup	4	0	2
Outgroup	1	3	2

joint profit matrix isolating MJP. With a 3 × 2 arrangement, it proved impossible to isolate MIP by itself and so it was always combined with MD or MJP. Parity or fairness was available to the subjects in every matrix. Examples of the two generic types of matrices and the baseline conditions (described below) for each type are given in Table 2. Note that the boxes represent the cards given to the subjects and that the three cards constituted one matrix.

Three of each type of matrix and its baseline were presented and so each subject was tested over twelve trials where each trial entailed a new combination of awards and penalties. In this experiment, each subject was given 24 trials and so the 12 original matrices were repeated in the same form.

The inclusion of baselines enabled a comparison to be made between the baseline response and a response on either the MD or MJP type matrices. This comparison represented the essence of the scoring system used to monitor the subjects' usage of the different strategies presented. By means of this comparison, a 'pull score' for each strategy could be calculated, where 'pull' refers to the subjects' utilization of a particular strategy. Table 3 illustrates how scale values were applied to the matrices and indicates how pull scores for each strategy (MD, MJP) and strategy combination (MD/MIP, MJP/MIP) were calculated from comparisons between the matrix types and the relevant baselines.

To give a concrete example of this scoring system, if a subject had chosen C for the MD baseline and then had chosen C again in the MD type matrix

Table 3. *Scale values for calculating pull scores in MD-type and MJP-type matrices*

	Matrix						
	Baseline: A B C				MD-type: A B C		
	2	0	4		2	3	1
	2	1	3		2	4	0
For MD	−1	−2	0		+1	0	+2
MJP/MIP	−1	−2	0		+1	+2	0
	Baseline: A B C				MJP-type: A B C		
	4	0	2		2	1	3
	1	3	2		2	4	0
For MJP	0	−2	−1		+1	+2	0
MD/MIP	0	−2	−1		+1	0	+2

Note: Ingroup payoffs are in the upper cells.

itself, he or she would then have a maximum score of +2 for the MD strategy and a score of 0 for the MJP/MIP strategy indicating that the subject had adopted an MD policy for that particular matrix. Similarly, with reference to the MJP type matrix, if a subject had chosen A on the baseline and then C for the MJP matrix, then he or she would have an MJP pull score of 0 and an MD/MIP pull score of +2 for that particular matrix. As there were 24 trials in the present experiment, a subject could build up to a maximum pull score for any strategy of +12 or alternatively a minimum score of −12.

This, then, was one method used to measure the subjects' behaviour. Other methods included calculation of total coin allocations to each group and usage of the parity strategy was assessed from this data. These methods are described in more detail in the Results section.

Before commencing the 24 trials of the experiment proper, each subject was given a practice matrix and the experimenter ensured that the child had understood the instructions. The experimenter also stressed that there was no correct way to divide up the money, but rather that it should be divided as the subject thought fit. Throughout, the experimenter refrained from any comment on the child's responses; she merely recorded behaviour and noted as well any comments made by the child.

Results

The results section is divided in relation to the different measures of the dependent variable: coin allocation, matrix strategy pull scores, and incidence of the parity strategy.

Table 4. *Mean number of coins allocated to In- and Outgroups by Polynesian and European girls and boys*

Experimental groups		Money allocation	
Ethnic group	Sex	Ingroup	Outgroup
European	Girls	85	71
	Boys	85	71
	Mean	85	71
Polynesian	Girls	87	74
	Boys	80	76
	Mean	83	75

Coin allocation to the groups   The mean numbers of coins subjects allocated to the ingroup and outgroup are presented in Table 4. A split-plot ANOVA for unweighted means revealed a significant main effect for coin allocation to the groups ($F = 54.46$, df $= 1,109$, $p < 0.01$), with all subjects regardless of ethnic group consistently awarding more coins to the ingroup. Two interaction effects became evident: ethnic group by sex interaction ($F = 4.03$, df $= 1,109$, $p < 0.05$) and ethnic group by coin allocation interaction ($F = 7.85$, df $= 1,109$, $p < 0.01$). Analysis of simple main effects for the first interaction revealed a significant ethnic difference for the female subjects ($F = 7.74$, df $= 1,109$, $p < 0.01$). Polynesian girls awarded more money to both groups than the European girls and this indicates use of the maximum joint profit strategy. The second interaction is of more theoretical interest, and here analysis of simple main effects demonstrated that Polynesian children were more generous to the outgroup than European children ($F = 11.56$, df $= 1,109$, $p < 0.01$), although the two ethnic samples did not differ in their allocation to the ingroup. Overall, then, it appears that both Polynesian and European children show ingroup favouritism but the Polynesians are less discriminatory towards the outgroup.

Matrix strategy pull scores   Table 5 shows the pull of the different strategies and strategy combinations for the Polynesian and European children. The two comparisons in Table 5 between MD and MJP and between MD/MIP and MJP/MIP were each subjected to a split-plot ANOVA for unweighted means.

First, the MD and MJP comparison: the only significant finding from the ANOVA was for the ethnic group by strategy usage interaction ($F = 9.78$, df $= 1,109$, $p < 0.01$). Further analysis of this interaction demonstrated that European children conformed to the pattern found for other

Table 5. *Mean pull scores for two individual strategies and two strategy combinations obtained from Polynesian and European girls and boys*

Experimental groups		Strategies			
		Comparison 1		Comparison 2	
Ethnic group	Sex	MD	MJP	MD/MIP	MJP/MIP
European	Girls	3.01	0.77	5.40	2.95
	Boys	2.99	0.87	5.56	3.95
	Mean	3.00	0.82	5.48	3.45
Polynesian	Girls	2.20	3.20	4.30	4.75
	Boys	1.28	2.61	−0.17	3.50
	Mean	1.74	2.91	2.07	4.13

Western groups and used MD more than MJP ($F = 8.13$, df $= 1, 109$, $p < 0.01$). In contrast, Polynesian children preferred MJP although they did not use this strategy significantly more frequently than MD. The differences between the samples for strategy use evident in Table 5 proved significant. European subjects used MD to a greater extent than Polynesian children ($F = 4.35$, df $= 1, 109, p < 0.05$), while Polynesian subjects used MJP more often than the Europeans ($F = 12.79$, df $= 1, 109, p < 0.01$). Therefore, Europeans prefer to discriminate in favour of the ingroup rather than maximize both groups' profit, while Polynesian children tend towards MJP, using this strategy to a greater extent than their European peers.

The second strategy comparison between usage of the MD/MIP and MJP/MIP strategy combinations yielded no significant main effects and also no significant interaction effects with the exception of the ethnic group by sex interaction ($F = 5.23$, df $= 1, 109, p < 0.05$). Analysis of simple main effects for this interaction showed a significant ethnic difference for the male subjects. The Polynesian boys used both these strategies to a lesser extent than the European boys ($F = 8.54$, df $= 1, 109, p < 0.01$) and also less than the Polynesian females ($F = 8.09$, df $= 1, 109, p < 0.01$). As Table 5 demonstrates, the Polynesian boys obtained a negative 'pull' score for MD/MIP and hence their low overall pull score for the strategy combinations. Because of the logic behind the matrices and pull score calculations, the negative number represents a pull score for the opposite strategy, and so Polynesian boys avoided MD/MIP and instead tended to choose the opposite (i.e. maximum difference in favour of the *outgroup* combined with maximum *outgroup* profit). Therefore, although Europeans and Polynesians do not appear to differ significantly in the way they implement

Table 6. *Percentages of European and Polynesian girls and boys using the parity strategy*

Ethnic group	Sex	Percentage
European	Girls	46
	Boys	33
	Mean	40
Polynesian	Girls	20
	Boys	39
	Mean	30

ingroup favouritism (whether MD/MIP or MJP/MIP), there is this indirect evidence that Polynesian males at least do not favour the more discriminatory MD/MIP strategy.

Incidence of parity   Usage of the parity strategy was measured by examining the total coin allocation made by each subject to the in- and outgroups and then deciding whether these total allocations fell within a range of fair scores represented by fiducial limits set at the 0.05 level of confidence which were established using the binomial expansion. An alternative method was also applied to check the accuracy of the fiducial limits procedure. Over the 24 trials, the number of times that a subject awarded more money to the ingroup was compared with the number of times he awarded less money to the ingroup than the outgroup. A sign test set at the 0.05 level of confidence (one-tailed) was used to compare the number of 'positives' against the number of 'negatives'. Only those subjects who did not deviate significantly from the parity mid-point on both tests were included in the number of subjects regarded as consistently using the parity strategy. Table 6 presents these figures in percentage form.

The two trends evident in Table 6 for Polynesian boys to use parity more than Polynesian girls and for Europeans to use parity more than the Polynesians did not prove significant in a chi-square analysis. An earlier experiment had similarly failed to demonstrate any sex differences in the use of this strategy for European children.

Summary and conclusions

The results demonstrate that there are cultural differences in responses to a minimal group situation. Both groups showed ingroup bias but the Polynesian children moderated their discrimination, displaying greater generosity to the outgroup and a preference for maximum joint profit rather than the establishment of maximum difference in favour of the ingroup. New Zealand European subjects behaved in much the same way as English children suggesting that the Polynesian/European response differences found in this experiment are the product of a non-Western value system. This value system and the implications of these findings for social identity theory will be examined in the discussion following the second experiment.

One finding of interest that will not be dealt with in the later discussion was the trend for Polynesian girls to use the MD/MIP and MJP/MIP strategy combinations more than the Polynesian boys. It is not clear what importance should be attributed to this sex difference or even whether it was the girls or the boys (or both) who were deviating from a typical pattern of MD/MIP and MJP/MIP responses. Given this uncertainty and the fact that the second experiment did not substantiate this finding, there seems little point in speculating about the reasons for this result.

The first experiment successfully demonstrated the feasibility of using the minimal group paradigm for cross-cultural investigation. The Polynesian children grasped the instructions as quickly as the European children and no severe language problems were encountered. The majority of the Polynesian children had attended New Zealand schools for several years and thus were quite accustomed to being divided into relatively arbitrary groups (e.g. for sports). One variable which could have affected the results was the experimenter's ethnic group (New Zealand European). However, there is some evidence (Vaughan, 1963) that the race of the experimenter has no effect upon young Polynesian children's choices in the more sensitive area of ethnic preferences and so it could be that this variable is not as salient for Polynesian children as it appears to be for Negro children.

To conclude, the advantages of this type of limited cross-cultural investigation appear to outweigh the disadvantages and it may be relevant to theoretically important behavioural differences. For this reason, the second experiment was conducted to extend the cross-cultural comparison.

3. Experiment 2: The European–Samoan–Maori comparison

As noted in the Introduction to this chapter, this experiment not only investigated the effects of cultural background, but also examined the response condition or dependent measure. Many of the minimal categorization studies conducted to date have used the matrix system to organize the subjects' responses. In this experiment, a free-choice responding condition was included as well as the matrix condition. The subjects in the free-choice condition freely allocated a prearranged number of coins to the ingroup and outgroup. The major difference between this and the matrix response situation is the lack of any response guidelines. The child in the free-choice condition has to make his own rules rather than choosing from a restricted range of strategies arranged by the experimenter.

All the children received both response conditions, matrices and free-choice; these were divided into two presentation orders. Half the children received the free-choice first and then the matrices (FC–M), while the other half responded in terms of the matrices and then freely (M–FC). No predictions were made concerning the direction of response in the free-choice condition or concerning the effect of the different presentation orders.

Predictions could be made about the effects of cultural group on the basis of the results obtained in the first experiment. It was hypothesized that the Maori and Samoan children would be more generous to the outgroup than European children, and that they would use the MJP strategy to a greater extent than the European children while adopting MD to a significantly lesser extent. No predictions were made concerning usage of the MD/MIP, MJP/MIP, and parity strategies.

Thus, the two independent variables in this experiment were the ethnic group and the experimental condition. Sex was not considered as a separate variable because preliminary analysis of the raw data did not reveal any consistent sex differences.

Method

Subjects

One hundred and ten European, Samoan and Maori subjects were tested. Subjects in all the groups had an average chronological age of eight years, and all came from suburbs ranked 6–7, low to very low socio-economic status, on an Auckland Regional Authority scale (1971). The school roll was used to determine the ethnic group of the children. The subjects were divided among the different cultural groups and the presentation orders in this manner:

European		Samoan		Maori	
M–FC	FC–M	M–FC	FC–M	M–FC	FC–M
20	20	20	20	15	15

In the schools used in this experiment, approximately 80 % of the children were of Polynesian origin; the Samoans were the largest ethnic group in the school while the Maoris and white Europeans were the next largest.

Procedure

Part One

On this occasion all the subjects were categorized on the basis of picture preferences. The same instructions were used in this experiment as in Experiment I.

Part Two

The effects of this categorization were measured in two ways. First, by means of the matrix arrangement described in Experiment 1, except that in Experiment 2 there were 12 matrix trials instead of 24. The second dependent measure was the 12 trials of the free-choice response condition. Here, the subjects were given a number of two-cent coins and asked to divide them between the groups as they thought fit. There were 12 free-choice trials, the number of coins given to the subjects on each trial ranged from six to one, and a prearranged random presentation of coins was used. On half the trials, the subjects were dividing an even number of coins between the groups and on the other six trials they were given an odd number of coins. The subjects arranged their coin allocation to the groups on one of the cards used for the matrix trials and then placed the coins in the two money boxes. As in the matrix response condition, they were told that they would not be getting any money for themselves as they would always be allocating it to other people in the two groups. The subjects were then given a practice trial and the instructions were repeated until they acknowledged comprehension. The experimenters recorded the number of coins allocated to each group and they were instructed not to offer any evaluative comment on the children's responses. Half the children received the matrices first and then the free-choice condition (M–FC), while the other half received the reverse presentation order (FC–M).

Results

The results of this comparison are presented in two sections. The first section examines the subjects' responses on the matrices and, as before, is further subdivided in relation to the various measures of the dependent variable: coin allocation, matrix strategy pull scores, and incidence of parity. The second section deals with the data from the 12 free-choice trials and looks at coin allocation and incidence of parity. All the ANOVAS mentioned were split-plot designs for unweighted means.

Matrix responses

Coin allocation in the matrices   Table 7 gives the means for the different ethnic groups across the two presentation orders. The clear-cut tendency for subjects to award more coins to the ingroup than to the outgroup proved to be significant ($F = 131.35$, df $= 1, 104$, $p < 0.01$). Secondary analysis showed that this held irrespectively of the cultural group of the subjects.

Table 7. *Mean number of coins allocated to the In- and Outgroups by European, Samoan, and Maori subjects in two different presentations orders over 12 matrix trials*

Experimental groups		Money allocation	
Ethnic group	Presentation order	Ingroup	Outgroup
European	M–FC	44	31
	FC–M	44	36
	Mean	44	33.50
Samoan	M–FC	44	39
	FC–M	43	39
	Mean	43.50	39
Maori	M–FC	41	37
	FC–M	44	34
	Mean	42.50	35.50

The ethnic groups did differ in the way they allocated the coins to the ingroup and outgroup, and this was reflected in a significant interaction effect ($F = 9.99$, df = 2, 104, $p < 0.01$). Analysis of simple main effects revealed that this difference concerned generosity to the outgroup ($F = 6.89$, df = 2, 104, $p < 0.01$), not allocation to the ingroup. An a priori comparison of the relevant means showed that, as predicted, Samoans were more generous to the outgroup than Europeans ($t = 7.66$, df = 104, $t_{0.05} = 1.98$, one-tailed); Maoris also awarded more to the outgroup than European children ($t = 3.28$, df = 104, $t_{0.05} = 1.98$, one-tailed), but they awarded less than the Samoan children ($t = 4.36$, df = 104, $t_{0.05} = 1.66$, two-tailed). These results confirm the trend evident in the first experiment: ingroup favouritism is the dominant response but culture does affects the degree of discrimination.

The picture is further complicated by a three-variable (ethnic group, presentation order, coin allocation) interaction which proved to be significant in the ANOVA ($F = 5.56$, df = 2, 104, $p < 0.01$). Analysis of this interaction produced the following conclusions: presentation order (M–FC or FC–M) does not affect the tendency to favour the ingroup over the outgroup, but ethnic differences in generosity to the outgroup only occurred in one presentation order, matrices first and then the free-choice. Samoans in the presentation order M–FC allocated more coins to the outgroup over the twelve matrix trials than European children (Tukey's test: $q = 4.03$, df = 104, $q_{0.05} = 2.80$); Maoris also awarded more than the Europeans in the M–FC order ($q = 2.95$, df = 104, $q_{0.05} = 2.80$) but there was no significant difference between the Maori and the Samoan

Table 8. *Mean strategy pull scores for two individual strategies and two strategy combinations obtained from European, Samoan, and Maori subjects in two different presentation orders*

Experimental groups		Strategies			
		Comparison 1		Comparison 2	
Ethnic group	Presentation Order	MD	MJP	MD/MIP	MJP/MIP
Europeans	M–FC	1.80	0.50	3.60	1.50
	FC–M	0.70	0.70	2.60	2.30
	Mean	1.25	0.60	3.10	1.90
Samoans	M–FC	0.75	1.15	1.15	3.35
	FC–M	−0.55	1.45	1.35	3.15
	Mean	0.10	1.30	1.25	3.25
Maoris	M–FC	1.20	0.40	0.87	1.47
	FC–M	0.67	1.07	2.67	1.73
	Mean	0.94	0.74	1.77	1.60

subjects in allocation to the outgroup ($q = 0.85$, df $= 104$, $q_{0.05} = 2.80$). This fact that ethnic differences in generosity to the outgroup only surfaced in one presentation order seems a result of the marked and contradictory influence that presentation orders had upon the European and Maori groups. European subjects were more generous to the outgroup on the matrices when they had the free-choice first and then the matrices ($F = 5.68$, df $= 2, 104$, $p < 0.05$) whereas the Maori children reversed the pattern and showed less ingroup bias and outgroup discrimination in the M–FC presentation order ($F = 7.60$, df $= 2, 104$, $p < 0.01$). For this reason, the difference between the Samoan and European groups in generosity to the outgroup was particularly evident in the M–FC presentation order.

Matrix strategy pull scores   Pull scores were calculated for the two individual strategies, MD and MJP, and for the two strategy combinations, MD/MIP and MJP/MIP. Table 8 gives the means for the three ethnic groups in the two presentation orders. Two three-way ANOVAS were performed on this data, the first compared usage of MD and MJP and the second usage of MD/MIP and MJP/MIP.

First MD and MJP: there were no significant main effects but one interaction effect for ethnic group combined with strategy usage ($F = 4.27$, df $= 2, 104$, $p < 0.05$). As Table 8 shows, the European and Maori children preferred the MD strategy to MJP whereas the Samoans used MJP more than MD. This differential strategy usage did not prove to be significant for the European and Maori groups in an analysis of simple main effects but the Samoans did use MJP more than MD ($F = 5.54$, df $= 1$, $p < 0.05$). The three ethnic groups differed from each other in the extent to which they used MD ($F = 3.48$, df $= 2, 104$, $p < 0.05$) but not in their utilization of MJP. An a priori comparison of means gave more information about these results from the analysis of simple main effects. It was discovered that, as hypothesized, Europeans used MD more than Samoans ($t = 4.96$, df $= 104$, $t_{0.05} = 1.98$, one-tailed). However, contrary to prediction, the Maori children did not differ from the Europeans in their use of MD ($t = 0.46$, df $= 104$, $t_{0.05} = 1.98$, one-tailed) and they used MD significantly more than the Samoans ($t = 4.16$, df $= 104$, $t_{0.05} = 1.66$, two-tailed). Thus, the trend noted in the first experiment for Polynesian children to prefer MJP rather than MD is confirmed for the Samoan children but the Maori children resemble the Europeans in their use of the different strategies, tending towards MD and away from MJP.

It must be noted that the strategy usage/presentation order interaction in this MD–MJP comparison ANOVA is significant at the $p < 0.10$ level ($F = 3.54$, df $= 1, 104$). Therefore, the pattern evident in the mean pull scores (Table 8) is tentatively confirmed. Subjects from all three ethnic groups in the M–FC presentation order tended to use MD more than subjects in the FC–M condition. The latter showed a greater inclination towards MJP. This finding parallels the finding in the coin allocation analysis, namely that European children tended to be more generous to the outgroup in the FC–M condition.

The other ANOVA performed on the pull score data concerned the MD/MIP and MJP/MIP comparison. It yielded one significant effect – for the ethnic group by strategy usage interaction ($F = 11.10$, df $= 2, 104$, $p < 0.01$). Analysis of simple main effects demonstrated that European children used MD/MIP more than MJP/MIP ($F = 5.99$, df $= 1, 104$, $p < 0.05$); Samoan children favoured MJP/MIP over MD/MIP ($F = 16.63$, df $= 1, 104$, $p < 0.01$); while Maori children showed no significant preferences. There were ethnic differences in use of both MD/MIP ($F = 5.83$, df $= 2, 104$, $p < 0.05$) and MJP/MIP ($F = 4.95$, df $= 2, 104$, $p < 0.05$). Further comparison of means revealed the following significant differences between the ethnic samples for the MD/MIP pull scores: Europeans used MD/MIP significantly more often than Samoan subjects ($q = 6.73$, df $= 104$, $q_{0.05} = 2.80$); whereas the Samoans and the Maoris did not differ ($q = 2.63$, df $= 104$, $q_{0.05} = 2.80$). For the MJP/MIP combination it was found that the Samoans used this strategy to a greater extent than Europeans ($q = 6.84$, df $= 104$, $q_{0.05} = 2.80$) and also more frequently than the

Table 9. *Percentages of European, Samoan, and Maori subjects in both presentation orders using the parity strategy over the 12 matrix trials*

Ethnic group	Presentation order	Percentage
European	M–FC	20
	FC–M	35
	Mean	27.5
Samoan	M–FC	25
	FC–M	40
	Mean	32.5
Maori	M–FC	47
	FC–M	33
	Mean	40

Maoris ($q = 8.35$, df $= 104$, $q_{0.05} = 2.80$), while the Maoris and the Europeans do not differ significantly ($q = 1.52$, df $= 104$, $q_{0.05} = 2.80$). In summary, then, it appears that cultural differences are expressed through utilization of the MD/MIP and MJP/MIP strategies. Samoan children prefer to temper their ingroup favouritism with MJP while the European children straightforwardly prefer MD/MIP and Maori children fall somewhere in-between these two response modes.

Incidence of parity in the matrix trials   The methods used to calculate reliable percentages of subjects using the parity strategy have already been described in the Results section for Experiment 1. The percentages for the three ethnic groups are given in Table 9. A chi-square analysis of this data showed that there were no significant ethnic differences in the use of the parity strategy. Presentation order also had no effect upon the responses of the Maori and European children. However, the Samoans did opt for parity more often in the FC–M condition than in the M–FC condition ($\chi^2 = 4.34$, df $= 1$, $\chi^2_{0.05} = 3.84$).

Responses in the twelve free-choice trials

Coin allocation in the free-choice trials   The number of coins each subject allocated to the in- and outgroups were totalled and the mean figures are displayed in Table 10. The ANOVA yielded a significant difference for coin allocation with all subjects awarding more money to the ingroup than to the outgroup ($F = 66.15$, df $= 1, 104$ $p < 0.01$). There were no significant interaction effects.

Table 10. *Mean number of coins allocated to In- and Out-groups by European, Samoan, and Maori subjects in two presentation orders over 12 trials*

Experimental groups		Coin allocation	
Ethnic group	Presentation order	Ingroup	Outgroup
European	M–FC	26	16
	FC–M	26	16
	Mean	26	16
Samoan	M–FC	25	17
	FC–M	23	19
	Mean	24	18
Maori	M–FC	25	17
	FC–M	23	19
	Mean	24	18

Further information on the free-choice responding becomes available when the coin allocations to the in- and outgroups are analysed in more detail. The 12 trials of the free-choice condition consisted of two types of trials: in six of the trials the subjects divided odd numbers of coins between the two groups and in the other six an even number were to be divided. Using Friedman's two-way analysis of variance by ranks (Siegel, 1956), the difference between the number of choices favouring the ingroup and the number favouring the outgroup could be examined, and for the even trials the number of choices favouring the ingroup and the number for the outgroup as well as the number of ties, or equal divisions, could be compared. Table 11 illustrates the percentages of different types of choice over the odd and even trials.

The statistical analysis demonstrated that in the case of trials with an odd number of coins, significantly more coins were awarded to the ingroup than to the outgroup. This outcome occurred consistently for all ethnic groups in both presentation orders with the exception of the Maori children in the FC–M presentation order. For the trials with the even number of coins, significant differences were found when comparing ingroup choices, outgroup choices and the number of ties in all cases, without exception. Table 11 indicates the direction of these significant differences for the groups concerned.

Summarizing this information, it is possible to conclude that division of an odd number of coins is conducive to ingroup favouritism, while the provision of an opportunity for equal division between the groups promotes use of parity. There are no consistent or clear-cut ethnic differ-

Table 11. *Percentages of choices made by European, Samoan, and Maori subjects in two presentation orders which favoured the ingroup, the outgroup, and ties respectively, for both the odd and even numbers of coins*

Experimental groups			Percentages		
Ethnic group	No. of coins	Presentation order	Ingroup	Outgroup	Ties
European	Odds	M–FC	77	23	
		FC–M	73	27	
		Mean	75	25	
	Evens	M–FC	42	8	51
		FC–M	39	8	53
		Mean	40.5	8	52
Samoans	Odds	M–FC	68	32	
		FC–M	63	37	
		Mean	65.5	34.5	
	Evens	M–FC	41	10	49
		FC–M	23	9	68
		Mean	32	9.5	58.5
Maoris	Odds	M–FC	68	32	
		FC–M	57	43	
		Mean	62.5	37.5	
	Evens	M–FC	35	11	55
		FC–M	31	9	60
		Mean	33	10	57.5

ences in this behaviour. Quick scanning of the percentages in Table 11 suggests that presentation order has some effect since the number of ties is larger in relation to the number of choices favouring the ingroup when subjects received the free-choice trials first.

Incidence of parity in the free-choice trials Using the procedures described in Experiment 1, the percentages of subjects consistently using parity were calculated for the three ethnic groups and are presented in Table 12. The percentages obtained for the 12 matrix trials are included also for comparison. A chi-square analysis of these data showed no significant presentation condition or ethnic effects. Comparison of the free-choice percentages with those obtained for the matrix trials demonstrates that for these subjects the free-choice condition engenders a higher incidence of parity.

4. Discussion

First, the cross-cultural comparison will be considered and its implications for the social identity theory, and then the methodological manipulation. The results from both experiments demonstrate conclusively that cultural

Table 12. *Percentages of European, Samoan, and Maori*
subjects in both presentation orders using the parity strategy

Experimental groups		Percentages	
Ethnic group	Presentation orders	Matrix trials	Free-choice
European	M–FC	20	70
	FC–M	35	70
	Mean	27.5	70
Samoan	M–FC	25	70
	FC–M	40	95
	Mean	32.5	82.5
Maori	M–FC	47	80
	FC–M	33	93
	Mean	40	86.5

background influences the degree of intergroup discrimination displayed in the minimal group experiment. MD and MD/MIP were the predominant European responses while MJP and MJP/MIP were the strategies favoured by the Polynesian sample in the first experiment and the Samoan children in the second experiment. This preference of Polynesian immigrant children was also reflected in their greater generosity to the outgroup as measured by total coin allocation. On the whole, the experimental hypotheses derived from the first experiment were confirmed in the second, although the Samoan utilization of MJP was not as strong as predicted. Also, contrary to prediction, the responses of the Maori children more often resembled those of the European children than those of the Samoan subjects. The intercultural similarities must also be stressed. All the groups displayed a significant amount of ingroup favouritism and, in fact, the groups differed mainly in the way this ingroup bias was expressed. The Samoan children, for example, preferred to combine ingroup profit with a 'most for all' approach, while the European children made sure that ingroup profit was achieved at the expense of the outgroup.

Despite the obvious similarities, it is evident that the children's behaviour was influenced by external cultural values. The differential usage of MD and MJP probably best sums up the most basic differences between the Polynesian and Western cultures. The MJP strategy involves awarding the most coins to *both* groups irrespective of which group actually wins. There are two facets to this response: it could be viewed as the ultimate in generosity and cooperation, a strategy which transcends the intergroup distinction, or it could be seen as an attempt to get as much money as possible out of the experimenter. Perhaps both attitudes determine the

Polynesian children's responses summed together in the 'best for all' approach to social interaction which is so characteristic of many institutionalized relationships in Polynesian society. In contrast to MJP, MD explicitly emphasizes group divisions; it implies the maximization of the monetary *difference* between the groups. With this strategy it is not enough to get the most for one's group; the aim is to *win* even if in doing so the ingroup is penalized.

Unlike Western societies, traditional Polynesian societies (and to a certain extent the modern immigrant communities) are based on cooperative institutions such as the extended kin group (the *'āiga*) (Beaglehole, 1957; Keesing and Keesing, 1973; Metge, 1976). This extended family group was and still is, in places, the dominant unit for economic activity. Most day-to-day activities revolved around this mode of communal organization which drew its strength from the institutionalization of the norms of generosity and cooperation. In general, personal relationships and individual achievement were overshadowed by the social organization and the collective good (Mead, 1930). The *'āiga* is still an important structuring principle in the modern Samoan migrant community (Ablon, 1971; Pitt and MacPherson, 1971, 1974) and Samoan children are continually exposed to situations organized on a cooperative group basis. To participate successfully within the *'āiga*, the individual must constantly consider the best outcome for the whole group. The New Zealand European child, in contrast, is more familiar with the norm of individual achievement and with the competitive principles at the basis of Western educational, legal, economic and political systems. Large communal groups play little part in his or her socialization. The urban Maori child lives in a 'grey' world between these two options. If the parents retain links with kin group members and if they consciously 'enculturate' the family in Maori ways, then the child may become familiar with the norms of generosity and cooperation stressed traditionally. Most urban Maori parents, however, are not familiar with these aspects of *Maoritanga* and they encounter few opportunities to engage in the communal gatherings which are still a feature of rural Maori life (Metge, 1976; Ritchie, 1964).

Ethnographic accounts, therefore, enable ready interpretation of the results. Moreover, the differences between the Maori and Samoan groups can be explained in terms of a rough acculturation continuum. The responses of the Samoan and European children represent the ends of the scale, and the responses of the Maori children appear to vacillate from the cooperative end to the competitive end. As the Samoans become more Westernized, no doubt they will also lose their distinctive attitudes to social interaction. It is in fact surprising that we did find evidence of cultural differences given that the majority of the Polynesian children, including the Samoans, were products of the New Zealand educational system. If the MJP-type behaviour does vary as a function of Westernization, this response style would presumably be more prevalent in the Islands than in New Zealand. One study (Graves and Graves, 1975) in the Cook Islands has confirmed the relationship between Westernization and the use of competitive strategies (in this case in an interpersonal coin game). The Graveses observed a developmental sequence in this type of behaviour. At 5–6 years of age, Cook Island children reached their most generous level and after that stage they became increasingly competitive with each successive year at school. The educational implications of this type of finding are obvious and N. Graves (1974) has argued that the cultural deficit assumptions which characterize educators' attitudes to the teaching of Polynesian children should be supplanted. It would seem that in this respect the European children could be seen as the unfortunate ones with the cultural deficit.

A question arises as to the generality of the MJP-type response. We have assumed that the Polynesian children and the Samoans in particular are acting in terms of recognizable and clear-cut cultural values which normally guide interindividual interaction within a large communal group and which also guide various forms of intergroup interaction (e.g. ritualized occasions such as the *tere* parties in Cook Islands' culture, the Maori *huis* for weddings and funerals, and the Samoan wedding feast within the modern migrant community. These are occasions where one kin group or larger grouping displays its generosity to other groups and to the community as a whole). We do not assume that the norms of generosity and cooperation would guide behaviour in all intergroup situations or that Samoan children asked to allocate coins to an ingroup and to a traditionally hostile outgroup would be any less competitive than European children in the same situation. The minimal group situation, with its group divisions which cut across a prior more important grouping (the school class), does seem to fit into a category of events relevant to cooperative norms and this finding does raise some questions for the social identity theory of intergroup relations which will be discussed later. There seems little point in asserting that we have tapped a generalized response to intergroup interaction.

A further related question concerns the meaning the Polynesian subjects attributed to the experimental situation. Did they see it as an intergroup situation at all? It was possible to check up on the manipulation of the independent variable through questioning the children once they had finished the task. As far as the experimenters could ascertain, the Polynesian children's comments indicated a clear understanding of the fact that they had been divided into two groups and were allocating money to these two groups.

Another possibility to be considered is that the experimental situation crossed and opposed two category memberships for the Polynesian children and thus inhibited intergroup discrimination (cf. Deschamps and Doise, 1978). In other words, the children were aware of being both members of the blue group and Polynesian or Samoan, for example, and that the 'red' group, the outgroup, contained many members of another ingroup (i.e., other Polynesians). While it is possible that criss-crossing of categories weakened intergroup discrimination and encouraged intergroup cooperation, it seems unlikely. The Polynesians were not in the minority in the school classes tested; in fact, these classes were all about 90 % Polynesian, and so the Polynesian/white European distinction probably did not interfere with their 'minimal' group identification. It certainly did not affect the behaviour of the European children who *were* in the minority. It also seems unlikely that various ethnic groups (e.g. Samoans) within the larger ethnic grouping of Polynesians would have noted any criss-crossing of group identities; that is, it is unlikely that the Samoans in the 'blue' group co-operated with the 'red' group because their social identity as a group of Samoans split between two other groups was salient. It was clear to the experimenters that the children themselves did not differentiate between the ethnic subgroups making up the Polynesian group and could not in fact usually identify whether a classmate was, for example, a Samoan, a Niuean or a Cook Islander. Also, there is now new evidence that criss-crossing works in a more complicated fashion than supposed and on some occasions does not reduce intergroup discrimination (Brown and Turner, 1979). All in all, then, there is little reason for supposing that cultural identity was more salient than minimal group categorization and that it weakened the Polynesian children's discrimination.

Although these cross-cultural findings are interesting in their own right, for the purposes of this chapter the importance of the results lies in their relevance to the evaluation of the social identity theory. The theory rests on three linked assumptions: (*a*) that individuals desire a positive self-evaluation; (*b*) that they will use their social identity as a group member as a source of self-evaluation, comparing ingroups with outgroups; and (*c*) in an intergroup situation, a positive social identity results from distinguishing the ingroup from the outgroup on some positively valued dimension. In terms of the minimal group paradigm, then, subjects discriminate between the groups in choosing the MD and MD/MIP strategies because these strategies allow the active establishment of a positively valued *difference* between the ingroup and the outgroup. Ingroup favour-itism alone would not be sufficient as it is the establishment of a distinction *between* the groups in favour of the ingroup on the positively valued dimension of money which is important. Why, then, do Polynesian subjects choose the MJP and MJP/MIP strategies which, in contrast, often award more coins to the outgroup? It would seem that social identity theory cannot explain the behaviour of the Polynesian children and thus the social categorization/self-evaluation/social comparison process is poten-tially limited as a theory of intergroup interaction.

A normative account, on the other hand, can explain the data. Through socialization, children internalize the norms of their social group. When faced with the experimental situation, they use these norms as guides to behaviour and for this reason children from different cultural groups act in different ways. The matrix strategies encapsulate different norms and thus the child's behaviour gives a clue as to which norm predominates. Prediction of behaviour is, therefore, only possible if the researcher has prior knowledge of the social background of his or her subjects.

This pessimism concerning the limitations of social identity theory as compared with a normative account ignores, however, one important possibility which has not been considered. As noted in the Introduction, Tajfel and Turner assume that the process they have identified is universal but that the form it takes in any given situation is socially determined. Specifically, the content of social identity and the value dimensions chosen for intergroup comparison are dependent upon the situation. Speculation about the value dimensions a Polynesian child might use for intergroup comparison suggests a way out for social identity theory. It is probable that the Polynesian children are using a different value dimension for self-evaluation and group differentiation and it is possible that this value dimen-sion involves generosity. Use of the MJP strategy may, in fact, represent a competition to appear the most generous.

In many Polynesian societies, generosity is associated with status, your *mana* or standing as a person is partly determined by how much you give away. As a result, a positive self-evaluation can be attained by placing everybody's interests before one's own and a positive social identity results from giving to other groups. Hence, apparently cooperative group inter-action may be motivated by competitiveness. The Polynesian child in the minimal group experiment is no doubt impelled by the same desire for a positive social identity as the European child. However, this motivation may be expressed by choosing the MJP and MJP/MIP strategies, as these strategies are traditionally associated with personal status. In fact, this type of behaviour would probably still receive the most praise in the modern Samoan migrant community.

It is, of course, an empirical question whether Polynesian children use MJP and MJP/MIP to differentiate between the ingroup and the outgroup on a generosity dimension. Further experimentation is required to elucidate the meaning of these strategies for the subjects. Whatever the case, a decision between normative accounts and the social identity model on these grounds must be postponed, perhaps indefinitely. The crucial experiment which can decide between the two theories is largely a mythical entity and theories are seldom evaluated on their performance in one setting. Social identity theory has a decided advantage over the looser normative accounts since it gives some understanding of the processes involved and thus enables coherent and productive analyses of many disparate phenomena (social change, minority groups, stereotypes, sociolinguistics). It is also associated with a large body of empirical research which has verified its postulates in these areas (e.g. Tajfel, 1978). For this reason it could be argued that a social identity model of the minimal group data is to be preferred. However, the dynamics behind the behaviour of both Polynesian and Western children in this situation are still largely obscured. It is possible further experimentation could reveal that the desire for a positive social identity and the subsequent impetus to differentiate are not involved in the children's decisions. Perhaps the least contentious conclusion is that normative pressures probably merge with the effects of social identification, so children discriminate between the groups (on whatever dimension) because they feel that this is the right way to behave in this situation and also because they are comparing the groups in an attempt to enhance their own social identity.

Thus, in summary, there seems to be little basis for rejecting a social identity account of these data and good reason for accepting this interpretation, but it is equally true that normative theories cannot be discounted and must still be taken seriously.

The application of social identity theory to the cross-cultural data clearly indicates the flexibility of the link between theories and the experiments which supposedly test their predictions. It was noted in the Introduction that Tajfel rejected normative accounts because they were too elastic and could explain any form of behaviour displayed in the minimal group situation. Turner, for example, maintains that normative theories are not truly predictive because of their potential circularity: the behaviour of the subjects in the experiment informs about and defines the norm which is operating. The present cross-cultural results indicate that social identity theory displays the same weaknesses. If MD, MJP, MIP and perhaps even parity choices can be replicated by assuming that each strategy involves a different comparative value dimension, what happens to the predictive value of the theory? It would seem that it also is in danger of becoming circular with the choices of the subjects defining the value dimensions selected for evaluating the ingroup. Normative accounts and social identity theory are, therefore, limited in exactly the same way as far as the minimal paradigm is concerned, calling into question any rationalization of the intrinsic advantages of the social identity models.

One point that does emerge from the consideration of the implications of the data for the social identity model is that the minimal group paradigm is not a particularly adequate means for testing the predictions of the theory in relation to predictions from other theories. One wonders if any experiment could serve this purpose. It should be clear that both normative accounts and social identity theory can only make predictions on the basis of a prior detailed analysis of the social context. This is to be expected in view of the dialectical relationship between individual psychology and the social context which should be captured in socio-psychological theories. As Tajfel (1972b) pointed out, experiments cannot be conducted in a social vacuum. Normative theories and social identity theory generally make the same predictions on the basis of an analysis of the social context but each account postulates a different process. It would seem difficult if not impossible to construct an experiment testing predictions derived from an understanding of psychological processes alone, since the process is always encapsulated in some socially given form. Thus, in the final analysis, the 'truth' of either approach will be determined by its applicability to the situation being studied and its general utility.

Finally, the methodological manipulation: generally, behaviour in the free-choice condition resembled behaviour in the matrix condition; when given a free choice, children still allocated more coins to the ingroup than to the outgroup. However, the parity strategy was used much more consistently in the free-choice condition and about 80 % of the subjects consistently adopted this strategy (more than twice the number obtained for the matrix response condition). The percentage of equal divisions made on the even trials in the free-choice condition probably gives an even more reliable indication of parity strategy adoption and for each ethnic group parity was the predominant strategy in these trials. This finding, combined with a slight tendency for subjects to be less competitive when they received the FC–M presentation order, suggests that the matrix methodology of Tajfel *et al.* encourages a competitive orientation.

This does not imply that this methodology creates a forced-choice situation as Gerard and Hoyt (1974) and other critics have claimed. The results of this experiment alone show that the subjects are not forced to compete; some Samoan children, in fact, freely choose not to compete by consistently adopting the MJP strategy. What it does seem to imply is that the matrix system, which gives clear guidelines on the different response alternatives, suggests to the children that competition is an approved way of responding. In the free-choice condition, such guidelines are not available, and as a result children are probably more reluctant to compete. Inevitably, structured response conditions, as opposed to naturalistic observation, show the subject the range of possibilities that the experimenter is prepared to accept as valid responses. In the matrix response condition, competitive choices are displayed among other types of choices, whereas in the free-choice condition there are more opportunities to be fair. Each response condition organizes the child's response in some way.

But even when they are given a free choice, children still compete. Therefore, the results of Tajfel *et al.* are not the product of a certain methodology even though by chance they may have chosen precisely the response condition which enhances and thus clearly demonstrates the behavioural tendencies. One study on attitudes to nationality (Middleton, Tajfel and Johnson, 1970) has indicated that children believe that fairness is the mature normative response. In a pilot study, Middleton *et al.* asked children to give their reasons for the way they allocated resources to other people in a simulated game and it emerged that a fair response was accepted as the most mature. A free-choice condition no doubt increases the salience of the fairness norm, the 'mature' response, and decreases the impact of categorization, and this might explain the differences between matrix and free-choice responding.

In conclusion, investigation of the effects of cultural background upon responses in the minimal group paradigm has revealed some interesting Polynesian/European differences which seem to derive from experience of different social structures. It even appears that the minimal group experiment could prove a useful tool for measuring degrees of Westernization. However, because of the intertwining of social context and psychological process, it proved impossible to decide whether social identity theory provided a better explanation of these differences than normative theory. The former theory certainly provides a tighter and on the whole more fruitful understanding of the processes involved although it is doubtful that its merits could be conclusively demonstrated by means of experimental studies. It was shown that both theories face the pitfalls of circularity in relation to the minimal group experiment. Finally, a methodological manipulation was discussed which illustrated the generality of ingroup favouritism across different response measures, although it also suggested that the matrix response condition encourages the clearest display of this tendency.

Notes

[1] This research was completed at Auckland University, New Zealand. I would like to thank Graham Vaughan for his supervision of this project and for his help with the statistical analysis, and also many fellow students, particularly Diane Mackie, Heather McDowell, Rob Leary, Lynne Tippett, and Kristen Patterson for their help in collecting the data.
[2] Because of the administrative requirements of the schools the children attended, it was impossible to make up even samples. The discrepancies between the samples were quite large and so it was decided to modify statistical procedures rather than discard data.
[3] This phrase refers to the belief that the money received by the subjects is dependent upon the money awarded by another ingroup member. Hence, if the subject awards the maximum amount of money to the ingroup, then he might expect others to do the same for mutual profit.

References

Ablon, J. 1971. Retention of cultural values and differential urban adaptation: Samoans and American Indians in a West Coast city. *Social Forces*, **49**, 385–93.
Auckland Regional Authority 1971. Social rank and familism of Auckland suburbs. Unpublished MS. Available from Auckland Regional Authority, Auckland, New Zealand.
Beaglehole, E. 1957. *Social change in the South Pacific*. London: Allen and Unwin.
Billig, M. and Tajfel, H. 1973. Social categorization and similarity in intergroup behaviour. *European Journal of Social Psychology*, **3**, 27–52.
Brown, R.C. and Turner, J.C. 1979. The criss-cross categorization effect in intergroup discrimination. *British Journal of Social and Clinical Psychology*, **18**, 371–83.
Deschamps, J.C. and Doise, W. 1978. Crossed category memberships in intergroup relations. In H. Tajfel (ed.), *op. cit.*
Doise, W. 1978. *Groups and individuals: Explanations in social psychology*. Cambridge: Cambridge University Press.
Doise, W., Csepeli, G., Dann, H.D., Gouge, C., Larsen, K. and Ostell, A. 1972. An experimental investigation into the formation of intergroup representations. *European Journal of Social Psychology*, **2**, 202–4.
Doise, W. and Dann, H.D. 1976. New theoretical perspectives in the experimental study of intergroup relations. *Italian Journal of Psychology*, **3**, 285–303.

Doise, W. and Sinclair, A. 1973. The categorization process in intergroup relations. *European Journal of Social Psychology*, **3**, 145–57.

Gerard, H.B. and Hoyt, M.F. 1974. Distinctiveness of social categorization and attitude towards ingroup members. *Journal of Personality and Social Psychology*, **29**, 836–42.

Graves, N.B. 1974. *Inclusive versus exclusive interaction styles in Polynesian and European classrooms*. Research Report, University of Auckland, No. 5.

Graves, N.B. and Graves, T.D. 1975. *The impact of modernization on the personality of a Polynesian people*. Research Report, University of Auckland, No. 7.

Jahoda, G. 1978. Cross-cultural perspectives. In H. Tajfel and C. Fraser (eds): *Introducing social psychology*. Harmondsworth: Penguin Books.

Keesing, F.M. and Keesing, M.M. 1973. *Elite communication in Samoa: A study of leadership*. New York: Octagon Books.

Mead, M. 1930. *Social organization of Manua*. Honolulu: Bernice P. Bishop Museum Bulletin, No. 76.

Metge, J. 1976. *The Maoris of New Zealand*. (Revised edition) London: Routledge and Kegan Paul.

Middleton, M.R., Tajfel, H. and Johnson, N.B. 1970. Cognitive and affective aspects of children's national attitudes. *British Journal of Social and Clinical Psychology*, **9**, 122–34.

Pitt, D. and MacPherson, C.J. 1971. *Voluntary separation and ethnic participation: Samoan migrants in urban New Zealand*. Nuffield Foundation Ethnic Relations Project, Report No. 1, November 1971.

Pitt, D. and MacPherson, C.J. 1974. *Emerging pluralism: The Samoan community in Auckland*. Auckland: Longmann Paul.

Ritchie, J. 1964. *Maori families*. Wellington: Victoria University Publications in Psychology, No. 18.

Sherif, M. 1966. *Group conflict and cooperation: Their social psychology*. London: Routledge and Kegan Paul.

Sherif, M. and Sherif, C.W. 1953. *Groups in harmony and tension*. New York: Harper and Row.

Siegel, S. 1956. *Nonparametric statistics for the behavioural sciences*. New York: McGraw Hill.

Steiner, I. 1974. What happened to the group in social psychology? *Journal of Experimental Social Psychology*, **10**, 93–109.

Tajfel, H. 1970. Experiments in intergroup discrimination. *Scientific American*, **223**, 96–102.

Tajfel, H. 1972a. La catégorisation sociale. In S. Moscovici (ed.): *Introduction à la psychologie sociale*. Paris: Larousse.

Tajfel, H. 1972b. Experiments in a vacuum. In J. Israel and H. Tajfel (eds): *The context of social psychology: A critical assessment*. European Monographs in Social Psychology, No. 2. London: Academic Press.

Tajfel, H. 1974a. Intergroup behaviour, social comparison and social change. Unpublished Katz-Newcomb lectures, University of Michigan, Ann Arbor.

Tajfel, H. 1974b. Social identity and intergroup behaviour. *Social Science Information*, **13**, 65–93.

Tajfel, H. (ed.) 1978. *Differentiation between social groups: Studies in the social psychology of intergroup relations*. European Monographs in Social Psychology, No. 14. London: Academic Press.

Tajfel, H., Flament, C., Billig, M. and Bundy, R. 1971. Social categorization and intergroup behaviour. *European Journal of Social Psychology*, **1**, 149–78.

Thomas, D.R. 1975. Effects of social class on cooperation and competition among children. *New Zealand Journal of Educational Studies*, **10**, 135–9.

Turner, J.C. 1975*a*. Social comparison and social identity: Some prospects for intergroup behaviour. *European Journal of Social Psychology*, **5**, 5–34.

Turner, J.C. 1975*b*. Social categorization and social comparison in intergroup relations. Unpublished Ph.D. thesis, University of Bristol.

Vaughan, G.M. 1963. The effect of the ethnic grouping of the experimenter upon children's responses to tests of an ethnic nature. *British Journal of Social and Clinical Psychology*, **2**, 66–70.

Vaughan, G.M. 1978. Social categorization and intergroup behaviour in children. In H. Tajfel (ed.), *op. cit.*

Vaughan, G.M., Tajfel, H. and Williams, J. 1981. Intergroup and interindividual discrimination in British children. *Social Psychology Quarterly*, **44**, (1), 37–42.

Wetherell, M.S. and Vaughan, G.M. 1979. Social class, sex, nationality and behaviour in minimal group situations. Unpublished MS, University of Auckland, Auckland, New Zealand.

Whiting, J. 1968. Method and problems in cross-cultural research. In G. Lindzey and E. Aronson (eds): *The handbook of social psychology*, Vol. 2. Reading, Mass.: Addison-Wesley.

9. Individuality and membership in the intergroup system

MURRAY HORWITZ AND JACOB M. RABBIE[2]

1. Introduction

In April 1942, during the German occupation of the Netherlands, individuals who happened to have at least three Jewish grandparents were required to wear a yellow star. People who met this criterion, including those who were unaccustomed to defining themselves as Jews at all, were suddenly marked off and isolated from the rest of the population. According to a Dutch historian of that period, reactions of Jewish and other Dutchmen varied a great deal (Presser, 1969). One thing was clear: many people who were categorized in this way shared an inescapable sense of belongingness to the Jewish group, mingled with fear and apprehension about what the future would bring them. These anxieties and fears were all too justified. Within a few months, deportations started. At the end of the war it was learned that about 100 000 Jews – men, women and children – had perished in the German death camps.

Impressed by very similar events, Kurt Lewin, a social psychologist and refugee from Nazi Germany, wrote at the time a number of papers on group belongingness and intergroup relations (Lewin, 1948). These papers were addressed primarily to the Jewish community in the United States. As a Jewish refugee, he was concerned about the lack of self-esteem and positive sense of group belongingness he observed among many American Jews. He had seen a similar lack of identification with the Jewish group among the Jews in pre-war Germany that left them completely unprepared for the terrible fate that awaited them. To Lewin, a sense of group belongingness provides a crucial component for a person's social identity and self-esteem.

Lewin tried to 'raise the consciousness' of the Jewish adolescents who were uncertain about their belongingness and identification with the Jewish group by pointing out to them that it is:

... not similarity or dissimilarity that decides whether two individuals belong to the same or to different groups, but *social interaction or other types of interdependence.* A group is best defined *as a dynamic whole based on interdependence rather than on similarity* ... regardless of whether the Jewish group is a racial, religious, national, or cultural one, the fact that it is classified by the majority as a distinct group is what counts ... the main criterion of belongingness is interdependence of fate. (Lewin, 1948, p184)

These experiences during the war and the formulations of Lewin have guided our research efforts on intergroup relations over the past 15 years. Working with groups of boys, Sherif, Harvey, White, Hood, and Sherif (1961) had demonstrated how easily intergroup competition erupts into intergroup hostility. The same effect was obtained by Blake and Mouton (1961) in training exercises with groups of adults. Adapting these exercises to intergroup cooperation, we found to our surprise that groups of adults still developed mutual antagonisms. The result led us to enquire into the minimal conditions that would produce ingroup–outgroup bias.

Our first experiment (Rabbie and Horwitz, 1969) examined the effects on group and member evaluations of arbitrarily assigning subjects to two differently designated groups. Subjects were strangers who were told that they would not interact with each other, but were being randomly assigned to Blue or Green groups for the experimenters' administrative convenience in obtaining first-impressions ratings of each other. Given the group assignment alone, we did not at the time detect any ingroup–outgroup bias as measured by differences between subjects' first-impression ratings of the individuals inside or outside their groups. We did, however, find significant differences favouring ingroup over outgroup members after one group won and the other lost a prize decided by the flip of a coin. The winners and losers both then rated ingroup members more favourably than outgroup members, the effects being most pronounced in the ratings made by winning girls and losing boys. Later, when asked to make sociometric choices of one another, winners and losers each tended to choose members of their own groups.

This bias effect in what has come to be called the 'minimal intergroup situation' has since proven to be a robust phenomenon (Brewer, 1979). It appears not only in the differential allocation of ratings to ingroup and outgroup members, but in the differential allocation of rewards to them. Tajfel, Billig, Bundy, and Flament (1971) designated groups only slightly less arbitrarily than we did, dividing subjects according to their preference for one of two abstract painters or their tendencies to over- or underestimate the number of dots on a screen. They found that subjects tended to allocate greater rewards to anonymous members of their own group than to those of the other group.

A number of explanations have been proposed for the effect. Our initial speculation focused on intermember relationships. We suggested that the differences between group outcomes caused subjects to feel more comfortable about interacting with ingroup members who had received the same outcome than with outgroup members who had received the opposite outcome.[3] The initial explanation by Tajfel *et al.* (1971) focused on members' views about group expectations. They suggested that subjects were responding to a generic group norm that one ought to favour the ingroup over the outgroup. Tajfel's subsequent explanations have emphasized possible intrapsychic processes. One is that subjects treat group membership as a component of their personal identities and favour their ingroups because they desire to compare favourably with others (Tajfel, 1978; Turner, 1978). Another is that the perception of cognitive unity with one's group engenders, through balance processes (Heider, 1958), more positive sentiments towards the ingroup than the outgroup (Rabbie and Wilkens, 1971; Ryen and Kahn, 1975).

The minimal intergroup system

The sample of possible interpretations given above suggests that there exist many possible relationships among persons and groups in the minimal intergroup situation, any of which may conceivably contribute to the emergence of intergroup bias. The subject in the intergroup situation can simultaneously perceive and may respond to such distinct relationships as that between himself and his ingroup, his outgroup, individual ingroup members, individual outgroup members, as well as to what he perceives as the relationship between the two groups as separate entities. His responses may be based not only on how he perceives his own place in this network of relationships but on how he believes that others perceive their place in relation to him. In short, the minimal situation places each subject within an intergroup system of interdependent relationships among numerous entities. Any of these relationships may impinge to a greater or lesser degree on his reactions.

The simple interposition of a group boundary between a collection of independent individuals transforms their relationships in a remarkable way. Figure 1 attempts to show the complexity of the transformation.

Figure 1(*a*) shows the relationships with which P may concern himself

(a) An individual 's (P) relationships with unaffiliated others prior to grouping

(b) A member's (G₁) relationships with other members after grouping

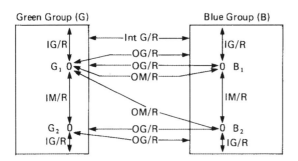

IG/R = Relationship to ingroup
OG/R = Relationship to outgroup
IM/R = Relationship to ingroup member
OM/R = Relationship to outgroup member
Int G/R = Relationship between groups

Figure 1. Effects of group boundaries on the system of relationships among individuals

in dealing with three unaffiliated and otherwise unrelated persons, Q, R, S. Figure 1 (b) simply introduces two new entities, a Green group and a Blue group in which the four individuals are included, not as independent persons, but as parts of the groups. P and Q now become identifiable members, G_1 and G_2, of the Green Group; R and S become identifiable members, B_1 and B_2, of the Blue group.

Most obviously, as Rice (1969) has noted, the introduction of the two groups as entities multiplies the number of relationships confronting the subjects, the number rising from three in Figure 1 (a) to a potential of thirteen in Figure 1 (b). Moreover, the qualities of the relationships change. In Figure 1 (a), P can view himself and believe he is viewed by others as behaving according to his own unconstrained individuality. In Figure 1 (b), however, the same person, G_1, may view himself and believe he is viewed by the others as behaving according to his interdependencies as an ingroup member (IG/R) of the Green Group and as an outgroup member (OG/R) of the Blue Group. Constraints on his relationships with the other persons appear as well; he may relate or believe he is seen as relating to some as ingroup members (IM/R) and to others as outgroup members (OM/R). He may also respond or believe he is seen as responding to the type of interdependence or non-interdependence that characterizes the intergroup relationship (Int G/R) between the groups themselves.

In order to understand what factors determine, very likely over-determine, the arousal of intergroup bias, it seems necessary to take account of the manifold system of relationships created by interposing group boundaries between individuals. In the minimal intergroup situation, the experimenter *simultaneously* affects a number of the subject's co-existing relationships with the ingroup, with the outgroup, with ingroup members, and with outgroup members. The single experimental intervention affects at once several interdependencies within a system of interrelated individual and group entities. If we have engendered an intergroup *system*, we are obliged to redefine such questions as 'what is the cause of ingroup/outgroup bias?' Instead, we ought to ask 'which of the various relationships within the system do or do not contribute to the bias and in what relative degree?'

Several issues follow from the view that the minimal intergroup situation creates a complex system characterized by different forms of interdependence among the group and member entities contained within the system. The issues considered below are: (1) Under what conditions will a classification or categorization of individuals be perceived by them as defining a group? (2) How might we conceptualize the interdependence between a member (or non-member) and the group as an entity? (3) What aspects of the intergroup system may contribute to ingroup–outgroup bias? (4) Can the foregoing shed light on the tendencies to depersonalize or dehumanize outgroup members, especially in the course of intergroup conflict?

2. Perceiving groups as entities

In Lewin's (1948) proposed definition of a group, the interdependence that characterizes it as a 'dynamic whole' may be based on social interaction within the group or between it and other groups. The definition implies an intergroup system in which the person is related not only to an ingroup but also to an outgroup. A subject's awareness of such a system depends in the first place on perceiving distinct and bounded entities of which individuals are parts, in Campbell's (1958) terminology, on perceiving group 'entitivity'.

We consider in this section what it is that is being perceived when a collection of individuals is seen as a group entity and what factors affect the likelihood of attaining such a perception. In Lewin's view, the segment of Jewish youth who were uncertain about their being part of the Jewish group were responding to the high costs of membership in a disadvantaged minority. By emphasizing the dissimilarities among individual Jews, they were, as Lewin saw it, turning away from recognizing that the Jewish group was subject to a common fate, if not by its own actions, then by the actions of the majority. The underlying assumptions are that in perceiving a group, as with any act of perception, there exists an actual stimulus to be perceived, that motivational factors may operate for or against attaining the group percept and, one may add, that there are likely to be differences in individual propensities for or against perceiving group entitivity.

The group as an object of perception

The question of what is being perceived when one perceives a collection of individuals as a group is difficult to investigate by direct inquiry. It is relatively easy to construe any set of individuals as constituting a group and merely putting the question invites the perceiver to search for how the aggregate may be apprehended as a group. One might examine the question by a projective test that ambiguously depicts individuals who may or may not constitute a group (Horwitz and Cartwright, 1953), but in the absence of a direct measure, one can try to gauge the perception of group entitivity through its presumed consequences.

In our original study (Rabbie and Horwitz, 1969), we sought to determine the minimal conditions engendering ingroup–outgroup bias. By now there is enough evidence (Brewer, 1979) to justify the working assumption that in the minimal intergroup situation, the stronger the perception of the ingroup as an entity, the more strongly will members favour their ingroup. The assumption must be limited to the minimal intergroup situation since motivational factors can obviously lead members to dislike the groups to which they belong, as in the case of minority self-hate (Lewin, 1948). With this provisional assumption, the degree of ingroup bias can be taken as an indicator of the degree of perceived group entitivity. From this altered angle, the various studies of ingroup–outgroup bias can be viewed as providing information about the conditions that affect the perception of groups as entities.

A finding of our first study (Rabbie and Horwitz, 1969), noted above, was that simply classifying subjects into 'Greens' and 'Blues' for 'administrative purposes only' did not evoke differences between the overall ratings given ingroups and outgroups. We concluded that 'group classification *per se* appears to be insufficient to produce discriminatory evaluations' (p272). If we now use the discriminatory evaluations as indicators of perceived group entitivity, we are led to the perhaps surprising conclusion that group classification was insufficient to produce the perception of the groups as distinct entities. Interestingly, the reactions to our finding have focused precisely on this point. As put by Tajfel *et al.* (1971):

> Rabbie's control conditions provide a useful guideline for tracing a baseline at which there is no reason whatever why differential intergroup behaviour should be expected to occur. Nothing in the manner adopted by the experimenter to classify the subjects, or in what happened subsequently, made the quality of 'group-ness' relevant to the situation. Judging the attributes of a few unknown, live and concrete individuals solely on the basis of where they sat would have been about just as sensible as doing the same to people sitting on the same and opposite benches in the compartment of a train. (p152)

As stated by Gerard and Hoyt (1974):

> ... randomly designating subjects as blues or greens, without attaching any psychological significance to the labels, leaves the classification transparent and without impact ... For labeling to be effective in producing we–they biasses, members of each ingroup must feel they have something in common, either in terms of differential outcomes or of some attributes or traits that distinguish them from outgroup members. (p837)

The statement by Tajfel *et al.* (1971) overlooks the fact that, unlike passengers in a train, the subjects in our control condition were designated as belonging to two distinct groups. Both quotations, however, appropriately raise the question as to whether group designations *per se* have any perceptible significance to the subjects. The original finding, suggesting they do not, was based upon a small number of subjects, eight boys and eight girls. Given the importance of the question, Rabbie (1972) ran 16 additional subjects in the identical control condition. As before, no reliable differences appeared between the summed ratings given ingroups versus outgroups either on the eight scales for individual members or for the groups themselves. With the enlarged number of subjects, however, significant differences in ratings did appear on single items. In the ratings of individual members, the items 'wanting to be friends with' and 'cordiality' showed a significant bias in favour of ingroup members.[4] In the ratings of the groups, the items 'wanting to be a member of the group' and 'familiarity among members' showed a similarly significant bias in favour of the ingroup.[5] The items on which ingroup–outgroup differences were displayed refer to subjects' desire for belonging (wanting to be a member, to be friends with) and their views about others' accessibility (familiarity among members, cordiality). The results indicate that the group designations alone must have created at least a rudimentary perception of the ingroup and outgroup as distinct entities.

Our experimental and control conditions differed in that the experimental groups received positive or negative outcomes while the control groups had at most only a potential for positive or negative outcomes. But they also differed in that individual subjects as well as the groups were rewarded or deprived in the experimental condition while individuals in the control condition were not. One may conjecture that it is the difference in individual outcomes rather than group outcomes that accounts for the greater bias displayed in the experimental than the control conditions. Conceivably, the evidence that there were sizeable payoffs for their participation led subjects in the experimental condition to attend more seriously than those in the control condition to the various features of the experiment, including their demarcation into 'Blue' and 'Green' groups. In order to pin down this possibility, Rabbie (1972) ran a second control in which 16 subjects assigned to the Blue or Green group were all rewarded for participating with movie tickets given to them as individuals rather than as group members.

The subjects in this second control behaved much as those in the first. They rated ingroup members significantly more favourably than outgroup members on the two items, 'wanting to be friends with' and 'cordiality', but not on the six other items. Again, as in the first control, they rated their ingroups significantly more favourably than their outgroups on the items, 'wanting to be a member' and 'familiarity among members' plus one other, 'group cohesion'. The presence or absence of individual reward or deprivation made little difference in subjects' responses within the control condition. Combining both controls, significant differences did appear in favour of the ingroup for the summed ratings of members and of groups. If one enlarges the N sufficiently, subjects' perception of the groups as entities in the controls can be clearly detected even with relatively insensitive items, although this perception is manifestly weaker than in the experimental conditions.

The high perceptibility of the groups as entities in the experimental conditions appears to be due to the groups' receiving positive or negative outcomes. What is the psychological significance of being randomly demarcated in the control conditions into blues and greens for the 'administrative convenience' of the experimenter with no opportunity for interaction? We propose that the group designations implied at least the potentiality for receiving group outcomes, either by action of the experimenter for whom the designations apparently had some importance or, conceivably, by action of the group members who, once the ratings were introduced, might be seen as inclined to rate one group better than the other. According to this interpretation, subjects' perceptions that the collection of individuals constituted a group entity were weaker where they perceived the entity as *potentially* receiving outcomes in the control conditions than *actually* receiving outcomes in the experimental conditions.

We propose the following in answer to the question of what is perceived when one perceives a group. A group is a bounded entity comprising individuals as parts (members) that is capable of locomotion or changes of position in its environment resulting in potential or actual outcomes that include group harms and benefits. The locomotions may be caused by its own action and that of members inside the group or by the action of other groups and individuals outside the group.

The view that a group is a social unit capable of acting or being acted upon, of moving, or being moved, towards or away from benefits or harms, should be distinguished from the view that a group is simply a social category, i.e. a collection of individuals who share at least one attribute in common that distinguishes them from others (van Leent, 1964). A group may provide the basis for categorizing individuals in that it distinguishes those who share common membership from those who do not. Moreover, individuals in a social category often perceive themselves as constituting a group, as suggested by Byrne's (1971) numerous demonstrations that subjects give higher evaluations to similar rather than dissimilar others. Nevertheless, if the group as a social unit is more than a social category, efforts to treat intergroup dynamics as an expression of category differentiation (Doise, 1978) must be incomplete at best. The evidence is fairly compelling that designating individuals as members of distinct groups easily overrides the effects of their perceiving each other as located in similar or dissimilar categories.

Two studies illustrate the point. Wilder and Allen (1974) assigned subjects to arbitrarily formed groups and informed them that the political preferences of their ingroup or outgroup members were either similar to or dissimilar from their own. They found the usual tendency by subjects to allocate greater rewards to ingroup than outgroup members even where subjects believed that their own political preferences differed from those of their ingroup members and agreed with those of their outgroup members. Rabbie and Huygen (1974) paired subjects who agreed with each other on a strongly felt religious and ethical issue, namely, whether to legalize euthanasia. Each dyad was told it would be given 10 minutes to discuss its position before joining another designated dyad to form a four-person group which would then meet to develop a group position on the issue in preparation for a competition with a second four-person group. The dyads composing each group were described as having opposing views in a heterogeneous group treatment and as having similar views in a homogeneous group treatment.

Immediately after these instructions and before any interaction occurred, subjects rated each other and the two groups. Their ratings varied according to group and subgroup structures, not according to similarity or dissimilarity of beliefs. Subjects rated their ingroups and ingroup members higher than the outgroups and outgroup members and rated homogeneous ingroups no higher than heterogeneous ingroups; they rated those in their dyadic subgroup higher than those in the other dyad within their group, but rated the other dyad no differently whether anticipating agreement or disagreement with it. All of these effects were amplified when the ratings were taken again after subjects had actually interacted within their dyads and within their four-man groups, despite the fact that the conflict within the heterogeneous groups was intense enough that the experimenter had to flip a coin to break deadlocks in about half the cases. After each group had arrived at its position, the experimenter announced that the outgroup had come to the opposite position, placing the outgroup on the side of the losing dyads within the heterogeneous groups. The losing dyads rated the outgroups more favourably than did the other subjects, suggesting that they saw the potential for forming a coalition with their outgroups based on similarity of views during the intergroup discussion to follow.

Insofar as subjects favoured own over other groups, the designations of group membership in these studies overrode the categorizations based on similarity or dissimilarity of belief. Nevertheless, almost any categorization of the type used by Byrne (1971) can be viewed by subjects as potentially defining a group entity that is subject to positive or negative outcomes. Similarity or dissimilarity in social attitudes, for example, may define individuals as belonging to the same or different political parties or ideological groups which can obviously achieve political gains or suffer political losses. Similarity or dissimilarity in interests may define individuals as belonging to the same or different social class or cultural subgroup to which group advantages or disadvantages may accrue. One can increase the likelihood that subjects will infer group membership from similarities and dissimilarities by 'consciousness raising' or reduce the likelihood as in the experiments just described. In the Rabbie–Huygen study, subjects could have seen themselves and others as belonging to pro- or anti-euthanasia groups, but the salience of such groups was reduced by the experimenter's defining the 'Blues' and 'Greens' as the entities whose outcomes would be affected in the experimental situation. In our view, a necessary condition for perceiving a collection of individuals as a group is that they be seen as capable of receiving good or poor outcomes as an entity or as members of an entity.

Some determinants of perceiving group entitivity

Several implications follow from the assumption that in perceiving a group subjects are perceiving an entity capable of receiving positive or negative outcomes. The perception of the group as an entity and of individuals as parts of this entity should be greater:
  (1) the greater the perceived value of the benefits that can be received or the costs that can be avoided by the group;
  (2) the greater the perceived likelihood that interaction among individuals inside the group boundary can serve to attain group benefits or avoid group costs;
  (3) the greater the perceived likelihood that action by an outgroup or by individuals outside the group boundary can affect the positive or negative outcomes received by the group.
In what follows we review experimental evidence pertaining to each of these propositions.

Differential value of group outcomes   In our first study (Rabbie and Horwitz, 1969), the experimental groups won or lost transistor radios. In a follow-up experiment, Rabbie (1972) reduced the value of the prize, using movie tickets rather than radios. The second study, like the first, evoked biased ingroup–outgroup ratings both on the summed scales for individual members and for the groups. However, the degree of bias expressed was less where movie tickets rather than radios were at stake. Taking single items, the radio treatment produced significant ingroup–outgroup differences among 11 of the 16 ratings; the movie-ticket treatment produced differences only in what we have already noted are the most sensitive items, namely, 'wanting to be friends with' and 'cordiality' for individuals and 'wanting to be a member of' and 'familiarity' for the groups. Likewise, when given the opportunity to make sociometric choices subjects favoured ingroup members more in the high win–loss treatment than in the low win–loss treatment. The data support the proposition that the perception of the group as an entity will be stronger, the greater the value of its actual or potential outcomes.

Mixed evidence for this proposition appears where the group mediates avoidance of negative outcomes rather than attainment of positive outcomes. In an experiment designed by Rabbie (1979), some subjects were led to expect (but did not actually receive) a high electric shock and others a low electric shock. In both these conditions, the subjects were then divided into 'Green' and 'Blue' groups. The next phase of the experiment consisted of two control and two experimental conditions. In the two control conditions (anticipation of 'high' and 'low' shock, respectively), the subjects rated each other and their group. In the two experimental conditions (also differing in the anticipated intensity of shock), these ratings were preceded by the experimenter's flipping of a coin in order to decide which of the two groups would or would not receive the shock. Consistent with the proposition being considered, subjects exhibited significantly more intergroup bias in the experimental conditions where shock or no shock was a group outcome than in the control conditions where shock was an individual outcome. Contrary to the proposition, however, subjects displayed about equal bias whether the groups could mediate avoidance of high or low shock. Lewin (1948) has observed that the costs of minority-group membership may have led the Jewish youths he addressed to avoid recognition of the Jewish group as an entity. A motivational process that can reduce the perceptibility of historically-based natural groups should be all the more likely to reduce the perceptibility of randomly established 'Blue' and 'Green' groups. If subjects had experienced heightened tendencies to perceive themselves as group members in the high-shock condition, these perceptual tendencies could have been offset by the aversiveness of the total situation in which they found themselves.

The shock experiment showed in addition a significant difference between the responses of boys and girls to their group's winning or losing, i.e. being spared or not spared the threatened shock. Exactly paralleling a previous finding (Rabbie and Horwitz, 1969), there was a significant interaction between sex of subject and their group's win or loss: among girls, intergroup bias was greater for winners than losers; among boys, intergroup bias was greater for losers than winners. An interpretation of this finding will be given below in the section examining individual differences in the propensity to perceive groups and group membership.

Action by the ingroup   Anticipated or actual social interaction within a group may be a sufficient condition for perceiving the group as an entity

(Lewin, 1948), but it is not a necessary condition, as shown by the foregoing experiments in which subjects were explicitly informed that, though designated as groups for administrative convenience, they would not be working together. Informing subjects that they will interact on a group task should increase the perception of the group as an entity. For the assignment of subjects to two groups distinguishes insiders who will work together from outsiders who will not, giving added definition to the group boundary. In addition, the group task implies that there are potential positive or negative outcomes for the group; it may do well or poorly on the task.

In the experiment reported next (Rabbie and Wilkens, 1971), the subjects, all boys, were assigned to Blue and Green groups and depending on the treatment were told they would or would not work together. Of those who anticipated working together, half expected to work on a construction task in competition with the other group; half expected to work independently of the other group. Subjects rated each other and their groups twice, once immediately before and once immediately after work on the task. Prior to beginning work, the subjects who anticipated working together rated ingroup members higher than did those who anticipated working separately. After the work was completed, those who had worked together elevated their ratings of ingroup members still further. The ratings rose about equally, whether the subjects expected to compete, or not compete, with the other group. Evidently both the anticipated and the actual ingroup interactions served to solidify subjects' perception of the group as a bounded entity and of themselves and others as members of the group.

Substantially the same result was obtained in an experiment (Rabbie and de Brey, 1971) in which the Blues and Greens were separately assigned a discussion problem and told that their group representatives would later meet to cooperate or compete for a prize. Subjects rated each other and their groups immediately before and after their respective discussions. The ratings given the ingroups were very significantly more positive after the members interacted than before; the competitive groups showed no greater rise in ingroup ratings than did the cooperative groups.

The finding that anticipated and actual ingroup interaction enhances ingroup evaluation might be interpreted as merely demonstrating what earlier findings have been construed to show, namely, that one's anticipation of interaction with other individuals raises one's evaluation of them (Darley and Berscheid, 1967). Our own view, however, is that the effect of anticipated interaction upon these evaluations is brought about by enhancing the subjects' perception of the ingroup as a distinct entity and of themselves as members. A straightforward test of this view can be made by comparing the effects of anticipated interaction where subjects view the interaction as confined within a group or crossing its boundaries. If interaction is confined to one's group it should strengthen the perception of the group as an entity and lead to relatively heightened evaluation of group members; if interaction crosses group lines, it should weaken the perception of the group as an entity and lead to relatively lowered evaluations of members.

In the relevant experiment (Rabbie, 1968), subjects were randomly divided into Blues and Greens and told they would work together on an unspecified task. Half were informed that the groups would work separately and half that the groups would work together on the task. Subjects then rated each other and the groups; the experimenter flipped a coin to decide which one of the two groups would receive transistor radios, after which, subjects repeated their ratings. The changes in the ratings given to ingroup members before and after the flip of the coin differed significantly between the two treatments. Subjects expecting to work with own groups alone raised their ingroup ratings; subjects expecting to work with both their own and the other group lowered their ingroup ratings. The subjects anticipated that they would interact with ingroup members in both treatments; what appears decisive in affecting their ratings is whether they perceived the form of social interaction to reinforce or diminish the strength of group boundaries.

There is ample evidence that the actual experience of intergroup competition strengthens group boundaries and increases ingroup solidarity (Sherif, 1966; Blake and Mouton, 1961). Yet, as noted above, the anticipation of competing with an outgroup for a prize rather than working independently for a prize produced no difference in ingroup ratings (Rabbie and Wilkens, 1971). The groups in that study worked side-by-side on construction tasks and could easily make comparisons between each other's products. It is possible that, like the subjects observed by Ferguson and Kelley (1964), these subjects made such comparisons, blurring the distinction between the independent and competitive treatments by transforming the independent treatment into a competition about which group was better. This possibility was ruled out in the experiment by Rabbie and de Brey (1971) in which the groups, working in separate rooms on discussion tasks, could not make comparisons about how well each was performing. Still, subjects who anticipated competing rated their ingroups no higher than did subjects who anticipated cooperating.

Anticipated competition and cooperation do appear to have differential effects on ingroup ratings depending on the form of social interaction within which the cooperation or competition is conducted. In the experiment by Rabbie and de Brey (1971), subjects were led to believe that the intergroup negotiations for the prize were to be conducted by group representatives, meeting privately in half the treatments, publicly in the other half. In the cooperative condition, the increase in preference for ingroup rather than outgroup membership was greater where subjects anticipated private rather than public negotiations; in the competitive condition, the increase was greater where subjects anticipated public rather than private negotiations. We have seen above that groups rate themselves higher where they anticipate separate rather than combined work on a task (Rabbie, 1968). For cooperative groups, private negotiations maintain the separation between the two groups while public negotiations move them in the direction of combined group work. Ingroup ratings should therefore be higher where cooperative groups anticipate private rather than public negotiations. By contrast, competitive groups probably anticipate that they will be more strongly divided from each other where they confront each other face-to-face rather than where they work alone. Ingroup ratings should therefore be higher for competitive groups where they anticipate interacting directly with their opponents rather than dealing through private negotiators.[6]

The effects of intergroup cooperation and competition on subjects' perceptions of the group as an entity and of themselves as members should be affected not only by their anticipations of different forms of social interaction, but by their anticipations of the consequences of these interactions for the group's outcomes. We have assumed that subjects will experience their membership more strongly the greater the perceived likelihood that their groups will attain positive outcomes or avoid negative outcomes. In a simulation of labour–management bargaining, three-person groups acting as union teams were instructed to prepare for competition or cooperation with management (Rabbie, Benoist, Oosterbaan, and Visser, 1974). In the competitive treatment, the teams were offered a reward depending on how much they gained for themselves at the expense of management; in the cooperative treatment, the reward depended on how well they and management could achieve a mutually satisfying agreement. Half the teams were given weak and half were given strong bargaining positions. Ratings taken immediately after the teams had prepared themselves for the negotiations (which did not actually occur) showed that regardless of treatment all groups felt more positively about their own groups than the management group. However, cooperative *versus* competitive relationships with the outgroup created larger differences in the ingroup ratings of subjects with weak rather than strong bargaining positions. The groups with weak bargaining positions rated themselves lower in the competitive than in the cooperative condition; they also expected most harm from management in the competitive condition and most benefit in the cooperative condition. Given their weakness, they must have anticipated less likelihood of gaining the reward where they were obliged to compete than to cooperate with the outgroup. By contrast, groups with strong bargaining positions rated themselves about the same in the competitive and cooperative conditions. Given their position of strength, they probably anticipated about equal likelihood of gaining the reward whether required to beat management in the competition treatment or negotiate a satisfying agreement with them in the cooperation treatment. The supposition that intergroup competition will engender stronger group identification than intergroup cooperation must be qualified. It appears to do so where the ingroup expects face-to-face interaction with the outgroup and where the ingroup does not anticipate poor outcomes from the transaction.

Action by the outgroup   The minimal intergroup situation presents subjects not only with an ingroup but with an outgroup that can itself be perceived as capable of action. The actions of the outgroup may be seen as affecting the ingroup's positive or negative outcomes as in the example just noted of members with weak bargaining positions anticipating harm from competitive outgroups or benefits from cooperative ones. The more that individuals perceive an outgroup as affecting their collective fate, the more should they perceive themselves as part of a group entity (Lewin, 1948).

Indeed, simply being 'marked off' by an outgroup (Herman, 1978) may lead individuals to perceive themselves as members of a bounded group. Doise (1978) compared college students' evaluations of each other when rating only themselves versus rating both themselves and apprentices. Their evaluations of fellow college students were very considerably higher when marked off than not marked off from the apprentices. Apprentices, despite their inferior social status, gave higher ratings in turn to fellow apprentices when marked off than not marked off from the students. With the outgroup made salient, both groups tended to rate ingroup members higher than outgroup members. If the elevated ratings express a heightened sense of group membership, the results show that awareness of the outgroup leads subjects to shift from viewing themselves as unaffiliated individuals toward viewing themselves as group members.

The sense of ingroup membership should be especially heightened where the outgroup can act to affect one's outcomes. Employing the Tajfel paradigm, Huff (1979) divided Boston College students into overestimators and underestimators and instructed them to allocate rewards between unknown persons in their own and the other group. In a treatment designed to reduce the perception that outgroup actions could affect ingroup outcomes, subjects were informed that their own rewards would be allocated by an ingroup member choosing between them and another ingroup member. In a treatment designed to heighten the perception that outgroup actions would affect ingroup outcomes, subjects were informed that their own rewards would be allocated by an outgroup member choosing between them and another outgroup member. Subjects then proceeded to make allocations between ingroup and outgroup members as well as to indicate their perceptions of the two groups.

Replicating Tajfel's findings, subjects gave significantly more favourable allocations to ingroup members than to outgroup members. As compared with subjects who could not be affected by the outgroup, those who could be affected rated themselves as feeling significantly more 'a part' of their group and as desiring significantly more to associate with ingroup rather than outgroup members. They also judged that outgroup allocators would significantly favour fellow outgroup members rather than themselves. Just as subjects tend to favour own groups, so they view outgroup members as tending to favour their groups.

Subjects not only expect outgroup members to discriminate against them in allocating rewards but in evaluating them as well. In order to examine subjects' reactions to acceptance and rejection by ingroup and outgroup members, Shake (1980) divided college women into overestimators and underestimators. Confederates planted in each group then publicly indicated whether they would prefer to get acquainted with a member of their own or the other group. In half the treatments, the confederates chose own members; in half, they chose the other members. Subjects then described their attributions about the confederate and their reactions to her choice.

Independently of the choice made, subjects estimated that the choosers evaluated the personal qualities of their ingroup members very significantly higher than those of their outgroup members. They viewed the chooser as motivated to choose her own member by virtue of: (*a*) having the same group membership; (*b*) being expected to do so by her group; and (*c*) being expected to do so by the individuals being chosen. The choosers obviously violated these expectations when they chose outsiders in preference to insiders. If subjects viewed the choosers as acting as autonomous, rational individuals, they should see them as expressing stronger personal preferences when they violated rather than conformed with external expectations (Jones, Davis and Gergen, 1961). Curiously, subjects judged that choosers evaluated the personal attractiveness of outsiders they accepted significantly *lower* than of insiders they accepted; they also judged that choosers evaluated the personal attractiveness of insiders they rejected *higher* than of outsiders they rejected. Subjects saw choosers who violated group expectations as feeling less 'a part' of their groups than choosers who conformed. Nevertheless, the subjects did not appear to ascribe the same rationality in making choices to them as they would to unaffiliated individuals. Instead, they seemed to view the choosers as in some degree automatically expressing group expectations.

Nor were the subjects themselves immune from these effects. They rated their ingroup choosers who accepted or rejected them significantly more favourably than outgroup choosers who respectively accepted or rejected them. Brewer (1979) has noted that in most reported studies the difference between ingroup and outgroup evaluations results from subjects elevating ingroup ratings rather than lowering outgroup ratings, a tendency we have noticed in our own studies as well. She suggests, incorrectly in our view, that future work on intergroup bias should therefore be focused on intragroup processes. But it is clear from the present results that subjects expect biased evaluations (and biased allocations) from outgroups in the minimal intergroup situation. These expectations cannot be plausibly excluded as possible determinants of the subjects' own bias.

The present experiment gives direct evidence that subjects' sense of group membership depends on outgroup action as well as ingroup action. As one would expect, subjects rated themselves as feeling significantly more 'a part' of their groups where their ingroup choosers accepted rather than rejected them; but they also rated themselves as feeling significantly more 'a part' of their groups where their *outgroup* choosers rejected rather than accepted them. (They felt least 'a part' of their group where their outgroup choosers accepted them.) The same pattern of results appears for subjects' ratings of the attractiveness of their groups. Most impressively, the pattern also appears for subjects' self-ratings. Subjects' evaluations of their own personal characteristics parallels their feelings of being 'a part' of the group. They rated their personal attractiveness higher where their ingroup chooser accepted rather than rejected them, but rated themselves higher where their *outgroup* chooser rejected rather than accepted them. These effects suggest that subjects were treating themselves as group members rather than as unaffiliated individuals and displaying the same tendencies toward heightened evaluations of themselves as group members that they displayed towards other ingroup members.

The more unresponsive the outgroup is to subjects' desires, the more impermeable should they view its boundary. An experiment by Giniger (1966) shows that the stronger the boundary created by the outgroup, the more strongly do subjects identify with their ingroup. Groups of college women were led to believe they were interacting with other groups (actually fictitious) using payoff matrices known to both. The fictitious outgroups repeatedly made choices that inflicted repeated and sizeable money losses on the subjects' groups. In one treatment, it would have cost the outgroups very little to have benefited the subjects' group; in a second treatment it would have cost the outgroups a very great deal. As the inter- action proceeded, the outgroups in the first treatment increasingly revealed themselves as giving very low weight to the subjects' desires and very high weight to their own (Horwitz, 1963; Horwitz, Glass, Giniger and Cohn, 1966). The outgroups in the second treatment, by contrast, could be seen as justifiably depriving subjects because so much more was at stake for themselves. With continuing trials, the unresponsive outgroups, but not the others, received increasingly negative ratings. The ratings subjects gave their ingroups were mirror images of their outgroup ratings: those interacting with the unresponsive outgroups gave their ingroups increas- ingly positive ratings; those interacting with the other outgroups did not. The fates of the ingroups in this experiment were entirely determined by the actions of outgroups. We have suggested that the more unresponsive the outgroup, the more it should be viewed as creating an impermeable boundary between itself and the ingroup. In a two-group system, the boundary defining the ingroup as an entity can be created by the outgroup as well as by the ingroup itself. The stronger the boundary created by the outgroup, the more do subjects appear to identify themselves as members of their ingroups.

Individual differences in thresholds for perceiving groups as entities Differences in the propensities to perceive collections of individuals as group entities should be most easily detected where, as in the minimal group situation, there is a relatively weak objective basis for perceiving a group. Convincing evidence for the existence of individual differences in the thresholds for perceiving groups is given in an experiment by Downing and Monaco (1979). Subjects attending skiing classes were given abbreviated forms of the F-test of authoritarianism and randomly assigned to Blue or Green groups for the alleged purpose of studying methods of ski instruction.

All subjects received the same instruction under three different treatments that varied the salience of the distinction between ingroups and outgroups. One treatment mixed the subjects within each class but led them to believe that they might later be working separately in Blue or Green groups; a second treatment physically separated the Blues and Greens in the same class, but discouraged ingroup interaction; the third treatment physically separated the groups and encouraged ingroup interaction. After the class instruction, subjects rated the performance of individual skiers wearing blue or green ribbons as they skied down the hill one at a time. As compared with subjects low in authoritarianism, the high authoritarians rated own-colour skiers significantly better, rated other-colour skiers significantly worse, and differentiated significantly more strongly between their ratings of own- and other-colour skiers. The low authoritarians showed little or no bias in favour of own-colour skiers over other-colour skiers. The results indicate that under conditions of weak ingroup – outgroup distinctiveness, high authoritarians have lower thresholds than low authoritarians for perceiving groups as entities and individuals as members of groups.

We have repeatedly found that girls favour winning groups more than losing groups, but that boys do not. A possible explanation is provided in findings by Schipani (1979), who compared the reactions of male and female college students to chance wins or losses under two conditions. In one treatment, subjects meeting eight at a time won or lost a prize by the experimenter's flipping a coin for each pair of subjects in turn; the prizes were placed next to each winner so that subjects could readily distinguish those who had won or lost. In a second treatment, the eight subjects in each session were divided into Blue and Green groups and won or lost a prize by the experimenter's flipping a coin between the pair of groups. Subjects in the Blue or Green groups showed no differences between their ratings of ingroup and outgroup members, suggesting they had developed little sense of membership in the designated groups, perhaps because of prior acquaintanceship as students in the same school. However, they rated the personal characteristics of winners higher than the personal characteristics of losers. Rabbie (1968) in a related study of girls' ratings of individual winners and losers found precisely the same result. Evidently, subjects view the good or bad fortune of individuals as 'belonging' to their persons, tending to evaluate lucky persons more positively than unlucky ones. In addition, the difference between the ratings of winners and losers was greater where winning and losing occurred in one-to-one competition rather than group-to-group competition. Subjects appear to view the good or bad fortune of other individuals as 'belonging' to them more where they have won or lost by virtue of their own individual luck than by the luck of a group to which they happen to be assigned. In general, where subjects view others as individuals rather than as members they rate winners higher than losers.

Although subjects did not appear to identify with the Blue or Green groups, they could also have defined ingroups and outgroups according to whether they and others had the same or opposite outcomes as winners or losers. Subjects clearly distinguished between those having the same and opposite outcomes from themselves. They anticipated significantly greater comfort in interacting with same-outcome others than opposite-outcome others and anticipated that the others would feel the same about interacting with them. That they tended to view same- and opposite-others as distinct groups is shown by their responses to a question about how much they 'positively identified' with each. Both winners and losers reported significantly greater positive identification with same-outcome others than with opposite-outcome others. However, males and females differed in their respective tendencies to distinguish the two groups. Males expressed a near-significantly greater identification than females with same-outcome others and a significantly lesser identification than females with opposite-outcome others. The result was that males differentiated significantly more sharply than females in how much they identified with others having the same or opposite outcomes. The pattern of these findings resembles that reported by Downing and Monaco (1979) for authoritarians and non-authoritarians. One might say that, like authoritarians, males are relatively predisposed to perceive aggregrates of individuals as groups; conversely, that females, like non-authoritarians, are predisposed to perceive aggregates of individuals as separate persons. Being disposed to view others as individuals, females rate others higher where they are winners rather than losers; being disposed to view others as members, males rate ingroup members higher than outgroup members regardless of winning or losing.[7]

Strong evidence that males and females differ in their proclivities to perceive groups as entities is given in the experiment by Huff (1979) described above. In that experiment, subjects reported feeling more 'a part' of their own groups where their outgroups had high salience, being able to affect the subjects' outcomes, rather than low salience, being unable to affect the subjects' outcomes. Males displayed greater intergroup bias than females in the low outgroup salience condition: they made significantly more biased allocations in favour of own members than did females; they anticipated that each group would be willing to inflict greater costs on the other group in order to benefit itself than did females. Males also displayed greater intergroup bias than females whether the outgroups were low or high in salience: they expected each group to make more biased allocations in favour of own members than did females; they saw both groups as less friendly toward each other than did females. Not only are males more predisposed than females to perceive themselves and others as group members, but they are more affected than females by the potentiality of outgroup action. Moving from low to high outgroup salience, males displayed a significant rise in feeling 'a part' of their group and near-significant rises in desiring to associate with own members and to avoid associating with other members. Females did not differ in their reactions to these items in the two conditions. Males appear to be more readily moved than females to perceive themselves as group members whether their outcomes can be affected by ingroup action or by outgroup action.

3. The interdependence of members and groups

If an aggregate of individuals is perceived as a group entity, the previously separated individuals become perceived as parts of a whole. We have treated groups, like the members who constitute their parts, as goal-seeking entities capable of receiving good or poor outcomes. In this section we shall consider how subjects view the interdependence that exists between group and member outcomes. Since the intergroup system also includes outgroups, we shall consider as well how subjects view their interdependence with the outgroup and its members.

Kelley and Thibaut have undertaken the most systematic effort to date to develop a theory of social interdependence (Thibaut and Kelley, 1959; Kelley and Thibaut, 1978). Interdependence between two parties is expressed in their theory by matrices that show how each party's outcomes are affected by the other's outcomes. A 'given' matrix contains the positive or negative evaluations of outcomes that each party would make if attending to own outcomes alone. An 'effective' matrix results from 'transformation rules' that the parties may apply in modifying their evaluations of own outcomes in the light of other's outcomes. In their first book (Thibaut and Kelley, 1959), the only transformation rule considered was that of judging the utility of one's own outcomes by comparing them with the outcomes of others. By this comparison process, the evaluation of own outcomes will rise if the outcomes are better than another's or fall if they are worse than another's.

A comparison process leads, in Heider's (1958) language, to relationships characterized by envy. The comparison rule implies that each will be more satisfied with own outcomes, the more dissatisfied the other is and that each will be more dissatisfied with own outcomes, the more satisfied the other is. While such relationships exist in abundance, Heider (1958) points out that there are relationships in which the parties 'positively identify' with each other's outcomes, being pleased by the other's good fortune and displeased by the other's misfortune. The latter, in our view, characterizes the relationship between members and ingroups with which they positively identify, the individual member being pleased with good group outcomes and displeased with poor group outcomes even though experiencing no personal benefit or harm. The former characterizes the relationship, for example, between members and outgroups with which they may negatively identify, the member being pleased with the outgroup's poor outcomes and displeased with its good outcomes.

Kelley (1979) has recently provided data demonstrating the positive identification of spouses and lovers with their partner's outcomes. For example, even where their respective outcomes were independent of one another, subjects enjoyed reading a liked book most if their partner was also reading a liked book, less if the partner was reading an indifferently valued book, and least if the partner was reading a disliked book. Conversely, subjects' dissatisfaction with reading a disliked book was greatest if the partner was also reading a disliked book, less if the partner was reading an indifferently valued book, and least if the partner was reading a liked book. Kelley (1979) proposes that the rule subjects applied in this relationship was that of algebraically adding the partner's given outcome to one's own given outcome in order to arrive at one's effective outcome. To deal with relationships of varying degrees of closeness, the rule would probably have to be modified so that one gives more or less weight to the other's given outcomes when adding them to one's own.

An alternative way of conceptualizing positive or negative identification with others is to broaden the assumption that persons are motivated within the 'given' matrix by own outcomes alone by including the fact that they can also be directly motivated by others' outcomes. Using the recall of unfinished tasks as a measure of the internalization of a goal, Horwitz (1954) found that members recalled more unfinished than finished group tasks for which they could claim no individual responsibility. The result was interpreted as showing that they had internalized the group's goal. More recently, Hornstein (1978) has shown parallel effects in a series of ingenious experiments concerning subjects' tendencies to help unknown persons to achieve their own or a group's goals. Subjects were led to believe that the unknown person either did or did not share group membership with them or was promoting a group aim of which subjects did or did not approve. The subjects displayed significantly greater helping behaviour where memberships were shared and group aims were approved than otherwise.

Positively identifying with another's outcomes implies that one desires that the other's desires be satisfied; negatively identifying with another's outcomes implies that one desires that the other's desires be unsatisfied. The degree of positive or negative identification with another's desires can be represented along a continuum of positive or negative weights applied as a multiplicative factor to the other's desires, the weights ranging from $+1$ (maximum positive identification) through 0 (absence of any identification) to -1 (maximum negative identification).

Any relationship one has with another party, whether an individual or a group, can be characterized by the weight one accords the other's desires (Horwitz, 1963). The clearest test of what weights are being accorded to another occurs where own and other desires are in conflict. Members may give varying degrees of weight to a group's desires *versus* their own desires as where they do or do not relinquish their own desires on behalf of the group's (Horwitz, 1954). They may give a weight of $+1.0$ to a group's desire and zero weight to their own as where a patriot is willing to die for his country, a religionist for his sect, or a partisan for his movement (Campbell, 1965). They give zero weight to a group's desires where they are indifferent to its fate. They may give a weight of -1.0 to a group's desires as where their antipathy is so great that they are prepared to sacrifice themselves to harm the group.

There is evidence, moreover, that groups and individuals view others' relationship with them in terms of the varying degrees of weight that others accord and ought to accord their desires (Horwitz, Glass, Giniger, and Cohn, 1966; Kelley, 1979). Individuals whose desires are equally frustrated by another will respond with anger if they believe the frustrating agent has given their desires less weight than they feel is due them, but with equanimity if they believe that the frustrating agent has given their desires the weight they deserve (Horwitz, 1963). Groups whose desires are equally frustrated by an outgroup will or will not react with hostility depending on whether they perceive the outgroup as reducing or not reducing their expected weight (Giniger, 1966).[8]

We propose the following as the nature of members' outcome interdependence with their ingroups and outgroups. Subjects who perceive themselves as group members give greater weight to the desires of their ingroups and of ingroup members than to the desires of the outgroups and of outgroup members. In addition, subjects who perceive others as group members anticipate that the others will give greater weight to the desires of the others' ingroups and ingroup members than to the desires of the outgroups and outgroup members.

A direct test of these propositions was made in the study by Huff (1979), described above, which examined allocations of rewards to ingroup versus outgroup members. Subjects were asked to indicate how much they would withhold or take away from outgroup members in order to benefit ingroup members by one cent. The average amount withheld or taken away was 5.6 cents. They were also asked to estimate how much typical members of their ingroup and outgroup would withhold or take away to benefit own members by a cent. They estimated the amounts as 6.6 cents for ingroup members and 8.9 cents for outgroup members. Subjects gave own members significantly less weight than they estimated other ingroup members would give, and very significantly less weight than they estimated outgroup members would give their own members, a finding that will be discussed below. But the subjects' tendency to give much higher weight to own members than to other members and to expect the same from members of both ingroups and outgroups is clearly manifested in these results.

The principle that members will give greater weight to the desires of own than other groups should apply not only to the allocation of rewards but to the allocation of ratings as well. We have so far treated subjects' ratings of own and other members or groups as simply expressing their feelings about those being rated. But it is almost certainly the case that if asked, subjects would say that the persons and groups being rated desired the most favourable possible evaluations. To that extent, differences in ratings should not only reflect how subjects feel about others but how much weight they give the others' desires to be rated well. In the experiment by Shake (1980) described above, subjects attempted to account for a chooser's selecting an ingroup member or an outgroup member as a friend. Prominent among these attributions were that the chooser believed: (a) that her ingroup expected her to choose its members more than her outgroup expected her to choose its members; (b) that as between the particular persons to be selected, the individual in her group had stronger expectations to be chosen by her than did the individual in the other group. These attributions indicate that subjects perceive the groups to have differential expectations about how much weight members ought to accord the desires of own *versus* other members to be favoured as a friend.

The study by Shake (1980) showed that subjects believed that choosers would rate ingroup members they chose more favourably than outgroup members they chose and even rate ingroup members they rejected more favourably than outgroup members they rejected. In a second experiment, Shake (1980) compared subjects' attributions about choosers who were either group members or unaffiliated individuals. Again, subjects indicated that they believed shared group membership would add a significant increment to one's ratings of others. Subjects estimated that group choosers would rate ingroup members they chose higher than unaffiliated individuals would rate unaffiliated individuals they chose; subjects also estimated that group choosers would rate ingroup members they rejected higher than unaffiliated choosers would rate unaffiliated individuals they rejected. The strongest determinant of subjects' views about the ratings that a chooser would give to another person was whether she did or did not choose that person. Yet so great was the impact of the chooser's acting as a member rather than as an individual that subjects believed that group choosers who *rejected* own members did not rate them lower than did unaffiliated choosers who *accepted* other unaffiliated individuals.

Subjects not only display ingroup–outgroup bias themselves but expect that others will do so as well. In holding these expectations, they may be functioning as naive balance theorists, believing that members will find other members attractive because unit-formation with others leads to heightened evaluations of them (Heider, 1958). Alternatively, they may be functioning as naive social-comparison theorists, believing that members' identities are defined by their groups and that members will enhance their ratings of other members in order to enhance their own self-esteem (Turner, 1978). An additional interpretation we would enter into the lists is that subjects believe that the persons or groups being rated desire as favourable ratings as they can get and that the raters will give greater weight to the desires of ingroup members than of outgroup members or unaffiliated individuals.

Viewed as social entities rather than social categories, groups can be seen as desiring some outcomes more than others. We view the interdependence between a member and the group entity as similar to that between two mutually responsive parties in a close relationship (Kelley, 1979). Giving greater weight to ingroup desires than to outgroup desires, members should evaluate and expect other members to evaluate their ingroups higher than their outgroups.

4. Attributions about individuality versus membership

Discussing the stereotypes that groups hold of one another, Campbell (1967) has noted the prevalence of the stereotype that 'we' are individuals, but 'they' are homogeneous. This disparity between the perception of ingroups and outgroups can be related to the fundamental attributional tendency to locate the causes of own behaviour in varying situations and the causes of others' behaviour in the constancies of their personal characteristics (Heider, 1958; Jones and Nisbett, 1971). Horwitz and Berkowitz (1975) have pointed out that interposing a group boundary between two persons enables each to perceive the other's behaviour as caused not only by personal but by group constancies, including such stable group characteristics as its culture, norms, leadership, conformity pressures, socialization practices, etc. Members should thus be inclined to view their own behaviour as varying according to different situations but outgroup behaviour as more or less fixed by membership characteristics.

There is evidence that in the minimal intergroup situation subjects view group membership as having differential impact on themselves, on ingroup members, and on outgroup members. The study by Huff (1979), noted above, measured the relative weights given own *versus* other members by how much one would deprive others in order to benefit own members by a fixed amount. As we have seen, subjects indicated that they believed outgroup members would give most weight to their own members, ingroup members would give next most weight, and subjects themselves would give least weight. When asked about favouring own members over others, subjects rated outgroup members as favouring own members most, ingroup members next, and themselves least. The greater the weight given one's group, the more should one be seen to be reacting as an extension of the group and the less should one be seen to be acting as an independent individual. The data therefore imply that subjects will perceive the relative potency of membership as greatest for outgroup members and the relative potency of individuality as greatest for themselves.

Evidence on this score was found in an unpublished interview study by Horwitz of peer groups among high school students and their teachers. Students were able to name numerous peer groups in the school. When asked to locate themselves and one friend in these groups, they readily placed the friend, but frequently stated that they themselves 'didn't belong to any group' or that they 'hung around with people in different groups'. Each friend in turn readily placed the students who denied group membership but then tended to deny his or her own group membership. Interviews with teachers elicited similar responses. Respondents were less likely to perceive themselves as group members than to be perceived as members by others. Conversely, they were more likely to perceive themselves as unaffiliated individuals than to be perceived as such by others.

The degree to which others' membership is perceived to determine their behaviour is well illustrated in the study by Shake (1980) described above. Subjects estimated that ratings given by members who chose own members were higher than the ratings given by unaffiliated individuals who chose other unaffiliated individuals. Subjects also believed that others would be significantly more pleased to be chosen by their group members than by unaffiliated individuals. However, they rated themselves as significantly more pleased when they themselves were chosen by unaffiliated individuals rather than by ingroup members, despite their anticipation of lower ratings from individuals than from members. The result suggests that subjects ascribe qualitatively different motivational processes to persons whom they perceive as individuals rather than as members. Perceiving themselves as individuals, subjects are more pleased to be selected for reasons of personal attractiveness rather than member attractiveness. Perceiving those in the outgroups as members, they believe these others are more pleased to be selected for reasons of member attractiveness rather than personal attractiveness. The effect goes beyond ingroup–outgroup bias; it suggests the emergence of tendencies toward 'depersonalization' of outgroup members even with the trivial separation of groups into overestimators and underestimators.

The process of depersonalization can be set in motion by the tendency to attribute others' behaviour to their stable characteristics, and in the case of outgroup members, to their stable characteristics as members. A concomitant is that outgroup members should be seen as relatively unaffected by the varying situations in which one must take account of others' desires, as in friendly rather than unfriendly interaction. Two studies show that outgroup members, defined by the usual trivial criteria, are perceived as very significantly less friendly to the subject's group than the subject's group is to the outgroup ... (Huff, 1979; Shake, 1980). Another study shows that outgroups are perceived as significantly more hostile to ingroups than *vice versa* (Rabbie, *et al.* 1974). Additional evidence that outgroups are viewed as less responsive than ingroups is given in Shake's (1980) finding that subjects reduce their identification with own groups when they are chosen by outgroup members, but view outgroup members as relatively impervious to actions by the subject's group, regarding them as remaining equally identified with their groups whether accepted or rejected by the subject's group.

Heider (1958) has noted that one is more likely to perceive others as animated by idiosyncratic personal characteristics, the stronger one's disagreement with them. However, Horwitz and Berkowitz (1975) have observed in workshops dealing with real-life disputes that the constancies attributed to one's antagonist often refer to member characteristics rather than to personal ones and that these attributions intensify the conflict. Both experimental and naturalistic observations suggest that hostility erupts more readily between group members than between individuals. Lindskold, McElwain, and Wayner (1977) found, for example, that groups sent more threatening messages than did individuals to opponents in a PDG game. While the result may reflect an increase in subjects' security to express hostility given group support, it may also reflect their tendency to depersonalize group opponents more than individual opponents.

A clear-cut demonstration of the central role of attributional processes in determining the course of intergroup conflict is given in an experiment by Flynn (1973) designed to alter ingroup and outgroup attributions. Pairs of groups with opposing positions on an issue were instructed to reach agreement. After the groups had deadlocked, they were administered one of three treatments. In one treatment, the groups were assigned the task of determining each other's self-attributions: the groups first wrote descriptions of 'how we see ourselves' and 'how they see themselves' and then discussed how well each group's judgement about the other's self-perception coincided with the other's actual self-perception. In a second treatment, the groups underwent the same procedure but wrote statements about 'how we see our reasons (for our position)' and 'how they see their reasons' and then discussed how well each group had judged the other's view of its reasons. In a control treatment, the groups separately discussed their reactions to the previous intergroup discussion in an otherwise unstructured format. Following these treatments the groups resumed negotiations for a specified period. Various measures pertaining to the resolution of the intergroup conflict were then obtained.

The groups dealing with each other's self-attributions exceeded the groups dealing with each other's reasons and these in turn exceeded the controls on each of the following measures: (a) positive versus negative characterizations given to the outgroup; (b) positive versus negative characterizations anticipated from the outgroup; (c) private ratings of each subject's own movement toward the outgroup position; (d) estimates of the probability of success in future negotiations between the two groups;

(e) relative frequencies with which pairs of groups actually reached agreement; (f) the degree of each subject's private acceptance of the compromise where group agreement was reached. The results show that mutual understanding of each other's self-attributions were more important than mutual understanding of each other's views about the issue in successfully resolving the intergroup conflict. Both treatments were more effective than the control condition. The relatively unstructured control condition allowed subjects to exercise their 'natural' tendencies to depersonalize outgroup members, to view their arguments as determined by membership characteristics, and to view them as unresponsive to what subjects probably perceived as their own rational arguments and reasonable concessions. Requiring the groups jointly to examine how each viewed itself probably offset these depersonalizing tendencies in two ways: in first judging how the outgroup sees itself, subjects were likely to conclude that 'they' probably see themselves much as 'we' see ourselves, namely, as flexible individuals capable of accommodating to others' desires in reaching a mutually satisfactory solution. In then communicating these views about the others' self-perceptions to the outgroups, subjects gave direct evidence that they could in fact understand and be responsive to the outgroups' own views. The results suggest that once the opponents perceived each other as being capable of breaking out of the constraints of membership and as capable of acting as responsive individuals, the attributional changes enabled the two groups to reach a relatively easy accommodation with each other.

This essay has attempted to grapple with the issues raised in our opening example of understanding not only ingroup bias but outgroup depersonalization. We began by considering the determinants of perceiving aggregates of individuals as group entities within an intergroup system and tried to indicate next how the nature of the interdependence between a member and a group can contribute to ingroup bias. We considered, finally, how the intergroup system might operate to depersonalize the attributions made about outgroup members. It is possible that these rudimentary tendencies toward depersonalization form the springs of outgroup dehumanization.

When Hitler first marked off the Jews from the rest of the population, a German might find that he was no longer merely a friend with a particular individual but a friend with a member of the Jewish group. If one can generalize from the findings reported above, he might continue to view another German friend in terms of his individuality, but the Jewish friend in terms of his membership. One might theorize that the attributions associated with outgroup membership would follow: he might see the Jewish friend as less friendly to Germans than to fellow Jews, as giving less weight to German concerns than to Jewish concerns, and, in general, as acting less as an individual and more as an extension of his group. It goes without saying that none of these attributions need be based on reality. In another context, Allport (1954) has eloquently described the progression by which antipathy can move to massacres. Implicit in his view is the assumption that it is easier to generate prejudice against groups than against individuals and that propaganda against an outgroup will spread easily to its depersonalized members. The evidences of incipient depersonalization of outgroup members described above may represent the seeds from which the extremes of dehumanization of others can grow, allowing a degree of brutalization of outgroup members that would be unthinkable if they were seen as unaffiliated individuals.

Notes

[1] Many of the studies reported here were supported by grants to the second author from the Netherlands Organization for the Advancement of Pure Research (ZWO), grant 57-7.
[2] For the academic year 1979–1980 Senior Fulbright Scholar at Boston College and Stanford University.
[3] The assumption regarding differential comfort with others having the same or opposite outcomes has been confirmed in an experiment directed by Horwitz (Schipani, 1979).
[4] The items not showing a reliable difference were responsibility, fearfulness, consideration, openness, and soundness of judgement.
[5] The non-significant items were goodness–badness of group, future cohesion, future performance, member similarity, hostility towards others, and pleasant atmosphere.
[6] Paralleling their ingroup attitudes, cooperative groups were more positive toward outgroups in the public than private conditions while competitive groups were less positive toward outgroups in the public than private conditions (Rabbie, 1980).
[7] A significant effect for females was that individual winners gave higher ratings to other individual winners than group winners gave to other group winners and that individual losers gave lower ratings to other individual losers than group losers gave to other group losers. This effect was not significant for males, being offset by their tendency to rate same-outcome others higher than opposite-outcome others without regard to how much the others' good or bad luck 'belonged' to them.
[8] The results of this study show that members view the strength of each group's desire for or against a given action as proportional to the algebraic *difference* between their respective outcomes from this action versus the alternative action. Where the parties give each other zero weight, their interdependence can be simply described in terms of the outcomes in each cell of the matrix (Thibaut and Kelley, 1959). Where they give each other more (or less) than zero weight, they must reckon with how much is at stake for each in taking one action rather than another, i.e. with the magnitudes and directions of the differences between the outcomes of each action for each party.

References

Allen, V.L. and Wilder, D.A. 1975. Categorization, belief similarity and inter-group discrimination. *Journal of Personality and Social Psychology*, **98**, 971–7.

Allport, G. 1954. *The nature of prejudice*. Reading, Mass: Addison-Wesley.

Blake, R.R. and Mouton, J.S. 1961. Reactions to intergroup competition under win–lose conditions. *Management Science*, **7**, 420–35.

Brewer, M.B. 1979. Ingroup bias in the minimal intergroup situation: A cognitive–motivational analysis. *Psychological Bulletin*, **86**, 307–24.

Byrne, D. 1971. *The attraction paradigm*. New York: Academic Press.

Campbell, D.T. 1958. Common fate, similarity and other indices of the status of aggregates of persons as social entities. *Behavioral Science*, **3**, 14–25.

Campbell, D.T. 1965. Ethnocentrism and other altruistic motives. In D. Levine (Ed.): *Nebraska Symposium on Motivation*, Vol. 13, Lincoln: University of Nebraska Press.

Campbell, D.T. 1967. Stereotypes and the perception of group differences. *American Psychologist*, **22**, (10), 817–29.

Campbell, D.T. 1975. On the conflicts between biological and social evolution and between psychology and moral traditions. *American Psychologist*, **30**, 1103–26.

Darley, J. and Berscheid, E. 1967. Increased liking caused by the anticipation of personal contact. *Human Relations*, **20**, 29–40.

Doise, W. 1978. *Groups and individuals: Explanations in social psychology*. Cambridge: Cambridge University Press.

Downing, L.L. and Monaco, N.R. 1979. Ingroup–outgroup bias formation as a function of differential ingroup–outgroup contact and authoritarian personality: A field experiment. (Mimeo.) Union College, Schenectady, N.Y.

Ferguson, C.K. and Kelley, H.H. 1964. Significant factors in the overevaluation of own group's product. *Journal of Abnormal and Social Psychology*, **69**, 223–8.

Flynn, L. 1973. Reducing intergroup conflict through attributional changes. Unpublished Ph.D. Dissertation, Boston College.

Gerard, H.B. and Hoyt, M.F. 1974. Distinctiveness of social categorization and attitude towards ingroup members. *Journal of Personality and Social Psychology*, **29**, 836–42.

Giniger, S. 1966. Relative deprivation and weight reduction in the arousal and reduction of intergroup conflict. Unpublished Ph.D. Dissertation, New York University.

Heider, F. 1958. *The psychology of interpersonal relations*. New York: Wiley.

Herman, S.N. 1978. *Jewish identity: A social psychological perspective*. London: Sage Publications.

Hornstein, H.A. 1978. Promotive tension and prosocial behavior: A Lewinian analysis. In L. Wispe (Ed.): *Altruism, sympathy, and helping: Psychological and sociological principles*. New York: Academic Press.

Horwitz, M. 1954. The recall of interrupted group tasks: An experimental study of individual motivation in relation to group goals. *Human Relations*, **7**, 3–38.

Horwitz, M. 1963. Hostility and its management in classroom groups. In, W.W. Charters, Jr. and N.L. Gage (Eds): *Readings in the social psychology of education*. Boston: Allyn and Bacon.

Horwitz, M. and Berkowitz, N. 1975. Attributional analysis of intergroup conflict. Paper presented at the meeting of the American Psychological Association, Chicago.

Horwitz, M. and Cartwright, D. 1953. A projective test for the diagnosis of group properties. *Human Relations*, **6**, (4), 397–410.

Horwitz, M., Glass, D.C., Giniger, S. and Cohn, A. 1966. The effects of frustrating acts upon the expectation of openness. *Human Relations*, 1965, 129–98.

Huff, E.D. 1979. Outgroup salience as a determinant of biased ingroup–outgroup attributions. Unpublished M.A. Dissertation, Boston College.

Jones, E., Davis, K. and Gergen, K. 1961. Role playing variations and their informational value for person perception. *Journal of Abnormal and Social Psychology*, **63**, 302–10.

Jones, E.E. and Nisbett, R.E. 1971. *The actor and the observer: Divergent perceptions of the causes of behavior*. Morristown, N.J.: General Learning Press.

Kelley, H.H. 1979. *Personal relationships: their structures and processes*. New York: Lawrence Erlbaum.

Kelley, H.H. and Thibaut, J.W. 1978. *Interpersonal relations: A theory of interdependence*. New York: Wiley-Interscience.

van Leent, J.A.A. 1964. *Sociologie, psychologie en sociale psychologie, hun opbouw, ontwikkeling en verhouding uit macro – micro oogpunt*. Arnhem/Zeist: W. de Haan/van Loghum Slaterus.

Lewin, K. 1948. *Resolving social conflicts*. New York. Harper and Row.

Lindskold, S., McElwain, D.C. and Wayner, M. 1977. Cooperation and the use of coercion by groups and individuals. *Journal of Conflict Resolution* **21**, 531–50.

Presser, J. 1969. *The destruction of the Dutch Jews*. New York: Dutton.

Rabbie, J.M. 1968. Effects of anticipated interaction within and between groups on intergroup bias. Unpublished manuscript. University of Utrecht.

Rabbie, J.M. 1972. Experimental studies of intergroup relations. Paper presented at a conference on the Experimental Study of Intergroup Relations, Bristol, England.

Rabbie, J.M. 1979. Vrees en in-en uitgroep differentiatie. Unpublished MS. University of Utrecht.

Rabbie, J.M. 1982. The effects of intergroup competition and cooperation on intra- and intergroup relationships. In V.I. Derlega and J. Grzelak (eds): *Cooperation and Helping behaviour. Theories and Research*. New York, Academic Press.

Rabbie, J.M., Benoist, F., Oosterbaan, H. and Visser, L. 1974. Differential power and effects of expected competitive and cooperative intergroup interaction on intra-group and outgroup attitudes. *Journal of Personality and Social Psychology*, **30**, 46–56.

Rabbie, J.M. and de Brey, J.H.C. 1971. The anticipation of intergroup cooperation and competition under private and public conditions. *International Journal of Group Tensions*, **1**, (3), 230–51.

Rabbie, J.M. and Horwitz, M. 1969. The arousal of ingroup–outgroup bias by a chance win or loss. *Journal of Personality and Social Psychology*, **69**, 223–8.

Rabbie, J.M. and Huygen, K. 1974. Internal disagreements and their effects on attitudes toward in- and outgroup. *International Journal of Group Tensions*, **4**, 222–46.

Rabbie, J.M. and Wilkens, G. 1971. Intergroup competition and its effects on intra-group and intergroup relations. *European Journal of Social Psychology*, **1**, 215–34.

Rice, A.K. 1969. Individual, group, and intergroup processes. *Human Relations*, **22**, (6), 565–84.

Ryen, A.H. and Kahn, A. 1975. Effects of intergroup orientation on group attitudes and proxemic behaviors. *Journal of Personality and Social Behavior*, **31**, 302–10.

Schipani, J. 1979. Interpersonal consequences of a group or individual chance win-loss. Unpublished M.A. Dissertation, Boston College.

Shake, A.M. 1980. Effects of attributions about acceptance and rejection between individuals and groups. Unpublished Ph.D. Dissertation, Boston College.

Sherif, M. 1966. *In common predicament*. Boston: Houghton Mifflin Co.

Sherif, M., Harvey, O.J., White, J., Hood, W.R., and Sherif, C.W. 1961. *Intergroup conflict and co-operation: The Robber's Cave Experiment*. Norman, Ok: University Book Exchange.

Tajfel, H. 1978. Introduction. In H. Tajfel (Ed.): *Differentiation between social groups: studies in the social psychology of intergroup relations*. London: Academic Press. European Monographs in Social Psychology, No. 14.

Tajfel, H., Billig, K., Bundy, R., and Flament, C. 1971. Social categorization and intergroup behavior. *European Journal of Social Psychology*, **1**, 149–75.

Thibaut, J.W., and Kelley, H.H. 1959. *The social psychology of groups*. New York: Wiley.

Turner, J. 1975. Social comparison and social identity: Some prospects for intergroup behaviour. *European Journal of Social Psychology*, **5**, 5–34.

Turner, J. 1978. Social categorization and social discrimination in the minimal group paradigm. In H. Tajfel (Ed.): *Differentiation between social groups: Studies in the social psychology of intergroup relations*. London: Academic Press. European Monographs in Social Psychology, No. 14.

Wilder, D.A. and Allen, V. 1974. Effects of social categorization and belief similarity upon intergroup behaviour. *Personality and Social Psychology Bulletin*, **1**, 281–3.

Part III
Contexts of social identity: Ethnicity and social differentials

10. Intergroup conflict in Northern Ireland

ED CAIRNS

1. Introduction

There has been a tendency to view the conflict in Northern Ireland as based upon a rational struggle for power in economic and political terms; yet, as Whyte (1978) and others (Darby, 1976; Moore, 1972; Rose, 1971; Schellenberg, 1977) have noted, in the last analysis the economic argument cannot account totally for the present conflict. As Whyte has put it: 'Anyone who studies the Ulster conflict must be struck by the intensity of feelings. It seems to go beyond what is required by a rational defence of the divergent interests which undoubtedly exist. There is an irrational element here, a welling-up of deep unconscious forces' (Whyte, 1978, p278). Or as McCann (1974) puts it, rather more succinctly: 'There is more to Irish politics than economics and reason'; there remain instead what Darby (1976) has labelled 'the unreal problems'. Thus, Carter in a 1972 postscript to Barritt and Carter (1972, first published in 1962) notes that while in 1962 Northern Ireland appeared to him to have real problems, yet 'much of the emotion centered on matters such as the holding of parades and the display of flags, which a less introspective community would long have recognized to be unimportant and even comic'.

To account for the irrational, the 'comic' behaviour of people in Northern Ireland, Whyte makes an appeal to what he terms the social psychological approach. However, social psychological theories, he notes, in contrast to the general literature on conflict, have been virtually ignored in relation to the conflict in Northern Ireland. Further, the few attempts at conceptualizing the Northern Irish conflict in psychological terms that do exist rely heavily on 'symptom' theories which postulate explanations at the individual level in an attempt to explain conflict between groups. This, however, is an approach which social psychologists are now actively rejecting because it is apparent that extreme sacrifice, such as that which is occurring almost daily in Northern Ireland, cannot be understood in terms of individual cost–benefit calculations (Laver, 1976) but rather must be seen from the outset 'as being inherently of an intergroup nature' (Tajfel, 1978*a*).

This distinction between interpersonal and intergroup explanations of prejudice and discrimination is no mere academic point; it has important consequences. Thus, Darby notes that the importance of considering theories about the conflict in Northern Ireland is that 'the way in which the administrator or legislator looks upon conflict will determine whether he will advocate the introduction of more soldiers or more factories or a charter of human rights' (Darby, 1976, p194). As Hogan and Emler (1978) have stated, the attempt to locate prejudice within the individual has encouraged for too long a search for solutions at this level and thus it distracted attention from the root causes of prejudice of which the individual expression is but a symptom. In fact, individual-level theories offer explanations but few remedies; people cannot 'undo their own childhood, but they are able to change collectively the nature of their society . . . The need therefore is for an avowedly social analysis of social phenomena' (Billig, 1976).

This chapter will therefore attempt to provide a social analysis of the conflict in Northern Ireland, structured in terms of Tajfel's (1978*b*) approach to intergroup relations. Tajfel's theory suggests that we tend to structure our social environment in terms of groupings of persons, or social categories, thus simplifying the world we live in. These categories are to some extent based upon our own experiences but are also largely determined by our society. Our knowledge of our own membership of various of these social categories is defined as our social identity and forms an important part of our self-concept. To enhance our social identity, we tend to behave in ways that make our own group acquire positive distinctiveness in comparison to other groups. If this is not possible we may seek to change our group membership; or if this is not possible, we may attempt a redefinition of the existing social situation so as to achieve a more positive social identity. This approach appears to have several major advantages over existing psychological theories. First, it is undoubtedly firmly based on a group-level approach in contrast to existing ego-psychology theories. Secondly, it has the advantage of taking a dynamic approach (Giles *et al.*, 1977) in which the relationships between groups are not seen as static. It would thus appear more likely to provide an explanation for the social changes which have occurred in Northern Ireland especially over the last decade, and which are still under way. Analysis in terms of Tajfel's theory should therefore help the present generation of observers to avoid Barritt and Carter's (1972) earlier mistake of reporting Northern Ireland as having a deeply divided, but stable, social structure.

2. Social categorization in Northern Ireland

Social categorization may be defined as 'the ordering of the social environment in terms of social categories, that is of groupings of persons in a manner which is meaningful to the subject' (Tajfel, 1974). While categorization *per se* is not seen by Tajfel as the sole cause of intergroup conflict, it does play a major role. This is because as Tajfel *et al.* (1971) have pointed out, there can be no intergroup behaviour without social categorization first occurring. In other words, 'in order for large numbers of individuals to be able to hate or dislike or discriminate against other individuals seen as belonging to a common social category they must first have acquired a sense of belonging to groups (or social categories) which are clearly distinct from ... those they hate, dislike or discriminate against' (Tajfel, 1978*b*, p6).

Social categorization is of course recognized as a fundamental process common to all people in all societies, which enables them to systematize and simplify their environment (Tajfel, 1978*b*). Therefore it would not be surprising to be able to present evidence for the existence of social categorization in Northern Ireland. What is important, however, is the extent to which this categorization is recognized as important by the people. Burton (1978), an English sociologist who has reported his observations made during an eight month stay in a Catholic, working-class area of Belfast, was obviously impressed by the level of categorization (or sectarianism) in Northern Irish society. So much so that he devotes almost one-quarter of his book to the topic which he feels, because of its 'pervasiveness and persistence', is 'one of the dominant ideological representations which feature in the Six Counties' (Burton, 1978, p67). This 'sectarian consciousness', he observed, is particularly expressed in the concern shown by people in Northern Ireland for 'the fundamental and almost overwhelming question – what is he?', a behaviour which he characterizes by the term 'telling'. Telling, he explains, 'constitutes the syndrome of signs by which Catholics and Protestants arrive at religious ascription in their everyday interactions' (Burton, 1978, p4). Burton suggests that the emphasis placed on 'telling' in Northern Ireland illustrates how thoroughly social categorization has permeated social consciousness.

Despite the fact that 'approximately 370 years of not living together have made the social construction of differences in Northern Ireland very sophisticated' (Burton, 1978, p49), little interest has been taken in this phenomenon by social scientists. The Royal Commission in 1864 when questioning the Chairman of the Belfast Police Committee regarding the small number of Catholics on that force, did express some mild scepticism of the claim that 'in this part of the country ... it is not very difficult to know a man's religion by his face', but beyond this the level of interest has barely risen during the past century. The onset of the recent 'troubles' led to some journalistic attempts to examine the subject and several authors have included anecdotal evidence of which Burton's (1978) work is the most colourful example.

Recently, however, Cairns (1980) has reported a series of studies which have attempted a more empirical approach. As a preliminary step, Catholic and Protestant adults were asked to list the cues they used to determine another's religion. The five most frequently listed cues by both groups were – area of residence (attesting to the geographic segregation in Northern Irish society), school attended (most children attend denominational schools), names (both first and last names were mentioned), appearance (which included references to clothing and especially to face) and speech (including both accent and content of speech). To date, some preliminary results concerned with accent have been reported (Cairns and Duriez, 1976) while a study is underway investigating the use of faces as a cue to denominational membership (Stringer and Cairns, 1978). However the bulk of the work reported by Cairns (1980) has involved the use of first names as cues and particularly the development of this knowledge in young children. These studies suggest that while some children have undoubtedly acquired this information by the age of seven years, (certain first names being associated with particular group membership), it is not till probably the age of 11 years that all children possess this information. This finding illustrates a major difference between religious ascription in Northern Ireland and racial categorization in the USA. Discrimination in Northern Ireland is based upon stereotyped cues which must be slowly learned as distinct from the more obvious perceptual cues in a racial context. This observation reinforces the thesis that the conflict in Northern Ireland does not have a 'racial' basis as some have suggested (for example Moore, 1972) but that the social categories in Northern Ireland are first and foremost a division of people, by people (Billig, 1976). In other words, as Burton (1978) has noted, what exists in Northern Ireland in many ways closely resembles a racial situation but it is essentially 'a social construction of ethnicity', which is historically based.

This construction of ethnicity leads to the assumption of two important conditions necessary for social categorization to assume important proportions (Tajfel, 1974). The first of these is that the division of the social world is made along lines which produce two clearly distinct and non-overlapping categories and the second is that there exists a serious difficulty, if not impossibility, of passing from one group to another. Given these two circumstances, then, Tajfel (1974, 1978b) has hypothesized that behaviour will be determined not in terms of self but rather in terms of group, thus bringing into play the processes of social comparison, social psychological differentiation and social identity.

In fact, one of the major characteristics of Northern Irish society is that it forms what LeVine and Campbell (1972) and others have termed a 'pyramidal–segmentary' structure. This is a structure totally lacking in categories which cut across each other; as a result, it is hardly possible for two or more loyalties to exist with contradictory demands. Thus, people in Northern Ireland 'do not perceive the world in terms of separate distinct spheres of work, religion, politics, education etc., but in terms of the two distinct spheres of Catholic and Protestant' (Easthope, 1976). And those categories which do exist apart from Catholic and Protestant are usually complementary to the two major categories, and not contradictory to them – for example, Protestant Church, Unionist Party, Orange Order (Roberts, 1971). Thus, the denominational categories provide what has been termed a 'terminal identity', that is one which embraces and integrates a number of lesser identities (Epstein, 1978). In fact, observers have been surprised to note that in Northern Ireland the potentially cross-cutting categories of sex and class are relatively unimportant. Thus, it has been observed that Northern Ireland is the region of the United Kingdom where class consciousness is lowest (Birrell, 1972; Rose, 1971) and Harris (1972) has even suggested that religious affiliation is a more important characteristic of an individual, normally outweighing even that of sex.

Northern Irish society similarly fulfils Tajfel's second important condition noted above – that of the difficulty or impossibility of passing from one group to the other. Of course, religious conversion is a possibility, but as Barritt and Carter (1972) observed, it is relatively rare and is opposed equally by both sides. Therefore, in Northern Ireland 'religious categorization is made at birth and maintained throughout life' (Easthope, 1976) and a change of group membership is thus virtually impossible, at least while an individual remains in Northern Ireland (Harris, 1972). Evidence for the strength of feeling regarding the sanctity of this dichotomous categorization can be obtained by noting the way in which people react to intermarriage between members of the two groups, such marriages being commonly referred to as 'mixed marriages'. Alexander Irvine (1921) writing of his own childhood in the late nineteenth century says this of his own parents' 'mixed' marriage: 'Not in the memory of man in that community had a wedding created so little interest in one way and so much in another. They were both 'turn-coats', the people said, and they were shunned by both sides' (p20).

There is little to suggest that the reaction to such marriages is any different today. In fact, the almost violent reaction to these marriages, particularly on the part of parents, suggests further that social categorization in Northern Ireland assumes the proportions of ethnicity. Fishman (1977) defines ethnicity as, at its core, an inherited constellation acquired from one's parents as they acquired it from theirs and so on back further and further *ad infinitum*. A mixed marriage then precipitates such a crisis, says Epstein (1978), precisely because this is a case where the parents were unsuccessful in transmitting their own attachment to the group; thus, responses to the threat of intermarriage reveal 'the affective power of ethnicity at its most naked'. This comment not only helps provide some insight into the mechanisms that help maintain social categorization in Northern Ireland, but also reveals the importance of this phenomenon, given that it has been suggested that ethnicity provides an example of the most powerful investments in which social man is involved (Fishman, 1977).

Social categorization, then, can safely be said not only to exist in Northern Ireland, but to fulfil the requirements for the norm of 'groupness' to operate – that is, where the social world is clearly dichotomized into 'us' and 'them'. Further, this is not simply a means by which the individual comes to understand the world, but also provides a guide to action (Tajfel, 1978b). The most obvious result of this is perhaps conformity, reinforced, as Easthope (1976) notes, by the fact that in Northern Ireland most social interaction occurs in small communities where individuals are highly visible and thus public deviation from group values is rare.

3. Social identity

One of the considerations on which Tajfel's theory is based is that a major task for the individual is to find, create and define his place in the existing networks (Tajfel, 1978b). That is, the individual will strive to develop a social identity, based on the knowledge that he belongs to certain social groups and not others and this will form a part of his view of himself or become, as Epstein (1978) states, 'an extension of the self'. The concept of identity is a difficult one. As Tajfel (1978*b*) has pointed out, it is unlikely to be resolved by any single discipline in the social sciences; and yet, as Moscovici and Paicheler (1978) have noted, 'the concept of identity is as indispensable as it is unclear'. Tajfel has tried to overcome or perhaps sidestep some of the problems revolving around the concept of identity by stressing that his view of social identity is essentially a dynamic one. It is not an attempt to view social identity for 'what it is' but rather to see it as an intervening causal mechanism in social situations. The complex dialectical relationship between social identity and social settings is stressed, in the sense that the salience of a particular social identity for an individual may vary from situation to situation and indeed from time to time within the same situation. Social identity, then, is a blanket term concealing the complexity of the relationship between the clarity of the awareness that one is a member of a group and the strength and nature of the emotional investments that derive from this identity (Tajfel, 1978*a*, 1978*b*).

Given a highly dichotomized society like that of Northern Ireland, the theory would certainly predict a high level of awareness of social identity defined in terms of the two predominant groups, plus a strong emotional investment in this identity.

Fortunately, at least some evidence is available concerning the salience of social identity in Northern Ireland. As Turner (1975) has pointed out, Tajfel's theory does not simply suggest that acceptance by an individual of a categorization is automatic. What is remarkable, therefore, in Northern Ireland is that failure to acknowledge membership of one of the two major groups is actually very rare. So much so that one can almost believe the joke which relates how a man stopped on the street in Belfast is asked his religion. When he replies 'Jewish' the rejoinder is 'Yes, but are you a Catholic Jew or a Protestant Jew?' Some empirical evidence comes from the 1971 census where the question about religious group membership was optional, yet over 90 % of the respondents chose to answer it and of these only some 0.11 % described themselves as atheist or agnostic (Darby, 1976). Similarly, when Cairns and Mercer (1978) asked some 900 adolescents to describe 'how you think about yourself' by completing a checklist consisting of 18 bipolar adjectives which consisted of nine personality traits (included as distractors) and nine possible social identities of interest in Northern Ireland such as Catholic–Protestant, Unionist–Nationalist etc., then only 3 % failed to describe themselves as either Catholic or

Protestant. These questionnaires were completed in a relatively informal non-school situation and are in fact typical of the response rate to such questions in other investigations by the same authors. It is also interesting to note that this study provides further evidence of the special use of these terms – Catholic and Protestant – in Northern Ireland. Sometimes outside observers are misled by the use of these terms into thinking that Northern Ireland is experiencing a 'holy' war. However the fact that in the Cairns and Mercer study almost half of those labelling themselves as Protestant and one third of those labelling themselves Catholic did *not* consider themselves to be 'religious' reveals the special ethnopolitical nature of these particular social identities in Northern Ireland.

The question of the strength of social identity in Northern Ireland is rather less well documented. However, given that almost every day people from both groups are risking their lives in situations which can only possibly benefit their group and not themselves, then presumably it can be safely assumed that, for some individuals at least, their social identity forms an important part of their view of themselves. Once again, the study by Cairns and Mercer (1978) throws some light on this question. After the adolescents had indicated which pole of the 18 bipolar adjectives best described how they thought about themselves, they were then asked to rank-order the 18 terms they had chosen. The most interesting result to emerge was that Catholics (but not Protestants) ranked the social-class label as less important than the label Catholic. Further, comparison of the Catholic and Protestant responses showed a tendency for the Catholic subjects to rank some of the ethnopolitical terms (particularly Gael/Planter, Celt/Anglosaxon and Protestant/Catholic) as more important to them.

It is, however, perhaps reassuring to note that all these Northern Irish young people regarded being happy, shy, calm etc. as clearly more im-portant than the various social identities presented to them. Of course, it should be pointed out that this study simply considered social identity as a static term and thus does not do justice to the dynamic concept envisaged by Tajfel. It would be interesting to obtain information in a similar fashion in different settings or at different times or among individuals who have shown differing degrees of commitment to their group. For example, Barritt and Carter (1972) observed that during the 'marching months' of July and August when Protestants take to the streets to commemorate old victories, friendly relationships between neighbours of different re-ligions are apparently often interrupted. At times like this, they noted, 'sectarian spirit' is at its height and therefore one could assume that at such times social identity in Northern Ireland assumes a heightened salience.

4. Social identity, social comparison, psychological distinctiveness

Where the dynamic nature of Tajfel's conception of social identity really comes into its own is when one considers the direction of the evaluation of social identity. He hypothesized that individuals will try to find and maintain a positive social identity. This social identity is always achieved, Tajfel's theory suggests, in contradistinction to an outgroup, that is, through the process of social comparison. Despite the criticism of the unsatisfactory nature of social identity as a motive force because of the vagueness of the 'concept of positivity' (Breakwell, 1978), this idea never-theless makes a major contribution towards understanding the 'groupness' or social loyalty prevalent in Northern Irish society.

As Laver (1976) has pointed out, although 'social loyalty' tends to be used as an explanatory concept, it really only explains why actions, once taken, are judged as they are. Tajfel's ideas at least provide an explanation for social loyalty, particularly in a society structured such as that in Northern Ireland. In other societies it may be possible for an individual who is dis-satisfied with the social identity supplied to him by his group simply to leave the group – the exit (Hirschman, 1970), or social mobility, option (Tajfel, 1976). If, however, as in Northern Ireland, leaving the group is virtually impossible, then other remedies must be sought via the process of social comparison, particularly for groups which Tajfel (1978*b*) describes as characterized by an 'insecure' social identity – one in which comparisons lead to the perception of 'cognitive alternatives' to the existing outcome (Turner and Brown, 1978). As Tajfel points out, a completely 'secure' social identity is hardly ever possible, as even the most consensually superior groups must work at maintaining their positive social identity by making social comparisons and maintaining their social psychological distinctiveness. It is the establishment of positively valued distinctiveness from other groups which Tajfel sees as the 'major outcome' of the sequence social categorization–social identity–social comparison (Tajfel, 1978*b*).

The way in which a group will act under pressure to achieve its aim of a positively valued psychological distinctiveness and hence an adequate social identity will depend upon whether the group perceives itself to be at present occupying a superior or an inferior position. The problem is how to classify the two main groups in Northern Ireland in terms of majority/minority status.

Generally, most writers, and certainly the media, have made the assumption based on the numbers of the respective groups in the population of Northern Ireland, that the Protestants form the majority group, the Catholics the minority. However, if one takes the population of Ireland as a whole, then of course the roles are reversed, the Protestants being the minority, and the Catholics the majority. Jackson (1971) has suggested what he calls 'the double minority model': Protestants see themselves as a minority within the whole island of Ireland while Catholics see themselves as a minority within Northern Ireland. For the sake of consistency, the reverse position must also be considered. It is possible to consider (though no one appears to have done so to date) that both groups see themselves as majorities, the Catholics in an all Ireland context, the Protestants in a Northern Irish context. Unfortunately, this question has not been approached empirically and therefore no direct evidence is available on what may be a crucial issue. This is a crucial issue as far as it relates to Tajfel's differing predictions for groups which are consensually superior and inferior, although he has of course stressed that the definition of a minority should not depend simply upon numerical criteria, but rather upon the perceptions by the individuals involved of the status of their group (Tajfel, 1978a).

In the case of a superior group, Tajfel (1978b) has suggested that a threat to its position may be perceived either because its superiority is perceived to be under attack or because group members are in conflict regarding the basis of the group's superiority, for example, if it is seen as being based upon some form of injustice. In these conditions, the predictions of interest to the Northern Ireland situation point to the intensification of existing distinctions with, in addition, the creation of new forms of psychological distinctiveness, which are perhaps designed to find new justifications for the maintenance of the *status quo* (Tajfel, 1978b).

For the inferior group with an insecure social identity, three basic options are open, according to Tajfel. They may attempt to redefine the attributes which contribute to the existing negative social comparison – for example 'black is beautiful'. Or they may attempt to create, through social action, new group characteristics which have a positively valued distinctiveness from the superior group. In practice, Tajfel suggests, some combination of these two tactics will actually be adopted. The third option involves becoming 'through action and reinterpretation of group characteristics more like the superior group' (Tajfel, 1978b). This is presumably the most important option, involving as it does the ultimate goal of social change where the inferior group in fact becomes either equal, or indeed superior to, the present superior group. It would appear that this option may be closely related to two other important dimensions related to the inferior group's perception of its relationship with the superior group. These involve the perceived legitimacy and stability of the *status quo*. Tajfel (1978*b*) suggests both these dimensions may vary independently to give four possible combinations of legitimacy and stability. Of these Tajfel notes that 'a combination of illegitimacy and instability would become a powerful incitement for attempts to change the intergroup *status quo* or to resist such changes on the part of the groups which see themselves as threatened by them' (Tajfel, 1978*b*, p52). This third option, which involves the inferior group becoming more like the superior group is also of interest because, in contrast to the first two options, it allows the value differential associated with a social comparison to be shared by two competing groups (Turner, 1975). In other words, it leads to the acknowledgement of, or at least implies the possible existence of, some dimensions of comparability, in fact of the existence of similarities between apparently highly dissimilar groups.

The evidence available regarding the operation of these processes in Northern Ireland is of course incidental, as no deliberate investigations of these processes have yet been undertaken. However, the limited evidence that is available will now be examined, first in an attempt to establish how the two groups in Northern Ireland have valued their social identity and then to establish if there is evidence that social comparisons leading to psychological distinctiveness have played a role in the conflict. Because the Catholic and Protestant groups are considered to occupy an inferior/superior status respectively, and therefore Tajfel's theory predicts different outcomes for them, the two groups will be discussed separately.

The Catholics

Implicit in Tajfel's theory is the idea that an inferior group will inevitably possess a negative social identity *at some time*. As he notes, 'there is fairly abundant evidence from many parts of the world that members of underprivileged groups engage quite often in ingroup devaluation or denigration and consequently show signs of outgroup favouritism' (Tajfel, 1978*b*, p16). Perhaps Irish Catholics did possess such a negative social identity at one time. Heslinga (1971) quotes one observer in the mid 19th century as remarking that 'the people were turning almost willingly into little Britons'. However, it would appear that cognitive alternatives to this situation were recognized early in Ireland and that the group began to establish for itself a more positive social identity.

Therefore, while virtually no empirical evidence exists on this point, observers during the more recent past appear to have concluded that the Catholics of Northern Ireland do in fact possess a positive social identity. Thus Barritt and Carter (1972, p1) writing originally in 1962 remarked that 'the Catholic community gathers to itself . . . the pride of a remote Celtic past'. Tajfel's idea that this positive social identity is related to an individual's image of himself has also been echoed by other observers of the Catholics of Northern Ireland. For example Harris (1972), remarking on the degree of self-identification with and among the minority group, suggests that this can only be explained in terms of 'some kind of self-advantage'. McCann (1974) writing of his own Catholic working class background in Derry also appears to have appreciated the relationship between social identity and self-concept: 'when a man lives in a world of bookies' slips, varnished counters and Guinness spits, he will readily accept an account of the past which tends to invest his living with dignity' (McCann, 1974, p119).

In fact, only one study provides any empirical evidence on this point. O'Donnell (1977) in the course of an investigation of stereotypes in Northern Ireland obtained information on the stereotypes held by Catholics about their own group and also how they evaluated these terms. Unfortunately, the study is flawed for several reasons (see Cairns, Mercer and Bunting, 1978, for a review). Nowhere in the book does the author indicate exactly when the study was undertaken. Also, a major problem is that the terms were not generated by representative members of the respective groups in Northern Ireland, but instead were chosen by a panel of six judges each of whom 'held at least a Master's university degree' (O'Donnell, 1977). Nevertheless, as the only information available on the subject, it does at least provide some insights. Particularly, it is interesting to note that of the ten terms most frequently chosen by Catholics to describe themselves, a majority of the panel rated four negatively (or it may have been three, depending on whether one follows Table 39, p144 or the text on p142). At any rate, the four terms which Catholics used to describe their own group but subsequently rated as negative were 'long-suffering', 'insecure', 'deprived' and 'unfortunate'. The remaining terms were, however, all rated by a majority as positive and (excluding two purely descriptive terms, Irish and Nationalistic) indicate a positive social identity – 'very ordinary people', 'decent', 'fine people', 'reasonable'. But, once again, this represents a static view of social identity. Burton (1978) has indicated one of the possible dynamics underlying social identity by suggesting that it is 'extremely obvious' to him that those Catholics he observed who were politically involved had a sense of purpose which was reflected in an often supremely confident presentation of self.

How then has this positive, or at least partially positive, social identity been achieved by the 'inferior' Catholic group? The primary method, it would appear, has been by creating a new ideology which involved positively valued distinctiveness from the superior group. This movement probably began in the second half of the 19th century and was either inspired by, or indeed itself inspired, the founding of the Gaelic Athletic Association (GAA) in 1884 and the Gaelic League in 1893. The GAA's main aim is to encourage Irish games and culture generally and at the same time to discourage 'foreign games' such as rugby, cricket and soccer. Until recently (the 1970s), it actually banned its members who participated in, or even attended, foreign games. As Darby (1976) notes, it has always had close links with political and cultural nationalism and today still will not accept members of the British armed forces or of the Royal Ulster Constabulary as members.

As many commentators have noted, this emphasis on Gaelic culture had the effect of excluding Protestants because the concept of a Gaelic Irish identity undoubtedly includes as one of its principal attributes the Catholic faith (Darby, 1976; Harris, 1972; Heslinga, 1971). It is interesting to note that today, about 100 years after the foundation of the GAA, the abhorrence of foreign games is apparently most keenly felt only in the North of Ireland. In the South are to be found schools which are keen proponents of rugby and cricket in particular, but in the North not a single Catholic school includes either of these games in its sports curriculum (Darby, 1973).

The other strategy of reinterpretation of 'inferior' characteristics has either been used less often or perhaps is rather more subtle and thus more difficult to observe. One possible example that has been recorded concerns the field of education and intellectual ability. Darby (1973) notes that there has been 'an occasionally repeated view that Catholic schools are academically less successful' than Protestant schools, a view which he points out is not substantiated by any evidence. Nevertheless it is interesting to note that one of the stereotypes consistently held by Catholic teachers of Protestant schools, according to the results of a recent survey by Darby *et al.* (1977), was that Protestant schools are 'cold, rigid, examination oriented and unfriendly', while Catholic schools were regarded as 'more friendly places . . . not obsessed with academic performance'.

Whatever the tactics of the past have been, the last decade appears to have heralded the emergence of a new strategy on the part of the minority group in Northern Ireland in their efforts to engage in social competition with the majority group. The emphasis on simply stressing distinctiveness based on different attributes from those valued by the majority has given way to efforts to compete on equal terms with the superior group. For approximately fifty years the segregationist policies of the Catholic political leadership resulted in little real progress in their group's relative position. In this context it is interesting to note that Billig (1976) has suggested the possibility that a positive social identity may actually serve an inferior group ill and this may indeed have been the case for the Northern Irish Catholics from at least 1920 to 1970. Recently, however, their goal has been epitomized in the phrase 'civil rights'. Tajfel (1978a) has pointed out that an important consequence of social competition may be that the so-called inferior group, while wishing to retain its own identity, at the same time wishes to become 'more like the majority in their opportunities of achieving goals and marks of respect which are generally valued by the society at large'. Thus, as Birrell (1972) observed, 'socio-economic deprivation in comparison to Protestants has been a main theme of Catholic grievances. The intensity of protests about such grievances can be explained in terms of the relative deprivation hypothesis. Perceived deprivation . . . is what is important' (Birrell, 1972, p338). Therefore, Birrell suggests, the newly emergent Catholic middle class in particular, seeing their desire for social mobility blocked, turned instead to more radical means, thus confirming Tajfel's (1978b) prediction that when individual social mobility is not possible, intergroup behaviour results. A concrete mark of the change of tactic was the total demise of the Nationalist Party which had represented an emphasis on Gaelic distinctiveness and advocated abstentionist politics in favour of a more radical party, the Social and Democratic Labour Party (SDLP). Recently, however, signs of rifts within the SDLP have been evident, particularly with the resignation of one of the founder members, Gerry Fitt. One of the issues appears to be a return to more 'green' policies and it may be that under stress there is a tendency to revert to former strategies.

Evidence for this on a more local level comes from Burton (1978). During his period of residence in the Catholic enclave in Belfast that he refers to as Anro, an assassination campaign by Protestant paramilitaries reached its height. At this time, he noted, there was within the Catholic community of Anro a tightening of community bonds which was particularly evidenced 'in the increased importance of celebrating things Irish' (Burton, 1978, p34).

However it seems likely that such reversion to previously tried tactics will only be temporary. The reason for this belief is that there can be no doubt that the change to direct social competition with the Protestants has led to considerable gains for the Catholic community which in turn have probably led to an increase in social distinctiveness. Therefore, it has been suggested by some observers that 'while the hearts and minds of the people of Ireland have never been united the sense of difference has, if anything, increased' (Brian Faulkner, former Prime Minister of Northern Ireland, quoted in Houston, 1978).

Perhaps the only remaining question on this topic is why it took the Catholics so long (at least 50 years) to change to a more direct confrontation with the Protestants. A possible explanation may be expressed in terms of legitimacy and stability. Undoubtedly the Catholic community had been in no doubt since 1920, if not before, of the illegitimacy of the Unionist/ Protestant regime in Northern Ireland. However it is possible that not until the late 1960s did they perceive the instability of this regime. As Tajfel has pointed out (1978b, p52) it is often this combination of illegitimacy and instability which 'will transform a potential and sometimes smouldering social conflict into one which is explicitly acknowledged as such by the groups involved'.

The Protestants

Northern Ireland watchers appear to have been in little doubt for some time that the Protestant community has enjoyed a positive social identity. Thus Barritt and Carter (1962, p57) observed that 'it seems clear to us that in general Protestants feel superior . . . The sense of superiority is, we think, to be found at all levels'. Further this sense of superiority has apparently existed for some time. Darby (1976) quotes Lecky in 1892 making exactly the same point: 'the most worthless Protestant, even if he had nothing else to boast of, at least found it pleasing to think that he was a member of the dominant race'. As with the Catholic group, this positive social identity appears to be based upon folk memories from the past, particularly related to what is seen as their triumphs in a struggle for freedom and conscience at 'Derry, Aughrim and the Boyne', battles linked with the name of William III, Prince of Orange (Barritt and Carter, 1972; Moore, 1972).

These triumphs are celebrated annually, particularly on the 12th of July when a mass turnout of Protestants 'serves the purpose of reinforcing group identity by emphasizing points of differences with rivals, however irrelevant' (Laver, 1976). The fact that these demonstrations were felt to be necessary, even when Protestant–Unionist power was at its height, indicates that the Protestant group never possessed a completely secure social identity, but instead felt it necessary to engage in continuous social competition in order to maintain positive social psychological distinc-

tiveness. Observers such as Rose (1971) have often pondered over the fact
that flying the Union Jack and singing the 'Queen' – the British national
anthem – are both carried out by Protestants in Northern Ireland with a
'frequency and fervour found nowhere else in the United Kingdom'.
While some have mistakenly simply seen these behaviours as irrelevant,
or even comic, others have perhaps read too much into them as symbolic
of the Protestants' desires to express their Britishness. It would appear
rather that a more parsimonious explanation may be offered in Tajfel's
terms, namely that these symbols chosen for historical reasons are now
used primarily to establish psychological distinctiveness and thus maintain
for the Protestant group a positive social identity. This hypothesis is
reinforced by observations that the annual commemorations of the battle
of the Boyne are not simply used to express hostility towards foes 'but a
local pride' (Harris, 1972) which pride Harbison (1960) in his autobiography
remembers as being linked to the fact that as a child he lived not in, but
simply near to Sandy Row in Belfast, 'the strongest Orange quarter'.

This is an important concept because it holds the key to understanding
what has proved for many observers the perplexing 'conditional' character
of the Loyalists' loyalty. When the British parliament assumed full control
of Northern Irish affairs in 1972 the fact was made obvious that many
Protestants who loudly proclaimed their loyalty to the Queen had distinct
reservations about submitting to her government. Nor is this a new
phenomenon. Darby (1976) quotes these lines from a nineteenth-century
Punch:

> Loyal to whom, to what
> To power to pelf,
> To place, to privilege, in a word to self.

Whether Protestants have always realized this inconsistency in their own
attitudes is not clear though the recent events noted above may have led to
greater self-awareness on this point. Thus Miller (1978) quotes a pamphlet
issued by one of the Protestant paramilitary organizations – the Ulster
Defence Association (UDA) – as declaring that the union with Britain had
'never been an end in itself' but 'was always a means to preserving Ulster's
British tradition and the identity of her loyalist people'.

Empirical evidence that this identity is essentially a positive one comes
from the study by O'Donnell referred to earlier. All the words chosen by
the Protestants as typical of their own group were subsequently rated by
a majority of the Protestants as positive rather than as negative terms. One
particular dimension of interest along which the Protestants feel they have

established superiority is that of cleanliness and/or neatness. This is evidenced in the colloquialism 'that's a bit more Protestant looking' said, for example, by a mother who has just tidied her child's hair or by a man who has just cut his lawn (Barritt and Carter, 1972; Nelson, 1975).

As one might expect, over the last decade some changes have been perceptible among the Protestant group who undoubtedly have felt their position of superiority to be threatened. Indeed, Miller (1978) has gone as far as to suggest that the Catholics have been winning consistently since 1968 and the resulting sense of humiliation has been keenly felt on the Protestant side. Under such conditions, as Tajfel (1978a) has suggested, a 'new consciousness of belonging' may arise. The creation of the Protestant paramilitary organizations such as the Ulster Defence Association and the Ulster Volunteer Force may be viewed in this way, and also the unsubstantiated rumours that the membership of the Orange Order has greatly increased of late. This increased affiliative behaviour may well be related to an increased insecurity of social identity. Turner and Brown (1978) suggest that the best example of an insecure relationship is where the subordinate group was itself previously dominant. While this reversal of status may not have actually happened yet, it may be that the Protestants feel that it is under way. An observation by Nelson may be relevant here. She remarked of the Protestants that 'the most striking characteristic of a community historically dominant, well organized and successful in so many walks of life is its singular lack of confidence in its own efficacy and power' (Nelson, 1975, p177). The time at which Nelson's research was carried out may be important. The others who commented on the obvious sense of superiority of the Protestants all carried out their fieldwork before 1960 while Nelson indicates that her work was completed in the 1970s. If her observation is correct then this could indicate a very interesting situation which would imply the development of other related changes, for example in the terms on which social comparisons will be based in future. Certainly it is a point worth pursuing in future empirical work.

Another change that observers have suggested may have occurred in the Protestant ranks is that a degree of divisiveness may have crept in (Laver, 1976). Whyte (1978) has stated this most strongly by suggesting that one of the most important features of the current conflict 'has been that Ulster Protestants are more deeply divided than at any time since the eighteen-eighties' and has in fact gone on to propose that it is because Protestant 'distrusts Protestant, not just because Protestant distrusts Catholic that the Ulster conflict is so intense' (Whyte, 1978, p279). These opinions are no doubt based on the proliferation of new political parties and splinter groups among the Protestants. Whether this represents a new fundamental categorization or not remains, of course, an empirical question as yet unanswered. Given the salience, strength and long history of Protestant group identity it is likely that it is merely a temporary phenomenon and already the 1979 general election has shown some signs of the closing of Protestant ranks.

5. Conclusion

One may safely conclude by noting that Northern Irish society is not only one in which social categorization is important and social identity salient but also that both groups appear to possess, or at least have in the past possessed, relatively positive social identities. Further, it would appear that these positive social identities have been achieved through a search for positive distinctiveness by both groups resulting in a tradition where there is a wish to emphasize differences 'without respecting them' (Barritt and Carter, 1972). Finally, it is clear that social comparison processes are still at work in a never-ending struggle to establish positive psychological distinctiveness. As the poet, Louis MacNeice, put it, writing of his native Northern Ireland:

And one reads black where the other reads white, his hope.
The other man's damnation.
(Autumn Journal, 1974).

Yet it can be argued from this conflict that something good develops – a positive social identity for the group which in turn contributes to a positive self-concept for the individual. Thus, as Harris (1972) astutely observed, 'the very binary opposition between the two religious groups gives the individual an unusual degree of importance...Individuals were seldom isolated' (Harris, 1972, p198). And, of course, the corollary also holds: a threat to the positive nature of the group's identity is seen as a personal threat. Nelson (1975) provides some evidence for this in her discussion of the Protestants' refusal to accept the existence of discrimination because it was viewed as 'an admission of personal complicity' which in turn was 'a serious threat to an individual's self-respect'.

Another interesting and perhaps relatively positive aspect of the conflict in Northern Ireland is the fairly low level of outgroup dislike. For example, O'Donnell (1977) remarked on the fact that while the stereotypes that each side holds of the other are negative, they are not as negative as might have been expected given the intensity and duration of the conflict.

Similarly, Miller (1977) has complained that overt questioning in his survey work in Northern Ireland had produced a 'high expression of moderate opinion'. Unfortunately, social scientists have been so embedded in the ethnocentrism syndrome with its attendant emphasis upon outgroup hostility that they have often failed to recognize its absence as a genuine phenomenon. In Northern Ireland apparently the major focus of bias had been ingroup bias, not outgroup devaluation, as evidenced in the fact that where discrimination existed, it was often not outgroup oriented but rather 'people looked after their own' (Nelson, 1975). In this respect, the evidence from Northern Ireland would appear to agree with the demonstration in the work deriving from Tajfel's conceptions that 'not only is ingroup favouritism in the laboratory situation not related to outgroup dislike, it also does not seem causally dependent on denigration of the outgroup' (Turner, 1978, p249).

This is just one of the many points raised by the present attempt to apply Tajfel's theory to the conflict in Northern Ireland which requires further empirical study – a mark of the value of this theory in the context of Northern Ireland. Nevertheless, one must not become overenthusiastic. As Tajfel (1978b) has pointed out, this is a 'modest' theory because social psychology 'is not and cannot be, by the nature of the questions it asks, in a position to provide more than a small part of the analysis of the relations between social groups'. However, it is precisely because the theory recognizes the powerful influences of economic and political processes, rather than attempting to exclude or ignore them as other psychological theories of conflict do, that it is likely to become a powerful conceptual tool in attempting to understand the conflict in Northern Ireland. Indeed, the theory's clearest contribution is undoubtedly that it attempts to provide 'the points of insertion of social psychological variables into the causal spiral' (Tajfel and Turner, 1979). The frightening prospect for Northern Ireland is that while the effects of these social psychological variables are undoubtedly determined by political and economic processes 'so they may also acquire in turn an autonomous function' (Tajfel and Turner, 1979).

References

Barritt, D.P. and Carter, C.F. 1972. *The Northern Ireland problem.* 2nd edition. Oxford: Oxford University Press.

Billig, M. 1976. *Social psychology and intergroup relations.* European Monographs in Social Psychology, No. 9, London: Academic Press.

Birrell, D. 1972. Relative deprivation as a factor in the conflict in Northern Ireland. *Sociological Review*, **20**, 321–43.

Breakwell, G. 1978. Some effects of marginal social identity. In H. Tajfel (ed.), *op. cit.*

Burton, F. 1978. *The politics of legitimacy*. London: Routledge and Kegan Paul.

Cairns, E. 1980. The development of ethnic discrimination in young children in Northern Ireland. In J. Harbison and J. Harbison (eds): *Children and young people in a society under stress*. London: Open Books.

Cairns, E. and Duriez, B. 1976. The influence of accent on the recall of Catholic and Protestant children in Northern Ireland. *British Journal of Social and Clinical Psychology*, **15**, 441–2.

Cairns, E. and Mercer, G.W. 1978. Adolescent social identity in Northern Ireland: The importance of denominational identity. Unpublished MS, New University of Ulster.

Cairns, E., Mercer, G.W. and Bunting, B. 1978. Northern Irish stereotypes: A review. *Bulletin of the British Psychological Society*, **31**, 331.

Darby, J. 1973. Diversiveness in education. *The Northern Teacher*, Winter, 3–12.

Darby, J. 1976. *Conflict in Northern Ireland*. Dublin: Gill and Macmillan.

Darby, J., Murray, D., Batts, D., Dunn, S., Farren, S. and Harris, J. 1977. *Education and community in Northern Ireland: Schools apart?* Coleraine: New University of Ulster.

Easthope, G. 1976. Religious war in Northern Ireland. *Sociology*, **10**, (3), 427–50.

Epstein, A.L. 1978. *Ethos and identity*. London: Tavistock.

Fishman, J. 1977. Language and ethnicity. In H. Giles (ed.): *Language, ethnicity and intergroup relations*. European Monographs in Social Psychology, No. 13. London: Academic Press.

Giles, H., Bourhis, R.Y. and Taylor, D.M. 1977. Towards a theory of language in ethnic group relations. In H. Giles (ed.): *Language, ethnicity and intergroup relations*. European Monographs in Social Psychology, No. 13. London: Academic Press.

Harbison, R. 1960. *No surrender*. London: Faber.

Harris, R. 1972. *Prejudice and tolerance in Ulster: A study of neighbours and strangers in a border community*. Manchester: Manchester University Press.

Heslinga, M.W. 1971. *The Irish border as a cultural divide*. Assen: Van Gorcum.

Hirschman, A. 1970. *Exit, voice and loyalty*. Cambridge, Mass.: Harvard University Press.

Hogan, R.T. and Emler, N.P. 1978. The biases in contemporary social psychology. *Social Science Research*, **45**, 478–534.

Houston, J. (ed.) 1978. *Brian Faulkner: Memoirs of a statesman*. London: Weidenfeld and Nicolson.

Irvine, A. 1921. *The souls of the poor folk*. London: Collins.

Jackson, H. 1971. *The two Irelands: A dual study of intergroup tensions*. London: Minority Rights Group, Report No. 2.

Laver, M. 1976. Cultural aspects of loyalty: On Hirschman and loyalism in Ulster. *Political Studies*, **24**, (4), 469–77.

LeVine, R.A. and Campbell, D.T. 1972. *Ethnocentrism: Theories of conflict, ethnic attitudes and group behaviour*. New York: Wiley.

MacNeice, L. 1974. Autumn journal XVI. In J. Montague (ed.): *The Faber book of Irish verse*. London: Faber.

McCann, E. 1974. *War in an Irish town*. Harmondsworth: Penguin Books.
Miller, D.W. 1978. *Queen's rebels: Ulster loyalism in historical perspective*. New York: Barnes and Noble.
Miller, R. 1977. Opinions on school desegregation in Northern Ireland. In A.E.C.W. Spencer and H. Tovey (eds): *Sociological Association of Ireland: Proceedings of First and Fourth Annual Conferences*. Belfast: Queen's University.
Moore, R. 1972. Race relations in the Six Counties: Colonialism, industrialization and stratification in Ireland. *Race*, **14**, 21–42.
Moscovici, S. and Paicheler, G. 1978. Social comparison and social recognition: Two complementary processes of identification. In H. Tajfel (ed.), *op. cit.*
Nelson, S. 1975. Protestant ideology considered: The case of discrimination. In I. Crewe (ed.): *British Political Sociology Yearbook*, Vol. 2, 155–87.
O'Donnell, E.E. 1977. *Northern Irish stereotypes*. Dublin: College of Industrial Relations.
Roberts, D.A. 1971. The Orange Order in Ireland: A religious institution. *British Journal of Sociology*, **22**, (3), 269–82.
Rose, R. 1971. *Governing without consensus: An Irish perspective*. London: Faber.
Schellenberg, J.A. 1977. Area variations of violence in Northern Ireland. *Sociological Focus*, **10**, 69–78.
Stringer, M. and Cairns, E. 1978. Protestant and Catholic children's ratings of stereotyped Protestant and Catholic faces. Paper read to the Annual Conference of the British Psychological Society, Northern Irish Branch.
Tajfel, H. 1974. Social identity and intergroup behaviour. *Social Science Information*, **13**, 65–93.
Tajfel, H. 1976. Exit, voice and intergroup relations. In L.H. Strickland, F.E. Aboud and K.J. Gergen (eds): *Social psychology in transition*. New York: Plenum Press.
Tajfel, H. 1978a. *The social psychology of minorities*. London: Minority Rights Group, Report No. 38.
Tajfel, H. (ed.) 1978b. *Differentiation between social groups: Studies in the social psychology of intergroup relations*. European Monographs in Social Psychology, No. 14. London: Academic Press.
Tajfel, H., Billig, M., Bundy, R.P. and Flament, C. 1971. Social categorization and intergroup behaviour. *European Journal of Social Psychology*, **1**, (2), 149–78.
Tajfel, H. and Turner, J.C. 1979. An integrative theory of intergroup conflict. In W.G. Austin and S. Worchel (eds): *The social psychology of intergroup relations*. Monterey, Calif.: Brooks/Cole.
Turner, J.C. 1975. Social comparison and social identity: Some prospects for intergroup behaviour. *European Journal of Social Psychology*, **5**, 5–34.
Turner, J.C. 1978. Social categorization and social discrimination in the minimal group paradigm. In H. Tajfel (ed.), *op. cit.*
Turner, J.C. and Brown, R.J. 1978. Social status, cognitive alternatives and intergroup relations. In H. Tajfel (ed.), *op. cit.*
Whyte, J. 1978. Interpretations of the Northern Irish problem: An appraisal. *The Economic and Social Review*, **9**, 257–85.

11. Problems of identity and social conflict: Research on ethnic groups in Italy[1]

DORA CAPOZZA, EMILIANA BONALDO AND
ALBA DI MAGGIO

1. Strategies for the affirmation of positive identity: The case of southern Italians

A brief analysis of social events is useful before introducing the data of the research done on southerners and northerners in Italy. Their relationship is to be considered according to the following points which, while not exhausting the problem, are important with regard to the theoretical framework adopted here:

(i) The problem of the South as an underdeveloped area began to be considered as such during the last century, about 1870. The *prise de conscience* of the problem determined the appearance of the differentiation between North and South, which was perceived as an opposition between progress and underdevelopment, in other words, between the typical qualities of a society becoming more and more industrialized and those of an agricultural society.

It is interesting to note the consensual nature of this differentiation, its persistence and that it is still to be found in socio-psychological research conducted at the end of the 1950s and the beginning of the 1960s[2] (Battacchi, 1972, p160 and pp139–53). According to these surveys, the southern group seemed to accept its inferiority: comparing itself to the other group, it placed itself at an inferior level both in socio-economic dimensions (such as social progress or income) and in psychological dimensions (characteristics such as laboriousness or self-control). From some of the work it also becomes evident that the southerners were trying to find a positive identity mainly using the strategies similar to (*a*) and (*c*) described below (Battacchi, 1972, p140; Capozza, 1968):

(*a*) The 'inferior' group members try to assume the positively valued traits of the other identity (*assimilation*). For example, we find that immigrants acquire, in the span of one generation, the linguistic standards of their adopted country (Giles *et al.*, 1977, p336).[3]

(b) When, for various reasons, assimilation is not possible, the 'inferior' group can use the strategy of transforming from negative to positive the value of those traits which define its own identity. Therefore, in the United States we find a re-evaluation of *négritude* on behalf of the negroes: the characteristic physical traits are accepted as positive and the typical expressions of the black culture (in language and in art) are accentuated (Tajfel, 1974; 1976, p33; 1978a, pp94–5).

(c) The impossibility of assimilation can give way to a third strategy which is the expression of *social creativity* (Giles *et al.*, 1977, p338). The 'inferior' group establishes new dimensions of comparison, never before used in comparisons with the 'superior' group, and through such new dimensions the group places itself in a pre-eminent position which assures it a satisfactory identity.[4]

(ii) The period immediately preceding 1963 was characterized in Italy by some important social changes. (Some relevant data come from a survey conducted by Capozza (1968) during that period.) Starting in 1956/7 there was, in fact, a change in public interest towards the South; this change was the consequence of both the benefits and the contradictions caused by the economic expansion of the North, and was evidenced by the impulse given to industrialization through introducing, for example, tax reductions for entrepreneurs and direct state participation in enterprises.

As far as agriculture was concerned, public interest was manifested by trying to guarantee, through an expenditure programme, security for the small property owner. Neither intervention has given positive results. In particular, industrialization was narrowly oriented, limiting the possibility of developing collateral activities. It was also organized into 'polar zones', conceived as future centres of expansion, but in reality not able to provide sufficient employment (Fissore and Meinardi, 1976, p193).

The difficulties of finding a solution to the southern problem and the unbalanced situation created by the 'economic miracle' of the North were both factors explaining the shift to the left in Italian politics. In 1963 the 'centre-left' was already active and, furthermore, the economic crisis had begun with a fall in investments and a rise in prices.

In order to outline, according to Tajfel's theory, the socio-psychological picture of the relationships between northerners and southerners in that year and during the preceding years, one must consider the following points:

(a) southerners and northerners constituted groups consensually considered to be 'inferior' and 'superior', respectively;

(b) the southerners, conscious of their 'inferior status', did not see the northerners as the cause of the South's underdevelopment. The

North and its social progress were seen as the solution – sometimes the only solution – to very serious economic problems;[5]

(c) the southern group accepted the interpretations common in the North of the dichotomy of underdevelopment in the South/progress in the North: this dichotomy was attributed either to the distinctive aspects of the southern character or to the geographical differences of the two environments;

(d) the northerners, on the other hand, though maintaining a predominant position, lived with the insecurity deriving from the continuous defence of their own identity: they saw danger in the southern immigration which, due to the great number of immigrants, could cause basic transformations in the northern culture.

(iii) The years following 1963 were characterized by a growing economic depression with only a few moments of standstill, such as 1968, when there seemed to be a slight increase in production. The depression, very serious at present, was (and is) apparent in a reduction of investments and of the rate of industrial development and was, in general, evidenced by a decline in the occupational level and by a reduction of the active population (Graziani, 1972, pp84–85). In 1977, the rate of inflation in Italy was 17 %, one of the highest in western Europe (*ILO Yearbook of Labour Statistics*).

The process of decline that followed the year 1963 seriously compromised the economic development of the South. The crisis was particularly felt during the period 1964–6 when northern and southern regional interests entered into open conflict for the following two reasons (Graziani, 1972, pp73–4):

(a) the search by the northern industry for unexploited markets in order to make up for the reduction in demand. Northern industry, therefore, turned its interests towards the southern markets but this outside competition created a critical situation for the small southern enterprises;

(b) the need, felt also by the North, for creating infrastructural public works. The intention was to involve, through such public works, the depressed zones of the North in the development of the 'industrial triangle'. On the political scene, the request for public works was turned into a firm opposition to the renewal of funds destined for the *Cassa del Mezzogiorno* (in 1965): the funds became available only after the institution of the same provisions for both North and South (Graziani, 1972, p73).

Today, in the midst of a general crisis, the problems facing the southern society are complex, both because of the presence of contradictions[6] and of the disintegration of the old structures. This disintegration is caused by factors such as the crisis of the small country farmer, the complete abandonment of vast areas and the rapid urbanization not accompanied by a stable occupational level (Fissore and Meinardi, 1976, pp196–7).

The events discussed form a picture which is helpful in fully understanding the evolution of relations between northerners and southerners. For this reason, before proceeding to the analysis of the data, a few additional considerations are necessary.

(a) We must note, first of all, how the 'superior' group (the northern group) has witnessed since 1963 a progressive crisis of the industrial society, that is, of its own social environment and culture. Furthermore, an attitude of ideological debate has spread through the entire nation, evidenced both by distrust in the institutions and by refusal to accept the way in which labour was organized (see Ronchey, 1977, chapter 1).

(b) A second consideration concerns the influence of 'objective' conflicts or conflicts of interest. Such conflicts have always existed between the northern and southern regions, as was the case with the industrial and public works discussed above. But these conflicts of interest have never been fully expressed or institutionalized. The factors which determined for the southerners and the northerners their self- and alter-evaluations were not the political–economic conflicts, but rather the resulting social conditions and the interpretation of such conditions.

2. The research

The strategies used by the southerners to give a positive value to their own identity are analysed here in two distinct periods: at the beginning of 1963 and at the end of 1978, beginning of 1979. In both surveys[7] the data were gathered using the technique of the semantic differential (Osgood, May and Miron, 1975) applied according to the procedures proposed by Hofstätter (1963, 1967), in which the meanings of critical concepts are determined by calculating their similarities with others functioning as paradigmatic terms: the similarity between concepts is obtained by correlating their respective profiles.[8]

Method

Procedure

The scales that were chosen and applied with the usual seven-step scale were as follows:

weak–strong; rough–smooth; active–passive; empty–full; small–big; cold–hot; clear–hazy; young–old; docile–rebel; sick–healthy; angular–rounded; tense–relaxed; sad–happy; beautiful–ugly; fresh–stale; cowardly–brave; near–far; variable–firm; progressive–conservative; shallow–deep; good–bad. To these, taken from Hofstätter (1963), were added distasteful–tasty; valuable–worthless.

For each scale a score of 1 was assigned to the extreme on the left and of 7 to the extreme on the right.

With regard to the concepts, besides 'Northerner', 'Southerner' and 'Italian', the following were used in 1978–9 both for the southern group and for the northern group:

Self-control	Passionateness	Fear
Intelligence	Impulsiveness	Anguish
Laboriousness	Vindictiveness	Sleep
Rationality	Superstition	Hero
Tenacity	Sweetness	Tyrant
Hospitality	Love	Male
Success	Hate	Female

The southerners evaluated, furthermore, 'Ideal Southerner' ('as I would like the southerner to be'); 'Southerner' ('as I think the northerners evaluate him'). The northerners evaluated 'Ideal Northerner' ('as I would like the northerner to be'); 'Northerner' ('as I think the southerners evaluate him').[9]

Subjects

The subjects (50 southerners and 50 northerners in both surveys) were male students following various courses of study at the University of Padua.[10] The northerners were mostly from the Venetian region; the southerners were from different regions in the South and lived in Padua during the academic year, returning to their home towns during the summer holidays. The subjects from both groups had been northerners and southerners for at least two generations. This 'objective' criterion of belonging to the group had to be confirmed by 'subjective' criteria: we chose only those subjects who, besides satisfying the aforementioned criterion, declared to feel themselves to be northerners or southerners.

The same experimenter performed both surveys.[11]

At this point, before proceeding to the analysis of the results, the following considerations should be made.

(i) First of all, we must note the indirect nature of the procedures used. The characterizations of a concept, for example, the description of a group as being 'rational' or 'self-controlled', are not determined by direct questioning but are deduced from the system of the similarities of the concept posed in relation to other paradigmatic concepts.

(ii) A second observation regards the subjects. They constitute a particular kind of group (they were young, with a high education level and were continuously in contact with the alien culture). Naturally, the mechanisms of identity evidenced by the data are valid for the selected population, but it would be difficult to extend them to other populations.

3. The results

The similarities with the paradigmatic concepts of ingroup and outgroup evaluations, that is, the correlations between the respective profiles, are summarized in Tables 1–4 in the Appendix to this chapter. For each concept, the profile corresponds to the scores on the 23 selected scales; each score is the average of n individual ratings ($n = 50$ for each group).

First of all we shall consider the data of the survey done in 1963. In the case of southerners, they exemplify the socio-psychological dynamics of an 'inferior' group at a time when the group's members consider as illegitimate such an evaluation of inferiority. We shall analyse these dynamics by confronting the ingroup with the outgroup evaluations, as described by the southerners.

The southern self-evaluation appears to be articulated into many different traits: occupying first place are characteristics such as affective vivacity which are associated with traits such as courage and generosity (see the correlations of SS in Table 1); the ingroup evaluation is defined, less intensively, by intelligence, laboriousness and, to a limited extent, by self-control (Table 1). This evaluation can be interpreted as a reaction to the stereotyped judgement of the northerners; in fact, the latter summarize the image of the outgroup by the simple attribute of impulsiveness (see the correlations of NS in Table 3). The southerners know of the alien evaluation (see the correspondence between the system of similarities of NS (Table 3) and that of SNS (Table 1)), but they do not accept it, unlike other southern subjects in different surveys taken during the same period.[12]

On the contrary, their own evaluation and that of others demonstrate the attempt to overcome the traditional characteristics and to establish a psychological distinctiveness that would satisfy the self-identity. The strategy used by the southerners is *social creativity*: when confronting the alien group, they use new dimensions, consensually positive, in which they place themselves in a pre-eminent position. These mechanisms appear from the comparison between the ingroup (SS) and the outgroup (SN) evaluations described by the southern subjects and from the comparison between such evaluations and the ideal image (IS).

	Hero	Male	Success	Love	Tenacity
SS	(0.87)	(0.84)	(0.79)	(0.78)	(0.77)
SN	(0.44)	(0.42)	(0.52)	(0.43)	(0.51)
IS	(0.86)	(0.87)	(0.87)	(0.86)	(0.88)

Also in the northerners they recognize a positive psychological distinctiveness: their self-control; in this dimension the southerner admits to the northerner's superiority:

Self-control: SN 0.73; SS 0.48; IS 0.79

As for the rest, both groups are attributed more or less the same positive qualities.

Following this analysis, we note that the southerner:

(1) overcomes the usual dichotomy of southern 'passionateness'/northern self-control and laboriousness;

(2) assigns to his own group a positive psychological distinctiveness which is obtained by using comparisons based on unused dimensions: strength, courage, constancy.

The southerners also tend to combine the typical mechanisms of social creativity with some of the dynamics of assimilation in order to preserve or improve their self-image. In fact, they recognize as ideal attributes the typical traits of the outgroup: laboriousness and self-control; and furthermore they consider not highly desirable the characteristic trait of their own culture, free expression of impulses, represented by the concept of impulsiveness.[13]

Impulsiveness: SS 0.76; IS 0.57

The northern attitudes are different. The northerners in fact:

(1) not only describe themselves in such a self-praising manner as almost to coincide with the ideal (see the comparison between NN and IN), but they place themselves in a pre-eminent position on every dimension of comparison;

(2) furthermore, they do not allow for any positive characterization of the outgroup (the southerner is only high on impulsiveness, see Table 3):

Intelligence	Practicality	Tenacity	Laboriousness
NN 0.95	NN 0.94	NN 0.92	NN 0.92
IN 0.94	IN 0.93	IN 0.92	IN 0.92
Self-control	Success	Male	Love
NN 0.92	NN 0.88	NN 0.83	NN 0.82
IN 0.84	IN 0.83	IN 0.90	IN 0.80
Hospitality	Hero	Sweetness	Impulsiveness
NN 0.82	NN 0.79	NN 0.73	NN 0.44
IN 0.73	IN 0.85	IN 0.56	IN 0.55

It is surprising how the northerners carry their attitude of superiority to the extreme. One can interpret this when considering that the intense southern immigration, perceived as dangerous, has caused the strengthening of the conceptions of northern superiority and cultural identity. It is interesting to note that a consequence of these mechanisms is the formation of irrational dynamics of projection (see the similarities of NSN in Table 3): the fact that the northerners think they are perceived as 'tyrants', which does not conform to the real outgroup judgement.

In conclusion, during the period of major social expansion (the economic crisis began at the end of 1963), the southerners[14] of relatively high status re-evaluate their own identity using strategies of social creativity and assimilation. The northerners show a strong attitude of superiority, to be interpreted as a reaction to the danger seen in the southern immigration and also possibly as a defence against the southern strategies of re-evaluation.[15]

Before proceeding to the analysis of the relationship between the two groups at the end of 1978 and the beginning of 1979, some additional points need to be made.

(i) The first concerns 'conflicts of interest'. One cannot exclude their intervention, that is, one cannot affirm that the southern strategies have only psychological causes. It is, in fact, possible that the objective of obtaining a socio-economic status equal or superior to that of the privileged group has produced the changes in evaluations described above. But the possible interference of 'objective' factors does not make it illegitimate to assume the contribution made to the data of the psychological mechanisms by which an 'inferior' group tries to overcome its own condition of inferiority. We have seen how our own data tend to confirm some of these hypotheses.

(ii) It is unlikely that either the southerners or the northerners in our sample were clearly aware of the socio-economic interests from which the underdevelopment of the South is derived. Therefore, the political – economic motives do not act directly upon the ingroup and outgroup evaluations, but indirectly through the objective conditions that they create and through the information spread by the dominant groups. In relationships characterized by conflicts of interest, the ingroup and out-group stereotypes are often the final result of solutions elaborated at a political level. (For some of the relationships between stereotypes and conflicts of interest, cf. Tajfel, 1978b, pp5–6.) It is certainly significant that the southerners have been, for a long time, described as 'passionate',[16] that is, incapable of self-control, since self-control is an attribute which is considered necessary for members of an advanced and industrialized society.

The above descriptions of the southern and northern stereotypes and evaluations need to be inserted into a functional analysis of stereotypes (Tajfel, 1981). The stereotypes are the result of comparisons in which the groups engage using dimensions which relate to personality and character traits. Other dimensions of comparison are also available, e.g. social prestige, political or economic power, the groups' artistic and cultural creations, the quality of their work, their collective actions, etc.

In 'insecure social comparisons' the re-evaluation mechanisms of the 'inferior' groups and the defence mechanisms of the 'superior' groups imply these dimensions, probably including most of them, and without a doubt including those corresponding to the attributes that lead to the formation of the stereotypes.

Ingroup and outgroup stereotypes can be, therefore, the result of psy-chological mechanisms that allow for a *differentiation* and a re-evaluation of the ingroup. In intergroup relations they also have other functions: the outgroup stereotypes can *justify* the actions against the alien groups; lastly, they make it possible to explain certain complex social phenomena which are attributed to characteristic traits in the alien groups (*social causality*) (cf. Tajfel, 1981).

The traits of the outgroup stereotype function as dimensions upon which comparisons which determine *differentiation* take place; at the same time, the derivation of such traits can be related to mechanisms of *justification* and *social causality*. The content of the stereotypes provides, therefore, a useful reflection of the socio-psychological dynamics active in intergroup relations.

The data gathered in 1979 outline a new picture of intergroup relations; it is characterized by a decline in the 'narcissistic' attitude of the northern group and by an end to the consensual nature of its superiority.

We shall begin by analysing the northern behaviour because the southern behaviour is, in fact, complementary to it.

First of all, the northern attitude is characterized by the novelty of some aspects of the ideal self-evaluation. From the correlations between IN and the paradigmatic concepts (Appendix, Table 4) and from the comparison with the ideal obtained from the first survey, it is evident that, instead of an ideal of social behaviour characterized by rationality, control of impulses, efficiency and male strength, there is a change of direction: the ideal is now in social behaviour in which intelligence, self-control and laboriousness are closely related to a certain softness and a kind disposition. Such a transformation of the ideal is particularly evident from the correlations between IN and the concepts of 'hospitality', 'love', 'sweetness' and, especially 'female' and 'sleep':

Data gathered in 1963[17]		Data gathered in 1979	
IN		IN	
Intelligence	0.94	Intelligence	0.94
Love	0.80	Love	0.92
Hospitality	0.73	Hospitality	0.88
Laboriousness	0.92	Laboriousness	0.85
Self-control	0.84	Self-control	0.84
Tenacity	0.92	Tenacity	0.82
Female	0.23	Female	0.80
Rationality	0.97	Rationality	0.77
Sweetness	0.56	Sweetness	0.76
Sleep	0.12	Sleep	0.73
Success	0.83	Success	0.70
Male	0.90	Male	0.68
Passionateness	0.33	Passionateness	0.58
Hero	0.85	Hero	0.53
Impulsiveness	0.55	Impulsiveness	0.35

At the same time, there is a lesser appreciation by the northerners of rationality and masculinity (see the correlations of IN with 'rationality', 'male' and 'hero') and a positive correlation of IN with the concept of 'passionateness'.

Such modifications of the ideal are evidenced, first of all, by the new meaning attributed to the concepts 'female' and 'male'.[18] The former, re-evaluated, adds to the traditional characteristics of sweetness, kind disposition and meekness, now attributed with greater intensity, the characteristics of intelligence, laboriousness, self-control and tenacity, all of which either had not been assigned or had been assigned to a minor degree. The latter – 'male' – is now less positive than in the past; its 'positive distinctiveness' is represented by the traits of tenacity and laboriousness; it is also defined by passionateness, love and, to a lesser degree, by intelligence and self-control. Therefore, in the latter survey, the high correlation between 'female' and the ideal image indicates the desire for an interpersonal behaviour characterized by sweetness and kind disposition.

The variations of the ideal, which is a synthesis of old attributes and new aspirations, derive from, and are the psychological counterpart to, the long social crisis still existing in Italy; the decline of the industrial world is, in fact, reflected in the decline of its values, and, while the personal need for self-realization is felt less strongly than in the past, there appears to be a strong need for solidarity. Therefore, the images strictly related to the old view of success, e.g. the image of masculinity, lose much of their importance, while such traits as passionateness, previously considered insignificant, acquire a positive value – even if a slight one. From the analysis of the profile and the correlations of this concept we can see, in effect, how passionateness is now considered to be a personality trait defined by efficiency and affective vivacity as well as by an absence of strict control of impulses.

It is now possible to outline the dynamics of the northern group's identity, a group that is 'superior' and has perceived the crisis of its own social environment and culture. We shall consider the following points.

(i) The socio-economic crisis and the 'ideological' one produced a decline in the strong self-praising attitude previously assumed by the northern group. As a consequence, the group shows a more critical attitude towards itself evidenced by the recognition of not possessing the qualities, thought to be ideal, to the right degree (compare the correlations of IN with those of NN in Table 4).

This diminishing positive significance of the self-identity can be seen even more clearly from the following data:

(a) The analysis of the NN profile: it is evident from it, in fact, how with respect to the previous survey the self-stereotype is, in almost every scale, less positive and nearer to the neutral point.

(b) The results of the factor analysis applied to the matrix of 'cross-products' between the concepts: the necessity to control by this analysis the results obtained from the matrices of the coefficients of correlation comes from some insufficiencies connected with the use of such coefficients. These insufficiencies are well-known, therefore we shall not analyse them here (see Osgood and Suci, 1952; Hofstätter, 1956; Nunnally, 1962). It is only necessary to remember that, in the case of our scales and concepts, the coefficient of correlation neglects only one source of information corresponding to the differences in variability between the profiles (in fact, in our data the differences between the averages of the profiles are only rarely significant).

Therefore, when there is a significant difference of variance, the high positive correlation indicates not a near-coincidence of the two profiles, but a similarity in their form, that is, a tendency of the respective concepts to assume the same meanings with a different intensity.

In order to control the effects of the variability (the variance of the profile of NN is, in some instances, statistically inferior to that of the paradigmatic concepts), we proceeded to factor-analyse the matrix of the cross-products between the concepts. In the obtained factor structure, the northern self-stereotype (NN) is loaded on the same factor on which IN, 'intelligence', 'love', 'self-control' and 'rationality' present a high loading; however, the correspondence between the factor composition of NN and the composition of such concepts is not as high as that to be found in the factor analysis of the correlations. This means that, if NN is characterized by meanings akin to those of 'intelligence', 'love', 'self-control' and 'rationality', the intensity with which such meanings are attributed to it is different and weaker.

(ii) The decline in self-appreciation of the 'superior' group does not cause a re-evaluation of the 'inferior' group. As in the previous survey, this last group is less appreciated than one's own group and perceived as void of ideal qualities (see the correlations of NN, NS and IN in Table 4). The 'inferior' group is perceived as void of any qualities and a singular image is attributed to it which has no significant correlation with any of the concepts.

Such a singularity does not indicate the absence of stereotype. In fact, even if there is less polarization in the single scales as compared with the previous survey, some of the scores maintain a clear distance from the neutral point.[19] We think that the absence of similarities is in effect to be attributed not to the disappearance of the stereotype but to its becoming more subdued and changed in its characteristics; the new stereotype finds no correspondence in the concepts that were used. It should be further noted how the re-evaluation of 'passionateness' cancels out its previous correspondence with the southern stereotype.

(iii) The affirmation of his traditional superiority remains for the northerner, even though he identifies himself to a lesser extent with his own group.

The fact that identity becomes less salient, as determined by the social events described earlier, and by the articulation of the society into many subgroups, often conflicting among themselves, produces a decrease in the importance attributed to the dichotomous categories, 'northerner' and 'southerner', and therefore a decrease in the processes of categorical differentiation. There is a reduction in the perception of oppositions between the two groups and in the agreement by which several traits are attributed to the ingroup and the opposite traits to the outgroup (see the research by Fonzi and Saglione, 1974).

We can now look at the evaluations expressed by the southern subjects. To be noted, first of all, is how the self-stereotype is positive, very similar to the one found in the first research. This becomes evident when confronting the results of the two surveys, in particular the profiles and the similarities of SS (see Appendix, Tables 1 and 2).[20] Even the ideal image corresponds on the whole: the exception consists, as for the northern subjects, of including now among the positive correlations 'female',[21] 'passionateness' and 'sleep' and, moreover, of being more pointedly described than in the past by traits of 'laboriousness' and 'self-control'.

What changes is the outgroup stereotype, which, as is evident in Table 2, is distinguished, although not to a high degree, by the most negative of concepts: superstition (see the correlation between IS and 'superstition': $r = -0.93$). SN is also, to a certain extent, the opposite of concepts implying dynamism and emotionality (Table 2). The southern attitude is evident in the geometrical configuration of Figure 1. It represents the factor plane defined by F_1 and F_2, factors which account for the largest amount of variance of the stereotypes.

What is interesting to note in Figure 1 is the position of the points which represent the self-evaluation (SS), the outgroup evaluation (SN) and the ideal self-evaluation (IS). Of these, SS is very near to the positive concepts – 'success', 'male', 'love' – and to those that indicate intense and uncontrolled expressions of emotionality. The southerners wish to subdue the latter in order to be characterized rather more by traits of intelligence, laboriousness, self-control, tenacity, hospitality, all of which are, in the figure, very near to IS. The attitude is, therefore, self-praising, clearly recognizing the possession of ideal qualities, but at the same time self-critical, wishing to subdue some attributes and to reinforce others.

However, the alien evaluation (SN) is negative, being placed in the same quadrant as 'superstition' and 'tyrant', in a position almost orthogonal, or in antithesis, to the ideal qualities.

The reactive attitude which used strategies of social creativity and assimilation is then replaced, in a moment of crisis and ideological conflict of the 'superior' group, by an attitude which cannot be traced back to either the one or the other of the hypothesized strategies. In the relations with

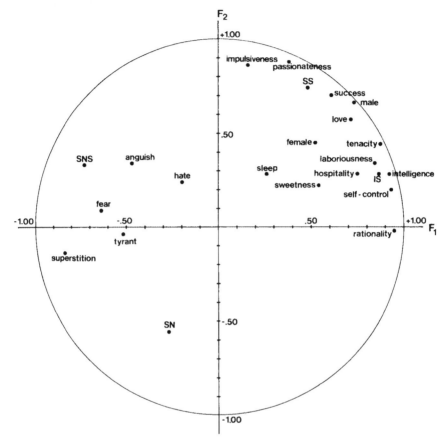

Figure 1. Factor plane determined by F_1 (intelligent dynamism and kind disposition) and F_2 (affective readiness) (southern group). For the meaning of 'SS', 'SN', 'SNS' and 'IS', see Tables 1 and 2

the 'superior' group, the southerner does not place himself in a position of equality by trying to be similar; he does not place himself in a position of equality or pre-eminence by trying to re-evaluate his own attributes; he does not try to overcome the outgroup in any specific aspect. The tendency is to deny the 'superior' group any positive qualities and to attribute only to his own group ideal models of behaviour. The specific aspiration to models corresponding to the traditional stereotype of the North (laboriousness, self-control, tenacity, rationality) makes one think of a strategy that is particular unto itself. Such a strategy consists of trying to emerge as superior exactly in those dimensions that were at the basis of the preceding alien superiority: 'Only we, maintaining our own attributes, can aspire to your past qualities'. This makes it a strategy of substitution which is almost like an exaggerated form of assimilation.

A few additional considerations are necessary.

(i) We argued above that the new strategy used by the southerners was not that of assimilation, because this, as a concept, implies that the 'superior' group maintains its own positive attributes. The strategy was also not one of a re-evaluation by the southerners of their own negative attributes, because the new evaluation of 'passionateness', also accepted by the northerners, is positive, but only in some of its aspects. It was also not a strategy of social creativity because, as related to the earlier data, there is no sign of new dimensions used for comparison, and the only thing that does change is the attitude towards the outgroup.

The various components of the southern attitude convey the idea of an additional strategy which we have termed the strategy of substitution.

(ii) A second consideration regards the socio-psychological determinants of the new southern attitude. These are as follows:

> (*a*) the perception of crisis in the alien social structure and of the conflict of values involving the outgroup members (note that it is a conflict which concerns interclass and not interethnic relations);
>
> (*b*) the outgroup's constant refusal to accept the southerners' attempts at re-evaluation of their own identity.

(iii) A final consideration regarding the future relations of the two groups, insomuch as they can be inferred from our data and insofar as such inferences allow for generalizations[22] leads us to the conclusions that: (1) the distinction North–South is of continuing importance to the southerners, and that this might help to revive the presently subdued northern differentiation between the categories; (2) that intense attitudes of reciprocal distrust (see the meaning of the two projective stereotypes, SNS and NSN, in Tables 2 and 4) are also continuing; and (3) that these psychological factors can produce further and intense intergroup conflicts.

4. Strategies of re-evaluation in the Italian ethnic group in South Tyrol

The data for the research which will now be reported were collected in 1975 in Bressanone in South Tyrol[23] where the majority of the population belongs to the German-speaking group. Before the data are presented, a brief description of the social background is necessary.

(i) In South Tyrol at present the German group (or South Tyrolese) has a pre-eminent status. In comparison with the others,[24] this group is characterized by numerical and socio-economic superiority. With the approval of the 'package deal',[25] a reform of the special statute granted to Trentino – South Tyrol, the German group acquired new advantages, of which the most important were guarantees of the defence and preservation of its ethnic separateness, and control over the development policies of the Province (Bolzano), consequent upon the transfer from the Regional to the Provincial government of the economic jurisdiction (Pristingher, 1978, p56).

(ii) The second point concerns the drive towards autonomy of the German group. The 'package' is, in fact, the result of a long struggle for autonomy conducted in Italy by the South Tyrolese minority. This struggle, following the war, was first caused by distrust which was due to the lack of legislative provisions in order to execute the special Statute (introduced by constitutional law in February 1948); it was then openly supported in 1955 by Austria which, at that time, gained from the Allies some power of decision in foreign policy. The conflict became acute in 1961 because of the lack of an international solution to the problem and of the rigid positions assumed by Austria and Italy. As a result, the struggle became terrorism. A commission was then established (*Commissione dei Diciannove*) to study the problem and to suggest solutions. The proposal of the new Statute became law after its approval by the *Südtiroler Volkspartei* (SVP), the dominating party in South Tyrol. (For an analysis of the South Tyrolese struggle, see Pristingher, 1978, pp45–57).

The ethnic solidarity in South Tyrol, already strong in the past, was accentuated by the pre-war fascist policies of assimilation. During that period, assimilation and exclusion from economic activities were jointly pursued; this came about as the result of policies tending to combine the use of drastic measures aimed at eliminating the South Tyrolese cultural attributes with the use of strategies which restricted the group to an economically marginal position (Pristingher, 1978, p30). The result was a stronger German opposition to the political plans of assimilation, which were perceived as dangerous both for the cultural and the economic survival of the German group.

The SVP's strategies were based on the idea of strong ethnic solidarity. In fact, the SVP, in its conception of such solidarity as being essential to the survival of the group and in proposing itself as the only organization capable of supporting it (see Pristingher, 1978, pp57–70), has until now assured itself the general consensus of the South Tyrolese group. Adherence to the party assumes a political choice which places ethnic interests above those of class.

(iii) The new Statute for the Trentino – South Tyrol has placed the South Tyrolese group in a pre-eminent socio-economic position with respect to the other groups. The latter, and in particular the Italian group, probably recognize the judicial legitimacy of such pre-eminence. The attitude towards cultural pre-eminence is different; it would, in fact, be difficult for the Italians to accept the German cultural pre-eminence, because they can refer to the national culture of the hinterland.

In our data, we shall analyse the dynamics of re-evaluation used by the Italian group: it is 'inferior' on 'objective' dimensions such as the extent of political and economic control and it is exposed to the 'superior' attitude of the antagonistic group.

5. The research

Procedure

This research has been conducted by using the techniques described earlier in this chapter. Twenty scales were used. The concepts were as follows:

Female	(Femminile)	(Weiblich)
Male	(Maschile)	(Männlich)
Blundering person	(Persona confusionaria)	(Wirrkopf)
Superstition	(Superstizione)	(Aberglaube)
Thief	(Ladro)	(Dieb)
Superficiality	(Faciloneria)	(Leichtfertigkeit)
Sweetness	(Dolcezza)	(Sanftheit)
Corruption	(Corruzione)	(Bestechung)
Impulsiveness	(Impulsività)	(Impulsivität)
Laboriousness	(Laboriosità)	(Arbeitsamkeit)
Disgust	(Disgusto)	(Widerwille)
Love	(Amore)	(Liebe)
Hate	(Odio)	(Hass)
Tyrant	(Tiranno)	(Tyrann)
Hero	(Eroe)	(Held)
Fear	(Paura)	(Furcht)
Intelligence	(Intelligenza)	(Intelligenz)
Self-control	(Autocontrollo)	(Selbstkontrolle)
Methodical person	(Metodicità)	(Methodiker)
Traditionalist	(Tradizionalista)	(Traditionalist)
Stubbornness	(Ostinatezza)	(Hartnäckigkeit)
Authoritarianism	(Autoritarismo)	(Autoritarismus)
Orderliness	(Persona ordinata)	(Ordentliche Person)
Aggressiveness	(Aggressività)	(Aggressivität)
Rationality	(Razionalità)	(Rationalität)
Harsh person	(Persona rude)	(Rauhe Person)
Italian	(Italiano)	(Italiener)
South Tyrolese	(Sudtirolese)	(Südtiroler)
Altoatesino		
German	(Tedesco)	(Deutscher)

The Italian subjects again evaluated the 'Ideal Italian' ('as I would like the Italian to be'); Italian ('as I think the South Tyrolese evaluate him'). The South

Tyrolese evaluated the 'Ideal South Tyrolese' ('as I would like the South Tyrolese to be'); South Tyrolese ('as I think the Italians evaluate him').

The translation of the concepts and the scales into German was done by a bi-lingual expert, resident in South Tyrol. We asked him to identify, for each Italian term, the one most conceptually similar in German. In some of the more complex cases, such as the translation of the concepts 'authoritarianism' and 'traditionalist', the solution was to use words not present in the lexicon but used regularly in the spoken language. For 'metodicità' ('methodical person'), which is a noun in Italian, we had to use the corresponding adjective as a noun ('Methodiker').

With respect to the concepts, a further observation must be made regarding 'Altoatesino', a term which exists only in the Italian form. Although not essential, it was inserted because of its different meaning from 'South Tyrolese': for the Italian-speaking subjects 'Altoatesino' indicates an inhabitant of South Tyrol ('South Tyrolese' indicates only the German group); naturally, it refers to the members of the German group more than to those of the Italian group. The South Tyrolese evaluation of this concept is a kind of projective hetero-stereotype, in other words, a self-evaluation determined in part by the presumed Italian judgement.

Subjects

There were 40 subjects (20 males and 20 females) for each of the two linguistic groups, aged between 18 and 30 years. They had a high level of education corresponding to a diploma or a degree; among the subjects the majority were University students. All of the subjects had resided in Bressanone for at least three years.

6. The results

The correlations of the ingroup and outgroup evaluations obtained from the South Tyrolese group are listed in the Appendix, Table 5. The self-evaluation is interesting (GG): the South Tyrolese characterize themselves by self-control, efficiency, intelligence, strength, tendency to behave according to rules, even with obstinacy, authoritarianism, little inclination towards tenderness. They place far from their own identity behaviour which consists of a violation of certain social norms ('corruption', 'thief') and which expresses weakness, irrationality, little control of impulses. (See the negative correlations of GG with 'superstition', 'fear', 'superficiality', 'blundering person', Table 5.) This self-evaluation has some attributes which present similarities to the ethnocentric traits analysed by Adorno et al. (1950). For example, the fear of losing control of one's affectivity, the importance assigned to strength, hostility and the strict, almost obsessive, observation of social rules.

The similarity between the ideal image and the ethnocentric traits indi-

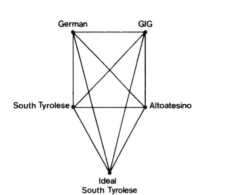

GIG = evaluation of the concept 'South Tyrolese' attributed to the Italian ethnical group.

Figure 2. Graph of the relations of likeness between ingroup and outgroup evaluations (German group). The dots represent the stereotypes, the lines the significant correlations equal to, or superior to, +0.56

cates the adhesion by the South Tyrolese to characteristic values of their own culture. These tend to be authoritarian values, originating from a variety of factors and, in particular, from complete devotion to the State during the Hapsburg domination, from the constant influence of the Church, from the agriculturally based economy and from the state of 'emergency' that involved the whole ethnic group during the struggle for autonomy.

The South Tyrolese ethnocentrism (cf. Gubert, 1976) is expressed by attitudes of differentiation and denigration towards the other group. The attitudes of differentiation are evident in Table 5 (see Appendix), and in Figures 2 and 3 which reproduce, respectively, the graph and the tree-diagram of the relations of likeness between the stereotypes. They have been obtained by the application of a different method of cluster analysis to the matrix of the correlations in Table 6: the graph results from the application of a hierarchical procedure which allows for, at each level of established likeness, intersections between the clusters (Peay, 1974, 1975); the tree-diagram results from the application of Johnson's Maximum Method (1967), a well-known procedure, equally hierarchical, but which does not allow for the possibility of intersections. (A procedure of rotation was applied to the results of this last method in order to eliminate the arbitrariness with which the terminal nodes of the tree are disposed; in Figure 3 they are placed in correspondence to $r = 1.00$ (Tzeng and May, 1976). If we consider as level of likeness $r \geqslant +0.56$ (coefficient of significant

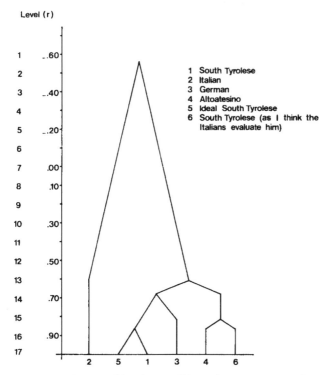

Level (r)

Figure 3. Dendrogram of the relations of likeness between ingroup and outgroup evaluations (German group). The levels of likeness in ordinate correspond to different levels of the coefficient of correlation

correlation with $\alpha = 0.01$ and df = 18), the results of both methods are the same: we find with both a clustering of the dots which indicates the drastic differentiation between the German and Italian worlds, experienced by the South Tyrolese.

For the South Tyrolese, the Italian group is furthermore, as we have said, negatively evaluated. This can easily be seen in Table 5: the Italian is characterized by disorder, superficiality and a tendency towards tenderness (which are all, in this context, negatively evaluated).

The South Tyrolese, therefore, combine the pre-eminence of socio-economic status with the tendency to affirm the superiority of their cultural attributes. The Italians do not accept this superiority and reveal an interesting attitude of re-evaluation, of which the most important aspects are analysed below (see Tables 7, 8, 9 and 10 in the Appendix.)

The Italian subjects, as a reaction to the presumed alien evaluation[26] which stresses in their identity the traits of superficiality and confusion, use the strategy of social creativity. The dimension of comparison on which they place themselves in a pre-eminent position is 'kind disposition' (tenderness) which is in turn positively evaluated as can be seen in the system of correlations of the ideal image.[27] The antagonistic group does not possess this attribute but nevertheless it is credited with 'positive distinctiveness': the quality of self-control and, to a lesser extent, those of laboriousness and orderliness. As for the rest, the Italians consider both groups far from the ideal; the ingroup because it does not possess positive attributes, excepting 'sweetness', and the other group because it possesses negative attributes (see Table 7).

The most interesting Italian attitude is, however, in the conception of an ideal,[28] in which the typical South Tyrolese characteristics, aside from self-control and rationality, have little importance (Table 7). The ideal image is different in many aspects from the one described by the other group (Tables 5 and 7). The Italian subjects express their rejection of the typical South Tyrolese characteristics and values, indicating their rejection of the other group's 'cultural' pre-eminence.

In reaction to the inferiority resulting from the intervening factors of an 'objective' nature (socio-economic) and to the outgroup's denigrating attitude, alien models of behaviour are rejected as negative, and alternative ones are proposed. The re-evaluation of one's own identity comes about by the assertion that one's own group, while maintaining a certain distance, is nearer to such ideal models than the alien group.

Before concluding this description, we shall consider some of the results obtained from the Italian group, which, although of minor importance, refer to the 'rapport' between the two groups and are helpful in understanding it.

First of all, for the Italian subjects the recognition that their own group is defined by an exclusive ideal attribute – 'kind disposition' – is apparent also in the results of factor analysis, to be found in Tables 8 and 9. Although to a lesser extent, the Italian self-stereotype is in fact loaded, as is the ideal self-stereotype, on F_1, a factor which means, at the positive pole, kind attitude.

A second point concerns the lesser appreciation of one's own group, shown by the Italian subjects as compared with the German subjects. This is evident in the lower correspondence between the similarities of the self-stereotype and those of the ideal self-stereotype (Tables 5 and 7; and in the difference between the two stereotypes, evidenced by the results of the cluster analysis, Figures 4 and 5). At the level of similarity equal to or superior to $r = 0.56$, the Italian ideal self-evaluation remains, in fact, an isolated concept without any significant similarity. On the same

Figure 4. Graph of the relations of likeness between ingroup and outgroup evaluations (Italian group). The dots represent the stereotypes, the lines the significant correlations equal to, or superior to, +0.56

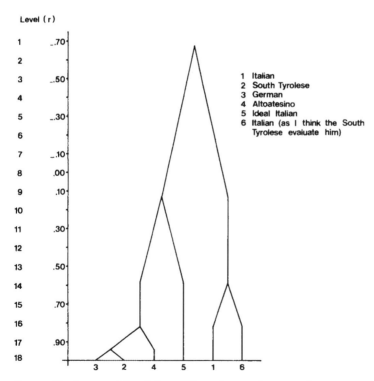

Figure 5. Dendrogram of the relations of likeness between ingroup and outgroup evaluations (Italian group). The levels of likeness in ordinate correspond to different levels of the coefficient of correlation

level, the German ideal self-evaluation is very close to the respective self-evaluation (Figure 3).

A final and general consideration concerns the relationship between identity and categorization. It can be seen that the concept of 'Italian' when evaluated by Italians living in South Tyrol (Table 7) is different from the same concept evaluated by southerners (Table 2) or by northerners (Table 4). The difference is greater when the South Tyrol data are compared with the southern data (see Tables 2 and 7). It is, of course, possible that this result is due to a variety of factors, such as the composition of the group examined (the Italian group in South Tyrol also included female subjects) and the period during which the research was conducted. One cannot, however, exclude the alternative that the different self-evaluation is the result of a different categorization. In the South Tyrolese context, the important social categories are the different ethnolinguistic groups and it is among these, especially the Italian and German groups, that the mechanisms of comparison, from which the distinctive traits of the two groups derive, take place. The most important comparative dimensions are those by which the two groups are diversified; it is on those dimensions that the perception of ingroup similarity is accentuated and therefore the uniformity and intensity of the corresponding attributions are also accentuated.

Outside of the South Tyrolese context, as the categorization changes, other intergroup relationships and other dimensions of comparison acquire importance. Consequently, the distinctive traits of the self-evaluation change.

Our data do not allow for ample generalizations; but it is possible to foresee that, with the growing influence of the new legislative powers, which lead to an accentuated German pre-eminence, the Italian attitudes towards the cultural re-evaluation will be respectively accentuated.[29] However, many factors can determine intergroup relations and it is therefore difficult to anticipate. This is particularly so with regard to the future influence of the SVP's politics and to the various transformations in class relationships which have, lately, involved the South Tyrolese group (see Pristingher, 1978, p112).

7. Discussion

Our data support the validity of some of the hypotheses formulated by Tajfel (1974, 1976, 1978*a*) on the psychological processes active in intergroup relations.

(1) First, we found some support for the hypothesis that during periods

of social change, when individual solutions are not possible, mechanisms of re-evaluation take place amongst members of 'underprivileged' groups; their function is to contribute to a more satisfactory social identity.

(2) Our data also support the assumptions concerning the various forms taken by such mechanisms. We found evidence for the functioning of two of the hypothesized strategies, those of assimilation and of social creativity.

With respect to the second point, we wish to note the need for an amplification of the system of hypotheses. Since the strategies of re-evaluation are sometimes connected with 'objective conflicts', since they evolve through processes of comparison with the 'superior' group, one should be able to formulate different hypotheses according to a prior analysis of the possible effects of the 'objective' determinants of the comparisons.

For example, the mechanisms of assimilation should not be found in intergroup relations where the motivation for change is 'material' and where the 'inferior' group desires 'goods' that are obtainable only by depriving the 'superior' group of them.

The strategies of re-evaluation depend, furthermore, on the characteristics that define the conditions of both the 'superior' and the 'inferior' groups. We can assume that the strategies are different when the dominating group is experiencing a period of exceptional economic prosperity (the case of the northerners at the time of the first research), and when it is experiencing conflicts connected with its own superiority or conflicts determined by a cultural and economic crisis (the northerners at the time of the second research). For each of these examples some strategies are possible, others must be excluded. The strategy of assimilation is possible during prosperity of the 'superior' group; it is no longer meaningful at the moment of its crisis. In the latter case, some new strategies may be used, such as the strategy of substitution which we found in the southern attitudes.

Naturally, no set of hypotheses formulated in advance can include the variety of cases that exist in real life. It would, therefore, be useful to collect an ample amount of data from which to infer the distinctive aspects of 'natural' relationships and the relevant characteristics of the context in which they evolve.

It should also be noted that the conceptual system discussed here allows for the enrichment, as compared with the traditional points of view, of the interpretation of relationships between groups as they can be inferred from stereotypes. Such images are, in fact, indications of dynamic processes activated by identity; from the strategies of comparison which these images allow to elicit, it is possible to foresee conflicts between groups and thereby some aspects of social change.

Notes

[1] Emiliana Bonaldo helped the first author with the research on relationships between northerners and southerners, and Alba Di Maggio helped with the research on relationships between the Italian ethnic group and the German ethnic group in South Tyrol.

[2] The most important studies carried out until 1972 on the problem of prejudice between southerners and northerners are to be found in the work of Battacchi (1972, p160). The most recent of these are referred to in the work of Quadrio (1967) and Barbiero (1969).

[3] For a detailed analysis of the factors that can impede the mechanism of *assimilation*, see Tajfel (1974; 1976, p33) and Giles *et al.* (1977, pp336–8).

[4] Giles, Bourhis and Taylor (1977, p339) hypothesize a fourth strategy, limited to groups having a certain level of *vitality*, in other words, characterized positively with regard to some of the following structural variables: status variables, such as economic status, social or socio-historical status; institutional variables, for example, formal or informal control of institutions; demographic variables such as the numerical entity of an 'ingroup' with respect to an 'outgroup' (Giles *et al.*, 1977, p309). Then, a subordinate group, which is distinguished by a certain *vitality*, can obtain a positive identity by using strategies of attack and provocation towards the dominating group. Giles, Bourhis and Taylor quote the example of the Welsh who, in order to affirm their own ethnic and linguistic identity, fought to satisfy the request for a greater number of channels and hours dedicated to Welsh television programmes. As their method of protest they used occupation of television stations and refusal of subscriptions (Giles *et al.*, 1977, p339).

The concept of *vitality* proposed for the ethno-linguistic groups can be extended to include any type of group.

[5] Southern immigration was very intense during those years to the area of the industrial triangle (Turin, Milan, Genoa).

[6] Poor areas are situated next to recently industrialized areas; 'isolated peasant' agriculture is situated next to capitalistic agriculture (Fissore and Meinardi, 1976, p196).

[7] The data of the research carried out in 1963 are taken from Capozza (1968).

[8] For a complete discussion of the method, see Capozza (1977, pp61–75).

[9] In the research carried out in 1963 the concepts were nearly the same:

Self-control	Impulsiveness	Fear
Intelligence	Vindictiveness	Anguish
Laboriousness	Superstition	Sleep
Tenacity	Sweetness	Hero
Hospitality	Love	Tyrant
Success	Hate	Male
Practicality	Jealousy	Female
Disgust	Loneliness	Guilt
Southerner		
Northerner		

Both groups also evaluated the southerners, 'Southerner' ('as I think the northerners evaluate him'); the northerners, 'Northerner' ('as I think the southerners evaluate him').

[10] Southern and northern students studying psychology were excluded from the survey taken in 1979 in order to maintain as much similarity as possible with the previous survey; in 1963 this course of study had not yet been founded.

[11] The experimenter was the first author of this chapter. In the survey done between the end of 1978 and the beginning of 1979, the subjects were examined with the help of Emiliana Bonaldo.

[12] The attitude largely adopted by the southern group, also found in Battacchi's research (1972), was during the period of this survey or immediately preceding it, the acceptance of the negative image prevalent in the northern environment. The different attitude of our subjects is most likely due to their cultural level (they are university students) and to their continuous contact with the alien culture (they live in Padua during the academic year).

[13] The southerners' devaluation of this trait is more clearly evidenced in Capozza (1968). In this work it is evident, in fact, how a second concept indicating the free expression of impulses, 'passionate', is correlated with the southern self-evaluation ($r = 0.66$) but not with the ideal self-evaluation ($r = 0.28$). (The correlations relative to the ideal images and to the concepts 'passionate' and 'national' (survey carried out in 1963) are taken from Capozza 1968.)

[14] Another condition which may have influenced our data concerns the geographical area of our survey; Padua and the whole Venetian region have never been the object of intense southern immigration.

[15] Contacts among the subjects (students at the University of Padua) of both groups leads us to believe that the northerners are familiar with the strategies of re-evaluation used by the southerners.

[16] With regard to this characterization, note that if the definition of an outgroup as 'emotive' allows for a justification of the group's exclusion from some forms of advanced production, a further enhancement of this attribute, that is, its transformation into 'passionate', accomplishes the function of accentuating, by differentiation, the positiveness of the self-evaluation.

[17] The data relative to the research carried out in 1963 are taken from Capozza (1968, p362). We have related, for each of the two surveys, all of the significant positive correlations of IN and, furthermore, the equivalents of the parallel survey. (In the first survey IN presented a very high correlation also with 'practicality' ($r = 0.93$), a concept not used later on.) It must be remembered that with regard to the data gathered for the first research. the correlations of IN were calculated considering 24 scales.

[18] The new meaning of the two concepts results both from their profile and from their correlations with the other concepts. (These data, not reported in this chapter, are available at the Institute of Psychology, University of Padua.)

[19] The southerner is, for example, evaluated as 'small', 'hot', 'variable', 'conservative', 'good'.

[20] When reading the two tables, one has to remember that in Table 1, where reference is made to data gathered in 1963, the concepts 'passionate' and 'rational' do not appear because at the moment of the parallel survey the corresponding profiles were no longer at our disposition. Listed in the same table are, on the other hand, the concepts 'practicality', 'guilt', 'loneliness', 'disgust' and 'jealousy' which were not used in the second research and therefore are not listed in Table 2.

[21] The concept 'female' has undergone, for the southern group, the same semantic changes that we observed in the northern group (see p308). This is not so for the concept 'male', which for the southerners remains unchanged. Consider, with regard to this, the positive correlations, statistically significant, of the two concepts and the corresponding correlations, obtained in the first survey:

MALE			FEMALE		
Data gathered in 1979		in 1963	Data gathered in 1979		in 1963
Tenacity	0.94	0.87	Love	0.87	0.58
Hero	0.93	0.95	Sweetness	0.83	0.77
Success	0.89	0.92	Sleep	0.83	0.74
Love	0.87	0.84	Hospitality	0.82	0.60
Intelligence	0.86	0.87	Laboriousness	0.77	0.50
Laboriousness	0.84	0.78	Intelligence	0.71	0.38
Passionateness	0.83	—	Success	0.70	0.42
Self-control	0.79	0.69	Male	0.63	0.19
Hospitality	0.72	0.69	Self-control	0.63	0.23
Impulsiveness	0.66	0.76	Tenacity	0.62	0.33
Rationality	0.65	—	Passionateness	0.60	—
Female	0.63	0.19	Hero	0.58	0.29
Sweetness	0.56	0.57	Rationality	0.50	—

[22] It will be remembered that it would be difficult to generalize our results beyond the populations of students from which they were obtained.

[23] The South Tyrol coincides with the Province of Bolzano.

[24] The Italian and the Ladin. In 1971 the German, Italian and Ladin linguistic groups represented, respectively, 62.9 %, 33.3 % and 3.7 % of the resident population in the Province of Bolzano (see Pristingher, 1978, p79).

[25] The unified version of the new special Statute for the region of Trentino-South Tyrol was published in the Official Gazette on November 20, 1972.

[26] Consider the correlations of IGI in Table 7. The evaluation that the Italians expect from the other group is only in part different to that which the South Tyrolese effectively describe (compare the correlations of IGI (Table 7) with those of GI (Table 5)).

[27] The following correlations of the self-stereotype and of the ideal self-stereotype (Table 7) should be considered:

II Female (0.86); Love (0.71); Sweetness (0.64)

Ideal I Female (0.69); Love (0.89); Sweetness (0.83)

[28] We assume that the subjects in this research, as did the northerners and southerners, when describing their own ideal image, are not really describing the ideal image of their own group but, in general, the ideal human being.

[29] This should mean a future increase in the similarity between the self-evaluation and the ideal self-evaluation described by the Italian subjects.

Appendix

Table 1. *Significant correlations of ingroup and outgroup evaluations with paradigmatic concepts (southern group, data relative to 1963)*

SS	Hero (0.87); Male (0.84); Success (0.79); Love (0.78); Tenacity (0.77); Impulsiveness (0.76); Intelligence (0.68); Laboriousness (0.67); Practicality (0.60); Hospitality (0.59); Sweetness (0.52); Self-control (0.48).
	Guilt (-0.65); Fear (-0.62); Superstition (-0.56); Loneliness (-0.44); Disgust (-0.43).
SN	Self-control (0.73); Practicality (0.69); Laboriousness (0.64); Intelligence (0.62); Sweetness (0.55); Hospitality (0.54); Success (0.52); Tenacity (0.51); Hero (0.44); Love (0.43); Male (0.42).
	Superstition (-0.67); Jealousy (-0.61); Vindictiveness (-0.58); Hate (-0.57); Fear (-0.50); Tyrant (-0.46); Anguish (-0.45); Guilt (-0.44).
SNS	Impulsiveness (0.53); Jealousy (0.42).

With $\alpha = 0.05$, r is significant if $\geq |0.41|$; with $\alpha = 0.01$, r is significant if $\geq |0.53|$ (df = 21).
SS   = southern evaluation of the concept 'Southerner'
SN   = southern evaluation of the concept 'Northerner'
SNS = southern evaluation of the concept 'Southerner (as I think the southerners evaluate him)'.

Table 2. *Significant correlations of ingroup and outgroup evaluations with paradigmatic concepts (southern group, data relative to 1979)*

SS	Male (0.86); Hero (0.82); Love (0.81); Success (0.79); Passionateness (0.79); Tenacity (0.77); Laboriousness (0.75); Hospitality (0.67); Intelligence (0.66); Impulsiveness (0.65); Self-control (0.65); Female (0.64); Sweetness (0.56); Sleep (0.48); Rationality (0.43). Superstition (−0.58); Tyrant (−0.47); Fear (−0.45).
IS	Intelligence (0.94); Laboriousness (0.90); Self-control (0.88); Tenacity (0.88); Love (0.87); Hospitality (0.86); Male (0.86); Hero (0.84); Sweetness (0.77); Rationality (0.77); Female (0.72); Success (0.71); Passionateness (0.56); Sleep (0.47). Superstition (−0.93); Fear (−0.74); Tyrant (−0.72); Vindictiveness (−0.57); Anguish (−0.54).
SNS	Superstition (0.54); Vindictiveness (0.44). Rationality (−0.70); Self-control (−0.57); Intelligence (−0.56); Sweetness (−0.44); Tenacity (−0.43); Hospitality (−0.42); Laboriousness (−0.41).
SN	Superstition (0.44). Love (−0.63); Male (−0.60); Passionateness (−0.56); Sweetness (−0.51); Tenacity (−0.50); Female (−0.50); Intelligence (−0.49); Success (−0.45); Laboriousness (−0.41).
Italian	Love (0.86); Success (0.84); Female (0.83); Passionateness (0.78); Male (0.76); Hospitality (0.76); Laboriousness (0.75); Sweetness (0.70); Hero (0.70); Sleep (0.66); Impulsiveness (0.65); Intelligence (0.64); Tenacity (0.64); Self-control (0.56). Superstition (−0.67); Tyrant (−0.64); Fear (−0.52); Anguish (−0.44).

With $\alpha = 0.05$, r is significant if $\geq |0.41|$; with $\alpha = 0.01$, r is significant if $\geq |0.53|$ (df = 21).
For the meaning of SS, SN, SNS, see Table 1.
IS indicates the ideal self-evaluation of the southern group.

Table 3. *Significant correlations of ingroup and outgroup evaluations with paradigmatic concepts (Northern group, data relative to 1963)*

NN	Intelligence (0.95); Practicality (0.94); Tenacity (0.92); Laboriousness (0.92); Self-control (0.92); Success (0.88); Male (0.83); Love (0.82); Hospitality (0.82); Hero (0.79); Sweetness (0.73); Impulsiveness (0.44). Superstition (−0.85); Fear (−0.73); Guilt (−0.55); Loneliness (−0.46); Vindictiveness (−0.42); Hate (−0.41).
NS	Impulsiveness (0.46).
NSN	Self-control (0.44); Tyrant (0.42).

With $\alpha = 0.05$, r is significant if $\geq |0.41|$; with $\alpha = 0.01$, r is significant if $\geq |0.53|$ (df = 21).
NN = northern evaluation of the concept 'Northerner'
NS = northern evaluation of the concept 'Southerner'
NSN = northern evaluation of the concept 'Northerner (as I think the northerners evaluate him)'.

Table 4. *Significant correlations of ingroup and outgroup evaluations with paradigmatic concepts (Northern group, data relative to 1979)*

NN	Tenacity (0.85); Self-control (0.83); Laboriousness (0.82); Rationality (0.79); Intelligence (0.79); Male (0.74); Hero (0.68); Love (0.66); Success (0.63); Passionateness (0.53); Hospitality (0.49); Impulsiveness (0.45); Female (0.43). Superstition (−0.68).
IN	Intelligence (0.94); Love (0.92); Hospitality (0.88); Laboriousness (0.85); Self-control (0.84); Tenacity (0.82); Female (0.80); Rationality (0.77); Sweetness (0.76); Sleep (0.73); Success (0.70); Male (0.68); Passionateness (0.58); Hero (0.53). Superstition (−0.96); Tyrant (−0.68); Fear (−0.54); Vindictiveness (−0.52); Anguish (−0.47).
NSN	Tyrant (0.58); Hate (0.54); Vindictiveness (0.53). Sweetness (−0.52); Female (−0.50); Sleep (−0.49).
NS	
Italian	Success (0.68); Passionateness (0.65); Female (0.62); Impulsiveness (0.58); Love (0.52); Sleep (0.52); Sweetness (0.44); Hospitality (0.43). Tyrant (−0.52).

With α = 0.05, r is significant if ⩾ |0.41|; with α = 0.01, r is significant if ⩾ |0.53| (df = 21). For the meaning of NN, NS, NSN, see Table 3.
IN indicates the ideal self-evaluation of the northern group.

Table 5. *Research done in South Tyrol: Significant correlations of ingroup and outgroup evaluations with paradigmatic concepts (German group)*

GG	Self-control (0.93); Laboriousness (0.92); Methodical person (0.88); Intelligence (0.85); Male (0.84); Stubbornness (0.84); Hero (0.84); Rationality (0.80); Orderliness (0.79); Authoritarianism (0.48); Hate (0.45); Love (0.44). Corruption (−0.90); Superficiality (−0.84); Superstition (−0.79); Fear (−0.78); Blundering person (−0.76); Thief (−0.64).
GI	Sweetness (0.69); Blundering person (0.59); Female (0.47); Superstition (0.45); Superficiality (0.45). Hate (−0.79); Tyrant (−0.72); Authoritarianism (−0.68); Rationality (−0.67); Stubbornness (−0.61); Methodical person (−0.59): Male (−0.58); Aggressiveness (−0.53); Traditionalist (−0.52); Laboriousness (−0.48); Harsh person (−0.48).
Ideal G	Intelligence (0.92); Hero (0.86); Laboriousness (0.86); Self-control (0.83); Orderliness (0.77); Methodical person (0.74); Male (0.74); Stubbornness (0.71); Love (0.71); Impulsiveness (0.52); Rationality (0.50); Female (0.47). Fear (−0.86); Superstition (−0.85); Corruption (−0.75); Thief (−0.68); Superficiality (−0.64); Blundering person (−0.60).
GIG	Laboriousness (0.78); Stubbornness (0.76); Male (0.74); Methodical person (0.73); Rationality (0.72); Hero (0.63); Self-control (0.62); Tyrant (0.58); Authoritarianism (0.55); Hate (0.54); Orderliness (0.49); Intelligence (0.47). Superstition (−0.84); Blundering person (−0.79); Superficiality (−0.79); Fear (−0.73); Corruption (−0.51).

With $\alpha = 0.05$, r is significant if $\geqslant |0.44|$; with $\alpha = 0.01$, r is significant if $\geqslant |0.56|$ (df = 18).
GG = German evaluation of the concept 'South Tyrolese'
GI = German evaluation of the concept 'Italian'
GIG = German evaluation of the concept 'South Tyrolese (as I think the Italians evaluate him)'
Ideal G = ideal self-evaluation of the German group.

Table 6. *Matrix of correlations between ingroup and outgroup evaluations (German group)*

		1	2	3	4	5	6
South Tyrolese	1		−0.44	0.81	0.76	0.86	0.72
Italian	2			−0.36	−0.45	−0.22	−0.57
German	3				0.67	0.67	0.61
Altoatesino	4					0.78	0.81
Ideal South Tyrolese	5						0.60
South Tyrolese (as I think the Italians...)	6						

Table 7. *Research done in South-Tyrol: Significant correlations of ingroup and outgroup evaluations with paradigmatic concepts (Italian group)*

II	Female (0.86); Love (0.71); Sweetness (0.64). Authoritarianism (−0.81); Tyrant (−0.68); Corruption (−0.59); Stubbornness (−0.59); Traditionalist (−0.57); Hate (−0.55); Methodical person (−0.55); Harsh person (−0.53); Disgust (−0.52).
IG	Harsh person (0.68); Stubbornness (0.60); Rationality (0.58); Self-control (0.57); Hate (0.55); Authoritarianism (0.53); Aggressiveness (0.51); Laboriousness (0.45); Tyrant (0.45); Orderliness (0.44). Superficiality (−0.44).
Ideal I	Intelligence (0.97); Laboriousness (0.89); Love (0.89); Hero (0.86); Male (0.83); Sweetness (0.83); Female (0.69); Rationality (0.62); Self-control (0.61); Orderliness (0.44). Superstition (−0.93); Corruption (−0.89); Traditionalist (−0.82); Fear (−0.71); Superficiality (−0.63); Authoritarianism (−0.54); Tyrant (−0.49); Disgust (−0.47); Blundering person (−0.45).
IGI	Superficiality (0.72); Blundering person (0.66). Self-control (−0.71); Rationality (−0.64); Hate (−0.64); Orderliness (−0.60); Laboriousness (−0.49); Harsh person (−0.47).

With $\alpha = 0.05$, r is significant if $\geq |0.44|$; with $\alpha = 0.01$, r is significant if $\geq |0.56|$ (df = 18).
II   = Italian evaluation of the concept 'Italian'
IG   = Italian evaluation of the concept 'South Tyrolese'
IGI   = Italian evaluation of the concept 'Italian (as I think the South Tyrolese evaluate him)'
Ideal I = ideal self-evaluation of the Italian group.

Table 8. *Factor structure of the concepts (Italian group)*

	F_1	F_2	F_3	F_4
Female	0.86	−0.36	0.17	−0.14
Hate	−0.21	0.83	−0.36	0.20
Blundering person	−0.06	−0.15	0.89	−0.08
Laboriousness	0.72	−0.01	−0.37	0.50
Methodical person	−0.71	−0.45	−0.29	0.21
Ideal Italian	0.88	−0.06	−0.30	0.29
German	0.00	0.26	−0.24	0.86
Italian	0.75	−0.27	0.45	−0.26
Male	0.76	0.39	−0.20	0.41
Stubbornness	−0.28	0.80	−0.10	0.40
Italian (as I think the South Tyrolese...)	0.07	−0.30	0.80	−0.36
South Tyrolese	−0.08	0.33	−0.17	0.86
Love	0.97	−0.06	−0.06	0.06
Authoritarianism	−0.78	0.46	−0.05	0.31
Sweetness	0.85	−0.44	−0.20	0.00
Orderliness	0.10	−0.35	−0.68	0.51
Rationality	0.33	0.14	−0.57	0.59
Aggressiveness	−0.07	0.93	−0.07	0.24
Impulsiveness	−0.03	0.68	0.63	−0.07
% total variance	32.68	21.42	18.32	16.84

Loadings $\geq |0.40|$ are in italics.

Table 9. *Results of the factor analysis applied to the cross-products between the concepts* (*Italian group*)

	F_1	F_2	F_3	F_4
Female	*5.1*	*−2.4*	1.6	−0.3
Hate	−1.8	*6.5*	−0.8	0.0
Blundering person	−0.9	−1.8	*2.8*	0.3
Laboriousness	*5.3*	1.9	−1.5	1.9
Methodical person	−1.9	−1.2	*−2.5*	0.9
Ideal Italian	*8.1*	1.3	−1.6	0.6
German	*−2.3*	*2.2*	−1.7	*3.3*
Italian	*3.0*	−1.6	*2.8*	−0.5
Male	*3.9*	*3.0*	0.6	1.9
Stubbornness	−1.6	*3.4*	0.1	1.8
Italian (as I think the South Tyrolese...)	−0.6	*−3.3*	*3.5*	−0.2
South Tyrolese	0.0	1.7	−1.1	*2.4*
Love	*7.4*	0.7	1.7	−0.7
Authoritarianism	*−5.6*	*3.0*	−1.4	*2.5*
Sweetness	*7.7*	*−2.1*	−0.6	−1.1
Orderliness	1.6	0.4	*−3.2*	0.7
Rationality	1.6	1.4	−1.5	1.2
Aggressiveness	−1.1	*4.9*	1.2	1.3
Impulsiveness	−1.3	1.2	*3.0*	1.1
% total sum of squares	50.61	22.81	12.08	6.71

Loadings $\geq$ |2.00| are in italics.

Table 10. *Matrix of correlations between ingroup and outgroup evaluations* (*Italian group*)

		1	2	3	4	5	6
Italian	1		−0.52	−0.53	−0.26	0.45	0.59
South Tyrolese	2			0.94	0.85	0.13	−0.61
German	3				0.82	0.23	−0.61
Altoatesino	4					0.42	−0.68
Ideal Italian	5						−0.25
Italian (as I think the South Tyrolese...)	6						

References

Adorno, T.W., Frenkel-Brunswick, E., Levinson, D.J. and Sanford, R.N. 1950. *The authoritarian personality*. New York: Harper.

Barbiero, M.C. 1969. Il pregiudizio regionale nei bambini napoletani. *Rivista di Psicologia*, **63**, 85–94.

Battachi, M.W. 1972. *Meridionali e settentrionali nella struttura del pregiudizio etnico in Italia.* Bologna: Il Mulino.

Capozza, D. 1968. Gli stereotipi del meridionale e del settentrionale rilevati e analizzati con la tecnica del differenziale semantico. *Rivista di Psicologia*, **62**, 317–67.

Capozza, D. 1977. *Il differenziale semantico: Problemi teorici e metrici.* Bologna and Padua: Patron.

Fissore, G. and Meinardi, G. 1976. *La questione meridionale.* Turin: Loescher.

Fonzi, A. and Saglione, G. 1974. Sul pregiudizio verso i meridionali. *Psicologia Contemporanea*, **I**, 13–19.

Giles, H., Bourhis, R.Y. and Taylor, D.M. 1977. Towards a theory of language in ethnic group relations. In H. Giles (ed.): *Language, ethnicity and intergroup relations.* European Monographs in Social Psychology, No. 13. London: Academic Press.

Graziani, A. 1972. Introduction. In A. Graziani (ed.): *L'economia italiana: 1945–1970.* Bologna: Il Mulino.

Gubert, R. 1976. *L'identificazione etnica.* Udine: Del Bianco.

Hofstätter, P.R. 1956. Dimensionen des mimischen Ausdrucks. *Zeitschrift für experimentelle und angewandte Psychologie*, **3**, 505–29.

Hofstätter, P.R. 1963. Über sprachliche Bestimmungsleistungen: Das Problem des grammatikalischen Geschlechts von Sonne und Mond. *Zeitschrift für experimentelle und angewandte Psychologie*, **10**, 91–108.

Hofstätter, P.R. 1967. Die Methode der Wortwahlen (Dargestellt am studentischen Stereotyp der evangelischen Kirche). *Kölner Zeitschrift für Soziologie und Sozialpsychologie*, **19**, 306–21.

Johnson, S.C. 1967. Hierarchical clustering schemes. *Psychometrika*, **32**, 241–54.

Nunnally, J. 1962. The analysis of profile data. *Psychological Bulletin*, **59**, 311–19.

Osgood, C.E., May, W.H. and Miron, M.S. 1975. *Cross-cultural universals of affective meaning.* Urbana: University of Illinois Press.

Osgood, C.E. and Suci, G.J. 1952. A measure of relation determined by both mean differences and profile information. *Psychological Bulletin*, **49**, 251–62.

Peay, E.R. 1974. Hierarchical clique structure. *Sociometry*, **37**, 54–65.

Peay, E.R. 1975. Nonmetric grouping: Clusters and cliques. *Psychometrika*, **40**, 297–313.

Pristingher, F. 1978. *La minoranza dominante nel Sudtirolo.* Bologna and Padua: Patron.

Quadrio, A. 1967. Giudizi e pregiudizi degli insegnanti sugli alunni immigrati. *Contributi dell'Istituto di Psicologia*, **29**, 126–41.

Ronchey, A. 1977. *Accadde in Italia 1968–1977.* Milan: Garzanti.

Tajfel, H. 1974. Social identity and intergroup behaviour. *Social Science Information*, **13**, 65–93.

Tajfel, H. 1976. Psicologia sociale e processi sociali. In A. Palmonari (ed.): *Problemi attuali della psicologia sociale.* Bologna: Il Mulino.

Tajfel, H. 1978a. The psychological structure of intergroup relations. In H. Tajfel (ed.): *Differentiation between social groups: Studies in the social psychology of intergroup relations.* European Monographs in Social Psychology, No. 14. London: Academic Press.

Tajfel, H. 1978*b*. Introduction. In H. Tajfel (ed.): *Differentiation between social groups: Studies in the social psychology of intergroup relations*. European Monographs in Social Psychology, No. 14. London: Academic Press.

Tajfel, H. 1981. *Human groups and social categories: Studies in social psychology*. European Studies in Social Psychology. Cambridge: Cambridge University Press.

Tzeng, O.C.S. and May, W.H. 1976. *On rotation of a Johnson hierarchical tree structure*. Urbana: University of Illinois.

12. Intergroup relations, ethnic identity and self-evaluation in Indonesia

J.M.F. JASPARS AND SUWARSIH WARNAEN

1. Introduction

In most developing countries problems of national integration are considered by many to be of extreme importance. Indonesia is a case in point. As Koentjaraningrat (1975) has recently shown, anthropological and sociological research activities became almost totally oriented towards the problems of nation building after 1965, when Indonesia committed itself fully to national development. The study of national integration, population pressure, socio-cultural change, transformation of the educational system, community development and the reorganization of the administration is considered as urgent anthropology. 'In the frame of national integration', Koentjaraningrat writes, 'the problems of interethnic relations, interracial relations and relations between religious groups, are of great interest to anthropologists as well as to sociologists and they are problems which can be studied in rural as well as in urban situations, with qualitative as well as quantitative methods' (Koentjaraningrat, 1975, p234).

Being an anthropologist writing for anthropologists, Koentjaraningrat should perhaps be forgiven for not mentioning that such problems are also of great interest to social psychologists, especially when he goes on to state that anthropologists can be of particular importance for the promotion of better understanding between ethnic groups in Indonesia by writing modern ethnographies. Not only can social psychology complement anthropological studies of separate ethnic groups based on intensive observation and qualitative study by large scale quantatitive studies of (perceived) relations between ethnic groups; it can also add to ethnographic and anthropological research a psychological explanation of the subjective representations of the relations between ethnic groups. More than ever, psychologists are beginning to realize that social problems like prejudice and discrimination can be understood neither solely as a function of individual characteristics, nor as a pure reflection of the 'objective' social relations between groups. What matters first of all is the realization that a *psychological* explanation should be sought at the *social* (group) and not at the individual level. Tajfel's theory of intergroup relations (Tajfel, 1978) strongly emphasizes this point of view and represents, as Eiser recently put it 'one of the most ambitious undertakings in research on group processes during recent years' (Eiser, 1980). There is no need to discuss it extensively here, since various discussions of it have appeared in recent publications (e.g. Tajfel, 1978; Eiser, 1980). The purpose of the present study is mainly to present a set of data based on a field study of ethnic stereotypes, conducted by the second author (Warnaen, 1979) in Indonesia, to test some of the hypotheses which have been, or can be, derived from Tajfel's theory. Before we present a summary of the relevant data we will discuss briefly those aspects of Tajfel's theory and some of the experimental work based upon it, which can elucidate the results obtained.[1]

2. Social categorization, social identity and social comparison

Classical theories of prejudice and discrimination (LeVine and Campbell, 1972) tend to view a person's social identity as an epiphenomenon (Billig, 1976; Turner et al., 1979) of intergroup relations and negatively evaluate the pursuit of a positive social self-definition through ethnocentric attitudes.

In a series of so-called minimal group experiments Tajfel and his colleagues have attempted to show that even a superficial categorization of individuals into groups without any realistic conflict or competition is *sufficient* to produce an ingroup – outgroup bias in the allocation of rewards or punishments (Tajfel et al., 1971; Billig and Tajfel, 1973; Tajfel, 1978; Turner et al., 1979).

Although Tajfel (1978) denies that these experiments are crucial for his theory and only admits that they served as crutches for further thinking about the issues involved, it is also important to notice that the minimal group experiments are interpreted as demonstrating the relationship between social categorization and the achievement of a positive social identity. Turner (1975) has probably expressed the potential significance of these experiments best by arguing that it is not the division into groups which causes discrimination in these experiments but rather the more basic motivation of positive self-evaluation which led the subjects to use the only existing social categorization in a discriminatory way. If Turner is right, this means, of course, that a categorization effect may be less strong when other means for achieving a positive self-evaluation are available or when there is less need to achieve a more positive self-evaluation.

Whatever the case may be, Tajfel (1978, p64) has argued later that 'an individual will tend to remain a member of a group and seek membership of new groups if these groups have some contribution to make to the positive aspects of his social identity'. Tajfel assumes, furthermore, that the individual will tend to leave a group if it does not satisfy this requirement, unless leaving is impossible for objective reasons, or if leaving conflicts with important values which are themselves part of his acceptable self-image. In the latter case Tajfel assumes that unwelcome features of one's group will be either justified or made acceptable through reinterpretation and/or that the individual engages in social action which would lead to desirable changes in the situation. Finally, Tajfel's theory postulates that positive aspects of social identity, reinterpretation of attributes and engagement in social action 'only acquire meaning in relation to, or in comparison with other groups'.

These ideas seem to capture a number of social and psychological processes which are illustrated almost continuously by existing social and political conflicts in the world today. However, as soon as one tries to apply these notions to the problem of the perception and evaluation of differences between ethnic groups, on which we shall report in this study, certain problems arise. The application of Tajfel's first hypothesis to ethnic groups immediately raises the problem that one does not choose one's ethnic group but is born into it, and that therefore the option of leaving the group is not possible. (Marrying outside one's own groups is perhaps a partial solution, but it is obvious that this is a special case which may lead to marginal membership of both groups.) It seems more appropriate to consider the case of ethnic groups as one where it is virtually impossible to leave for 'objective' reasons. It would seem to follow therefore that a reinterpretation of the unwelcome attributes or engagement in social action are to be expected when we are concerned with ethnic groups. Whether this will indeed happen is, however, a moot question. At one point Tajfel also suggests that an individual may leave the group at least symbolically (Tajfel, 1978) when it does not contribute positively to his or her social identity. One way in which an individual would be able to do this might be by regarding himself as not being a typical member of the group to which he or she belongs. Codol's *primus inter pares* (PIP) principle (Codol, 1975) does suggest that it is a fairly universal phenomenon for group members to think of themselves as being better than the average group member. It seems therefore that there is an easy way out for the individual. The P.I.P. principle suggests that unwelcome features are seen as characteristics of the average member of the group and do not apply to oneself. If such a process of dissociation of individual and social identity takes place one could argue that this is a case of symbolically leaving the group. In addition to this, one would expect that the tendency to dissociate oneself from the group should be stronger the more negative is the social identity implied by group membership.

3. A generalized social comparison model

The comparative nature of the evaluative judgement discussed by Tajfel raises still another problem. If positive differentiation from other groups is what the members of the ingroup want, exactly which comparison does this imply? The minimal intergroup experiments suggest that one compares the judgement of the ingroup by ingroup members with the judgement of the outgroup by the ingroup members. There are, however, two other comparisons possible which do not necessarily have to lead to the same comparative evaluation. The second comparison which seems relevant is the comparison between the judgement of the ingroup by the ingroup and the judgement of the ingroup by the outgroup. Does Tajfel's theory also imply that we think better of ourselves than others think of us? The third possibility which presents itself logically is the comparison between the judgement of the outgroup by the ingroup with the judgement of the outgroup by itself. In other words do we have a more negative opinion of 'them' than they have of themselves? The last two possibilities involve, of course, formally the same comparisons, depending upon which group is defined as ingroup or outgroup, but for each group of a pair the two judgements do not imply the same comparisons.

This is especially important if one considers groups which are of unequal status. This point can perhaps best be illustrated with reference to a recent study conducted by van Knippenberg (1978a, b). Van Knippenberg asked students of a Dutch polytechnic and a Dutch university to judge themselves and each other on a large number of traits under two different (relevant–not relevant) conditions. The group means for the first axis produced by the canonical discriminant analysis of the data are presented in Table 1.

As can be seen in Table 1 the judgements of own and other group made by the university and polytechnic students are quite different. The university students appear to behave as one would predict on the basis of the minimal intergroup studies. They show a strong ingroup bias in the sense

Table 1. *Projected group means on first canonical axis (Scientific, Status v Practical, Human) for judgements made by polytechnic and university students (after van Knippenberg, 1978a relevant condition only)*

Groups Judging	Groups Judged	
	University Students	Polytechnic Students
University Students	+1.33	−3.18
Polytechnic Students	+3.97	−1.85

that they regard themselves as superior to the polytechnic students on the 'scientific status' dimension. This is, however, not the case for the poly-technic students. What is even more remarkable is that the polytechnic students do not only rate the university students as superior to themselves on this dimension, they even give them higher ratings than the university students assign to themselves. Or, to look at this result from the point of view of the university students: they regard themselves as less scientific than they are seen by the polytechnic students. Similar findings have been reported by Doise and Sinclair (1973) and Turner and Brown (1978).[2] The same appears to hold for the relationship between majority and minority groups (Gerard and Hoyt, 1974; Moscovici and Paicheler, 1978) but high status in a particular respect (creativity) apparently interacts with the majority effect (Moscovici and Paicheler, 1978).

We should be careful, however, in interpreting these results as indicating a stronger degree of ingroup favouritism or outgroup discrimination in higher status groups. A much more obvious interpretation, which has nothing to do with discrimination, is that both high and low status groups share a common representation based on the objective relationship between both groups, but use a different comparison level to make these judgements. Ingroup favouritism or outgroup discrimination enter into this process by changing the comparison level when judgements are made about one's own or another group.

This point can be readily illustrated by analysing the projected group-means on the first canonical axis of van Knippenberg's study. A simple analysis of variance on the means shows a strong main effect of the status of the group to be judged (86 % of the variance), a small effect of the status of the group which makes the judgement (13 % of the variance) and virtually no effect at all of a bias (1 %). The regression equation for the group-means which summarizes this analysis allows us to represent

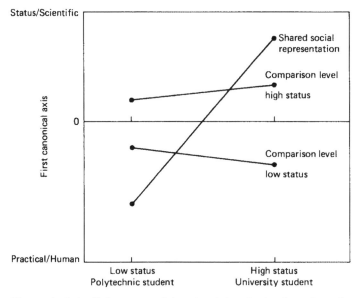

Figure 1. Analysis of judgements made by polytechnic and university students of own and other group (after van Knippenberg, 1978a)

the data of van Knippenberg using the different comparison levels for both groups.

As can been seen in Figure 1 the actual judgement can be interpreted as the difference between the comparison levels for each of the groups and the shared representation of the status of the two groups. There are two points worth noting in this figure. The first one is that the comparison level for the high status (HS) group is much higher than the comparison level for the low status (LS) group; and, secondly, the comparison level appears to be nearly the same for the judgement of one's own and the other group in this particular study. The first of these points brings immediately to mind the notion, introduced in Festinger's social comparison theory, that non-objective individual self-evaluation takes place by comparing one's own abilities or opinions with those of others who are not too different from oneself. Or, to put it in another way, the comparison level for individual self-evaluation is a function of the person's own abilities or opinions. As such, Festinger's social comparison theory can be seen as a special case of a more general adaptation-level theory. The results obtained by van Knippenberg suggest that the same adaptation or comparison level may be used by Ss when judging their own group and the outgroup.

Table 2. *A generalized social comparison model*

		Group judged	
		HS	LS
Group judging	HS	$\dfrac{H}{H + \delta_1}$	$\dfrac{L}{H + \delta_2}$
	LS	$\dfrac{H}{L + \delta_3}$	$\dfrac{L}{L + \delta_4}$

HS indicates high-status group
LS indicates low-status group
H, L are the actual levels of perceived characteristics
$\delta_{1,2,3,4}$, indicate the discrepancy between actual and comparison levels.

This idea is analogous to models developed in economics for the study of individual and group welfare functions. In a number of studies it has been shown that the subjective evaluation of income can be described by a lognormal distribution function, where the mean of the distribution is a logarithmic function of the income to be judged, family size, own income and the average income of one's reference group. Two characteristics of this model are important. The first one is that individual evaluation of income apparently has to be corrected both for an individual and a social comparison level, which suggests that the same might be the case for the judgement of other characteristics of individuals and groups. Secondly, the fact that all parameters are expressed in the form of logarithms suggests that social comparison judgements are not based upon a perceived difference between the individual or social level of comparison and the perceived real level but upon the ratio of the two. This may seem a rather technical and therefore uninteresting point but the consequence of it is that the differences perceived by lower status groups should be larger than those perceived by higher status groups. Assuming e.g. that the social comparison level for each group is always slightly higher than the actual level of the characteristics to be judged, as Festinger suggests for abilities, we would get the following judgements for high- and low-status groups.

From Table 2, if $H > L$ and $\delta_1 = \delta_2 = \delta_3 = \delta_4$ it follows that

$$\frac{H}{H + \delta} > \frac{H}{L + \delta} > \frac{L}{L + \delta} > \frac{L}{H + \delta}$$

which is precisely the result obtained by van Knippenberg. It also follows
from this formulation that

$$\frac{H-L}{H+\delta} < \frac{H-L}{L+\delta}$$

i.e. the differences perceived by the lower status group should be larger
than those perceived by the higher status group. Again, this is precisely
what van Knippenberg shows to be the case.

It should be realized, however, that the difference between the actual
and the comparison level is constant in the simple version of the model,
which is in line with Festinger's theory that each individual uses the next
'higher' person to compare himself with. Nevertheless it is unlikely that
this would in general be the case because the evaluation of the higher status
group by the lower status group is not always higher than the judgement
of the higher status group of itself.

The analysis illustrated above permits us to test in a field study both
Tajfel's social identity theory and a generalized social comparison model,
presented here. If intergroup evaluations can be interpreted as the result
of two main effects (i.e. shared social representation and stable comparison
level) there is no need to assume that such evaluations represent a search
for a positive social identity through discriminatory social categorization.
If the generalized social comparison model holds, one would not expect
Ss to feel a need to redefine unwelcome characteristics of their own group.
It would be sufficient to have a lower comparison level to resolve the social
identity problem or maintain an individual comparison level which is
distinct from the social comparison level.

In the second part of this chapter we shall present data obtained in a study
of ethnic stereotypes in Indonesia, which allow us to test some of the
alternative hypotheses formulated above. The emphasis will be on the perception and evaluation of differences between six major ethnic groups,
both in Jakarta and in the original locations in the various islands. This
comparison is important both from a theoretical and a practical point of
view. It seems reasonable to assume that, in a cosmopolitan urban environment, differences between ethnic groups become more salient, especially
in Indonesia where the social contact between ethnic groups, living sometimes thousands of miles apart, has been minimal and increasing migration
and urbanization are bound to make interethnic relations more salient.
Theoretically one would therefore expect social differentiation to increase
rather than decrease (Tajfel, 1978).

4. Ethnic stereotypes in Indonesia

Introduction

'Bhinneka Tungal Ika' (Unity in diversity), the Indonesian motto, expresses in a few words, perhaps better than any scientific analysis, the dilemma and the hopes of Indonesia today. The total population of Indonesia, estimated at 124 million in 1972, consists of 300 separate ethnic groups, which speak 250 different languages, but is united in a nation which has a dominant religion (90 % of the population professes Islam) and a national language based on a previously widely used *lingua franca*. The ethnic composition of Indonesia has been discussed at length by anthropologists (Bruner, 1972) but the perceptions that the various major ethnic groups have of themselves and each other have not been subjected to systematic scientific investigation, (Koentjaraningrat, 1975). Although there is a vast body of ethnographic literature, describing many of the ethnic groups in Indonesia, most of the data are by now obsolete, because they were largely obtained before World War II. They are, moreover, not easily accessible because most of the information is in Dutch and, finally, the earlier writings produced by travellers, sailors, missionaries, explorers and colonial administrators are obviously of dubious reliability and show a strong cultural bias. In particular, the statements about the personality of ethnic groups are based on biased subjective impressions and personal experiences gained by the authors in their dealings with individuals from the respective groups, rather than on objective psychological methods of investigation. More objective studies of culture and personality in Indonesia are extremely limited in number and, despite the fact that some have been conducted by well known anthropologists like Mead, Bateson and du Bois, no psychologist would nowadays dare to subscribe to Mead's conclusion based on the observation of eight infants over a period of a year, that 'one of the determining aspects of Balinese character formation is strongly like ... the character displayed by schizophrenics' (Koentjaraningrat, 1975). One wonders to what extent the observations made by anthropologists sometime reflect the social stereotypes which are prevalent in the society to which they belong.

To illustrate this point it is, for instance, quite revealing to compare the stereotypes of the six ethnic groups which we shall discuss in this chapter with ethnographic descriptions given by experts. As one example, the stereotype of the Sundanese, based on 17 groups of Ss of different ethnic composition, both in Jakarta and outside Jakarta, consists of the following traits: 'polite', 'good natured', 'friendly', 'honest' and 'hospitable'. A Dutch ethnographic description from 1920 contains exactly these same traits, but also a fair number of more negative characteristics, which seem to reflect a bias emerging from cross-cultural contact between colonial authorities and the autochthonous population: 'lazy', 'superficial', 'susceptible', 'mendacious', 'ingratiating', 'hypocritical', 'wasteful', 'immoral' and 'imitative'. Apart from anything else, the value of a study like the one conducted by Warnaen (1979) is that it finally presents us with a solid descriptive basis of ethnic stereotypes free from Western biases, upon which an analysis of intergroup relations can be based.

Although our main interest is in the general issue of intergroup relations, ethnic identity and self-evaluation, we have to say at least a few words about the specific ethnic groups and their political, social, cultural and historical background, without which it would be hard to understand some of the results which will be reported. However, we cannot do much justice to the social and historical background in this chapter, and refer the reader to Koentjaraningrat (1975), Kennedy (1974), McVey, and le Bar et al. (in Koentjaraningrat, 1975).

It has been pointed out above that there are many different ethnic groups in Indonesia, but the majority of these groups fall into 15 to 20 major cultures which have similar customs, languages and systems of common law. A widely accepted basis for major ethnic distinctions is the classification developed by van Vollenhoven, over a period of 30 years, of the separate *adat* law regions of Indonesia.

As can be seen in Figure 2, the ethnic groups included in the present analysis inhabit areas which are sometimes thousands of miles apart. The choice of the major ethnic groups in Warnaen's study (1979) was guided to some extent by the consideration of the possibilities of direct social contact which let to a selection of ethnic groups in pairs from three of the main islands of Indonesia: Javanese and Sundanese from Java, Bataks or Tapanuli and Minangkabau from Sumatra, the Buginese or Maskassarese and the Minahassan from Sulawes (Celebes). In addition to these groups, a group of Maluku (Moluccans) from Ambon was included. The samples in all groups consist of 100 boys and girls, in approximately equal numbers, between the ages of 16 and 20, attending high-school. Similar size samples of the same ethnic groups (except for the Buginese) were obtained from high-schools in Jakarta. In addition, the total Jakarta sample also contained a group of Chinese subjects ($N = 72$) and various groups of mixed ethnic

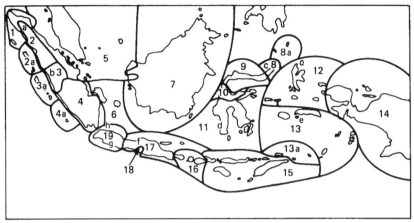

Source: Koentjaraningrat: *Anthropology In Indonesia*, 1975 p 91.

Regions used in the study		Location of samples	
2	Bataks–Tapanuli	a	Pematang Siantar
3	Minangkabau	b	Bukittinggi
8	Minahassa	c	Menado
11	Makassar–Buginese	d	Ujang Pandang
13	Moluccans	e	Ambon
17	Javanese	f	Yogjakarta
19	Sundanese	g	Bandung
		h	Jakarta

Figure 2. *Adat* Law regions of Indonesia

origin, the number of Ss in the total sample being 1291. What can not be appreciated from Figure 2 is the difference in size and culture of the various groups. In interpreting the data we shall present, it is important to remember that the Javanese represent the dominant ethnic group in Indonesia and that the Sundanese are the second largest group. All the other ethnic groups included in the study can be considered more or less as minority groups.

It is perhaps useful to point out that of the various ethnic groups included in the analysis, the Minahassa from North Sulawesi have been strongly influenced by Western culture through the impact of Western missionary activity. The strong ties of the Maluku with the Dutch during the colonial period are of course well known, but in interpreting the data one should also remember that many Moluccans emigrated to the Netherlands after Indonesia obtained its independence. It is also important to remember that in the past internal migration, sometimes forced, has taken place in

Indonesia. The migration of the Javanese from the densely populated island of Java to the north of Sumatra should be mentioned in particular.

Social contact, perceived similarity and stereotypes: descriptive results

The study conducted by Warnaen (1979) consisted of four types of questionnaires. The first questionnaire (the contact questionnaire) was designed to gather biographical information, including the ethnic group to which the individual and his or her parents belonged, information about personal contact experienced with other ethnic groups and the amount of knowledge about other ethnic groups. We shall refer here to the data about social contact only in passing, since an analysis of the relationship between social contact and ethnic stereotypes will be published elsewhere.

The similarity questionnaire (questionnaire 2) consisted of 55 paired combinations of 11 labels. Eight of the labels referred to the various ethnic groups already mentioned (Java, Sunda, Minangkabau, Tapanuli, Minahassa, Maluku, Makassar and Tionghoa (Chinese)) and three to the concept 'myself' (*saja sendiri*), Jakarta and Indonesia. Subjects were asked to judge the similarity between each pair by making a mark on an 11 cm straight line on one end of which was written 'very similar' (*sangat sama*) and on the other end 'very dissimilar' (*sangat berbeda*). This questionnaire was adapted from Taylor *et al.* (1972).

The stereotype questionnaire (questionnaire 3) was adapted from Katz and Braly (1933). The same labels which were used in the similarity study were presented again to the subjects, one label on each page. Subjects were asked to select from a list of 62 traits which ones they thought were appropriate to each label. The Ss were allowed to add other traits which were not on the list.

The fourth questionnaire contained the same list of 62 traits as in questionnaire (3). This time the Ss were asked to evaluate each trait on a five-point scale, where 5 means 'very good' and 1 means 'very bad'. All the materials were written in Indonesian and all testing was conducted in the same language by one investigator (Suwarsih Warnaen).

Perceived similarity   To obtain some insight into the overall structure of perceived similarities and differences between ethnic groups, the data obtained were subjected to an individual-differences scaling analysis as developed by Carroll and Chang (1970) in which the 19 different samples (7 outside Java, 12 in Jakarta) were treated as 'individuals'. Such an analysis presupposes that the perceived differences between the various ethnic groups are essentially the same, or at least shared to such an extent that any differences which may exist can be represented by weighting the perceived similarities differently. By and large this happens to be the case, since the perceived similarity matrices for the separate groups do not differ greatly, as is evident from the similar weights obtained in the Carroll and Chang analysis. One exception should, however, be mentioned in this respect. We also included in the analysis the concept of self and thus analysed the perceived similarity between self and all the ethnic groups. The perceived similarity between self and own ethnic group is usually greater than the similarity perceived between oneself and any other ethnic group or Indonesia and Jakarta. This result is not evident from the individual-differences scaling analysis since it presents the average result for all groups and thus gives the impression that the perceived similarity between the self and the dominant ethnic groups, as well as with Jakarta and Indonesia, is always smaller than with any of the other ethnic groups. This is, however, simply an artefact which is due to almost half of the total sample being from Jakarta; secondly, concepts like Jakarta and Indonesia very often end up in second place for separate ethnic groups in the ratings of the similarity to self. Averaged over all ethnic groups, this leads to greatest perceived similarity to the central concepts just mentioned.

Apart from this aspect, Figure 3 gives a relatively clear idea of the shared subjective representations of the perceived differences between the various ethnic groups. As can be seen in Figure 3, the first dimension appears to distinguish between the two dominant ethnic groups (Javanese and Sundanese) and all other Indonesian ethnic groups in the sample. Of course this implies simultaneously a geographical distinction between the central island of Java and the (sometimes) so-called outer islands. The second dimension appears to emphasize almost exclusively the distinction between all Indonesian ethnic groups and the Chinese (*Tionghoa*), which is perhaps not surprising since it is the only ethnic group of foreign origin included in our study. Interesting in this respect is that the matrix of weights, which indicates to what extent the general structure has to be transformed to obtain the perceived structure for the separate groups, shows the highest weight for the Chinese Ss from Jakarta on dimension (1) and the lowest for dimension (2). The implication of this finding is that for the Chinese Ss the structure of the perceived similarities almost reduces to a one-dimensional distinction which does not assign a qualitatively different position to the Chinese, but perceives the Chinese 'merely' as defining one end of the continuum which is characterized at the other end by

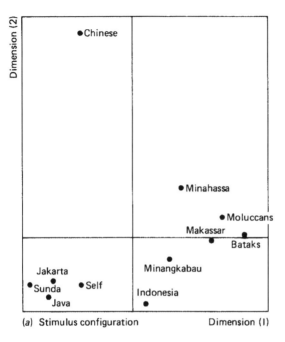

(a) Stimulus configuration   Dimension (I)

(b) Weights

| | Outside Jakarta | | Jakarta | |
	Dimension (1)	Dimension (2)	Dimension (1)	Dimension (2)
Sundanese	0.59	−0.59	0.68	−0.53
Javanese	0.55	−0.60	0.67	−0.53
Minangkabau	0.48	−0.60	0.62	−0.54
Chinese			0.75	−0.17
Bataks	0.31	−0.52	0.59	−0.45
Makassar	0.44	−0.56		
Minahassa	0.48	−0.49	0.55	−0.45
Moluccans	0.39	−0.50	0.52	−0.45

Figure 3. Indocal analysis similarity ratings of all groups (data from Warnaen, 1979). (a) Stimulus configuration. (b) Weights

the dominant ethnic groups of Javanese and Sundanese (see Figure 3).

Another feature of this analysis worth noting is the fact that the dimension (1) weights for the ethnic groups from Jakarta are always larger than for the comparable ethnic groups outside Jakarta. This means that the subjects from the Jakarta sample see the perceived differences between the various ethnic groups as larger than the Ss belonging to the same ethnic groups, living outside Jakarta. If the samples from Jakarta and from the other locations are otherwise comparable this result gives us an indirect confirmation of the hypothesis that relations between ethnic groups are more salient in an urban environment.

Ethnic stereotypes   The results obtained with the questionnaire (2) are more difficult to summarize since the raw data consist of traits assigned by the members of each group to all groups, which leads to 880 462 ratings. A summary of the stereotypical descriptions of each group and the self-descriptions shared by the majority of the groups in the sample is presented in Table 3.

The traditional descriptive form in which the stereotype data are presented in Table 3 is of rather limited value, but the table gives a general impression of the way in which each of the ethnic groups in Indonesia is seen in general. Inspection of the clusters of traits assigned to the various ethnic groups shows, however, that some descriptions are much more alike than others. In order to reveal the structure which is implied by the inter-relationships of the various stereotypes, a non-metric multidimensional scaling analysis (Coombs, 1964) was made of the matchings between the stereotypes, where each stereotype was defined as consisting of the 12 traits which were most frequently used by each of the groups in the sample (Warnaen, 1979).

A two-dimensional structure developed, in which the first factor explained 70 % of the triadic relationships and the second factor 25 %. The ethnic stereotypes of the various groups appear to form three clusters. The stereotypes of the Javanese and the Sundanese are very similar and show almost no overlap with the stereotypes of the Moluccans and the Bataks which in turn resemble each other. The first stereotype is characterized by such common traits as 'politeness', 'honesty', 'friendliness', 'hospitality' and 'good naturedness', whereas the latter can be summarized by the traits 'emotional', 'quick-tempered', 'gregarious' and 'loyal to family'. The Minangkabau, Minahassans and Buginese of Makassar form an intermediate group with some of the characteristics of the first, and some of the second group. The second dimension is mainly defined by the unique stereotype of the Chinese who are in general described as 'deceitful', 'stingy', 'industrious', 'suspicious' and 'slovenly'.

The interrelationships between the stereotypes obviously show a structure which is essentially similar to the one found in the previous analysis of perceived similarities between ethnic groups. To illustrate this overall similarity we have calculated the correlations between the positions of the

Table 3. *Stereotypes of ethnic groups in Indonesia shared by the majority of ethnic groups* (*Warnaen, 1979*)

Sundanese		Javanese		Minangkabau	
polite	17	polite	17	loyal to family	17
friendly	17	honest	14	old fashioned	14
good natured	16	traditional	14	traditional	14
honest	13	friendly	14	stingy	14
hospitable	13	old fashioned	11	deceitful	13
opinionated	10	superstitious	11		
materialistic	10	good natured	11		
neat	10	industrious	10		
Tapanuli		Makassarese		Minahassans	
emotional	17	emotional	17	pleasure loving	17
pleasure loving	17	rude	16	fond of parties	15
loyal to family	17	loyal to family	15	aggressive	13
quick tempered	17	quick tempered	15	gregarious	12
stubborn	11	old fashioned	14	polite	10
gregarious	11	traditional	13	hospitable	10
		polite	13	happy go lucky	10
		ambitious	10		
		deceitful	10		
		industrious	10		
Moluccans		Chinese		Indonesians	
fond of parties	16	deceitful	18	polite	19
rude	16	stingy	18	imitative	18
gregarious	16	industrious	17	friendly	18
emotional	14	suspicious	13	hospitable	17
aggressive	12	slovenly	13	traditional	17
ambitious	12	loyal to family	10	honest	14
quick tempered	12			loyal to family	14
happy go lucky	10			nationalistic	14
loyal to family	10				
Jakartans		Self			
humouristic	16	honest	19		
polite	13	opinionated	19		
fond of parties	12	polite	18		
old fashioned	11	hospitable	17		
friendly	11	humouristic	17		
aggressive	10	reliable	14		
hospitable	10	happy go lucky	11		
bad	10				
happy go lucky	10				

The figures indicate the number of groups (maximum 19) for which a trait is included in the stereotype.

ethnic groups on the two dimensions of the perceived similarity structure and the rank orders of assignment of the traits to the various ethnic groups.

This analysis shows that the perception of similarity is not only based on geographical or social criteria but also on a shared representation of psychological characteristics. The two major dimensions revealed by the analysis are relatively easy to interpret. The first dimension appears to reflect a distinction between groups which are regarded as more controlled, civilized or cultured *versus* groups which are seen as more primitive and uncontrolled. The stereotype of the Sundanese and Javanese is very positive whereas the stereotype of the 'primitive' ethnic groups is typically ambivalent containing some moderately unfavourable and moderately favourable traits. The second dimension which characterizes mainly the difference with the Chinese in Indonesia shows the familiar prejudice against a minority group engaged in business and commerce.

It is important to point out, however, that the stereotypes described here are only the dominant views shared by the majority of the groups in our sample. This sample is heavily weighted towards an urban population which constitutes approximately half of our Ss. Over and above this it seems reasonable to expect that differences between auto- and hetero-stereotypes (Triandis, 1972) will exist and so far these have not been taken into account. A differential analysis of the intergroup perceptions and evaluations is, however, the main purpose of the present chapter. We turn to it in the next section.

5. Differentiation between ethnic groups

According to both Tajfel's theory of intergroup relations (Tajfel, 1978) and classical theories of prejudice and discrimination (LeVine and Campbell, 1972; Billig, 1976) we would have to expect that the members of a particular ethnic group would attempt to achieve a positive differentiation with respect to other ethnic groups. As we have already pointed out in section 3 of this chapter, such a differentiation can be achieved in at least three different ways, depending upon which stereotypes are compared. A further complication is that we cannot simply compare the extent to which various ethnic groups attribute particular traits to their own and other groups because group members may be inclined, as Tajfel has suggested, to re-evaluate or reinterpret particular attributes which constitute unwelcome features of their own ethnic group.

We shall analyse therefore first of all the extent to which Ss are inclined to accept unwelcome features as part of the stereotype they have of their own group. In order to do so we have combined the data for all groups which were tested outside Jakarta and compared the evaluative ratings of the traits which were part of the autostereotype of an ethnic group but not part of the dominant heterostereotype, with the evaluative ratings of the traits which were part of the heterostereotype but not accepted as part of the autostereotype. If Ss are inclined to reject negative aspects of their social identity one would expect that the latter ratings would be more negative than the former ones. This, however, turns out not to be the case. The mean for the pure autostereotype ratings is $AS = +0.36$, whereas the mean for the pure heterostereotype ratings is $HS = +0.78$ on a scale from -2 to $+2$, a difference which is not significant. The mean for traits which are part of both auto- and heterostereotypes appears to fall in-between, i.e. $S = +0.64$.

This is only a fairly crude test of differentiation between own and other ethnic groups, because we have not taken into account the extent to which a particular trait is accepted as part of a stereotype. Following Katz and Braly (1933), a stereotype was defined as the set of the most frequently assigned traits which comprises 50 % of the total response. If there is considerable agreement among subjects in a particular subsample, relatively few traits are needed to reach this criterion and Katz and Braly have developed a stereotype index which is based upon this notion. One striking finding of the present study is that there appears to be much more agreement among Ss in assigning traits to one's own ethnic group than to other ethnic groups. If fewer traits are used to describe one's own ethnic group this means of course that each of those traits must have been chosen more often to complete the stereotype as defined by Katz and Braly. Although those fewer traits which are included in the stereotype of one's own group are not more positive than the ones which are assigned to one's group by other groups, the fact that they are chosen more often may make the overall autostereotypes more positive than the heterostereotype. To show that this is indeed the case we have analysed the difference between the frequency with which all traits belonging to auto- or heterostereotypes are assigned to all ethnic groups by those groups and by all other groups. Overall, the difference between the frequency with which stereotype traits are assigned to one's own group is slightly higher than the frequency with which other groups assign the same traits to one's group (8.22 %). This difference is slightly larger for the more positive traits (9.96 % v 6.48 %) a result which is marginally significant ($\chi^2 = 4.64$, df $= 1$) if one chooses the most advantageous cut-off point.

The picture which emerges from these preliminary analyses can be summarized in the following points:

(i)   The features which are accepted as part of one's autostereotype or social identity are not more positive than the features which are attributed to the group by others.

(ii) There is a tendency to describe one's own group in a more stereo-typical manner than other groups. In other words there is more agreement among the members of an ethnic group about the features which are characteristic of the group than about the traits which are assigned to other groups and to the own group by others.

(iii) The tendency to ascribe stereotypical traits to one's own group with greater frequency is slightly stronger for positive traits. In general a more positive autostereotype arises, however, from the fact that in the present study the content of most stereotypes is predominantly positive, so that the higher frequency with which traits are accepted in general can still result in a positive differentiation of one's own group from other groups.

It is important to stress that these conclusions are based upon the overall results for all the ethnic groups in the sample. The next question one should ask is to what extent these conclusions hold for each of the groups we have studied. One could argue that the rejection or redefinition of unwelcome features only becomes a necessity to preserve a positive social identity when the attitude of other groups towards one's own group becomes predominantly negative. The only group which meets this criterion is the Chinese. In this group we find indeed that the Ss strongly reject such characteristics as deceitful, suspicious and slovenly, which are attributed to them by the majority of the other ethnic groups.

When the heterostereotype others hold of one's own group is predominantly positive, but contains one or only a few negative traits the reaction of most people appears to be more subtle. In general such negative traits appear to be accepted as part of the stereotype of one's own group, but there is a tendency to exclude them from one's self-description. In order to show this we have compared the self-descriptions of Sundanese, Bataks and Chinese with their autostereotypes since these three groups form the extremes of the two stereotype dimensions which we described in the previous section. In the case of the Chinese we do not find a clear discrepancy between the self-description and the autostereotype since the most negative traits have already been rejected at the group level. A few other less negative traits, like 'conservatism', 'stinginess' and 'superstition' are, however, rejected at the individual level. It is interesting to note that, although most positive traits are overemphasized in the individual self-description as compared with the autostereotype, there are two positive traits which are part of the autostereotype, but which the Chinese Ss strongly reject at the individual level. They are 'industriousness' and 'loyalty to the family'.

In the case of the Bataks we find the clearest indication of an attempt to differentiate the self-description from the group stereotype in a positive way. All negative traits are regarded as less characteristic of oneself than of the group, and most positive traits are seen as more typical of oneself than of the group. There is only one clear exception which is again 'loyalty to the family'. This is seen as a typical positive characteristic of Bataks but does not seem to apply to the individual Batak's self-description. The Sundanese, who have a very positive auto- and heterostereotype show an interesting effect in the opposite direction. The most positive characteristics of the group are also seen as part of one's self-description but in general the judgement is less extreme.

Evaluative differentiation between ethnic groups

After these preliminary remarks we are ready to consider the way in which the various ethnic groups achieve overall an evaluative differentiation from each other. In order to obtain a sensitive measure of intergroup perception which takes into account the fact that the content of auto- and hetero-stereotypes may be different and that each of the features which are part of a stereotype may be evaluated differently by different groups, an overall measure of preference was constructed. This consists of the mean of the evaluations of the traits of a stereotype, differentially weighted according to the frequency with which a trait is assigned to a particular group.

The results are presented in Table 4 both for the Ss in Jakarta and for the groups outside Jakarta.

Table 4 shows immediately that evaluation of other groups is not always less positive than the evaluation of one's own group. If we compare the evaluation by each group of itself with the overall evaluation of all other groups, we see that for three groups outside Jakarta other groups are evaluated more positively than one's own group. For the groups in Jakarta, where such a comparison is possible, the difference is, however, always in favour of one's own group although it is sometimes very small. Occasionally we found that, in the Jakarta sample, members of an ethnic group would evaluate an outgroup as more positive. Overall, however, the difference between the evaluation of one's own group and of the other groups is larger in Jakarta (3.65 v 3.15) than outside Jakarta (3.61 v 3.43), indicating a stronger degree of intergroup differentiation.

A slightly different result is found when one compares the evaluation of the ingroup with the evaluation of the own group by other groups. This is a comparison which is in fact a summary of the preliminary analyses we

Table 4. *Evaluative differentiation between ethnic groups in Indonesia (data from Warnaen, 1979)*

Groups judging	Groups judged										
Outside Jakarta	R	I	A	S	J	B	T	M	H	K	O
1 S	4.09	3.82	3.07	4.03	3.29	3.03	2.53	3.21	3.26	3.15	2.76
2 J	4.04	3.85	3.15	3.37	3.82	3.39	2.73	3.40	3.63	3.38	2.69
3 B	4.34	4.02	3.36	4.12	3.53	4.05	2.99	3.72	3.71	3.46	3.01
4 T	3.74	3.54	3.66	3.91	3.57	3.14	3.04	3.44	3.44	3.53	3.16
5 M	4.25	4.01	3.66	3.92	3.69	3.88	2.73	3.40	3.51	3.28	2.96
6 H	4.11	4.05	3.62	3.77	3.80	3.76	3.18	2.76	3.77	3.56	3.09
7 K	4.10	4.04	3.66	4.08	3.92	3.86	3.15	2.60	3.36	3.20	2.99
Mean	4.09	3.90	3.45	3.88	3.66	3.63	2.90	3.21	3.52	3.36	2.95
Jakarta											
8 Sa	3.86	3.53	2.96	3.93	3.54	2.95	2.52	3.11	3.16	2.87	2.80
9 Ja	3.83	3.75	3.01	3.41	3.96	2.85	2.65	3.17	3.20	2.96	2.86
10 Ba	3.90	3.71	3.11	3.61	3.50	3.56	2.79	3.41	3.40	3.17	2.81
11 Ta	3.61	3.53	3.27	3.43	3.68	2.92	3.46	3.20	3.23	3.04	2.93
12 Ha	3.39	3.36	3.20	3.24	3.46	2.66	2.70	2.80	3.34	3.23	2.67
13 Ka	3.79	3.57	2.81	3.17	3.64	2.61	2.44	2.62	2.76	3.51	2.84
14 Oa	4.03	3.23	3.12	3.55	3.39	3.03	2.60	2.90	3.47	2.95	3.65
15 La	4.02	3.70	3.47	3.56	3.57	3.22	2.76	3.15	3.33	3.19	3.03
16 J/S	3.90	4.03	3.14	3.81	4.16	2.88	2.74	3.13	3.18	3.14	2.68
17 J/L	3.67	3.69	3.04	3.44	3.94	2.96	2.72	3.24	3.09	3.18	3.20
18 S/L	3.77	3.52	3.00	3.72	3.52	2.80	2.72	2.85	3.08	3.12	2.90
19 C/L	3.59	3.42	3.03	3.33	3.31	2.84	2.63	3.00	3.16	3.10	3.11
Mean	3.78	3.60	3.09	3.51	3.63	2.94	2.72	3.04	3.21	3.12	2.95
Overall mean	3.89	3.71	3.22	3.65	3.64	3.19	2.79	3.11	3.33	3.21	2.95

Scores range from 1 to 5. Higher scores indicate higher preferences.
S, Sa = Sundanese; J, Ja = Javanese; B, Ba = Minangkabau; T, Ta = Tapanuli; M = Makassar; H, Ha = Minahassa; K, Ka = Moluccans; O, Oa = Chinese; La = Other groups; J/S = Javanese/Sundanese; J/L = Javanese/Other; S/L = Sundanese/Other; C/L = Other/Other; R = Self; I = Indonesia; A = Jakarta.

have reported in the previous subsection. In this case we find for all groups, both inside and outside Jakarta, except for the Moluccans from Ambon, that the evaluation of own group is more positive than the evaluation of one's own group by other groups. In short 'we' always seem to have a more positive opinion of our own group than others have of 'us', but it is not always the case that 'we' have a more positive opinion of our own group than we have of other groups.

356   J.M.F. Jaspars & Suwarsih Warnaen

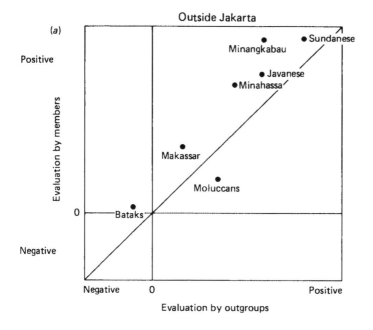

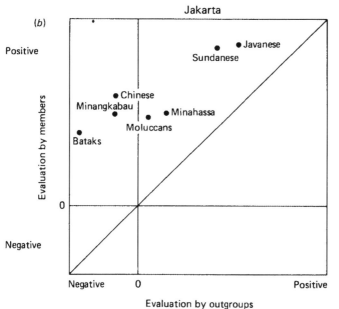

Figure 4. Relationship between evaluations of ingroup by members and by outgroups (data from Warnaen, 1979). (a) Groups outside Jakarta. (b) Groups in Jakarta

Also in line with the findings of the preliminary analyses we find that own group evaluations are clearly related to 'hetero' evaluations. The data for Jakarta and the provinces are presented separately in Figure 4.

As can be seen in Figure 4 there is an interesting difference between the result for Jakarta and the results for the groups outside Jakarta. In the latter case there is an almost perfect correlation between the two sets of evaluations ($\rho = 0.93$), whereas the correlation is $\rho = 0.71$ for the Jakarta data. In all cases except one, the evaluation of one's own group is more positive than the heteroevaluation, as we have seen already. Nevertheless there is more differentiation between these evaluations in Jakarta than for the groups outside Jakarta.Whereas the Javanese and Sundanese retain approximately the same positive evaluations in Jakarta as outside Jakarta, the Minakabau and the Minahassa are much less highly evaluated in Jakarta by both ingroup and outgroup members. The two groups with the lowest evaluations outside Jakarta (Bataks and Moluccans) also receive positive evaluations in Jakarta from other groups but their own group evaluations have become much more positive.

The explanation of this difference in intergroup evaluations can only be speculative at this moment, but it does not seem far-fetched to suppose that the lowest evaluation in Jakarta of all the groups which come from outside Java is related to the fact that Jakarta is more or less home territory for the Javanese and the Sundanese. The immigrant groups of Bataks and Moluccans seem to react to this treatment by raising the evaluation of their own group, but the evaluation of the Minahassa and the Minangkabau by the ingroup is lower in Jakarta. It is interesting to note, however, that all immigrants in Jakarta differentiate themselves much more strongly from other groups than the comparable groups in the provinces, whereas the Javanese and Sundanese show a small reverse effect with respect to each other and a slight increase in differentiation with respect to the minority groups. The differentiation in the latter case was already fairly strong as can be seen in Table 5.

In the analysis of the evaluative differentiation of ethnic groups we should also consider the self-evaluation of the individuals who constitute the various groups as we have suggested before, because it seems that people are sometimes willing to accept a negative image of their own group as long as they can differentiate their own self-image from the group stereotype.

In Figure 5 we have plotted the group-evaluations for the seven ethnic groups in Jakarta and outside Jakarta in combination with the self-evaluations.

358   J.M.F. Jaspars & Suwarsih Warnaen

Table 5. *Positive social differentiation between own and other ethnic groups in Indonesia (data from Warnaen, 1979)*

	Groups judging	Groups judged	
		Majority groups	Minority groups
Outside Jakarta	Majority groups	+0.60	+0.83
	Minority groups	−0.34	+0.17
Jakarta	Majority groups	+0.48	+1.02
	Minority groups	+0.08	+0.63

Scores range from −2 to +2. A positive score indicates that the own group receives a more positive evaluation than the other group; a negative indicates the reverse. Majority groups are Javanese and Sundanese. Minority groups are all other ethnic groups.

There is again, as we can see in Figure 5, a clear difference between the results for Jakarta and the results obtained outside Jakarta. It appears that for the latter groups the evaluation of the groups by the ingroup members follows fairly closely the evaluation by other groups, but the self-evaluation appears to be divorced from the group evaluation especially for the four lowest evaluated minority groups. In Jakarta the ingroup evaluation of the four lowest groups is, as was pointed out above, much more positive than the heterostereotype and more in line with the self-evaluation. However, it does not necessarily follow that the content of the stereotype of one's own group changes in the direction of the self description. If one compares directly the traits which are chosen in both cases it appears that there is about an equal amount of overlap for the two descriptions in the Jakarta sample and the sample from the provinces. Typically, the self-description includes a number of traits which are not included in the stereotype one has of one's own group. Thus the more positive social identity which is characteristic of the Jakarta sample does not develop because of the desocialization of the stereotype which becomes more individual. The change in content which accompanies the higher ingroup-evaluation appears to be of a different nature. This becomes clear when one compares the autostereotypes for those minority groups which have been tested both in Jakarta and outside Jakarta (Minangkabau, Batak, Minahassa and Moluccans). The typical change is one in which more traits disappear than are added. Overall, as is to be expected, the evaluative ratings of the traits which are added are slightly higher than the valence of the traits which disappear from the autostereotype (3.66 v 3.52). It is interesting to note, however, that quite a few positive traits also disappear

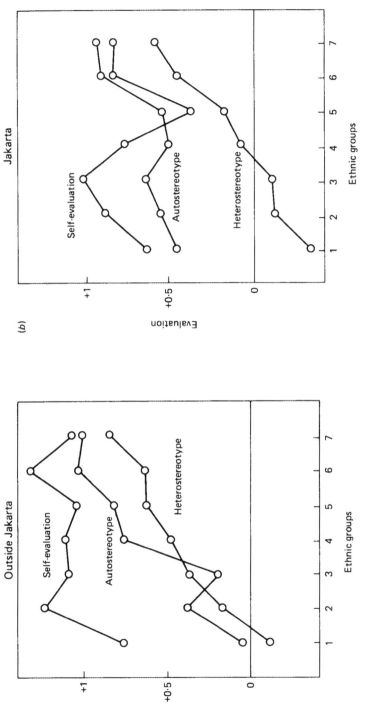

Figure 5. (a) Autostereotypes, heterostereotypes and self-evaluations for seven ethnic groups outside Jakarta. (b) Autostereotypes, heterostereotypes and self-evaluations for seven ethnic groups in Jakarta. (Data from Warnaen, 1979)

from the provincial stereotype, such as 'polite', 'friendly', 'honest' and 'hospitable' along with such 'primitive' traits as 'emotional', 'rowdy', 'slovenly', 'rude' and 'stubborn', and are replaced by traits like 'aggression', 'ambition', 'openness', 'imagination', etc.

We should not forget that the differences between the urban and the provincial samples are first of all relative differences, i.e. differences in comparison with the evaluation of one's own group by others. In fact in two of the groups (Minangkabau and Minahassa) the stronger positive differentiation is entirely relative since the autostereotypes in the urban samples are more negative than in the provincial samples, but the hetero-stereotypes change even more in the negative direction. In the case of the Bataks and the Moluccans the more positive differentiation in Jakarta is due both to more positive autostereotypes and more negative heterostereotypes.

Finally, it should be noted that in an absolute sense the self-evaluations of the individuals belonging to the various ethnic groups are significantly lower in Jakarta than outside Jakarta.

It is not easy to summarize these findings and it is even more difficult to give a precise interpretation. The main finding of the comparison between the urban and the provincial samples is that, in the former case, there is an increased evaluative differentiation between the various ethnic groups. This is mainly due to the fact that heterostereotypes become more negative which provides ingroup members with a more positive social identity in a relative sense. One possible interpretation of the pattern of results could be as follows: The dominant majority groups of Javanese and Sundanese appear to differentiate themselves in Jakarta more from the immigrant minority groups than they do outside Jakarta. This results in lower self-evaluation of minority group members, to which they in turn react by a more negative evaluation of outgroups. Consequently, there is a positive differentiation of one's own group which allows for the develop-ment of a positive social identity in a relative sense.

This interpretation seems to fit Tajfel's theory of intergroup relations quite well. But before this conclusion is drawn, we should consider whether the results can be understood by assuming that the Ss judgements mainly reflect a shared social representation of the Indonesian society modified perhaps by the differences in comparison level against which each ethnic group is evaluated. If Tajfel is correct in assuming that intergroup relations have, at least in part, the function of a search for a positive social identity, we would expect to find an intergroup effect over and above the social representation and social comparison effects mentioned above. In order to test this idea we have conducted an analysis of variance on the data presented

Table 6. *Analysis of variance of means of intergroup evaluations (data from Warnaen, 1979)*

Source of Variance	Jakarta				Outside Jakarta			
	SS	df	MS	$\hat{V}\%$	SS	df	MS	$\hat{V}\%$
Groups judged (social representation effect)	3.18	5	0.636	54	3.15	5	0.630	60
Groups judging (social comparison effect)	0.39	5	0.078	0	0.88	5	0.176	13
Residue (social differentiation effect)	2.00	25	0.080	46	1.17	25	0.047	28

$\hat{V}\%$ = Estimated variance components in percentages.
SS = Sum of squares
df = Degrees of freedom
MS = Mean square

in Table 4 for the six ethnic groups which are represented in the sample for Jakarta and outside Jakarta.[3] The results are presented in Table 6.

As can be seen in Table 6, by far the most important effect is the influence of the shared social representation of the relationship between the various groups. Apparently this factor is somewhat more important for the groups outside Jakarta, which indicates that comparison levels become more nearly equal when we move to a situation of closer cultural contact. The least important factor in understanding the overall pattern of intergroup evaluations is the process of positive social differentiation, if we can indeed interpret the residual term as such. This factor appears to be equally important in both samples but this is a somewhat misleading result. Although the interaction-error term is equally strong in both cases it is clear from inspection of the residual matrix that the deviations from row- and column-means show a clear pattern for the data in Jakarta but not in the case of the sample from outside Jakarta. In the Jakarta data the residual evaluations of the own group are always positive whereas in all cases except two the evaluations of other groups are negative, indicating a clear social differentiation in favour of the ingroup. For the data from the provinces we find a much less clear pattern with e.g. negative residual ingroup evaluation for the Moluccans and quite often positive evaluations of outgroups. One could argue, therefore, that the close cultural contact of the cosmopolitan environment of Jakarta brings about a stronger social differentiation but, as we have shown in the analysis above, by far the most important factor appears to be the view of the social structure shared by the various ethnic groups.

6. Conclusions

In this chapter we have argued that field studies of intergroup relations are of great significance both from a practical and from a theoretical point of view. For many (developing) countries relations between ethnic groups are of paramount importance for the achievement of a national identity and are therefore regarded as social problems urgently in need of research.

Classical theories of prejudice and discrimination have paid little attention to the relationship between such relations and problems of social identity. It is for this reason that Tajfel's theory of intergroup relations should be considered carefully because it is the only theory developed so far which deals explicitly with this relationship. However, only a few studies have been conducted which attempt to test some of Tajfel's ideas with natural groups outside the laboratory.

As Tajfel (1978) and others have shown, discrimination between social groups may arise under minimal conditions of interaction and interdependence: its function is to develop a positive social identity. With real groups, which occupy positions of unequal status in the social structure of which they are part, it is more difficult to show that discrimination may arise for similar reasons. (Evaluative) judgements about one's own (ethnic) and other (ethnic) groups may reflect the combined effect of a shared representation of the social structure and the group members' social comparison level which is itself a function of the position of the group in the social structure. It is argued that ingroup favouritism and outgroup discrimination which may arise in intergroup evaluations and perceptions should not be confused with the effect of a group's stable comparison level on intergroup judgements. Ingroup favouritism and outgroup discrimination represent an effect over and above the effect of the generalized comparison level, and can be conceived of as a change in such a comparison level when judgements of outgroups are made as compared with ingroup judgements. The greater discrepancy between evaluative judgements of in- and outgroup for groups of higher social status may therefore not be an indication of outgroup discrimination but simply of a different comparison level.

Whatever the reasons may be for comparatively negative evaluations, the effect of such judgements may be, as Tajfel has suggested, that group members will redefine, reinterpret and re-evaluate the unwelcome features which are ascribed to them by outgroups. It is conceivable, however, that group members will attempt to resolve a threat to their positive social identity by making a clear differentiation between their personal and their social identity.

The data presented in this chapter allow us to answer some of these questions at least in part. It was found first of all that significant differences existed in the perception of differences between ethnic groups in the cosmopolitan sample from Jakarta and a sample of Ss taken from the original locations of the ethnic groups in Indonesia. Perceived differences in Jakarta were larger, as one would expect on the basis of Tajfel's theory which suggests that saliency will increase perceived differences between groups. The perception of intergroup differences was overall, however, remarkably similar, indicating a strongly shared social representation.

The only group which appeared not to have a similar representation of intergroup relations in Indonesia was a group of subjects from a Chinese sample in Jakarta. In contrast to its perception by all other ethnic groups, this group did not perceive its own position as qualitatively different from other minority groups. In other words, the Chinese Ss appear to redefine their own position as similar to other national minorities rather than as a distinct (foreign) outgroup. The Chinese Ss also constituted the only ethnic group which clearly rejected the unwelcome features assigned to them by other groups. All other groups appeared to accept unwelcome features as part of the stereotype of their own group, but individuals typically rejected such features as part of their own self-descriptions. One possible interpretation of this finding is that for all own groups (except the Chinese) such negative characteristics were relatively rare and hence did not pose a threat to one's social identity. By denying these features as part of one's own self-image one can still maintain a positive self-concept and at the same time benefit from the overall positive identification with the group.

The crucial results of the present study pertain, however, to the differential evaluative judgements of the various ethnic groups, both in Jakarta and in the provinces. It appeared that in both cases groups do not necessarily evaluate outgroups more negatively than their own group. They do however, in general, have a more positive view of themselves than other groups have of them. Analysis of variance shows that these effects are to a large extent the result of a shared view of the relations between ethnic groups in Indonesia. In the sample of groups outside Jakarta (groups which have little direct contact with each other) differences in comparison level appear to play some role in the intergroup judgements. In Jakarta, however, we see that virtually all the remaining variance can be explained by ingroup favouritism and outgroup discrimination, when one estimates the variance components in the population. These results suggest that Tajfel's theory is indeed, as he suggested (Tajfel, 1978), more relevant when intergroup relations become more salient, as one might expect they are in an urban environment like Jakarta. When there is virtually no direct social contact as in our non-urban samples, it appears that intergroup judgements reflect much more a shared view of the social structure which is somewhat modified by differences in standard of comparison, but is less affected by problems of positive social differentiation since there is no direct confrontation with other ethnic groups. These results cast, therefore, serious doubt upon the value of classical stereotype studies, which very often are concerned with the description of groups which are not in direct contact with each other. Our analysis suggests that it may not be appropriate to predict what will happen when such groups are brought into contact with each other through increased urbanization. This becomes even clearer when we take into account, not only the group-evaluations, but also the self-evaluations which were made by the Ss in both cases. Comparing the results obtained in Jakarta and outside we see that the self-evaluations in Jakarta are significantly lower than for the groups outside Jakarta. This is especially true for the minority groups. What could have caused this change? The data suggest that this difference is not due to a change in social identity since the evaluative autostereotypes remain virtually the same for both majority and minority groups. There is, however, a significant change in heterostereotypes which is almost identical to the change in self-evaluation. The explanation of this apparent relationship is difficult since the change in heterostereotype can be both cause and effect of the change in self-evaluation. Group members who are discriminated against in Jakarta may develop a lower self-evaluation, which may lead to a lower evaluation of outgroups, i.e. a more negative heterostereotype, in order to maintain the positive social identity in a comparative sense. Such an explanation would be very similar to the one offered by Turner (1978) on the basis of experimental data. However, the present data do not allow us to conclude with certainty whether this explanation is valid in the present study. Only a field study which would include differences in time might possibly resolve this issue. We hope to have shown, however, that even with such complex data as we have presented here, it is to some extent possible to arrive at conclusions which have some theoretical relevance and are at the same time potentially of genuine social significance.

Notes

[1] We hesitate to present the results of the stereotype study as a strict test of Tajfel's theory, because the data were not collected for that purpose. It is even questionable whether a test of the theory is possible with data obtained in what is essentially a descriptive field study. We do believe, however, that the theory is capable of rendering the results intelligible, something which goes beyond most survey studies of social stereotypes.

[2] Opposite results were obtained by Branthwaite and Jones (1975) for English and Welsh students at the University of Cardiff but in this study there is good reason to believe that the higher status group (the English students) consisted of selected students who were probably already positively disposed towards the 'outgroup' as Eiser (1980) has pointed out.

[3] We have some doubt about the legitimacy of calculating variance components in this particular case, since it is not clear to which population of ethnic groups one is generalizing. If we define the population as the existing ethnic groups in Indonesia, and especially Jakarta, it is obvious that the seven groups we have included in our analysis constitute a very large part of the existing population since they are numerically the largest groups. Whatever the case may be, it is clear from the results, even if one only considers the mean squares, that social comparison processes are more important than the social differentiation effect in the rural sample whereas the converse is true in the urban sample. The variance component analysis brings out this difference more clearly.

References

Billig, M. 1976. *Social psychology and intergroup relations.* European Monographs in Social Psychology, No. 9. London: Academic Press.

Billig, M. and Tajfel, H. 1973. Social categorization and similarity in intergroup behaviour. *European Journal of Social Psychology*, **3**, 27–52.

Branthwaite, A. and Jones, J. 1975. Fairness and discrimination: English versus Welsh. *European Journal of Social Psychology*, **5**, 323–38.

Bruner, E.M. 1972. *The expression of ethnicity in Indonesia.* Seadag Papers. New York: The Asian Society.

Carroll, J.D. and Chang, J.J. 1970. Analysis of individual differences in multi-dimensional scaling via an *N*-way generalization of Eckert–Young decomposition. *Psychometrika*, **35**, 283–319.

Codol, J.P. 1975. On the so called 'Superior Conformity of the Self': twenty experimental investigations. *European Journal of Social Psychology*, **5**, 457–501.

Coombs, C.H. 1964. *A theory of data.* New York: Wiley.

Doise, W. and Sinclair, A. 1973. The categorization process in intergroup relations. *European Journal of Social Psychology*, **3**, 145–57.

Eiser, J.R. 1980. *Cognitive social psychology.* London: McGraw Hill.

Gerard, H.B. and Hoyt, M.F. 1974. Distinctiveness of social categorization and attitude toward ingroup members. *Journal of Personality and Social Psychology*, **29**, 836–42.

Katz, D. and Braly, K. 1933. Racial stereotypes of one hundred college students. *Journal of Abnormal and Social Psychology*, **28**, 280–90.

366   J.M.F. Jaspars & Suwarsih Warnaen

Kennedy, R. 1974. *Bibliography of Indonesian peoples and cultures*. New Haven, Connecticut: Yale University Press. South East Asia Studies, 2nd revised edition.
van Knippenberg, A. 1978*a*. Perception and evaluation of intergroup differences. Unpublished Ph.D. thesis, University of Leiden.
van Knippenberg, A. 1978*b*. Status differences, comparative relevance and intergroup differentiation. In H. Tajfel (ed.), *op. cit.*
Koentjaraningrat. 1975. *Anthropology in Indonesia: A bibliographical review*. The Hague: Nijhoff.
LeVine, R.A. and Campbell, D.T. 1972. *Ethnocentrism: Theories of conflict, ethnic attitudes and group behaviour*. New York: Wiley.
Moscovici, S. and Paicheler, G. 1978. Social comparison and social recognition: Two complementary processes of identification. In H. Tajfel (ed.): *Differentiation between social groups: Studies in the social psychology of intergroup relations*. European Monographs in Social Psychology, No. 14. London: Academic Press.
Tajfel, H. (ed.) 1978. *Differentiation between social groups: Studies in the social psychology of intergroup relations*. European Monographs in Social Psychology, No. 14. London: Academic Press.
Tajfel, H., Flament, C., Billig, M. and Bundy, R. 1971. Social categorization and intergroup behaviour. *European Journal of Social Psychology*, **1**, 149–75.
Taylor, D.M., Simard, L.M. and Aboud, F.E. 1972. Ethnic identification in Canada: A cross-cultural investigation. *Canadian Journal of Behavioural Science/Rev. Canad. Sci. Comp.*, **4**, 1.
Triandis, H. 1972. *Analysis of subjective culture*. New York: Wiley.
Turner, J.C. 1975. Social comparison and social identity: Some prospects for intergroup behaviour. *European Journal of Social Psychology*, **5**, 5–34.
Turner, J.C. 1978. Social categorization and social discrimination in the minimal group paradigm. In H. Tajfel (ed.), *op. cit.*
Turner, J.C. and Brown, R.J. 1978. Social status, cognitive alternatives and intergroup relations. In H. Tajfel (ed.), *op. cit.*
Turner, J.C., Brown, R.J. and Tajfel, H. 1979. Social comparison and group interest in ingroup favouritism. *European Journal of Social Psychology*, **9**, 187–204.
van Vollenhoven, C. 1918/1933. *The adat law of the Netherlands–Indies*. Leiden: Brill, Vols. I–III.
Warnaen, S. 1979. Steretip etnik di dalam Suatu Bangsa Multietnik. Unpublished Ph.D. Thesis, University of Indonesia.

13. The Swedish-speaking Finns: A case study of ethnolinguistic identity

KARMELA LIEBKIND

1 The Swedish-speaking Finns

(a) Ethnolinguistic vitality of a minority group

Howard Giles describes the ethnolinguistic vitality of a minority group as something that helps ethnolinguistic communities to survive and makes the whole group likely to behave as a distinct collective entity in intergroup situations (Giles et al., 1977, p308). According to Giles, there are at least three kinds of variables supporting the overall vitality of a group: (A) status variables; (B) demographic variables; and (C) variables of institutional support.

In the following sections, the vitality of the Swedish-speaking population in Finland will be examined in reference to this taxonomy. Of special social psychological interest in this case are the status variables, which will be analysed in greater detail than the others.

$A1$, economic status, refers to the group's degree of control over its own economic destiny. If a minority group is economically exploited by a majority group, the vitality of the former is severely restricted. $A2$, social status, refers to the degree of esteem ascribed to the group in general. This has consequences for the self-esteem of the group. If low, it saps the group's morale, and if high, it bolsters morale (Giles et al., 1977, p310). $A3$, socio-historical status, is of special importance in the case of the Swedish-speaking Finns, as will later become evident. Historical events can be used as mobilizing symbols to inspire individuals to bind together in the present. But if these events are lacking, or if they are only of a demobilizing nature, people tend to neglect or hide their linguistic identity, thereby diluting the vitality of the group as a collective entity (Giles et al., 1977, p311).

After a short excursion into the meaning of $A4$, the other variables ($A1$, $A2$ and $A3$) will be examined in greater detail in subsequent sections.

A taxonomy of the structural variables affecting
ethnolinguistic vitality

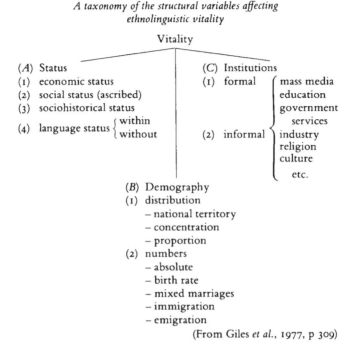

(From Giles *et al.*, 1977, p 309)

(b) The prestige value of the Swedish language in Finland

$A4$, status of the language itself, is a complicated question and also of special relevance to the present case. Minorities who speak an international language of high status are advantaged compared to those who speak a language with less prestige value. But within the boundaries of a certain territory – a commune, a country – the respective status of the languages used can be reversed. The prestige value of a language can be said to determine in part whether the language is a source of pride or of shame for its user (Giles *et al.*, 1977, p312).

According to Giles, speech accommodation is a means of expressing values, attitudes and intentions towards another person. Social approval and disapproval is communicated by a shift towards or away from the other person's language, called convergence and divergence respectively. Generally, the more the other's approval is desired, the more a person converges – upwards, if the other speaks a high-status language, and downwards, if the other speaks a low-status language. Of course, up to a certain point convergence is totally dependent upon sufficient language ability. But divergence away from the other's language can also be used by linguistic groups as a tactic for showing that the other's approval is not necessary and not wanted. In a sense, divergence as a strategy explicitly communicates pride in one's own language (Giles *et al.*, 1977).

The linguistic behaviour of Swedish-speaking and Finnish-speaking Finns in interaction with each other tends to vary according to whether it takes place in unilingual Swedish or bilingual areas. An increasing proportion of Swedish-speaking Finns live in a bilingual environment. In bilingual areas, some general tendencies have been discerned: Finnish is usually spoken even when the majority of the company is Swedish-speaking, and Swedish-speaking and Finnish-speaking persons who are both bilingual tend to speak Finnish together (Grönroos, 1978). It is not likely that these language shifts are due to practical reasons or ability only. Until very recently Finns have learnt Swedish in secondary school as their second domestic language (cf. the legislative situation, p371). As Giles has pointed out, language shifts are also dependent on attitudes towards the language and its speakers. A general reluctance on the part of the Finns to speak Swedish in Swedish-speaking company seems to be accompanied by a readiness on the part of the Swedish-speaking Finns to use Finnish as soon as ability permits. The situation becomes different when both interacting persons are unilingual. But even then various degrees of convergence and divergence are possible.

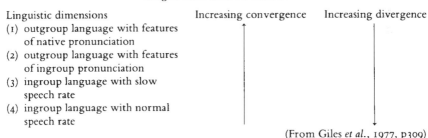

Variants of convergence and divergence in a
bilingual communicative situation

Linguistic dimensions	Increasing convergence	Increasing divergence
(1) outgroup language with features of native pronunciation		
(2) outgroup language with features of ingroup pronunciation		
(3) ingroup language with slow speech rate		
(4) ingroup language with normal speech rate		

(From Giles *et al.*, 1977, p309)

In this way, attitudes towards the outgroup language and its user can be communicated by varying the pronunciation of outgroup language or the speech rate of ingroup language. So far, this kind of communicative study has not been carried out in Finland, but the strategies above may represent a natural continuation of the tendencies discerned in communicative situations mentioned earlier, where both parties are bilingual.

Another clue to the overall prestige value of the Swedish language in

Finland is the language retention rate of Swedish in mixed marriages. The more prestige value Swedish has, the higher this rate is. However, only 39 % of the children in bilingual families in Finland become Swedish-speaking. In spite of the small size of the Swedish-speaking minority in Finland, this language retention rate seems to reflect general attitudes towards Swedish as well as an objective minority situation. This will become even more evident when the other status variables which obviously influence the status of the language itself are examined.

(c) 'The Swedo – Finns': definition and number

There are two main language groups in Finland, a Finnish-speaking majority and a Swedish-speaking minority. The official calculations of the size of the Swedish-speaking minority are based on decennial population censuses, in which the citizens are simply asked to report their main language. No alternative answer (for instance, bilingualism) is available.

Naturally, the number of Swedish Finns varies according to the operational definition adopted. It has been noted that the number of the answers 'Swedish' increases by 5 % when the term 'mother tongue' is used instead of 'main language' (Schalin, 1977). In a study carried out in 1969, the number of Swedish-speaking Finns, bilinguals and Finnish-speaking Finns was calculated in three communities. A comparison of these results with the census of 1970 leads to the conclusion that almost all bilinguals in these communities must have reported Finnish as their main language in the census (Sandlund, 1970, pp22–3, *Population Census* 1970, XVII A, pp42–65).

The census can thus be said to apply a 'minimum principle' to the definition of the Swedish-speaking population of Finland. In contrast, the definition of a Sámi (also called Lapp) in the 1970 census includes those who have had at least one parent or grandparent who has learnt Sámi as his first language, as well as those who have themselves learnt Sámi as their first language.

According to the 1970 census, the Swedish-speaking minority accounts for 6.6 % of the total population in Finland. There has been a slow decline in this proportion both over the centuries and during the last decades.

The main reasons for the decline have been the following:
(i)   emigration, primarily to Sweden and primarily during the last decades. Emigration has been considerably higher among the Swedish-speaking than among the Finnish-speaking Finns;
(ii)   lower birth rates than in the general population;

Table 1. *The Swedish-speaking population in Finland 1610–1975 (From Fougstedt, 1951, Klövekorn, 1960, Forsberg, 1975, Allardt, 1977)*

Year	Number	As percentage of the total population	Source based on
1610	73 000	17.5	estimates
1749	87 200	16.3	estimates
1815	160 000	14.6	estimates
1880	294 900	14.3	parish registers
1890	322 000	13.6	parish registers
1900	349 000	12.9	parish registers
1910	339 000	11.6	parish registers
1920	341 000	11.0	parish registers
1930	342 900	10.1	parish registers
1940	354 000	9.5	parish registers
1950	348 300	8.6	population census
1960	330 500	7.4	population census
1970	303 400	6.6	population census
1975	302 700	6.4	Population and Housing Census,* 1975

*Hereafter abbreviated *PHC*.

(iii) a high rate of intermarriage, with the result that the children adopt Finnish more often than Swedish as their main language;

(iv) language shifts due to entry into an entirely Finnish-speaking environment (Allardt, 1977, cf. p90).

(d) Formal institutional support of the Swedish language

According to Finland's Constitution Act of 1919, Finnish and Swedish are the national languages of the Republic of Finland. In this Act, the general principle of equality of the two main languages was established. The practical legal applications are given mainly in the Language Act of 1922, as amended in 1935, 1962 and 1975. The basic unit of language policy is the primary unit of local government, the commune. Communes can be officially bilingual, although individuals cannot. The basic rule is that a commune is unilingual (Finnish or Swedish) if the minority (Swedish-speaking or Finnish-speaking respectively) either constitutes less than 8 % of the population or is composed of less than 3000 persons. If the minority exceeds the 8 % level or 3000 persons, the commune is regarded as bilingual. There are some additional rules applied when the proportions of the language groups are changing: bilingual communes do not become unilingual unless the minority falls below 6 % and unilingual communes do not become bilingual until the minority reaches 12 % (Allardt, 1977; Miemois, 1978).

The linguistic status of the commune has consequences for local administration as well as for larger administrative units in which the communes are included. The linguistic status of each commune is reviewed after each decennial census, which, despite its ambiguity, is the only source for calculation of the size of the language groups. At the beginning of 1976, the linguistic status of the communes was as follows:

Table 2. *The linguistic status of communes in Finland (From Statistical Yearbook of Finland, 1975, p11)*

	Urban	Rural	Total
Unilingual Swedish communes	1	28	29
Bilingual communes	17	25	42
Unilingual Finnish communes	67	337	404
	85	390	475

The Swedish and the bilingual communes are all located on the southern, south-western and western coasts of Finland and in the Åland Islands. It should be stressed that the choice of main language contains a clear subjective element which makes the choice basically a question of subjective identity. However, the language identification issue is related to domestic cleavages only, in the sense that the national identity of the Swedish-speaking Finns is tied to Finland and not to Sweden. Internationally, Swedish-speaking Finns are Finns. There is a clear identification with Swedish as their mother tongue and with Finland as their homeland (Allardt, 1977).

(e) Demographic factors influencing the overall vitality of the Swedish-speaking minority in Finland

As was noted above, several factors account for the decrease of the Swedish-speaking population. Here they are examined in greater detail.

(i) *Emigration*: According to various estimates, 20–25 % of the 250 000 persons who have moved from Finland to Sweden since World War II are Swedish-speaking Finns. The hope of a better standard of living is part of the motivation of all emigrants, but an already-existing knowledge of

Table 3. *The Swedish-speaking population in Finland according to the linguistic status of their home communes (From Broo, 1978)*

The linguistic status of the commune	Number of persons			As percentage of the total Swedish-speaking population in Finland		
	1950	1960	1970	1950	1960	1970
Unilingual Swedish	92 822	79 943	69 540	26.6	24.2	23.0
Bilingual:						
Swedish majority						
– Finns < 1/3	85 982	67 443	50 732	24.7	20.4	16.7
– Finns > 1/3	33 160	53 722	45 246	9.5	16.2	14.9
Finnish majority						
– Swedes > 1/3	27 847	1 905	24 978	8.0	0.6	8.2
– Swedes < 1/3	93 786	115 978	103 855	27.0	35.1	34.2
Unilingual Finnish	14 689	11 547	9 055	4.2	3.5	3.0
Total	348 286	330 538	303 406	100.0	100.0	100.0

Swedish is certainly an accelerating factor in making the final decision to move to Sweden, especially if skill in Finnish is bad as well. (ii) *Low birth rates*: Especially in earlier decades, there was a much lower birth rate among the Swedish-speaking than among the Finnish-speaking Finns, and this has had a clear effect on the age structure of the group. The fact that the usual emigrant is young also adds to the lopsided age-structure. (iii) *Mixed marriages*: Intermarriage is increasing, but it is still rarer than can be expected on the basis of purely random selection. It has been clearly demonstrated that the dominant language of the community has a decisive influence on the choice of language in bilingual families. It has been estimated that approximately 11.1 % of the Swedish-speaking Finns live in bilingual families, and only 39.2 % of the children born in these families become Swedish-speaking. This language retention rate is to some extent influenced by the education of the parents. But generally, the more Finnish the commune, the more probable are intermarriages, and the more probable it is that children of bilingual families become unilingual Finns. (iv) *Language shifts*: Language shifts over a lifetime occur when people enter completely Finnish environments, usually through the labour market. This effect on the decrease of the Swedish-speaking Finns seems to be smaller than the effect of intermarriage (Allardt, 1977; Grönroos, 1978; Broo, 1978; Reitz, 1974).

Considering the facts presented above, the future of the Swedish-speaking minority in Finland seems to be closely connected to problems encountered in bilingual or Finnish environments. The fact that, by now, more than 75 % of all Swedish-speaking people in Finland live in bilingual or Finnish communes cannot be ignored.

(f) Status and support in an historical perspective

Historians are not unanimous in regard to the date of the first Swedish settlement in Finland. According to some, there was a population movement from the west as early as between the 5th and the 9th centuries AD. This can be stated as a certainty only for the Åland Islands. It is certain that Swedish settlement occurred before and during the 13th century in connection with Swedish crusades and with the colonization of Finland. Since that time there have been two historically important and distinct parts to the Swedish-speaking minority in Finland: the rural part, consisting of farmers, fishermen and persons engaged in coastal shipping on the southern and western coasts of Finland, and the upper classes, which earlier consisted of the higher estates of the bourgeoisie and the nobility in the country. The stability of the borderline between the Swedish-speaking and the Finnish-speaking communities in Finland has been remarkable. It is only in the 20th century that the language borders in the countryside have blurred.

From the time of the Swedish colonization to the last decades of the 19th century, the ruling class of Finland was Swedish-speaking. Contrary to the Swedish-speaking rural population, over the centuries this class was recruited from several different groups: (1) officials, merchants, military officers and nobles moving from Sweden to Finland; (2) upwardly mobile individuals from the Finnish-speaking peasantry who, by moving into the upper classes, had to adopt Swedish as their language; (3) upwardly mobile individuals from the Swedish-speaking peasantry; and (4) merchants and artisans from all over the Baltic regions who, for one reason or another, settled in Finland and because of their position adopted the Swedish language (Allardt, 1977). However, the great majority of the Swedish-speaking Finns had little or no contact with the political and economic elite. Up to the last decade of the 19th century, language was no basis for social bonds between the two distinct parts of the Swedish-speaking population. In contrast, Finnish nationalism became a social force in the middle of the 19th century. The so-called Fennocization movement, which demanded equal rights for the Finnish language, and later on at times complete Fennocization, was originally created and led by members of the upper classes who at the time were Swedish-speaking. In this way, the rights and interests of the Swedish-speaking rural population tended to be overlooked, for instance in the area of primary education (Allardt, 1977; Broo, 1978).

Nationalism as a popular movement among the Swedish-speaking Finns thus started as a reaction to the Finnish nationalist popular movement, and it resulted in a unification of the Swedish bourgeoisie and the Swedish lower classes. This tendency towards unification has been reflected in many ways in the cultural and practical life of the Swedish Finns. The political expression of this tendency has been the Swedish People's Party which, according to various estimates, has been given around 75 % of the Swedish votes throughout the years (Allardt, 1977).

2. The interaction between horizontal and vertical interests

(a) The socio-economic status of the minority group

It should be quite clear from the foregoing that the Swedish-speaking upper class has played a crucial role in Finnish history. It remained in a dominant position throughout the Russian annexation, 1809–1917, and thus was still the dominant class when industrialization and other great social changes began at the end of the 19th century. Members of this group acted as leaders in these developments and also acquired important roles in new social sectors (university education, culture, etc.) (Allardt, 1977).

It is therefore easy to see how the misconception of Swedish-speakers as generally and exclusively upper class was born. But the fact is that the main body of the Swedish Finns never did, and does not now, belong to the upper classes. The majority of the Swedish-speaking population has always had manual occupations in farming, fishing, transportation and industry. It would be wrong to infer from the historical background that Swedish-speakers today are strongly overrepresented in the upper classes. There is no rationale for speaking about a 'cultural division of labour' in this context, as the Finnish-speaking majority dominates all social strata (Miemois, 1978, p25). The Finnish-speaking population has very rapidly become culturally, politically, socially and economically mobilized. In the following table the Swedish-speaking population is divided into socio-economic groups on the basis of both occupational status and type of industry:

Table 4. *The Swedish-speaking and the total population in Finland by socio-economic groups in 1970 (From Forsberg, 1975, p39)*

Socio-economic groups	Swedish-speaking population (%)	Total population (%)
Employers	3.6	3.2
– in agriculture	1.2	1.1
– other	2.4	2.1
Self-employed entrepreneurs	16.3	16.0
– in agriculture	12.9	13.1
– other	3.4	2.9
Managerial, administrative and professional occupations	11.3	6.9
Clerical and related occupations	20.9	17.8
Skilled workers	21.7	31.9
– in agriculture	1.7	2.6
– others	20.5	28.8
Unskilled workers	4.3	6.8
Pensioners	20.2	16.3
Students	1.5	1.4
Unknown	0.3	0.2

It is obvious that the lower strata composed of workers, farmers and lower white-collar workers form the majority in both the Swedish and the Finnish-speaking population. However, it is also true that the workers are underrepresented while both higher and lower white collar occupations are overrepresented among the Swedish Finns. In any case, the Swedish-speaking population no longer dominates the elite and does not show upper-class characteristics. If anything, the socio-economic difference of Swedish-speaking Finns lies in their slight overrepresentation in the middle class. Looking at statistics of the occupational structure of the Swedish-speaking population, it can be noted that it is somewhat overrepresented in commerce and transportation, which fits its middle-class socio-economic features. This has an historical–geographical explanation. The first towns were established on the southern and western coasts of Finland, because this facilitated transportation and commerce. These areas were Swedish-speaking, and so parts of the Swedish-speaking population became urbanized earlier than the Finnish-speaking population. This is also reflected in the average educational level, which is slightly higher in the Swedish-speaking minority than in the Finnish-speaking majority. In both groups, however, the majority has completed elementary school only (Allardt, 1977; Broo, 1978; Schalin, 1976).

Despite the observable differences, the most striking feature when comparing the social stratification of the Swedish-speaking population with that of the Finnish-speaking population, is in the structural similarities between the two language groups (Miemois, 1978). The primary reasons for the tenacious retention in Finland of the popular stereotype of the Swedish-speaking minority as an upper-class population must be sought more in the historical symbol value of this image than primarily in statistical facts. The memory of the necessity in the past for Finns to adopt the Swedish language in upward social mobility does not fade away as quickly as the objective cultural, political, social and economic mobility of the Finnish-speaking population actually has taken place. Once a stereotype based on the perceived differences between two groups is firmly established, even a minor existing difference will suffice for its maintenance or revival (Campbell, 1967).

(b) The effect of the subjective assessment of vitality on objective vitality

People want to belong to groups which give them satisfaction and pride. If group membership offers more shame than pride, more discomfort than satisfaction, attempts at leaving the group are undertaken (Tajfel, 1978). A very effective strategy of maintaining a positive social identity within a specific linguistic minority is involvement in direct competition with the majority group on control over linguistic affairs. In this way, cultural pluralism is actively fought for, and the accommodative process becomes in itself a way to a satisfactory social identity. Competition issues may be concerned with e.g. the control over mass media (number of TV channels, hours on the air, etc.), education (number of schools, school levels, unilingual v bilingual educational institutions, etc.), and the provision of unilingual and bilingual facilities in services (both governmental and private). All these issues have been relevant to the political process involving the Swedish-speaking minority in Finland, although strong disagreements within the minority as to which claims are the most urgent are not infrequent.

However, direct competition on specific language issues is possible only when the overall vitality of a linguistic minority is experienced as high, i.e. when the minority feels secure. If minority members experience the vitality of their group as low, no direct challenge to the majority group can be afforded without fear of losing previously achieved privileges. A subjective assessment of the group's vitality by its members may thus be as important as its objective vitality. It therefore becomes clear that the information about objective vitality factors reaching both majority and minority members through the mass media can be manipulated according to the interests of the communicators, either to support or to attenuate the perception of the minority group's vitality (Giles *et al.*, 1977).

Historically, it can be assumed that no cultural group whose majority represents the upper classes can survive very long, i.e. cultures based primarily on the dominant position of members in society are likely to vanish along with historical development. It was noted previously that the popular stereotype of the Swedish-speaking population distorts its factual class composition for obvious historical reasons. Consequently, a strengthening of the popular image of this minority group will only have demobilizing effects on all those minority members who realize that the future vitality of their group is dependent on its broad class composition.

In analysing the strategies available for mass media communicators to maintain outgroup images intact, Husband (1977) states that one of the most important criteria for selecting news about minority groups seems to be the notion of consonance. In this context it means that events will be selected for news reporting in terms of their agreement or consonance with pre-existing images – the news of the event will conform to earlier ideas (Husband, 1977, p217). There is some evidence that the Finnish press follows this pattern by tending to support the stereotype of the Swedish-speaking population in Finland and to give a very gloomy picture of its future (see e.g. Professor Allardt's comment in *Helsingin Sanomat*, Jan. 5, 1978 on this matter).

Whenever the presented historical symbols of a minority group are experienced as negative, a psychological need to hide the linguistic identity may be created. This, in turn, actually dilutes the vitality of the group as a collective entity and factually contributes to its extinction by increasing subjective motivation to leave the group whenever possible (Giles *et al.*, 1977). Considering the manifold consequences for the objective vitality of the whole Swedish-speaking minority of, for example, an easy switch in official linguistic identification in the decennial censuses, the prevailing stereotypes cannot be neglected.

(c) Objective vitality and linguistic orientations

The objective vitality of the Swedish-speaking population in Finland is high in institutional support but decreasing in demographic variables and very ambiguous in status variables because of the distinct historical backgrounds of the separate Swedish-speaking subgroups.

The Swedish-speaking population in Finland is represented both in developed and in underdeveloped areas of the country (Miemois, 1978). The problem of emigration is most acute in the less developed rural areas along the western coast, whereas the Fennocization problem is more relevant in the densely populated, industrialized and urbanized south. The rural areas along the coast are also traditionally the most unilingual Swedish ones, while the Swedish-speaking population in the coastal towns has experienced a bilingual environment for a longer period of time. Swedish-speaking groups living in rural and urban unilingual Swedish and bilingual (or totally Finnish) communes in the more peripheral areas of Finland, or close to the capital, in upper or lower socio-economic classes etc., are bound to have very different objective problems of vitality (*Samhällsforskning*, 1977).

For the rural Swedish areas the survival of the traditional livelihoods – fishing and agriculture – directly influences the vitality of the Swedish-speaking population. However, whenever the old occupations have to be replaced by new industrial ones, the lack of knowledge of Finnish so typical of these unilingual Swedish areas becomes a severe problem. It is impossible to succeed in the labour market in Finland with Swedish only. Naturally, the demands presented from these areas are concerned with very concrete survival questions common to all inhabitants of underdeveloped areas, as far as the economic development of the area is concerned. As a result of the primarily unilingual Finnish labour market, the specific linguistic demands from these unilingual Swedish areas tend to emphasize the *right to learn Finnish properly* whenever industrialization is advocated (e.g. Olof Granholm in *Folktidningen Ny Tid* – hereafter abbreviated *FNT* – Jan. 5, 1978). This linguistic demand thus arises from an emphasis on *social equality* between the language groups.

Looking at the situation of the Swedish-speaking Finns in the industrialized, urbanized and bilingual or Finnish areas, the problems of vitality become different. Language loyalty breeds in contact and it becomes salient when linguistic identity is threatened (Giles *et al.*, 1977, p329). With increasing bilingualism the right and motivation to *maintain the Swedish language* becomes the crucial question. This linguistic demand has its roots in a quest for *cultural pluralism* (cf. p11, *FNT* leading article, April 13, 1978; Grönroos, 1978).

Although a fairly large percentage of the Swedish Finns still live in predominantly Swedish communes, the general social development (and bad regional planning) is rapidly increasing the percentage of Swedish Finns living in bilingual or Finnish environments. It therefore seems crucial to investigate the possibilities for the Swedish language to survive in

Finland. If the bilingualism created by the general social development is detractive, it will not prevail but, instead, it constitutes an intermediate stage towards Finnish unilingualism (Skutnabb-Kangas, 1978).

Those who emphasize the territorial criteria as the crucial one for the vitality of the Swedish-speaking population in Finland tend to view bilingualism in this way, as an intermediate stage. According to this view, only a strong regional bond can preserve conditions for survival of the minority (Sandlund, 1976; Salmén, 1976). Others argue that linguistic criteria are the most crucial ones, and that it is quite possible to remain fluently bilingual and to maintain bilingualism in generations to come if there is enough motivation to do so. In this perspective the survival of the Swedish-speaking minority is totally dependent on the retention of Swedish as a living language in Finland. In turn, these conditions could be fostered, for instance by ending the view of Swedish as a language reserved exclusively for minority members, and by making allowances for an official bilingual identity in the decennial censuses. But even this proposal finds its opponents, primarily among unilingual Swedes from rural areas who want to maintain the identity of the Swedish-speaking population in Finland intact (Grönroos, 1978).

(d) The consequences of competing loyalties

The overall situation of the Swedish-speaking minority gives rise to a number of disagreements within the minority group as to which vitality factors have priority in the political process. These conflicts are also reflected in the culture of the group as a whole. According to some external evaluations, the culture of the Swedish-speaking population seems very much alive at the moment, but the exceptional ideological heterogeneity so typical of it seems to reflect regional and social contrasts, and splinters this already small language group into different camps.

This, of course, is detrimental to the objective vitality of the group and makes it vulnerable to any manipulative strategies from outside aiming at directing the development of the minority in one direction or another. The subjective position taken by individuals and groups is decisive for membership in any ethnic group, and especially for the Swedish-speaking minority in Finland. Within this group it is evident that the various levels of consciousness (Sandlund, 1976) can become easy targets for competing external influences. There is also enough disagreement within the minority to set the stage for ambivalent identifications.

So far salience and primacy of ethnic allegiance, for the great majority of the Swedish-speaking Finns, has implied voting for the Swedish People's

Party. Structural and ideological changes in Finnish society have, however, made this fact a matter of controversy. As was previously seen (see Table 4), the lower socio-economic strata form the majority of the Swedish-speaking population as well as of the Finnish-speaking population. As the political structure of Finland is characterized by an approximately equal proportion of socialist and non-socialist representation in Parliament, and as the Swedish People's Party is classified as a non-socialist one close to the centre, it becomes clear that the salience of class aspects above ethnic allegiances for a majority of Swedish-speaking Finns could imply a reluctance to vote for a non-socialist party. In this way, membership in the Swedish-speaking minority is made a direct target for public potential competition.

Considering that the prevailing stereotype of the minority distorts its real class composition, and that this interacts with the cross pressures created by the political constellations described above, it is no wonder that an activation of class aspects in most of the minority causes a strong escape mechanism in which minority membership has to be denied or undermined. This becomes likely despite the fact that the simultaneous aims of social equality and cultural pluralism as such are not in conflict with each other. It can thus be assumed that the assimilation of Swedish-speaking Finns into the Finnish population is at its strongest in the lower social classes in bilingual or Finnish communes. A recent survey in the Helsinki region actually shows that it is the working class which, more than other classes, changes its linguistic identity from Swedish to Finnish (Miemois, 1978, p24).

These lower social classes are likely to experience the highest simultaneous salience of language loyalty and class solidarity and thus the strongest cross-pressure. The identity conflicts arising from this situation seem to reduce individual motivation to retain bilingualism and minority identification, and the resulting assimilation thus acquires strong escapist features. This biased development could, in the end, produce just the kind of linguistic minority which the majority group always believed it to be – upper class. All other minority members, in this case, could become motivated to assimilate or emigrate. This would exemplify only too well the old notion of the self-fulfilling prophecy.

3. An empirical study of intergroup identification

(a) The commune of Pyhtää: 'The outpost in the east'

The provinces in which the Swedish-speaking population lives in Finland are very different in both degree and nature of development. They cannot be treated as a whole. The scattered pattern of residence clearly favours the use of case studies as a principal method of research on the Swedish-speaking population in Finland (Miemois, 1978).

The commune of Pyhtää is located in the unilingual Finnish province of Kymi, on the coast of the Bay of Finland. Pyhtää is the easternmost of all unilingual Swedish and bilingual communes in Finland. This commune is still officially bilingual, but the Swedish-speaking population does not exceed one-third of the total population of Pyhtää. Although the largest percentage of the Swedish-speaking Finns live in communes with this linguistic structure (34.2 %, cf. Table 3), 20 of these communes are urban and only five are rural. Pyhtää is one of these five rural communes (*Statistical Yearbook of Finland*, 1975, p11).

In 1970 the Swedish-speaking population of Pyhtää constituted 54.1 % of all Swedish-speaking Finns in the province of Kymi. As all unilingual Swedish communes of the Finnish mainland are rural ones, and as the bulk of the Swedish-speaking population in Finland is to be found in the south-western and western parts of the country, Pyhtää is in many respects a 'border area'. The Swedish-speaking Finns have, therefore, sometimes called Pyhtää 'the outpost in the east'.

As the research carried out in Pyhtää was a pilot study with an emphasis on the development of methodology, the bilingual and 'border' characteristics of the commune were the main reasons for choosing it: language loyalties breed in contact and the salience of social categories increases in border areas (Giles et al., 1977). In Pyhtää the objective lack of demographic vitality factors accentuates the problematic aspects of assimilation (cf. Tajfel, 1976). To some extent, this heightened level of identification problems counterbalances the small size of the Pyhtää sample, but it also puts an even clearer limit to the generalization of the results to the rest of the Swedish-speaking Finns.

The land area of Pyhtää is 285.3 km^2 and in 1975, when the study was carried out, it had 4894 inhabitants, 786 (16.1 %) of whom were Swedish-speaking (PHC, 1975). Pyhtää is situated 17 km west of the nearest city, Kotka, which is unilingual Finnish, and 130 km east of the bilingual capital, Helsinki. By the end of the 14th century, the Pyhtää area was already permanently settled by both a Swedish-speaking and a Finnish-speaking population. Historians seem to disagree as to which of the language groups actually came first, but this has only marginal relevance for the present study.

Today the commune includes 15 villages, four of which are rather densely populated. Three-fifths of the population in Pyhtää live in these four

Table 5. *The population of Pyhtää 1950–1975 (From communal report of Pyhtää 1975, PHC 1975)*

Year	Total	Swedish-speaking N	%	Source
1950	5544	1285	23.2	Population census
1960	5449	1229	22.6	Population census
1970	5038	870	17.3	Population census
1975	4893	786	16.1	PHC

villages. All 15 villages are to be found by their present names by the end of the 16th century, and they are located quite far from each other, separated by large areas of woods and fields. The commune is nonetheless more industrialized than the average rural commune in Finland, and there is a telephone and/or a car in almost every household.

Many inhabitants of Pyhtää go to work outside the commune in the surrounding industrial centres. The change of the industrial structure of Pyhtää itself from primarily agrarian to its present degree of industrialization is of a very recent date and has been a rapid process. This has caused a typical decrease in the population, especially in its Swedish-speaking part.

With the Swedish-speaking population shrinking at this pace, Pyhtää is not likely to be able to maintain its official bilingual status for very long. In any case, the immediate surroundings of the Swedish-speaking population in Pyhtää are rapidly becoming 'Fennocized', partly because Pyhtää has, to some extent, become a suburb area of the industrialized city of Kotka. In this situation, the subjective position taken by the Swedish-speaking population in Pyhtää towards its historically determined linguistic identity will be a reflection of a rapidly changing immediate intergroup context.

(b) The two-generation sample

The primary aim of the Pyhtää study was the development of an adequate methodology for studying group identity. The Swedish-speaking population in Pyhtää is facing a need to reconstruct its linguistic group identity according to a rapidly changing intergroup context. The Pyhtää study also illustrates the changing identification patterns in the Swedish-speaking group by means of a sample of two generations: 15–17 year old adolescents and their parents.

The adolescents of 15–17 years of age are of special interest for two reasons: (1) general identity formation is in its most vulnerable stage (e.g. Erikson, 1968); and (2) at this age decisions have to be made as to further education and vocational training. The starting point of the systematic sample was two school classes at strategic levels of the Finnish school system.

Within the National Board of General Education of Finland there is a Swedish division. The general principle is that Swedish and Finnish children go to schools of their own language throughout their stay in school (Allardt, 1977). The school system in Finland, however, is undergoing fundamental changes. Education is compulsory until the age of 16, and the former public elementary schools (ages 7–10) and private (lower) secondary schools (ages 11–15) are being rapidly replaced by so-called comprehensive schools (ages 7–15).[1]

Naturally, comprehensive schools require a broader population base than public elementary schools, and in sparsely settled areas several communes may have to share one school. When it comes to Swedish comprehensive schools in linguistic 'border' areas, this problem is, naturally, accentuated. Consequently, there is no Swedish comprehensive school in Pyhtää, and only one Swedish elementary school. The closest Swedish secondary school is in the city of Kotka, in spite of Kotka's official unilingual Finnish status.

In this situation, the choice of a Swedish secondary school seems to imply that the Pyhtää family in question identifies quite strongly with its own language group. To the extent that this choice also requires additional material and other resources, however, it is also bound to bias the socioeconomic structure of a Swedish-speaking sample based on families with children in a Swedish secondary school as compared to the whole Swedish-speaking population in Pyhtää. As will be seen in the next section, this has, to some extent, been the case with the sample of this study.

The starting point of the systematic sample in Pyhtää was all Swedish-speaking pupils from this commune in the last grade of lower secondary school (equivalent to the last grade of comprehensive school) and in the first grade of the higher level of secondary school.

For the Finnish children in Pyhtää, there is one comprehensive school and five elementary schools. There are also Finnish-speaking pupils from Pyhtää in the Finnish secondary schools in Kotka. As all the Swedish-speaking pupils in the sample went to school in Kotka, the matching sample of Finnish-speaking adolescents from Pyhtää in the equivalent school grades was taken both from the last grade of the Finnish comprehensive school in Pyhtää and from the equivalent grade and the next two

Table 6. *The sample from Pyhtää*

	Men	Women	Total
Adolescents	18	33	51
Swedish-speaking	6	8	14
Finnish-speaking	12	25	37
Adults	34 (+2)	41 (+2)	75 (+4)
Swedish-speaking	11	13	24
Finnish-speaking	23 (+2)	28 (+2)	51 (+4)

grades of a Finnish secondary school in Kotka. In this way, the socio-economic structure of the two language groups in the sample were matched more closely. The parents of all the pupils formed the adult generation in the sample.

The adults were given both a questionnaire on background variables and a Role Construct Repertory Grid, in that order. The adolescents were only given the grid. Four of the adults completed only the questionnaire (noted in parentheses in Table 6). The grids were given to the adolescents in the school during class, and all the pupils completed the test. The adults were tested and interviewed individually in their homes, both parents simultaneously but separately by different interviewers. Excluded from the sample numbers above are seven parents who refused to take part and one who was ill.

Five adolescents (three of them Swedish-speaking) had only one parent alive or living at home, one had a stepfather and one lived with her grandmother.

The language groups in Table 6 are formed on the basis of a language index. This means that some Swedish parents may have their children in a Finnish school. However, this is the case only when one of the parents is Finnish-speaking. In this case, the child is classified as Finnish-speaking. If a child of a 'mixed' marriage goes to a Swedish school, however, he is classified as Swedish-speaking. There were two adolescents in the Swedish school from totally Finnish families, one of them because the family had lived several years in Sweden. These adolescents were classified as Finnish-speaking.

The Swedish-speaking adults thus constituted 32 % of the total grid sample of adults. The corresponding percentage for the Swedish-speaking adolescents in the sample is 27.4 %.

(c) Who is a 'Swedo-Finn'? Problems of categorization

There are some clearly conceptual and definitional problems in studying the Swedish-speaking Finns. There is a comparatively high degree of movement from the Swedish-speaking to the Finnish-speaking group, and the number of mixed marriages and bilingual individuals is constantly increasing (cf. above and also Miemois, 1978; Grönroos, 1978).

The actual ability to speak a specific language cannot be a sufficient criterion of membership in an ethnolinguistic group (Sandlund, 1976, p8). The subjective positions taken by individuals have to be acknowledged, but ethnolinguistic identity is also an historical process. The primary agent forming cultural consciousness is the family, which gives ethnolinguistic identity its historical dimension (Sandlund, 1976, p108).

The direct subjective position of the adults in the Pyhtää sample towards their linguistic group membership was obtained both from the question-naire and from the grid test. In both of these, the person was asked to indicate his mother-tongue. In the questionnaire, the alternatives were: Finnish, Swedish and bilingual, but in the test Finnish and Swedish only. The adolescents were only given the test.

In connection with the test, however, both adults and adolescents were asked to indicate the mother-tongue of their parents, and the adults were asked to indicate the same for their spouse and child as well. In this way, the mother-tongue of three generations was obtained, although only indirectly for the oldest generation. Therefore, the number of 'mixed' marriages could be determined for two generations.

Table 7. *Number and linguistic structure of marriages in the sample*

	Finnish marriages		'Mixed' marriages		Swedish marriages	
	N	%	N	%	N	%
The adults included in the sample	27	58.7	12	26.1	7	15.2
Their parents	49	62.1	17	21.5	13	16.4
Chi-square – test ns.						

The number of mixed marriages was not significantly higher among the adults included in the sample than among their parents, but high enough to influence the adults' subjective definitions of their linguistic group membership and that of other family members. Looking more closely at the two sources of information on the adults' mother-tongue, and the information obtained from different family members on their own mother-tongue and that of other family members, considerable inconsistencies can be found.

The inconsistencies are due to the different number of alternative answers available in the two sources of information. In the questionnaire, 56 persons gave Finnish and 15 persons Swedish as their mother-tongue. Eight persons indicated themselves to be bilingual. In the test 57 gave Finnish and 22 Swedish as their mother-tongue. Consequently, there was a clear tendency to give a more 'Swedish' answer in the test; seven of the eight bilinguals gave Swedish as their mother-tongue in the test. This reflects the demographic situation of the Swedish-speaking population in Pyhtää: the smaller the Swedish-speaking minority in a commune, the fewer the bilinguals 'recruited' from the Finnish-speaking and the more from the Swedish-speaking group (Sandlund, 1972).

As for information from different family members, either the spouse or the child or both could disagree in any direction with a particular adult as to his mother-tongue, but parents usually agreed upon the mother-tongue of their child. Although in itself interesting, this complicated network of subjective linguistic identifications definitely called for a more 'objective' assessment of linguistic identity. The change of linguistic group identification among the Swedish-speaking Finns has been found to depend primarily on family background and marital partner (Sandlund, 1972). Therefore, a language index based on the linguistic structures of a person's primary and secondary families (as perceived by the person himself) was formed for each adult in the sample.

The structure of the language index for adults in the sample

Index variable	Index score		
	'Finnish'	'Bilingual'	'Swedish'
Mother-tongue, questionnaire	1	2	3
Mother-tongue, test	1	—	3
Mother's language	1	—	3
Father's language	1	—	3
Spouse's language	1	—	2
Child's language	1	—	2
(= the adolescent included in the sample)			

The maximum score in this index is thus 16 (very 'Swedish') and the minimum score is 6 (very 'Finnish'). For the adolescents, only two variables

Table 8. *The adults in the sample according to the language index score and the language of the child's school*

	Language index scores	Number of adults with their child in a Swedish school	Number of adults with their child in a Finnish school	Total
N = 55 (51 grids)	6	4 (3 grids)	38 (35 grids)	42 (39 grids)
Finnish-speaking	7	—	4	4
Finns	8	4*	5†	9
N = 24	9	—	1	1
Swedish-speaking	10	—	1	1
Finns ('Swedo–Finns')	11	—	2	2
	12	1	—	1
	13	4	1	5
	14	3	1	4
	15	1	—	1
	16	9	—	9
		26 (25 grids)	53 (50 grids)	79 (75 grids)

* Members of the Finnish-speaking majority, whose spouse and child are Swedish-speaking. 'Acculturated Finns' (no change of reference group).
† Finnish-speaking persons, whose father or mother was Swedish-speaking, and whose secondary family is totally Finnish. 'Assimilated Swedo–Finns' (change of reference group).

were considered when determining their language group: their mother-tongue and the language of the school. Only when these two did not coincide were the language indexes of both parents used to determine the language group of the adolescent. There were four adolescents in the Swedish school who considered their mother-tongue to be Finnish. On the basis of their parents' language indexes only two of these were classified as Finnish-speaking, the other two as Swedish-speaking. All the pupils in the Finnish schools gave Finnish as their mother-tongue and were classified as Finnish-speaking.

Only one adult who consistently gave Finnish as her mother-tongue both in the questionnaire and in the test was nonetheless classified as Swedish-speaking: both her parents were Swedish, and her child gave Swedish as his mother's language. She had 10 points in the language index, and only scores of 6–8 points were classified as Finnish. The parents were classified according to the school language of their child as shown in Table 8.

The division of the sample into Finnish-speaking and Swedish-speaking Finns according to the index above is based upon the assumption that those who are 'objectively' Finns do not become 'subjectively' Swedo-Finns, but the opposite is possible. The majority members do not assimilate into the minority, although they may be acculturated to it (i.e. speak Swedish). In accordance with the historical nature of the linguistic identities, therefore, the index conditions for being 'objectively' a Finn instead of a Swedo-Finn have been restricted: the subjective self-identification of being a Swedo–Finn has been considered to be a sufficient, but not a necessary condition for 'objectively' being a Swedo–Finn.

This kind of definition, based primarily on descent, naturally maximizes the number of Swedish-speaking Finns in the sample. In this respect the definition adopted here clearly opposes the minimizing principle of the definition of a Swedish-speaking Finn adopted in the population census, but it resembles the definition used in the census to define a Sámi person.

(d) General characteristics of the language groups

Clearly a sample of this size and structure cannot be properly representative in a statistical sense of the Swedish-speaking population in Pyhtää as a whole. For the purpose of this study, however, it is more important that the language groups in the sample are comparable to each other. Furthermore, the sample will be treated according to its generational structure as representing a specific age group of the Pyhtää population.

Table 9. *Age structure of the adolescent sample compared to the corresponding age group in Pyhtää*

	Number in Pyhtää:*			Number in sample:		
Age	Swedish-speaking	Finnish-speaking	Total	Swedish-speaking	Finnish-speaking	Total
15	12	73	85	6	7	13
16	17	64	81	6	14	20
17	15	64	79	2	9	11
18	(16)	(61)	(77)	—	7[†]	7
	44 (+16)	201 (+61)	245 (+77)	14	30 (+7)	51

*(PHC 1975).
[†] The age of the adolescents had no effect on the test results: the Finnish-speaking 18 year old pupils were therefore included in the analysis.

The 14 Swedish-speaking adolescents in the sample represent *circa* 32 % of their age group in Pyhtää. The corresponding percentage for the Finnish-

Table 10. *Age structure of the adult sample compared to the corresponding age group in Pyhtää*

	Number in Pyhtää*			Number in sample		
Age	Swedish-speaking	Finnish-speaking	Total	Swedish-speaking	Finnish-speaking	Total
35–39	37	243	280	5	7	12
40–44	43	246	289	9	15 (−1)	24 (−1)
45–49	53	277	330	6	13 (−1)	19 (−1)
50–54	52	271	323	—	11 (−1)	11 (−1)
55–59	47	234	281	2	8 (−1)	10 (−1)
60	14	49	63	1	—	1
	246	1320	1566	23	54 (−4)§	79 (−4)§
(66	13	55	68	1†	1‡	2)

*(PHC 1975).
† A stepfather.
‡ A grandmother.
§ Those who completed the questionnaire only.

speaking group is 15. The 23 Swedish-speaking parents (in the 35 to 60 age group) represent 9.4 % of their total age group in Pyhtää (the corresponding percentage for the Finnish-speaking parents is 4.1). If the unmarried are excluded from the analysis there are 209 Swedish-speaking and 1163 Finnish-speaking persons in Pyhtää in the 35 to 60 age group. The sample of Swedish-speaking adults represents 11 % of the former, and the matching Finnish-speaking sample 4.6 % of the latter group. Despite the fact that the parents of the 18 year old pupils cause the average age of the Finnish-speaking adults to rise above that of the Swedish-speaking adults, the age structures of the two adult language groups do not differ significantly from each other.

The analysis of the social stratification of the Pyhtää sample is not directly comparable with the information obtained from the 1970 population census, because different classifications were used in the Pyhtää questionnaire. However, the extensive nationwide study (PHC) made by the Central Statistical Office of Finland covered both language groups on the commune level. The comparable data for the Pyhtää sample were obtained from this study. The data from the 1975 census are not as trustworthy as those based on the population census in 1970, because unlike the 1970 data they are not based on direct inquiries. In 1975 the information was obtained from several different secondary sources, and in most tables the

Table 11. *Swedish-speaking and Finnish-speaking persons in the 35 to 60 age group* by social status in 1975*

Status level	In Finland[†] Swedish-speaking %	Finnish-speaking %	In Pyhtää[†] Swedish-speaking N	%	Finnish-speaking N	%	In the sample Swedish-speaking N	%	Finnish-speaking N	%
I	16.2	9.4	19	9.1	81	7.0	4	17.4	8	16.0
II	36.3	30.1	65	31.1	288	24.8	11	47.8	17	34.0
III	28.1	38.6	77	36.8	480	41.2	8	34.8	21	42.0
IV	7.6	12.0	24	11.5	142	12.2	—	—	4	8.0
unknown	11.8	9.9	24	11.5	172	14.8	—	—	—	—
	100	100	209	100	1163	100	23	100	50	100

* Excluding the unmarried
[†] (PHC 1975)

amount of 'unknown' is considerably high. The *PHC* tables of this study concerning Pyhtää are unpublished and directly ordered from the Central Statistical Office of Finland. In Table 11 however, the population and housing census of 1975 deviates from the classification of status levels below and classifies pensioners as 'unknown', whereas in the sample pensioners are classified according to their former occupation. The statistics presented should, therefore, be interpreted with caution.

The classification of social status used in Table 11 (with the exception mentioned above) combines different types of industry and gives the general social status only. It is based on research done by Rauhala in 1966, and was used for the first time in the 1970 census. The classification contains the following status levels:

(i) managers and other higher administrative or clerical employees, farmers who own more than 50 hectares land;

(ii) lower administrative or clerical employees, small-scale entrepreneurs, farmers who own 15–49.9 hectares land;

(iii) skilled or specialized workers, farmers who own 4–14.9 hectares land;

(iv) labourers, farm and forestry workers, small farmers, pensioners whose former occupation is unknown. (Rauhala, 1966, *PHC* 1975, Vol. VII).

Table 11 shows that in both language groups of the sample there is a clear overrepresentation of the higher social classes as compared to the

Table 12. *The Swedish-speaking and the Finnish-speaking grid-samples by type of industry*

Code*	Swedish-speaking		Finnish-speaking		Total	
	N	%	N	%	N	%
02 + 03	5	20.9	14	27.5	19	25.3
04 + 07 + 09	1	4.2	13	25.5	14	18.7
05	9	37.5	3	5.9	12	16.0
08	3	12.5	14	27.4	17	22.7
10 + 11	6	25.0	7	13.7	13	17.3
	24	100	51	100	75	100

Chi-square = 16.69, df = 4, $p < 0.005$

*Codes (From *Pohjoismainen ammattiluokittelu* – *Scandinavian classification of occupations*, 1973)
02 Arts and professions
03 Administrative and clerical work
04 Commerce
05 Agriculture and forestry, fishing
07 Transportation
08 Industrial work
09 Services
10 Pensioners
11 Housewives

whole country and to the whole population of Pyhtää. As the Swedish secondary school in Kotka was the base for the sample, this was to be expected. However, the difference between the language groups in the sample fails to reach the level of statistical significance and does not exceed the differences observable in the whole country or in Pyhtää.

Other results from the analysis of the questionnaire show that the differences between the two language groups in the sample are clearly of a 'vertical' rather than a 'horizontal' nature. There is no significant difference observable in the educational level ($r = 0.02$, $N = 79$) between the Swedish-speaking and the Finnish-speaking adults in the sample, and not in family income ($r = 0.01$, $N = 64$), either. Furthermore, there is no difference between the language groups studied as to political attitude if this is classified according to the position on the left–right continuum of the political parties supported. In the comparison, the 12 political parties of Finland were divided into three groups: left, centre and right ($r = 0.05$, $N = 66$).

The differences that do appear in the sample concentrate on the occupational structures of the language groups. However, the classification used in the Pyhtää study for type of industry was not included in the Population and Housing Census of 1975.

Considering the significant overrepresentation of the Swedish-speaking group in the agrarian occupations above, it is hardly surprising that they also differ significantly from the Finnish-speaking group in occupational status; the Swedish-speakers are significantly more often self-employed entrepreneurs than the Finnish-speakers in the Pyhtää sample ($r = 0.34$, $N = 79$, $p < 0.005$). Contrary to the situation of the Swedish-speaking population in the whole country, however, the Swedish-speaking sample from Pyhtää shows no more middle-class features than does the Finnish-speaking sample: it is not overrepresented in commerce and transportation, and its educational level is not higher than that of the Finnish-speaking group. The analysis of the questionnaire also shows that the Swedish-speaking adults of the sample have lived a significantly higher proportion of their lives in Pyhtää than have the Finnish-speaking adults ($r = 0.23$, $N = 79$, $p < 0.05$). It seems possible to conclude that at least part of the Finnish-speaking sample has moved into rural Pyhtää from the industrial centre nearby (Kotka), which is virtually unilingual Finnish.

4. Identity research and the Role Construct Repertory Grid

(a) Formal characteristics of grid methodology

The Role Construct Repertory Grid ('the grid') can be seen as a sorting task which gives primary data in the form of a matrix (Bannister and Mair, 1968). Originally, the grid technique developed explicitly from G.A. Kelly's theory of personal constructs, but later on a more generalized grid technique has also emerged, especially in Great Britain (Kelly, 1955). General grid technique encompasses all test situations in which a subject is asked to judge or evaluate a number of stimuli on a number of attributes. In a general grid-matrix A (i,j) the columns represent the stimuli, the rows the attributes, and each cell a_{ij} represents the value of stimulus i on attribute j (Chetwynd, 1973).

In spite of its Kellian roots, grid methodology has been used extensively outside the realm of personal construct theory. The grid has proved to be a reliable measuring instrument and it has been used extensively to elicit important constructs from individuals. The grid technique has been successfully used in psychological research on dependency, stereotypical thinking, identification, etc. But it has also been used within social anthropology (Orley, 1976), social policy (Stringer, 1976) and sociology (Simons, 1976; Bonarius, 1965; Adams-Webber, 1970; Seaman and Koenig, 1974; Bannister and Mair, 1968; Fransella and Bannister, 1977; Slater, 1976, 1977).

The formal characteristics of the grid resemble those of the tables of scores from psychological tests. Kelly called the stimuli to be judged 'elements', and the attributes on which to judge them 'constructs'.

In psychometric experiments interest usually focuses on the relationships between various tests, i.e. operators. In this case, the subjects are not considered individually, as they collectively form a representative sample of the population being investigated. Usually, there are many more subjects than tests. In the context of semantic differential experiments, the major dimensions of the meaning-space are considered to be well-established, and interest centres on the relationships between the concepts, i.e. operands. The experiments carried out within grid methodology can focus on either of these, and in addition the relationships between the constructs and the elements may be investigated.

It has to be emphasized that the grid technique basically represents a method, not a ready-made test. This means that the use of a grid involves all the problems confronted in designing an experiment. The problems concern the nature of the elements to be used, forms of construct elicitation and the grid format, various forms of grid analysis, etc. (Fransella and Bannister, 1977).

The more idiographic, i.e. specially constructed for each individual, the chosen grid test is, the more difficult it becomes to compare individual grid results with each other. In a typical clinical grid, used for therapeutic rather than research purposes, both constructs and elements are specific for each individual. If the demands for phenomenological validity are less acute, it is possible to construct totally nomothetic grids, in which both elements and constructs are supplied by the investigator (Slater, 1969, 1977). In a social psychological study of identity, however, the nomothetic usefulness of a grid has to be combined with its unique idiographic sensitivity in order to reach an optimal level of identity analysis.

As the essential feature of the grid technique is that the subject compares a list of elements on a list of constructs, the basic requirement of a grid test is that the elements must be comparable. They have to be either (e.g.) people, ideologies, vegetables or behavioural alternatives, but they cannot encompass all of these in the same grid. If the elements consist of people, the self can be included as one element, and the grid can be used in identity research (Ryle, 1975; Weinreich, 1975, 1977, 1978, 1979).

Morse (1966) operationalized three forms of personal identity by means of the grid technique. He also found that patterns of identity structure correlated with patterns of identity content. Jones (1961) studied identification patterns in neurotics, schizophrenics and normals with the grid technique, and he found significant over- and underidentifications in the psychiatric groups as compared with the normals. In the seventies, Maklouf-Norris, Jones and Norris have studied the self-systems of obsessional neurotics with the grid technique (Maklouf-Norris, Jones and Norris, 1970; Maklouf-Norris and Norris, 1972; Norris and Maklouf-Norris, 1976). The psychological identity studies have concentrated basically on psychiatric patients, and the grid forms used have been very idiographic. They cannot, therefore, be applied directly to a social psychological study of group identification.

Grid technique is not the only method used in attempts to define identity empirically. Zavalloni has developed a series of research methods for the study of the cognitive content of social identity, called the Focused Introspection Technique (FIT) and the Associative Network Analysis (ANA) (Zavalloni, 1975). The aim of her studies has been to analyse the subjective reactions of individuals to various group memberships and to discover the content of individual coding systems of reality, i.e. construct systems. From her subjects Zavalloni obtained free descriptions of eight membership groups and she then quantified the variables through content analysis techniques. The elicited descriptions were also used to generate more detailed information through a multistage focused introspection, and together with the subsequent ANA-stage each interview lasted four to six hours (Zavalloni, 1973, 1975).

The first serious attempt at developing a grid technique for studying group identification was not made until 1975 by Peter Weinreich at the Research Unit on Ethnic Relations at the University of Bristol. Weinreich carried out a comparative study of identity development in West Indian, Asian and native white adolescents in Bristol. The sample consisted of 32 West Indian, 13 Asian and 37 native school leavers in Bristol in the 15–16 age group (Weinreich, 1975, 1977, 1979). The emphasis of this research project was on understanding the internal psychodynamics of the adolescents at an individual case-study level.

The Pyhtää study was carried out simultaneously and without knowledge of the Bristol study.

The crucial task of any investigator carrying out grid testing is to provide for, or elicit from, the subject taking the test a list of comparable elements and relevant and useful constructs. How these lists are achieved will ultimately determine the balance between idiography and nomotheticity, and between the projectivity and objectivity of the grid test. Generally, the more the subject provides his own elements and constructs, the more his identity will be revealed (Ryle, 1975).

(b) The grid test used in the Pyhtää study

In the Bristol study both the elements and the constructs of the study were elicited from the subjects during a semistructured probing interview which ranged across various areas of life experience. During the interview, notes were made of all significant others mentioned. The subjects were then presented at another occasion individually with their own constructs and, using rating scales, were asked to evaluate systematically the full range of significant others and themselves. The investigator, in analysing the data, then selected only the ethnically relevant elements for inclusion in the study (Weinreich, 1975, 1977, 1979).

In the Pyhtää study the test situation was more structured and less time-consuming. The elements were given to the subjects in the form of a role-title list, containing the self and significant others in a manner close to Kelly's original grid technique. The role titles of significant others included persons of different age, sex and emotional significance (cf. Appendix 1 at the end of this chapter), but the linguistic group membership of the role figures was not predetermined by the investigator. The subject was asked to fill the list with real persons which he knew or had known personally. There had to be one separate individual for each role title, so that 10 different elements, including the self, were obtained.

Naturally, the subject had not much choice with the role titles referring to 'myself' and various family members, but the names of the other element figures could be concealed from the interviewer as long as the subject kept the same element persons in mind throughout the test. In this way the interviewer and the subject cooperated in the elicitation of the concrete elements to be evaluated.

Only after having completed the filling of the role title list was the subject asked to indicate the mother-tongue of all elements, including the self. Naturally, the amount of elements from the linguistic outgroup would have increased considerably for each subject if the elements had been originally defined in the role-title list according to linguistic group membership (e.g. 'your best Finnish-speaking friend'). The outgroup elements would also have been more equally distributed among the subjects. But a predetermination of this kind would have revealed the purpose of the study and changed the level of investigation completely.

The next step in the test was to elicit the constructs, and here the value of leaving as much as possible to the subject was considered to be even greater than with the elements. Therefore, the classic triadic method developed originally by Kelly (1955) was adopted. The subject was presented with three elements at a time (six times) and asked, each time, to *specify some important way in which two of them are alike and thereby different from the third* (cf. Appendix 2). Having recorded the reply, the subject was asked *in what way the third person differed from the other two*.

This method for eliciting constructs is based on the bipolar nature of constructs. We make sense of our world by simultaneously noting similarities and differences. By saying that someone is honest, we usually mean that he is not a crook, or not false, or not a thief, but we do *not* mean that he is not a battleship or a chrysanthemum, although we may agree that the judged person is none of these things, either.

The contrast of an applied construct pole is not normally specified or verbalized as it is in a grid, but it nevertheless exists as the other end of a cognitive dimension. Kelly's triadic method of construct elicitation has been found to be too complex for children under 10 or 12 years of age, the mentally handicapped, the deaf, and those who are not fluent in the tester's language (Fransella and Bannister, 1977, p54). In the Pyhtää study it caused no special problems. The test was carried out by bilingual interviewers in the language chosen by the subject.

In order to insure that all the elicited constructs were personally relevant and applicable to the self, the element 'myself' was included in all triads. During the eliciting of constructs, however, the tester must know which part to play or not to play in prompting as to which type of constructs may be included in the test. In this study, the only restrictions used were those originally recommended by Kelly (cf. Appendix 3, Fransella and Bannister, 1977). The verbalization of the constructs was not altered in any way; the constructs were recorded in the subject's own words.

After this, the completion of the test only required that the subject was asked to compare (i.e. to rate) all the element persons, including the self, on all the constructs. The elicited constructs were written alongside a matrix, the columns of which represented all the 10 elements of the role-title list, 'myself' being the first column. The languages of the element persons were not visible in this matrix (cf. Appendix 2).

The similarity poles of the constructs, characterizing two of the persons in the triads, were written on the left side, and the contrast poles on the right side of a line regardless of construct content. The constructs were then presented as dimensions, defined by a rating scale of from 1 to 7 (cf. Appendix 2). The subjects were asked to rate all elements on one construct at a time so that those resembling the contrast pole of the construct received a higher score than those resembling the similarity pole (i.e. emergent pole). For each construct, the poles were verbalized separately in the subject's own terms and the scaling procedure was clarified. The subjects were told that, for each construct dimension, any score from 1 to 7 could be used and that the same score could be given to several persons on the same construct dimension (cf. Appendix 4).

(c) The projective nature of grid technique

Most nomothetic attempts at measuring identity have been based on verbal self-evaluation within the realm of Q-methodology. This means that the subject is asked to classify himself on a number of attributes supplied by the investigator (Nunnally, 1967; Gordon and Gergen, 1968). However, a supplied list of attributes cannot insure the personal relevance and applicability of the chosen characteristics; phenomenological problems of validity are bound to arise. Consequently, the use of individually elicited constructs will insure that the subjects evaluate themselves on personally relevant dimensions.

Part of the validity problem is the question of the level of consciousness to be investigated. How deep into the identity structure will the measurement reach? This will also determine the psychological relevance of the identity content to be measured. Psychoanalytic research usually favours unstructured, 'projective' techniques, with open responses, over more structured 'objective' ones. In this way more subconscious levels of identity may be reached and the sensitivity of the instrument is increased.

The level of identity measured by the grid technique is clearly deeper than the level reached by ordinary Q-methodology. The 'projective' v 'objective' characteristics of the grid technique can be expressed as follows:

If a focus on the subject's structuring of his environment in personal terms is considered to be the essence of projective tests, then clearly the grid is projective. But if ambiguous stimuli and unrestricted speculative freedom for the experimenter are considered to be the hallmark of projective tests, then the grid is not projective. If we argue that mechanical scoring systems which give absolute inter-judge agreement are the essence of objective tests, then clearly the grid is objective. But if we argue that predetermined dimensions and a supporting substructure of normative data are essential to objective tests, then the grid is not always objective. (Bannister and Mair, 1968, p151)

The possibility of presenting a view of the self which is distorted by defensiveness or by the wish to please cannot be ruled out in the grid. By having the self evaluated in a comparative way together with other objects of evaluation, however, the tendency towards defensive bias influencing the self-rating diminishes as compared to having the self rated separately on a range of supplied attributes (Ryle, 1975).

The grid method is direct inasmuch as the subject is aware of the purpose of the measurement, but the type of response is open, there are no right or wrong answers, and the task is unstructured in that the subject is free to use his own construct dimensions (Pervin, 1970, p344). In the Pyhtää study, the projectivity of the grid was deliberately heightened by leaving the question on the mother-tongue of the elements until *after* the subject had chosen the persons to fit the role titles. Naturally, this reduced the amount of elements from the linguistic outgroup for each subject, but it also concealed the ultimate purpose of the test. Consequently, the comparisons between the elements were less *consciously* influenced by the language of the element figures. In this way, a psychological 'deep structure' of group identification could be reached (Dašdamirov, 1977, p9).

(d) Methods of grid analysis

The object of any mathematical analysis of a grid must be to reveal the structure in the grid, not to impose the experimenter's structure upon it. All grids contain relationships between the individual ratings in it which are accessible to mathematical analysis and related to underlying psychological processes.

Full analysis of the essential properties of a grid in terms of the relationships between constructs, the relationship between elements and the interaction of elements and constructs demands computer analysis. There are simpler methods available for grids based on dichotomization of elements instead of rating scales, but there seems little advantage in using them where more comprehensive use can be made of the data by fuller analysis (cf. e.g. Bannister and Mair, 1968; Fransella and Bannister, 1977; Ryle, 1975; Slater, 1976, 1977).

In the research on adolescent identity carried out by Weinreich, a comprehensive computer programme was devised for grid analysis. This programme was specially developed to calculate the indices of identity conflict using operational definitions of current identification and counter-identification (i.e. negative identification).

In the Bristol study, the elements included both 'myself as I am' (current self-image) and 'myself as I would like to be' (ideal self). The current identifications of the adolescents were obtained by comparing their construals of their current self-images with their construals of the other elements: the more an element shared the characteristics, good or bad, of the current self, the stronger the identification with this element (Weinreich, 1975, 1978, 1979).

However, in order to define the adolescent's counter identifications (negative identifications), something had to be known about the subjects' value systems; the recording of existing similarities was not sufficient. Consequently, in the Bristol study the positively and negatively valued construct poles of the adolescents were determined by reference to their construals of their ideal self. The counter-identifications of the adolescents could then be calculated as the extent to which they attributed negative characteristics to the object of current identification. Correspondingly, conflicts of identification were assessed by taking the product of the subjects' simultaneous current and counter-identifications with each significant other (Weinreich, 1978).

Slater has developed successive programmes for grid analysis, which now form the grid analysis package (GAP). Full details of the procedures involved in the various programmes are available, for instance, in Slater (1977). The Pyhtää data were analysed at the Grid Unit with a standard GAP programme called INGRID 72.

The main output of INGRID is concerned with: (a) The relationships between the elements, i.e. how similar or different any two elements in the grid are in terms of their ratings on all the constructs. This is expressed as element distances. (*b*) The relationships between the constructs expressed as correlations and angular distances. This indicates how far one construct tends to 'go with' another. (*c*) The underlying components of the variation in construct–element interaction (Ryle, 1975; Slater, 1977).

Two elements receiving precisely the same rating on every construct must be perceived by the subject as indistinguishable in terms of the constructs used. Conversely, two elements rated at the opposite extremes on each construct must be regarded as highly dissimilar. In the output of INGRID, overall similarity of any two elements is indicated by a measure of distance which indicates where, between these two extremes, any two elements lie in relation to each other, taking into account the degree to which they are rated similarly or differently on all the constructs used in the grid (Ryle, 1975; Slater, 1977). The distance between 'self' and other persons, therefore, gives a measure of current identification with them.

In the INGRID programme, the value for the distance between elements is calculated in such a way that two elements drawn at random from a grid of the same size would stand at a distance of 1 from each other. The overall similarity of any two elements in the grid can be obtained from the table of element distances in the INGRID printout. Values for the distances between elements have a lower limit of 0 and an upper limit of the square root of $N - 1$ where N = the number of elements in the grid. Analysis of a large number of grids shows that the distribution of values of element distances are virtually normal with a mean of just below 1 (Ryle, 1975; Slater, 1977).

5. General structure and content of minority identity

(a) The structural properties of core construct systems

The analysis of the grid results in the Pyhtää study focuses on four basic sample groups: the Swedish-speaking adolescents, the Swedish-speaking adults, the Finnish-speaking adolescents and the Finnish-speaking adults. Throughout the study, the various grid data of these four groups are treated as separate units of investigation and compared with each other.

The grid measures most extensively used in the Pyhtää study are the element distances of the INGRID output. These measures form the basis for analysing the patterns of intergroup identification to be found below. But before going into the specific identification patterns defined by the element distances, the total structural variance of the grids will be analysed in greater detail. As was pointed out earlier, the structure and the content of identity are not independent of each other. The cognitive strategies of unification and divisiveness may result in patterns of over- and/or under-identification, reflected in identity content.

Quite a number of various grid measures have been developed separately in research on cognitive differentiation and cognitive integration. The study of so-called 'cognitive complexity' has developed into a virtually independent area of research (Bieri, 1966). Most of the grid measures in this area overlap, most of them correlate with each other and most of them pose some problems of interpretation (Adams-Webber, 1970; Fransella and Bannister, 1977). Basically, these problems stem from a frequent lack of theoretical underpinning, but they are also due to the temptation to invent so complex methods of analysis that the psychological meaning of the original data is lost (Fransella and Bannister, 1977).

In the Pyhtää study the primary analysis of the general structural properties of the grids was restricted to the size of the construct correlations in the INGRID output. These correlations indicate how closely knit the constructs are, i.e. how much they tend to 'go together'. As is the case with more complicated measures of 'cognitive complexity', the raw correlations measure, strictly speaking, cognitive differentiation, not cognitive integration. Complexity or 'intensity' measures of this kind cannot tell anything about how the various constructs are integrated with each other, only whether or not this is the case. Grid measures of cognitive integration do exist, but they are much more complicated than the 'complexity' measures. They have been developed by Hinkle (the Implications grid, 1965) and Maklouf-Norris, Jones and Norris (the Articulation grid, 1970) among others.

The basic assumption of the structural measure used here is that there is a relationship between the size of correlations obtained from a grid and the notions of 'tight' and 'loose' construing.

Bannister has developed a so-called Intensity score – not far from Bieri's complexity score – which measures the 'tightness' or 'looseness' of construing. Using ranked grids, the operational definition of the Intensity score is simply the absolute value of the sum of all relationship scores ($rho^2 + 100$) for all constructs. Bannister's Intensity score is one of the measures that have been shown to discriminate between thought-disordered schizophrenics (when they are construing people), on the one hand, and other psychiatric and normal groups on the other. The lower the Intensity score (i.e. the lower the correlations) the more disordered (loose) one's thinking is (Fransella and Bannister, 1977).

In the Pyhtää study, the correlation coefficients from the INGRID output were not summed as such for each individual, but the absolute values were arranged into a frequency table with nine classes of correlation size across individuals within the basic sample groups (cf. Appendix 5). The percentage distributions of the construct correlations within the groups were then compared with each other. They were also compared to a random distribution of construct correlations, obtained from the GRANNY programme of the GAP (cf. Appendix 5). This programme generates 100 random grids of requested size against which the variance of the experimental grids can be contrasted (in this case 6 × 10 grids rated on a seven-point scale – Ryle, 1975).

The most general feature of the figure in Appendix 5 is that the structures of all the experimental grids differ significantly from the structure of the random grids; human grid structure reflects underlying psychological meaning. There are significant correlations between the constructs in all sample groups, whereas the distribution of the correlations of the random grids is approximately normal.

But also, the experimental grids differ significantly from each other in the groups studied. Generally, the adolescents' construing is in some direction structurally more extreme than that of the adults, which should be expected as a reflection of a typical developmental characteristic of their age (generation difference, $p < 0.001$ in the Finnish-speaking, and <0.01 in the Swedish-speaking group). The highest percentage of high correlations and the lowest percentage of low correlations are both found among the Finnish-speaking adolescents. However, the Swedish-speaking adolescents display quite the opposite pattern; the difference between the language groups among the adolescents is really remarkable ($p < 0.001$, cf. Appendix 5).

The adult language groups show less extreme distributions, but nonetheless differ significantly from each other ($p < 0.05$). The difference here, however, goes in another direction than in the case of the adolescents; the Swedish-speakers' distribution is more U-shaped than that of the Finnish-speakers, who display the least extreme correlations (cf. Appendix 5).

Following the interpretation of construct correlations presented above then, the Finnish-speaking adolescents display the 'tightest' construing of the sample groups, and the Swedish-speaking adolescents the 'loosest' construing. The group of Swedish-speaking adults display both 'loose' and 'tight' construing, while the distribution of construct correlations is the flattest among the Finnish-speaking adults.

Structurally, it seems as if the Swedish-speaking adolescents would react to possible invalidation of core constructs with increased differentiation which loosens the relationships between the constructs. The Finnish-speaking adolescents, on their part, seem to maintain a fairly tight construct

Table 13. *Mean percentages of the variance accounted for by the first principal component within sample groups*

	Adolescents		Adults	
	Swedish-speaking	Finnish-speaking	Swedish-speaking	Finnish-speaking
N	14	37	24	51
M	46.16	51.80	54.62	48.66
D	8.95	7.75	11.25	9.80

F-test for two-way analysis of variance:
A = language index grouping
B = generation
$F = 3.37$, df = 3,122, $p < 0.025$

Source under the null hypothesis:	F	df	p
AB	9.40	1, 122	<0.01
B, AB	4.71	2, 122	<0.05
A, AB	5.05	2, 122	<0.01

Note: N = number in sample; M = mean %; D = standard deviation.

system. It seems reasonable to suppose that developmental differences may be important to the level of structural complexity in a grid. Various grid studies have shown that complexity, i.e. differentiation, increases with age until it drops again after 60 (Chetwynd, 1977). The tight construing of the Finnish-speaking adolescents can be assumed to represent a 'normal' adolescent structure around a satisfying identity content, in contrast, the apparent looseness of construing among the Swedish-speaking adolescents clearly points towards an experienced need for reconstruction. The distribution of construct correlations among minority adults suggests more varying cognitive structures around current identity content.

In some cases the percentage of variation in the grid accounted for by the first principal component of the INGRID output has been used to measure general cognitive simplicity, i.e. tight construing (e.g. Chetwynd, 1977). Comparing the group mean percentages of the variation accounted for by the first component with each other shows the general conclusions drawn from the raw construct correlations to be confirmed.

The same general structural characteristics can be observed in Table 13 as in Appendix 5. The first principal components of the Swedish-speaking adolescents account for the smallest average percentage of grid variation. The highest average percentage is, however, not that of the Finnish-speaking adolescents – although they come close to it – but that of the Swedish-speaking adults. Considering their higher deviation score, however, the U-shape of their curve in the figure is confirmed, and the high average percentage must indicate that those tight in construing among the Swedish-speaking adults are even 'tighter' than the average Finnish-speaking adolescent.

(b) General emotional significance of outgroup members

In the Pyhtää study the distances between the elements, expressed as d $(i; j)$ (the distance between elements i and j) constituted the basic unit of the identification patterns studied. The element distances were submitted to further analysis at the Computer Centre of Helsinki University. They were treated as basic data and divided into two main groups as follows:
  (i) Distances between self and others: $d(1; 2, \ldots, 10)$
  (ii) Distances between others: $d(2, \ldots, 10; 2, \ldots, 10)$

The distances between element number 1 (the self) and elements number $2, \ldots, 10$ (the other element figures) were treated as measures of *current identification* in the same way as the corresponding measure was used by Weinreich in the Bristol study (Weinreich, 1977, 1978). The distances between the other elements were treated as the subjects' perceptions of the similarities and differences between other people and analysed according to their internal relationships in the language groups.

The very first impression of the general intergroup attitudes of the adult sample was not obtained from the element distances, but from the sheer number and nature of the significant others chosen into the emotionally defined element roles: four of the elements were defined according to their (positive or negative) emotional significance, and these were analysed separately: 'my best friend', 'a person I admire', 'an enemy', and 'a pitied person'.

Of the adults, 51.9 % had no representative of the linguistic outgroup in these particular element roles, and 16.5 % had chosen outgroup members into both positive and negative element roles as defined above. Only 8.9 % of the adults had chosen outgroup members into positive element roles only, as opposed to 19 % who had chosen them into negative element roles only. As was expected, the total amount of choices across the language groups in all element roles was significantly higher among the Swedish-speaking than among the Finnish-speaking group in both generations.

The predetermined emotional valence (positive or negative) of the four elements in question influenced the number of cross choices among the adults only. And, for the adults, the patterns of cross-choices in these element roles differed in the two language groups, as shown in Table 14.

Table 14. *Number of linguistic cross-choices among the adults according to the predetermined emotional significance of the element role*

EGO language:	Swedish		Finnish		
ALTER language:	Swedish	Finnish	Swedish	Finnish	Total
ALTER (element) role					
Friend	18	6	5	46	75
Admired	9	15	5	46	75
Enemy	8	16	11	40	75
Pitied	11	13	3	48	75
	46	50	24	180	300
	$\chi^2 = 9.88$		$\chi^2 = 6.80$		
	$df = 3, p < 0.025$		$df = 3, p < 0.10$		

Finnish-speaking adults have significantly more cross-choices in the element role of 'enemy' than in any other of the four elements above. The Swedish-speakers, however, have chosen almost as many 'admired' persons as 'enemies' from the linguistic outgroup. Most of the 'friends' are chosen from the linguistic ingroup in both language groups. Generally, the tendency is for the Swedish-speakers, who have more cross-choices, to have few Finnish-speaking 'friends', whereas the Finnish-speakers with fewer cross-choices tend to have more Swedish-speaking 'enemies' than any other emotionally defined element figures.

(c) Identification under pressure towards assimilation

If the intergroup situation of the Swedish-speaking minority and the Finnish-speaking majority in Finland is treated as a historical process, the majority population can be said to have moved, objectively, from an 'insecure' towards a 'secure' position (cf. the classification of Moscovici and Paicheler, 1978). Correspondingly, the minority can be perceived as having moved in the opposite direction.

Subjectively, however, the Finnish-speaking majority may still find cause to define the minority in terms which aim at diminishing an experienced threat and, consequently, show identification patterns characteristic of an insecure majority. Correspondingly, part of the minority may be assumed to display identification patterns characteristic of a secure minority.

In Pyhtää, however, the rapid changes in the demographic structure of the linguistic groups are likely to create a pressure towards assimilation for the minority. Inasmuch as the Finnish-speaking majority members are unaware of, or unaffected by, these changes in linguistic demography, they will continue to display 'insecure' majority identification patterns. Correspondingly, members of the minority group who are not affected by the changes will continue to display 'secure' minority identification patterns. The possibility cannot be ruled out, however, that such identification patterns may also reflect more or less deliberate intention, in the case of the majority, to foster assimilation, or, in the case of the minority, to resist it.

However, in a commune of the size and structure of Pyhtää, the younger minority generation can hardly avoid experiencing the pressure towards assimilation. Assuming that the changed situation of the Swedish-speaking Finns in Pyhtää is reflected mainly in the identification patterns of minority youth, a set of general hypotheses was formulated. The hypotheses were expressed as functions of the group means of element distances between self and other. The element distances were analysed separately in the two generations and in the two language groups of the sample, and the sums of all distances between the self and other elements were compared with each other across individuals within the four basic sample groups.

If 'd' stands for the group mean of element distances between self and others, 'S' for Swedish-speaking, 'F' for Finnish-speaking, 'c' for children (adolescents) and 'a' for adults, the hypotheses concerning general patterns of group identification can be specified as follows:

The mean distances between 'self' and 'others' according to generation and language group

	(A) Adolescents (c)	(B) Adults (a)	(C) Generational differences
I (S;S)	$d(S;S) > d(F;F)$	$d(S;S) < d(F;F)$	$d_c(S;S) > d_a(S;S)$
II (S;F)	$d(S;F) < d(S;S)$	$d(S;F) > d(S;S)$	$d_c(S;F) < d_a(S;F)$
III (F;F)	$d(F;S) > d(S;F)$	$d(F;S) < d(S;F)$	$d_c(F;S) < d_a(F;S)$
IV (F;F)	$d(F;F) < d(F;S)$	$d(F;F) < d(F;S)$	$d_c(F;F) < d_a(F;F)$

The hypotheses can be restated as follows:
(I)   The Swedish-speakers' identification with other Swedish-speakers is:
       in (A)   weaker than that of the Finnish-speakers with other Finnish-speakers;

in (B) stronger than that of the Finnish-speakers with other Finnish-speakers;

in (C) weaker among the adolescents than among the adults.

(II) The Swedish-speakers' identification with the Finnish-speakers is:

in (A) stronger than their identification with other Swedish-speakers;

in (B) weaker than their identification with other Swedish-speakers; and

in (C) stronger among the adolescents than among the adults.

(III) The Finnish-speakers' identification with the Swedish-speakers is:

in (A) weaker than the Swedish-speakers' identification with the Finnish-speakers;

in (B) stronger than the Swedish-speakers' identification with the Finnish-speakers; and

in (C) stronger among the adolescents than among the adults.

(IV) The Finnish-speakers' identification with other Finnish-speakers is:

in (A) and (B) stronger than their identification with the Swedish-speakers in both generations; and

in (C) generally stronger among the adolescents than among the adults.

In the next section the support for these hypotheses will be analysed.

(d) Patterns of overall intergroup identification

Generally, the adolescents' identifications and dissociations are more extreme than those of the adults. This is especially true for the emotionally defined element roles; the adolescents dissociate themselves more strongly from their 'enemies' and 'pitied' persons than do the adults, and they also identify more strongly with their 'friends' and 'admired' persons (cf. Appendix 6). This should be expected as a reflection of their structural extremism revealed in the construct correlations. In this respect, the language groups do not differ significantly from each other.

But when all the elements are classified according to their linguistic group membership and the identification patterns are analysed according to these, group differences emerge. In Table 15 the mean distances between the self and all other elements are calculated separately for the two language groups and the two generations according to the mother-tongue of the objects of identification.

Table 15. *Mean distances between self (language index grouping) and all others (reported mother tongue grouping)*

	Adolescents:				Adults:			
	$d(S;S)$	$d(S;F)$	$d(F;S)$	$d(F;F)$	$d(S;S)$	$d(S;F)$	$d(F;F)$	$d(F;F)$
Number of distances	77	49	30	301	124	90	41	415
Mean valve	93.4	84.6	93.2	93.2	87.0	97.8	95.4	94.9
Deviation	31.9	33.7	34.9	35.9	35.8	34.6	35.0	30.9

F-test for two- way analysis of variance within the Swedish-speaking sample:
A = generation
B = mother tongue of the object of identification
$F = 2.45$, df $= 3,336$, $p < 0.10$
Source under the null hypothesis:

	F	df	p
AB	6.23	1, 336	<0.05
B, AB	3.59	2, 336	<0.05
A, AB	3.18	2, 336	<0.05

F-test for two- way analysis of variance within the Finnish-speaking sample:
A = generation
B = mother tongue of the object of identification
$F = 0.17$, df $= 3,783$, ns.

Taken in turn, the general hypotheses formulated above are supported as follows (all *t*-tests below are one-tailed):

(IA) Not supported by the analysis above: generally, the Swedish-speaking and the Finnish-speaking adolescents identify equally with their own linguistic group. Surprisingly, however, the Swedish-speaking adolescents identify significantly more strongly with outgroup members than the Finnish-speaking adolescents with their ingroup members ($t = 1.65$, df $= 348$, $p < 0.05$).

(IB) Supported ($t = 2.22$, df $= 537$, $p < 0.025$): Swedish-speaking adults identify more strongly with ingroup members than do Finnish-speaking adults.

(IC) Supported, but only at the level of $p < 0.10$ ($t = 1.32$, df $= 199$): Adult Swedish-speakers tend to identify more strongly with ingroup members than do the adolescents.

(IIA) Supported, but only at the level of $p < 0.10$ ($t = 1.44$, df $= 124$): Swedish-speaking adolescents tend to identity more with outgroup than with ingroup members.

(IIB) Supported ($p < 0.025$, $t = 2.22$, df $= 212$): Swedish-speaking adults identify more with ingroup than with outgroup members.

(IIC) Supported ($p < 0.025$, $t = 2.17$, df $= 137$): Swedish-speaking adolescents identify more strongly with outgroup members than do Swedish-speaking adults.

(IIIA) Not supported. The mean distance between the Finnish-speaking adolescents and all other elements is not affected by alter language. The Finnish-speaking adolescents do, however, identify significantly less with outgroup members than do the Swedish-speaking adolescents ($p < 0.01$, $t = 2.56$, df $= 77$).

(IIIB) Not supported. The mean distance between the Finnish-speaking adults and all other elements is not affected by alter language.

(IIIC) Not supported. The Finnish-speaking generations do not differ in their mean distances to all other Finnish-speaking elements. (Note, however, the difference in deviation caused by the more extreme identification patterns of the adolescents.)

6. Conclusions

The empirical study of intergroup identification conducted in the commune of Pyhtää aimed primarily at developing an adequate methodology for identity research. Pyhtää was chosen because of its rapidly changing linguistic demography, which accentuates the problematic aspects of ethnolinguistic identity. The two-generation samples of Pyhtää were drawn from both language groups so that they matched each other. Numerically, however, the whole sample is too small to allow for generalizations to the rest of the Swedish-speaking minority in Finland. All the results presented should therefore be perceived to be merely tentative.

The social structure of the whole sample is upwardly lopsided. However, the two language groups are comparable to each other. As competing loyalties and the pressure towards assimilation have been found to be strongest in the lower social classes, the probability of secure minority identities should be increased in the present sample, and partly counterbalance the pressure towards assimilation caused by demographic factors.

The routes to ethnolinguistic redefinition include partial identification with the outgroup, which very few minority members in Pyhtää have been able to avoid. The specific nature of ethnolinguistic redefinitions depends, however, on the awareness open to individuals, given their patterns of identification with significant others (Weinreich, 1978). For the measurement of these patterns, a fairly projective kind of grid test was designed, combining nomothetic usefulness with idiographic sensitivity. As the measure of element distances used in this study only indicates the amount of current identification, identification conflicts were not directly calculated in the manner done in the Bristol study (Weinreich, 1977).

The structural properties of the core construct systems and the identification patterns involving emotionally significant others indicate the specific stage and the general direction of the ongoing identity processes. The value connotations associated with the threatened core constructs exert a decisive influence on the strategy adopted to diminish this threat: a loosening process is more readily started if the value connotations of the threatened constructs are negative than if they are positive. In the latter case, increased tightening is more likely to occur.

Generally, the structural properties of the construct systems and the identification patterns were more extreme, in one way or another, among the adolescents than among their parents. This was to be expected as a reflection of general adolescent identity development. In spite of the increased probability for a secure minority identity, however, the minority adolescents displayed an apparent looseness in construing as opposed to the very tight construing of the majority adolescents. The minority youth also showed a clear orientation towards the majority group in their identification patterns.

This suggests an ongoing process of assimilation (i.e. change of reference group) on the part of the minority adolescents which acquires some escapist features in the light of additional results: generally the minority adolescents identified more strongly with majority members than did the majority adolescents themselves. The current identifications of minority adolescents with outgroup members included, however, persons of both positive and negative emotional significance. Consequently, the possibility of identification conflicts cannot be excluded. To some extent, the minority adolescents also tended to identify more with outgroup than with ingroup members. In sum, the identification patterns of the Swedish-speaking adolescents pointed towards an insecure minority identity in an ongoing process of assimilation.

The fairly dramatic differences in ethnolinguistic identification patterns observed between the two Swedish-speaking generations in Pyhtää – and which were totally lacking in the matching Finnish-speaking group – suggest a stronger intergenerational conflict within the minority than within the majority. Most of the adult minority members identify quite strongly with their ingroup and dissociate themselves from the outgroup. Together with a fairly tight structure of core constructs, this suggests a fairly secure minority identity. The clearly U-shaped distribution of construct correlations within this sample group and the identification patterns within the 'mixed' marriages indicated, however, a diversity of identity strategies adopted among adult minority members. The high degree of tightness in construing among those of the group choosing to define their system more clearly around current identity content indicated some amount of assertiveness of defensiveness in this part of the minority.

In the analysis of the patterns of intergroup perception (the data are not reported in this chapter) among the adults, however, no evidence was found of stereotypical outgroup perceptions among the minority members. If anything, they held stereotypical perceptions of themselves. Although the linguistic outgroup played a fairly negligible role in the overall identifications of the Finnish-speaking adults, the role it played in the specific identifications was the same for both majority generations; it usually increased the element distances. The Finnish-speaking adults also tended to perceive minority members stereotypically. They also perceived the difference between ingroup and outgroup members to be considerably larger than did adult minority members. The adolescents from both language groups shared the perceptions of the adult majority members of these major differences. No adolescents displayed, however, any stereotypical perceptions of either language group.

New ethnolinguistic coherence between individuals is developed through shared and self-chosen values, when these arise from self-esteem based on common elements in ethnolinguistic redefinitions. If, however, individual group members find heterogeneous solutions to their identification conflicts, no new coherence is to be expected (Weinreich, 1978).

In the light of the tentative results from the Pyhtää study, the splitting tendencies within the Swedish-speaking minority in Finland described in the previous sections seem to be at work within the two generations of the socially homogeneous sample of this study. Minority adolescents – and probably part of the minority adults, too – display insecure minority identities, while part of the minority adults display secure minority identities.

The overall significance of the outgroup is considerably smaller for the majority than for the minority. The significance that does appear, however, points towards predominantly insecure majority identities in both majority generations.

As far as grid technique is concerned, it seems perfectly possible to extend it in order to develop an adequate device for social psychological identity research. The projective nature of the technique allows for a deeper level of identity to be investigated without making it too complicated for use even in larger samples than that of the Pyhtää study.

Notes

[1] The last three grades of secondary school (ages 16–18) which, in Finland, lead to university, up to now have been directly connected with the lower classes of secondary school. Now they are to be separated from the comprehensive school and, in this respect, set on a more equal standing with other vocational schools.

Appendix 1. The grid test used in the Pyhtää study: list of significant others

Adolescents   mother-tongue

(1) (myself)	F/S
(2) father (or equivalent)	F/S
(3) mother (or equivalent)	F/S
(4) a person of the opposite sex, approx. the same age, whom I like ('boy friend or girl friend')	F/S
(5) a teacher	F/S
(6) a classmate	F/S
(7) my best friend (same sex)	F/S

        is she/he: a relative

                 a neighbour

                 a school friend, a member of the same club
                    or hobby circle as you

                 a childhood friend

                 something else, what . . . ?

(8) an 'enemy' or a person with whom I disagree a lot	F/S
is she/he: (same list as above)	
(9) a person that I admire	F/S
is she/he: (same list as above)	
(10) a person that I pity	F/S
is she/he: (same list as above).	

Parents

(1) (myself)	F/S
(2) father (or equivalent)	F/S
(3) mother (or equivalent)	F/S
(4) husband/wife	F/S
(5) employer ('boss') (now or before; if none: a teacher)	F/S
(6) daughter/son in the age of 15–17 (child included in study)	F/S
(7) my best friend (same sex)	F/S

        is she/he: a relative

                 a neighbour

                 a colleague

                 a childhood friend, a member of the same club
                    or hobby circle as you

                 something else, what . . . ?

(8) an 'enemy' or a person with whom I disagree a lot	F/S
is she/he: (same list as above)	
(9) a person that I admire	F/S
is she/he: (same list as above)	
(10) a person that I pity	F/S
is she/he: (same list as above).	

Appendix 2. The grid test used in the Pyhtää study: Triads

Adolescents	Parents
(1) myself father mother	(1) myself father mother
(2) myself person of opposite sex whom I like father/mother (parent of opposite sex)	(2) myself wife/husband father/mother (of opposite sex)
(3) myself best friend (same sex) 'enemy'	(3) myself best friend (same sex) 'enemy'
(4) myself a class-mate person of opposite sex whom I like	(4) myself daughter/son (15–17 in study) wife/husband
(5) myself person I admire teacher	(5) myself person I admire 'boss'
(6) myself 'enemy' person I pity	(6) myself 'enemy' person I pity

The same question was presented for each triad: 'In what way are any two persons of these three alike, and in this respect different from the third?' (= emergent pole). 'In what way is the third person different (in this respect)?' (= contrast pole).

The Grid:

Scale range

1...2...3...4...5...6...7   persons no:

	A		B	1	2	3	4	5	6	7	8	9	10
(1)	emergent pole	–	contrast pole										
(2)	emergent pole	–	contrast pole										
(3)	emergent pole	–	contrast pole										
(4)	emergent pole	–·	contrast pole										
(5)	emergent pole	–	contrast pole										
(6)	emergent pole	–	contrast pole										

Scales

Note: Values (1–7) obtained from the scales (1–6) are placed in the grid. See Appendix 4 for a full explanation of the use of the grid.

Appendix 3. The restrictions for construct elicitation recommended by Kelly (1955) and adopted in the Pyhtää study

(1) *Excessively permeable constructs*

> e.g. 'These two are alike, they are both men.'
> The response is recorded, but additional questions are asked: 'That is one way in which they are alike. Can you tell me some specific characteristics in their both being men that makes them alike, or can you tell me any other way in which they are alike?'

(2) *Situational constructs*

> e.g. 'These two are alike; they are both from the same town.'
> The procedure used in (1) was used.

(3) *Excessively impermeable constructs*

> e.g. 'These two are tool makers and the other is a die maker.'
> Again, the same procedure as above was used.

(4) *Superficial constructs*

> e.g. 'They both have the same colour eyes.'
> Again, as above.

(5) *Vague constructs*

> e.g. 'They are both O.K.'
> The subject was asked to explain further and to give possible examples of other people who are O.K.

(6) *Constructs which are a direct product of the role title or element*

> e.g. 'I like them both.'
> Additional questions like: 'Is there something about their being likable which seems to be alike?' were added.

(Fransella and Bannister 1977).

Appendix 4. The grid test used in the Pyhtää study: grid instructions

(1) Forget the triads, but keep the same persons in mind.

(2) When evaluating the persons, consider all ten of them simultaneously.

(3) Consider only one row at a time, independently of each other.

(4) Give scores from 1 to 7 to all persons on each row as follows:
  - a person who is most like part A of a dimension gets 1 point (independently of the content of the dimension).
  - a person who is close to being like part A of a dimension gets 2 points
  - a person who is somewhat more like part A than part B of a dimension gets 3 points
  - a person who is midway between part A and part B of a dimension gets 4 points
  - a person who is somewhat more like part B than part A of a dimension gets 5 points
  - a person who is close to being like part B of a dimension gets 6 points
  - a person who is most like part B of a dimension gets 7 points

(5) You can give any number of points you want to any of the persons.

(6) Give *every person* points according to the rules above, but consider *each row separately*!

416   Karmela Liebkind

Appendix 5. Percentage distributions of construct correlations across individuals within sample groups

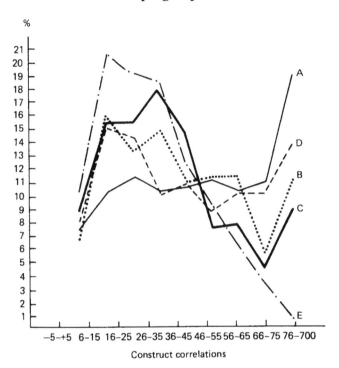

Construct correlations

A	————————	Finnish-speaking adolescents
B	··············	Finnish-speaking adults
C	▬▬▬▬▬	Swedish-speaking adolescents
D	– – – – – –	Swedish-speaking adults
E	·—·—·—·	'GRANNY'-grids (simulated random grids)

Distributions compared with each other:	χ^2:	df:	p:
A : C	33.51	8	< 0.001
A : B	31.31	8	< 0.001
C : D	21.38	8	< 0.01
B : D	18.17	8	< 0.05

Appendix 6. Mean distances between self and specific others (disregarding other's language) across individuals within sample groups

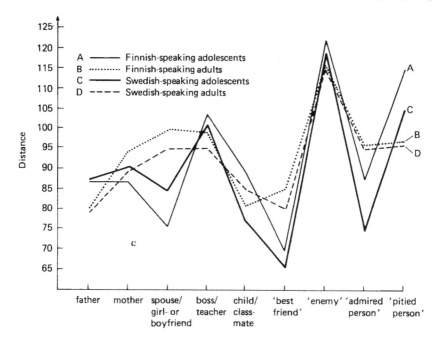

Appendix 7. Specific sources under the null hypothesis in the F-tests for two-way analysis of variance within the language groups

	The Swedish-speaking sample:	The Finnish-speaking sample:
Specific element distances:		
(1) 'self'–'partner'	(a) $F = 0.00$ ns	(a) $F = 1.25$ ns
	(b) $F = 0.00$ ns	(b) $F = 7.59$ $p < 0.01$
	(c) $F = 0.00$ ns	(c) $F = 0.72$ ns
(2) 'self'–'best friend'	(a) $F = 0.72$ ns	(a) $F = 1.75$ ns
	(b) $F = 0.44$ ns	(b) $F = 5.77$ $p < 0.01$
	(c) $F = 0.53$ ns	(c) $F = 0.88$ ns
(3) 'self'–'admired person'	(a) $F = 0.13$ ns	(a) $F = 1.85$ ns
	(b) $F = 0.13$ ns	(b) $F = 3.46$ $p < 0.05$
	(c) $F = 0.46$ ns	(c) $F = 1.08$ ns
(4) 'self'–'pitied person'	(a) $F = 0.14$ ns	(a) $F = 1.05$ ns
	(b) $F = 0.78$ ns	(b) $F = 2.82$ $p < 0.10$
	(c) $F = 0.11$ ns	(c) $F = 0.87$ ns
(5) 'self'–'enemy'	(a) $F = 0.00$ ns	(a) $F = 0.16$ ns
	(b) $F = 0.21$ ns	(b) $F = 0.28$ ns
	(c) $F = 0.00$ ns	(c) $F = 0.00$ ns
(6) 'self'–'pitied person' + 'enemy'	(a) $F = 0.83$ ns	(a) $F = 0.00$ ns
	(b) $F = 0.54$ ns	(b) $F = 0.25$ ns
	(c) $F = 0.70$ ns	(c) $F = 2.88$ $p < 0.10$
	(a) AB; df $= 1, 34$	(a) AB; df $= 1, 84$
	(b) B, AB; df $= 2, 34$	(b) B, AB; df $= 2, 84$
	(c) A, AB; df $= 2, 34$	(c) A, AB; df $= 2, 84$

A = Generation, and
B = Mother-tongue of the object of identification

References

Adams-Webber, J.R. 1970. An analysis of the discriminant validity of several grid indices. *British Journal of Psychology*, **61**, (1), 83–90.

Allardt, E. 1977. Finland's Swedish-speaking minority. University of Helsinki, Research Group for Comparative Sociology, *Research Reports*, No. 17.

Bannister, D. and Mair, M. 1968. *The evaluation of personal constructs*. London: Academic Press.

Bieri, J. 1966. Cognitive complexity and personality development. In O.J. Harvey (ed.): *Experience, structure and adaptability*. New York: Springer.

Bonarius, J.C.J. 1965. Research in the Personal Construct Theory of G.A. Kelly: Role Construct Repertory Test and basic theory. *Progress in experimental personality research*, 2. New York: Academic Press.

Broo, R. 1978. The Swedish-speaking Finns – quite an ordinary people. In C. Laurén (ed.): *Finlandssvenskan: Fakta och debatt*. Porvoo: Söderströms.

Chetwynd, J.S. 1973. Generalized grid technique. Mimeo, Academic Department of Psychiatry, St. George's Hospital, London.

Chetwynd, J.S. 1977. The psychological meaning of structural measures derived from grids. In P. Slater (ed.), *op. cit.*

Dašdamirov, A.F. 1977. Social psychological aspects of the ethnic–national specificity of individuals. *Sovietskaja Etnografija*, **3**, 3–13.

Erikson, E.H. 1968. *Identity: Youth and crisis*. London: Faber and Faber.

Forsberg, K.E. 1975. *The Swedish-speaking Finns according to the 1970 population census*. Svenska befolkningsförbundet i Finland, publikation no. 17.

Fougstedt, G. 1951. *The Swedish population in Finland 1936–1945*. Helsinki: Finska Vetenskapssocieteten.

Fransella, F. and Bannister, D. 1977. *A manual for repertory grid technique*. London: Academic Press.

Giles, H., Bourhis, R.Y. and Taylor, D.M. 1977. Towards a theory of language in ethnic group relations. In H. Giles (ed.): *Language, ethnicity and intergroup relations*. European Monographs in Social Psychology, No. 13. London: Academic Press.

Gordon, C. and Gergen, K. 1968. *The self in social interaction*. New York: Wiley.

Grönroos, M. 1978. The Swedish-speaking Finns and their language. In N. Ahlberg (ed.): *Kulttuuri-identiteetin ongelmia: Suomen kulttuurivähemmistöt*. The Finnish National Commission for UNESCO, Publication Series No. 14.

Hinkle, D. 1965. The change of personal constructs from the viewpoint of a theory of construct implications. Unpublished Ph.D. thesis, Ohio State University.

Husband, C. 1977. News media, language and race relations. In H. Giles (ed.): *Language, ethnicity and intergroup relations*. European Monographs in Social Psychology, No. 13. London: Academic Press.

Jones, R.E. 1961. Identification in terms of personal constructs: Reconciling a paradox in theory. *Journal of Consulting Psychology*, **25**, (3), 276.

Kelly, G.A. 1955. *The psychology of personal constructs*, Vols. I and II. London: Methuen.

Klövekorn, M. 1960. *The linguistic structure of Finland 1880–1950*. Helsinki: Finska Vetenskapssocieteten.

Liebkind, K. 1979. The Social Psychology of Minority Identity. A case study of intergroup identification. Theoretical refinement and methodological experimentation, University of Helsinki, Department of Social Psychology, Research Reports, No. 2, second revised edition.

Maklouf-Norris, F., Jones, H.G. and Norris, H. 1970. Articulation of the conceptual structure in obsessional neurosis. *British Journal of Social and Clinical Psychology*, **9**, 264–74.

Maklouf-Norris, F. and Norris, H. 1972. The obsessive–compulsive syndrome as a neurotic device for the reduction of self-uncertainty. *British Journal of Psychiatry*, **27**, 277–88.

Miemois, K.J. 1978. Changes in the structure of the Swedish-speaking population in Finland 1950–1970. University of Helsinki, Research Group for Comparative Sociology, *Research Reports*, No. 19.

Morse, E.L. 1966. An exploratory study of personal identity based on the psychology of personal constructs. *Dissertation Abstracts*, **27**, 3291–B.

Moscovici, S. and Paicheler, G. 1978. Social comparison and social recognition: two complementary processes of identification. In H. Tajfel (ed.) *Differentiation between social groups: Studies in the social psychology of intergroup relations*. European Monographs in social psychology, No. 14. London: Academic Press.

Norris, H. and Maklouf-Norris, F. 1976. The measurement of self-identity. In P. Slater (ed.), *op. cit.*

Nunnally, J. 1967. *Psychometric theory*. New York: McGraw Hill.

Orley, J. 1976. The use of grid technique in social anthropology. In P. Slater (ed.): *op. cit.*

Pervin, P.A. 1970. *Personality: Theory, assessment and research*. New York: Wiley.

Population and Housing Census 1975. *1978 Official Statistics of Finland* VI C: 105. Vol. III. Households and families, Vol. VII Tabulation programme. Central Statistical Office of Finland, Helsinki.

Population Census 1970. *Official Statistics of Finland* IV C: 104. Vol. IX, Vol. XVII A.

Rauhala, U. 1966. *The social stratification of Finnish society*. Helsinki: WSOY.

Reitz, J.G. 1974. Language and ethnic community survival. *Canadian Review of Sociology and Anthropology*, 104–23.

Ryle, A. 1975. *Frames and cages: The repertory grid approach to human understanding*. Brighton: Sussex University Press.

Salmén, L. 1976. The national question. SOIHTU's svenska skriftserie 'Facklan'. *Socialistiska studentförbundet SOL, ASS*, No. 1–76, **2**, 1–55.

Social research on the future of Swedish Finland 1977. Symposium in Turku, October 1976. Publications of the Research Institute of the Abo Akademi Foundation, No. 15, 78.

Sandlund, T. 1972. Language and group identification in Pargas, Lovisa and Gamlakarleby. Svenska Litteratursällskapets i Finland nämnd för samhällsforskning, *Research Reports*, No. 8.

Sandlund, T. 1972. Language use and identification with language groups in Finland. In B. Loman (ed.): *Språk och samhälle*. Lund: Gleerup.

Sandlund, T. 1976. Social classes, ethnic groups and capitalist development: An outline of a theory. Svenska Litteratursällskapets nämnd för samhällsforskning, *Research Reports*, No. 24.

Schalin, W. 1976. *Swedish Finland: Short notes based on the 1970 census*. Borgå: The Association of Swedish Finland.

Schalin, W. 1977. Perhaps half a million Swedish-speaking Finns. *Folktingsnytt*, May 14.

Seaman, J.M. and Koenig, F. 1974. A comparison of measures of cognitive complexity. *Sociometry*, **37**, 375–90.

Simons, J. 1976. Measuring the meaning of fertility control. In P. Slater (ed.): *op. cit.*

Skutnabb-Kangas, T. 1978. Hide and seek in Sweden: How the transitional model of education hides the exploitation of language and camouflages the conflict with sweet harmony. In N. Ahlberg (ed.): *Kulttuuri-identiteetin ongelmia: Suomalaiset kulttuurivähemmistöt*. The Finnish National Commission for UNESCO, Publication Series No. 14.

Slater, P. 1969. Theory and technique of the repertory grid. *British Journal of Psychiatry*, **115**, 1287–96.

Slater, P. (ed.) 1976, 1977. *Explorations of intrapersonal space: The measurement of intrapersonal space by grid technique*, Vols I, II, London: Wiley.

Statistical Yearbook of Finland 1975. Central Statistical Office of Finland: Helsinki.

Stringer, P. 1976. Repertory grids in the study of environmental perception. In P. Slater (ed.), *op. cit.*

Tajfel, H. 1976. Exit, voice and intergroup relations. In L. Strickland, F. Aboud and K. Gergen (eds): *Social psychology in transition*. New York: Plenum Press.

Tajfel, H. 1978. *The social psychology of minorities*. London: Minority Rights Group.

Weinreich, P. 1975. Identity diffusion in immigrant and English adolescents. Paper presented at the Annual Conference of the British Psychological Society, Nottingham, April 1975.

Weinreich, P. 1977. Socialization and ethnic identity development. Paper presented at the conference on 'Socialization and social influence', European Association of Experimental Social Psychology and the Polish Academy of Sciences, Warsaw, September 1977.

Weinreich, P. 1978. Ethnicity and gender in identity conflict and redefinitions of self. Paper presented at the European Laboratory of Social Psychology, Colloquium on Social Identity, Rennes, December 1978.

Weinreich, P. 1979. Ethnicity and adolescent identity conflicts. In V.S. Khan (ed.): *Minority families in Britain*. London: Macmillan.

Zavalloni, M. 1973. Social identity: Perspectives and prospects. *Social Science Information*, **12**, 65–91.

Zavalloni, M. 1975. Social identity and the recoding of reality: Its relevance for cross-cultural psychology. *International Journal of Psychology*, **10**, (3), 197–217.

14. Intergroup perceptions in British higher education: A field study[1]

RICHARD Y. BOURHIS AND PETER HILL

The aim of this field study was to examine the dynamics of a real-life intergroup situation using concepts derived from Tajfel's Social Identity Theory (Tajfel, 1974a, 1978; Tajfel and Turner, 1979). As in some other studies using real groups to investigate aspects of this theory (e.g. Doise and Sinclair, 1973; van Knippenberg, 1978; Turner and Brown, 1978), group members selected for the present study were recruited from educational institutions of different social prestige; in this case universities and polytechnics in Britain. The main focus of this study was on the lecturing staff of polytechnics and universities rather than on the more transient student population of these insitutions. Lecturers in universities and polytechnics do a similar type of work, have a comparable social standing and salary, and may be regarded as members of the same profession. They do, however, occupy distinctively different status positions within the British higher education system. As will be seen later, important structural and status changes in the relationship between polytechnics and universities in the past decades make lecturers from these two types of institutions especially suited for a field study using a dynamic approach to intergroup relations (Tajfel, 1978).[2]

This chapter is divided into three sections. The first section deals with a discussion of some of the historical and structural characteristics of polytechnics and universities in British higher education. The second section deals with a brief overview of selected aspects of Tajfel's identity theory which guided the research questions addressed in the field study. The third section consists of a report of the findings obtained in the field study proper.

1. Universities and polytechnics in the United Kingdom: background of the two groups

Traditionally, the British further education system has been based on three types of institution: the universities, initially developed for the academic education of fee-paying upper- and middle-class students, together with some working-class students of exceptional ability; the teacher training colleges, conceived as academically inferior to the universities; and the technical colleges operating as an amalgam of education beyond school, incorporating vocational training for workers and also overflow from the universities. For the purposes of this account, we shall not look at the teacher training colleges but instead consider the growth and reorganization of the technical colleges into polytechnics and the growth of universities.

The universities, though the oldest sector of higher education, have been the slowest to expand since World War II. The most rapid expansion in the post-war years took place in the technical colleges for three reasons. Firstly, there was pressure from employers for better trained workers and from employees for better jobs. Secondly, the Government scheme of grant aid for ex-servicemen (the FET Scheme) placed an unprecedented demand on the universities for places, ones which they could not supply, so the Government allowed the FET scheme to be tenable in the technical colleges, encouraging for the first time growth of university degree level work in these colleges. Thirdly, there was the Government's encouragement of technological advancement after the war to keep up with the technology revolutions occurring in other countries. In 1945 the Percy Committee on Higher Technological Education was appointed to consider the needs of higher technological education in England and Wales and the respective contributions to be made thereto by universities and technical colleges. The Committee took the view that industry should look mainly to the universities for the supply of scientists and to the technical colleges for technical assistants and craftsmen. Since neither the universities nor the technical colleges were at that time designed to produce trained technicians and engineers, this difficulty was to be resolved in technical colleges by creating new three-year courses made up of alternate periods of full-time study and practical work experience known as 'sandwich courses'. However, it was not until 1956 that these courses got under way, the intervening years being taken up by much feuding between the universities and technical colleges as to whether the award for the new courses should be designated as a 'degree' or a 'diploma'. Universities argued that since only courses taken in universities could lead to the granting of a 'degree', courses taken in technical colleges could only lead to the granting of a 'diploma'. Technical colleges argued that university level courses should lead to the granting of a 'degree' regardless of whether it was taken in a university or a technical college. However, this period did see the technical colleges involved in high-level work, recruiting new staff and enjoying the status associated with university level work.

Following these 10 years of controversy between the universities and the technical colleges, the Government in its 1956 White Paper decided to rationalize the organization of non-university technical education. As a result, in 1957, seven technical colleges (instead of a proposed 24) were upgraded into Colleges of Advanced Technology (CAT) with a national student catchment area and a concentration on university level work. These seven CATs were at the top of a pyramidical structure with a' broad base of about 300 regional technical colleges. Whilst the technical colleges were to retain their function of dealing with full-time and part-time students over a wide range of course work, the CATs were soon to drop their lower level work and their interest in part-time students. Eventually as a result of recommendations made by the Robbins Report (1963) the seven CATs received Royal Charters making them fully fledged universities in 1967. Meanwhile, the remaining technical colleges obtained their own degree-granting body in accordance with the principle of 'equal academic awards for equal performance' laid out in the Robbins Report.

In spite of the Robbins Report recommendations to upgrade more technical colleges into universities, the Labour Government in April 1965 announced that there was to be no more expansion of the universities; subsequent expansion was to be concentrated in the technological colleges. This was the 'binary' principle which meant in essence that there should be two systems in British higher education; the universities in the autonomous sector and the colleges in the publicly controlled sector. The White Paper in 1966 (DES, 1966) institutionalized this binary plan by proposing that technological training should be concentrated in 'strong centres' to be given the name 'polytechnics'. The binary policy was, for the most part, a reaction to the shortcomings of the universities as technological institutions.

Firstly, the universities were seen as unwilling to develop applied studies on a large enough scale and correspondingly were remote from industry and commerce. The universities' approach to education did not fit well with the need for training part-time students on day release from industry or with the 'sandwich course' concept. The Government also felt that the new polytechnics would be more in line with the sort of qualifications and attitudes that the young 'bright' working class would have. The Government did not like the autonomy of the universities and wanted the new polytechnics to be under more public control and hence responsible to each local authority. The new polytechnics were also designed to produce graduates more economically than would the universities. From these points can be drawn three characteristics (not counting the economic ones) that were to differentiate the polytechnics from the universities: greater heterogeneity of levels and types of courses, greater concentration on part-time courses and a more explicit concern with 'vocationally oriented' education.

The binary plan went ahead. Sixty colleges of technology were combined into 30 polytechnics. The polytechnics were to be independent of the universities, governed under a different status, financed through a system of central and local government grants, and legally responsible to the education authority of their locality.

How have the new polytechnics progressed? A White Paper published in 1972, *Education: a framework for expansion* (DES, 1972) assumed that there should be a 70 % expansion in the number of students in non-university institutions between the years 1971/72 and 1981, and stated that 'the Government will look to the local education authorities and the governing bodies and staffs of the polytechnics to ensure that they can play the *key* role in this expansion' (paragraphs 141–2).

Since 1972 the major event affecting the relationship between the universities and the polytechnics has been the Houghton Report on the salaries of non-university teachers, published in December 1974 (Houghton, 1974). It was only after the publication and implementation of the Houghton Report that polytechnic staff were paid on a par with their university counterparts. Until this point, they were receiving considerably less. The recommendations of the Houghton Committee were based on the principle that lecturers recruited to do comparable work should be paid comparable wages. Following Houghton and a cost of living rise in 1975, polytechnic lecturers' salaries would seem to have jumped ahead of university lecturers'. In 1976, the starting salary of university lecturers began at £3330 while that of polytechnic lecturers started at £3700 or more. The comparison between the two in terms of salary, however, is not simple as the nature of the scales is different, and although polytechnic lecturers were better off, at the time of this study, at the bottom points of the scales, it is worth noting, whilst comparing salaries, that the situation was different further up the scales with one-third of university lecturers earning over £6400 compared with only about one-fifth of polytechnic lecturers.

'Houghton' had a dramatic effect upon the relationship between university and polytechnic lecturers. The *Times Higher Education Supplement*, during 1975, printed many letters from university and polytechnic lecturers arguing the merits and demerits that Houghton had brought about – a situation that the *THES* itself commented upon when reviewing the year 1975: 'Our abiding memory of 1975 is of the bickering and peevishness that disfigured the relationship between universities, colleges and poly-technics.... Universities in 1975 felt threatened by what they imagined as the Government's preference for polytechnics, shown by the treatment of their salary claim.'

What, then, were the differences between the two institutions? The 1966 White Paper, laying the foundations of the binary system of higher edu-cation, stated in what ways the two institutions were designed to be different, or in other words, how the new polytechnics were meant to be distinct from the already existing and well-established universities. The White Paper intended that 'they [the polytechnics] would be distinguished from other institutions providing higher education by the comprehensive range and character of work, especially their commitment to non-degree students and to part-time courses [and] . . . they will, as a whole, have more direct links with industry, business and the professions' (DES, 1966). We should therefore expect differences in the range and nature of the courses offered and in the range of students taking these courses. These differences will be looked at presently; other differences will be considered in the areas of finance; course validation; lecturers' qualifications, pay, promotion and tenure; facilities; time for research; and teaching load.

(a) Range and nature of courses

Whereas the universities teach almost exclusively degree and post-degree courses, the polytechnics have a much wider range of courses. Beside degree courses the polytechnics are involved with part-time courses, sandwich courses, courses leading to professional qualifications, such as nursing and law, and many lower level courses. With their vocational interest the polytechnics do courses at a degree and post-degree level in 'specialized' areas rarely replicated by universities: post-graduate studies in marketing, for example.

The polytechnic degree courses are usually four-year courses, compared with three years at universities. Other polytechnic courses vary in duration as much as they do in nature; some are short courses of only several weeks, some of one year or two.

(b) Validation of courses and financing

Whereas each university has its own charter to issue degrees, polytechnic degrees are issued by a single council, the Council for National Academic Awards (CNAA). The CNAA operates nationally and awards degrees from B.A. and B.Sc. to M.Phil. and Ph.D., acting as an inspecting and supervising body judging the adequacy of courses that the polytechnics themselves set up. Although there is a clear-cut difference between the two institutions, it is difficult to determine where the advantages lie. Whereas the CNAA is more able to act in a regulating manner, maintaining high standards for all the courses it approves, it would seem that such national 'machinery' makes course validation for the polytechnics an arduous process. Indeed, the experts sitting on the review panels of the CNAA are usually lecturers from the university sector who tend to use university standards as a criterion of academic respectability for the polytechnics. Each new course at a polytechnic has to be passed firstly by the academic board of the polytechnic, secondly by the local education authority, thirdly by the Regional Education Advisory Council, then by the DES and finally by the CNAA. Here can be seen the extent of outside control of the polytechnics as opposed to the autonomy of the universities. The major difference, fundamental to the Government policy which set up the polytechnics, makes the polytechnics dependent on the local education authorities for their finance. The running of the polytechnic, then, will be part of the day-to-day financial matters of the local education authority which at the same time must finance the primary, secondary and further education sectors. In contrast, university finances are completely independent from local education authority control. Instead, universities obtain their operating funds from the University Grants Committee (UGC) which in turn obtains its money directly from the Treasury.

(c) Facilities

Without figures for the quality of facilities in the two institutions, objective differences between university and polytechnic facilities cannot easily be listed. However, there are important trends that affect the distribution of facilities. Firstly, the recent inauguration of the polytechnics has meant difficulties in setting up good libraries. There has not been the time to build up libraries with the completeness of university libraries. Secondly, the amalgamation of many small colleges into one new polytechnic is a very expensive process as far as buildings and equipment are concerned. In the particular polytechnic looked at in this study, centralization into one site was at the time only partly completed due to lack of money, leaving many parts of the polytechnic widely spread across the city, and in some cases expanding into make-shift buildings.

Details of scientific equipment, secretarial back-up, social facilities, etc.

Table 1. *Qualifications of lecturing staff in polytechnics and universities in the UK (Source: Whitburn, Mealing and Cox, 1976)*

Degree or award	Polytechnic staff (%)	University staff (%)
BA or BSc	41	>95
MA or MSc	(not available)	37
PhD	16	51
Professional qualifications	67	—

are difficult to obtain but there is some consensus that universities do overall have better facilities than polytechnics (Whitburn, Mealing and Cox, 1976).

(d) Lecturing staff: qualifications, union representation, salary, promotion, and allocation of time

As can be seen in Table 1, university lecturers had, in general, higher academic qualifications than polytechnic lecturers, with 51 % of all university lecturers having PhDs compared with 16 % in polytechnics. However, since the emphasis of the two institutions is different it is important to include other factors such as professional qualifications. A high percentage of polytechnic lecturers have some professional qualification relevant to specific areas of industry, management, etc. (Whitburn, Mealing and Cox, 1976).

The great majority of higher education lecturers belong to two main professional unions. University lecturers have their own organization, the Association of University Teachers (AUT). Polytechnic lecturers are mostly represented by the National Association of Teachers in Further and Higher Education (NATFHE) and to a lesser extent by the AUT. In having separate unions, the fates of the lecturers in these two institutions are recognized to be separate to some extent and this is reflected in the range of salaries each group has negotiated with the Government.

A comparison of polytechnic and university lecturer salaries is presented in Table 2.

A few points concerning this comparison need to be made. Both university and polytechnic lecturers were divided into three groups: university lecturers into (1) lecturers, (2) senior lecturers and readers, and (3) professors; polytechnic lecturers into (1) lecturers grades 1, 2 and senior lecturers, (2) principal lecturers, and (3) heads of department. Hence university lecturers in category (1) and polytechnic lecturers in category (1)

Table 2. *Salary comparisons of equivalent grades of lecturers in universities and polytechnics for 1972, 1974 and 1976*

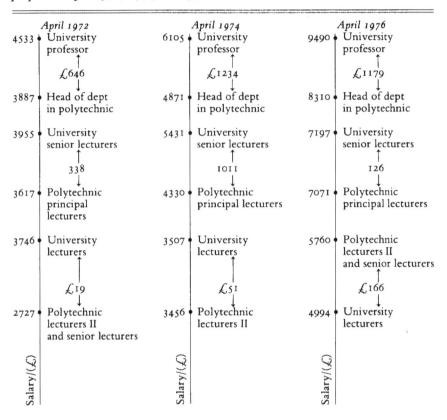

were seen to be equivalent in seniority and representing broadly the same percentage of the total lecturing staff. For salary comparison purposes the mean of the salary scales for each category of lecturers was computed and it is this mean that makes up the 'statistic' used for the comparison. Polytechnic lecturers grade 1 were not included in the calculation of this mean of salary scales since a very small fraction of polytechnic lecturers occupy this grade (6 % compared with 75.8 % grade 2 and senior lecturers, April 1973) and it was felt that inclusion of this minority would skew the mean unrealistically. The comparisons have been made for April 1972, April 1974, immediately before Houghton, and April 1976, after the changes brought about by the report.

A few trends seen in Table 2 should be briefly mentioned. Firstly, our category 1 lecturers. In 1972 university lecturers were £19 per annum

Table 3. *Number of hours spent on average per week by lecturers* on teaching/administration and on research*

	Polytechnic lecturers (hours/week)	University lecturers (hours/week)
Teaching and administration	32	27
Research	3	11
TOTAL	35	38

* Source: Whitburn *et al.*, 1976. As these figures were obtained in a survey, these self-reports may be somewhat biased.

better off than the comparison polytechnic lecturers; by 1974 this was slightly increased for university lecturers being £51 per annum ahead. The effect of Houghton reversed this situation and in 1976 the polytechnic lecturers in category (1) were ahead by £166 per annum. Considering category (2), the university senior lecturers had a differential of £338 in 1972, £1011 in 1974, which was reduced to £126 by Houghton. A smaller reduction of differential, favouring university professors, also occurred with Houghton, where a 1974 lead by professors of £1238 was only slightly reduced to £1174 in 1976.

However, such comparisons minimize the lead that university lecturers had prior to Houghton. In 1974 polytechnic senior lecturers were earning on average about £1500 less than university senior lecturers (£3868 v. £5341) and were only slightly ahead of the average of university lecturers category (1) (£3507). It is these comparisons, unfavourable for polytechnics, which produced the recommendations for comparability with university lecturers embodied in the Houghton report.

Broad differences in promotion potentials between university and polytechnic lecturers can be gleaned by the differences in expansion of the two sectors. The expansion of the polytechnics has been very rapid, and the creation of new degree level courses has meant that the polytechnics had a large demand for lecturers with quick promotion for those with the appropriate qualifications. With the filling of senior posts by young men and women this fast promotion may well now be slowing down.

Table 3 shows the number of hours spent on average by lecturers on the two areas of teaching/administration and research. The table shows a difference in emphasis in the way lecturers spend their time, polytechnic lecturers doing less research and more teaching than university lecturers.

It should be noted that three hours/week for research is the norm granted by local education authorities to polytechnic lecturers.

(e) Students in universities and polytechnics

Comparisons between students in universities and polytechnics can only be approximate due to the great range of types of students in polytechnics. However, comparing degree course students, these being the most educationally qualified of the polytechnic students, Whitburn, Mealing and Cox (1976) find that, of their sample of 4122 polytechnic students on degree courses, 2352 had three or more 'A' levels (57 %), equivalent to the usual minimum entry standard for universities. It would seem, then, that compared to university students, polytechnic students are of a lower academic standard. Whitburn *et al.* also add 'it may be inferred that in many cases the polytechnics do serve as a 'safety net' for students who wish to acquire a degree but who do not obtain the 'A' level grades required by Universities' (p73).

(f) Perceived status of the two groups

How do the two groups compare in terms of their status? University lecturers (henceforward abbreviated 'ULs') have traditionally held high status. How do polytechnic lecturers (PLs) compare? The question was asked therefore whether or not there was consensus on this assumed status difference.

A pilot study was carried out to investigate the perceived status of both universities and polytechnics and of the lecturers working within them. The pilot study was carried out in the city in which the field study proper took place. Fifty people were interviewed in two shopping areas of the city, a predominantly middle–class area and a centrally located shopping precinct. They were asked if they could help by answering a few questions concerning education. The questions were as follows:

   (i)   If you had the chance to send your child for further education after school would you send him/her to a polytechnic or a university?

  (ii) If you wanted to make sure that your child got a good job would you rather send him/her to a polytechnic or a university?

 (iii) Which job do you think has the higher status – a lecturer in a polytechnic or a lecturer in a university?

 (iv) Which institution do you think is the most highly regarded: a polytechnic or a university?

Table 4. *Results of the 'status questionnaire' with a sample of the 'general public' (N = 50)*

		University	Polytechnic	Don't know
Q_1	Where would you send your child for a degree in higher education?	41/50 (82 %)	7/50 (14 %)	2/50 (4 %)
Q_2	Where would you send your child if the emphasis was on getting a job after graduation?	29/50 (58 %)	17/50 (34 %)	4/50 (8 %)
Q_3	Which type of lecturer has the higher status?	49/50 (98 %)	1/50 (2 %)	—
Q_4	Which institution has the most prestige?	50/50 (100 %)	—	—

Table 5. *Answers with respect to the social class of respondents to the question: 'Where would you send your child if the emphasis was on getting a job after graduation?'*

	University	Polytechnic	Don't know
Working class respondent* N = 26	11	13	2
Middle class respondent* N = 24	18	4	2

$\chi^2 = 7.85$, df = 1, $p \leqslant 0.01$ (excludes 'Don't know')

*Determined by respondent's stated occupation

The results can be seen in Table 4. Questions 3 and 4 dealing more overtly with status show 99 % agreement on the higher status of universities and university lecturers. Indeed, overall, of 200 comparisons (50 Ss × 4 comparisons) 178 or 89 % gave universities higher status than polytechnics.

As seen in Table 5, answers to question 2 were analysed according to the social class of the respondents (determined by the repondent's occupation). The results show that working class respondents were more likely to prefer polytechnics when considering ulterior job prospects than middle-class respondents.

This pilot study was repeated with 50 university and polytechnic students interviewed in their respective Student Union buildings. The results shown in Table 6 replicate those obtained with the adult respondents. They indicate that polytechnic students share the notion that, in general, uni-

Table 6. *Results of the 'status questionnaire' with a sample of university*
(N = 25) and polytechnic (N = 25) students

		University	Polytechnic	Don't know
Q$_1$	Where would you send your child for a degree in higher education?	39/50 (78 %)	7/50 (14 %)	4/50 (8 %)
Q$_2$	Where would you send your child if the emphasis was on getting a job after graduation?	19/50 (38 %)	29/50 (58 %)	2/50 (4 %)
Q$_3$	Which type of lecturer has the higher status?	47/50 (94 %)	—	3/50 (6 %)
Q$_4$	Which institution has the most prestige?	49/50 (98 %)	—	1/50 (2 %)

versities and their lecturers enjoy more prestige and status than polytechnics.

The results obtained with students and adults suggest that the status relationship between polytechnics and universities is fairly consensual. The majority of respondents felt that ULs enjoy a higher social status than PLs. Nevertheless, for close to half the respondents, polytechnics, by virtue of their more vocational orientation, were perceived to have the advantage of increasing the chances of obtaining a job after graduation. A comparison of the relative advantages and disadvantages of each group suggests that, overall, ULs are advantaged relative to PLs on a number of important dimensions. Nevertheless, from a historical perspective, PLs and their predecessors have made steady progress relative to ULs on a number of dimensions including salaries and the granting of university level degrees in the polytechnics.

2. The theoretical approach of the study

Given the changing nature of the relations between PLs and ULs, what attitudes and perceptions do polytechnic and university lecturers have of themselves and of each other as group members? How do polytechnic and university lecturers perceive their respective roles in British higher education? Answers to these and other questions become particularly interesting when they are considered in the context of Tajfel's Social Identity Theory.

Distinctions between Tajfel's theory and other important approaches to intergroup relations such as Sherif's (1966) Realistic Group Conflict Theory have been discussed elsewhere by Billig (1976), Tajfel (1978) and

Tajfel and Turner (1979). In its simplest terms Tajfel's theory involves a series of interrelated social psychological processes described as social categorization, social identity, social comparison and psychological distinctiveness. Each of these will be briefly discussed as they apply to the relationship between polytechnic and university lecturers in this study.

Social categorization This is a cognitive tool which allows individuals to define and organize their social world into meaningful units (Tajfel, 1970). Numerous studies have shown that the mere categorization of persons as ingroup and outgroup is sufficient to trigger ingroup favouritism and outgroup bias (Tajfel *et al.*, 1971 Tajfel, 1972*b*; Doise and Sinclair, 1973; Billig and Tajfel, 1973; Gerard and Hoyt, 1974; Doise, 1978; Turner, 1978*a*, 1978*b*).

Although polytechnic and university lecturers fulfil a complementary role in British higher education, each group can be clearly distinguished by virtue of the institutions they serve and by various other characteristics. One purpose of the field study was to establish how these category boundaries are perceived by polytechnic and university lecturers themselves, and whether *implicit* and *explicit* categorizations could lead to different patterns of intergroup bias in the field setting (Doise, 1972; Doise and Sinclair, 1973).

Social identity and social comparison Tajfel (1974*b*) proposed that individuals define and evaluate themselves in terms of the social group to which they belong. Thus membership in a social category can contribute to a person's identity. This social identity may be positive or negative depending on the value people attach to their category membership. But social identity only acquires meaning by comparison with other social groups (Tajfel, 1974*b*). A group's position may thus depend on the outcome of comparisons between the ingroup and relevant outgroups. These comparisons take place on valued dimensions which may be objective or subjective (Tajfel, 1972*a*). Thus differences between ingroup and outgroup perceived to favour the ingroup (positively discrepant comparisons) may result in a positive social identity, whereas group differences in favour of the outgroup may result in a negative social identity. It was shown in the pilot study that both students and members of the general public perceived PLs to have less status than ULs. Comparisons on other dimensions listed in other tables also suggest that the PLs may be disadvantaged relative to ULs. The field study was carried out to investigate aspects of the social identity of polytechnic and university lecturers. To the degree that polytechnic and university lecturers identify with their own group and perceive each other as relevant comparison groups one may find that PLs have a less positive identity than ULs.

Psychological distinctiveness   A major proposition of Tajfel's theory is that group members cannot be satisfied with a negative social identity and thus engage in various strategies to define themselves positively in relation to other social groups. The assumption is that to restore the self-esteem of their members, social groups must establish a positively valued distinctiveness from relevant comparison groups. At least four types of distinctiveness strategies can be used to restore or maintain positive social identity. These are individual mobility, social creativity, choice of social comparison group and social competition.

Individual mobility   Group members may leave their own group and attempt to 'pass', as individuals, to a high-status group. Thus an individual may achieve a more positive social identity by succeeding to pass from a low-status to a high-status group. According to Tajfel (1975) group members have a social mobility belief system to the degree they perceive that *individuals* can readily move from one social group to the other within the intergroup hierarchy. These variables were investigated in the field study where PLs and ULs were interviewed concerning the perceptions of, and desires for, social mobility within and outside of the British higher education system.

But in some intergroup situations, social mobility and 'passing' may be quite difficult, if not impossible (e.g. colour bars, caste or rigid class systems). Individuals will have a 'social change' belief system to the degree they perceive they can only change their position in the intergroup hierarchy by acting as *group members* through social creativity or social competition.

Social creativity   In cases where social mobility appears limited or loyalty to the ingroup is high, group members may achieve positive distinctiveness by altering or redefining the dimensions of social comparison with the outgroup. Lemaine (1966, 1978) has documented how disadvantaged groups can restore positive social identity by *creating* new dimensions of social comparisons that ensure favourable comparison with relevant outgroups. In addition, group members may achieve positive distinctiveness by changing their values so that comparisons perceived negatively in the past are *redefined* positively in the present (e.g. the 'Black is Beautiful'

movement, cf. Hraba and Grant, 1970; the Welsh and Québécois movements, cf. Bourhis, Giles and Tajfel, 1973, Bourhis, Giles and Lambert,
1975; Maoris in New Zealand, cf. Vaughan, 1978, etc.).

Some evidence already suggests that these two strategies can be used to
restore positive group identity (Brown, 1978; Lemaine, 1966); the polytechnic and university setting provides an ideal intergroup context to
gain further insights into the functioning of these strategies in the field
setting. Given the wide range of dimensions differentiating polytechnics
and universities, both social creativity and redefinition could be used by
polytechnic and university lecturers as strategies of positive distinctiveness.
While one group of lecturers may use one series of dimensions to distinguish
themselves positively from the outgroup, the latter may denigrate or
minimize the values of these dimensions and claim their own as being more
relevant (Tajfel, 1972b, 1978). Thus, strategies of creativity and redefinition
can introduce new dimensions of positive social identity which, once
accepted by ingroup members, can become salient dimensions of differentiation from the outgroup. Dimensions of positive social identity were
investigated in the field study by asking polytechnic and university lecturers to list and evaluate advantages and disadvantages of being PLs and
ULs in British higher education.

Choice of social comparison group   The choice of social comparison group
remains central to any theory of social comparison processes (Hyman and
Singer, 1968, Austin, 1977). Group members may feel more or less satisfied
in being members of their own group depending on who they consider
to be their relevant comparison outgroup (Kidder and Stewart, 1975;
Runciman, 1966; Sears and McConahay, 1970). According to Tajfel and
Turner (1979) and Turner, Brown and Tajfel (1979), group members can
maintain a positive social identity by avoiding unfavourable comparisons
with 'advantaged' outgroups. Thus, group members may maintain a
positive social identity by comparing with outgroup members that are
of lower status than themselves (positively discrepant comparisons, e.g.
Asher and Allen, 1969). An alternative strategy which needs to be further
integrated within Tajfel's intergroup approach is that in which group
members compare with higher status outgroups as a way of gaining some
legitimate claim to the advantages enjoyed by higher status outgroups.
Indeed, anecdotal (Guimond, 1979)[3] as well as empirical evidence (Patchen,
1968) shows that lower status groups may actively seek unfavourable
comparisons with higher status outgroups (negatively discrepant comparisons) as a way of justifying claims for improving their own *material*

conditions. Negatively discrepant comparisons can be made without threatening positive social identity under the following two conditions: first, such unfavourable comparisons may pose little threat to positive identity as long as ingroup members do not blame themselves as the cause of their unfavourable position *vis-à-vis* the outgroup. Indeed, Giles, Bourhis and Taylor (1977, p333) suggest that ingroup claims for greater parity with outgroup advantages can be particularly forceful if ingroup members blame 'relevant' outgroups as the cause the ingroup's plight. Support for this notion was obtained by Gurin *et al.* (1969) in which radical black American youths could maintain a positive self-esteem by attributing their plight not to a lack of personal skill or effort but to external factors such as the USA system of racial discrimination. Secondly, one can propose that given an attribution of blame to some outgroup, negatively discrepant comparisons may pose *little* threat to social identity as long as such comparisons occur on 'material' dimensions rather than on 'social' ones related to the group's own options, abilities, values and dimensions of psychological distinctiveness. This may be the case especially since it seems much easier to blame an outgroup for one's own plight on 'material' dimensions such as poverty, inadequate resources and lack of institutional support (Giles, Bourhis and Taylor, 1977) than it is to blame an outgroup for one's own opinions, values and abilities. Ultimately, awareness of negatively discrepant comparisons on material dimensions may help group members to obtain parity with advantaged outgroups and contribute to a more positive social identity based on a wider range of salient comparison dimensions. The interview protocol used with polytechnic and university lecturers was arranged to investigate the dynamics of these social comparison strategies.

Social competition   Group members may achieve positive social identity through direct competition with the outgroup. This implies a direct attempt to reverse the relative position of the groups on some salient dimension of comparison such as power, status, attributes, etc. To the extent that this process involves a redistribution of scarce resources, Tajfel and Turner (1979) suggest that this strategy would generate overt conflict and antagonism between the groups. Interview questions dealing with the respective role of polytechnics and universities in British higher education were designed to assess if social competition strategies were used by respondents in this study.

   To the degree that the low-status PLs emerge with a less positive social identity than ULs, one could expect the above strategies to be more prevalent amongst PLs than amonst ULs. Nevertheless, Tajfel (1974) proposed that high-status groups will also adopt strategies of group distinctiveness when confronted with low-status groups who threaten their superiority. Thus ULs may also adopt group distinctiveness strategies when reminded of the recent advances achieved by lecturers in the polytechnics.

Intergroup perceptions, group distinctiveness strategies and intergroup bias According to Turner and Brown (1978), the choice of group distinctiveness strategies adopted to restore or maintain positive social identity will also depend on the perception group members have of the intergroup situation. Thus group members who perceive the intergroup status relationship to be stable and legitimate may adopt different strategies of group distinctiveness than members who view the intergroup situation to be unfair and susceptible to change. An important aim of the field study was not only to investigate how university and polytechnic lecturers perceived the legitimacy and stability of the intergroup situation (i.e. impact of the Houghton Report) but also to determine how these perceptions could influence the choice of group distinctiveness strategies adopted by these groups.

In the laboratory study by Turner and Brown (1978) it was also found that patterns of ingroup bias varied depending on how low- and high-status group members perceived the legitimacy and stability of the intergroup situation. Another aim of the field study was to investigate the degree of intergroup bias PLs and ULs would display given their perceptions of their own intergroup situation. Both groups of lecturers were given the opportunity to display intergroup bias on a number of dimensions differentiating the two groups. Other measures of intergroup bias were obtained by asking PLs and ULs to choose from various combinations of ingroup–outgroup salary structures to be negotiated in the next round of collective bargaining with the government.

3. The study

The Institutions

The study was carried out in a university and a polytechnic both located in a large city in England. The university was academically well established and was situated near the city centre. Enrolment in the university was over 6000 students with a lecturing and research staff of about 1200. The polytechnic, created in 1971, occupied a new site a few miles from the city centre as well as other older sites throughout the city. The polytechnic student enrolment was approximately 9000 students (including 5000 part-time students) while the lecturing staff was

650. Both institutions can be described as typical in terms of the range of courses and facilities offered. In addition both institutions occupy roughly equivalent prestige positions within their respective pecking orders in the university and polytechnic sectors.

Participants

A random sample of lecturers from both institutions were contacted by letter asking for their cooperation in an interview about higher education. Respondents included in the study were 48 ULs and 48 PLs, all of whom were tenured in their respective institutions. An equal number of Arts and Science lecturers were interviewed in each institution, no professors or heads of department were included in the sample. Each lecturer was interviewed in his or her office for about 60 minutes. The interviews were conducted over a period of two months from February to April 1977.

Interview procedure

The interview was in five parts and was tape-recorded throughout.

Part I: Introduction and personal background

The interview began with the interviewer explaining the aims of the research, which were described as 'an interest in aspects of higher education and in how lecturers feel about their jobs'. In the first and second part of the interview no mention was made by the interviewers of polytechnics, if the respondent was a UL, or of universities, if the respondent was a PL. If queried, the interviewer presented himself as a researcher on a grant from the SSRC. Respondents were assured that their individual responses would be kept anonymous. They were informed that the survey was not meant to tap their factual knowledge of higher education issues, but simply aimed at obtaining their candid opinions and feelings concerning education matters. Lecturers were then asked a number of questions concerning their background including the respondent's position in the institution, academic and professional qualifications, previous employment, career expectations, job satisfaction, etc.

Part 2: Implicit categorization, social identity and group distinctiveness strategies

Without ever mentioning PLs or ULs as comparison outgroups, respondents were queried on aspects of their category membership as lecturers. Firstly, respondents were asked why and under what circumstances they became lecturers in their respective institutions. Secondly, they were asked how satisfied they were with their job and how much they identified as members of their own group. Thirdly, they were asked to describe the advantages and disadvantages of being lecturers in their respective institutions. Fourthly, they were asked to describe what aspects of their job made them feel most proud to be lecturers. The final question was: 'When comparing your present position as a polytechnic (university) lecturer, which other group or groups do you find you compare yourself with?' Lecturers could name any group or groups they felt served as a meaningful comparison group and were urged to explain why such comparisons were appropriate.

Part 3: Explicit categorization, social identity and group distinctiveness strategies

In this part of the interview, explicit mention of the outgroup was made by the interviewer. Five questions were asked. They concerned: advantages and disadvantages of being lecturer in the outgroup institution, distinctions between the characteristics of polytechnic and university lecturer's jobs, and role and goals of the two institutions in higher education and the ultimate aims of the Government in its treatment of the two sectors of education in Britain.

Part 4: Perception of mobility and desire to pass

Respondents were given copies of an assisted questionnaire. Each question was read out loud by the interviewer. In addition to responding to each question with comments and observations, lecturers were also asked to qualify their answers using a seven-point rating scale. The questions were explicitly concerned with comparing the perceived mobility of ULs and PLs from one sector of higher education to the other: e.g. 'How easy do you feel it is for a polytechnic lecturer to become a lecturer in a university? How often does this take place? How qualified are they to move?' etc. Similar questions were asked for the movement of university lecturers to polytechnics. Lecturers were also asked how satisfied they felt members of each group were, how linked the two institutions had been and how much more linked they should be.

Finally, respondents were asked whether they would like to move to the other group, i.e. for a polytechnic lecturer to become a university lecturer, and vice-versa. Reasons for subject's decision were also noted.

Part 5: Intergroup bias

The last part of the interview consisted of questions which gave respondents the opportunity to display intergroup bias on a number of dimensions. (1) *Salary matrices:* Respondents were given four sets of salary scales shown in Table 7. Each of the four sheets represented combinations of salary scales for mid-range lecturers in polytechnics and universities. Respondents were asked to choose the salary combination on each sheet which they felt would be most appropriate for PLs and ULs as an outcome of salary negotiations with the Government. The salary matrices were designed for field use by Brown (1978) from the original matrices developed for laboratory studies by Tajfel *et al.* (1971). (2) *Education cuts:* Respondents were asked to imagine themselves in a position where they would have to distribute a government cut of 100 parts in six areas of education. These six areas were: university teaching; university research; polytechnic teaching; polytechnic research; secondary education; and further education colleges. The cuts were to be made as if *per capita* to overcome problems of different student enrolment in each education sector. Using a similar form, respondents were asked to distribute the cuts the way they thought the Government would in a period of economic depression. (3) *The questionnaire:* At the end of the interview respondents were given a questionnaire which they could complete immediately or in their own time. Using seven-point rating scales respondents were asked to compare universities and polytechnics on fourteen relevant comparison dimensions. Questions included quality of teaching in the

Table 7. *Salary matrices: Combinations of
Government annual pay awards to mid-range
lecturers in polytechnic and university presented to
each respondent*

A		B	
Polytechnic	University	Polytechnic	University
£4650————4500		£4200————4050	
4550————4450		4250————4150	
4450————4400		4300————4250	
4350————4350		4350————4350	
4250————4300		4400————4450	
4150————4250		4450————4550	
4050————4200		4500————4650	

C		D	
Polytechnic	University	Polytechnic	University
£4300————4300		£4000————4600	
4350————4250		4050————4550	
4400————4200		4100————4500	
4050————4150		4150————4450	
4500————4100		4200————4400	
4550————4050		4250————4350	
4600————4000		4300————4300	

two types of institutions, prestige of the two institutions five years ago and
'today', quality of research and of facilities in the two institutions, quality of
working atmosphere between colleagues, quality of graduates, etc. A number
of these dimensions were obtained from pilot interviews with PLs and ULs.

Results and discussion

Implicit categorization, social identity and group distinctiveness strategies   First,
both groups of respondents readily categorized themselves as lecturers in
their respective institution. Relative to any other occupational groups in
Britain, both PLs and ULs rated themselves to be highly satisfied with their
present occupation (on a seven-point scale: PLs = $\bar{x}$: 6.00; ULs = $\bar{x}$: 6.17).
In addition, both PLs and ULs identified moderately with their respective
ingroup (PLs = $\bar{x}$: 4.44; ULs = $\bar{x}$: 4.25).

Interesting patterns of results emerged when PLs and ULs described
the circumstances which brought them to their respective institutions.
The results show that more ULs (39/48) could be categorized as giving
an internal attribution for becoming a UL (e.g. 'I always wanted to do
research in a university setting') than PLs (16/48). Conversely, more PLs

Table 8. *Total number of advantages and disadvantages listed by all lecturers concerning their own job*

	Advantages	Disadvantages	Ratio of advantages to disadvantages	Total number of features listed
Polytechnic lecturers $N = 48$	173	118	+1.47	291
University lecturers $N = 48$	183	77	+2.38	260

(25/48) could be categorized as giving an external attribution for becoming a PL (e.g. 'I ended up in a polytechnic at a time when the Government was expanding the polytechnic sector and recruiting from industry') than ULs (1/48). These results reflect the fact that polytechnics are new institutions within higher education in the UK and that the career background of PLs is more varied than that of ULs.

The social identity of group members may be influenced by the number of advantages and disadvantages individuals perceive in being members of their own group. Respondents were asked to enumerate the advantages and disadvantages they perceived in being lecturers in their respective institutions. The results obtained are summarized in Table 8.

A computation of the ratio of advantages (+) and disadvantages (−) listed by each group indicates that a positive ratio in favour of advantages emerged for both PLs and ULs. Nevertheless, the results show that ULs had a higher positive ratio (+2.38) than PLs (+1.47), suggesting that it may be easier for ULs to maintain a positive social identity than for PLs. The difference between PLs and ULs was mostly due to the high number of disadvantages PLs were 'forced' to acknowledge compared to ULs. This latter trend does reflect the 'objective' position of each group as previously described. Of greater interest is the fact that PLs listed as many advantages in being lecturers in polytechnics as did lecturers in the university sector. Tajfel (1978) proposed that when faced with a disadvantaged group position, low-status group members can maintain positive social identity by creating new dimensions of positive group identity. The first job advantage mentioned by each lecturer in the polytechnic and university sectors is listed in Table 9.

As seen in Table 9, PLs did mention a greater variety of advantages in being members of their own group (23 different ones in all) than did ULs

Table 9. *First type of advantage listed by each lecturer concerning their own job*

	First Type of Advantage Listed for Own Job
Polytechnic lecturers $N = 48$	Freedom of movement★ (8 PLs)
	good salary (5 PLs)
	wide range of teaching experience (5 PLs)
	20 different other types of advantages (30 PLs)
University lecturers $N = 48$	Freedom to pursue own research and academic interests (28 ULs)
	freedom of movement★ (10 ULs)
	5 different other types of advantages (10 ULs)

★'Freedom of movement' include items such as flexible hours of work and degree of control over own work and holidays.

Table 10. *Pls' and ULs' response to the question 'Which aspect of your job makes you feel most proud to be a lecturer in the university/polytechnic sector?'*

Main dimension given by each respondent	Polytechnic lecturers $N = 48$	University lecturers $N = 48$
Teaching	22	30
Special applied teaching	18	0
Research	2	17
None	6	1

(only seven different types of advantages). Although a proportion of these PL advantages may actually represent a creativity strategy, it must be noted that PLs by virtue of their greater applied and vocational interests may already have had more varied dimensions of differentiation at their disposal than ULs.

On which dimension of group distinctiveness did the two groups prefer to base their positive social identity? Answers to the interview question 'Which aspect of your job makes you feel 'proud' to be a lecturer in a university (polytechnic)?' are presented in Table 10. Only the first dimension mentioned by each respondent is presented in Table 10. Whereas both 'teaching' and 'research' emerged as positive distinctiveness dimensions for ULs, only 'teaching' emerged as an important dimension of positive identity for PLs. But 18/40 PLs gave a special meaning to the 'teaching' dimension. Indeed these PLs were keen to *redefine* the 'teaching' dimension by emphasizing both the distinctively applied nature of their teaching and the specialized pedagogical skills they developed in dealing with a broader range of educationally qualified students. As one PL put it: 'I'm proud of

Table 11. *PLs' and ULs' responses to the question 'Which group do you find you compare yourself with?'*

Number of PLs who gave the following as relevant comparison groups ($N = 48$)		Number of ULs who gave the following as relevant comparison groups ($N = 48$)	
University lecturers	= 26	Scientific civil servants (15) and professionals (11)	= 26
Social workers	= 4	Polytechnic lecturers	= 3
Teachers in higher education generally	= 3	Teachers in higher education generally	= 4
Secondary school teachers	= 2		
Other groups	= 5	Other groups	= 6
No comparison groups	= 8	No comparison groups	= 9

the applied aspects of our teaching. I'm not pretending to be an academic.' As a net effect, 17 ULs managed to distinguish themselves clearly and positively by stressing pride in their university research, while 18 PLs managed to do likewise by emphasizing the special applied nature of the teaching they dispensed in the polytechnic sector.

As regards to choices of social comparison groups, it has been suggested by Tajfel (1978) that low-status group members may achieve a positive social identity by selecting the group they compare themselves with. A low-status group may avoid using high-status groups as relevant comparison groups (Turner and Brown, 1978) and maintain group identity by comparing favourably with 'inferior' outgroups. Alternatively group members may maintain their distinctiveness by refusing to consider groups immediately below them as relevant comparison groups. Finally it was suggested that groups may seek *negatively discrepant* comparisons with 'superior' outgroups as a strategy for justifying claims to the advantages enjoyed by high status outgroups.

As can be seen in Table 11, both PLs and ULs adopted the strategy of comparing themselves with groups of higher status than their own. PLs compared themselves with university lecturers, while ULs compared themselves with scientific civil servants and with professions such as physicians and lawyers.

The main reasons given by PLs for comparing with ULs were: (1) because the work was of an equivalent nature and level (mentioned by 16 PLs); and (2) in order to link salary structures (mentioned by 6 PLs). Reasons given by ULs for comparing with professionals and scientific civil servants were: (1) in order to link salary structures (mentioned by

7 ULs); and (2) because the work was of an equivalent nature (mentioned by 12 ULs). This latter reason appears suspect since professionals and civil servants seldom teach, and professionals by virtue of their applied work rarely do any research. These latter results suggest that ULs may have been comparing upwards in order to differentiate themselves further from the more comparable, and perhaps threatening, PLs (Turner, 1978*b*). Indeed, this seems to be borne out by the AUT policy of 1976–1977 which argued that ULs' salaries should be linked to those of the 'more comparable' scientific civil servants rather than to those of polytechnic lecturers.

More important, the social comparison results obtained from both the university and polytechnic lecturers show that under some circumstances group members do actively seek unfavourable (negatively discrepant) comparisons with advantaged outgroups. Reasons given by both groups for comparing upwards indicate that negatively discrepant comparisons may be used as a strategy for justifying claims for improving a group's financial and material position *vis-à-vis* relevant outgroups. These results corroborate those obtained by Patchen (1968) who found that numerous oil refinery workers who compared upwards did so in order to justify higher pay claims relative to 'higher status' outgroup workers whom they felt had equal or lower qualifications and workloads than their own. The role of negatively discrepant comparison strategies will be explored further in the discussion of the 'intergroup bias' results.

The above results suggest that status differences between the two groups had an impact on their respective social identities and had some influence on their strategies of group distinctiveness. The aim of the next part of the study was to investigate group distinctiveness strategies when the comparison between PLs and ULs was made quite explicit and salient to the respondents in the interview setting (Doise and Sinclair, 1973).

Explicit categorization, intergroup perceptions and group distinctiveness strategies
Since PLs compared more with ULs than did ULs with PLs, one could expect PLs to be more aware of university affairs than ULs of polytechnic affairs. Table 12, however, shows that *both* groups were able to list many features of the outgroup environment. Of these, PLs saw mostly advantages of being a UL (62 % of total or a ratio of +1.65), while ULs saw mostly disadvantages of being a PLs (68 % of the total, or a ratio of −0.48). These ratios contrast with those obtained for self-ratings in Table 9: whereas PLs gave themselves a ratio of advantages/disadvantages of +1.47, ULs only gave PLs a ratio of −0.48; while ULs gave themselves a ratio of +2.38, PLs only gave ULs a ratio of +1.65. These patterns suggest that

Table 12. *Total number of advantages and disadvantages listed by all lecturers concerning the outgroup job*

	Advantages of outgroup job	Disadvantages of outgroup job	Ratio of advantages to disadvantages	Total number of features listed
Polytechnic lecturers $N = 48$	126 (62 %)	76 (38 %)	+1.65	202 (100 %)
University lecturers	65 (32 %)	135 (68 %)	−0.48	200 (100 %)

Table 13. *Main outgroup advantages and disadvantages listed by PLs and ULs*

	Advantages of outgroup job	Disadvantages of outgroup job
Polytechnic lecturers ($N = 48$)	More time for research in University (14 PLs) Lighter teaching load (9 PLs) Higher status (5 PLs) Other different advantages (16 PLs) Don't know (4 PLs)	More academic pressure in University (9 PLs) Academic back-biting (8 PLs) Difficult promotion (4 PLs) Lower pay (4 PLs) None (5 PLs) Other different disadvantages (14 PLs) Don't know (4 PLs)
University lecturers ($N = 48$)	Better salary in polytechnics (24 ULs) Other different advantages (13 ULs) None (4 ULs) Don't know (7 ULs)	Heavy teaching load in polytechnics (15 ULs) No time for research (18 ULs) Lower standard of students (5 ULs) Other different disadvantages (10 ULs)

both groups had a tendency to minimize some of the advantages enjoyed by the outgroup, perhaps as an attempt to compare more favourably with the outgroup on at least some dimension of social comparison.

The main characteristics listed by each group as advantages and disadvantages of the outgroup are listed in Table 13. A few points can be raised about these perceptions. Although PLs could not deny the very real advantages enjoyed by ULs, they did list 'greater academic pressure' and 'academic back-biting' as important disadvantages associated with the 'academic careerism' of the University sector. That these disadvantages were listed by PLs and not by ULs suggests that PLs may have been seeking and finding disadvantages in the university sector. Again, these

Table 14. *Main advantages of each sector given by polytechnic and university lecturers*

Main advantages in the university sector given by	
University lecturers	Polytechnic lecturers
Freedom to pursue own research and academic interests (28 ULs)	More time for research (14 PLs)
	Lighter teaching load (9 PLs)
Freedom of movement (10 ULs)	Greater status (5 PLs)
Other different advantages (10 ULs)	Other different advantages (16 PLs)

Main advantages in the polytechnic sector given by	
University lectures	Polytechnic lecturers
Better salary (24 ULs)	Freedom of movement (8 PLs)
Other different advantages (13 ULs)	Better salary (5 PLs)
	Wider range of teaching experience and students (5 PLs)
	Other different advantages (10 PLs)

perceptions may allow PLs to compare more favourably with ULs. Conversely, ULs had a tendency to list as disadvantages of being a PL absence of those characteristics that ULs used to define their own superiority: i.e. lack of time for research, less academically qualified students, etc. Although many ULs gave 'better pay' as the main advantage of being a PL, many ULs perceived this 'advantage' as an 'unfair' erosion of their salary differentials *vis-a-vis* PLs.

How consensual were the two groups in acknowledging each other's positive dimensions? Table 14 combines results from Tables 13 and 9. PLs tended to agree with ULs on the advantages of being a UL, with 'lighter teaching load' and 'more time for research' being equivalent to ULs' freedom of interest and movement. In contrast, ULs did not agree with PLs about the advantages of being a PL. PLs listed 'range of teaching', 'freedom of movement' and 'better pay' as advantages of being PLs, while ULs only acknowledged PLs' higher salaries as being an advantage. ULs, it would seem, felt that the advantage of 'freedom of movement' was distinctive to them only and not for PLs. In addition, only two ULs saw 'broader range of teaching' as a possible advantage of being a lecturer in a polytechnic. This suggests that ULs had difficulty in evaluating dimensions of the PLs' work as advantages.

To test further the impact of explicit comparisons on the lecturers' social identity, lecturers were asked to describe the distinctiveness of their

Table 15. *Number of lecturers assigned to each category of group distinctiveness*

	Positive distinctiveness	Negative distinctiveness	Neutral
Polytechnic lecturers $N = 48$	20	10	18
University lecturers $N = 48$	34	1	13

own work relative to that of the outgroup lecturers. The distinctions given by each respondent were categorized as positively valued, negatively valued or neutral. Table 15 represents the number of lecturers who were assigned to each category of group distinctiveness. Positive distinctiveness meant a lecturer differentiating from the outgroup on a majority of dimensions favouring the ingroup; negative distinctiveness meant differentiating from the outgroup on dimensions favouring the outgroup while neutrality meant differentiating from the outgroup on dimensions which were not explicitly valued.

As can be seen in Table 15, more group members could be categorized as distinguishing themselves *positively* from the outgroup than *negatively*. These results confirm the trends obtained earlier, suggesting that in *both groups*, the majority of lecturers identified themselves positively. However, fewer PLs identified themselves positively than ULs. As expected, attemps to maintain positive distinctiveness could be more difficult for the low-status PLs than for the high-status ULs. Whereas ULs positively valued the distinctive academic and research oriented university environment, PLs positively valued the applied and innovative nature of their teaching in the polytechnic sector.

Considering the status relationship between polytechnics and universities, it could be expected that polytechnic and university lecturers would perceive the role of the two institutions differently. Would PLs, being the low status group, be more likely to seek changes in the present role of each institution in higher education? From the interview results, lecturers' views on the role of the universities and polytechnics in higher education could be classified in the following categories:

(1) The binary system of higher education is fair, universities and polytechnics have *complementary* roles.

(2) The binary system is a fact, but it makes the polytechnics into second-rate universities and this is *wrong*.

(3) The polytechnics embody what higher education should be, i.e.

Table 16. *Lecturers' perceptions of the role of polytechnics and universities in higher education*

	(1) The binary system is fine	(2) The binary system is a fact but it makes polytechnics into second-rate universities	(3) Polytechnics mean higher education for all: universities should be scaled down
Polytechnic lecturers N = 48	23 (48 %)	9 (19 %)	16 (33 %)
University lecturers N = 48	46 (96 %)	2 (4 %)	0

higher education for everyone, and therefore the universities should be *scaled down* to allow for the expansion of the polytechnic sector.

The desire for social change embodied in these statements increases from category one to three. The third statement represents a social competition strategy since it advocates a direct attempt to reverse the intergroup situation in favour of polytechnics to the detriment of the university sector. As seen in Table 16, lecturers could be readily classified on the basis of their views of the role of polytechnics and universities in higher education. While the majority of ULs (96 %) were satisfied with the binary system, less than half (48 %) of the PLs were satisfied with the status quo. As the high-status group, ULs felt the intergroup situation was fair and legitimate and should not change. PLs were either dissatisfied with the present status relationship (19 %) or advocated a strategy of social competition (33 %) by proposing to scale down the universities to allow for further expansion of the polytechnic sector.

Lecturers' views of the Government's aims in dealing with the polytechnic and university sectors were also obtained. Since the Government has ultimate control over both the polytechnic and university sector, one can illustrate this relationship as follows:

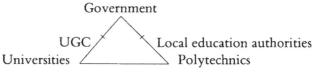

Government

UGC   Local education authorities

Universities   Polytechnics

Lecturers from both groups were asked to respond to the following question: 'What do you see to be the ultimate aim of the present Government (Labour) in dealing with the polytechnics and universities?' As can be seen

Table 17. *Lecturers' perceptions of the aim of the Government in dealing with the university and polytechnic sectors*

	Government favours the ingroup	Government favours the outgroup	No Government favouritism	Don't know
Polytechnic lecturers $N = 48$	20 (42 %)	12 (25 %)	9 (19 %)	7 (14 %)
University lecturers $N = 48$	9 (19 %)	20 (42 %)	13 (28 %)	6 (11 %)

in Table 17 lecturers' responses were classified according to whether the government was seen to favour the ingroup or the outgroup, or neither group.

The results show a tendency for lecturers in both groups to see the Government as favouring the polytechnic sector more than the university sector. Both groups saw the intergroup situation to be unstable to some extent. Interview results showed that Government policy changes based on the 1974 Houghton Report were perceived as a threat by many ULs. For these ULs, the threat was perceived especially in terms of the erosion of their salary differentials *vis-à-vis* PLs.

Individual mobility and desire to pass   Although group members may achieve positive social identity by 'passing' as individuals from a low- to a high-status group, the possibility of such movement may be limited by numerous factors. Polytechnic and university lecturers were asked a number of questions dealing with the perceived social mobility of lecturers in higher education. Table 18 represents results of a 2 × 2 ANOVA on three questions with factors: (1) ratings made by PLs/ULs; and (2) whether the movement was from polytechnic to university or from university to polytechnic.

Although PLs and ULs perceived very little mobility for lecturers across the two sectors of higher education in absolute terms, PLs perceived more mobility in general than did ULs ($F = 6.57$, df 1, 391, $p \leqslant 0.05$). In addition, both groups of lecturers felt that movement from the university sector to the polytechnic sector was more frequent than the converse ($F = 11.19$, $p \leqslant 0.01$). Both groups of lecturers also felt it was easier for lecturers to move to the polytechnic sector from the university sector than to move to the university sector from the polytechnic sector ($F = 280.7$, $p \leqslant 0.01$).

Table 18. *Perception of mobility in higher education, means and significant F values for four questions (2 × 2 ANOVA)*

Social mobility questions	Lecturer (PLs/ULs) main effect (df = 1, 391)	Institution (poly/uni) main effect (df = 1, 391)	Lecturer × institution interaction (df = 1, 391)
Frequency movement	PLs: $\bar{x} = 2.5^{\dagger}$ ULs: $\bar{x} = 2.0$ $F = 6.57^{\star}$	Poly to uni: $\bar{x} = 2.00$ Uni to poly: $\bar{x} = 2.50$ $F = 11.19^{\star\star}$	ns
Ease of movement	ns	Poly to uni: $\bar{x} = 2.3$ Uni to poly: $\bar{x} = 5.2$ $F = 280.70^{\star\star}$	ns
Academic qualification to move	ns	Poly to uni: $\bar{x} = 3.7$ Uni to poly: $\bar{x} = 4.8$ $F = 32.97^{\star\star}$	$F = 5.53^{\star}$
How easy for yourself to move to the outgroup sector	PLs: $\bar{x} = 2.4$ ULs: $\bar{x} = 3.8$ $F = 16.31^{\star\star}$	ns	ns

$^{\star}p \leqslant 0.05$
$^{\star\star}p \leqslant 0.01$
†The higher the mean rating (seven-point scale), the higher the rating on the item.

Also both groups of lecturers agreed with the notion that lecturers from the university sector were more academically qualified to move to the polytechnic sector than vice versa. ($F = 32.9$, $p \leqslant 0.01$). A significant interaction on this last item indicates that this difference was emphasized by ULs compared to PLs.

When lecturers were asked how easy it would be for themselves to move to the outgroup sector, ULs felt such moves would be easier ($\bar{x} = 3.8$) than did PLs ($\bar{x} = 2.4$; $F = 16.30$, df 1, 391, $p \leqslant 0.01$). The general lack of social mobility in British higher education was reflected by the finding that both university and polytechnic lecturers reported that they rarely searched for positions outside their own type of institution.

Though little actual mobility was reported, ULs and PLs did agree that lecturers from universities have greater potentials for mobility than lecturers from polytechnics.

Since members of the university high-status group could only lose status by moving to the polytechnic sector, it was expected that desire to 'pass' to the outgroup sector would be lower for ULs than for PLs. On the assumption that PLs value the higher status enjoyed by ULs, PLs would

Table 19. *Desire for social mobility amongst polytechnic and university lecturers*

	Desire to move to the outgroup sector	No desire to move to the outgroup sector	Don't know
Polytechnic lecturers N = 48	19 (40 %)	28 (58 %)	1 (2 %)
University lecturers N = 48	1 (2 %)	47 (98 %)	0

$\chi^2 = 23.81$, df $= 1$, $p \leqslant 0.001$ (excludes 'Don't know')

have much to gain by 'passing' to the university sector. The results shown in Table 19 support the expectation held for ULs: 47 out of 48 ULs expressed *no* desire to move to the polytechnic sector. The reasons given by ULs for remaining in the university sector were directly related to the advantages of being a lecturer in the university sector as opposed to being a lecturer in the polytechnic sector.

The results obtained for PLs indicate that whereas the *majority* of PLs expressed no desire to move to the university sector (28/48), two-fifths of the PL sample (19/48) did express such a desire. Did PLs who had a desire to 'pass' have different career backgrounds and expectations from lecturers who had no desire to 'pass' to the university sector? No differences in status position, and academic qualifications differentiated PLs who wanted to 'pass' from those who did not. Nevertheless, PLs who had no desire to move tended to have more seniority than those who did. As expected, PLs with a desire to 'pass' had higher career expectations than those with no desire to move.

Differences between PLs with a desire to 'pass' and those with a desire to remain in the polytechnic sector did emerge on important attitudes concerning the advantages and disadvantages of being a lecturer in higher education. As can be seen in Table 20, PLs with a desire to 'pass' to the university sector were more dissatisfied with conditions in higher education than were PLs who had no desire to move. PLs with a desire to move to the university sector felt there was less time for research and less of a fair deal from the government in higher education in general than did PLs who had no desire to 'pass'. While PLs who wanted to stay in the polytechnic sector emphasized the 'niceness' of the working atmosphere in polytechnics ($\bar{x} = 5.6$) relative to that in the university sector ($\bar{x} = 4.2$),

Table 20. *Intergroup perceptions of PLs who have and do not have a desire to 'pass' to the university sector (2 × 2 ANOVA)*

Intergroup attitudes N = 47	Desire to pass: (yes/no) main effect df = 1, 187	Institution (in poly/uni) main effect df = 1, 187	Desire x institution interaction (df 1, 187)
Time for research	Yes = $\bar{x}$ = 3.6[†] No = $\bar{x}$ = 4.1 F = 7.92**	ns	ns
Fair deal from the Government	Yes = $\bar{x}$ = 3.9 No = $\bar{x}$ = 4.6 F = 5.00**	ns	ns
Quality of working atmosphere	ns	ns	$F = 4.78$*

* $p \leqslant 0.05$
** $p \leqslant 0.01$
[†] The higher the mean rating (seven-point scale) the higher the rating on the item.

PLs who had a desire to 'pass' did not emphasize such differences between the polytechnic ($\bar{x} = 4.9$) and university sector ($\bar{x} = 4.6$; $F = 4.78$, $P \leqslant 0.05$).

In addition, PLs who wished to move to the university sector did not identify as strongly with their ingroup ($\bar{x} = 3.70$) as did PLs who had no desire to 'pass' ($\bar{x} = 4.71$, $F = 5.60$, df = 1, 187, $p \leqslant 0.05$). From comments gathered during the interviews, PLs who wanted to move to the university sector felt research was an important dimension of their activity and felt frustrated about the lack of time available for research in the polytechnic sector. This pattern of results corroborates results obtained by Whitburn et al. (1976) where it was found that PLs who were most active in research were also those who were most likely to want to move to the university sector.

When examining the reasons PLs gave for wanting to stay in the polytechnic sector the following trends emerged:

(1) PLs were satisfied with various aspects of their job in the polytechnic sector.

(2) PLs gave reasons indicating their commitment to the polytechnic ideals as set out in the Robbins Report.

(3) PLs asserted they would lose in salary if they moved to the university sector.

Reasons classified as satisfaction with the job were related to the quality of the working life in polytechnics relative to other occupations in the UK, including university lecturing. PLs who wished to stay in the polytechnic sector also stressed their satisfaction with teaching in applied fields to a broad range of students. As seen earlier and from comments gathered during the interviews, PLs who wished to stay in the polytechnic sector identified more strongly with their ingroup than lecturers who wished to move to the university sector. From comments gathered in the interviews, it seems that part of these PLs' identity was to 'opt out' of research so that unfavourable comparisons with ULs on this dimension became somewhat irrelevant since no claim was made about interest in research. No other differences emerged in the attitudes of PLs who wished to stay in the polytechnic sector compared to those who wished to pass to the university sector (including attitudes sampled in the intergroup bias questionnaire).

The results obtained so far suggest that the status differentials between polytechnic and university lecturers did have an effect on their respective social identity and did influence their choice of group distinctiveness strategies. The results suggest the following.

As the high-status group, ULs did exhibit a positive social identity on the various dependent measures. ULs were quite satisfied with the intergroup status relationship, felt moderately threatened by recent government policy changes in favour of PL salaries, and showed no desire whatsoever to move to the polytechnic sector. The ULs did engage in accentuating some aspects of their positive group distinctiveness *vis-à-vis* PLs. In spite of the inherent similarities between ULs and PLs, and perhaps because of this similarity (Turner, 1978*b*), ULs did not acknowledge PLs as a relevant comparison group. In addition to emphasizing their own dimensions of positive distinctiveness *vis-à-vis* PLs, ULs displayed outgroup bias by refusing to acknowledge the 'positive dimensions' of polytechnic lecturers except 'higher pay' which they perceived as somewhat illegitimate anyway.

While acknowledging the advantages of the university sector over the polytechnic sector on numerous dimensions, PLs adopted numerous strategies to maintain a positive social identity including individual mobility, social creativity and social competition.

While recognizing the difficulty of PLs moving to the university sector, two-fifths of the PLs in this survey expressed a desire to 'pass' to the university sector. Thus, in spite of a virtual freeze in the mobility of lecturers from the polytechnic to the university sector, 'passing' as an individual was still perceived as a viable alternative for many PLs. Polytechnic lecturers who wanted to 'pass' to the university sector did not identify strongly as polytechnic lecturers, were concerned with research and were dissatisfied with the lack of opportunities for doing research in the polytechnic sector.

One-third of the PLs were keen to define positively the applied nature of their work and the uniqueness of the pedagogical skills they *created* whilst teaching to a broad range of academically endowed students.

Finally, numerous PLs saw the intergroup status relationship to be both unstable and illegitimate. One-third of the PLs interviewed in this survey adopted a *social competition* strategy by advocating that the polytechnic sector symbolizes what higher education should be in Britain, and that consequently the university sector should be scaled down to allow polytechnics to expand further.

These interview results show that more than one group-distinctiveness strategy can be used by different members of a social group to maintain a positive social identity. This was especially the case for PLs who, by virtue of their low-status position and their perception of the intergroup situation, adopted a number of different strategies to maintain positive distinctiveness. As the high-status group, ULs did have a tendency to show more ingroup favouritism than PLs (Doise and Sinclair, 1973; Turner and Brown, 1978). The aim of the last part of the interview was specifically designed to investigate patterns of intergroup bias displayed by PLs and ULs.

Intergroup bias   The status relationship between PLs and ULs as well as their respective belief systems concerning the legitimacy and stability of the intergroup relation situation had an impact on patterns of intergroup bias (Tajfel, 1978). As seen earlier, ULs perceived their high-status position in the binary system to be quite fair and legitimate. In addition, ULs felt the intergroup situation was slightly unstable due to recent increases in Government pay awards to PLs. Government policy changes made PLs feel that the intergroup situation in higher education was somewhat unstable. Only half of them felt that the relationship between polytechnics and universities was fair and legitimate, the others felt it was unfair and illegitimate. How did these different intergroup perceptions interact with lecturers' status positions to affect patterns of intergroup bias?

Salary matrices   As explained earlier, PLs and ULs were given the opportunity to display intergroup bias through their choice of appropriate pay awards to lecturers from each group using the salary matrices shown in Table 7. As in the study by Brown (1978) salary matrices were constructed so that choices made by lecturers could reflect various strategies of intergroup bias including: maximum differentiation (MD); a combination of maximum ingroup profit and maximum differentiation (MIP + MD); fairness (F); and a combination of maximum ingroup profit with maximum joint profit (MIP + MJP).

Table 21. *Education cuts*

(a) How lecturers themselves cut each area of education

Education sector	Polytechnic lecturers (N = 48)	University lecturers (N = 48)
University teaching	16 % ⎫ 42 %	14 % ⎫ 32 %
University research	26 % ⎭	18 % ⎭
Polytechnic teaching	14 % ⎫ 32 %	15 % ⎫ 37 %
Polytechnic research	18 % ⎭	22 % ⎭
Secondary education	6 %	11 %
Further education (adult)	20 %	20 %

(b) How lecturers saw possible Government cuts

Education sector	Polytechnic lecturers (N = 48)	University lecturers (N = 48)
University teaching	14 % ⎫ 34 %	14 % ⎫ 35 %
University research	20 % ⎭	21 % ⎭
Polytechnic teaching	14 % ⎫ 31 %	12 % ⎫ 31 %
Polytechnic research	17 % ⎭	19 % ⎭
Secondary education	13 %	10 %
Further education (adult)	23 %	24 %

The results indicate that, on the salary matrices, neither group showed any significant tendency towards using strategies of psychological differentiation such as MD or MIP + MD. Both groups displayed a slight pull towards ingroup profit combined with joint profit (MIP + MJP), but this effect did not reach statistical significance. The predominant strategy employed by both groups was that of fairness. Both groups showed large pulls on 'fairness' ($\bar{x} = 5.5$ for PLs and $\bar{x} = 4.7$ for ULs), with PLs being significantly more 'fair' than ULs ($F = 5.02$, df $= 2, 96$, $P \leqslant 0.05$). The greater pull on 'fairness' displayed by PLs reflected their desire to have their salaries linked with those of ULs through parity. Though ULs also strove for 'fairness', their lower score on this measure reflects their concern about the erosion of salary differentials *vis-à-vis* PLs.

Education cuts   PLs and ULs were given the opportunity to display ingroup bias by being given the task of distributing education cuts across various sectors of secondary and higher education. Table 21 (a) shows how lecturers themselves distributed cuts in the six areas of education.

Combining the areas of research and teaching for each institution, it can be seen that each group preferred to cut the outgroup more than the ingroup. This bias occurred more in the area of research than in teaching, mainly because cuts in teaching were perceived as generally less defensible. Looking at lecturers' perceptions of how the Government would distribute the cuts (Table 21b), both groups saw the Government as tending to cut universities more than polytechnics. This result supports the earlier findings in which both groups saw the Government as favouring the polytechnics more than the universities. These trends are due to the fact that both groups of lecturers perceived polytechnics as being ideologically more aligned with the Government's emphasis on the development of the technological aspects of higher education rather than universities.

Intergroup bias questionnaire   Polytechnic and university lecturers were asked to compare universities and polytechnics on the following comparison dimensions:

  (a) Prestige of the two types of institutions today; and five years ago; academic standards of the lecturers; and of the student intake; quality of graduates; and of the research produced in the two types of institutions.

  (b) The quality of facilities in the two types of institutions; the teaching load in the two types of institutions; time for research; lecturers' salaries and fair deal from the Government.

  (c) Quality of the working atmosphere in the two types of institutions; quality of teaching; importance placed on teaching; and job satisfaction.

As was seen earlier, some dimensions listed above clearly favour either the university sector or the polytechnic sector, while others can be valued differently by each group of lecturers. The question arises whether each group will acknowledge each other's advantages or will show outgroup bias by denigrating, minimizing, or claiming as their own, the 'advantages' held by the outgroup (Tajfel, 1978; Tajfel and Turner, 1979).

Lecturers' ratings on each comparison dimension were subjected to a 2 × 2 ANOVA consisting of a 'lecturer' factor (PL v UL) and an 'institution' factor (rating the polytechnic v the university sector). The results obtained for the first series of dimensions are presented in Table 22. A 'lecturer' main effect on four dimensions indicates that in general, PLs rated the academic standards in higher education institutions (universities *and* polytechnics) to be higher than ULs rated them to be. More interestingly, significant 'institution' main effects indicate that both groups of lecturers recognized that universities were 'superior' to polytechnics on the following dimensions:

Higher 'prestige' today ($F = 242.8$, df $= 1, 391, p \leqslant 0.01$) and five years ago ($F = 641.3, p \leqslant 0.01$).

Table 22. *Intergroup bias: questionnaire results for dimensions (a):*
(2 × 2 ANOVA)

Intergroup attitudes N = 98	Lecturer PL/UL main effect (df = 1, 391)	Institution poly/uni main effect (df = 1, 391)	Lecturer × institution interaction (df = 1, 391)	
Prestige today	PLs: $\bar{x} = 5.0^†$ ULs: $\bar{x} = 4.5$ F = 10.42**	in poly: $\bar{x} = 3.7$ in uni: $\bar{x} = 5.7$ F = 242.77**	ns ns	
Prestige five years ago	ns	in poly: $\bar{x} = 2.7$ in uni: $\bar{x} = 6.1$ F = 614.30**		
			in poly	*in uni*
Academic standards of lecturers	PLs: $\bar{x} = 5.2$ ULs: $\bar{x} = 4.8$ F = 6.24*	in poly: $\bar{x} = 4.3$ in uni: $\bar{x} = 5.8$ F = 175.60**	PLs $\bar{x} = 4.6$ ULs $\bar{x} = 3.8$ F = 13.65**	$\bar{x} = 5.7$ $\bar{x} = 5.8$
			in poly	*in uni*
Quality of student intake	ns	in poly: $\bar{x} = 13.4$ in uni: $\bar{x} = 5.4$ F = 277.19**	PLs $\bar{x} = 3.8$ ULs $\bar{x} = 3.0$ F = 24.69**	$\bar{x} = 5.2$ $\bar{x} = 5.6$
			in poly	*in uni*
Quality of graduates	PLs: $\bar{x} = 5.3$ ULs: $\bar{x} = 4.5$ F = 24.79**	in poly: $\bar{x} = 4.3$ in uni: $\bar{x} = 3.5$ F = 118.70**	PLs $\bar{x} = 5.0$ ULs $\bar{x} = 3.5$ F = 46.68**	$\bar{x} = 5.5$ $\bar{x} = 5.5$
			in poly	*in uni*
Quality of research	PLs: $\bar{x} = 5.2$ ULs: $\bar{x} = 4.6$ F = 15.58**	in poly: $\bar{x} = 4.1$ in uni: $\bar{x} = 5.7$ F = 134.91**	PLs $\bar{x} = 4.6$ ULs $\bar{x} = 3.5$ F = 10.54**	$\bar{x} = 5.8$ $\bar{x} = 5.7$

*$p \leqslant 0.05$
**$p \leqslant 0.01$
† The higher the mean rating (seven-point scale) the higher the rating on the item.

Higher academic standards of *lecturers* and undergraduate *students* in the universities than in the polytechnics ($F = 176.7$, p $\leqslant$ 0.01 and $F = 134.9$, $P \leqslant 0.01$ respectively).

Although PLs 'acknowledge' the high academic standards of lecturers, students, graduates and research in the university sector, interaction effects on these four dimensions show that there was less consensus concerning standards in the polytechnic sector. On each of these dimensions ULs rated the academic standards of polytechnics less favourably than did PLs themselves. These results suggest that, as the high-status group interested in maintaining its position, ULs asserted their group distinctiveness by accentuating the academic 'inferiority' of PLs relative to ULs (Turner and Brown, 1978).

Results obtained in the second series of dimensions are presented in Table 23. Highly significant 'institution' main effects show that lecturers

Table 23. *Intergroup bias: questionnaire results for dimensions (b):*
(2 × 2 ANOVA)

Intergroup attitudes N = 98	Lecturer PL/UL main effect (df = 1, 391)	Institution poly/uni Dain effect (df = 1, 391)	Lecturer × institution interaction (df = 1, 391)	
			in poly	*in uni*
Quality of facilities	ns	in poly: $\bar{x} = 3.91$[†] in uni: $\bar{x} = 5.3$ $F = 87.31$**	PLs $\bar{x} = 3.7$ ULs $\bar{x} = 4.0$ $F = 8.12$**	$\bar{x} = 5.6$ $\bar{x} = 5.1$
			in poly	*in uni*
Teaching load	PLs: $\bar{x} = 4.3$ ULs: $\bar{x} = 4.6$ $F = 4.15$*	in poly: $\bar{x} = 5.6$ in uni: $\bar{x} = 3.3$ $F = 267.64$**	PLs $\bar{x} = 5.7$ ULs $\bar{x} = 5.4$ $F = 16.42$**	$\bar{x} = 2.9$ $\bar{x} = 3.7$
			in poly	*in uni*
Time for research	PLs: $\bar{x} = 3.9$ ULs: $\bar{x} = 3.6$ $F = 6.22$*	in poly: $\bar{x} = 2.3$ in uni: $\bar{x} = 5.2$ $F = 809.60$**	PLs $\bar{x} = 2.2$ ULs $\bar{x} = 2.3$ $F = 13.77$**	$\bar{x} = 5.5$ $\bar{x} = 4.7$
			in poly	*in uni*
Importance placed on teaching	ns	in poly: $\bar{x} = 6.0$ in uni: $\bar{x} = 4.1$ $F = 138.12$**	PLs $\bar{x} = 6.3$ ULs $\bar{x} = 5.7$ $F = 16.76$**	$\bar{x} = 3.8$ $\bar{x} = 4.5$
			in poly	*in uni*
How well paid	ns	in poly: $\bar{x} = 5.2$ in uni: $\bar{x} = 4.2$ $F = 51.23$**	PLs $\bar{x} = 5.0$ ULs $\bar{x} = 5.5$ $F = 27.23$**	$\bar{x} = 4.7$ $\bar{x} = 3.8$

*$p \leqslant 0.05$
**$p \leqslant 0.01$
[†] The higher the mean rating (seven-point scale) the higher the rating on the item.

felt that the university sector has better facilities ($F = 87.3$, df = 1, 391, $p \leqslant$ 0.01), lighter teaching loads ($F = 267.6$, $p \leqslant$ 0.01) and more time for research ($F = 809.6$, $p \leqslant$ 0.01) than the polytechnic sector. Nevertheless both groups of lecturers felt polytechnic lecturers were better paid than university lecturers ($F = 51.23$, $p < 0.01$; for comparisons of actual pay differentials see Table 2).

Interaction effects also emerged on these ratings. Though both groups of lecturers tended to agree about the disadvantages of the polytechnic sector, Table 23 shows there was less consensus regarding the relative advantages of the university sector on these dimensions. PLs rated the facilities of the university sector to be better than ULs reported them to be ($F = 8.12$, df = 1, 391, $p \leqslant$ 0.01); PLs rated the teaching load in the university sector to be lower than ULs rated it to be ($F = 16.4$, $p < 0.01$) and PLs considered that ULs had more time for research than ULs themselves said they had ($F = 13.77$, $p \leqslant$ 0.01).

Table 24. *Intergroup bias: questionnaire results for dimensions (c):*
(2 × 2 ANOVA)

Intergroup attitudes $N = 98$	Lecturer PL/UL main effect (df = 1, 391)	Institution poly/uni main effect (df = 1, 391)	Lecturer × institution interaction (df = 1, 391)	
			in poly	*in uni*
Quality of working atmosphere	ns	ns	PLs: $\bar{x} = 5.3$ ULs: $\bar{x} = 4.8$ $F = 26.12$**	$\bar{x} = 4.5$[†] $\bar{x} = 5.4$
			in poly	*in uni*
Quality of teaching	PLs: $\bar{x} = 4.8$ ULs: $\bar{x} = 4.4$ $F = 6.25$*	ns	PLs: $\bar{x} = 5.3$ ULs: $\bar{x} = 4.2$ $F = 40.83$**	$\bar{x} = 4.0$ $\bar{x} = 4.8$
			in poly	*in uni*
Fair deal from Government	ns	ns	PLs: $\bar{x} = 4.0$ ULs: $\bar{x} = 4.7$ $F = 31.69$**	$\bar{x} = 4.8$ $\bar{x} = 4.0$
			in poly	*in uni*
Job satisfaction	ns	ns	PLs: $\bar{x} = 5.3$ ULs: $\bar{x} = 4.7$ $F = 29.20$**	$\bar{x} = 5.0$ $\bar{x} = 5.7$

*$p \leqslant 0.05$
**$p \leqslant 0.01$
[†] The higher the mean rating (seven-point scale) the higher the rating on the item.

In each of these cases, it seems that PLs were exaggerating the advantages of the university sector as a strategy for claiming that their low-status position on items like those included in Table 24 was not due to any inherent inferiority of their own, but could be attributed externally to the illegitimate 'material' advantages (Table 23) enjoyed by lecturers in the university sector. The previous results on choice of social comparison group gave some support for the notion that groups may actively seek negatively discrepant comparisons with advantaged outgroups as a strategy for justifying claims for improving a group's own conditions (Patchen, 1968). The present results suggest that unfavourable comparisons on 'material' dimensions (Table 23) may be used (or exaggerated) to 'explain away' unfavourable comparisons on 'social' dimensions such as abilities, group products (Table 22), opinions and values. Seeking negatively discrepant comparisons and viewing outgroup 'material' advantages as somewhat illegitimate has the advantage of justifying claims for 'improving' one's own group position relative to the outgroup, without threatening the ingroup's social identity.

Conversely, ULs as the high-status group 'forced' to compare with PLs, may have had vested interests in minimizing the 'material' advantages inherent in their own group position as a strategy for maintaining the legitimacy of their position *vis-à-vis* PLs. Interestingly enough, an inter-action effect emerged on salary, the only dimension on which PLs were perceived to compare favourably with ULs. On this dimension, ULs rated polytechnic salaries higher (see Table 2 for real differences) than what PLs reported themselves ($F = 27.23, p \leqslant 0.01$). This result suggests that, as with PLs on the other dimensions included in Table 23, ULs may have been exaggerating pay differentials in *favour* of PLs so as to make this difference appear more illegitimate. In addition, ULs may have been exaggerating the salary advantages of PLs in order to 'demonstrate' that this group was adequately compensated for their relative disadvantages on other comparison dimensions. Finally, both PLs and ULs perceived the outgroup as getting a better deal from the Government than the in-group ($F = 31.7, p \leqslant 0.01$). Again, this pattern of results suggests that both groups of lecturers could be exaggerating the extent of the outgroup advantages as a strategy to make the outgroup position appear less legiti-mate. In this case, it appears that both groups found it convenient to 'blame the Government' as the source of perceived inequity between these two sectors of higher education.

As can be seen in Table 24, no consensus emerged over the 'superiority' of either the polytechnics or the universities on the last series of social comparison dimensions.

Significant interaction effects revealed ingroup favouritism on valued dimensions of both groups' identity including 'quality of working atmo-sphere' ($F = 26.2$, $df = 1,391$, $p \leqslant 0.01$), 'job satisfaction' ($F = 29.2, p \leqslant 0.01$) and 'quality of teaching' ($F = 40.8, p \leqslant 0.01$). Although both groups of lecturers perceived that more importance was placed on teaching in the polytechnic sector than in the university sector ($F = 138.12, p \leqslant 0.01$), an interaction effect on this important dimension of both groups' social identity still emerged ($F = 16.76, p \leqslant 0.01$). The interaction effect indicates that PLs rated the importance of teaching in the university sector to be lower than what ULs actually reported. Conversely, ULs tended to rate the importance placed on teaching in the polytechnic sector to be lower than what PLs reported themselves. These results suggest that both groups were attempting to maintain their positive distinctiveness by minimizing the importance of this dimension in the outgroup. The significant inter-action effect for 'quality of teaching' reflects PLs' special emphasis on this dimension of group distinctiveness. Although both groups of lecturers showed ingroup favouritism on this dimension, PLs showed more ingroup favouritism by rating the quality of PL teaching higher than ratings made by ULs for university teaching.

The above results show that status position and beliefs concerning the intergroup situation had an effect on patterns of intergroup bias for both university and polytechnic lecturers. As the high-status group perceiving the intergroup situation to be legitimate but slightly unstable, ULs did show more ingroup bias than PLs (Turner and Brown, 1978). Whereas PLs acknowledged the academic 'superiority' of universities over 'poly-technics' on numerous dimensions (Table 22), ULs displayed ingroup bias by accentuating the academic 'inferiority' of polytechnics on these dimensions. In addition, ULs displayed less fairness on the salary matrices than did PLs.

On other less objectively defined dimensions of comparisons such as 'quality of working atmosphere', 'quality of teaching', etc. (Table 24), both ULs and PLs showed distinct patterns of ingroup favouritism.

As with strategies of intergroup distinctiveness, the above patterns of intergroup bias reflected each group's need to maintain a positive social identity *vis-à-vis* the outgroup on at least some dimensions of social comparison. Nevertheless, while ULs could base much of their positive social identity on consensually acknowledged dimensions such as quality of research, academic excellence and social prestige (Table 22), PLs had to 'struggle' (through group-distinctiveness strategies and bias) to maintain their positive social identity on non-consensually acknowledged dimen-sions such as 'quality of teaching', 'quality of working atmosphere' and 'job satisfaction'. The fact that these social comparison attributes were not consensual indicates that social competition was occurring between the groups on these valued dimensions (Tajfel and Turner, 1979).

4. Concluding notes

Though our two groups of lecturers could have stressed their common task of providing students with a training in higher education, instead, both groups were keen to differentiate themselves positively from each other on valued comparison dimensions. Although PLs acknowledged their disadvantaged position relative to ULs on numerous attributes, both groups emerged with a positive social identity: ULs on dimensions like 'pure research' and 'academic excellence', while numerous PLs based their positive identity on the innovative and applied nature of their teaching.

As the low-status group striving to maintain a positive social identity,

PLs did adopt distinctiveness strategies such as 'individual passing', 'social creativity' and 'social competition' (Tajfel, 1978). As proposed by Tajfel and Turner (1979), the choice of these strategies was influenced by the lecturers' beliefs concerning the stability and legitimacy of the intergroup relation situation. As the high-status group perceiving the intergroup situation to be quite legitimate though somewhat unstable, ULs were keen to assert their superiority over PLs on their own dimensions of positive distinctiveness. Although PLs achieved positive distinctiveness on the 'relevance' of their teaching, the positive nature of this distinctiveness was denied by ULs who saw such emphasis as coinciding with the teaching of poor students, heavier teaching load and lack of time for the 'more important' task of research. Hence PLs' positive distinctiveness was devalued by ULs (Tajfel, 1974a).

Finally, without threatening their positive social identities, both groups of lecturers attempted to justify their claims for better material conditions by seeking negatively discrepant comparisons with 'relevant' advantaged outgroups. On the intergroup bias measures, both groups of lecturers showed ingroup favouritism; this was the case especially on valued dimensions of each group's social identity. When forced to compare with each other on the intergroup bias measures, both groups managed to maintain a positive identity on valued *social* dimensions by exaggerating the extent of the 'unfair' *material* advantages enjoyed by the outgroup.

The results of this field study are encouraging. They indicate that Tajfel's theoretical concepts are applicable to a complex intergroup situation. They also reflect, and hopefully may contribute to, the renewed interest (e.g. Austin and Worchel, 1979; Sherif, 1966; Tajfel, 1978) in the testing of propositions of this kind in a variety of field studies. Although such studies may not be able to 'prove' or 'disprove' conclusively a hypothesis, they are obviously of considerable importance in ordering a large amount of data in terms of systematic articulations, and in extending the range of 'natural' social processes to which social psychological theory can be applied.

Notes

[1] This research was supported by a grant from the Social Science Research Council (SSRC) to Professor Henri Tajfel for a programme of research on intergroup relations at Bristol University. The first author is now an assistant professor in the psychology department at McMaster University. We are grateful to Henri Tajfel, John Turner and Rupert Brown for their most valuable comments during various phases of this study. We also wish to thank Peter Archibald, Serge Guimond, Peter Graf, Charles Husband, Herb Jenkins,

David Lang, and Richard Thorn for their very useful comments on previous drafts of this chapter.

[2] The data for the study on which this chapter is based were collected some five years ago. There is no doubt that some of the 'objective' and 'subjective' relations between the two types of institution and their staff, as described in the chapter, do not obtain any more, particularly in view of the recent heavy cuts in the allocation of funds to higher education. Nevertheless, the chapter was included in the book for three reasons: (i) the study was conducted in an interesting field setting using highly sophisticated respondents; (ii) despite this sophistication, results do not differ considerably from those often obtained with more 'usual' respondents; and (iii) the data can provide an interesting basis for comparison with later studies conducted in today's and tomorrow's drastically changed circumstances. (Editor's note).

[3] Guimond (1979) provides two Canadian examples of this phenomenon. In a document entitled *Égalité et Indépendance* (Editeur du Québec 1978) Québécois women systematically compare their position with that of Québécois men on a multitide of 'material' comparison dimensions including salary, promotion and representation and services offered, in cultural, political and economic agencies. On each of these comparison dimensions Québécois women compare unfavourably with Québécois men. In a document entitled *The heirs of Lord Durham: Manifesto of a vanishing people* the federation of Francophones outside of Québec (FFHQ, 1978a) systematically compare the position of Francophone minorities with the position of Anglophone majorities in each of the nine 'English' provinces of Canada. The results of these comparisons show that Francophone minorities compare unfavourably with Anglophone majorities on each 'ethnolinguistic vitality' dimension (Giles, Bourhis and Taylor, 1977). Finally, in a more recent publication entitled *Deux poids deux mesures: les francophones hors Québec et les Anglophones au Québec, un dossier comparatif,* the Federation of Francophones outside Québec (FFHQ, 1978b) deliberately and systematically compare their legal, educational, economic, cultural and political position with that of the 'comparable' English Canadian minority inside Québec. On every dimension of comparison Francophone minorities outside Québec are shown to compare very unfavourably with the position of the English Canadian minority inside Québec. These three documents provide evidence for the notion that low status groups can actively seek unfavourable comparisons (negatively discrepant comparisons) with an advantaged outgroup. The concluding remarks included in each of these documents point out the unfair and illegitimate nature of these unfavourable comparisons and use these negatively discrepant comparisons to justify claims for improving their own position *vis-à-vis* the advantaged outgroup.

References

Asher, S.R. and Allen, V.L. 1969. Racial preferences and social comparison processes. *Journal of Social Issues*, **25**, 157–66.

Austin, W. 1977. Equity theory and social comparison processes. In J. Suls and R. Miller (eds): *Social comparison theory: Theoretical and empirical perspectives.* Washington, D.C.: Hemisphere Press.

Austin, W.G. and Worchel, S. 1979. *The social psychology of intergroup relations.* Monterey, Calif.: Brooks/Cole.

Billig, M. 1976. *Social psychology and intergroup relations.* European Monographs in Social Psychology, No. 9, London: Academic Press.

Billig, M. and Tajfel, H. 1973. Social categorization and similarity in intergroup behaviour. *European Journal of Social Psychology*, **3**, 27–52.

Bourhis, R.Y., Giles, H. and Lambert, W.E. 1975. Social consequences of accommodating one's style of speech: A cross-national investigation. *International Journal of the Sociology of Language*, **6**, 53–71.

Bourhis, R.Y., Giles, H. and Tajfel, H. 1973. Language as a determinant of Welsh identity. *European Journal of Social Psychology*, **3**, 447–60.

Brown, R. 1978. Divided we fall: An analysis of relations between sections of a factory workforce. In H. Tajfel (ed.): *Differentiation between social groups: Studies in the social psychology of intergroup relations*. European Monographs in Social Psychology, No. 14. London: Academic Press.

DES 1966. *A plan for polytechnics and other colleges*. London: HMSO Cmnd 3006.

Deschamps, J.C. 1978. La perception des causes du comportement. In W. Doise, J.C. Deschamps and G. Mugny (eds): *Psychologie sociale expérimentale*. Paris: Colin.

Doise, W. 1972. Rencontres et représentations intergroupes. *Archives de Psychologie*, **41**, 303–20.

Doise, W. 1978. *Individuals and groups: Explanations in social psychology*. Cambridge: Cambridge University Press.

Doise, W. and Sinclair, A. 1973. The categorization process in intergroup relations. *European Journal of Social Psychology*, **3**, 145–57.

Éditeur de Québec 1978. *Égalite et indépendance*. Québec: Gouvernement du Québec.

FFHQ 1978a. *The heirs of Lord Durham: Manifesto of a dying people*. Ottawa: La Fédération des Francophones hors Québec.

FFHQ 1978b. *Deux poids, deux mesures: Les Francophones hors Québec et les Anglophones au Québec: Un dossier comparatif*. Ottawa: La Fédération des Francophones hors Québec.

Gerard, H.B. and Hoyt, M.F. 1974. Distinctiveness of social categorization and attitude towards ingroup members. *Journal of Personality and Social Psychology*, **29**, 836–42.

Guimond, S. 1979. L'intérprétation des inégalités économiques et sa relation au mécontentement social et à la perception de différences culturelles. Unpublished M.Sc. thesis, Department of Psychology, Université de Montréal.

Gurin, P., Gurin, R.L. and Beattie, M. 1969. Internal–external control in the motivational dynamics of Negro youth. *Journal of Social Issues*, **25**, 23–54.

Houghton 1974. *Report of the Committee of Enquiry into the pay of non-university teachers*. London: HMSO Cmnd 5848.

Hraba, J. and Grant, C. 1970. Black is beautiful: A re-examination of racial preference and identification. *Journal of Personality and Social Psychology*, **16**, 398–402.

Hyman, H.H. and Singer, E. 1968. *Readings in reference group theory and research*. New York: The Free Press.

Kidder, L.H. and Stewart, V.M. 1975. *The psychology of intergroup relations*. New York: McGraw Hill.

van Knippenberg, A. 1978. Status differences, comparative relevance and intergroup differentiation. In H. Tajfel (ed.): *Differentiation between social groups: Studies in the social psychology of intergroup relations*. European Monographs in Social Psychology, No. 14. London: Academic Press.

Lemaine, G. 1966. Inégalité, comparaison et incomparabilité: Esquisse d'une théorie de l'originalité sociale. *Bulletin de Psychologie*, **20**, 24–32.

Lemaine, G., Kastersztein, J. and Personnaz, B. 1978. Social differentiation. In H. Tajfel (ed.): *Differentiation between social groups: Studies in the social psychology of intergroup relations*. European Monographs in Social Psychology, No. 14. London: Academic Press.

Patchen, M. 1968. A conceptual framework and some empirical data regarding comparisons of social rewards. In H.H. Hyman and E. Singer (eds): *Readings in reference group theory and research*. New York: The Free Press.

Percy 1945. *Report of the Percy Committee on Higher Technological Education*. London: HMSO.

Perkin, H. 1969. *Key profession: The history of the Association of University Teachers*. London: Routledge and Kegan Paul.

Robbins 1963. *Report of the Committee on Higher Education*. London: HMSO Cmnd 2154.

Runciman, W.G. 1966. *Relative deprivation and social justice*. London: Routledge and Kegan Paul.

Sears, D.O. and McConahay, J.P. 1970. Racial socialization: Comparison levels and the Watt riot. *Journal of Social Issues*, **26**, 121–40.

Sherif, M. 1966. *Group conflict and cooperation: Their social psychology*. London: Routledge and Kegan Paul.

Tajfel, H. 1970. Experiments in intergroup discrimination. *Scientific American*, **223**, (5), 96–102.

Tajfel, H. 1972a. Experiments in a vacuum. In J. Israel and H. Tajfel (eds): *The context of social psychology: A critical assessment*. European Monographs in Social Psychology, No. 2. London: Academic Press.

Tajfel, H. 1972b. La catégorisation sociale. In S. Moscovici (ed.): *Introduction à la psychologie sociale*. Paris: Larousse.

Tajfel, H. 1975. The exit of social mobility and the voice of social change: Unpublished Katz–Newcomb Lectures, Ann Arbor: University of Michigan.

Tajfel, H. 1974b. Social identity and intergroup behaviour. *Social Science Information*, **13**, 65–93.

Tajfel, H. 1975. The exit of social mobility and the voice of social change: Notes on the social psychology of intergroup relations. *Social Science Information*, **14**, 101–18.

Tajfel, H. 1978. The psychological structure of intergroup relations. Part I in H. Tajfel (ed.): *Differentiation between social groups: Studies in the social psychology of intergroup relations*. European Monographs in Social Psychology, No. 14. London: Academic Press.

Tajfel, H., Flament, C., Billig, M. and Bundy, R.P. 1971. Social categorization and intergroup behaviour. *European Journal of Social Psychology*, **1**, 149–78.

Tajfel, H. and Turner, J.C. 1979. An integrative theory of intergroup conflict. In W.G. Austin and S. Worchel (eds), *op. cit.*

Turner, J.C. 1978a. Social categorization and social discrimination in the minimal group paradigm. In H. Tajfel (ed.): *Differentiation between social groups: Studies in the social psychology of intergroup relations*. European Monographs in Social Psychology, No. 14. London: Academic Press.

Turner, J.C. 1978*b*. Social comparison, similarity and ingroup favouritism. In H. Tajfel (ed.): *Differentiation between social groups: Studies in the social psychology of intergroup relations*. European Monographs in Social Psychology, No. 14. London: Academic Press.

Turner, J.C. and Brown, R. 1978. Social status, cognitive alternatives and intergroup relations. In H. Tajfel (ed.): *Differentiation between social groups: Studies in the social psychology of intergroup relations*. European Monographs in Social Psychology, No. 14. London: Academic Press.

Turner, J., Brown, R.J. and Tajfel, H. 1979. Social comparison and group interest in ingroup favouritism. *European Journal of Social Psychology*, **9**, 187–204.

Vaughan, G.M. 1978. Social change and intergroup preferences in New Zealand. *European Journal of Social Psychology*, **8**, 297–314.

Whitburn, J., Mealing, M. and Cox, C. 1976. *People in polytechnics*. University of Surrey: Society for Research into Higher Education.

15. Open conflict and the dynamics of intergroup negotiations[1,2]

CLAUDE LOUCHE

1. Introduction

In professional negotiations, delegates representing the wage-earners meet the representatives of the management of an enterprise. The resulting encounter usually leads to the definition of a new equilibrium in the conflicts of interests and power between the work-force and the management. There is no doubt that the meaning of the negotiations varies from one country to another depending upon historical situations and the choices which are open to the organizations which confront each other. For example, the negotiation could simply be defined as a provisional armistice in the irreducible antagonism between social classes. Or it could also appear as an alternative to open conflict and the means to insure a harmonious resolution of a conflict of interests between social groups. Independently of negotiations tending towards one or the other of these two models, they must always be seen in relation to a process of conflict which is at the background of the exchange of moves and counter-moves between the negotiators. Power, defined as the capacity to influence the outcome of the negotiation, is a major variable in this situation. Raven and Kruglanski (1970) distinguished between various forms of power in conflict situations: the power of persuasion, of relevant expertise, of legitimate claims and, finally, the power based on reward and on coercion.

This chapter is mainly concerned with coercive power. It presents the results of a field study concerned with the analysis of the role played by the use of coercive power in the negotiations about collective agreements in enterprise settings in France. For the purposes of this analysis, comparisons will be made between negotiations which take place in the absence of open conflict and those which are conducted during a strike. A strike constitutes, in this context, the implementation of a coercive form of power designed to cause damages to those against whom it is directed.

Social psychologists have conducted many laboratory studies aiming to elucidate the role of coercive power in bargaining. The most important results of these studies will be summarized in order to evaluate them in the context of a real social situation.

2. Some aspects of the research on threats and negotiation

As previously mentioned, the role of coercive power in negotiation has been the subject of a great deal of laboratory research. Several reviews of this research have been published (e.g. Tedeschi, 1970; Apfelbaum, 1974). What are its results? Rubin and Brown (1975) attempted in their book to formulate, on the basis of an analysis of the published material, a number of global propositions about the influence of coercion. They distinguished between several aspects of this influence.

First, the equal or unequal distribution of power between the negotiators. Rubin and Brown (p199) conclude with regard to this variable that 'under conditions of unequal relative power among bargainers, the party with high power tends to behave exploitatively, while the less powerful party tends to behave submissively'.

Second, in the case of an unequal distribution of power, the effects of the extent of inequality are considered. Finally, when there is an equal power distribution, Rubin and Brown compare the situations in which the power of the negotiators is high with those when it is low. This variable is crucial for the research described in this chapter. Rubin and Brown attempt to prove the notion that 'the smaller the amount of power in the system, the more effectively bargainers are likely to function' (p199).

This conclusion which implies that power, and particularly coercive power, constitutes an obstacle to the rapid resolution of a conflict, seems to be shared by Raven and Kruglanski (1970, p89) who wrote: 'Possessing coercitive capabilities may lead the sides in conflict to perceive each other as hostile and thus unlikely to resolve the incompatibilities involved in reasonable unaggressive ways ... In other words, superimposing coercive potentials on the structure of conflict is likely to enhance "subjective" conflict.' According to these authors, the possession by the negotiators of means of pressure causes the development of hostility, it reduces considerably the amount of communication exchanged between the parties, and it directs the contents of the communication towards the formulation of threats, blocking at the same time the exchange between the negotiators which would be directed towards the resolution of the conflict.

This negative role played by coercion in negotiations was mainly stressed as a result of the well-known experiments by Deutsch and Krauss (1960). Their research was based on the following ideas:

(i) in a conflict situation, a threat, if it is available, will be used to force the opponent to yield;

(ii) if the threat is used, it will provoke a counter-threat and a display of greater resistance by the threatened party.

In such conditions, an agreement will be made easier when no negotiator has threats available to him than when there is a bilateral availability of threats.

When one only of the negotiators has the capacity to threaten, an agreement will be reached more easily than in the bilateral situation. These hypotheses were confirmed in the 'Acme Bolt Trucking Game' (Deutsch and Krauss, 1960). This was a situation in which the subjects were made to simulate driving a truck to a certain destination. They had two routes at their disposal: a longer route which was reserved solely for each of the subjects; and a shorter single-track route which was available to both subjects. The use of the longer route penalized the subjects financially: the amount of their reward increased as the time they took to reach their destination became shorter. But the possibility to use the shorter, single-track route placed them in a situation where they had to negotiate about the right of way. In the experiments, the disponibility of threat was operationalized through each of the subjects having the control of a gate which enabled them to deny to the opponent the availability of the single-track route. As a conclusion of his study, Deutsch (1973) wrote: 'It is dangerous for bargainers to have weapons at their disposal'.

The conclusions that the availability and use of coercive power constitute an obstacle to the development of negotiations deserve further discussion. Kelley (1965) questioned the conclusions reached by Deutsch and Krauss about the relationship between the availability of coercive power and the development of more acute competition. The measure of the difficulty of reaching an agreement adopted by Deutsch and Krauss consisted of the amount of gain that was realized. But it is possible that the small gains realized in the situation of bilateral threat may have been due to the amount of time spent in taking the longer route; in other words, that they were the result of the experimental procedures rather than necessarily providing evidence that a conflict has developed. Borah (1963) confirmed this interpretation. Using the same procedure as Deutsch and Krauss, he found – as they did – that bilateral threat is associated with smaller gains as compared with a situation in which there is no coercive power. But if, instead of gains, the time spent in compelling the opponent or in resisting the constraint is taken as a measure of the extent of competition, no significant effect of threat was shown. In addition, the existence in the experimental arrangements of the second and longer route creates other problems: it allows the subjects the possibility of avoiding all confrontation.

For this reason, Shomer, Davis and Kelley (1966) studied the effect of threats with and without the availability of the longer route. They also distinguished between threats expressed in the intention of harming the opponent and their implementation which consisted of inflicting actual harm. This distinction had not been made in the Deutsch and Krauss study. Shomer *et al.* were able to show that the availability of threat did not by itself reduce the gains made by the subjects. The authors also considered the possibility that if threat is bilaterally available, it need not become an 'undesirable component' of interpersonal relations.

There are other studies which also suggest that the availability of means of pressure may be a factor which favours the reaching of an agreement. Thus, Thibaut and Faucheux (1964, p241) obtained experimental data which showed that contractual activities became possible when the level of threats was high. As they wrote: 'We have shown that the possibility of entering into a valid contract depends upon the capacity of the parties to give up their threat potentials on the basis of a mutual recognition of these respective potentials and of reciprocal renouncing of their implementation. It is obvious that this compensating of abstention on one side by abstention on the other side cannot take place unless the threat potentials are important and approximately equal'. Hornstein (1965) also conducted an extensive study of threat in a commercial negotiation. He distinguished between the capacity to harm, the uttering of threat and its realization. These three levels were also distinguished by Deutsch and Krauss, but only on the conceptual level and not in their experimental design.

Hornstein proposed the following criteria for classifying these situations: (i) whether the negotiators had equal or unequal power; (ii) in the case of unequal power, whether the inequality was more or less accentuated; and (iii) in the case of equal power, whether this power was strong or weak.

It appears that when negotiators have strong power which is equally balanced between the two parties, threats are expressed the least frequently and provoke the least number of counter-threats. The results also show that, in situations of equal power, there is a greater number of agreements when these reciprocal powers are strong. In these situations, threats are implemented the least frequently. These conclusions have also been confirmed when other types of experimental paradigms were used (e.g. Morrison *et al.*, 1971, using the Prisoner's Dilemma Game).

The conclusion which can be drawn from all this research is that coercive power is not harmful to the development of interaction in the framework of a negotiation; on the contrary, it may contribute to the reaching of an agreement through encouraging the parties to engage in an exchange of views. This was the hypothesis we intended to test in field research in which the dynamics of negotiations between management and the unions were affected by the absence or presence of a strike representing coercive power. But, as always, in the transition from the laboratory to the 'field', the variables lose their simplicity both at the level of definitions and of the effects they have. It was therefore necessary to undertake an analysis of two negotiation contexts which were to be compared. The aim of this analysis was to arrive at an understanding, in each of the two situations, of the nature of the power available to each of the social agents and of its effects.

3. Description of the research

A negotiation in an enterprise may proceed in a situation of latent conflict. It may also follow as a consequence of a stoppage of work by the labour-force. In what ways does this affect the stands taken in the meetings of the representatives of both sides in the context of negotiations in France?

A negotiation conducted without a strike is one in which there is a disequilibrium of power. The management enters the discussions from a position of strength since, in an enterprise, it has as its disposal the unilateral power of decision. If and when an agreement about wages and conditions of work is signed as a result of a negotiation, the decision becomes contractual and the power of decision is shared. From a review of collective negotiations in France (Louche, 1977), the conclusion was drawn that new contractual arrangements following negotiations are by no means the usual outcome. In fact, there is nothing to prevent the management from transferring its unilateral power of decision to the level of group negotiation. The relevant legal framework does not create, in this situation, any constraints for the social agents in interaction. It does not forbid the management the use of delaying tactics or of a unilateral decision; at the same time, it does not impose on the unions the obligation to enter into a contractual arrangement. It is possible that this legal framework is perfectly adapted to the French social situation in which social relations are characterized by acute conflicts. It is difficult to see the French management accepting to lose a share of their powers of decision or the unions peace. But this juridical framework does not strengthen, in its effects, the position of the unions in discussions in which there is parity between the negotiators. This framework does not include a definition of 'disloyal practices', as is the case in the United States, where unilateral decisions are not legally admitted. Thus, when there is no strike, the management can preserve the option of temporizing, of letting the discussions drag on, or even of stopping them altogether unilaterally. These aspects of the situation were stressed by an observer of negotiations (Rocard, 1965) who wrote that in many cases 'there are management decisions instead of negotiations about the claims of the workers. When the management representatives refuse to discuss wages, the choice consists of either proceeding to the next point of the agenda or going away ... The only remaining question is to decide whether one wishes to break the negotiations or to yield.' The only power that remains to the unions is the power of the weak, i.e. not to sanction by their signature an agreement which is disadvantageous to them.

But there also exists the possibility of re-establishing an equilibrium of power through strike and action. Through strike, the union causes a financial damage to its opponent. The losses are not, however, limited to the economic level alone. They are also reflected in a possible deterioration of the brand image of the enterprise and in undermining the authority structure of the organization. As a result, strike represents pressure which gives the union the means of affecting the decisions and preventing unilateral decisions. The trial of strength becomes a factor in making decisions contractual and a powerful incitement for engaging in discussions. This has also been the conclusion reached by an observer from the management side who wrote: 'It is in confrontation and, in practice, in the relationship of strength between the management and union organizations that collective agreements are developed. Such a diversity of elements cannot reach an equilibrium, so many snags cannot be avoided unless there is a certain amount of tension.' (De Calan, 1965).

It must, however, be clear that coercion inflicts costs on the union which initiates it as well as on those who are at its receiving end. It is well known that a successful strike is an important factor in unionization. In contrast, a failure disrupts the organization of the wage-earners and deprives the union of all possibility of action for a long period of time. It is therefore important for the union to achieve as quickly as possible through negotiation an acceptable solution to the open conflict. Thus, it can be said that – paradoxically – an open conflict provides the union and management negotiators with common interests. From this analysis, the following hypotheses can be formulated:

(*a*) An open conflict facilitates negotiations. When it exists, the negotiations proceed in a climate of relatively low conflict.
(*b*) An open conflict insures equilibrium in the gains which are achieved and the results which are accepted.

After initial contacts with trade union organizations, a questionnaire was constructed. For methodological reasons, the questionnaire was designed to obtain data which were basically factual. At any time when negotiations in an enterprise reached a conclusion in our region, a member of the union described, in the framework of the questionnaire, the negotiation in which he had just participated. We were able to analyse the progress of nine negotiations without strike and eight in which a strike was involved.

4. Results

(a) Open conflict as a facilitating factor in negotiations

We hypothesized that, in creating common interests, open conflict facilitates the course of a negotiation. This hypothesis was confirmed in a number of ways.

(*i*) *The time required to engage in discussions* This indicator is interesting in the French context of professional relations because the legal framework exerts no constraint on the parties involved to engage in negotiations within any specified limit of time. Thus, in the first stage of the conflict, the aim is to reach the point of opening negotiations as a preliminary to any discussion of the claims. These delays are distributed as follows:

Table 1. *Period of time between request for negotiation presented by the union and the opening of discussions*

	Less than 15 days	More than 15 days
No open conflict	3	6
Open conflict	6	2

Thus, with the exercise of coercive power in an open conflict, negotiations are initiated more rapidly.

(*ii*) *The results of negotiations* A negotiation may reach an outcome which is acceptable to both parties or it may be concluded by a unilateral decision taken by the negotiator who is in a position of strength. In the case of negotiations which finish with a satisfactory agreement, it seems that there are two ways of achieving this:

First, through a compromise which constitutes an intermediate position between the initial positions of the parties.

Or, second, through innovation; this presupposes the discovery by the negotiating representatives of a new solution which transcends the initial opposing points of view. The innovation which goes beyond the initial cleavages implies the existence of a constructive climate of discussions and of problem-solving activity.

We have been able to conclude that agreement through innovations intervened more frequently in conditions of strike (it applied to 22.7 % of the points which were debated) than without a strike (5.7 %). This seems to show that in the case of open conflict the negotiating group develops more often a form of activities which are of a problem-solving nature than is the case in latent conflict. Thus, it seems that the use of coercive power facilitates communication within the negotiating group. This conclusion finds a further confirmation.

(iii) *Forms of communication between the negotiators*   The tactics employed by the negotiators around the table were analysed, particularly in relation to the use of verbal coercion in exchanges between them (e.g. personal aggression, warnings, threats of breakdown). The results confirm the hypotheses as they show that these coercive tactics are employed less frequently when there is a strike. Paradoxically, it is when the underlying conflict is an open one that the conflict within the negotiating group is the least acute.

(b) The results of the negotiation

(i) *The outcome of the discussions*   We have formulated the hypothesis that a negotiation related to a latent conflict leads to unbalanced results. Under the pressure of a strike, the gains are more satisfactory for both groups of representatives and less unequal. In order to assess the results of the negotiations, we asked the trade unionists to inform us how the negotiation ended in relation to each of the points on the agendas of the meetings.

The following range of outcomes was suggested to the respondents: a breakdown of discussions; unilateral decision consisting of one of the parties imposing fully its point of view; a compromise solution which represents a balance between the initial positions; the creation of a committee, i.e. of a working party whose task is to find a solution for some of the issues under discussion; and finally, innovation which creates a new solution.

Table 2. *Percentage of agreements and unilateral decisions in agenda points*

	Agreements	Breakdowns or unilateral decisions
Open conflict	90 % $n = 18$	10 % $n = 2$
No open conflict	62 % $n = 18$	37.9 % $n = 11$

We assumed that unilateral decisions by the management or the break-down of negotiations led to outcomes which were unsatisfactory for the union, and to a disequilibrium in the gains which were achieved after the management had imposed its views. Compromise, innovation and the creation of a working party represented gains which were more balanced and more satisfactory to both parties. Three types of outcome imply, in fact, the agreement and the participation of both the management and the union. In Table 2 they appear in the column of 'agreements'.

This is a marked difference which appears to be determined by the nature of the situation underlying the negotiation. The acceptability and level of satisfaction in negotiations conducted during an open conflict is confirmed in the answers to the question described below.

(*ii*) *Acceptance of the outcome*   The attitude of the union towards the results of the negotiation was assessed at the end of the process. It may be expected that, in a situation of unbalanced power, the union could refuse to sanction by its signature an agreement in which it finds no satisfaction. Therefore, the negotiators were asked whether their delegates have or have not agreed to sign the minutes of the meetings. Of the eight open-conflict negotiations which were considered, six sets of minutes were signed. Out of the nine cases of latent conflict, four only of the sets of minutes were signed.

5. The articulation in negotiations of behaviour and social representations

The field research just presented describes two different situations forming the basis of negotiations. In the absence of open conflict, discussions take a long time to get started and they are conducted in an atmosphere of conflict. They often result in unilateral decisions which are not acceptable to the unions. In the case of open conflict, the dynamics of negotiations are very different: after an early start, the negotiations take their course with little conflict between the parties directly involved which even develop some forms of problem-solving activities. It seems, therefore, that in a situation of open conflict the negotiating group develops in its behaviour a certain cooperativeness. No doubt, the meaning of this cooperativeness must be understood as remaining limited to its particular circumstances and it is by no means based on a deeper convergence. It must not be forgotten that the most important French trade unions locate their actions in the context of the class struggle. This certainly remains the case in the actions observed in latent conflicts in which the initial cleavages between the management and the unions are rarely left behind.

Our field observations yielded contrasting results which in turn led us to conduct further experimental studies. While the power relationships exerted their influence on the behaviour of the participants, our results also showed that this was not the case for intergroup perception and stereotypes. Whether the actions are tough or conciliatory, the social representations remain fixed. It seems that there is no correspondence between the evolution of behaviour and the evolution of representations. Therefore, the problem of the articulation between behaviour and representations in the intergroup context needs to be considered.

Previous research on intergroup relations suggests that there is a close interdependence in the evolution of the behavioural and the perceptual forms of differentiation. For example, in the work of Sherif (e.g. 1966) when a behavioural divergence was created as a result of the development of competition between two groups, perceptual differentiations favourable to the ingroup also appeared. Behavioural convergence and alternation of the conflict reduced these perceptual differentiations. The same phenomenon was also found as soon as contacts with an outgroup were anticipated (Doise and Weinberger, 1973). Conversely, the establishment on a psychological level of a distinction between ingroup and outgroup, based on a social categorization, elicited behavioural differentiations consisting of favouring the ingroup at the expense of the outgroup (Tajfel et al., 1971). All these results show that a divergence at a behavioural level induces a perceptual divergence just as a divergence at the level of representations leads to behavioural differentiation. This was stressed by Doise (1976, p147) who wrote that 'when there is differentiation at one of the three levels (behavioural, evaluative and representational), there is a tendency for corresponding differentiation to occur at the other two levels'.

As this correspondence between behaviour and representations was not found in our data on negotiations, several subsequent experiments were conducted to test the hypothesis of an independent variation in these two levels of differentiation. In an unpublished report, two experimental situations were defined as follows: (i) a situation of behavioural convergence in which negotiators were encouraged towards conciliation; and (ii) a situation of behavioural divergence where intransigent behaviour was elicited.

In both these situations, the negotiators found themselves in an irreducible conflict with their employer. They were then requested to describe the tactics they would use and the tactics which would be adopted by their opponents during the discussions. The results showed that in the case of behavioural convergence the perceptual differentiations between self and the opponent were significantly more marked than in the case of behavioural divergence. In a situation of irreducible conflict, a negotiator who adopts a moderate course of action shows a higher differentiation from the opponent on a representational level than the negotiator who remains firm in his actions. Thus, it appears that in negotiations, the relationship between behaviour and representations evolves in a way which is the inverse of the development observed in the previously mentioned research on intergroup relations.

How can these results be explained? Sherif's theory of the objective conflicts of interests is not able to provide a satisfactory explanation. The theory would have to maintain that, whatever may be the tactical needs of the moment which would push towards firmness or conciliation while negotiating, the fundamental conflict between the groups would remain. The prediction from the theory would be that when negotiation intervenes in a situation of intergroup conflict, conciliation on a tactical level should not be associated with a decrease in perceptual differentiation. For example, beyond the provisional common interests in ending a strike, the divergences between the groups persist.

This explanation stressing the long-term incompatibility between the aims of the groups would have been satisfactory if perceptual differentiations were found to be similar in our two experimental conditions. This is not the case: the intergroup perceptions do not remain static and, as mentioned earlier, they show a movement which is in a direction opposite to that of the actions which are undertaken. This movement is difficult to interpret within the theoretical framework of an objective conflict of interests. But the results fit in very well with assumptions about linkages between social categorization and social identity (Tajfel, 1972).

Let us consider from this point of view the position of the respondents to the questionnaire. The negotiating situation leads to an encounter of members of two social categories which are in conflict: the management and the trade union representing the wage-earners. The conflict concerns more than just a distribution of resources between the relevant categories. The wage-earners deny in principle the validity of the social position and of the very existence of the other category, since their union is the carrier of a project of a society in which that category would be suppressed as a dominant group. Differentiations between the two groups are therefore likely to be strongly accentuated, particularly as they are based on a system of values in which there is a good deal of emotional investment. They will also tend to be accentuated because the syndicalist group can preserve its identity as a group only as long as it is strongly differentiated from the management; this difference is at the core of its identity. When in the course of the study the subjects moderate the mode of their discussions with the opposite party, they attenuate the differentiation between the two categories. It is therefore necessary for them to compensate at the psychological level of representations for the differentiation which has become fuzzy at the level of actions. This is one possible reason why, in the framework of negotiations, the behavioural and perceptual differentiations do not conform to a dynamics which resemble what happens in those instances of intergroup relations in which the social identity of the individuals involved is not directly under threat.

6. Conclusion

There exists an established trend of research in which negotiation is conceived as an isolated and self-sufficient phenomenon (cf. Louche, 1978). On one side there is conflict, and on the other negotiation, the aim of which is to provide the resolution of the conflict. In this perspective, the dynamics of negotiation are seen as linked to cooperative motivations of the negotiators. Consequently, the use of coercive power would constitute an obstacle to the development of negotiation. This conception does not stand up to an examination of social reality. When this is done, one finds that the process of negotiation needs to be redefined. Negotiation is not an alternative to intergroup conflict; it is one of the forms in which conflict is expressed. It does not eliminate the play for power and the test of strength. This being the case, pressures can be considered as a facilitating factor in the development of discussions between opponents. They create common interests for the negotiators: in an open conflict, intergroup negotiations develop in a 'cooperative' climate. At the same time, an accentuation of the perceptual intergroup differences can be observed. These differentiations re-establish the fact that two opposing social categories find themselves face to face (or 'eyeball to eyeball') in the negotiation. The gap remains in order to stress the fact that cooperation is highly transitional since it is based on no more than a provisional convergence of interests.

Notes

[1] Some of the data reported in this chapter are reproduced with the kind permission of the Éditions du CNRS.
[2] Translated from the French by Henri Tajfel.

References

Apfelbaum, E. 1974. On conflicts and bargaining. In L. Berkowitz (ed.): *Advances in experimental social psychology*, Vol. 7. New York: Academic Press.
Borah, L. 1963. The effects of threat in bargaining. *Journal of Abnormal and Social Psychology*, **66**, 37–44.
De Calan, P. 1965. *Les professions*. Paris: Éditions France Empire.
Deutsch, M. 1973. *The resolution of conflict*. New Haven: Yale University Press.
Deutsch, M. and Krauss, R.M. 1960. The effect of threat upon interpersonal bargaining. *Journal of Abnormal and Social Psychology*, **61**, 181–9.
Doise, W. 1976. *L'articulation psychosociologique et les relations entre groupes*. Bruxelles: De Boeck.
Doise, W. and Weinberger, M. 1973. Représentations masculines dans différentes situations de rencontres mixtes. *Bulletin de Psychologie*, **26**, 649–57.
Hornstein, H. 1965. The effects of different magnitudes of threat upon interpersonal bargaining. *Journal of Experimental Social Psychology*, **1**, 282–93.
Louche, C. 1977. *Pouvoir et délégation dans les négociations professionnelles*. Paris: Éditions du CNRS.
Louche, C. 1978. La négociation comme processus interactif. *Psychologie française*, **23**, (3) and (4), 261–8.
Morrison, B., Enzle, M., Henry, T., Dunaway, D., Griffin, M., Kneisel, K. and Gimperling, J. 1971. The effects of electrical shock and warning on cooperation in a non-zero-sum-game. *Journal of Conflict Resolution*, **15**, 105–8.
Raven, B.H. and Kruglanski, A.W. 1970. Conflict and power. In P. Swingle (ed.): *The structure of conflict*. New York: Academic Press.
Rocard, M. 1965. La négociation de la convention collective des industries metallurgiques et mécaniques du territoire de Belfort. In A. Tiano, M. Rocard, and H. Désiré Ogrel: *Expériences françaises d'action syndicale ouvrière*. Paris: Éditions Ouvrières.
Rubin, J.Z. and Brown, B.R. 1975. *The social psychology of bargaining and negotiation*. New York: Academic Press.
Sherif, M. 1966. *Group conflict and cooperation: Their social psychology*. London: Routledge and Kegan Paul.
Shomer, H., Davis, A. and Kelley, H. 1966. Threats and the development of coordination. *Journal of Personality and Social Psychology*, **4**, (2), 119–26.
Tajfel, H. 1972. La catégorisation sociale. In S. Moscovici (ed.): *Introduction à la psychologie sociale*, Vol. I. Paris: Larousse.
Tajfel, H., Flament, C., Billig, M.G. and Bundy, R.P. 1971. Social categorization and intergroup behaviour. *European Journal of Social Psychology*, **1**, 149–78.

Tedeschi, J.T. 1970. Threats and promises. In P. Swingle (ed.): *The structure of conflict*. New York: Academic Press.

Thibaut, J. and Faucheux, C. 1964. L'approche clinique et expérimentale de la génèse des normes contractuelles dans différentes conditions de conflit et de menace. *Bulletin du CERP.*, **13**, 225–343.

16. Instrumentality, identity and social comparisons

HENRI TAJFEL

The chapters of this book do, or should, speak for themselves. It cannot be the purpose of these few concluding pages to return to the detail of their arguments or their data in order to discuss all the agreements or disagreements one may have with the conclusions reached, or all the differences and similarities of the various points of view. It would be presumptuous to aim at a 'conclusion' which would encompass the diversity of the issues raised, to which reference has already been made in the Introduction. There are, however, some general themes which clearly emerge. The aim of this chapter is to draw attention to them.

Some years ago the Minority Rights Group in London published as one of their reports a text about the social psychology of minorities (Tajfel, 1981),[1] parts of which were based on the ideas about social identity to which reference has been made, in one way or another, in most chapters of this book. The text was seen by two distinguished reviewers before it was published. Both made the same point: there was very little in the conclusion of the report which provided a basis for optimism about the future course of minority–majority relations or, more generally, about future possibilities of eliminating the more acute forms of intergroup tensions. The reviewers were right. The perspective briefly outlined in several chapters of this book as the 'social identity theory' (or under other similar designations), and more fully described in several previous publications, can be seen as often leaving us stuck in a spiral of conflict between groups from which it is not easy to see an escape. This is why Brian Caddick referred to the theory in chapter 5 as a 'pessimistic' one, and contrasted it from this point of view with some aspects of equity theory from which, it appears, it is easier to draw certain more optimistic conclusions.

Some of the arguments and data presented in this book also seem to support a more optimistic perspective. For example, there is little evidence from Karmela Liebkind's study in Finland (chapter 13) of acute tensions or unfavourable outgroup stereotypes in the relations between the Finnish-speaking majority and the Swedish-speaking minority. Margaret Weth-erell's data from New Zealand (chapter 8) show that the Samoan and Polynesian children discriminate less against the outgroups in a 'minimal categorization' study than do children from a cultural background of Western values; and all of the children with whom she worked (including New Zealanders of European descent) show a strong tendency to be fair to the outgroup when the situation is so arranged that they have a clear opportunity to do it.[2] From one at least of the many experiments described by Murray Horwitz and Jaap Rabbie (chapter 9), it appears that if one provides competing groups with a chance to engage in certain forms of interaction, the 'depersonalization' of members of an outgroup can dis-appear, or at least it can be considerably reduced. As Horwitz and Rabbie wrote: 'once the opponents' perceived each other as being capable of breaking out of the constraints of membership and as capable of acting as responsive individuals, the attributional changes enabled the groups to reach a relatively easy accommodation with each other' (p270). The members of several ethnic groups in Indonesia who were the respondents in the study by Jos Jaspars and Suwarsih Warnaen (chapter 12) seem to be living in a paradise of mutually favourable stereotypes. With the exception of one target group (the Chinese), almost everyone thinks almost nothing but good about almost everyone else.

Where, then, have all the tensions gone? It is true that several other chapters come up with starker images of intergroup relations. Jean-Claude Deschamps (see chapter 3) would certainly argue that, despite the views expressed in chapter 9, 'attributional' interaction between individual members of 'dominant' and 'dominated' groups, however reasonable it might be, would not eliminate certain forms of depersonalization *generally* apply-ing to members of peripheral groups until and unless the cognitive reflec-tions of power differentials between the groups were also removed. Sik Hung Ng's experiments (chapter 7) show that naked power *will* be exercised towards an outgroup when it can be. Miles Hewstone and Jos Jaspars (chapter 4) abundantly illustrate the systematic biases in attribution which occur when people assess the behaviour of others who belong to outgroups as contrasted with ingroups. Rupert Brown and Fred Ross (chapter 6) demonstrate the strong reactions which occur when one group does not win its 'battle' to gain from another the legitimacy of its claims to self-respect. There is no need to dwell on the acuity of the Northern Irish conflict discussed by Ed Cairns in chapter 10; or on the reality of the tensions in the North–South Italian context and in the regional context of South Tyrol, as they are both described by Dora Capozza, Emiliana Bonaldo and Alba Di Maggio in chapter 11. Claude Louche, writing about industrial conflicts in chapter 15, goes as far as to state that 'negotiation is not an alternative to intergroup conflict; it is one of the forms in which conflict is expressed' (p480). And in chapter 9 by Murray Horwitz and Jaap Rabbie many examples are provided of how easy it is to trigger off intergroup bias and discrimination.

It is possible to derive from these two sets of examples a generalization which is admittedly very rough and very approximate, but could have some uses. Before this is done, however, it may be worthwhile to return to the truism that social groups are not 'things'; they are processes. This is meant in the sense that they are cognitive constructions shared by the individuals involved (see Part I), and/or result from a perception of shared interests (see e.g. chapter 9). It is hardly true that 'a group is a group'. As has often been said in the past, and reiterated in some chapters of this book, the psychological existence of a group for its members is a complex sequence of appearances and disappearances, of looming large and vanishing into thin air; it also includes all the intermediate stages between these two extremes. A very large number of variables is responsible for these increases and decreases in the *prise de conscience* that one is a group, acting as member of it, *and consequently* that other groups are around. These variables will not be discussed here in any detail (see Tajfel, 1981, particularly chapter 11). It will be sufficient for our purposes to make a distinction between a static and a dynamic conception of groups and of relations between them. In the static conception, the groups are seen as 'being there' side by side, almost like herrings packed in a box, coming to life to 'perceive' each other whenever prodded into doing so by the researchers. In the dynamic conception, groups (and intergroup relations) come to life when their *potential* designations as such have acquired a psychological and behavioural reality. Some requirements for research arising from this 'dynamic' view are discussed in chapter 6.

The rough generalization referred to at the beginning of the previous paragraph is based on this distinction between the static and the dynamic approaches. Although it would be impossible (and quite incorrect) to divide the two sets of examples mentioned earlier into two neat and separate packages, it appears true that the peace and harmony of the first of the two sets derives *in some cases* from the static conception. This possibly underlies the difference between the psychological significance of the two methods employed in the experiments described in chapter 8. It is unlikely that the results either from the 'free choice' method or the matrices, both employed by Margaret Wetherell in her cross-cultural studies, can be considered as 'artefacts' inherent in the methods themselves. It is more likely that one of the methods leads more directly than the other to a direct awareness of comparisons with an outgroup, and that both sets of results she obtained reflect different 'real-life' conditions of interaction between groups. The static view can also not be imputed to the Finnish study (chapter 13) in which socio-psychological differentiations between the groups are undoubtedly shown to exist, while at the same time not only is it true that the relations between the two groups are not characterized by acute tensions but – in addition – views held by one of them are affected by a substantial trend towards assimilation with the other.

On the other hand, certain 'static' extrapolations are undoubtedly made in the 'attribution-depersonalization' experiment mentioned above (which is a small part of chapter 9) about the effectiveness of individual contacts in reducing the depersonalization of large social groups by other groups. This consists of assuming that certain kinds of attributions about *individual* members of an outgroup can become the *cause* of changes in the relations between large groups without corresponding changes having occurred in the intergroup situation which had first set into motion the process of depersonalization.

This is a crucially important issue. When introducing the description of the above experiment, Horwitz and Rabbie refer to it as 'a clear-cut demonstration of the central role of attributional processes in determining the course of intergroup conflict' (p269). There is no quarrel with the view that depersonalization of outgroups (and some of its horrifying effects) must depend upon the perception of the members of an outgroup not as individuals but as 'extensions of their group'. But some of the underlying processes are discussed in the chapter in attributional terms, even when the concern is with such collective issues as the treatment of Jews in Nazi Germany (p271). It was hardly the perception of Jews as 'unresponsive' to German interests, or as 'giving less weight to German concerns than to Jewish concerns' which played a central role, or could even be seen as 'incipient', in what happened to millions of people, Jews and others, during the Second World War. The 'marking off' from the rest of the population, to which Horwitz and Rabbie refer, applied to uncounted numbers of Russians, Poles, Gypsies, Jews (German or not), mentally retarded, and many other categories of human beings. They were not so much marked off from the rest of the population, as from their definition as being human, and all that this entails. It is not that attributions of some kind or another were made about the motives of all those people.

No attributions needed to be made at all, no more than attributions are made about insects subjected to a DDT treatment. This was a social psychological consequence of a historical process which led to the redefinition of vast categories of people as being inescapably and inherently at an immense distance from any considerations or attributions about their motives which could imply any form of potential reciprocity with the 'definers'. One example: Horwitz and Rabbie mention in their chapter the fate of Dutch Jews under the Nazi occupation. There is little doubt that the occupiers must have perceived *also* the non-Jewish Dutch population as being 'unresponsive' to German interests and giving them 'less weight' than they gave to Dutch interests. And yet, there was an immense difference between the treatments meted out to Dutch Jews and to other Dutch citizens. This difference can certainly not be accounted for by subtle, or even unsubtle, differences in the 'attributions' made about the Jewish and the non-Jewish Dutch. In the former case, it was the extreme of the process of the deprivation of individuality, of the *complete* definition of human beings through categories to which they belong, some aspects of which are discussed by Deschamps in chapter 3.

It must be made clear that the concern at this point is with one particular aspect of the much wider and more complex argument developed in their chapter by Horwitz and Rabbie. We shall return later to some of the more general perspectives which the chapter formulates. The relevance of the depersonalization issue at this stage is that it illustrates in its own way the static view of intergroup relations. The assumption about the central role played by attributional processes in intergroup conflict has the merit of drawing attention to the functioning of certain psychological processes in *some conditions* of intergroup relations (in which, as can be seen in chapter 4, they do undoubtedly play a part); but it also neglects to specify these conditions and, because of this, the more basic and non-attributional determinants of the conflict are made to disappear. In some conflicts, attributions about motives can become very important; in others their various forms systematically *follow* the way in which the underlying intergroup situation is defined by the contestants. What happens then is that changes in attributions of the kind described in the experiment by Flynn, as summarized in chapter 9, are either not allowed to pass through the protective gates of powerfully selective biases against an outgroup; or if they are allowed through, they are ineffective in changing the definition of the intergroup situation: 'some of my best friends are X, but . . .'.

It is possible that similar distinctions between *types* of intergroup conflict might also help to resolve the predicament in which Caddick finds himself in chapter 5 when comparing alternative interpretations of intergroup behaviour, one of which derives from equity theory and the other stresses the functioning of social categorization, social identity and social comparison. As he writes, equity theory is an 'intragroup' or interindividual theory, or at least it 'is essentially concerned with transactions between individuals or subunits of a common culture' (p147). This is undoubtedly the case in the experiments described in chapter 5. The subjects all come from the same background and the only intergroup differences which exist are introduced by the experimenters. Even in these cases, it is not entirely clear – as is shown in Caddick's discussion – that the interindividual principles of equity theory are directly applicable to conflicts between groups. As will be remembered, Caddick's concern is mainly with the role that the perceived illegitimacy of the arrangements regulating the relations between the groups plays in the development of intergroup bias and discrimination. 'Illegitimacy' can be translated in terms of equity theory as a form of inequity, and therefore – according to the theory – tendencies to eliminate it, either actually or psychologically, should come into play. One of the questions which Caddick asks in chapter 5 is: 'under what conditions will a group which holds an illegitimately ascendant position within a web of intergroup relationships accept or actively work towards an improvement in the standing or circumstances of a group (or groups) less well placed?' (p150). The answer is to be found in the results of the studies reported by Ng in chapter 7: when the ascendant group is not entirely sure of its power to impose its decisions on the outgroup. As Caddick adds: 'Of course, there are answers to this question which would not involve social identity processes at all', and indeed this appears to be the case in Ng's studies on power.

This leads to the conclusion that, in a properly 'dynamic' perspective on relations between groups, the variables deriving from presumed tendencies towards achieving equity, from social identity and from power differentials should be considered *simultaneously*. It is fully possible that, as Caddick suggests, equity does play a role when the groups in conflict share an identical background. But even when this is the case, the size of the discrepancies in power intervenes as an important variable. Ng refers to the early social categorization experiments as characterized by a 'tacit, bilateral and equal power relation' between the groups (p181); and he suggests that it is this absence of power differentials which 'not only makes discrimination possible' in these situations 'but also makes it necessary for the preservation or achievement of a positive social identity' (p181).

It follows from these views that when the size of power differentials leaves no doubt about one group's capacity to deal as it wishes with another group, social identity is not much of a preoccupation in the solidly based superiority which allows for the establishment of any differences from the weaker group which are seen as useful or desirable. In other words, the greater is the relative power of a group, the more secure will it feel in its ascendance and the less need does it have to draw upon its psychological resources. At the same time, groups which are in conflict do not live in a vacuum. Other groups are also around, and this wider social context of the conflict may sometimes force the playing-to-the-gallery presentations of equity-type 'excuses' for the exercise of naked power. This does not necessarily lead to the conclusion that inequity causes distress and therefore it tends to be eliminated, as is assumed by the equity theorists. In inter*group* situations, in which very often the 'supreme good' is normatively identified with benefits accruing to the ingroup (this not being normatively the case for individual benefits) the social *instrumentality* of justifications is a more parsimonious explanation of their use than are considerations about equity (see Tajfel, in press, for a more extensive discussion).

All this leads to the conclusion that the socio-cultural context of justifications is crucial and must always be taken into account. A further consideration of that same context leads to two fundamental questions, both of which are discussed in various chapters of the book. Under what conditions do groups *need* to engage in social comparisons with other groups? And: How is the nature of these comparisons affected by the social and cultural milieu in which they are made?

Both these questions require another brief return to the issues of depersonalization and inequity. As mentioned above, the groups of subjects in the studies described in chapter 5 did not differ culturally or in any *general* way apart from the differences between them introduced in the experiments; and therefore it is possible that, in the case of these 'subunits of a common culture', the need for justifications intervened in their behaviour. As has been pointed out, even this does not require an explanation using the assumptions of equity theory. By contrast, in the acute forms of depersonalization, discussed by Horwitz and Rabbie in chapter 9, members of groups which persecute other groups have no *need* to achieve their individual resolutions of problems which might be created for them not just by inequity but, in some cases, by much more than that: massacres and liquidation of outgroups. The principles of conduct applying within a cultural milieu do not extend in these cases beyond it, and the work of justification is done by powerful and pervasive social and cultural myths. Equity theory is concerned with attempts by *individuals* to resolve contradictions between values and actions which arise in interpersonal conduct. It was argued earlier that even in conditions of cultural homogeneity, the range of application of the theory to intergroup relations is fairly restricted. It finds hardly any application at all in the extreme cases of depersonalization which are one of the major concerns of chapter 9.

The effects of the socio-cultural context on the nature of comparisons with outgroups are clearly shown in a simple and elegant way in the experiments described by Wetherell in chapter 8. As the chapter contains a full discussion of the results obtained, there is no need to return to them here. Ingroup bias *is* shown by all the groups of children, but so is 'parity' in some of the conditions. Perhaps the most interesting aspect of Wetherell's results is in the clear indications they provide that very subtle forms of interaction between experimental procedures and cultural context need to be taken into account in the interpretation of much of our data. In the case of the studies reported in chapter 8, this is clear, since cross-cultural comparisons were their purpose. There is, however, little doubt that the same applies to other experiments in which the differences in cultural background of the subjects or respondents are not one of the independent variables. As I wrote some years ago (see Tajfel, 1981, chapter 2), *all* social psychological experiments are 'cultural'. Most of them appear not to be so only because they are conducted by, with and amongst 'insiders'.

Several interrelated issues have been, so far, briefly discussed in these notes. They included the 'optimism' and 'pessimism' about intergroup relations; the possibility that some of the optimism may be due to a 'static' view of relations between groups, in the sense that the fundamental features of the conflicts dividing them are transposed onto a different plane in which mutual accommodations appear easier than they often are in reality; and the socio-cultural context of relations between large-scale groups, i.e. the values, myths and widely shared beliefs which sometimes powerfully affect ideas about who should or should not be the recipient of equitable treatment, who may or may not be made an un-person, and what kinds of comparisons can or need to be made with what kinds of other people. The discussion of these issues will continue in this chapter, its guidelines remaining closely connected to the points of view presented in the various chapters of the book.

It seems that the Indonesian multi-ethnic situation, as it is described in chapter 12 by Jaspars and Warnaen, presents a case (as one might infer from the data) in which comparisons of one's own group with others do not fulfill any important self-enhancing functions, stereotypes are overwhelmingly positive and there is very little, if any, evidence of representational effects of intergroup tensions. We shall return later to the differences between the provinces and Jakarta, and to the Chinese who are an exception to the findings concerning other groups.

What happens then to generalizations about the social groups' search for a positive distinctiveness which is based on certain comparisons with other social groups? It seems that the Indonesian data (at least from the provinces) present an exception which is theoretically of considerable importance. One of the major underlying conditions, often specified in the past, (e.g. Tajfel, 1981, chapter 11; Tajfel and Turner, 1979), for members of groups to act *as* members of groups rather than as individuals (and thus, also to engage in certain intergroup comparisons) had to do with the existence of a widely shared belief within a group that 'passing' to another group is undesirable, impossible or very difficult.

As Jaspars and Warnaen wrote: 'The application of Tajfel's first hypothesis to ethnic groups immediately raises the problem that one does not choose one's ethnic group but is born into it, and that therefore the option of leaving the group is not possible' (p337). As they state later in the chapter: 'These results suggest that Tajfel's theory is indeed, as he suggested, more relevant when intergroup relations become more salient, as one might expect they are in an urban environment like Jakarta' (p364). This is a considerable understatement. In several publications describing various aspects of the theoretical perspective which we attempted to formulate, the importance of the 'salience' of intergroup relations was not merely a 'suggestion', but the corner-stone of the whole edifice (cf., e.g. Tajfel, 1981, chapter 3 and Part IV; Turner, 1975; Brown and Turner, 1981). The fact that people 'cannot leave their ethnic groups' may seem to be the case in Indonesia but is not by any means universal – there exist innumerable instances of ethnic assimilation. It seems from the data of chapter 12 that the respondents have no reason or wish either to pass into another group or to establish any form of psychologically structured relationship with it *as a group*. This represents almost a theoretical baseline. It is the kind of baseline which always seems difficult to find, and for which the prediction from the theoretical perspective of 'social identity' is exceedingly simple: very little or nothing should happen with regard to attempts at achieving positive group distinctiveness from other groups. This is so because this distinctiveness does not seem relevant to the formation of the self-image or of a 'positive social identity'. The reason may be that either the existence of the other groups has little psychological impact, or the individuals' membership of their own group is not for them a matter of great significance; in other words, the *external* designations of the groups as such have very little, if any, correspondence with the development and existence of internal (i.e. psychological) criteria for their membership (Tajfel, 1981, chapters 11 and 15).

It seems *from the data*[3] that, at least in the Indonesian provinces (but also to some extent in Jakarta), Jaspars and Warnaen found just such a situation. The theoretical importance of their data is obvious on the usual methodological grounds: the finding of negative instances for predictions when the conditions in which these predictions are supposed to work are not fulfilled. There is a good deal of suggestive evidence in chapter 12 that there is a low identification of the respondents with their ethnic groups in the provinces, and that this is higher, but not considerably so, in Jakarta. (The concern here is *not* with the possibility, which always needs to be taken into account, that this may not really be the case, but with the logic of the *internal* relationships within the data. See note 3.) As Jaspars and Warnaen wrote: 'It is conceivable . . . that group members will attempt to resolve a threat to their positive social identity by making a clear differentiation between their personal and their social identity' (p363). And: ' . . . for all our groups (except the Chinese) such negative characteristics were relatively rare and hence did not pose a threat to one's social identity. By denying these features as part of one's self-image one can still maintain a positive self-concept and at the same time benefit from the overall positive identification with the group' (p363).

Indeed, Jaspars and Warnaen found that the few negative traits which were assigned by outgroups to an ingroup were generally accepted by its members, but there was 'a tendency to exclude them from one's self-description'. Outside Jakarta, 'the evaluation of the groups by the ingroup members follows fairly closely the evaluation by other groups, but the self-evaluation appears to be divorced from the group evaluation' (p358). The major conclusion of Jaspars and Warnaen – that the threat to the self-image is averted in their data by the respondents' falling back on their *own* differences from their groups – is undoubtedly justified; there seems to be little intensity to 'the overall positive identification with the group'.

The relevance of this field study to the questions posed earlier in this chapter about the conditions underlying the need for certain kinds of intergroup comparisons and about the way in which social context determines their character is not limited, however, to the potential importance of the negative instance just mentioned. The study contains three levels of salience of group membership, and in this way it presents possibilities of some fairly systematic comparisons which are not often found in field settings. The lowest level of this salience – in the provinces – has just been discussed.

In Jakarta, where many ethnic groups continually rub against each other, it is higher. It is still higher with regard to the Chinese (who are regarded as alien) both as a target group for stereotyping by outsiders and as an object of ingroup-stereotyping. The data of the chapter show that, as this level of salience increases from one of these contexts to the next, so the usual patterns of social comparisons, described in some of the other chapters of this book and elsewhere, increasingly make their appearance. The Chinese case presents a much more marked salience of group membership; consequently, Jaspars and Warnaen 'do not find a clear discrepancy between the self-description and the auto-stereotype since the most negative traits have already been rejected at the group level' (p353).

One detail of the Chinese data is particularly interesting from the point of view of cross-cultural comparisons. The Chinese strongly *reject* the two presumably 'positive' traits assigned to them by others: industriousness and loyalty to the family. It has been argued elsewhere (Tajfel, 1981, chapter 7) that we badly need the long-neglected analysis of *social* (or group) functions of stereotypes (see also chapter 4 in this book). This is particularly so in view of the fact that there exists at large only a limited variety of the *types* of stereotypes. It appears from the data of chapter 12 that the Chinese living in Indonesia are the object of what might be called 'Jewish' type of ascriptions by others (which also seems to have been the case for Asians in East Africa and seems to exist in an incipient stage for Palestinians in some of the Arab countries). This tends to apply to groups which have been particularly active in trade and professional occupations. In such cases, 'industriousness' and 'loyalty to the family' are by no means unambiguously positive. They also imply an eagerness to get on as quickly as possible and an exclusion of others from mutual help which applies to the ingroup. The evaluation attached to any one particular trait of a stereotype cannot be assessed with any certainty if it is divorced from the total pattern within which the stereotyped characteristics acquire their significance.

This is one of the many important ways in which the Chinese group differs in the Jaspars and Warnaen data from the groups located in the provinces for which there is evidence of 'the *desocialization* of the stereotype which becomes more individual' (p358, my italics). As the authors wrote earlier in the chapter, 'one could argue that the rejection or redefinition of unwelcome features only becomes a necessity to preserve a positive social identity when the attitude of other groups towards one's own group becomes predominantly negative' (p353). Indeed, we have argued this in the past over and over again, mainly in terms of a distinction between a 'secure' and an 'insecure' social identity of a group. Several chapters of this book return to a discussion of this distinction and of its relevance to the predictions that can be made about ingroup bias and intergroup discrimination.

This 'insecurity', as discussed, for example, in chapters 5 and 6, is probably one of the crucial determinants of the *need* to engage in certain forms of social comparisons with selected outgroups. In other words, it is amongst the issues most directly relevant to the questions about the conditions for, and the nature of, social comparisons which were asked earlier in this chapter. Here again, one of the issues raised by Jaspars and Warnaen in their chapter provides an excellent point of departure for an attempt at a clarification of some of the basic aspects of intergroup comparisons. This has to do with the 'generalized social comparison model' presented in chapter 12 (pp338–342). In their quantified model, Jaspars and Warnaen stress the weight of the relative *levels* at which comparisons are made and of the use of individual self-evaluations. The data presented in chapter 12 support this 'generalized model' and, in this particular case, the groups' attempts to create distinctiveness from other groups in order to achieve a more positive social identity account for a relatively small part of the general variance.

This may well be the case, for reasons already argued, because of the 'desocialization' of stereotypes found in much of the data of chapter 12. But when this desocialization is not as widespread as it seems to be amongst the respondents of Jaspars and Warnaen, some general issues immediately arise. They concern: the existence of consensual value systems in multi-group societies; the background and functions of 'ingroup devaluation' (i.e. of relatively low evaluation of a group by its own members); and the forms that these ingroup devaluations may take.

As Jaspars and Warnaen write: the assumption of 'a stronger degree of ingroup favouritism or outgroup discrimination in higher status groups' need not be made in order to explain their establishment of large perceived differences from other groups. 'A much more obvious interpretation which has nothing to do with discrimination is that both high- and low-status groups share a common representation based on the objective relationships between both groups, but use a different comparison level to make these judgements' (p339). A similar point about a 'common representation', which includes systems of values shared by social groups differing in their status and other attributes, is made by Deschamps in chapter 3 and was also discussed by Turner (1975) when he introduced the notion of 'social competition'. A quotation from chapter 3 will be useful here: 'Groups exist within a system of mutual dependence; they acquire a reality which is defined in and through their interdependence. They are not pre-existing closed spheres each of which would be able to engender its own specific system of meanings. It cannot therefore be said that each group has its own interpretations and values; groups exist as something which is concrete and 'objective' only in the context of some values which are common to the society as a whole' (p87).

From this point of departure, Deschamps develops in chapter 3, as will be remembered, his ideas about some effects of this interdependence. Differences in power between groups determine the degrees of opportunities to achieve full 'individuality' which are open to various individual members of the various groups. One need not, however, agree with Deschamps about the distinction he proposes between these ideas about interdependence and other definitions of groups quoted in his chapter which he deems to be insufficient because they assume no more than 'coexistence or juxtaposition' in the relations between groups. Although, as Ng also pointed out in chapter 7, the early experiments on social categorization were based on arrangements of 'juxtaposition', all of the later discussions and much of the research on social identity, social comparisons and social competition explicitly took into account status and other differences between groups *within a shared system of values*. Discussions, such as that of Turner (1975), about groups competing to achieve positive distinctiveness on shared dimensions of values would have made no sense without the inescapable acknowledgement that groups within a social system *cannot* be 'closed spheres each of which would be able to engender its own specific system of meanings' (p87).

These definitional misunderstandings are not, however, very important. Much more to the point is the basic agreement underlying the arguments of Deschamps in chapter 3, of Jaspars and Warnaen in chapter 12, of Turner's discussion in 1975, of some of the other chapters in this book, and of some previous discussions about social minorities (e.g. Mugny, 1981; Tajfel, 1981, chapter 15) that 'high- and low-status groups share a common representation based on the objective relationships between the groups'. Starting from this unexceptionable point of origin, it may be worthwhile to attempt a clarification of some of the processes and conditions which may be responsible for the fact that *sometimes* high-status groups perceive *certain* intergroup differences unfavourable to them as being larger than do low-status groups; and other differences, favourable to them, as being smaller;

and that *sometimes* exactly the same is true for lower status groups on various dimensions of intergroup differences when their perceptions are compared with those of higher status groups.

This is an important area of problems which undoubtedly requires very much more research despite the fact that a great deal already exists. It seems that a selective functioning (and sometimes an interaction) of one or more amongst at least three underlying principles is involved in this diversity of intergroup comparisons in which some groups of higher or lower status accentuate or minimize some differences between them in some conditions. These principles seem to be: level of comparison adopted by a group as a function of its status; effects on self-images of consensual and pervasive value systems; and the perceived instrumentality of certain comparisons. We shall discuss briefly each of these three principles.

The first of them seems to operate (perhaps in the form of a 'generalized social comparison model') in the data presented in chapter 12. As mentioned earlier, this seems particularly clear in the chapter when the individuals did their best to dissociate their self-evaluations from the evaluations applying to their groups as a whole.

There is a large amount of evidence (for reviews and examples, see e.g. Katz, 1973; Milner, 1975; Tajfel, 1981, chapters 5 and 15) showing the deleterious effects that consensual and pervasive value systems may have on the self-images and the conceptions of their groups held by members of disadvantaged or minority groups. As Hewstone and Jaspars write in chapter 4 of this book: 'In many studies such minority group members as blacks, working class adolescents etc. have been found to devalue their own group and their own language. In attributional terms this leads to the prediction that members of such objectively "inferior" groups will show a more favourable pattern of attribution for outgroup members than for ingroup members' (pp115–16).

Some of these data also seem concordant with the 'generalized social comparison model' which is apparently able to encompass the fact that in the study by van Knippenberg (1978a and b) 'the polytechnic students, who are consensually "lower" than the university students on the dimension of "scientific", not only rate the university students as superior to themselves on this dimension; they even give them higher ratings than the university students assign to themselves' (p339). It is possible (but unlikely, as we shall argue below) that, in the case of these students, we need to do no more than look at the combined effects of the level of comparison adopted by each of the groups and a shared social representation of the differences between them on the dimension of 'scientific'. If this is all we did in innumerable other instances, we would have to ignore a great deal of accumulated evidence about the self-derogation of disadvantaged groups. This seems to have very little to do with 'generalized comparison levels' and a great deal to do with the acceptance by the members of a group of the image of their group imposed upon them by more powerful groups which stand higher in the social pecking order (see Tajfel, 1981, chapter 15).

The attempts by a group to achieve a positively valued distinctiveness from other groups cannot be assumed to consist of some kind of an autistic process which would ignore stark social realities and would thus enable a group to insist that they are 'superior' on certain dimensions of comparison on which they are quite obviously inferior. This is why Turner's statement in chapter 1 that 'any characteristic which defines the ingroup as different from other groups will tend to be evaluated positively' (pp34–5) is something of an oversimplification. On the other hand, Turner is correct in pointing to the importance of *evaluations* when social comparisons are considered. These evaluations of characteristics which define for the ingroup its differences from an outgroup must be considered from two points of view. One of them concerns the maintenance, protection or creation, *whenever possible*, of positively valued differences from certain outgroups on certain dimensions of comparison. The other concerns the *instrumentality* of comparisons and of the evaluations which are associated with them.

A good example of the functioning of the principle of instrumentality can be found in the extensive study by van Knippenberg (1978*a* and *b*) to which reference is also made in chapter 12. His respondents came from two Dutch institutions of higher learning, where they studied engineering. These institutions clearly differed in their social and scientific prestige. The study included two methods of eliciting from the respondents descriptions of the characteristics of the ingroup and the outgroup: the 'non-relevant' condition (NR) in which one of the groups was described without the respondents knowing that they would have to describe the other group afterwards; and the 'relevant' condition (R) in which one of the groups was described in the knowledge that the other one would have to be described afterwards. The aim of using these two conditions was to attempt to elicit social comparisons at two levels of their salience; it was assumed that the R condition would lead to a keener awareness of the differences between the groups and of their relevance to the respondents.

One of the analyses of data conducted by van Knippenberg concerned the differences between the NR and the R conditions in the *evaluations* of the various clusters of traits in which the respondents consensually assumed the groups to be clearly different from one another. These included 'status' and, as Jaspars and Warnaen wrote in their chapter, the degree to which the groups were 'scientific'. There was agreement from both groups that in both these clusters one of the groups, studying in an institution of university level, was higher than the other whose institution was more like a technical college.

The two clusters fared very differently in their passage from NR to R condition. The evaluation of 'status' *decreased* for the higher status group and *increased* for the lower status group; the converse happened to the evaluation of 'scientific' (van Knippenberg, 1978*b*, p192). The first of these findings is obviously in contradiction with any simplistic ideas about groups enhancing *whatever* differences happen to be favourable to them, and minimizing all the unfavourable differences. When, however, one takes into account the facts that the difference in 'status' is clearly visible to both groups, that it is unwelcome to the lower status group and that the higher status group would prefer to preserve it, then the pattern of changes in the evaluations becomes *instrumentally* clear: reducing the value of the difference which is to their advantage is likely to serve the interests of the higher group; enhancing it and drawing attention to it can serve the purposes of the lower group – on the assumption that the status difference is perceived as not entirely legitimate when applied to the future professional work in which both groups will be engaging. As van Knippenberg (1978*b*) wrote: 'At the same time, the Higher Status group downgraded "status". This pattern of evaluations can be interpreted as an action which is strategic, though not necessarily deliberate. Its purpose is to foster the preservation of the existing status relationships' (p197). As to the upgrading of status by the Lower Status group, 'as subjective likelihood of change increases, perceived legitimacy will decrease ... When the difference in status between the two groups is seen as one that can be changed (beyond certain criteria of probability) the intergroup relationship has reached a stage in which attempts toward change – and subsequent defense – are made. This will, among other things, result in the evaluative tendencies described before' (p199).

The opposite pattern of changes in the evaluation for 'scientific' is almost overdetermined: in enhancing its value, the higher group at the same time defend a positive difference from the outgroup and make a statement about its relevance to their future work; in minimizing it, the lower group at the same time defend their self-concept and reduce the relevance of the difference in 'scientific' for future professional competition. An analysis of similar biases can be applied to the evaluations of the two other clusters of traits which van Knippenberg elicited from his respondents.

It is of direct interest to this argument that Bourhis and Hill report in chapter 14 a very similar pattern of data for some dimensions of comparison between their two groups of respondents who are also consensually of different status: university and polytechnic lecturers in Britain. As Bourhis and Hill summarized this aspect of their data: 'under some circumstances, group members do actively seek unfavourable (negatively discrepant) comparisons'. These comparisons 'may be used as a strategy for justifying claims for improving a group's financial and material position *vis-à-vis* relevant outgroups' (p446). At the same time, it was found that the 'university lecturers rated polytechnic salaries higher than what polytechnic lecturers reported themselves'. They 'may have been exaggerating the salary advantages of polytechnic lecturers in order to "demonstrate" that this group was adequately compensated for their relative disadvantages on other comparison dimensions' (p462). There is at the same time abundant evidence in the chapter that on the dimensions of comparison on which the reduction of a difference favourable to the ingroup or the increase of a difference unfavourable to it are not likely to be relevant to future instrumental advantages, comparisons continue to enhance the positive distinctiveness of the ingroup.

There exists therefore strongly suggestive evidence that intergroup comparisons reflect a pattern in which both instrumentality and social identity must be taken into account. As we once wrote (Tajfel and Turner, 1979), the perspective stressing the functioning of social categorization, social identity and social comparison in intergroup relations must be conceived as *complementary* to the views emphasizing the importance in these relations of the 'objective' conflicts of interests, rather than as aiming to be a substitute for these views.

It is interesting to see that the same important complementarity between instrumentality and identity appears in this book in the chapters directly concerned with the processes of group formation (chapters 1, 2 and 9); it can also be found in Cairns's discussion in chapter 10 of the Northern Irish conflict. One of the merits of Turner's argument in chapter 1 is that it specifies what processes might be responsible for the individuals' identification with large-scale social groups or categories, which is difficult to conceive as an accumulation of face-to-face interpersonal contacts. Reicher was able in chapter 2 to start from this basis in order to provide a useful analysis of crowd behaviour which, like other forms of 'large-scale social behaviour cannot be seen as arising out of, and hence as being constrained by, intra- and interpersonal behaviour' (p77).

In parallel with the previously made distinction between identity and instrumentality in social comparisons, Turner's argument in chapter 1 stresses the processes of identity in group formation, while Horwitz and Rabbie in chapter 9 place their bets on instrumentality. The results of this juxtaposition are complex, and we can do no more here than provide a rough outline of some questions raised by both perspectives and of the promise they present in their potential complementarity.

But before this is done, a semantic confusion must be got out of the way, not only because it leads to misunderstandings, but also because it creates a rigid distinction between the two perspectives which does not, in fact, exist. Horwitz and Rabbie contrast in chapter 9 a group which is 'a social unit capable of acting or being acted upon' with 'the view that a group is simply a social category, i.e. a collection of individuals who share at least one attribute in common that distinguishes them from others' (p249). This definition of a 'social category' as not transcending similarities between its members is then stressed again in the chapter: 'if the group as a social unit is more than a social category, efforts to treat intergroup dynamics as an expression of category differentiation (Doise, 1978) must be incomplete at best' (p249).

We have no disagreement whatever with this view and the distinction it implies between a static and a dynamic conception of intergroup relations which was already discussed earlier in this chapter. The confusion arises from the variety of uses to which the term 'social category' has been put. There is no doubt that Horwitz and Rabbie are correct in stating that a 'social category' has often meant no more than a collection of individuals who share a common attribute or attributes distinguishing them from other such collections. In this sense, all people using a certain brand of toothpaste may be a 'category', although they are highly unlikely to become a 'group'. It is just as true, however, that the term 'social category' has often been used by some of us in clear distinction from such collections of individuals. Billig (1976) was at pains to point out in his book on intergroup relations why simple 'similarity' was an insufficient criterion for categorizing people together in ways which would be socially meaningful. Other lengthy discussions can be found (e.g. Tajfel, 1981, chapters 3, 11, 12, 14 and 15) in which definitions of social groups or social categories are made either in terms of internal criteria of membership, or in terms of a *conjunction* between the internal criteria (such as awareness of membership and evaluations which go with it) and external criteria (such as designations as a 'group' by other people). Billig and Tajfel (1973) ran an experiment precisely to show that interindividual similarity was not enough to elicit group or social category behaviour. A 'dynamic' definition of a social group or a social category is Turner's major preoccupation in chapter 1 of this book, and Reicher's in chapter 2.

It is entirely true that categorial differentiation alone (even when it is based simultaneously on several criteria) does not create 'groups'. The confusion comes from the often interchangeable use of the terms 'social group' and 'social category' which was adopted in several of the publications mentioned in the previous paragraphs. There was a reason for this confusing interchangeability of terms: this was the need to stress as often as possible that the concern of these various discussions was at least as much with large-scale social groupings as with small face-to-face groups which were the traditional subject matter of much of social psychology. Thus, 'social category' was clearly distinguished in them from a 'collection' of individuals based on no more than some criteria of similarity, and – in turn – it strongly resembles the conception of 'social group' as it is discussed in chapter 9. To these previous criteria Deschamps in chapter 3 and (by implication) Ng in chapter 7 add the differentials of power. It is questionable whether *all* group formation or *all* processes of intergroup discrimination must involve power differentials, but as Ng wrote in chapter 7, 'instead of asking what causes intergroup discrimination' he was asking 'what makes it possible' (p180). There is little doubt that if the semantic confusions just discussed can be resolved or ignored, we are likely to reach agreement about a generally acceptable conception of 'social groups' or 'social categories' which is dynamic in its implications and remains close to the social realities of group functioning.

There is one important point in common in the discussions of group formation which are the subject of chapters 1, 2 and 9 of this book. They agree that it is neither simple 'similarities', nor various forms of 'cohesion' (such as mutual liking of individuals who then become members of an ingroup), nor personal interactions, which can provide the *first* basis from which the formation of groups can be understood. The fundamental and *sine qua non* condition for the group process to be set into motion is to be found, according to Horwitz and Rabbie, in the group members' perception of their interdependence of fate – a notion taken over from Kurt Lewin (e.g. 1948). In contrast, for Turner in chapter 1, and in the application of the same views by Reicher in chapter 2, this basic condition for group formation needs to be sought in social identity conceived as 'the cognitive mechanism which makes group behaviour possible' (p21). This is so because 'what matters is how we perceive and define ourselves and not how we feel about others' (p16). As a result, 'we may not, after all, tend to join people we like so much as like people that we perceive outselves joined to' (p17). If we return to the issue of identification with large-scale groupings as compared with small face-to-face groups, the consequence is that the former 'do not seem to be based on, but seem to precede and encourage social and psychological interdependence between individuals' (p22). This is particularly so in conditions of salience of group membership in which 'we perceive or stereotype ourselves and others in terms of the common or criterial attributes of the categories to which we and they belong' (p26). It will be obvious from reading chapter 1 that this is not a return to a simple and passive notion of 'categorial differentiation' based on similarities; group or category belongingness is seen by Turner as the result of an active process of social identification which is described in detail in his chapter.

It is not, however, our purpose at this point to provide a detailed summary of the arguments presented in these chapters; they do the job for themselves. One of the few privileges associated with the task of an editor consists perhaps of being able to look back from some small distance at the various arguments developed in a book in order to see if some kind of a common perspective can sometimes emerge from viewpoints which appear to be diametrically opposed. For most of the chapters in this volume this was hardly necessary: despite a number of disagreements about a number of issues, there is in the book a common underlying perspective to which reference has been made in the Introduction and also earlier in this chapter. This does not appear to be the case for the two conceptions of group formation which concern us at present. And yet, it is very possible that this is so because each of them concentrates on a different *stage* of the same process which is then treated as if this one stage amounted to the total sequence. It is fully possible that each of these conceptions needs to take the other one into account in order to provide a more complete overview of the whole process. This issue will be discussed here briefly and in a very general way; a return to the chapters themselves offers the possibility of reconsidering from this point of view the great variety of more detailed points which are made in them.

Thus, starting from this general view, it would appear that Turner's description in chapter 1 of the sequence of events ending in the formation of a group, which is seen as a convergence of social identifications, leaves out a preliminary stage that might perhaps be referred to as the pre-history of group formation. As already mentioned, Turner's is a view which starts from the processes of social identity, the individuals' subjective location in the network of social relationships of which they are a part. The 'referent informational influence' (see chapter 1) provides then the elements from which individuals can construct their group identifications. It is this process which can be conceived as being in the middle and not at the beginning of the sequence. The question arises as to the *conditions* in which this construction of group identification will be initiated, as to when and why should people be propelled to seek and construct such identifications. Turner is not unaware of the need to specify these conditions. In the third section of his chapter, he suggests that in order 'to understand how social groups are formed', the traditional focus on interpersonal attraction should be replaced by, amongst others, 'variables such as similarity, common fate, proximity, shared threat and other unit-forming features which function as cognitive criteria for the segmentation of the social world into discontinuous social categories' (p27). He returns to the issue in the conclusion to chapter 1 when he stresses the need to clarify 'the conditions under which a social identification is "switched on" to become a salient basis for cognition and behaviour' (p36).

In chapter 9, Horwitz and Rabbie find these conditions in the existence and perception of the 'interdependence of fate' by which individuals are united. Just as Turner's view (and the part of the sequence with which his discussion is concerned) focuses on processes of social *identity*, so the process underlying the perception of interdependence of fate can be seen as the *instrumentality* which is involved in forming or joining a group. This is done by individuals, in Horwitz and Rabbie's argument, in order to achieve gains and/or avoid losses. For them, as for Turner, this basic instrumentality of group formation is theoretically prior to the various possible effects of face-to-face interaction or interpersonal attraction. In this way chapter 9 provides one possible (and highly plausible) view as to what 'switches on' the processes of social identification discussed by Turner. But then, just as the beginning of the sequence is missing in Turner's argument and is possibly supplied in what is being said in chapter 9, so Horwitz and Rabbie clarify the starting point and seem to be getting into difficulties when they consider the later stages of group formation and of relations between groups. It is quite obviously very often *not* the case that remaining in a group, or refusing to move to another group, provides individuals with gains or keeps them safe from losses. Remaining loyal to a group is sometimes a very difficult decision to take, precisely *because* it may involve a great deal of suffering, risks of great losses or missing some potential benefits.

Just as Turner is aware in chapter 1 of the missing link at the beginning of his sequence, so Horwitz and Rabbie do not ignore the difficulties, such as those just discussed, in the later stages of their sequence. They attempt to resolve these difficulties by assuming that interdependence of fate leads to greater liking for people who are in the ingroup than for those who are in the outgroup, and that, in this way, pleasant or unpleasant things happening to *other* members of the ingroup acquire an affective significance which can then be subsumed under personal gains or losses (see, for example, the discussion in chapter 9 of Kelley's ideas about close personal relationships and their application to group processes, p263). This attempt to resolve the problem creates two difficulties, one of which is factual and the other conceptual.

The factual difficulty is that, particularly in the case of large-scale social groups or categories, there is no need to like the members of the ingroup in order for it to remain and survive as a focus of intense affiliation. As a matter of fact, the opposite is often the case. An appropriate example recently heard from a journalist ran approximately as follows: 'Israel is a democracy which has as many parties as a democracy can afford, and some more'. Intense and sometimes extreme dislikes amongst the members or subgroups of this particular 'group' co-exist with the persistence of a very powerful common affiliation which is 'switched on' in a large variety of situations. As a matter of fact, the disagreements, rivalries and dislikes, which exist in this case and many other such cases, are often based on the perception of oneself or one's subgroup as being the most appropriate and effective representatives of the common group affiliation. Phenomena of this kind closely converge with Codol's (e.g. 1979) views and research about the PIP (*primus inter pares*) normative process, in which, according to him, individuals consider themselves, together with others, as members of their group but also as being rather better at it (or symbolizing more faithfully its attributes) than is the case for the 'average' members. In sum, powerful group affiliations or identifications are capable of a robust persistence despite the vagaries of intense likes or dislikes felt towards some or many members of the ingroup. A similar argument can be found in chapter 1.

The second difficulty in the Horwitz and Rabbie discussion, which is conceptual, concerns the subsuming of affective phenomena under the rubric of interdependence of fate. They need to do this in order to encompass the abundant evidence from common experience, already mentioned above, that people often remain in their groups and refuse to 'cross' to other groups despite the high cost of staying or the possible benefits of leaving. Suggestive evidence that this happens is also contained in some of the studies summarized in chapter 9. The only way in which this costly staying in or not moving out can be encompassed within the instrumental conception of interdependence of fate, based as it is on gain/loss calculations, is to assume that the *affective* gains of staying or losses of leaving are greater than any of the 'objective' risks involved in staying (which may sometimes be immense) or in not crossing over. It is undoubtedly true that these intense affective affiliations must, in these cases, be more powerful than any other considerations. Otherwise these personal sacrifices could not have been made, some Buddhist monks would not have set fire to themselves, some prisoners in Northern Ireland would not have starved themselves to death, and innumerable examples of lesser but still very substantial personal offerings at the altar of the ingroup would not have existed. It does not seem very useful to assign these powerful expressions of ingroup loyalty to their presumed basis in a perceived matrix of gains and losses. This can only he done at the cost of stretching the meaning of 'gain' and 'loss' so far as to cause it to lose most of its heuristic value or significance. There exists here a substantial danger of ending up with a tautology: when the individuals' calculation or assessment of 'objective' gains or losses, however large they may be, is not capable of determining social behaviour, *then* the other (affective) gains or losses must be, by definition, more important. When this does not happen, then the case must have been that the objective gains and losses were more important. It is not easy to imagine how the appropriate weights for this affective–objective balancing of factors could ever be established *before* the event; they can only be used in a circular fashion as a *post facto* explanation.

It seems therefore that, just as interdependence of fate is needed to establish the locus of origin for the development of social identity, so the processes of social identification – which can reach great heights of intensity – need to be used as an explanation for the continuing, long-lasting group affiliations which often contain motives and beliefs that are contradictory and conflicting. It is not at all certain that Turner's emphasis in chapter 1, which is primarily cognitive, can do full justice to these occasional heights of intensity. It is, however, a beginning of what appears to be a promising direction of search. It is also interesting to see that, as Reicher points out in chapter 2, a concept of social identification, although admittedly a very different one, was used by Freud (1922) when he was confronted with the same problem of intense group affiliations. We are only at the beginning of considering the *entire* sequence involved here in ways which are capable of being directly linked to convincing empirical research; there is no doubt that a wider and fuller synthesis will be required in the future.

The aim of this concluding chapter was not to discuss all of the wide variety of themes which make their appearance in this book, and even less to attempt a summary (a fairly impossible task) of all of the chapters. The selection of the issues raised in the chapter was entirely determined by *some* of the questions which remained open and seemed important to at least one (careful) reader of all the contributions; and also by some of the ambiguities which seemed to remain unresolved. Themes which are no less important have not been returned to in this chapter precisely because they would have been simply 'returned to' after what the authors of the other chapters had already written. It is my conviction that all these themes taken together – whether or not mentioned in this concluding discussion – provide most of the elements we need for the construction of a comprehensive social psychological theory of intergroup relations. If this conviction is justified, then the book has achieved its aim.

Notes

[1] See Introduction, note 1.
[2] On the other hand, a recent study by Locksley *et al.* (1980) in which a method of 'free distribution' was used, very similar to the procedures employed by Wetherell, showed strong ingroup favouritism. The experiments were conducted with American undergraduates, and therefore the problem remains whether cultural and/or age differences were responsible for the different results obtained in the two studies.
[3] This is italicized here because there exists a good deal of historical evidence that the process of nation-building in Indonesia has been by no means a smooth progression, but rather has been characterized by acute – and often bloody – conflicts and tensions.

References

Billig, M. 1976. *Social psychology and intergroup relations.* European Monographs in Social Psychology, No. 9. London: Academic Press.

Billig, M. and Tajfel, H. 1973. Social categorization and similarity in intergroup behaviour. *European Journal of Social Psychology,* 3, 27–52.

Brown, R.J. and Turner, J.C. 1981. Interpersonal and intergroup behaviour. In J.C. Turner and H. Giles (eds): *Intergroup behaviour.* Oxford: Blackwell.

Codol, J.P. 1979. *Semblables et différents: Recherches sur la quête de la similitude et de la différenciation sociale.* Aix-en-Provence: Université de Provence.

Doise, W. 1978. *Groups and individuals: Explanations in social psychology.* Cambridge: Cambridge University Press.

Freud, S. 1922. *Group psychology and the analysis of the ego.* London: Hogarth Press.

Katz, I. 1973. Alternatives to a personality-deficit interpretation of Negro under-achievement. In P. Watson (ed.): *Psychology and race.* Harmondsworth: Penguin Books.

van Knippenberg, A.F.M. 1978a. *Perception and evaluation of intergroup differences.* Leiden: University of Leiden.

van Knippenberg, A.F.M. 1978*b*. Status differences, comparative relevance and intergroup differentiation. In H. Tajfel (ed.): *Differentiation between social groups: Studies in the social psychology of intergroup relations.* European Monographs in Social Psychology, No. 14. London: Academic Press.

Lewin, K. 1948. *Resolving social conflicts.* New York: Harper and Row.

Locksley, A., Ortiz, V. and Hepburn, C. 1980. Social categorization and discriminatory behaviour: Extinguishing the minimal intergroup discrimination effect. *Journal of Personality and Social Psychology,* **39,** 773–83.

Milner, D. 1975. *Children and race.* Harmondsworth: Penguin Books.

Mugny, G. 1981. *El poder de las minorias.* Barcelona: Rol.

Tajfel, H. in press. Psychological conceptions of equity: The present and the future. In P. Fraisse (ed.): *Psychologie de demain.* Paris: Presses Universitaires de France.

Tajfel, H. 1981. *Human groups and social categories: Studies in social psychology.* Cambridge: Cambridge University Press.

Tajfel, H. and Turner, J.C. 1979. An integrative theory of intergroup conflict. In W.G. Austin and S. Worchel (eds): *The social psychology of intergroup relations.* Monterey, Calif.: Brooks/Cole.

Turner, J.C. 1975. Social comparison and social identity: Some prospects for intergroup behaviour. *European Journal of Social Psychology,* **5,** 5–34.

Subject index

OSA *see* objective self-awareness
outgroup action, 256–9
outgroup advantages and disadvantages, *447*
outgroup communication, *166*
outgroup depersonalization *see* depersonalization
outgroup discrimination *see* discrimination
outgroup dislike, 294–5
outgroup evaluation *see* ingroup and outgroup evaluation
outgroup favouritism *see* favouritism
outgroup jobs, *447*
outgroup language, pronunciation of, 369
outgroup members, general emotional significance of, 403–4
outgroup stereotypes, 484; *see also* ingroup and outgroup stereotypes
outgroups, 7, 305, 410, 484–6; *see also* dichotomization of ingroup and outgroup *and* depersonalization

Paris commune, 47
parity, *215–16, 220, 227, 230, 236–7*
parity choices, replication of, 236
'pay-off matrix', structure of, *156*; *see also* profit strategies *and* matrices
perceived status *see* status
perceptual differences, in attribution, 116
performance conditions, 202
performance factors, *200–1*
personal identity, 20, 110, 111; *see also* identity
personal relationships, 504
pessimism, 483, 490
physical reality, contrasted with social reality, 102, 119–20
PIP *see primus inter pares* effect
Poles, marked off from the rest of the population, 486
political bias, 5; *see also* biases
political causality, 8; *see also* causality *and* psychological effects
political mobility, 377
political mobilization, 375
political parties, in Finland, 392
politics, Irish, 277; Italian, 300
Polynesian children, and discrimination, 484; and European children, 212–221
Polynesian cultural background, contrasted with Western cultural background
Polynesian societies, 231
Polynesian/European differences, 237–8
polytechnic facilities, 428–9
polytechnic lectures, 10, 45, 499; and intergroup perceptions, *454*; and social mobility, *453*; and status, 432–4
polytechnic sector, advantages of, *448*; and Government, *451*
polytechnic students, 338–9, 432, 496; among groups judged, *339–40*

polytechnics, historical and structural characteristics of, 423–34; as proposed, 425; role of, *450*; study of, 439–63
positional responses, 91
positive differentiation *see* differentiation
positive distinctiveness *see* distinctiveness
positive intergroup differentiation *see* intergroup differentiation
'post-test' only methodological orthodoxy *see* methodological orthodoxy
potential designations, 485; *see also* groups
power, disequilibrium of, 473–94; equal or unequal, 472; equal or unequal distribution of, 468; equilibrium of, 474; *see also* social power *and* property
power conditions, *192*
power differentials, 488–9
power factors, *201*
prejudice, 118–119, 126, 278, 335–6; cognitive analysis of, 125
pressure, availability of means of, 472
prestige, 30
primus inter pares (PIP), 75, 337–8, 504
prise de conscience, 485
Prisoner's Dilemma, 159, 472; *see also* strategic options
privilege conditions, *192, 202*
privilege factors, *200–1*
privilege variable, *196*
prize, 183–4, 191
profit, mutual, 238
profit strategies, 208, 212–38
progress, 301
property, 180, 182–4, 191, 200–2, 204
'Protestant individualism' ideology, 107
Protestants, 286, 291–4
psychodynamic ideas, 54
psychological criteria, 492
psychological crowds *see* crowds *and* crowd psychology
psychological distinctiveness, 285–94, 305, 436; *see also* distinctiveness
psychological effects, of conflict, 8
psychological equity restoration *see* equity restoration
psychological explanation, 49
psychological processes, 68
psychological reductionism *see* reductionism
public works, 301
Pyhtää, commune of, 381–3; population of, *383*; *see also* Role Construct Repository Grid, INGRID, grid analysis package *and* intergroup identification

Q-methodology *see* Role Construct Repository Grid
qualifications, of lecturing staff, *429*
Québécois, 465

Author index

2468472R00274

Printed in Great Britain
by Amazon.co.uk, Ltd.,
Marston Gate.